College Student Alcohol Abuse

A Guide to Assessment, Intervention, and Prevention

Christopher J. Correia
James G. Murphy
Nancy P. Barnett

WILEY

JOHN WILEY & SONS, INC.

Copyright © 2012 by John Wiley & Sons, Inc. All rights reserved.
Published by John Wiley & Sons, Inc., Hoboken, New Jersey.

Published simultaneously in Canada.

Library of Congress Cataloging-in-Publication Data:

College student alcohol abuse : a guide to assessment, intervention, and prevention / [edited by] Christopher J. Correia, James G. Murphy, Nancy P. Barnett.
   p. cm.
   Includes index.
   ISBN 978-1-118-03819-2 (pbk.)
   1. College students--Alcohol use. 2. Alcoholism–Prevention. I. Correia, Christopher J. II. Murphy, James G. III. Barnett, Nancy P.
   HV5135.C65 2012
   362.292084'2—dc23

                                        2012010598

Printed in the United States of America

10 9 8 7 6 5 4 3 2 1

College Student Alcohol Abuse

Contents

Preface

According to the U.S. Surgeon General and the U.S. Department of Health and Human Services, heavy episodic drinking among college students represents a "major national health problem" (USDHHS, 2000). A number of sources have also noted recent increases in the use of drugs like marijuana and nonmedical use of prescription medications. Misuse of alcohol and other drugs can lead to many well-documented negative outcomes, including injuries and fatalities, social and interpersonal difficulties, and problems related to academic performance. Substance misuse also results in increased violence, property destruction, sexual assaults, and other problems that affect the entire college community. Recent reports by the Task Force of the National Advisory Council on Alcohol Abuse and Alcoholism (NIAAA, 2002, 2007) noted that widespread heavy drinking and associated consequences on campuses place colleges and universities in the challenging position of developing programs and policies that will adequately protect students from harm.

The impetus for this book was our shared recognition of the need for a comprehensive resource on how to address substance use among college students. Our primary goal was to bring together experts from across the United States to create a thought-provoking, hands-on, and user-friendly book that practitioners, administrators, and researchers will find valuable in their day-to-day work with college students. The book is useful to a variety of professions and professionals in training who work primarily with college students and young adults, including psychologists, counselors, and other mental health practitioners; physicians and nurses; those involved in higher education administration; researchers with an interest in substance abuse or clinical interventions; and students who aspire to join one of these exciting professions.

The text is divided into two major sections. Part I, "Epidemiology, Consequences, and Risk Factors," consists of four chapters that provide a primer on substance use among college students. The initial chapters give readers a firm understanding of the prevalence of alcohol and drug use and associated negative consequences, the populations (e.g., Greek members, student athletes), and activities and events (e.g., spring break, drinking games) associated with increased risk of misuse, and the latest theories used to explain substance use among college students.

In Part II, "Assessment, Intervention, and Prevention Strategies," 10 chapters translate the latest theories and research findings related to college student substance abuse into clear and evidence-based strategies for assessing and treating college students who are abusing alcohol and other drugs. Consistent with a public health approach to college drinking prevention, the book covers a continuum of prevention and intervention modalities, ranging from campus-wide and community-based prevention programs, to brief and easily disseminated computerized and web-based interventions, to more intensive small group and individual approaches utilizing both peer and professional counselors. Each chapter provides clear suggestions about how to implement the strategies and interventions that have been shown to be most effective.

Many people contributed to making this book a reality. We would like to thank all of the authors for their excellent contributions. We would also like to thank our colleagues and students, too many to name individually, who continue to challenge and excite us with new perspectives. Finally, we thank the people of Wiley for supporting this project, with special acknowledgment to Marquita Flemming and Sherry Wasserman for seeing us through from start to finish.

REFERENCES

National Institute on Alcohol Abuse and Alcoholism. (2002). *High-risk drinking in college: What we know and what we need to learn. Final report on the panel on contexts and consequences.* National Advisory Council on Alcohol Abuse and Alcoholism Task Force on College Drinking. USDHHS.

National Institute on Alcohol Abuse and Alcoholism. (2007). *What colleges need to know now: An update on college drinking research.* National Advisory Council on Alcohol Abuse and Alcoholism Task Force on College Drinking. USDHHS.

U.S. Department of Health and Human Services. (2000). *Healthy people 2010* (conference ed., Vol. II, pp. 26–29). Washington, DC: author.

Contributors

Brooke J. Arterberry, MS
University of Missouri
Columbia, MO

Rachel L. Bachrach, MS
University at Buffalo, The State University
of New York
Buffalo, NY

Nancy P. Barnett, PhD
Brown University
Providence, RI

Todd M. Bishop, MS
Syracuse University
Syracuse, NY

Brian Borsari, PhD
Department of Veterans Affairs Medical
Center
Providence, RI

Julia D. Buckner, PhD
Louisiana State University
Baton Rouge, LA

Jennifer M. Cadigan, BA
University of Missouri
Columbia, MO

William Campbell, MS
The University of New Mexico
Albuquerque, NM

Kate B. Carey, PhD
Brown University
Providence, RI

Amy L. Copeland, PhD
Louisiana State University
Baton Rouge, LA

Christopher J. Correia, PhD
Auburn University
Auburn, AL

Anthony H. Ecker, BS
Louisiana State University
Baton Rouge, LA

Darin J. Erickson, PhD
University of Minnesota
Minneapolis, MN

Anne M. Fairlie, MA
University of Rhode Island
Kingston, RI

Nicole Fossos, BS
University of Houston
Houston, TX

Dawn W. Foster, MPH
University of Houston
Houston, TX

Raluca M. Gaher, PhD
University of South Dakota
Vermillion, SD

Eliza J. Hart, BA
Syracuse University
Syracuse, NY

Reid K. Hester, PhD
Behavior Therapy Associates, LLP
Albuquerque, NM

Ralph W. Hingson, ScD, MPH
National Institute on Alcohol Abuse and
Alcoholism
Bethesda, MD

Jason R. Kilmer, PhD
University of Washington
Seattle, WA

Melissa A. Lewis, PhD
University of Washington
Seattle, WA

Diane E. Logan, MS
University of Washington
Seattle, WA

Stephen A. Maisto, PhD
Syracuse University
Syracuse, NY

Matthew P. Martens, PhD
University of Missouri
Columbia, MO

Nadine R. Mastroleo, PhD
Brown University
Providence, RI

James G. Murphy, PhD
University of Memphis
Memphis, TN

Clayton Neighbors, PhD
University of Houston
Houston, TX

Jennifer P. Read, PhD
University at Buffalo, The State University
of New York
Buffalo, NY

Ryan N. Reed, BS
University of South Dakota
Vermillion, SD

Erica Eaton Short, MA
Brown University
Providence, RI

Jeffrey S. Simons, PhD
University of South Dakota
Vermillion, SD

Ashley E. Smith, MA
University of Missouri
Columbia, MO

Meredith A. Terlecki, PhD
Louisiana State University
Baton Rouge, LA

Aaron M. White, PhD
National Institute on Alcohol Abuse and
Alcoholism
Bethesda, MD

Mark D. Wood, PhD
University of Rhode Island
Kingston, RI

Tyler B. Wray, MS
University of South Dakota
Vermillion, SD

College Student Alcohol Abuse

PART I

Epidemiology, Consequences, and Risk Factors

1

Prevalence and Consequences of College Student Alcohol Use

Ralph W. Hingson and Aaron M. White

Since 1976, when the National Institute on Alcohol Abuse and Alcoholism (NIAAA) issued its first report on abusive drinking by college students, research advances have transformed our understanding of alcohol abuse and related problems among college students. Several national surveys indicate that about 80% of college students drink alcohol each year. Many first-year students come to college with an established pattern of drinking developed in high school and even middle school. Further, we now know that a broad array of factors affect college student drinking behaviors and the consequences that follow. These factors include an individual's genetic susceptibility to the positive and negative effects of alcohol, campus norms related to drinking, expectations regarding the benefits and detrimental effects of drinking, penalties for underage drinking, parental attitudes about drinking while at college, whether one is member of a Greek organization, and conditions within the larger community that determine how accessible and affordable alcohol is. Together, these influences and others contribute to a culture of drinking that, in the end, can be more damaging and deadly than previously recognized.

HEAVY DRINKING AT COLLEGE

Research suggests that a large percentage of college students who drink do so to excess. National surveys indicate that from 1999 to 2007 (Substance Abuse and Mental Health Services Administration, 2000, 2002, 2006, 2008) the percent of 18- to 24-year-old college students who drank five or more drinks on an occasion in the previous 30 days increased from 41.7% to 43.8%, a significant 5% proportional increase.

Among 18- to 24-year-olds not in college, the percent increased from 36.5% to 40.7%, a significant 12% proportional increase.

For the majority of drinkers, five drinks in a 2-hour period, often referred to as heavy episodic or binge drinking, would produce a blood alcohol concentration (BAC) at or above 0.08%, a level at which driving-related abilities are markedly impaired, decision making and impulse control are dulled, and memory starts to fail. This is the legal limit of intoxication for adults in all 50 states. The odds of a fatal car crash are elevated significantly here, as are the chances of suffering from alcohol blackouts, being sexual assaulted, physically injured, and suffering various other harms (Hingson & White, 2010).

A greater percentage of 18- to 24-year-old college students compared with noncollege respondents engage in binge drinking. However, because only 36% of 18- to 24-year-olds are in college, the number not in college who consumed five or more drinks on an occasion in 2007 exceeded the number of college students who did so by a large number (7,705,578 vs. 4,564,861). From 1999 to 2007, among 18- to 24-year-olds, the proportion of college students who drove under the influence of alcohol decreased slightly from 26.1% to 25.2%. Among those in the same age-group who are not in college, the proportion increased significantly from 19.8% to 21.0%.

Those old enough to drink legally drink more heavily and are more likely to drink and drive than students who are underage based on current law (i.e., < 21 years old). The largest increase in binge drinking occurred among 21- to 24-year-olds (43% in 1999 and 48% in 2007), not 18- to 20-year-olds (38% in 1998 and 39% in 2007), who currently are prohibited from drinking legally. Similarly, the percentages of those who drove under the influence were highest in the 21- to 24-year-old group at 30% in both 1999 and 2007. In the 18- to 20-year-old group, the percent declined from 24% to 21% during those years.

Concerns have been raised that the legal drinking age of 21 drives drinking by underage persons into unsupervised settings where very heavy drinking is apt to occur. Analyses of the National Longitudinal Alcohol Epidemiologic Study (NLAES) and National Epidemiologic Study on Alcohol and Related Conditions (NESARC) national surveys conducted 10 years apart in 1991 to 1992 and 2001 to 2002 reveal increases in consuming 10 or more drinks or 21 or more drinks, the latter being the equivalent of one fifth of distilled spirits, occurred among 21- to 24-year-olds, particularly those in college, not 18- to 20-year-olds (see Figure 1.1). Among 21- to 24-year-old college students, the percentages consuming 10 or more drinks on an occasion rose from 27% to 40%, and the percent consuming 21 or more drinks on an occasion rose from 8% to 15%.

ALCOHOL-RELATED CONSEQUENCES

Drinking to intoxication leads to widespread impairments in cognitive abilities, such as decision making and impulse control, and impairments in motor skills, such as balance and hand-eye coordination, thereby increasing the risk of injuries and various

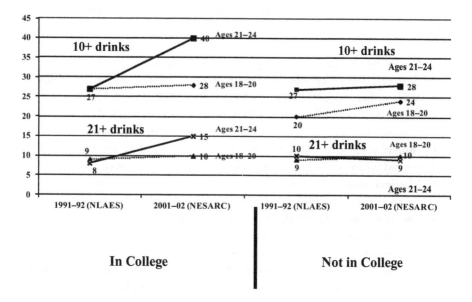

Figure I.I Consumption of 10+ Drinks or More or 21+ Drinks on an Occasion in Past Year by U.S. 18- to 20-year-olds and 21- to 24-year-olds, 1991–1992 versus 2001–2002

other harms. Among 18- to 24-year-old college students, deaths from all alcohol-related unintentional injuries, including traffic and other unintentional injuries, increased from 1,442 in 1998 to 1,870 in 2007, corresponding to a 1% increase in rates of death among students per 100,000 from 18.5 to 18.6. Among all 18- to 24-year-olds, alcohol-related unintentional injury deaths increased from 4,809 in 1998 to 5,502 in 2007. Most of the injury deaths resulted from traffic crashes involving alcohol (1,395 among college students ages 18 to 24 and 4,103 among all individuals in that age group) in 2007. Alcohol-related traffic deaths involving college students increased from 1,135 to 1,395 and from 3,783 to 4,103 among all 18- to 24-year-olds. Nontraffic unintentional injury deaths increased from 308 to 531 among 18- to 24-year-old college students and from 1,026 to 1,562 among all persons that age. Most of that increase resulted from increases in poisoning deaths involving alcohol, up from 62 to 262 among college students and from 207 to 770 among all 18- to 24-year-olds from 1998 to 2007.

NIAAA reports have documented that heavy-drinking college students not only place their own health at risk, they jeopardize the well-being of others. As many as 46% of the 4,553 people killed in 2007 in crashes involving 18- to 24-year-old drinking drivers were people other than the drinking driver. Further, a national survey in 2001 indicated that more than 690,000 college students that year nationwide were hit or assaulted by a drinking college student, and 97,000 students were the victim of a date rape or assault perpetrated by a drinking college student (Hingson & Zha, 2009).

Below are recent statistics summarizing alcohol-related harm involving college students:

- **Death:** More than 1,800 college students between the ages of 18 and 24 die each year from alcohol-related unintentional injuries, including motor vehicle crashes (Hingson, Heeren, Winter, & Wechsler, 2005; Hingson, Zha, & Weitzman, 2009, Hingson & White, 2010). Nearly one half of people 18 to 24 who die in crashes involving alcohol are persons other than the drinking driver.
- **Injury:** 599,000 students between the ages of 18 and 24 are unintentionally injured under the influence of alcohol (Hingson et al., 2005).
- **Physical assault:** More than 696,000 students between the ages of 18 and 24 are assaulted by another student who has been drinking (Hingson et al., 2005).
- **Sexual assault:** More than 97,000 students between the ages of 18 and 24 are victims of alcohol-related sexual assault or date rape (Hingson et al., 2005).
- **Unsafe sex:** 400,00 students between the ages of 18 and 24 had unprotected sex and more than 100,000 students between the ages of 18 and 24 report having been too intoxicated to know if they consented to having sex (Hingson, Heeren, Winter, & Wechsler, 2003).
- **Health problems/suicide attempts:** More than 150,000 students develop an alcohol-related health problem (Hingson, Heeren, Zakocs, Kopster, &Wechsler, 2002) and between 1.2% and 1.5% of students indicate that they tried to commit suicide within the past year due to drinking or drug use (Presley, Leichliter, & Meilman, 1998).
- **Drunk driving:** 2.7 million students between the ages of 18 and 24 drove under the influence of alcohol last year.
- **Memory loss:** National estimates suggest that 10% of nonbinge drinkers, 27% of occasional binge drinkers, and 54% of frequent binge drinkers reported at least one incident in the past year of blacking out, defined as having forgotten where they were or what they did while drinking (Wechsler, Lee, Kuo, & Lee, 2000; White, 2003).
- **Property damage:** More than 25% of administrators from schools with relatively low drinking levels and more than 50% from schools with high drinking levels say their campuses have a "moderate" or "major" problem with alcohol-related property damage (Wechsler, Dowdall, Maenner, Gledhill-Hoyt, & Lee, 1998).
- **Police involvement:** About 5% of 4-year college students are involved with the police or campus security as a result of their drinking (Wechsler et al, 2002) and an estimated 110,000 students between the ages of 18 and 24 are arrested for an alcohol-related violation such as public drunkenness or driving under the influence (Hingson et al., 2002). A more recent national study reported 8.5% were arrested or reported other trouble with the police because of drinking (Presley & Pimentel, 2006).

- **Alcohol abuse and dependence:** 31% of college students met criteria for a diagnosis of alcohol abuse and 6% for a diagnosis of alcohol dependence in the past 12 months, according to questionnaire-based self-reports about their drinking (Knight et al., 2002).

Clearly, alcohol use by college students is viewed by some people as normative, but alcohol is associated with a variety of negative outcomes on college campuses. We explore some of these negative outcomes in detail in this chapter.

ACADEMIC PERFORMANCE

About 25% of college students report academic consequences of their drinking including missing class, falling behind in class, doing poorly on exams or papers, and receiving lower grades overall (Engs, Diebold, & Hanson, 1996; Presley, Meilman, & Cashin, 1996a; Presley, Meilman, Cashin, & Lyerla,1996b; Wechsler et al., 2002). Although some published research studies have not found a statistically significant association between binge drinking and academic performance (Howland et al., 2010; Paschall & Freisthler, 2003; Gill, 2002; Wood, Sher, & McGowan, 2000), studies linking binge drinking to poorer academic performance outnumber the former studies 2 to 1. Presley and Pimentel (2006) report that, in a national survey of college students, those who engaged in binge drinking and drank at least three times per week were 5.9 times more likely than those who drank but never binged to perform poorly on a test or project (40.2% vs. 6.8%), 5.4 times more likely to have missed a class (64.4% vs. 11.9%), and 4.2 times more likely to have had memory loss as a result of drinking (64.2% vs. 15.3%) (Thombs et al., 2009). Singleton (2007) and Singleton and Wolfson (2009), in separate prospective studies, both found negative associations between heavy alcohol use and grade point average. Jennison (2004), based on a national prospective study reported binge drinkers in college were more likely to drop out of college, work in less prestigious jobs, and experience alcohol dependence 10 years later. Wechsler et al. (2000) and Powell et al. (2004), based on a national survey of full-time students at four year colleges and universities, found frequent binge drinkers were six times more likely than nonbingers to miss class and 5 times more likely to fall behind in school. White, Jamieson-Drake, and Swartzwelder (2002) observed that the number of blackouts, a consequence of heavy drinking, students reported was negatively associated with GPA. Collectively, the existing research suggests that heavier drinking is associated with poorer academic success.

ALCOHOL BLACKOUTS

Heavy episodic drinking can lead to a form of memory impairment known as a blackout. Blackouts are periods of amnesia during which a person actively engages in behaviors (e.g., walking, talking) but the brain is unable to create memories for the events. Blackouts are quite different from "passing out," which means either falling asleep from excessive drinking or literally drinking oneself unconscious. During blackouts, people are capable of participating in events ranging from the mundane, such as eating food, to the emotionally charged, such as fights and even sexual intercourse, with little or no recall (Goodwin, 1995). Like milder alcohol-induced short-term memory impairments caused by one or two drinks, blackouts are primarily "anterograde," meaning that they involve problems with the formation of new memories rather than problems recalling memories made prior to intoxication. For this reason, during a blackout, an intoxicated person is able to discuss events that happened before the drinking session commenced even if the discussion itself is not stored in memory.

Blackouts are quite common among college students who consume alcohol. White et al. (2002) reported that half (51%) of roughly 800 college students who had ever consumed alcohol at any point in their lives reported experiencing at least one alcohol-induced blackout, defined as awakening in the morning not able to recall things one did or places one went while under the influence. The average number of total blackouts in those who experienced them was six. Of those who had consumed alcohol during the 2 weeks before the survey was administered, 9% reported blacking out.

Blackouts tend to occur following consumption of relatively high doses of alcohol. In a study by White, Signer, Kraus, and Swartzwelder (2004), in which students with a history of blackouts were interviewed about their most recent blackout, estimated peak BACs during the night of the last blackout were generally similar for males (0.30%) and females (0.35%). A study of amnesia in people arrested for either public intoxication, driving under the influence or underage drinking found that the probability of a blackout was 50% at BAC levels of 0.31% or higher (Perry et al., 2006). In their study of blackouts in college students, Hartzler and Fromme (2003) noted a steep increase in the likelihood of blackouts above a BAC of 0.25%. Thus, from existing research, it appears the odds of blacking out increase as BAC levels climb and become quite common at BAC levels approaching or exceeding 0.30%, which is almost 5 times the legal limit for operating a motor vehicle for those aged 21 and older. As such, the high prevalence of blackouts in college students points to the magnitude of excessive consumption that occurs on college campuses.

ALCOHOL AND ADOLESCENT NEUROCOGNITIVE DEVELOPMENT

Although acute alcohol use produces short-term impairments in cognitive functions, such as attention and memory, related to academic success, a growing body of research suggests that heavy drinking during the adolescent years could produce lingering deficits that might further compromise academic achievement. In a longitudinal study,

Squeglia, Spadoni, Infante, Myers, and Tapert (2009) assessed cognitive functions in healthy subjects at ages 12 to 14 and then during a follow up session on average 3 years later. For females, more drinking days in the year before follow-up and more drinks per month predicted deficits in visuospatial memory. For males, greater hangover symptoms in the year before the follow-up predicted impairments in attention. In a longitudinal study beginning when subjects were ages 13 to 18 and spanning the next 10 years, Hanson, Medina, Padula, Tapert, and Brown (2011) reported that greater alcohol use independently predicted declines in verbal memory over time relative to controls. In a cross-sectional study of college students, Parada et al. (2011, 2012) observed that, compared to controls, students with a history of recent binge drinking exhibited deficits in the ability to remember items on lists, a fundamental skill critical to academic achievement.

Brain research is beginning to shed light on the potential mechanisms underlying the lingering cognitive deficits observed in heavy drinking adolescents, though such work remains in the early stages. Some researchers report decreased activity in frontal lobe regions during tests of memory in binge drinking adolescents compared to controls (Crego et al., 2010), while others report increased activation the frontal lobes in binge drinkers compared to controls (Schwiensburg, Mcqueeny, Nagel, Eyler, & Tapert, 2010). Anatomically, a wide array of structural changes have been observed in adolescents who drink heavily, including reduced frontal lobe gray and white matter volumes in females (Medina et al., 2008; Squeglia, 2011) and increased gray and white matter volumes in males (Medina et al., 2008; Squeglia et al., 2011).

Collectively, the findings of this relatively new area of research suggest that alcohol can impact academic-related cognitive functions long after acute intoxication wears off and that such impairments might stem from alcohol-induced changes in brain morphometry and function during adolescent development.

ALCOHOL AND DRUG USE AMONG COLLEGE STUDENTS

A smaller percentage of college students use either illicit drugs or misuse prescription drugs than engage in binge drinking. However, compared with students who do not binge drink, those who do are considerably more likely to engage in prescription drug misuse or use illicit drugs. More than one third of binge drinkers also use drugs, and the combination of alcohol with prescription or illicit drugs can increase significantly the risk of harm. See Table 1.1.

ALCOHOL OVERDOSES

When consumed in large quantities during a single occasion, such as a binge episode, alcohol can cause death directly by suppressing brain stem nuclei that control vital reflexes, like breathing and gagging to clear the airway (Miller & Gold, 1991). Even

Table 1.1 Drug Use Among College Students and College Students Who Binge Drink, Ages 18–25

		1999	2001	2005	2007	2009
All Respondents	Prescription Drug Misuse*	4				
	Total	3	5	7	6	7
	College	4	5	6	5	6
	Non-College		6	7	7	7
	Illicit Drug Use†					
	Total	19	21	22	21	23
	College	20	22	21	21	24
	Non-College	18	21	22	22	23
	Any Drug Use					
	Total	20	23	24	24	26
	College	21	23	23	23	26
	Non-College	20	23	25	24	26
Respondents Who Binge	Prescription Drug Misuse*					
	Total	6	8	10	9	10
	College	6	7	9	8	10
	Non-College	7	9	10	10	10
	Illicit Drug Use†					
	Total	30	32	31	31	34
	College	32	33	32	31	36
	Non-College	29	31	30	31	33
	Any Drug Use					
	Total	32	34	34	35	37
	College	33	34	35	34	39
	Non-College	31	34	34	35	36

National Household Survey on Drug Use and Health, 2011

*Illicit drug use: marijuana, cocaine, crack, heroin, hallucinogens, and inhalants

†Prescription drug misuse: pain relievers, tranquilizers, and stimulants/sedatives

a single session of binge drinking causes inflammation and transient damage to the heart (Zagrosek, Messroghli, Schulz, Dietz, & Schultz-Menger, 2010). The acute toxic effects of alcohol in the body can manifest in symptoms of alcohol poisoning, which include vomiting, slow and irregular breathing, hypothermia, mental confusion, stupor and death (NIAAA, 2007; Oster-Aaland, Lewis, Neighbors, Vangsness, & Larimer, 2009). Using data from the Global Burden of Disease study, the World Health Organization (WHO) estimated that, in 2002, alcohol poisoning caused 65,700 deaths worldwide, with 2,700 poisoning deaths occurring in the United States (WHO, 2009b). It has become increasingly common to read news stories about alcohol overdoses among college students and their non college peers, a fact that is perhaps not surprising given the tendency toward heavy drinking in this age group.

Alcohol interacts with a wide variety of illicit and prescription drugs, including opioids and related narcotic analgesics, sedatives and tranquilizers (NIAAA, 1995; Tanaka, 2002). Importantly, blood alcohol concentrations (BAC) required for fatal overdoses are lower when alcohol is combined with prescription drugs. An analysis of 1,006 fatal poisonings due to alcohol alone or in combination with other drugs revealed that the median postmortem BAC in those who overdosed on alcohol alone was 0.33%, compared to 0.13% to 0.17% among those who overdosed on a combination of alcohol and prescription drugs (Koski, Ojanperä, & Vuori, 2003; Koski, Vuori, & Ojanperä, 2005). The combined use of alcohol and other drugs peaks in the 18- to 24-year-old age group (McCabe, Cranford, & Boyd, 2006).

To investigate the prevalence of hospitalizations for alcohol overdoses—which stem from excessive intoxication or poisoning—among college-aged young people in the United States, White and colleagues (2011) examined rates of inpatient hospitalizations for 18- to 24-year-olds between 1999 and 2008 using data from the Nationwide Inpatient Sample, which contains hospital discharge records from roughly 20% of all hospitals in the country. Hospitalizations for alcohol overdoses without any other drugs involved increased 25% among 18- to 24-year-olds from 1999 to 2008, highlighting the risks involved in heavy drinking. In total, nearly 30,000 young people 18 to 24, more males (19,847) than females (9,525), were hospitalized for alcohol overdoses in 2008. Hospitalizations for overdoses involving drugs only increased 55% over the same time period, while those involving alcohol and drugs in combination rose 76%. All total, 59,000 hospitalizations in 2008 of 18- to 24-year-olds for alcohol overdoses only or in combination with drugs occurred (nearly 30,000), approximately one third of whom were college students, 35.6% of the population that age.

Data from the Drug Abuse Warning Network (DAWN) indicate that emergency department (ED) visits for alcohol-related events exhibited increases similar to those observed for inpatient hospitalizations. Among those ages 18 to 20, ED visits for alcohol-related events with no other drugs increased 19% from 67,382 cases in 2005 to 82,786 cases in 2009. Visits related to combined use of alcohol and other drugs increased 27%, from 27,784 cases in 2005 to 38,067 cases in 2009. In 2009, 12% of ED visits related to alcohol involved use of alcohol in combination with other drugs (Substance Abuse and Mental Health Services Association, 2011).

The above findings reflect the fact that heavy consumption of alcohol quickly can become a medical emergency. One does not need to get behind the wheel of a car after drinking or jump off a balcony into a swimming pool on a dare to risk serious harm. Simply drinking too much alcohol is enough to require hospitalization and potentially cause death. Further, combining alcohol with other drugs can increase substantially the risk of requiring medical intervention. Thus, efforts to minimize the consequences of alcohol-related harms on college campuses should not lose sight of the fact that alcohol often is combined with other drugs and, when this is the case, the risks can be greater than when alcohol or drugs are used alone.

STUDENTS AT HIGH RISK

The proportion of college students who drink varies depending on where they live. Drinking rates are highest in fraternities and sororities, followed by on-campus housing (e.g., dormitories, residence halls) (Presley et al., 1996a, 1996b; Wechsler et al., 1998; Wechsler et al., 2000a). Students who live independently off-campus (e.g., in apartments) drink less, while commuting students who live with their families drink the least (O'Hare, 1990; Wechsler et al., 2002).

A number of environmental influences working in concert with other factors may affect students' alcohol consumption (Presley et al., 2002). Colleges and universities where excessive alcohol use is more likely to occur include schools where Greek systems dominate (i.e., fraternities and sororities), schools where athletic teams are prominent, and schools located in the Northeast (Presley et al., 1996a, 1996b; Wechsler, Kuh, & Davenport, 1996; Wechsler, Davenport, Dowdall, Grossman, & Zanakos, 1997; Wechsler et al., 1998; Wechsler et al., 2000b; Werner & Greene, 1992).

Among college student males, Caucasians, members of fraternities and sororities, and athletes have the highest percentages of students who drink the most (Johnston, O'Malley, & Bachman, 2001a, 2001b; Meilman, Leichliter, & Presley, 1999; Meilman, Presley, & Lyerla, 1994; Presley et al., 1996a, 1996b; Presley & Pimentel, 2006; Wechsler et al., 1996, 1997, 1998, 2000b). The least amount of drinking occurs in 2-year schools, religious schools, commuter schools, and historically black colleges and universities (Meilman, Presley, & Cashin, 1995; Presley et al., 1996a, 1996b; Wechsler et al., 2000a, 2000b).

Some first-year students who live on campus may be at particular risk for alcohol misuse. During their high school years, those who go on to college tend to drink less than their noncollege–bound peers. But during the first few years following high school, the heavy drinking rates of college students surpass those of their noncollege peers, and this rapid increase in heavy drinking over a relatively short period of time can contribute to difficulties with alcohol and with the college transition in general (Schulenberg et al., 2001; Timberlake et al., 2007). Anecdotal evidence suggests that the first 6 weeks of enrollment are critical to first-year student success. Because many students initiate heavy drinking during these early days of college, the potential exists for excessive alcohol consumption to interfere with successful adaptation to campus life. The transition to college is often so difficult to negotiate that about one third of first-year students fail to enroll for their second year (Upcraft, 2000).

INTERVENTIONS TO REDUCE COLLEGE DRINKING

The increase in the past 7 years in alcohol-related traffic and other unintentional injury deaths among 18- to 24-year-olds, both in college and not in college, underscores the need for colleges and their surrounding communities to expand and strengthen interventions demonstrated to reduce excessive drinking among college students and those in the same age-group who do not attend college. Numerous individually oriented counseling approaches, web-based educational programs, environmental interventions, and comprehensive community interventions can reduce drinking and related problems among college students and the college-aged population. Information on individually oriented interventions, web-based educational programs, family interventions, and campus/community comprehensive interventions are covered in detail in other chapters of this book. This chapter examines environmental policy intervention.

Environmental interventions: Legal drinking age of 21. In 1984, when 17 states had a legal drinking age of 21, the U.S. Congress passed legislation that would withhold highway construction funding for states that did not make it illegal to sell alcohol to people younger than age 21. By 1988, all states adopted the law (Fell, Fisher, Voas, Blackman, & Tippetts, 2009).

However, there are some important exceptions. In 24 states, individuals under 21 can possess alcohol with parental or guardian consent and/or presence. In 31 states, parents can legally furnish alcohol to their children who are under 21. Only 31 states and the District of Columbia explicitly prohibit consumption by a person under 21. In 47 states, people under 21 can serve alcohol (NIAAA, 2010).

In August 2008, a group of 130 college presidents called for a debate about whether the drinking age should be lowered to age 18. Some suggested, after receiving education about safe drinking levels, that 18-year-olds should be given drinking licenses that would be rescinded if their drinking posed dangers to themselves or others. Given this widely publicized challenge to the legal drinking age of 21, it is worth reviewing evidence on the topic. Figure 1.2 examines trends in the frequency of binge drinking from 1982 to 2007 (five or more drinks on an occasion) from Monitoring the Future, a yearly survey assessment of the attitudes, behaviors, and values of nearly 50,000 8th, 10th, and 12th graders (Johnston, O'Malley, Bachman, & Schulenberg, 2007). According to the survey data, binge drinking among high-school seniors dropped from 40% to just over 25%. Among individuals 1 to 4 years past high school, the declines were less, from 40% to just under 35%. Little change was seen among full-time college students. Figure 1.3 examines trends in alcohol-related traffic fatalities among individuals aged 18 to 20 targeted by the drinking age changes and those aged 21 to 24 not targeted. Both groups experienced proportional declines, but the declines were greater in the 18- to 20-year age group than in the 21- to 24-year age group (60% vs. 44%).

A review of 49 studies of the legal drinking age changes revealed that in the 1970s and 1980s, when many states lowered the drinking age, alcohol-related traffic crashes among people younger than 21 increased 10%. In contrast, when states increased the legal drinking age to 21, alcohol-related crashes among people younger than 21 decreased 16% (Shults et al. 2001). Wagenaar and Toomey (2002) reviewed 48 studies of the effects of drinking-age changes on drinking and 57 studies on traffic crashes. They concluded that increases in the legal age of alcohol purchase and consumption

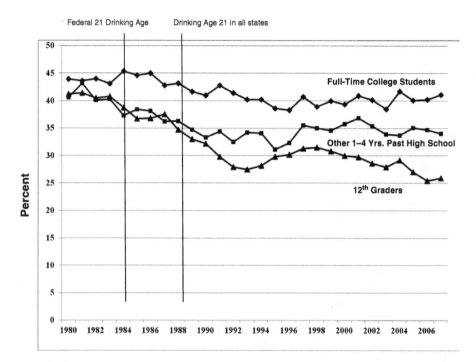

Figure 1.2 Alcohol: Trends in 2-Week Prevalence of 5 or More Drinks in a Row Among College Students versus Others 1–4 Years Beyond High School
Source: Monitoring the Future, 2007.

have been the most successful interventions to date in reducing drinking and alcohol-related crashes among people under 21.

Miron and Tetelbaum (2009) found significant declines in traffic fatalities among individuals under 21 in states that changed the minimum legal drinking age to 21 prior to the 1984 federal mandate to raise the drinking age to 21. However, in states that raised the drinking age after the federal legislation, the minimum legal drinking age increases were not associated with significant declines in traffic deaths. Miron and Tetelbaum's analyses controlled for whether states had a seatbelt law, the legal blood alcohol limit, beer taxes, and vehicle miles traveled. Of note, Miron and Tetelbaum did not explore whether the traffic deaths were alcohol-related. After adjusting for changes in the population for that age during the time period 1982 to 2007, alcohol-related traffic fatalities among people aged 16 to 20 declined 64%, whereas those that did not involve alcohol increased 17% (see Figure 1.4) (Hingson & White, 2010).

In 2009, Fell, Fisher, Voos, Blackman, and Tippetts examined trends in the ratio of drinking to nondrinking drivers in fatal crashes in each state annually from 1982 to 2004 (unlike Miron and Tetelbaum's [2009] analyses). This analysis controlled for

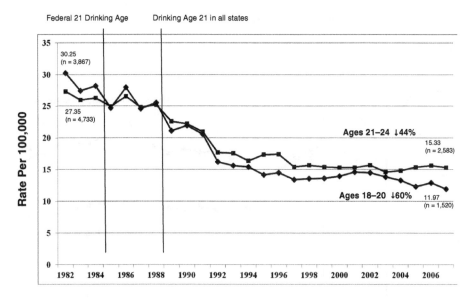

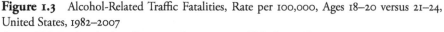

Figure 1.3   Alcohol-Related Traffic Fatalities, Rate per 100,000, Ages 18–20 versus 21–24, United States, 1982–2007

Source: U.S. Fatality Analysis Reporting System, 2009; U.S. Census Bureau, 2009.

zero-tolerance laws, graduated license night restrictions, and use/lose laws that target drivers under 21 and could influence their involvement in alcohol-related crashes. Fell et al. (2009) also controlled for 0.10% and 0.08 BAC per se laws, legal limits, mandatory seatbelt laws, per capita beer consumption, unemployment rates, vehicle miles traveled, frequency of sobriety checkpoints, number of licensed drivers, and the ratio of drinking to nondrinking drivers aged 26 or older in fatal crashes.

Fell et al.'s (2009) findings are quite informative. Adoption of the minimum legal drinking age of 21 was associated with a 16% decline in the ratio of drinking to nondrinking drivers in fatal crashes involving those under 21, even after controlling for all the other factors listed above. Of note, other laws targeting drivers under 21 independently predicted lower involvement of drinking drivers in fatal crashes. Use/lose laws and zero-tolerance laws were each associated with 5% declines. Further, laws aimed at adult drivers also independently contributed to declines in the ratio of drinking to nondrinking drivers in fatal crashes: 0.08% BAC laws were independently associated with an 8% decline, 0.10% BAC laws a 7% decline, administrative license revocation a 5% decline, and seatbelt laws a 3% decline. Thus, the preponderance of evidence suggests that raising the drinking age to 21 reduced alcohol involvement in fatal crashes involving drivers under 21 and that other laws aimed at drivers of all ages can also reduce alcohol-related fatal crashes involving drivers under the age of 21.

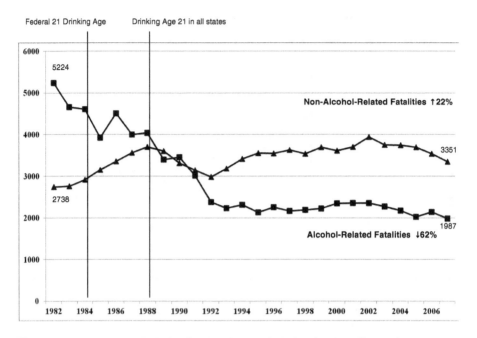

Figure 1.4 Trends in Alcohol-Related and Non–alcohol-Related Traffic Fatalities, Persons Ages 16–20, United States, 1982–2007
Source: U.S. Fatality Analysis Reporting System, 2009.

Carpenter and Dobkin (2011) explored data from 1975 to 1993 from the Fatality Analysis Reporting System and Vital Statistics. They also looked at national annual Monitoring the Future survey data. They found that lowering the drinking age was associated with a 17% increase in 18- to 20-year-old involvement in nighttime fatal crashes, the fatal crashes most likely to involve alcohol. Daytime fatal crash rates did not change. No other age group experienced an increase in nighttime fatal crashes. In the 18- to 20-year-old age group, suicides increased 10%, past month drinking increased 17%, and binge drinking increased 3%. Because suicides are not consistently tested for alcohol, any direct causal link between drinking age and that outcome should be cautiously interpreted.

Of note, an analysis (Norberg, Bierut, & Grucza, 2009) of more than 33,000 adult respondents in two national surveys 10 years apart compared respondents who grew up in states where they legally were allowed to drink prior to age 21 with respondents who grew up in states where the legal drinking age was 21. The analysis, which controlled for numerous potential confounding variables, found that those allowed legally to drink prior to age 21 were more likely as adults to meet alcohol and drug use disorder criteria.

Zero-tolerance laws. Zero-tolerance laws, which make it illegal in every state for those under the age of 21 to drive after any drinking, also have contributed to declines in alcohol-related traffic deaths among people younger than 21 (Hingson, Heeren,

& Winter, 1994; Liang & Huang, 2008; Voas, Tippetts, & Fell, 2000; Wagenaar, O'Malley, & Lafond, 2001). Unfortunately, despite their demonstrated benefits, legal drinking age and zero-tolerance laws generally have not been vigorously enforced (Jones & Lacey, 2001). Young drivers are substantially underrepresented in the driving-while-intoxicated (DWI) arrest population relative to their contribution to the alcohol-related crash problem (Voas & Williams, 1986). Stepped-up enforcement of alcohol purchase laws aimed at sellers and buyers has been shown to be effective in reducing alcohol misuse and related problems (Preusser, Ulmer, & Preusser, 1992; Wagenaar, Murray, & Toomey, 2000). More enforcement could further reduce college drinking problems.

Price of alcohol. The majority of published studies have reported an inverse relation between the tax on or price of alcohol and alcohol misuse and related negative health outcomes. The National Academy of Sciences (National Research Council Institute of Medicine of the National Academies, 2004) reviewed the literature on price of alcohol and alcohol-related problems and recommended that Congress and State legislatures raise excise taxes to reduce underage alcohol consumption and to raise additional revenues to reduce underage drinking problems.

Three recent extensive literature reviews examined the relation of alcohol price and tax with consumption and related harms (Elder et al., 2010; Wagenaar, Salois, & Komro, 2009; World Health Organization Regional Office for Europe, 2009). Wagenaar et al.'s (2009) analysis of 1,003 separate estimates from 112 studies reported "overwhelming evidence of the effects of alcohol prices on drinking. Price affects drinking of all types of beverages and across the population of drinkers, from lightest to heavy drinkers." They concluded, "We know of no other preventive intervention to reduce drinking that has the numbers of studies and consistency of effects seen in the literature on alcohol taxes and prices." Minimal research regarding price and alcohol has examined college students. Further research is needed about the effects of price increases on (1) college students relative to others the same age and (2) college-age people relative to older people. Similar to Wagenaar et al. (2009), Elder et al.'s (2010, p. 226) review of 78 alcohol tax studies found "consistent evidence that higher alcohol prices and taxes are associated with reductions in both excessive alcohol consumption and related subsequent harms. Results were robust across different countries, time periods, study designs, analytic approaches, and outcomes."

A World Health Organization review (2009) concluded,

> When other factors are held constant, such as income and the price of other goods, a rise in alcohol prices leads to less alcohol consumption and less alcohol-related harm, and vice versa. . . . Policies that increase alcohol prices delay the time when young people start to drink, slow their progression towards drinking large amounts, and reduce their heavy drinking and volume of alcohol drunk on an occasion. (p. 13)

Although very high prices for alcohol might stimulate illegal production, in the United States alcohol prices have not kept pace with inflation over the past 60 years.

Alcohol outlet density. Higher alcohol outlet density has been associated with increased alcohol-related problems in both cross-sectional and prospective studies, and reducing outlet density may reduce drinking-related problems (Campbell et al., 2009). Alcohol outlet density around college campuses has been found to be related to higher levels of alcohol problems among college students (Reboussin, Song, & Wolfson, 2011; Scribner et al., 2008; Weitzman , Folkman, Folkman, & Wechsler, 2003), including higher campus rape offense rates (Scribner et al., 2010) and in one study, was linked to alcohol misuse prevention programs having lower positive benefit (Scribner et al., 2011). Prospective research is needed to specifically test whether reducing outlet density will reduce consumption, related problems, and specific effects on college students.

CONCLUSIONS

Alcohol misuse on college campuses continues to be a significant problem, and one complicated by the increase in prescription and illicit drug use among students, and the combination of alcohol with these substances. Despite considerable expansion of the scientific literature and knowledge base regarding how to reduce drinking and related harms among college students, binge drinking, driving under the influence of alcohol, and unintentional injuries attributable to alcohol have not declined. An important research question is how to translate our new knowledge into reductions in alcohol misuse and related problems in the future. Research also is needed in colleges and universities that serve minority populations, an area that has been underrepresented in college research initiatives.

As documented in other chapters in this book, there is now a sizable scientific literature, which demonstrates that individually oriented approaches such as screening and brief motivational interventions can reduce drinking not only among students who voluntarily seek out these programs but also among those mandated to receive counseling because of alcohol-related disciplinary actions. Unfortunately, these interventions are not reaching a sizeable portion of college students with problematic drinking practices. Persons age 18 to 24 nationwide are least likely to be asked by physicians about their drinking and advised about drinking patterns that pose risk to health (Hingson, Heeren, Edwards, & Saitz, 2011).

Although nearly 20% of college students meet *DSM-IV* alcohol dependence or abuse criteria, less than 5% of them have sought counseling or treatment (NIAAA, 2007). An important challenge is to sufficiently expand screening and counseling so that these effective individually oriented interventions can achieve general population-level effects. Establishing alcohol screening and brief intervention as a routine part of student health service encounters and use of the Internet screening and advice might help remedy this situation.

Also, a variety of environmental policy interventions that reduce availability of alcohol and deter driving while impaired by alcohol have been shown to be effective in reducing drinking and driving and alcohol-related crash involvement of college-aged individuals. These policies must, however, be implemented and enforced at the community level. Recent research evidence now indicates that colleges and universities can reduce harmful drinking and drinking and driving among college students through the use of comprehensive cooperative college–community multicomponent approaches that include heightened enforcement of the legal drinking age and other laws aimed to reduce drinking and driving.

But clearly colleges by themselves cannot resolve the alcohol problems of all college-aged people. For every 18- to 24-year-old college student, two 18- to 24-year-olds are not in college. Further, many college students develop problematic drinking habits before they enter college. Analyses of the national College Alcohol Survey indicates that the younger college students were when they first drank to intoxication, the greater the likelihood that they experienced alcohol dependence while they were in college, rode with drinking drivers, drove after drinking, were injured under the influence of alcohol, and had unplanned and unprotected sex after drinking (Hingson, Heeren, Winter, & Wechsler, 2003; Hingson, Heeren, Zakocs, Kopster, & Wechsler, 2002). Hence, community conditions and the availability of alcohol to those under 21 contribute to college drinking problems. Further, many of the problems experienced as a result of excessive college student alcohol consumption affect people other than the college drinkers themselves.

Consequently, colleges and surrounding communities need to work together to implement multifaceted programs at various levels of intervention. Collectively, they need to involve multiple departments of city government as well as concerned private citizens and organizations and multiple sectors of the college community, presidents, deans, other administrators, campus security, residence counselors, health service providers, alumni, faculty, and students if they want to most effectively reduce harmful drinking and the myriad of health and social problems linked to harmful drinking.

REFERENCES

Campbell, C. A., Hahn, R. A., Elder, R., Chattopadhyay S. K., Fielding, J., Naimi T., ...Task Force on Community Preventive Services (2009). The effectiveness of limiting alcohol outlet density as a means of reducing excessive alcohol consumption and alcohol-related harms. *American Journal of Preventive Medicine, 37*(6), 556–569. PMID: 19944925

Carpenter, C., & Dobkin, C. (2011). The minimum legal drinking age and public health. *Journal of Economic Perspectives, 25*(2), 3–156.

Crego, A., Rodriguez-Holguín, S., Parada, M., Mota, N., Corral, M., & Cadaveira, F. (2010). Reduced anterior prefrontal cortex activation in young binge drinkers during a visual working memory task. *Drug Alcohol Dependence, 109*(1–3), 45–56.

Elder, R. W., Lawrence, B., Ferguson, A., Naimi, T. S., Brewer, R. D., Chattopadhyay, S. K., ...Task Force on Community Preventive Services. (2010). The effectiveness of tax policy interventions for reducing excessive alcohol consumption and related harms. *American Journal of Preventive Medicine, 38*(2), 217–229. PMID: 20117579

Engs, R.C., Diebold, B.A., & Hanson, D. J. (1996). The drinking patterns and problems of a national sample of college students, 1994. *Journal of Alcohol Drug Education, 41*, 13–33.

Fell, J., Fisher, D. A., Voas, R. B., Blackman, K., & Tippetts, A. S. (2009). The impact of underage drinking laws on alcohol-related fatal crashes of young drivers. *Alcoholism: Clinical and Experimental Research, 33*(7), 1208–1219. PMID: 19389192

Gill, J. S. (2002). Reported levels of alcohol consumption and binge drinking within the UK undergraduate student population over the last 25 years. *Alcohol and Alcoholism, 37*(2), 109–120.

Goodwin, D. W. (1995). Alcohol amnesia. *Addiction,* 90, 315–317.

Hanson, K. L., Medina, K. L, Padula, C. B, Tapert, S. F, & Brown, S. A. (2011). Impact of adolescent alcohol and drug use on neuropsychological functioning in young adulthood: 10-year outcomes. *Journal of Child & Adolescent Substance Abuse, 20*(2), 135–154.

Hartzler, B., & Fromme, K. (2003). Fragmentary blackouts: Their etiology and effect on alcohol expectancies. *Alcoholism: Clinical and Experimental Research, 27*(4), 628–637.

Hingson, R. W., Heeren, T., Edwards, E.M., & Saitz, R. (2011). Young adults at risk for excess alcohol consumption are often not asked or counseled about drinking alcohol. *Journal of General Internal Medicine.* Epub ahead of print.

Hingson, R., Heeren, T., & Winter, M. (1994). Lower legal blood-alcohol limits for young drivers. *Public Health Reports, 109*(6), 738–744. PMID: 7800781

Hingson, R., Heeren, T., Winter, M. R., & Wechsler, H. (2003). Early age of first drunkenness as a factor in college students' unplanned and unprotected sex attributable to drinking. *Pediatrics 111*(1), 34–41. PMID: 12509551

Hingson, R., Heeren, T., Winter, M., & Wechsler, H. (2005). Magnitude of alcohol-related mortality and morbidity among U.S. college students ages 18–24: Changes from 1998 to 2001. *Annual Review of Public Health, 26*, 259–279.

Hingson, R., Heeren, T., Zakocs, R., Kopster, A., &Wechsler, H. (2002). Magnitude of alcohol-related mortality and morbidity among U.S. college students ages 18–24. *Journal of Studies on Alcohol, 63*(2), 136–144.

Hingson, R., Heeren, T., Zakocs, R., Winter, M., & Wechsler, H. (2003). Age of first intoxication, heavy drinking, driving after drinking and risk of unintentional injury among U.S. college students. *Journal of Studies on Alcohol, 64*(1), 23–31. PMID: 12608480

Hingson, R., & White, A. (2010). Magnitude and prevention of college alcohol and drug misuse: U.S. college students ages 18–24. In J. Kay & V. Schwartz (Eds.), *Mental health in the college community.* London, England: Wiley.

Hingson, R., Zha, W., & Weitzman, E. R. (2009). Magnitude of and trends in alcohol-related mortality and morbidity among U.S. college students ages 18–24, 1998–2005. *Journal of Studies on Alcohol and Drugs, Supp. 16*, 12–20. PMID: 19538908

Howland, J., Rohsenow, D. J., Greece, J. A., Littlefield, C. A., Almeida, A., Heeren, T., ... Hermos J. (2010). The effects of binge drinking on college students' next-day academic test-taking performance and mood state. *Addiction, 105*(4), 655–665.

Jennison, K. M. (2004). The short-term effects and unintended long-term consequences of binge drinking in college: A 10-year follow-up study. *American Journal of Drug and Alcohol Abuse, 30*(3), 659–684.

Johnston, L. D., O'Malley, P. M., & Bachman, J. G. (2001a). *Monitoring the future national survey results on drug use, 1975–2000. Vol. I: Secondary school students.* NIH Publication No. 01–4924. Bethesda, MD: National Institute on Drug Abuse.

Johnston, L. D., O'Malley, P. M., & Bachman, J. G. (2001b). *Monitoring the future national survey results on drug use,1975–2000. Vol. II: College students and adults ages 19–40.* NIH Publication No. 01–4925. Bethesda, MD: National Institute on Drug Abuse.

Johnston, L. D., O'Malley, P. M., Bachman, J. G., & Schulenberg, J. E. (2007). *Monitoring the future national survey results on drug use, 1975–2006. Vol. II: College students and adults ages 19–45.* Bethesda, MD: National Institute on Drug Abuse. (NIH Publication No. 07–6206)

Jones, R., & Lacey, J. (2001). *Alcohol and highway safety 2001: A review of the state of knowledge.* Washington, DC: National Highway Traffic Safety Administration. (Report No. DOT HS–809–383)

Knight, J. R., Wechsler, H., Kuo, M., Seibring, M., Weitzman, E. R., & Schuckit, M.A. (2002). Alcohol abuse and dependence among U.S. college students. *Journal of Studies on Alcohol, 63*(3), 263–270.

Koski, A., Ojanperä, I., & Vuori, E. (2003). Interaction of alcohol and drugs in fatal poisonings. *Human and Experimental Toxicology, 22*, 281–287.

Koski, A., Vuori, E., & Ojanperä, I. (2005). Relation of postmortem blood alcohol and drug concentrations in fatal poisonings involving amitriptyline, propoxyphene and promazine. *Human and Experimental Toxicology, 24*, 389–96.

Liang, L., & Huang, J. D. (2008). Go out or stay in? The effects of zero tolerance laws on alcohol use and drinking and driving patterns among college students. *Health Economics, 17*(11), 1261–1275. PMID: 18219708

McCabe, S. E., Cranford, J. A., & Boyd, C. J. (2006). The relationship between past-year drinking behaviors and nonmedical use of prescription drugs: Prevalence of co-occurrence in a national sample. *Drug Alcohol Dependence, 1*, 281–288.

Medina, K. L., Mcqueeny, T., Nagel, B. J., Hanson, K. L., Schweinsburg, A. D., & Tapert, S. F. (2008). Prefrontal cortex volumes in adolescents with alcohol use disorders: Unique gender effects. *Alcoholism: Clinical and Experimental Research, 32*(3), 386–394.

Meilman, P. W., Leichliter, J. S., & Presley, C.A. (1999). Greeks and athletes: Who drinks more? *Journal of American College Health, 47*(4), 187–190.

Meilman, P. W., Presley, C. A., & Cashin, J. R. (1995). The sober life at the historically black colleges. *Journal of Blacks in Higher Education, 9*, 98–100.

Meilman, P. W., Presley, C. A., & Lyerla, R. (1994). Black college students and binge drinking. *Journal of Blacks in Higher Education, 8*, 70–71.

Miller, N. S., & Gold, M. S. (1991). *Alcohol.* New York, NY: Plenum Press.

Miron, J. A., & Tetelbaum, E. (2009). Does the minimum legal drinking age save lives? *Economic Inquiry, 47*(2), 317–336.

National Institute on Alcohol Abuse and Alcoholism. (1995). Alcohol-medication interactions. *Alcohol Alert, 27.*

National Institute on Alcohol Abuse and Alcoholism. (2007). *Parents—Spring break is another important time to discuss college drinking.* Bethesda, MD: National Institutes of Health, DHHS. (NIH Publication No. 05–5642)

National Institute on Alcohol Abuse and Alcoholism. (2007). *What colleges need to know now: An update on college drinking research.* Bethesda, MD: National Institutes of Health, DHHS. (NIH Publication No. 07–5010)

National Institute on Alcohol Abuse and Alcoholism. (2010). *Alcohol policy information system.* Available at www.alcoholpolicy.niaaa.nih.gov/

National Research Council Institute of Medicine of the National Academies. (2004). *Reducing underage drinking: A collective responsibility.* Washington, DC: National Academies Press.

Norberg, K. E., Bierut, L. J., & Grucza, R. A. (2009). Long-term effects of minimum drinking age laws on past-year alcohol and drug use disorders. *Alcoholism: Clinical and Experimental Research 33*(12), 2180–2190. PMID: 19775322

O'Hare, T. M. (1990). Drinking in college: Consumption patterns, problems, sex differences and legal drinking age. *Journal of Studies on Alcohol, 51*(6), 536–541.

Oster-Aaland, L., Lewis, M. A., Neighbors, C., Vangsness, J., & Larimer, M. E. (2009). Alcohol poisoning among college students turning 21: Do they recognize the symptoms and how do they help? *Journal of Studies on Alcohol and Drugs, Suppl 16*, 122–130.

Parada, M., Corral, M., Caamaño-Isorna, F., Mota, N., Crego, A., Holguín, S. R., & Cadaveira, F. (2011). Binge drinking and declarative memory in university students. *Alcoholism Clinical and Experimental Research, 35*, 1475–1484.

Parada, M., Corral, M., Mota, N., Crego, A., Rodríguez Holguín, S., & Cadaveira, F. (2012). Executive functioning and alcohol binge drinking in university students. *Addictive Behaviors, 37*(2), 167–172.

Paschall, M. J., & Freisthler, B. (2003). Does heavy drinking affect academic performance in college? Findings from a prospective study of high achievers. *Journal of Studies on Alcohol, 64*, 515–519.

Perry, P. J., Argo, T. R., Barnett, M. J., Liesveld, J. L., Liskow, B., Hernan, J. M., Trnka, M. G., & Brabson, M. A. (2006). The association of alcohol-induced blackouts and grayouts to blood alcohol concentrations. *Journal of Forensic Science 51*(4), 896–899.

Powell, L. A., Williams, J., & Wechsler, H. (2004). Study habits and the level of alcohol use among college students. *Education Economics, 12*(2), 135–149.

Presley, C. A., Leichliter, J. S., & Meilman, P. W. (1998). *Alcohol and drugs on America college campuses: A report to college presidents. Third in a series: 1995, 1996, and 1997.* Carbondale, IL: Core Institute, Southern Illinois University.

Presley, C. A., Meilman, P. W., & Cashin, J. R. (1996a). *Alcohol and drugs on American college campuses: Use, consequences, and perceptions of the campus environment. Vol. IV: 1992–94.* Carbondale, IL: Core Institute.

Presley, C. A., Meilman, P. W., Cashin, J. R., & Lyerla, R. (1996b). *Alcohol and drugs on American college campuses: Use, consequences, and perceptions of the campus environment. Vol. III: 1991–93.* Carbondale, IL: Core Institute.

Presley, C. A., Meilman, P. W., & Leichliter, J. S. (2002). College factors that influence drinking. *Journal of Studies on Alcohol, Suppl 14*, 82–90.

Presley, C. A., & Pimentel, E. R. (2006). The introduction of the heavy and frequent drinker: A proposed classification to increase accuracy of alcohol assessments in postsecondary educational settings. *Journal of Studies on Alcohol, 67*(2), 324–331.

Preusser, D., Ulmer, R., & Preusser, C. (1992). *Obstacles to enforcement of youthful (under 21) impaired driving.* Washington, DC: National Highway Traffic Safety Administration. (DOT HS 807–878)

Reboussin, B. A., Song, E. Y., & Wolfson, M. (2011). The impact of alcohol outlet density on the geographic clustering of underage drinking behaviors within census tracts. *Alcoholism: Clinical and Experimental Research, 35*(8), 1541–1549.

Schulenberg, J., Maggs, J. L., Long, S. W., Sher, K. J., Gotham, H. J., Baer, J.S., Kivlahan, D. R.,... Zucker, R. A. (2001). The problem of college drinking: Insights from a developmental perspective. *Alcoholism: Clinical and Experimental Research, 25*(3), 473–477.

Schweinsburg, A. D., Mcqueeny, T., Nagel, B. J., Eyler, L. T., & Tapert, S. F. (2010).A preliminary study of functional magnetic resonance imaging response during verbal encoding among adolescent binge drinkers. *Alcohol, 44*(1), 111–117.

Scribner, R. A., Mason, K. E., Simonsen, N. R., Theall, K., Chotalia, J., Johnson, S., . . . DeJong, W. (2010). An ecological analysis of alcohol outlet density and campus-reported violence at 32 U.S. colleges. *Journal of Studies on Alcohol and Drugs, 71*, 184–191. PMID: 20230715

Scribner, R., Mason, K., Theall, K., Simonsen, N., Schneider, S. K., Towvim, L.G., & DeJong, W. (2008). The contextual role of alcohol outlet density in college drinking. *Journal of Studies on Alcohol and Drugs, 69*(1), 112–120.

Scribner, R. A., Theall, K., Mason, K., Simonsen, N., Schneider, S. K., Towvim, L. G., & DeJong, W. (2011). Alcohol prevention on college campuses: The moderating effect of the alcohol environment on the effectiveness of social norms marketing campaigns. *Journal of Studies on Alcohol and Drugs, 72*(2), 232–239.

Shults, R. A., Elder, R. W., Sleet, D.A., Nichols, J. L., Alao, M. O., Carande-Kulis, V. G., ... Task Force on Community Preventive Services. (2001). Reviews of evidence regarding interventions to reduce alcohol-impaired driving. *American Journal of Preventive Medicine, 21, Supp l 4*, 66–88. PMID: 11691562

Singleton, R. A. (2007). Collegiate alcohol consumption and academic performance. *Journal of Studies on Alcohol and Drugs, 68*, 548–555.

Singleton, R. A. Jr., & Wolfson, A. R. (2009). Alcohol consumption, sleep, and academic performance among college students. *Journal of Studies on Alcohol and Drugs, 70*(3), 355–363.

Squeglia, L. M., Spadoni, A. D., Infante, M. A., Myers, M. G., & Tapert S. F. (2009). Initiating moderate to heavy alcohol use predicts changes in neuropsychological functioning for adolescent girls and boys. *Psychology of Addictive Behaviors, 23*(4), 715–722.

Squeglia, L. M., Sorg, S. F., Schweinsburg, A. D., Wetherill, R. R., Pulido, C., & Tapert, S. F. (2011). Binge drinking differentially affects adolescent male and female brain morphometry. *Psychopharmacology.* [Epub ahead of print]

Substance Abuse and Mental Health Services Administration. (2000). *Summary of findings of the 1999 national household survey on drug abuse.* Rockville, MD: Substance Abuse and Mental Health Services Administration. (DHHS Publication No. SMA 003466)

Substance Abuse and Mental Health Services Administration. (2002). *Results from the 2001 national household survey on drug abuse: Volume 1: Summary of national findings.* Rockville, MD: Substance Abuse and Mental Health Services Administration, (DHHS Publication No. SMA 02-3758, 2002)

Substance Abuse and Mental Health Services Administration. *Results from the 2005 National Survey on Drug Use and Health: National Findings.* Rockville, MD: Substance Abuse and Mental Health Services Administration, 2006 (DHHS Publication No. SMA 06-4194).

Substance Abuse and Mental Health Services Administration. (2008). *Results from the 2007 national survey on drug use and health: National findings.* NSDUH Series H-34, DHHS Publication No. SMA 08-4343. SAMHSA, Rockville MD.

Substance Abuse and Mental Health Services Administration. (2011). *The DAWN Report: Trends in Emergency Department Visits Involving Underage Alcohol Use: 2005 to 2009.* Rockville, MD.

Tanaka, E. (2002). Toxicological interactions between alcohol and benzodiazepines. *Journal of Toxicology: Clinical Toxicology, 40,* 69–75.

Thombs, D. L., Olds, R. S., Bondy, S. J., Winchell, J., Baliunas, D., & Rehm, J. (2009). Undergraduate drinking and academic performance: a prospective investigation with objective measures. *Journal of Studies on Alcohol and Drugs, 70*(5), 776–785.

Timberlake, D. S., Hopfer, C. J., Rhee, S. H.; Friedman, N. P., Haberstick, B.C., Lessem, J. M., & Hewitt, J. K. (2007). College attendance and its effect on drinking behaviors in a longitudinal study of adolescents. *Alcoholism: Clinical and Experimental Research, 31*(6), 1020–1030.

Upcraft, M. L. (2000). *Today's first-year students and alcohol.* Paper prepared for the Task Force on College Drinking, National Advisory Council on Alcohol Abuse and Alcoholism, Bethesda, MD.

Voas, R. B., & Williams, A. F. (1986). Age differences of arrested and crash-involved drinking drivers. *Journal of Studies on Alcohol, 47*(3), 244–248. PMID: 3724162

Voas, R. B., Tippetts,A. S., & Fell, J. (2000). The relationship of alcohol safety laws to drinking drivers in fatal crashes. *Accident Analysis and Prevention, 32*(4), 483–492. PMID: 10868751

Wagenaar, A. C., Murray, D. M., & Toomey, T. L. (2000). Communities mobilizing for change on alcohol (CMCA): Effects of a randomized trial on arrests and traffic crashes. *Addiction, 95*(2), 209–217. PMID: 10723849

Wagenaar, A. C., O'Malley, P. M., & Lafond, C. (2001). Lowered legal blood alcohol limits for young drivers: Effects on drinking, driving, and driving-after-drinking behaviors in 30 states. *American Journal of Public Health, 91*(5), 801–804. PMID: 11344892

Wagenaar, A. C., Salois, M. J., & Komro, K. A. (2009). Effects of beverage alcohol price and tax levels on drinking: A meta-analysis of 1003 estimates from 112 studies. *Addiction, 104*(2), 179–190. PMID: 19149811

Wagenaar, A. C., & Toomey, T. L. (2002). Effects of minimum drinking age laws: Review and analyses of the literature from 1960 to 2000. *Journal of Studies on Alcohol, Suppl 14,* 206–225. PMID: 12022726

Wechsler, H., Davenport, A. E., Dowdall, G. W., Grossman, S. J., & Zanakos, S.I. (1997). Binge drinking, tobacco, and illicit drug use and involvement in college athletics. A survey of students at 140 American colleges. *Journal of American College Health, 45*(5), 195–200.

Wechsler, H., Dowdall, G. W., Davenport, A., & Castillo, S.. (1995). Correlates of college student binge drinking. *American Journal of Public Health, 85*(7), 921–926.

Wechsler, H., Dowdall, G. W., Maenner, G., Gledhill-Hoyt, J., & Lee, H. (1998). Changes in binge drinking and related problems among American college students between 1993 and 1997. Results of the Harvard School of Public Health College Alcohol Study. *Journal of American College Health, 47*(2), 57–68.

Wechsler, H., Kuh, G., & Davenport, A. E. (1996). Fraternities, sororities and binge drinking: Results from a national study of American colleges. *NASPA Journal, 33*(4), 260–279.

Wechsler, H., Lee, J. E., Kuo, M., & Lee, H. (2000). College binge drinking in the 1990s: A continuing problem: Results of the Harvard School of Public Health 1999 College Alcohol Study. *Journal of American College Health, 48*(5), 199–210.

Wechsler, H., Lee, J. E., Kuo, M., Seibring, M., Nelson, T. F., & Lee, H. (2002). Trends in college binge drinking during a period of increased prevention efforts. Findings from 4 Harvard School of Public Health College Alcohol Study surveys: 1993–2001. *Journal of American College Health 50*(5), 203–217.

Weitzman, E. R., Folkman, A., Folkman, M. P., & Wechsler, H. (2003). The relationship of alcohol outlet density to heavy and frequent drinking and drinking-related problems among college students at eight universities. *Health Place, 9*(1), 1–6.

Werner, M.J., & Greene, J.W. (1992). Problem drinking among college freshman. *Journal of Adolescent Health*, 13, 487–492.

White, A. M. (2003). What happened? Alcohol, memory blackouts, and the brain. *Alcohol Research and Health, 27*(2), 186–196.

White, A. M., Hingson, R. W., Pan, I. J., & Yi, H. Y. (2011). Hospitalizations for alcohol and drug overdoses in young adults ages 18–24 in the United States, 1999–2008: Results from the nationwide inpatient sample. *Journal of Studies on Alcohol and Drugs, 72*(5), 774–786.

White, A. M., Jamieson-Drake, D. W., & Swartzwelder, H. S. (2002). Prevalence and correlates of alcohol–induced blackouts among college students: Results of an e-mail survey. *Journal of American College Health, 51*, 117–131.

White, A. M., Signer, M. L., Kraus, C. L., & Swartzwelder, H. S. (2004). Experiential aspects of alcohol–induced blackouts among college students. *American Journal of Drug and Alcohol Abuse 30*(1), 205–224.

Wood, M. D., Sher, K. J., & Mcgowan, A. K. (2000). Collegiate alcohol involvement and role attainment in early adulthood: Findings from a prospective high-risk study. *Journal of Studies on Alcohol 61*(2), 278–289.

World Health Organization Regional Office for Europe. (2009). Evidence for the effectiveness and cost–effectiveness of interventions to reduce alcohol-related harm. Copenhagen, Denmark: World Health Organization.

Zagrosek, A., Messroghli, D., Schulz, O., Dietz, R., & Schultz-Menger, J. (2010). Effect of binge drinking on the heart as assessed by cardiac magnetic resonance imaging. *Journal of the American Medical Association, 304*, 1328–1330.

2

College Student Drug Use

Prevalence and Consequences

Jeffrey S. Simons, Raluca M. Gaher, Tyler B. Wray, and Ryan N. Reed

The typical college student falls in the 18- to 23-year-old age bracket variously described as older adolescents, young adults, or emerging adults (Arnett, 2000). This is a developmental period characterized by increased exploration associated with a highly active reward-seeking system that is not yet fettered by a fully developed system of executive control (Steinberg, 2008; Wiers et al., 2007). This heightened tendency to explore is developmentally advantageous. Young adults have energy, enthusiasm, and an interest in trying new things, which facilitate learning and skill development. Parting with convention, they question the world around them and bring new answers to long-standing truths and social mores. Young adulthood brings newfound legal rights and responsibilities not afforded to minors; as such, it is a time of both enhanced freedom and accountability. For most college students who live independent of parental supervision for the first time, this developmental period is commonly accompanied by a sudden and dramatic change in their social groups and freedom (Arnett, 2000; Schulenberg & Maggs, 2002). This creates an ideal context for heightened risk taking in all forms. It should come as no surprise, then, that college students use drugs.

This chapter reviews prevalence estimates of common drugs of abuse and research on related negative consequences among college students. Risks and consequences of drug use should be viewed in light of appreciation for the positive aspects of impulsivity, risk taking, and reward seeking. As the introduction suggests, increased impulsivity and risk taking during this period is not entirely negative (Gullo & Dawe, 2008). Like alcohol, experimentation and low-level illicit drug use are intertwined with normative developmental transitions and a number of positive psychosocial aspects such as social cohesion, enjoyment, and relaxation (Lee, Maggs, Neighbors, & Patrick, 2011; Maggs, 1997; Park, 2004; Schulenberg & Maggs, 2002; Simons & Arens, 2007; Simons, Dvorak, & Lau-Barraco, 2009). Heightened risk taking among college students may serve an important role in development, and some of these risks involve drugs and alcohol.

Prevalence estimates of drug use produce a number of distinct values that represent different aspects of drug-taking behavior. The literature abounds with estimates of current, past year, or lifetime use, percent of individuals in treatment for various drugs, and rates of hospital admissions that are drug-related. Similarly, there are estimates of prevalence of any use, problematic use, and substance use disorders. Each of these estimates may tell a different story. Estimates of lifetime use are quite high for several illicit drugs, yet rates of current use and use-related problems are markedly lower. All too often (or perhaps fortunately), public perception may overestimate the scope of drug use among college students. Given the well-established associations between social norms (i.e., perceptions of peer use) and drug use (Martens et al., 2006; Neighbors, Geisner, & Lee, 2008; Perkins, Meilman, Leichliter, Cashin, & Presley, 1999), it is important that drug use among college students is not portrayed as more commonplace than the data indicate. When possible, this review seeks to provide multiple prevalence estimates in order to portray and integrate diverse perspectives on the scope of college student drug use.

Estimates of consequences of drug use also take many forms. An accurate understanding of the severity of the problem requires consideration of consequences at multiple levels and, depending on one's goal (e.g., individual risk assessment, education, or intervention versus prevention programming), consideration of prevalence of use of the drug in the population. From a population-wide prevention standpoint, the relative merits of reducing use of a prevalent drug with minor negative consequences versus reducing use of a rarely used drug with severe negative consequences needs to be considered. In this regard, our review considers acute problems associated with intoxication as well as short- and long-term, or future, consequences associated with regular use.

This book focuses on both prevention and treatment of excessive alcohol use in college students. As such, it is important for a review of drug use to consider the costs and benefits in terms of the individual, the public at-large, and relative to other drugs (e.g., alcohol) that may be the target of limited prevention and treatment resources. Considering these issues with respect to the range of drugs that college students use, this book's focus on alcohol is well justified. Alcohol consumption is far more widespread than even the most commonly used illicit drug (i.e., marijuana), and only the less prevalent drugs, such as heroin, prescription medications, and cocaine, incur risk for overdose like alcohol does. Considering the rate of use and the consequences across the population, all illicit drugs combined pose less of a threat to the health of college students than alcohol.

Nonetheless, alcohol and illicit drug use frequently co-occur and combined use is associated with compounded problems (McCabe, Knight, Teter, & Wechsler, 2005; Midanik, Tam, & Weisner, 2007; Simons & Carey, 2006). In addition, though alcohol may pose the greatest risk to student health due to its prevalence and associated health risks, the prevalence of other drug use and associated problems is substantial. Thus, illicit drug use needs to be addressed in prevention and intervention programs. In some respects, secondary or tertiary alcohol interventions are an ideal venue for addressing use of other drugs as the target population for those interventions is at heightened risk for use of drugs aside from alcohol.

Structure of the chapter. The initial portion of this chapter is organized by drug and reviews the prevalence of use, and the acute, short-term and long-term consequences of each, including epidemiological data about the prevalence of diagnoses for substance use disorders. Although a comprehensive review of the health-related consequences of each drug is beyond the scope of this chapter, a brief overview of potential consequences and common associated features is provided. However, because causal associations between drugs and particular negative outcomes are frequently not established, it is worth pointing out that some "consequences" may be more accurately labeled *associated problems.* Nonetheless, these are psychosocial problems and health risks known to be elevated in users of the drugs and warrant attention. The second portion of the chapter reviews data on demographic and other factors associated with use prevalence. Finally, we present a summary of the chapter and discuss differences in substance use as a function of college enrollment.

PREVALENCE AND CONSEQUENCES

This section provides an overview of the prevalence, consequences, and problems associated with common drugs of abuse.

Marijuana

Marijuana is by far the most commonly used illicit drug among U.S. college students (see Table 2.1 for prevalence of marijuana and other selected drugs). Across several national epidemiological surveys, approximately half of U.S. college students and young adults report having used marijuana. Lifetime prevalence of marijuana use increases from 47.3% (for those ages 18 to 20) to 55.6% for those ages 21 to 25 (Substance Abuse and Mental Health Services Administration [SAMHSA], 2010a). Estimates from the Monitoring the Future (MTF) study are similar, with 47.5% of college students reporting having used marijuana in their lifetime (Johnston, O'Malley, Bachman, & Schulenberg, 2010a). The results from the CORE survey indicate 45.1% of college

Table 2.1 Prevalence of Select Drugs by College Enrollment Status in the 2009 NSDUH

		Lifetime	Annual	Past Month	Abuse or Dependence[a]
Marijuana	College Students	49.0	34.7	20.2	6.2
	Others 18–22	52.4	33.2	19.0	6.6
Methamphetamine	College Students	1.5	0.5	0.2	*
	Others 18–22	3.8	1.1	0.3	*
Prescription Stimulants[b]	College Students	15.8	9.7	3.0	0.3
	Others 18–22	13.5	5.9	1.8	0.6
Cocaine	College Students	9.3	5.3	1.7	0.5
	Others 18–22	15.5	6.1	1.3	1.2
Heroin	College Students	0.9	0.4	0.2	0.2
	Others 18–22	1.9	0.6	0.2	0.3
Prescription Pain Relievers	College Students	20.2	11.4	4.5	1.2
	Others 18–22	25.6	13.1	5.5	2.3
Sedatives	College Students	1.5	0.6	0.2	0.0
	Others 18–22	1.6	0.5	0.3	0.2
Tranquilizers	College Students	9.7	5.5	1.9	0.3
	Others 18–22	13.4	5.8	1.9	0.6
Ecstasy	College Students	9.1	5.2	1.3	*
	Others 18–22	13	5.4	1.4	*
Hallucinogens[c]	College Students	15.4	9.4	2.6	0.4
	Others 18–22	19.1	8.4	2.2	1.0
Ketamine, Rohypnol, GHB	College Students	1.4	0.5[d]	0.2[d]	*
	Others 18–22	2.1	0.2[d]	0.0[d]	*
Inhalants	College Students	8.5	1.9	0.5	0.1
	Others 18–22	11.5	2.4	0.5	0.3
Tobacco	College Students	64.4	48.3	34.1	6.7[e]
	Others 18–22	69.6	55.6	46.1	20.8[e]

Note. College students means students aged 18–22 enrolled full time. Figures are percentages. *Estimates are unavailable. [a]Indicates individuals meeting criteria for either dependence or abuse in the past year. [b]NSDUH includes methamphetamine in these estimates. The category includes non medical use of medications such as Adderall, Ritalin, etc. [c]These estimates include ecstasy as well LSD, PCP, and other hallucinogens. [d]Estimates include only Ketamine and GHB. [e]Estimates based on dependence criteria according to the Nicotine Dependence Syndrome Scale (NDSS) and the Fagerstrom Test of Nicotine Dependence (FTND) for individuals reporting cigarette smoking in the past month. NSDUH-National Survey on Drug Use and Health students have tried marijuana (CORE Institute, 2010). In contrast, approximately 16% of 8th graders, 32% of 10th graders, and 42% of 12th graders reported using marijuana in their lifetime (Johnston, O'Malley, Bachman, & Schulenberg, 2010b). Thus, as students transition into high school, the percent who have tried marijuana roughly doubles, and is followed by a steady increase in lifetime use prevalence each year through age 25. These figures suggest that although the greatest increase in use initiation occurs during the early teen years, a fair number try marijuana for the first time while in college (Gledhill-Hoyt, Lee, Strote, & Wechsler, 2000). Despite this, past-year prevalence for 18- to 25-year-olds lies at a much lower 30.6%, and past-month use at 18.1% in the 2009 National Survey on Drug Use and Health (NSDUH). Past-month use by college students 18 to 22 has increased slightly from approximately 17.9% in 2008 to 20.2% in 2009 (SAMHSA, 2010a). Similar rates are found in both the 2008 CORE survey and the 2009 Monitoring the Future survey, with past-month use in college students estimated at 17.3% and 18.5%, respectively. The 2008 CORE survey indicates 6.7% of college students use marijuana three times a week or more. In summary, about half of college students have experimented with marijuana; however, a much smaller percentage report using it in the past month and an even smaller proportion report using it three times a week or more. This suggests that a relatively small percentage of those who experiment with the drug transition to using it regularly (Beck et al., 2009; Johnston, O'Malley, & Bachman, 2002). Results from the MTF study suggest that lifetime, past year, and past month prevalence of marijuana use among college students is slightly less than their noncollege peers. For example, 18.5% of college students versus 21.8% of noncollege peers report having used marijuana in the past 30 days. Whereas annual use prevalence is similar across the groups, daily use among college students (4.9%) is considerably less than among noncollege peers (7.9%).

The prevalence of marijuana use may be high, in part, because the perceived risk of marijuana use is relatively low. For example, only 15% of college students in the 2008 CORE survey indicated there was "great risk" in occasional marijuana use, though 43% considered regular use to be of "great risk." Results from the 2009 MTF survey are similar, indicating that 18% to 27% of 18- to 26-year-olds consider occasional marijuana use to be of great risk and roughly 43% to 52% reported regular use to be of great risk (Johnston et al., 2010a). Interestingly, despite the relatively high prevalence of marijuana use, the data suggest that marijuana use is not socially sanctioned. In the 2008 CORE survey, 44% indicated their friends would disapprove of trying marijuana once or twice.

Marijuana use is not without negative consequences. Though the extent, severity, and nature of associated problems is a matter of debate, marijuana use is associated with a number of health-related problems, including respiratory problems, such as lung cancer (Aldington, et al., 2007; Aldington et al., 2008; Earleywine & Barnwell, 2007; Hall & Degenhardt, 2009; Looby & Earleywine, 2007), deficits in areas of cognitive functioning, such as verbal learning, working memory, and response per-severation (Hanson et al., 2010; Lane, Cherek, Tcheremissine, Steinberg, & Sharon, 2007); mental health–related problems (Buckner, Ecker, & Cohen, 2010; Looby & Earleywine, 2007); and impaired impulse control and error monitoring (Hester, Nestor, & Garavan, 2009; Lane, Cherek, Tcheremissine, Lieving, & Pietras, 2005; McDonald, Schleifer, Richards, & de Wit, 2003). The acute and long-term effects of marijuana on cognitive functioning may contribute to other health-risk behaviors.

Indeed, marijuana use is associated with a number of behavioral consequences. For example, marijuana use is positively associated with sexual risk behavior (Griffin, Botvin, & Nichols, 2006; Simons, Maisto, & Wray, 2010), traffic accidents (Hall & Degenhardt, 2009), and poor academic performance (Buckner et al., 2010). College students perceive less risk and are more tolerant of driving under the influence of marijuana relative to alcohol (McCarthy, Lynch, & Pederson, 2007). Though there is some evidence that individuals may be more effective in compensating for the degree of impairment from marijuana relative to alcohol (Ligouri, Gatto, & Jarrett, 2002), like alcohol, marijuana impairs driving abilities and increases the risk of ac-cidents (Bedard, Dubois, & Weaver, 2007; Hall & Degenhardt, 2009; Ronen et al., 2008; Sewell, Poling, & Sofuoglu, 2009). Use is also associated with poor academic performance (Buckner et al., 2010). Academic impairment likely is a function of both individual difference factors as well as effects of marijuana interfering with academic performance and cognitive functioning. However, longitudinal examina-tion of associations between marijuana use and educational attainment shows little effect (Bachman et al., 2007). In respect to sexual risk behavior, it is unclear whether associations between marijuana use and sexual behavior are due to correlated indi-vidual difference factors (i.e., people who use marijuana are more likely to engage in sexual risk behaviors) or to the acute effects of marijuana. The results of laboratory studies regarding marijuana's effects on risk taking (e.g., Lane et al., 2005) suggest that marijuana may have a causal association with sexual risk behavior, but further evidence from laboratory studies is still needed.

Among young adults 18 to 25, 5.5% met criteria for a marijuana use disorder in 2009 (SAMHSA, 2010a). Table 2.2 presents consequences associated with marijuana use in a sample of 438 college students who reported using marijuana at least once in the past 6 months. As can be seen, reported problems are quite common, and more than a third of respondents reported trying to reduce their use. Though more than a third report efforts to try to control their use and more than one quarter report their use interfering with schoolwork or other responsibilities, only 10% would consider that they have a "problem" with marijuana. As such, even individuals who recognize marijuana use interfering with their functioning may be unlikely to seek treatment. Prevention and intervention programs that focus on increasing motivation for change

Table 2.2 Marijuana Consequences Among 438 College Students Who Reported Any Marijuana Use in the Past 6 Months

Consequence	Percent Endorsed in Past 6 Months
1. Went to work or school high	35.84
2. Neglected your responsibilities	34.25
3. Tried to cut down or quit smoking marijuana	34.03
4. Had a bad time	30.43
5. Not able to do homework or study for a test	26.71
6. Felt that you needed more marijuana than you used to use in order to get the same effect	26.48
7. Tried to control your marijuana use by trying to smoke only at certain times of the day or certain places	21.00
8. Kept smoking marijuana when you promised yourself not to	20.14
9. Felt you were going crazy	18.08
10. Missed out on other things because you spent too much money on marijuana	17.12
11. Missed a day (or part of a day) of school or work	16.44
12. Was told by a friend or neighbor to cut down on smoking marijuana	13.50
13. Noticed a change (for the worse) in your personality	13.01
14. Suddenly found yourself in a place you could not remember getting to	12.81
15. Caused shame or embarrassment to someone	11.42
16. Felt physically or psychologically dependent on marijuana	10.53
17. Felt that you had a problem with marijuana	10.50
18. Had a fight, argument, or bad feelings with a friend	7.78
19. Passed out or fainted suddenly	6.86
20. Got into fights, acted bad, or did mean things	5.48
21. Had a fight, argument, or bad feelings with a family member	5.03
22. Had withdrawal symptoms, that is, felt sick because you stopped or cut down	4.57
23. Relatives avoided you	3.88

Note. Simons 2010, unpublished data.

and avoiding traditional connotations associated with substance use disorder treatment may be advantageous to promote adaptive change in this population.

Methamphetamine, Amphetamine, and Prescription Stimulants

In recent years, there has been considerable alarm regarding methamphetamine use due to its rapid increase in prevalence in certain areas of the country, its high potential for addiction, and dramatic pernicious effects (Grant et al., 2007; Rawson, Gonzales, & Ling, 2006; Rawson, Gonzales, McCann, & Ling, 2007). In 2006, National Geographic featured a show on methamphetamine with the title, "The World's Most Dangerous Drug." There were an estimated 731,000 current users of methamphetamine in the United States aged 12 or older (0.3% of the population) in 2006, with young adults age 18 to 25 being the most likely to have used methamphetamines in the past year (SAMHSA, 2007). The highest rates of past year use were reported on the West coast and rural areas (as high as 4.6% in Wyoming) and lowest rates on the East coast (0.3% in New York; 0.4% in Connecticut; SAMHSA, 2006a). Nationally, from 1995 to 2005, methamphetamine treatment admissions increased from 30 to 68 per 100,000 population (SAMHSA, 2008). Notably, in 2005, Hawaii, Oregon, Iowa, and Washington had a treatment admission rate of 220 or more per 100,000 population (SAMHSA, 2008). Likewise, methamphetamine-related admissions to emergency rooms nationwide increased by 54% between 1995 and 2002 (Drug Abuse Warning Network, 2003). Finally, methamphetamine accounted for 32% of substance use treatment admissions in rural counties and 26% of admissions in the most urban counties (SAMHSA, 2006a). Though these statistics are dramatic, the prevalence of use in absolute terms has remained low. For instance, in 2005, past-month prevalence of methamphetamine use in the general population was 0.2% and this rate had not significantly changed since 2002 (SAMHSA, 2006b), although there was a significant increase among full-time college students aged 18 to 22 from 0.2% in 2004 to 0.5% in 2005 (SAMHSA, 2006b).

The 2009 National Survey on Drug Use and Health indicates a decline in rates of past month methamphetamine use among individuals 12 and older between 2006 and 2008 and a slight increase to 0.2% in 2009 (SAMHSA, 2010a). Treatment and emergency room admissions due to methamphetamine use have also declined in recent years (SAMHSA, 2009; SAMHSA, 2010b). Rates of current methamphetamine use among young adults 18 to 25 have dropped from 0.6% in 2002 to 0.2% in 2009 (SAMHSA, 2010a). Among college students, 0.7% to 1% report lifetime use of methamphetamine or crystal meth (Johnston et al., 2010a). In some regions of the country, however, estimates are higher. For example, in a large rural Midwest sample, 5% of college students had used methamphetamine in their lifetime and 1.6% reported using it in the past 6 months (Simons, Dvorak, & Batien, 2008). Although elevated prevalence rates in certain regions of the country are certainly a concern, the prevalence rates among young adult college students, even in the more affected areas, are low, and are considerably lower than one might intuit based on media reports. Decreases in methamphetamine use may be the result of increased awareness of health consequences.

Methamphetamine abuse is associated with tremendous short- and long-term health consequences. Methamphetamine is characteristically smoked, injected, snorted, or taken orally (Meredith, Jaffe, Ang-Lee, & Saxon, 2005). Acute effects can include paranoia, agitation, violent behavior, anxiety, and hallucinations (National Institute on Drug Abuse [NIDA], 2002). The rapid development of tolerance to methamphetamine's effects may lead to using at extremely high frequencies and quantities over time (Davidson, Gow, Lee, & Ellinwood, 2001; Meredith et al., 2005). Using at such high levels puts chronic methamphetamine users at increased risk for overdose (Angrist, 1994; Hong, Matsuyama, & Nur, 1991). Repeated methamphetamine use may result in deleterious effects across a wide variety of bodily systems. Widespread vasoconstriction may lead to serious cardiac or neurological events, including myocardial infarction, spontaneous intra-cerebral and retinal hemorrhages, or acute kidney failure (Lineberry & Bostwick, 2006). In summary, negative consequences of methamphetamine abuse are widely recognized (Castro, Barrington, Walton, & Rawson, 2000; Rawson et al., 2006), but fortunately the use of methamphetamine among college students is relatively low.

In contrast to the relatively low use of forms of methamphetamine, lifetime use of other amphetamines is considerably higher. Lifetime use of amphetamines increased from 2008 to 2009, from 9.1% to 11.8% (Johnston et al., 2010a). Results from the CORE survey are similar, with 11.1% reporting amphetamine use in their lifetime, 5.0% reporting use in the past year, 2.4% reporting use in the past 30 days, and 1.2% reporting using three times per week or more (CORE Institute, 2010). Much of reported amphetamine use in these national surveys is illegal use of prescription stimulants. Misuse, or illicit use, of prescription drugs may be defined as use of a controlled substance without a prescription, using more than prescribed, or using the drug for purposes other than prescribed. For example, a large web-based survey indicated past-year prevalence of illicit use of prescription stimulants to be 5.9%, with approximately 75% of these students reporting use of an amphetamine-dextroamphetamine drug, such as Adderall (Teter, McCabe, LaGrange, Cranford, & Boyd, 2006). In the 2009 Monitoring the Future study, annual prevalence rates for college students were 7.9% (Adderall), 1.6% (Ritalin), and 0.2% (Provigil).

The 2009 NSDUH survey reports that, among those age 18 to 25, lifetime use of stimulants, such as methamphetamine, desoxyn, or methedrine is 4.5%, prescription diet pills is 2.1%, amphetamine, dextroamphetamine, and phentermine products is 4.2%, and bethylphenidate or dexmethylphenidate products is 5.3% (SAMHSA, 2010a). Adderall should fall into the amphetamine-dextroamphetamine category. However, it does not appear to be included as a core drug for the computation.

Adderall is one of the more common prescription stimulants that are misused. Results from the 2009 NSDUH indicate the past-year prevalence of misuse of prescription stimulants including Adderall among college students to be 9.7%, a rate significantly higher than their non–college attending peers (5.9%). Recent studies warn about the widespread availability of prescription stimulants on college campuses, as well as increases in recreational use of these drugs among college students from their freshman to sophomore year (Arria, Caldeira, O'Grady, et al., 2008a; Arria & DuPont, 2010). Arria and colleagues (2008a) reported an increase in lifetime nonmedical prescription stimulant use of more than 318% over the course of the first two years of college to 22.6% of sophomores in their sample.

Nonmedical use of prescription stimulants by college students is often motivated by perceived benefits, such as weight control or enhancement of educational performance (Bogle & Smith, 2009; Outram, 2010; Teter et al., 2006; White, Becker-Blease, & Grace-Bishop, 2006) and by social and recreational purposes (De-Santis, Webb, & Noar, 2008; Labbe & Maisto, 2010; White et al., 2006). Though use may be thought to enhance academic performance, evidence for this is mixed (Greely et al., 2008; Outram, 2010) and nonmedical prescription stimulant use is inversely associated with GPA (McCabe et al., 2005a). As prescription drugs, these may be perceived as relatively safe and lacking the stigma associated with illicit drug use (DeSantis et al., 2008). However, some results indicate that, although prescription stimulants are perceived as carrying less risk than cocaine, they are perceived as more risky than marijuana and more risky than moderate to heavy weekly alcohol use (Arria, Caldeira, Vincent, O'Grady, & Wish, 2008b). Approximately 25% of college students reported perceiving occasional nonmedical use of prescription stimulants as having "great risk" (Arria et al., 2008b). In contrast, approximately 7% reported occasional marijuana use as posing "great risk" (Arria et al., 2008b). In spite of these perceptions of risk, recent reports have suggested that an increasing number of college students may manipulate the route of administration of prescription stimulants in order to increase the effects (Bright, 2008). Examples include crushing or "cooking" pills (mixing them with water and heating them) to snort or inject them (Bright, 2008; Hall, Irwin, Bowman, Frankenberger, & Jewett, 2005; White et al., 2006). Increasing the intensity of the drug has its own dangers and snorting and injection add the associated risks of these methods of administration (e.g., damage to mucous membranes, infection; Strang et al., 1998).

Acute intoxication and prolonged use of stimulants, including prescription stimulants, is associated with several negative consequences, including difficulty sleeping, increased aggressiveness, anxiety, tension, paranoia, and irritability (Berman, Kuczenski, McCracken, & London, 2009; Caplan, Epstein, Quinn, Stevens, & Stern, 2007; Sommers, Baskin, & Baskin-Sommers, 2006). Serious or life-threatening complications may result, including seizures, hyperthermia, and serotonin syndrome (a potentially deadly reaction resulting in highly elevated levels of serotonin in the brain)

(Caplan et al., 2007). Sudden deaths and adverse cardiovascular effects have been reported as a result of prescription stimulant use and have led to increased FDA warnings and safety review (FDA, 2011; Gould et al., 2009; Smith, 2006; Sussman, Pentz, Spruijt-Metz, & Miller, 2006). Illicit use of prescription stimulants is positively associated with other drug use and related problems (McCabe et al., 2005a; McCabe & Teter, 2007), verbal memory deficits (Reske, Eidt, Delis, & Paulus, 2010) and depression (Teter, Falone, Cranford, Boyd, & McCabe, 2010). Mixing stimulants with alcohol leads to a diminished subjective sense of drunkenness (Barrett & Pihl, 2002). This can result in the ingestion of larger quantities of alcohol, while missing the warning signs of intoxication that would normally signal a person to stop drinking (Caplan et al., 2007). Moreover, combining high doses of alcohol and prescription stimulants may have toxic effects (Caplan et al., 2007; Markowitz, Logan, Diamond, & Patrick, 1999). The concurrent use of prescription stimulants and alcohol is particularly relevant to college students because this population is characterized by high rates of drinking. Several studies have also shown that college students who use stimulants are also more likely to binge drink (see Arria & DuPont, 2010, for review). Finally, there are legal consequences that may result from using nonprescribed stimulants. Often, college students are unaware of the legal ramifications involved in sharing prescription drugs with others or using medication not prescribed to them (Arria & DuPont, 2010). This lack of awareness can further increase college students' risk of legal problems. Taken together, these findings indicate a wide variety of negative effects associated with the illicit use of prescription stimulants, including physiological, psychological, and social consequences.

Cocaine

Approximately 8% to 9% of college students report lifetime use of cocaine (CORE Institute, 2010; Johnston et al., 2010a). Use has been fairly stable in the past decade and is dramatically less than in the mid-1980s when more than 20% of students reported having tried cocaine. Use in the past year is about 4% to 5%, and 1% to 2% report using cocaine in the past 30 days (CORE Institute, 2010; Johnston et al., 2010a). Reported use of crack cocaine is quite low, with 0.1% of college students reporting use of crack cocaine in the past 30 days (Johnston et al., 2010a). Cocaine is both highly addictive and poses substantial risk of overdose (Pottieger, Tressell, Inciardi, & Rosales, 1992) that can result in cardiac arrest or respiratory depression (Maraj, Figueredo, & Lynn Morris, 2010; Tseng, Derlet, Stark, & Albertson, 1991). Cocaine use is associated with both acute and long-term cognitive deficits in decision making, attention, learning, and memory (Lundqvist, 2005, 2010; Verdejo-Garcia et al., 2007). Depending on the route of administration, individuals who use cocaine are at increased risk for HIV infection, destruction of the nasal septum, or respiratory problems (Brand, Gonggrijp, & Blanksma, 2008; Devlin & Henry, 2008; Restrepo et al., 2007; Tyndall et al., 2003).

Long-term use of the stimulant can lead to cardiac problems (Maraj et al., 2010), and extended use and withdrawal are associated with depression, which carries its own risks (Bohnert & Miech, 2010; Helmus, Downey, Wang, Rhodes, & Schuster, 2001; Sofuoglu & Kosten, 2005). Though cocaine use has considerable acute and long-term health risks, its use on college campuses is fortunately relatively low. Nonetheless, given that up to 5% of college students report using cocaine in the past year, it poses a significant risk for student health.

Opiates, Prescription Pain Killers, Tranquilizers, and Sedatives

In recent years, lifetime use of heroin among college students peaked at 1.7% in 2000, declined to 0.5% in 2005, and increased to 0.8% in 2009 (Johnston et al., 2010a). Past month heroin use among college students is quite low, estimated at 0.1% in 2009 (Johnston et al., 2010a). Although heroin has considerable risk for dependence, overdose, and associated health problems (especially if used intravenously), the low prevalence indicates it is not a substantial problem on college campuses. In contrast, lifetime use of narcotics other than heroin is substantial and has steadily increased since the early 1990s, peaking at 14.6% in 2006 (Johnston et al., 2010a). Lifetime use of narcotics was estimated at 14% in 2009, representing a 1.6% increase since 2008. Use in the past 30 days is considerably lower, with 2.7% reporting having used narcotics other than heroin in the past 30 days in 2009 (Johnston et al., 2010a). Reports from the NSDUH appear higher, with an increase in past month nonmedical use of prescription pain killers among college students age 18 to 22 from 3.6% in 2008 to 4.5 % in 2009 (SAMHSA, 2010a).

Experimentation with sedatives (e.g., Quaaludes or barbiturates) and tranquilizers (e.g., Valium, Ativan, or Flexeril) among college students is common. Data from the MTF survey indicates 6.0% report using barbiturates and related sedatives and 9.2% report using tranquilizers nonmedically in their lifetime (Johnston et al., 2010a). Results from the NSDUH estimate the lifetime nonmedical use of benzodiazepines at 12.2% and muscle relaxants at 3.6% among young adults 18 to 25 (SAMHSA, 2010a). Use of sedatives and tranquilizers in the past month are relatively low and somewhat less common than use of narcotics. The MTF study estimates that in 2009 1.2% of college students used sedatives and 2.2% used tranquilizers in the past 30 days, both of which appear to be slightly decreasing in popularity since 2002, though there was an increase in use of tranquilizers between 2008 and 2009.

Broadly, misuse of these drugs is associated with substantial risk for developing dependence (Catalano, White, Fleming, & Haggerty, 2011; McCabe, West, Morales, Cranford, & Boyd, 2007) and potentially increases the risk for mood disorders and suicide (Catalano et al., 2011; Goodwin & Hasin, 2002). A study by Catalano and colleagues (2011) reported that, whereas nonmedical prescription opiate (NMPO) use was associated with higher use of other drugs, NMPO use was minimally associated with increased negative consequences beyond what could be explained by the use of other illicit drugs. The simultaneous use of alcohol and sedatives or tranquilizers among college students is associated with experiencing more problems related to both categories of drugs (McCabe, Cranford, Morales, & Young, 2006) and misuse of prescription drugs is associated with increased alcohol-related problems, including associated risk behaviors and interpersonal problems (Hermos, Winter, Heeren, & Hingson, 2009). For college students, perhaps the greatest risk is that of accidental overdose due to synergistic effects with alcohol (Garnier et al., 2009; Wilson & Saukkonen, 2004). In sum, although heroin use is very low among college students, use of painkillers, sedatives, and tranquilizers is considerably higher. Among these, the narcotics other than heroin, such as Vicodin and OxyContin, have the highest lifetime prevalence rate (14%), followed by tranquilizers (9.2%) and, finally, sedatives (6%; Johnston et al., 2010a). In the past year, 7.3% of college students report using OxyContin and 8.4% using Vicodin (Johnston et al., 2010a). The 2009 NSDUH data indicates 0.6% of college students used OxyContin in the past month, a significant increase from the 0.2% estimate from 2008 (SAMHSA, 2010a).

Ecstasy

Use of ecstasy (MDMA) steadily increased among young adults across the 1990s. The MTF study estimated 3.3% had used ecstasy in their lifetime in 1989 and this increased to 7.1% by 1999 (Johnston et al., 2010a). In the year 2000, 11.6% reported lifetime use of ecstasy and this continued to increase to 16% by 2004. Since 2004, there has been a gradual decrease, with the most recent MTF estimate being 11.5% in 2009. However, recent results from the 2010 MTF study of adolescents indicates a recent increase in ecstasy use in 8th to 12th grade, suggesting that its popularity may be on the rise again (Johnston, O'Malley, Bachman, & Schulenberg, 2011).

The popularity of ecstasy through the 1990s and early 2000s may, in part, be due to low perceptions of its risk. These perceptions may have been driven by its early therapeutic uses, status as a legal drug until 1985, and its yet unclear risks for overdose, dependence, or negative experiences (Benzenhöfer & Passie, 2010; Grob, 2000; Pentney, 2001; Walters, Foy, & Castro, 2002). Use of MDMA has profound effects of euphoria, with users indicating heightened feelings of love and well-being. It is no wonder that young adults' perceptions of the drug were similarly positive and accepting. In 1997, approximately one third of 18-year-old respondents indicated they viewed using ecstasy once or twice as associated with significant risk for harm (Johnston et al., 2010a). This contrasts sharply with the nearly 54% of respondents who viewed trying cocaine as having substantial risk, though is clearly higher than the 15% who viewed trying marijuana as posing great risk. Perceived risk of using ecstasy once or twice increased to 60% in 2005 among 18-year-olds (Johnston et al., 2010a). This corresponded with increasing recognition of negative consequences, both acute and long term, in the scientific literature and popular media. Media reports of ecstasy-related deaths at raves and concerns about the potentially wide range of other chemical compounds that may be found in drugs sold as MDMA contributed to increased recognition of the dangers associated with ecstasy use (Parrott, 2004; Patel, Wright, Ratcliff, & Miller, 2004; Schifano, 2004).

Acute negative consequences from ecstasy use include increased risk of seizures, profound and potentially life-threatening hyperthermia and dehydration, serotonin syndrome, and sympathomimetic overstimulation (e.g., tachycardia, hypertension) (Parrott, 2002; Schifano, 2004; Vuori et al., 2003). Severe acute effects of the drug may be compounded by use of other drugs (including alcohol) and/or medications (Kaye, Darke, & Duflou, 2009; Upreti, Eddington, Moon, Song, & Lee, 2009). Thus, the role of ecstasy itself in fatalities is often difficult to ascertain due to concurrent use of other drugs and environmental risk factors (Kaye et al., 2009; Schifano, 2004; Upreti et al., 2009). Nonetheless, MDMA toxicity can have fatal consequences (Kaye et al., 2009). Long-term users of ecstasy exhibit a wide range of neurological impairments, including problems with working memory, associative memory, and attention, as well as behavioral problems including impulsivity, disturbances in sleep, and mood and anxiety problems (Jager et al., 2008; Lundqvist, 2005, 2010; Montoya, Sorrentino, Lukas, & Price, 2002). Despite these risks, the perceived danger of use has been gradually falling (Johnston et al., 2010a) as a new generation of students not exposed to concerns associated with ecstasy's previous rise and fall in popularity enters college.

Nicotine

Like alcohol, nicotine is a legal drug in the United States, and is commonly packaged and sold in the form of cigarettes, cigars, and chewing or pipe tobacco. Cigarettes are the most common form of tobacco use among college students (SAMHSA, 2010a). Nicotine's legal status, in conjunction with its highly addictive properties, contribute to its being one of the most widely used drugs among young adults. Cigarettes and alcohol are often among the first drugs that young people experiment with (Degenhardt et al., 2010). Consequences of smoking contribute to an estimated 443,000 deaths each year in the United States (Centers for Disease Control, 2008).

In the 2009 MTF survey, approximately 30% of college students reported smoking cigarettes in the past year (Johnston et al., 2010a). This rate is considerably lower than their noncollege counterparts, more than 40% of whom report smoking in the past year. These figures are somewhat lower than findings from the NSDUH survey, which indicated 38.8% of college students and 50% of their same aged noncollege peers smoked cigarettes in the past year (SAMHSA, 2009). Whereas 30% of college students in the MTF survey report smoking in the past year, approximately 18% report smoking in the past 30 days, and 8% report daily smoking (Johnston et al., 2010a). About 4% of college students report smoking a half pack or more a day. Thus, the majority of college student smokers are occasional smokers, "light and intermittent smokers," or "chippers" (Shiffman, 2009). Even occasional smoking can have substantial health consequences (An et al., 2009), yet the greatest concern is the potential for the establishment of a lifelong pattern of smoking and developing dependence. Approximately 14% to 18% of "occasional" smokers progress to regular smoking and nicotine dependence over the course of 4 to 7 years (McDermott, Dobson, & Owen, 2007; Wetter et al., 2004). Tobacco use has well-known and severe long-term health consequences including lung cancer, emphysema, heart disease, and a wide array of other health complications (National Institute on Drug Abuse, 2009). The rates of death due to cancer are two or more times greater among smokers relative to nonsmokers (National Institute on Drug Abuse, 2009).

On the positive side, the prevalence of smoking has been dropping dramatically. Since 1999, 30-day prevalence among college students has dropped from 31% to 18% and daily prevalence has dropped from 19% to 8% (Johnston et al., 2010a). A substantial proportion of students who smoke report only doing so when drinking or in other social settings (Jackson, Colby, & Sher, 2010; Krukowski, Solomon, & Naud, 2005; Sutfin, Reboussin, McCoy, & Wolfson, 2009). The increasingly prevalent smoking bans in bars and restaurants may further decrease the adoption of "casual" smoking among this group. Smoking is often not discussed with quite the same alarm as drugs such as methamphetamine or cocaine. However, nicotine is a highly addictive drug with severe health consequences, its use is far more prevalent than many illicit drugs, and hence represents a great public health risk.

Hallucinogens

Use of hallucinogens, such as LSD or psilocybin mushrooms, is common among college students; only marijuana and nonmedical use of prescription medications rank higher in terms of prevalence. Recent estimates from the Monitoring the Future study for college students indicate a lifetime prevalence of 8% (Johnston et al., 2010a). However, estimates from the NSDUH are substantially higher, with lifetime estimates for college students (or former students) aged 18 to 25 to be approximately 17% to 19% (SAMHSA, 2010a). These figures are more consistent with the MTF estimate of 14% for the general young adult population (Johnston et al., 2010a). In the MTF study, noncollege peers report substantially higher lifetime prevalence (13.3%) of hallucinogen use than their college peers. One of the difficulties interpreting these prevalence rates is that both of these surveys include ecstasy in the hallucinogen class, and this is one of the more common drugs endorsed. For example, lifetime prevalence estimates for LSD range from 3.3% to 8.5% and PCP 1.6% to 1.9%. LSD has steadily decreased in popularity among college students in the past decade. Estimates from the MTF study indicate a decrease in lifetime use from approximately 12% to 3% between 2000 and 2009. In recent years, annual prevalence of Salvia, a short-acting hallucinogenic plant, has become more common than LSD among college students (5.8% vs. 2.0%; Johnston et al., 2010a). Although hallucinogens are a popular type of drug to try, regular use is quite low with only 1% to 2.6% of college students reporting having used a hallucinogen in the past month (Johnston et al., 2010a; SAMHSA, 2010a).

Although hallucinogens such as LSD and psilocybin mushrooms can have powerful effects, negative consequences associated with these drugs are relatively few. As indicated above, most individuals use them sporadically. The development of dependence on these drugs is rare (American Psychiatric Association, 2000) and their infrequent use reduces the risk of long-term consequences. Of greatest concern is the association with panic reactions and potential psychosis in vulnerable users (Abraham & Aldridge, 1993).

Ketamine, Rophynol, GHB

Ketamine, Rohypnol, and gamma hydroxybutyrate (GHB) are in a loosely defined class of "club drugs" (National Institute on Drug Abuse, 2010a). Annual ketamine use among college students is fairly low (0.1%) compared to use among individuals not enrolled in college (2%; Johnston, O'Malley, & Bachman, 2003). Ketamine (also called "special K") is a dissociative anesthetic sold for veterinary uses. In humans, the effects of ketamine are dependent on the dose, and range from a sense of detachment from reality and impairment in attention and memory at low doses, to hallucinations at medium doses, and delirium, amnesia, and possible fatal respiratory failure at high doses (Jansen & Darracot-Cankovic, 2001). Rohypnol is a benzodiazepine that can be lethal when combined with alcohol. Also called *roofies*, it commonly produces sedation and anterograde amnesia, and has garnered national attention due to its use in sexual assaults (NIDA, 2010). It has been termed the *date rape drug* as it is colorless and odorless when dissolved and thus may be undetected in a drink. Victims may begin to feel relaxed and disinhibited before becoming extremely intoxicated, incapacitated, and passing out. Due to its effects on memory (Saum & Inciardi, 1997), individuals may awake unable to remember the event (Calhoun, Wesson, Galloway, & Smith, 1996; Maxwell, 2005).

MTF data estimate that past-year Rohypnol prevalence is less than 0.05% for college students, compared with 0.8% among noncollege peers (Johnston et al., 2010a). College student use of GHB, a central nervous system depressant that is also implicated in many incidences of sexual assault (Nicholson & Balster, 2001), is similarly rare, with annual use estimated at less than 0.05% among college students and 0.4% among noncollege student young adults (Johnston et al., 2010a). GHB was legal in the United States until 2000, and was used both for its euphoric effects as well as a dietary supplement to promote muscle growth (Camacho, Matthews, Murray, & Dimsdale, 2005; NIDA, 2001). A sharp increase in GHB-related medical emergencies in the late 1990s caused concern for a potential new drug epidemic; however, its use among college students has remained low (i.e., annual use < 1%) for the past decade (Johnston et al., 2010; NIDA, 2001). High doses of these drugs can lead to seizures, loss of consciousness, loss of muscle control, vomiting, slowed heart rate, hypothermia, and respiratory depression (Chin, Sporer, Cullison, Dyer, & Wu, 1998; NIDA, 2001; Romanelli, Smith, & Pomeroy, 2003; Smith, Larive, & Romanelli, 2002). Like tranquilizers, opiates, and sedatives, these drugs exhibit amplified depressant effects and thus increased dangers when co-ingested with alcohol (Chin et al., 1998; NIDA, 2001).

Inhalants

Inhalants represent substances that produce a chemical vapor that can be inhaled to produce a "high," and which are not normally taken in any other manner (National Institute on Drug Abuse, 2010b). Because these drugs are solely categorized based on their route of administration rather than their pharmacologic properties, inhalants are a highly heterogeneous class of drugs in terms of included substances, acute effects, and use-related consequences (Brouette & Anton, 2001). The term *inhalant* has been used to refer to breathing household chemicals and cleaning agents, fuels, nitrates, and nitrous oxide, among others (National Institute on Drug Abuse, 2010b). Lifetime use of these substances among young adults is relatively prevalent when compared with many other drugs, including ecstasy, heroin, and methamphetamine, and is slightly less prevalent among college students than their non–college attending peers (6.9% versus 9.7%; Johnston et al., 2010a). However, current and annual use prevalence is quite low among college students, 0.1% and 1.2%, respectively (Johnston et al., 2010a). Whereas current and annual use for many drugs increases across adolescence and into young adulthood, inhalants exhibit a different pattern. Younger adolescents are more likely to report past year use of inhalants. For example, 8.1% of 8th graders report use of inhalants in the past-year (Johnston et al., 2010b). The popularity of inhalants among young adolescents reflects that these are often readily available household items. In contrast, availability and use of alcohol and other drugs increases in young adulthood. Inhalants used by college students are more likely to be nitrous oxide or nitrates ("poppers") rather than glue, gasoline, and so on (National Institute on Drug Abuse, 2010b).

The low frequency of inhalant use among college students is fortunate, given the devastating consequences of both acute intoxication and prolonged use of many inhalants (Brouette & Anton, 2001; National Institute on Drug Abuse, 2010b). Specifically, although the sensation of inhalant intoxication is similar to alcohol intoxication, overdose produces a rapid generalized loss of sensation, unconsciousness, and ultimately, death (NIDA, 2010c). Long-term effects of use are severe and include irreparable cerebral and cerebellar damage, increased risk for sudden cardiac death, and renal failure (Brouette & Anton, 2001; Kurtzman, Otsuka, & Wahl, 2001).

AT-RISK GROUPS

With few exceptions, prevalence rates for each of the drugs reviewed in the previous chapters are higher for men versus women. For example, annual prevalence rates of LSD, cocaine, narcotics, and tranquilizers are 1.5 to 3 times higher in men than women (Johnston et al., 2010a). In contrast, annual prevalence rates of drugs such as marijuana, barbiturates, cigarettes, and methamphetamine exhibit far less gender disparity.

Similar to gender differences in illicit drug use prevalence, there are some substantial differences as a function of race and ethnicity (SAMHSA, 2010a). For example, among young adults 18 to 25, past-month prevalence of any illicit drug is similar across some racial groups: Black or African American (20.5%) or White (23.4%). In contrast, rates among American Indian or Alaskan Native (30.5%) and multiracial individuals (30.9%) tend to be higher, while those among Asian (9.4%) and Hispanic or Latino (16.3%) tend to be lower. Notably, the pattern of racial and ethnic differences in illicit drug use may be different in college populations (SAMHSA, 2009; see Table 2.3 for a summary).[1] For example, in the 2009 NSDUH data among full-time college students ages 18 to 22, prevalence of past month illicit drug use is only 14.5% for Native Americans or Alaskan Natives. This is less than half the prevalence of use among Native American/Alaskan natives in this age range who are not full-time students. This is also considerably less than the use prevalence for non-Hispanic White college students (25.2%). Full-time college status has little association with past-month illicit drug use for non-Hispanic Whites, is *positively* associated with use prevalence for Hispanics, and inversely associated with past-month illicit drug use prevalence for other racial groups. Finally, there is some evidence of increased risk of club drug (e.g., GHB, Rohypnol, Ecstasy, Ketamine) use among gay/lesbian and bisexual men and women (Fendrich, Wislar, Johnson, & Hubbell, 2003; Gorman, Nelson, Applegate, & Scrol, 2004; Parsons, Kelly, & Wells, 2006).

Use of alcohol and other drugs tend to covary. For example, individuals who use marijuana tend to drink more, begin drinking at a younger age, and are more likely to use methamphetamine than individuals who do not use marijuana (Collins, Bradizza, & Vincent, 2007; Midanik et al., 2007; Simons & Carey, 2006; Simons et al., 2008; Simons et al., 2010). Similarly, nonmedical use of stimulants is linked to greater use of alcohol, marijuana, cigarettes, ecstasy, and cocaine (McCabe et al., 2005a). Thus, heavy use of alcohol may be an indicator of potential other problematic drug involvement as well. For this reason, known indicators of heavy drinking may

---

[1] We note that the described pattern of use as a function of race and college enrollment status varies across years in the NSDUH surveys. For example, the marked difference in illicit drug use for Native Americans as a function of college enrollment is quite pronounced in the 2007 and 2009 surveys, but not in the 2006 and 2008 surveys. However, for most years back to 2002, the observed difference in illicit drug use by Native American college students does exhibit this pattern.

Table 2.3 Thirty-Day Prevalence of Illicit Drug Use by College Enrollment and Race/Ethnicity

Race	Percent Reporting Illicit Drug Use in the Past 30 Days	
	Full-Time College Students Aged 18–22	**Other Individuals Aged 18–22**
Non-Hispanic White	25.2	25.5
Non-Hispanic Black/African American	17.1	22.1
Non-Hispanic American Indian/ Alaskan native	14.5	30.3
Non-Hispanic Native Hawaiian/ Other Pacific Islander	27.8	30.7
Non-Hispanic Asian	9.8	15.2
Non-Hispanic multiracial	28.8	31.4
Hispanic	20.9	16.0
Total	22.7	22.8

Note. Source 2009 NSDUH data.

also be useful for identifying young adults at risk for problems with other drugs. For example, fraternity and sorority membership is a predictor of heavy alcohol use as well as nonmedical use of stimulants, marijuana, and other substances (McCabe et al., 2005a; McCabe et al., 2005b; Park, Sher, & Krull, 2008).

There are important regional differences in drug use that should be considered. For example, estimates of past-month marijuana use in areas of the South and Midwest are less than 15%, whereas the prevalence in some Western states and New England are 20.5% to 26.6% (SAMHSA, 2010a). Cocaine use also varies widely across regions with 4% of young adults in New England reporting past month use compared to 0.5% in East South Central states (SAMHSA, 2010a). Thus, though there are clear national trends in prevalence of drug use, local characteristics need to also be considered in prevention programming.

Finally, substance use disorders are highly comorbid with other mental health disorders, including mood, anxiety, psychotic, and personality disorders (Compton, Thomas, Stinson, & Grant, 2007; Westermeyer, 2006). For example, approximately 26% of adults with a serious mental illness in the past year have co-occurring alcohol or other substance abuse or dependence, a significant increase over the 6.5% without a serious mental illness (SAMHSA, 2009). Similarly, past-year prevalence of mood (19.67% vs. 8.13%) or anxiety disorders (17.71% vs. 10.39%) is markedly higher among those with a substance use disorder than for individuals without a substance use disorder (Grant et al., 2004). Associations in college populations are similar, with 12.9% of individuals with a mental disorder reporting a comorbid illicit drug use disorder, compared to 5.2% among individuals without a mental disorder (SAMHSA, 2009). Thus, incorporating routine screening and integrated treatment options in psychological clinics on college campuses is clearly warranted.

SUMMARY

This chapter provided a brief overview of the prevalence of common substances used on college campuses and a review of associated consequences and risk factors. Approximately 36% to 39% of college students report some illicit drug use in the past year, which is equivalent to or slightly less than their noncollege peers (Johnston et al., 2010a; SAMHSA, 2009). A distant second to alcohol, marijuana is by far the most commonly used illicit drug, and some estimates indicate that use within the past 30 days is currently slightly more prevalent than cigarette smoking (Johnston et al., 2010a). Whereas past-year prevalence of marijuana use is similar for college students and their noncollege peers, current daily use is less prevalent among college students (Johnston et al., 2010). Along with alcohol, nonprescription use of Adderall, Ritalin, and OxyContin is higher among college students (Johnston et al., 2010a). However, prevalence rates for other illicit drugs are often lower among college students than among their noncollege peers (Johnston et al., 2010a). There are some differences across surveys, and 30-day prevalence rates for full-time college students versus others aged 18 to 22 are often similar in the 2009 NSDUH. Interestingly, although college enrollment is associated with lower annual prevalence rates for several illicit drugs in the MTF survey, this is largely due to pronounced differences in women. Whereas use among men varies less as a function of college enrollment, use among women college students tends to be much lower compared with their peers not attending college (Johnston et al., 2010a). Finally, college students exhibit lower rates of past year illicit drug abuse or dependence relative to their noncollege peers (7.6% vs. 9.5%; SAMHSA, 2009).

The most commonly used drug, marijuana, is associated with diverse psychosocial problems as well as potential long-term health consequences. Due to the prevalence of use and association with comorbid problems and consequences, its use warrants attention on college campuses. However, its potential for severe acute consequences (e.g., overdose), as well as progression to dependence and long-term health consequences, is notably lower than other commonly used drugs, such as alcohol and nicotine, or the less commonly used drugs, such as opiates and stimulants (Swift, Copeland, & Lenton, 2000; Zimmer & Morgan, 1997). Experimentation and light use of marijuana with few associated negative consequences is the normative pattern among college students and, despite its prevalence, most students appear to negotiate the college years without incurring significant harm. Nonetheless, its association with impairments in learning and psychosocial risk behaviors is cause for concern.

With few exceptions, at-risk groups in college are similar to known risk factors in the general population. Men tend to use and abuse drugs more than women, abuse of alcohol and other drugs tend to covary, and risk for substance use disorders are higher among those with other comorbid mental health problems. However, college attendance may be associated with lower levels of use in certain groups, including women, Native Americans, and Alaskan Natives. Whether this reflects a selection effect or effects of the environment is unclear, and there were some inconsistencies in this pattern across years.

Common drugs rise and fall in popularity as new generations enter college. In addition, there is a constant emergence of recreational drugs (e.g., salvia; Lange, Reed, Croff, & Clapp, 2008), new prescription drugs, and synthetics (e.g., mephedrone; Schifano et al., 2011). This, combined with the characteristic "openness" to experimentation among young adults, suggests that the landscape of drug use on college campuses, and thus the targets of prevention programs, will be in constant flux. Fortunately, most students navigate the myriad of drug choices during their college years without incurring significant consequences, and illicit drug involvement naturally declines as they age and enter new social roles (Staff et al., 2010). However, a minority of college students *do* fall victim to tragic accidents, incur life altering legal problems, or develop longstanding substance use problems. By virtue of the developmental period, college students, like their noncollege peers, are at heightened risk for using a wide variety of drugs and incurring related harm. Campus policy, prevention programs, and treatment options on college campuses can reduce drug-related harms, while appreciating that drug use is occurring within the context of a developmental period that fosters exploration, growth, and risk taking.

REFERENCES

Abraham, H. D., & Aldridge, A. M. (1993). Adverse consequences of lysergic acid diethylamide. *Addiction, 88*(10), 1327–1334.

Aldington, S., Harwood, M., Cox, B., Weatherall, M., Beckert, L., Hansell, A., ...Beasley, R. (2008). Cannabis use and risk of lung cancer: a case-control study. *European Respiratory Journal, 31*(2), 280–286.

Aldington, S., Williams, M., Nowitz, M., Weatherall, M., Pritchard, A., McNaughton, A., . . . Beasley, R. (2007). Effects of cannabis on pulmonary structure, function and symptoms. *Thorax, 62*(12), 1058–1063.

American Psychiatric Association (2000). *Diagnostic and statistical manual of mental disorders, fourth edition, text revision.* Washington, DC: American Psychiatric Association.

An, L. C., Berg, C. J., Klatt, C. M., Perry, C. L., Thomas, J. L., Luo, X., . . . Ahluwalia, J. S. (2009). Symptoms of cough and shortness of breath among occasional young adult smokers. *Nicotine & Tobacco Research, 11*(2), 126-133. doi: 10.1093/ntr/ntp015

Angrist, B. (1994). Clinical variations of amphetamine psychosis. In A. K. Cho & D. S. Segal (Eds.), *Amphetamines and its analogs: Psychopharmacology, toxicology, and abuse.* San Diego, CA: Academic Press.

Arnett, J. J. (2000). Emerging adulthood. A theory of development from the late teens through the twenties. *American Psychologist, 55*(5), 469–480.

Arria, A. M., Caldeira, K. M., O'Grady, K. E., Vincent, K. B., Fitzelle, D. B., Johnson, E. P., & Wish, E. (2008a). Drug exposure opportunities and use patterns among college students: Results of a longitudinal prospective cohort study. *Substance Abuse, 29,* 19–38.

Arria, A. M., Caldeira, K. M., Vincent, K. B., O'Grady, K. E., & Wish, E. D. (2008b). Perceived harmfulness predicts nonmedical use of prescription drugs among college students: Interactions with sensation-seeking. *Prevention Science, 9*(3), 191–201.

Arria, A. M., & DuPont, R. L. (2010). Nonmedical prescription stimulant use among college students: Why we need to do something and what we need to do. *Journal of Addictive Diseases, 29*(4), 417–426.

Bachman, J. G., Freedman-Doan, P., O'Malley, P. M., Schulenberg, J. E., Johnston, L.D., & Messersmith, E. E. (2007). *Education-drug use relationships: An examination of racial/ethnic subgroups.* Ann Arbor, MI: Institute for Social Research.

Barrett, S. P., & Pihl, R. O. (2002). Oral methylphenidate-alcohol co-abuse. *Journal of Clinical Psychopharmacology, 22*(6), 633–634.

Beck, K. H., Caldeira, K. M., Vincent, K. B., O'Grady, K. E., Wish, E. D., & Arria, A. M. (2009). The social context of cannabis use: relationship to cannabis use disorders and depressive symptoms among college students. *Addictive Behaviors, 34*(9), 764–768.

Bedard, M., Dubois, S., & Weaver, B. (2007). The impact of cannabis on driving. *Canada Journal of Public Health, 98*(1), 6–11.

Benzenhöfer, U., & Passie, T. (2010). Rediscovering MDMA (ecstasy): The role of the American chemist Alexander T. Shulgin. *Addiction, 105*(8), 1355–1361.

Berman, S. M., Kuczenski, R., McCracken, J. T., & London, E. D. (2009). Potential adverse effects of amphetamine treatment on brain and behavior: A review. *Molecular Psychiatry, 14,* 123–142.

Bogle, K. E., & Smith, B. H. (2009). Illicit methylphenidate use: a review of prevalence, availability, pharmacology, and consequences. *Current Drug Abuse Review, 2*(2), 157–176.

Bohnert, A. S., & Miech, R. A. (2010). Changes in the association of drug use with depressive disorders in recent decades: The case of cocaine. *Substance Use and Misuse, 45*(10), 1452–1462.

Brand, H. S., Gonggrijp, S., & Blanksma, C. J. (2008). Cocaine and oral health. *British Dental Journal, 204*(7), 365–369.

Bright, G. M. (2008). Abuse of medications employed for the treatment of ADHD: Results from a large-scale community survey. *Medscape Journal of Medicine, 10*(5), 111–117.

Brouette, T., & Anton, R. (2001). Clinical review of inhalants. *American Journal on Addictions, 10*(1), 79–94.

Buckner, J. D., Ecker, A. H., & Cohen, A. S. (2010). Mental health problems and interest in marijuana treatment among marijuana-using college students. *Addictive Behaviors, 35*(9), 826–833.

Calhoun, S. R., Wesson, D. R., Galloway, G. P., & Smith, D. E. (1996). Abuse of flunitrazepam (rohypnol) and other benzodiazepines in Austin and South Texas. *Journal of Psychoactive Drugs, 28,* 183–189.

Camacho, A., Matthews, S. C., Murray, B., & Dimsdale, J. E. (2005). Use of GHB compounds among college students. *American Journal of Drug and Alcohol Abuse, 31*(4), 601–607.

Caplan, J. P., Epstein, L. A., Quinn, D. K., Stevens, J. R., & Stern, T. A. (2007). Neuropsychiatric effects of prescription drug abuse. *Neuropsychology Review, 17*(3), 363–380.

Castro, F. G., Barrington, E. H., Walton, M. A., & Rawson, R. A. (2000). Cocaine and methamphetamine: Differential addiction rates. *Psychology of Addictive Behaviors, 14*(4), 390–396.

Catalano, R. F., White, H. R., Fleming, C. B., & Haggerty, K. P. (2011). Is nonmedical prescription opiate use a unique form of illicit drug use? *Addictive Behaviors, 36*(1–2), 79–86.

Centers for Disease Control. (2008). Smoking-Attributable Mortality, Years of Potential Life Lost, and Productivity Losses—United States, 2000–2004. *MMWR Weekly, 57*(45), 1226–1228.

Chin, R. L., Sporer, K. A., Cullison, B., Dyer, J. E., & Wu, T. D. (1998). Clinical course of Gamma-hydroxybutyrate overdose. *Annals of Emergency Medicine, 31*(6), 716–722.

Collins, R. L., Bradizza, C. M., & Vincent, P. C. (2007). Young-adult malt liquor drinkers: Prediction of alcohol problems and marijuana use. *Psychology of Addictive Behaviors, 21*(2), 138–146.

Compton, W. M., Thomas, Y. F., Stinson, F. S., & Grant, B. F. (2007). Prevalence, correlates, disability, and comorbidity of DSM-IV drug abuse and dependence in the United States: Results from the national epidemiologic survey on alcohol and related conditions. *Archives of General Psychiatry, 64*(5), 566–576.

CORE Institute (2010). *2006–2008 National data*. Carbondale, IL: Southern Illinois University Carbondale.

Davidson, C., Gow, A. J., Lee, T. H., & Ellinwood, E. H. (2001). Methamphetamine neurotoxicity: Necrotic and apaptotic mechanisms and relevance to human abuse and treatment. *Brain Research Reviews, 36*(1), 1–22.

Degenhardt, L., Dierker, L., Chiu, W. T., Medina-Mora, M. E., Neumark, Y., Sampson, N., ... Kessler, R.C. (2010). Evaluating the drug use "gateway" theory using cross-national data: consistency and associations of the order of initiation of drug use among participants in the WHO World Mental Health Surveys. *Drug and Alcohol Dependence, 108*(1–2), 84–97.

DeSantis, A. D., Webb, E. M., & Noar, S. M. (2008). Illicit use of prescription ADHD medications on a college campus: A multimethodological approach. *Journal of American College Health, 57*(3), 315–324.

Devlin, R. J., & Henry, J. A. (2008). Clinical review: Major consequences of illicit drug consumption. *Critical Care, 12*(1), 202.

Drug Abuse Warning Network (2003). *Marijuana-related Emergency Department Visits by Youth*. Rockville, MD: U.S. Department of Health and Human Services.

Earleywine, M., & Barnwell, S. S. (2007). Decreased respiratory symptoms in cannabis users who vaporize. *Harm Reduct J, 4*, 11.

FDA (2011). Communication about an ongoing safety review of stimulant medications used in children with attention-deficit/hyperactivity disorder (ADHD). Retrieved from http://www.fda.gov/Drugs/DrugSafety/PostmarketDrugSafetyInformationforPatientsandProviders/DrugSafetyInformation-forHeathcareProfessionals/ucm165858.htm

Fendrich, M., Wislar, J. S., Johnson, T. P., & Hubbell, A. (2003). A contextual profile of club drug use among adults in Chicago. *Addiction, 98*(12), 1693–1703.

Garnier, L. M., Arria, A. M., Caldeira, K. M., Vincent, K. B., O'Grady, K. E., & Wish, E. D. (2009). Nonmedical prescription analgesic use and concurrent alcohol consumption among college students. *American Journal of Drug and Alcohol Abuse, 35*(5), 334–338.

Gledhill-Hoyt, J., Lee, H., Strote, J., & Wechsler, H. (2000). Increased use of marijuana and other illicit drugs at US colleges in the 1990s: results of three national surveys. *Addiction, 95*, 1655–1667.

Goodwin, R. D., & Hasin, D. S. (2002). Sedative use and misuse in the United States. *Addiction, 97*(5), 555–562.

Gorman, E. M., Nelson, K. R., Applegate, T., & Scrol, A. (2004). Club drug and poly-substance abuse and hiv among gay/bisexual men: Lessons gleaned from a community study. *Journal of Gay & Lesbian Social Services: Issues in Practice, Policy & Research, 16*(2), 1–17.

Gould, M. S., Walsh, B. T., Munfakh, J. L., Kleinman, M., Duan, N., Olfson, M., ... Cooper, T. (2009). Sudden death and use of stimulant medications in youths. *American Journal of Psychiatry, 166*(9), 992–1001.

Grant, B. F., Stinson, F. S., Dawson, D. A., Chou, S. P., Dufour, M. C., Compton, W., ... Kaplan, K. (2004). Prevalence and co-occurrence of substance use disorders and independent mood and anxiety disorders: results from the National Epidemiologic Survey on Alcohol and Related Conditions. *Archives of General Psychiatry, 61*(8), 807–816.

Grant, K. M., Kelley, S. S., Agrawal, S., Meza, J. L., Meyer, J. R., & Romberger, D. J. (2007). Methamphetamine use in rural Midwesterners. *American Journal on Addictions, 16*(2), 79–84.

Greely, H., Sahakian, B., Harris, J., Kessler, R. C., Gazzaniga, M., Campbell, P., & Farah, M. J. (2008). Towards responsible use of cognitive-enhancing drugs by the healthy. *Nature, 456*(7223), 702–705.

Griffin, K. W., Botvin, G. J., & Nichols, T. R. (2006). Effects of a school-based drug abuse prevention program for adolescents on HIV risk behavior in young adulthood. *Prevention Science, 7*(1), 103–112.

Grob, C. S. (2000). Deconstructing Ecstasy: The politics of MDMA research. *Addiction Research, 8*(6), 549–588.

Gullo, M. J., & Dawe, S. (2008). Impulsivity and adolescent substance use: Rashly dismissed as "all-bad"? *Neuroscience & Biobehavioral Review, 32*(8), 1507–1518.

Hall, K. M., Irwin, M. M., Bowman, K. A., Frankenberger, W., & Jewett, D. C. (2005). Illicit use of pre-scribed stimulant medication among college students. *Journal of American College Health, 53*(4), 167–174.

Hall, W., & Degenhardt, L. (2009). Adverse health effects of non-medical cannabis use. *Lancet, 374*(9698), 1383–1391.

Hanson, K. L., Winward, J. L., Schweinsburg, A. D., Medina, K. L., Brown, S. A., & Tapert, S. F. (2010). Longitudinal study of cognition among adolescent marijuana users over three weeks of abstinence. *Addictive Behaviors, 35*(11), 970–976.

Helmus, T. C., Downey, K. K., Wang, L. M., Rhodes, G. L., & Schuster, C. R. (2001). The relationship between self-reported cocaine withdrawal symptoms and history of depression. *Addictive Behaviors, 26*(3), 461–467.

Hermos, J., Winter, M., Heeren, T., & Hingson, R. (2009). Alcohol-related problems among younger drinkers who misuse prescription drugs: Results from the national epidemiologic survey of alcohol and related conditions (NESARC). *Substance Abuse, 30*(2), 118–126.

Hester, R., Nestor, L., & Garavan, H. (2009). Impaired error awareness and anterior cingulate cortex hypoactivity in chronic cannabis users. *Neuropsychopharmacology, 34*(11), 2450–2458.

Hong, R., Matsuyama, E., & Nur, K. (1991). Cardiomyopathy associated with the smoking of crystal methamphetamine. *Journal of the American Medical Association, 265*, 1152–1154.

Jackson, K. M., Colby, S. M., & Sher, K. J. (2010). Daily patterns of conjoint smoking and drinking in college student smokers. *Psychology of Addictive Behaviors, 24*(3), 424–435.

Jager, G., de Win, M. M., van der Tweel, I., Schilt, T., Kahn, R. S., van den Brink, W., . . . Ramsey, N. F. (2008). Assessment of cognitive brain function in ecstasy users and contributions of other drugs of abuse: results from an FMRI study. *Neuropsychopharmacology, 33*(2), 247–258.

Jansen, K. L. R., & Darracot-Cankovic, R. (2001). The nonmedical use of ketamine, part two: A review of problem use and dependence. *Journal of Psychoactive Drugs, 33*(2), 151–158.

Johnston, L. D., O'Malley, P. M., & Bachman, J. G. (2002). *Monitoring the Future national survey results on drug use, 1975–2001* (Vol. 1). Bethesda, MD: National Institute on Drug Abuse.

Johnston, L. D., O'Malley, P. M., & Bachman, J. G. (2003). *Monitoring the future national survey results on drug use, 1975–2002. Volume II: College students and adults ages 19–40.* (NIH Publication No. 03-5376). Bethesda, MD: National Institute on Drug Abuse.

Johnston, L. D., O' Malley, P. M., Bachman, J. G., & Schulenberg, J. E. (2010a). *Monitoring the future national survey results on drug use, 1975–2009. Volume II: College students and young adults ages 19–50* (NIH Publication No. 10–7585). Bethesda, MD: National Institute on Drug Abuse.

Johnston, L. D., O'Malley, P. M., Bachman, J. G., & Schulenberg, J. E. (2010b). *Monitoring the future national survey results on drug use, 1975–2009. Volume I: Secondary school students* (NIH Publication No. 10–7584). Bethesda, MD: National Institute on Drug Abuse.

Johnston, L. D., O'Malley, P. M., Bachman, J. G., & Schulenberg, J. E. (2011). *Monitoring the Future national results of adolescent drug use: Overview of key findings, 2010.* Ann Arbor: Institute for Social Research, University of Michigan.

Kaye, S., Darke, S., & Duflou, J. (2009). Methylenedioxymethamphetamine (MDMA)-related fatalities in Australia: demographics, circumstances, toxicology and major organ pathology. *Drug and Alcohol Dependence, 104*(3), 254–261.

Krukowski, R. A., Solomon, L. J., & Naud, S. (2005). Triggers of heavier and lighter cigarette smoking in college students. *Journal of Behavioral Medicine, 28*(4), 335–345.

Kurtzman, T. L., Otsuka, K. N., & Wahl, R. A. (2001). Inhalant abuse by adolescents. *Journal of Adolescent Health, 28*(3), 170–180.

Labbe, A. K., & Maisto, S. A. (2010). Development of the stimulant medication outcome expectancies questionnaire for college students. *Addictive Behaviors, 35*, 726–729.

Lane, S. D., Cherek, D. R., Tcheremissine, O. V., Lieving, L. M., & Pietras, C. J. (2005). Acute marijuana effects on human risk taking. *Neuropsychopharmacology, 30*(4), 800–809.

Lane, S. D., Cherek, D. R., Tcheremissine, O. V., Steinberg, J. L., & Sharon, J. L. (2007). Response perse-veration and adaptation in heavy marijuana-smoking adolescents. *Addictive Behaviors, 32*(5), 977–990.

Lange, J. E., Reed, M. B., Croff, J. M., & Clapp, J. D. (2008). College student use of Salvia divinorum. *Drug and Alcohol Dependence, 94*(1–3), 263–266.

Lee, C. M., Maggs, J. L., Neighbors, C., & Patrick, M. E. (2011). Positive and negative alcohol-related consequences: associations with past drinking. *Journal of Adolescence, 34*(1), 87–94.

Ligouri, A., Gatto, C. P., & Jarrett, D. B. (2002). Separate and combined effects of marijuana and alcohol on mood, equilibrium, and simulated driving. *Psychopharmacology 163*, 399–405.

Lineberry, T. W., & Bostwick, J. M. (2006). Methamphetamine abuse: A perfect storm of complications. *Mayo Clinic Proceedings, 81*(1), 77–84.

Looby, A., & Earleywine, M. (2007). Negative consequences associated with dependence in daily cannabis users. *Substance Abuse Treatment, Prevention, and Policy, 2*, 3.

Lundqvist, T. (2005). Cognitive consequences of cannabis use: Comparison with abuse of stimulants and heroin with regard to attention, memory and executive functions. *Pharmacology Biochemistry and Behavior, 81*(2), 319–330.

Lundqvist, T. (2010). Imaging cognitive deficits in drug abuse. In D. W. Self & J. K. Staley (Eds.), *Behavioral neuroscience of drug addiction.* (pp. 247–275). New York, NY: Springer.

Maggs, J. L. (1997). Alcohol use and binge drinking as goal-directed action during the transition to postsecondary education. In J. Schulenberg & J. L. Maggs (Eds.), *Health risks and developmental transitions during adolescence* (pp. 345–371). New York, NY: Cambridge University Press.

Maraj, S., Figueredo, V. M., & Lynn Morris, D. (2010). Cocaine and the heart. *Clinical Cardiology, 33*(5), 264–269.

Markowitz, J. S., Logan, B. K., Diamond, F., & Patrick, K. S. (1999). Detection of the novel metabolite ethylphenidate after methylphenidate overdose with alcohol coingestion. *Journal of Clinical Psychopharmacology, 19*(4), 362–366.

Martens, M. P., Page, J. C., Mowry, E. S., Damann, K. M., Taylor, K. K., & Cimini, M. D. (2006). Differences between actual and perceived student norms: An examination of alcohol use, drug use, and sexual behavior. *Journal of American College Health, 54*(5), 295–300.

Maxwell, J. (2005). Party drugs: Properties, prevalence, patterns, and problems. *Substance Use & Misuse, 40*(9–10), 1203–1240. doi: 10.1081/JA-200066736

McCabe, S. E., Cranford, J. A., Morales, M., & Young, A. (2006). Simultaneous and concurrent polydrug use of alcohol and prescription drugs: Prevalence, correlates, and consequences. *Journal of Studies on Alcohol and Drugs, 67*(4), 529–537.

McCabe, S. E., Knight, J. R., Teter, C. J., & Wechsler, H. (2005a). Non-medical use of prescription stimulants among US college students: Prevalence and correlates from a national survey. *Addiction, 100*(1), 96–106.

McCabe, S. E., Schulenberg, J. E., Johnston, L. D., O'Malley, P. M., Bachman, J. G., & Kloska, D. D. (2005b). Selection and socialization effects of fraternities and sororities on US college student substance use: a multi-cohort national longitudinal study. *Addiction, 100*(4), 512–524.

McCabe, S. E., & Teter, C. J. (2007). Drug use related problems among nonmedical users of prescription stimulants: A web-based survey of college students from a midwestern university. *Drug and Alcohol Dependence, 91*(1), 69–76.

McCabe, S. E., West, B. T., Morales, M., Cranford, J. A., & Boyd, C. J. (2007). Does early onset of non-medical use of prescription drugs predict subsequent prescription drug abuse and dependence? Results from a national study. *Addiction, 102*(12), 1920–1930.

McCarthy, D. M., Lynch, A. M., & Pederson, S. L. (2007). Driving after use of alcohol and marijuana in college students. *Psychology of Addictive Behaviors, 21*(3), 425–430.

McDermott, L., Dobson, A., & Owen, N. (2007). Occasional tobacco use among young adult women: a longitudinal analysis of smoking transitions. *Tobacco Control, 16*(4), 248–254.

McDonald, J., Schleifer, L., Richards, J. B., & de Wit, H. (2003). Effects of THC on behavioral measures of impulsivity in humans. *Neuropsychopharmacology, 28*(7), 1356–1365.

Meredith, C. W., Jaffe, C., Ang-Lee, K., & Saxon, A. J. (2005). Implications of chronic methamphetamine use: A literature review. *Harvard Review of Psychiatry, 13*(3), 141–154.

Midanik, L. T., Tam, T. W., & Weisner, C. (2007). Concurrent and simultaneous drug and alcohol use: results of the 2000 National Alcohol Survey. *Drug and Alcohol Dependence, 90*(1), 72–80.

Montoya, A. G., Sorrentino, R., Lukas, S. E., & Price, B. H. (2002). Long-term neuropsychiatric consequences of "ecstasy" (MDMA): a review. *Harvard Review of Psychiatry, 10*(4), 212–220.

National Institute on Drug Abuse (2001). *Conference highlights increasing GHB abuse.* Bethesda, MD: National Institutes of Health.

National Institute on Drug Abuse (2002). *Research report series: Methamphetamine abuse and addiction.* Bethesda, MD: National institutes of Health.

National Insititue on Drug Abuse (2009). *Tobacco addiction.* (NIH Publication Number 09–4342). Bethesda, MD: U.S. Department of Health and Human Services.

National Institute on Drug Abuse (2010a). *Club drugs (GHB, Ketamine, and Rohypnol).* Rockville, MD: National Institutes of Health.

National Institute on Drug Abuse (2010b). *Inhalants.* Rockville, MD: National Institutes of Health.

National Institute on Drug Abuse (2010c). *Inhalants.* Rockville, MD: National Institutes of Health.

Neighbors, C., Geisner, I. M., & Lee, C. M. (2008). Perceived marijuana norms and social expectancies among entering college student marijuana users. *Psychology of Addictive Behaviors, 22*(3), 433–438.

Nicholson, K. L., & Balster, R. L. (2001). GHB: A new and novel drug of abuse. *Drug and Alcohol Dependence, 63,* 1–22.

Outram, S. M. (2010). The use of methylphenidate among students: The future of enhancement? *Journal of Medical Ethics, 36*(4), 198–202.

Park, A., Sher, K. J., & Krull, J. L. (2008). Risky drinking in college changes as fraternity/sorority affiliation changes: A person-environment perspective. *Psychology of Addictive Behaviors, 22*(2), 219–229.

Park, C. L. (2004). Positive and negative consequences of alcohol consumption in college students. *Addictive Behaviors, 29*(2), 311–321.

Parrott, A. C. (2002). Recreational Ecstasy/MDMA, the serotonin syndrome, and serotonergic neurotoxicity. *Pharmacology Biochemistry and Behavior, 71*(4), 837–844.

Parrott, A. C. (2004). Is ecstasy MDMA? A review of the proportion of ecstasy tablets containing MDMA, their dosage levels, and the changing perceptions of purity. *Psychopharmacology, 173*(3–4), 234–241.

Parsons, J. T., Kelly, B. C., & Wells, B. E. (2006). Differences in club drug use between heterosexual and lesbian/bisexual females. *Addictive Behaviors, 31*(12), 2344–2349.

Patel, M. M., Wright, D. W., Ratcliff, J. J., & Miller, M. A. (2004). Shedding new light on the "safe" club drug: Methylenedioxymethamphetamine (Ecstasy)-related fatalities. *Academic Emergency Medicine, 11*(2), 208–210.

Pentney, A. R. (2001). An exploration of the history and controversies surrounding MDMA and MDA. *Journal of Psychoactive Drugs, 33*(3), 213–221.

Perkins, H. W., Meilman, P. W., Leichliter, J. S., Cashin, J. R., & Presley, C. A. (1999). Misperceptions of the norms for the frequency of alcohol and other drug use on college campuses. *Journal of American College Health, 47*(6), 253–258.

Pottieger, A. E., Tressell, P. A., Inciardi, J. A., & Rosales, T. A. (1992). Cocaine use patterns and overdose. *Journal of Psychoactive Drugs, 24*(4), 399–410.

Rawson, R. A., Gonzales, R., & Ling, W. (2006). Methamphetamine abuse and dependence: An update. *Directions in Psychiatry, 26*(3), 221–236.

Rawson, R. A., Gonzales, R., McCann, M., & Ling, W. (2007). Use of methamphetamine by young people: Is there reason for concern? *Addiction, 102*(7), 1021–1022.

Reske, M., Eidt, C. A., Delis, D. C., & Paulus, M. P. (2010). Nondependent stimulant users of cocaine and prescription amphetamines show verbal learning and memory deficits. *Biological Psychiatry, 68*(8), 762–769.

Restrepo, C. S., Carrillo, J. A., Martinez, S., Ojeda, P., Rivera, A. L., & Hatta, A. (2007). Pulmonary complications from cocaine and cocaine-based substances: imaging manifestations. *Radiographics, 27*(4), 941–956.

Romanelli, F., Smith, K. M., & Pomeroy, C. (2003). Use of club drugs by HIV-seropositive and HIV-seronegative gay and bisexual men. *Topics in HIV Medicine, 11*(1), 25–32.

Ronen, A., Gershon, P., Drobiner, H., Rabinovich, A., Bar-Hamburger, R., Mechoulam, R., . . . Shinar, D. (2008). Effects of THC on driving performance, physiological state and subjective feelings relative to alcohol. *Accident Analysis and Prevention, 40*(3), 926–934.

Saum, C. A., & Inciardi, J. A. (1997). Rohypnol misuse in the United States. *Substance Use & Misuse, 32*(6), 723–731.

Schifano, F. (2004). A bitter pill. Overview of ecstasy (MDMA, MDA) related fatalities. *Psychopharmacology (Berlin), 173*(3–4), 242–248.

Schifano, F., Albanese, A., Fergus, S., Stair, J. L., Deluca, P., Corazza, O., ... Ghodse, A. H. (2011). Mephedrone (4-methylmethcathinone; 'meow meow'): chemical, pharmacological and clinical issues. *Psychopharmacology (Berlin), 214*(3), 593–602.

Schulenberg, J. E., & Maggs, J. L. (2002). A developmental perspective on alcohol use and heavy drinking during adolescence and the transition to young adulthood. *Journal of Studies on Alcohol and Drugs, Suppl14,* 54–70.

Sewell, R. A., Poling, J., & Sofuoglu, M. (2009). The effect of cannabis compared with alcohol on driving. *American Journal on Addictions, 18*(3), 185–193.

Shiffman, S. (2009). Light and intermittent smokers: background and perspective. *Nicotine & Tobacco Research, 11*(2), 122–125.

Simons, J. S., & Arens, A. M. (2007). Moderating effects of sensitivity to punishment and sensitivity to reward on associations between marijuana effect expectancies and use. *Psychology of Addictive Behaviors, 21*(3), 409–414.

Simons, J. S., & Carey, K. B. (2006). An affective and cognitive model of marijuana and alcohol problems. *Addictive Behaviors, 31,* 1578–1592.

Simons, J. S., Dvorak, R. D., & Batien, B. D. (2008). Methamphetamine use in a rural college population: associations with marijuana use, sensitivity to punishment, and sensitivity to reward. *Psychology of Addictive Behaviors, 22*(3), 444–449.

Simons, J. S., Dvorak, R. D., & Lau-Barraco, C. (2009). Behavioral inhibition and activation systems: differences in substance use expectancy organization and activation in memory. *Psychology of Addictive Behaviors, 23*(2), 315–328.

Simons, J. S., Maisto, S. A., & Wray, T. B. (2010). Sexual risk-taking among young adult dual alcohol and marijuana users. *Addictive Behaviors, 35,* 533–536.

Smith, K. M., Larive, L. L., & Romanelli, F. (2002). Club drugs: Methylenedioxymethamphetamine, flunitrazepam, ketamine hydrochloride, and gamma-hydroxybutyrate. *American Journal of Health-System Pharmacy, 59*(11), 1067–1076.

Smith, M. (2006). Cardiovascular safety warning added for stimulants for ADHD. Retrieved from http://www.medpagetoday.com/ProductAlert/Prescriptions/tb2/3987

Sofuoglu, M., & Kosten, T. R. (2005). Novel approaches to the treatment of cocaine addiction. *CNS Drugs, 19*(1), 13–25.

Sommers, I., Baskin, D., & Baskin-Sommers, A. (2006). Methamphetamine use among young adults: Health and social consequences. *Addictive Behaviors, 31*(8), 1469–1476.

Staff, J., Schulenberg, J. E., Maslowsky, J., Bachman, J. G., O'Malley, P. M., Maggs, J. L., & Johnston, L. D. (2010). Substance use changes and social role transitions: proximal developmental effects on ongoing trajectories from late adolescence through early adulthood. *Development and Psychopathology, 22*(4), 917–932.

Steinberg, L. (2008). A Social Neuroscience Perspective on Adolescent Risk-Taking. *Developmental Review, 28*(1), 78–106.

Strang, J., Bearn, J., Farrell, M., Finch, E., Gossop, M., Griffiths, P.,... Wolff, K. (1998). Route of drug use and its implications for drug effect, risk of dependence and health consequences. *Drug and Alcohol Review, 17,* 197–211.

Substance Abuse and Mental Health Service Administration (2006). *State estimates of past year methamphetamine use.* Rockville, MD: Office of Applied Studies, Substance Abuse and Mental Health Services Administration.

Substance Abuse and Mental Health Services Administration (2006a). Methamphetamine/amphetamine treatment admissions in urban and rural areas: 2004. *DASIS report*(27).

Substance Abuse and Mental Health Services Administration (2006b). *Results from the 2005 national survey on drug use and health: National findings.* Rockville, MD.

Substance Abuse and Mental Health Services Administration (2007). *Results from the 2006 National Survey on Drug Use and Health: National Findings. Office of Applied Studies, NSDUH Series H-32, DHHS Publication No. SMA 07–4293.* Rockville, MD.

Substance Abuse and Mental Health Services Administration (2008). *The DASIS Report–Geographic differences in substance abuse treatment admissions for methamphetamine/Amphetamine and marijuana: 2005.* Rockville, MD.

Substance Abuse and Mental Health Services Administration (2009). *National Survey on Drug Use and Health (NSDUH), 2009.*

Substance Abuse and Mental Health Service Administration (2009). *Treatment episode data set (TEDS). Highlights—2007. National admissions to substance abuse treatment services.* Rockville, MD.

Substance Abuse and Mental Health Service Administration (2010a). *Results from the 2009 national survey on drug use and health: Volume I. Summary of national findings.* Rockville, MD.

Substance Abuse and Mental Health Service Administration (2010b). *The DAWN report: Emergency department visits involving methamphetamine: 2004 to 2008.* Rockville, MD.

Sussman, S., Pentz, M. A., Spruijt-Metz, D., & Miller, T. (2006). Misuse of "study drugs": prevalence, consequences, and implications for policy. *Substance Abuse Treatment, Prevention, and Policy, 1,* 15.

Sutfin, E. L., Reboussin, B. A., McCoy, T. P., & Wolfson, M. (2009). Are college student smokers really a homogeneous group? a latent class analysis of college student smokers. *Nicotine & Tobacco Research, 11*(4), 444–454.

Swift, W., Copeland, J., & Lenton, S. (2000). Cannabis and harm reduction. *Drug and Alcohol Review, 19*(1), 101–112.

Teter, C. J., Falone, A. E., Cranford, J. A., Boyd, C. J., & McCabe, S. E. (2010). Nonmedical use of prescription stimulants and depressed mood among college students: Frequency and routes of administration. *Journal of Substance Abuse Treatment, 38*(3), 292–298.

Teter, C. J., McCabe, S. E., LaGrange, K., Cranford, J. A., & Boyd, C. J. (2006). Illicit use of specific prescription stimulants among college students: Prevalence, motives, and routes of administration. *Pharmacotherapy, 26*(10), 1501–1510.

Tseng, C.-C., Derlet, R. W., Stark, L. G., & Albertson, T. E. (1991). Cocaine-induced respiratory depression in urethane-anesthetized rats: A possible mechanism of cocaine-induced death. *Pharmacology Biochemistry and Behavior, 39*(3), 625–633.

Tyndall, M. W., Currie, S., Spittal, P., Li, K., Wood, E., O'Shaughnessy, M. V., & Schechter, M. T. (2003). Intensive injection cocaine use as the primary risk factor in the Vancouver HIV-1 epidemic. *AIDS, 17*(6), 887–893.

Upreti, V. V., Eddington, N. D., Moon, K. H., Song, B. J., & Lee, I. J. (2009). Drug interaction between ethanol and 3,4-methylenedioxymethamphetamine ("ecstasy"). *Toxicology Letters, 188*(2), 167–172.

Verdejo-Garcia, A., Benbrook, A., Funderburk, F., David, P., Cadet, J. L., & Bolla, K. I. (2007). The differential relationship between cocaine use and marijuana use on decision-making performance over repeat testing with the Iowa Gambling Task. *Drug and Alcohol Dependence, 90*(1), 2–11.

Vuori, E., Henry, J. A., Ojanpera, I., Nieminen, R., Savolainen, T., Wahlsten, P., & Jantti, M. (2003). Death following ingestion of MDMA (ecstasy) and moclobemide. *Addiction, 98*(3), 365–368.

Walters, S. T., Foy, B. D., & Castro, R. J. (2002). The agony of ecstasy: Responding to growing MDMA use among college students. *Journal of American College Health, 51*(3), 139–141.

Westermeyer, J. (2006). Comorbid schizophrenia and substance abuse: A review of epidemiology and course. *American Journal of Addictions, 15,* 345–355.

Wetter, D. W., Kenford, S. L., Welsch, S. K., Smith, S. S., Fouladi, R. T., Fiore, M. C., & Baker, T. B. (2004). Prevalence and predictors of transitions in smoking behavior among college students. *Health Psychology, 23*(2), 168–177.

White, B. P., Becker-Blease, K. A., & Grace-Bishop, K. (2006). Stimulant medication use, misuse, and abuse in an undergraduate and graduate student sample. *Journal of American College Health, 54*(5), 261–268.

Wiers, R. W., Bartholow, B. D., van den Wildenberg, E., Thush, C., Engels, R. C. M. E., Sher, K. J., ... Stacy, A. W. (2007). Automatic and controlled processes and the development of addictive behaviors in adolescents: A review and a model. *Pharmacology, Biochemistry and Behavior, 86*(2), 263–283.

Wilson, K. C., & Saukkonen, J. J. (2004). Acute respiratory failure from abused substances. *Journal of Intensive Care Medicine, 19*(4), 183–193.

Zimmer, l., & Morgan, J. P. (1997). *Marijuana myths: Marijuana facts.* New York, NY: Lindesmith Center.

3

Windows of Risk

Events and Contexts Associated With Extreme Drinking

Clayton Neighbors, Dawn W. Foster, Nicole Fossos, and Melissa A. Lewis

T his chapter considers etiology and prevention of college drinking from contextual and event-level perspectives. Events may include holidays or academic periods common to all students, or they can be personal events or celebrations of occasions that occur for only some students or for all students at varying times. Contexts may include pregaming, parties, and drinking games. A primary distinction between events and contexts presented in this chapter is that events are planned and occur on prespecified dates that can be anticipated, whereas contexts are more diffuse and not necessarily designated for a specific date or time. The distinction between events and contexts can be ambiguous in some cases. For example, sporting events are a high-risk context but a specific sporting event such as March Madness or an annual rivalry football game is an event. Similarly, parties are contexts but parties may be held to celebrate specific events such as Halloween, New Year's Eve, or 21st birthdays. These parties would be considered events. Moreover, high-risk drinking contexts are often evident during specific windows of risk such as the start of the school year. Thus, the distinction between contexts and events is made to facilitate helping us think about windows of risk and not because there is a clearly defined boundary between them in reality. Accordingly, we have divided the chapter into two major sections: the first focuses on events associated with excessive drinking and the second focuses on contexts associated with excessive drinking.

EVENTS ASSOCIATED WITH EXTREME DRINKING

Much of the content in this section encompasses an emerging prevention paradigm known as Event Specific Prevention (ESP). We review work that identifies specific holidays and windows of time that have been associated with elevated drinking. We also provide an overview of the conceptualization of ESP and its potential to augment existing prevention efforts, which include empirically supported general interventions and well intentioned but nonempirically supported efforts to provide alcohol programming for specific events. We further review the existing available literature covering specific event etiology and prevention where available. This includes 21st birthdays and Spring Break, where the majority of ESP efforts have focused to date. We also provide some consideration of other specific events where data have been relatively limited.

Why consider specific events. At an event level, windows of risk can be defined as specific periods of time or specific events in which risks of adverse consequences are elevated. Similarly, ESP refers to attempts to reduce risks within specific windows or during specific events. We begin by asking why one might want to consider preventing drinking during specific windows of risk. There are multiple perspectives from which we attempt to answer this question, for example, proverbial, historical, and practical. Considering these three in turn, we begin with a parable that may be familiar to many readers.

There was a man who was walking around under a streetlight peering intently at the ground. Another man came up to him and asked him what he was doing. The first man said he was looking for his keys. The second man asked, "Did you drop your keys here under the streetlight?" The first man replied, "No, actually I dropped them over there across the street, but there is more light over here." The parable illustrates the tendency for us to look for answers where we feel comfortable looking. In many ways, the typical methods for studying college drinking and other behavioral phenomena are analogous to looking for keys under the streetlight. For example, it is easier to ask students how much they drink than to observe their drinking directly. Similarly, it is easier to ask students how much they drink during an average week than to assess their daily drinking. We cannot see into people's minds and directly evaluate their motivations for drinking. Yet, the farther away we get from direct observations and/or assessment of real, concrete, specific events, the greater the risks of distortion and misinterpretation. Practical barriers prevent us from the acquisition of perfect measures of drinking, but it is important for us to consider why we are asking the questions in the first place and to recognize the limitations of our examination strategies.

Historically, for us at least, much of the work on ESP, and 21st birthday specifically, which will be reviewed, was precipitated by a series of tragedies that occurred in North Dakota in 2003. In the spring of 2003, three near-deaths occurred in North Dakota within a short period of time as a result of excessive drinking during 21st birthday celebrations. These events inspired an empirical investigation into the phenomenon of 21st birthday drinking. An extensive review of the literature at that time did not reveal even a single published paper in the peer-reviewed literature related to 21st birthday drinking. In fact, the only research-related work regarding 21st birthday drinking being done at that time was a program initiated at Michigan State University (MSU). The B.R.A.D. (Be Responsible About Drinking) program was inspired by Cindy McCue, whose son Brad died as a result of drinking on his 21st birthday. The B.R.A.D. program sent birthday cards to MSU students turning 21 as a tribute to Brad McCue. The cards include a brief description of Brad, encouragement to celebrate responsibly, and alcohol poisoning information. This program inspired several subsequent studies reviewed below. The point here is that the focus was inspired by a desire to address an observed problem in the real world that had not received empirical attention. It was not inspired by the desire to test some preexisting theory about why individuals may engage in extreme drinking during specific windows of time or on specific events. Those thoughts came later. Thus, one might want to study drinking during specific windows of risk because it provides an opportunity to address real problems that arise from extreme drinking during specific events.

A related reason for focusing on specific windows of risk is that it may provide a more focused and precise view of data that have traditionally been studies at broader levels of abstraction. For example, a student who drinks an average of 14.7 drinks per week almost certainly does not drink 14.7 drinks every week. Moreover, 14.7 drinks per week will almost certainly not correspond to drinking 2.1 drinks each day. Rather, a student who drinks an average of 14.7 drinks per week probably varies considerably in his or her drinking, depending on what is going on in his or her life (e.g., whether it is a "normal" week; the week of finals; holidays; the beginning of a new romantic relationship). A student who drinks 14.7 drinks in a given week probably consumes most of them on the weekend in the context of social interactions with specific others who are consuming alcohol. Scientific explorations often examine phenomena by averaging across many contexts to identify general principles. Among the costs of this macro focus is the loss of potentially important contextual information, which may be critical in advancing theoretical understanding. In addition, alcohol-related negative consequences in this population usually result from acute heavy drinking episodes rather than from chronic heavy use over an extended period (Hingson, Heeren, Winter, & Wechsler 2005; Turner & Shu, 2004). Thus, in addition to providing an opportunity to address real problems, the study of drinking during specific windows of risk also provides a more focused description of how drinking actually occurs in real life, which should be helpful in theory development.

Windows of risk may fundamentally differ from typical time periods in multiple ways that make them worthy of study. First, by definition, many windows of risk can be anticipated. With a few mouse clicks, we can determine when Spring Break is scheduled on any campus well in advance. We have 21 years notice for when people will celebrate their 21st birthdays. New Year's Eve happens on the same date every year (usually December 31). Moreover, most events or windows of risk associated with holidays or academic periods are known in advance. Relatedly, these types of windows of risk tend to be time limited. Spring Break usually lasts no more than 10 days, depending on whether students include the weekend before and after. Most students celebrate their 21st birthday on a single day, though some may spread the celebration over a few days. New Year's lasts until the party is over; for most, this is not much later than the wee hours of January 1.

Some features of specific windows of risk, such as being predetermined and time-limited, work in our favor, in that they make the timing of assessment and intervention efforts straightforward. Other aspects of specific windows of risk may not work in our favor. Specifically, social norms for drinking during specific events may promote heavier drinking (Neighbors, Oster-Aaland, Bergstrom, & Lewis, 2006). Research reviewed below suggests that students overestimate peer drinking during specific windows of risk (e.g., Spring Break, 21st birthdays, and football games) and that these perceptions are higher than their perceptions of nonspecific drinking days. Norms in the college population, and among college age youth more generally, may become insulated from outside perspectives. Drinking 21 shots while celebrating one's 21st birthday has somehow become a good idea in the minds of many students, even though this may provide a lethal dose of alcohol. Similarly, students who strongly disapprove of getting drunk and having sex with a stranger may see this behavior as less unacceptable during Spring Break. Windows of risk may be viewed as "time outs" from normal self-regulation. Furthermore, it may be that drinking is harder to change during some windows of risk than others, though research has yet to directly evaluate this question.

In sum, the study of drinking during specific events and windows of risk may provide a more accurate picture of high-risk drinking and may provide us with insights into how to reduce risks associated with specific events and windows. Research has begun to consider the context in which college drinking occurs, with greater emphasis on specific days, windows of risks, and patterns of drinking within weeks and across weeks of the academic calendar.

Twenty-First Birthday

The 21st birthday marks the transition to the legal drinking age in the United States and is often considered a rite of passage among young adults. As such, the prevalence and quantity of alcohol consumed during this celebratory event is quite high. Approximately 90% of college students report drinking alcohol during their 21st birthday (Neighbors, Spieker, Oster-Aaland, Lewis, & Bergstrom, 2005; Neighbors et al., 2011), and 72% engage in heavy episodic drinking (at least 4 drinks for women and 5 drinks for men) on this occasion (Neighbors et al., 2005). Nearly 70% of students drink more than they intend to consume on their birthday (Brister, Wetherill, & Fromme, 2010) and roughly half of all 21st birthday drinkers consume more alcohol on this occasion than on any prior occasion (Rutledge, Park, & Sher, 2008). Moreover, the 21st birthday outranks all other holidays for the greatest proportion of students who drink and the highest blood alcohol concentrations (BACs) reached among college students (Neighbors et al., 2011). Recent work has shown that 21st birthday drinking is grossly elevated in comparison with other holidays (Foster, Rodriguez, Neighbors, DiBello, & Chen, 2011; Neighbors et al., 2011).

More concerning than the amount of alcohol consumed on the 21st birthday are the consequences associated with extreme drinking. Engaging in dangerous drinking practices such as the "power hour" whereby the birthday celebrant attempts to consume 21 shots between midnight and 1 a.m. on their 21st birthday, or attempting to consume 21 drinks over the course of a night, have led to fatal consequences on numerous college campuses across the nation (e.g., B.R.A.D. Foundation, 2008). Rutledge and colleagues (2008) found that engaging in these drinking practices is relatively common on college campuses, with 12% of students in their sample reporting consuming 21 or more drinks over the course of their 21st birthday celebration. Alarmingly, nearly one quarter of college students report drinking at levels corresponding to BACs at or above 0.25% (Neighbors et al., 2005), and nearly 40% of students report blacking out as a result of drinking for their 21st birthday (Wetherill & Fromme, 2009), putting them at risk for dangerous, and in some cases lethal harms. Lewis, Lindgren, Fossos, Neighbors, and Oster-Aaland (2009) reported that half of the students in their sample indicated experiencing at least one alcohol-related consequence during the 21st birthday, with the most commonly reported alcohol-related consequences being hangovers (44%), vomiting (35%), and not remembering part or parts of the evening before (31%).

Given the prevalence, quantity, and consequences associated with drinking during 21st birthday celebrations, research has begun to evaluate risk factors for extreme drinking and related negative consequences experienced on these occasions to inform intervention efforts. One line of research in this area has evaluated the role of perceived social norms on drinking during the 21st birthday. Perceived norms for drinking take the form of descriptive (perceived frequency or quantity of consumption) or injunctive (perceived approval of drinking) norms. Young adults and college students in particular tend to overestimate the amount that other students typically consume and the degree to which other students approve of drinking in general. Thus, social norms have frequently been used as a target of preventive interventions for typical drinking behavior among college students. However, students also tend to overestimate drinking norms for 21st birthdays, and exaggerated normative beliefs about drinking during 21st birthdays have been associated with increased drinking on this occasion (Day-Cameron, Muse, Hauenstein, Simmons, & Correia, 2009; Neighbors et al., 2006). Additionally, the more closely connected one is to the reference group, the stronger the influence perceived drinking norms have on behavior (Patrick, Neighbors, & Lee, 2012). Thus, close friends have a stronger influence on one's drinking in comparison to students on one's campus, who have a stronger influence on one's drinking than people in general.

Another line of research has begun to evaluate what factors in the immediate drinking context influence the amount one consumes on the 21st birthday. Brister and colleagues (2010) examined situational characteristics that contribute to drinking more than intended on one's 21st birthday, and found that celebrants who drank shots of liquor and drank at a faster pace, engaged in drinking traditions (e.g., 21 run, drinking at midnight), and had peers present who encouraged their drinking, showed the greatest discrepancies between intended and actual drinking.Additionally, typical drinking patterns have been found to predict drinking over one's 21st birthday, such that typically heavy drinkers tend to drink more during their 21st birthday celebrations than students who typically drink at lower or moderate levels. However, students at greatest risk for experiencing negative consequences are those who were not typically heavy drinkers but drank heavily on their birthdays (Lewis et al., 2009). Thus, interventions that only focus on typically heavy drinkers might miss an important subgroup of students who do not typically drink heavily, but drink heavily and experience consequences because of their drinking during their 21st birthday celebration.

Recent media stories have highlighted the lethal dangers associated with engaging in drinking traditions, with 21st birthday alcohol-related deaths reported on college campuses across the United States. Prevention efforts on college campuses have begun to target 21st birthday drinking and have most often entailed sending a birthday card to students prior to their birthday that incorporates encouraging messages of moderation or abstinence for drinking during the celebrant's birthday. The pioneers of this approach developed the Be Responsible About Drinking (B.R.A.D.) program and drew their inspiration from the death of a Michigan State University student, Bradley McCue, who consumed 24 drinks, reaching a BAC of 0.44 on his 21st birthday. The B.R.A.D Birthday Card intervention consists of sending students a birthday card the week prior to their 21st birthday with the message telling of the tragedy of Bradley McCue and a reminder to drink responsibly during their birthday celebration so that they can be around for their next birthday. The B.R.A.D. card is currently used by more than 130 colleges and universities spanning 31 states (B.R.A.D. Foundation, 2008). Research evaluating the B.R.A.D. card has produced mixed findings. Hembroff, Atkin, Martell, McCue, and Greenamyer (2007) found that sending the B.R.A.D. card can reduce amount of alcohol consumed on the 21st birthday, but only when the card is received before the birthday, is read, and is remembered by the birthday celebrant. Smith, Bogle, Talbott, Gant, and Castillo (2006) evaluated the B.R.A.D. card in comparison to a neutral birthday card, a card containing social norms information, a card containing harm-reduction information (e.g., tips to avoid negative consequences), and a card that combined the social norms and harm reduction information. This study found that none of the birthday cards had any significant effects on drinking or alcohol-related negative consequences. Thus, the support for utilizing a birthday card incorporating a message of caution without other components is minimal and it may not be the most effective stand-alone approach for curbing drinking during this event.

Neighbors and colleagues (Neighbors et al., 2005; Lewis, Neighbors, Lee, & Oster-Aaland, 2008) designed a birthday card that took a different approach from the B.R.A.D. card. A humorous, nonthreatening message encouraged moderation of drinking while celebrating the 21st birthday. Results revealed that although students reported liking the card, the card had no impact on their drinking or plans for their birthday. Lewis et al. (2008) expanded on this approach to incorporate personalized normative feedback into a birthday card. The card asked students to write down the number of drinks they intended to consume on their birthday and the number of drinks they believed other students consume on their 21st birthday and then presented them with the average number of drinks students actually consume on their campus (6.95 drinks) on their 21st birthday. These three pieces of information, taken together, allow students to make two key comparisons: the amount they believe the typical student drinks (perceived descriptive norm) compared with the actual amount typical students drink during their 21st birthday (actual descriptive norm) on their campus *and* the amount typical students actually drink compared with their own drinking intentions for their 21st birthday. These comparisons highlight the discrepancies between the student's drinking intentions/perceived norms and how much others are actually drinking on their campus. Results of this study revealed that the card did not have an impact on drinking or alcohol-related consequences during the 21st birthday, but did reduce normative misperceptions for drinking during the 21st birthday, which has previously been found to mediate changes in drinking in a social norms intervention targeting general drinking behavior (Neighbors et al., 2010). Glassman, Dodd, Sheu, Rienzo, and Wagenaar (2010) tested the efficacy of four different electronic birthday cards that either contained: (1) alcohol education information and alternatives to drinking on the 21st birthday, (2) a social norms message about 21st birthday drinking, (3) harm-reduction messages to avoid negative consequences while drinking during the 21st birthday, or (4) a combination of alcohol education information, social norms messages, and harm-reduction messages about 21st birthday drinking, and found no impact of the cards on drinking during the birthday. However, the social norms message used in the social norms card and combined card was not personalized (e.g., "Most [insert school mascot here] have 0 to 4 Drinks on their Birthday"). Thus, no explicit information was communicated about the recipient's own drinking or his or her perceptions of typical drinking. In addition, students appeared to question the accuracy of drinking norms information that was provided.

LaBrie, Migliuri, and Cail (2009) evaluated the efficacy of a 21st birthday card campaign on drinking and related consequences among residence hall students using a harm-reduction approach with a card emphasizing moderate drinking among those who chose to drink (rather than recommending abstinence). The card incorporated multiple components, including a list of alternative options for celebrating that did not involve alcohol, tips and protective behavioral strategies the celebrant could use if they chose to drink, and a normative message about typical drinking on campus. Contrary to the majority of birthday card intervention studies, students who received the birthday card consumed fewer drinks and reached lower estimated BACs (eBAC) than students who did not receive the card. Specifically, male students who received the card reported consuming 23.4% fewer drinks and had a 22.1% lower eBAC level than the males who did not receive the card. Female students who received the card consumed 40.2% fewer drinks and reached a 46.4% lower eBAC level in comparison to the females in the control condition.

Neighbors, Lee, Lewis, Fossos, and Walter (2009) also designed a multicomponent Web-based approach to 21st birthday intervention delivery, whereby students turning 21 were randomized to either receive a Web-based multicomponent feedback intervention or attention control feedback one week prior to their 21st birthday. The 21st birthday intervention feedback was adapted from the feedback utilized in the Brief Alcohol Screening and Intervention for College Students (BASICS; Dimeff, Baer, Kivlahan, & Marlatt, 1999; Marlatt et al., 1998) and incorporated personalized information about the student's drinking intentions, BAC information that included a personalized BAC chart that students could use to calculate their eBAC, personalized normative feedback about their drinking intentions and perceptions compared with other students' drinking behavior on the 21st birthday, and protective behavior strategies that incorporated the students, own expectations for effects and consequences of drinking on their birthday. The students in the intervention feedback condition reported lower BAC on their 21st birthday, and this effect was mediated by reductions in perceived 21st birthday drinking norms. Additionally, the intervention was particularly effective among those who had previously intended to reach higher levels of intoxication. Thus, this study provides support for an adapted, yet established intervention (e.g., BASICS) delivered over the Web in reducing intended and actual BACs on the 21st birthday.

In an extension of this study, Neighbors and colleagues (in press) expanded their approach to evaluate whether delivering the 21st birthday-specific BASICS intervention in-person with a trained intervention facilitator versus over the web increased the efficacy of the intervention. In addition, they incorporated friend involvement as an active intervention component among half of those randomized to the 21st birthday specific interventions. A general BASICS group and an attention control group were also included as comparisons. Thus, students were randomized to one of six intervention conditions: 21BASICS, 21BASICS + Friend Intervention, 21WEB-BASICS, 21WEBBASICS + Friend Intervention, General BASICS, or Control. The 21st birthday intervention materials for both the in-person and web interventions were similar in content to the intervention in Neighbors et al. (2009). Additionally, friends of participants who participated in the Friend Intervention were provided with general tips for helping their friend have a safe and fun 21st birthday celebration as well as information about BAC that was personalized based on the participant's gender and weight (although the friend was not told the participant's weight). Results of this study showed that all five treatment groups reported fewer drinks on the 21st birthday relative to the control group, though none of the differences were statistically significant. General BASICS participants had the strongest reduction (14% decrease), followed by 21WEBBASICS (13% decrease) and 21BASICS + Friend Intervention (9% decrease) relative to control, and each of these comparisons approached significance (p-values between .05 and .10).

Similarly, all five treatment groups reported lower mean peak eBAC on the 21st birthday relative to the control group, with 21WEBBASICS showing the largest significant difference (0.05), followed by general BASIC (0.048 difference). In addition, all five intervention groups reported fewer alcohol-related negative consequences on the 21st birthday, relative to the control group, with participants in the General BASICS condition and 21BASICS + Friend Intervention reporting 22% and 21% significantly fewer alcohol-related negative consequences than the control group, respectively. Findings from this study indicate that specificity of the intervention (birthday-specific vs. general), mode of intervention delivery (in-person vs. Web), and whether friends are involved in the intervention, may play an important role in the efficacy of interventions on alcohol-related outcomes. These results, however, do not provide unequivocal support for either inclusion of friends or specificity of content. They may simply suggest that doing something is better than doing nothing, and which options are included are a matter of preference. It is also possible that timing of the intervention is a critical element, though this was not varied in the study. Future research is needed to evaluate whether an intervention administered immediately before a specific event is more effective than one that is delivered far in advance. Another important future step is to further evaluate how these interventions impact drinking over time and across different events.

In sum, with respect to specific events, the 21st birthday represents the heaviest reported drinking day among college students (Neighbors et al., 2011) and has received considerable research and media attention. Previous work has found that perceived social norms, typical drinking behavior, and situational factors all contribute to the amount that one drinks on his or her 21st birthday. Additionally, prevention efforts have begun to target 21st birthday drinking on many college campuses, often utilizing a birthday card intervention approach utilizing harm reduction and/or normative messages about drinking during the 21st birthday. In general, birthday cards and approaches that do not provide personalized feedback have not been effective to date. Recent efforts have begun to utilize a multicomponent approach to curb drinking during this event, incorporating alcohol education, social norms/personalized normative feedback, harm reduction, and/or personalized BAC information components. These approaches have shown more promise. Future research should aim to evaluate which components are most effective at reducing drinking during this high-risk event to better inform intervention efforts targeting drinking during the 21st birthday on college campuses. Future research is also needed to distinguish the extent to which intervention content or timing is most critical in determining efficacy.

Spring Break

Previous research has found that college student drinking is highly variable over the course of an academic year (Del Boca, Darkes, Greenbaum, & Goldman, 2004; Greenbaum, Del Boca, Darkes, Wang, & Goldman, 2005). One window of risk that was identified by Del Boca and colleagues is Spring Break. From vacation packages and destinations promoted heavily through advertising and the media (e.g., MTV), Spring Break drinking has received an excess of media attention (Josiam, Hobson, Dietrich, & Smeaton, 1998). In addition, research has found that many students use college Spring Break vacations to travel with the intent to engage in extreme party behaviors, including excessive alcohol use, other drug use, and related sexual risks (Josiam et al., 1998; Maticka-Tyndale & Herold, 1997). To examine Spring Break drinking, Smeaton, Josiam, and Dietrich (1998) used beachfront convenience samples in Panama City beach in Florida, and found that men reported drinking 18 drinks and women 10 drinks the previous day; the majority of students surveyed had engaged in heavy episodic drinking. In another study, Sönmez et al. (2006) found that a large proportion of students reported getting drunk over Spring Break (51% males, 40% females) as well as having three or more drinks in one sitting (52% males, 45% females).

Additional research examining Spring Break has found that trips place individuals at greater risk for engaging in high-risk drinking. The proportion of students who go on Spring Break trips likely varies across campuses and as a function of socioeconomic status but few studies have taken these factors into account. In addition, trips have not always been defined in a manner distinguishing trips to exotic destinations versus trips to visit parents. For example, Lee, Maggs, and Rankin (2006) found elevated drinking during Spring Break, but primarily among students who went on Spring Break trips, where trips were not specifically defined. Furthermore, this study found that students who went on Spring Break trips reported higher levels of drinking both during Spring Break and in general. Grekin, Sher, and Krull (2007) reported similar findings, such that students who went on vacation with friends during Spring Break had larger increases in Spring Break drinking, relative to typical drinking, than students who did not vacation with friends. Additionally, this study found that students who went on vacation with friends drank more during non–Spring Break weeks than students who stayed with parents. When examining students' motivations for selecting Panama City Beach to celebrate their Spring Break, Smeaton et al. (1998) found that students' motivations were associated with alcohol use such that students who selected Panama

City Beach because of its "good party reputation," drank more and were intoxicated more often compared to students who selected Panama City Beach for other reasons, such as the cost of the trip. Together, findings from Lee, Lewis, and Neighbors (2009); Grekin, Sher, and Krull (2007); and Smeaton, Josiam, and Dietrich (1998) suggest a possible selection effect for Spring Break drinking, where heavier drinking students may seek out opportunities or activities, such as going on Spring Break vacations with friends, with the intent of engaging in extreme drinking.

Time-limited occasions, such as Spring Break, are associated with elevated risks for a majority of students, even for ones who would typically be categorized as low or infrequent drinkers. For example, Greenbaum et al. (2005) found that most students, including typical light drinkers, evidenced increased drinking during specific events, including Spring Break. Furthermore, as found with 21st birthday drinking (Lewis et al., 2009), Lee et al. (2009) found that typically lighter drinkers who drank during Spring Break were *more* likely to have reported negative consequences than heavier drinkers. Findings suggest that those who do not normally drink heavily and those who have lower tolerance may be especially at risk on occasions where they drink much more than they would normally, such as Spring Break. An alternative explanation is that lighter drinkers may be more likely than heavier drinkers to report alcohol-related negative consequences.

In addition to Spring Break being associated with problematic drinking, this window of time has also been related to risky sexual behavior (Matika-Tyndale et al., 1998; Ragsdale, Difranceisco, & Pinkerton, 2006). For example, Apostolopoulos, Sönmez, and Yu (2002) examined college students' drinking and sexual behaviors during Spring Break vacation, and found that approximately half of all students reported getting drunk, and a third reported having sex with someone they met on their vacation. Furthermore, this study found that although more than half of all students reported either having condoms with them or having access to them, less than a quarter of students who had casual sex reported regular condom use. In another study, Sönmez et al. (2006) examined drinking and sexual behavior during Spring Break. Of the male and female students who reported having casual sex during Spring Break (30% and 31%, respectively), the majority of students (79% of men, and 84% of women) reported irregular condom use (i.e., never, rarely, or sometimes using condoms). Additionally, a large proportion of students reported having had sex as a result of drinking (49% males, 38% females). When considering the low rates of condom use, it is alarming that most students had sex with a partner that they knew less than one week (84% males, 96% females). Students who rarely or never used a condom indicated it was because they never or rarely worried about STIs/HIV (74% males, 87% females). It is important to note that this research examined the general global relationship between drinking and sexual behavior during Spring Break; drinking in relation to sexual behavior during this window of risk has not been examined at the event level. In other words, although it might be predicted, it is not known whether alcohol use and risky sexual behavior occur at the same time (e.g., Cooper, 2002; Weinhardt & Carey, 2000). Thus, research has yet to determine the influence of excessive drinking on sexual behavior during Spring Break.

Another study conducted by Patrick, Morgan, Maggs, and Lefkowitz (2010) examined drinking and sexual behavior over Spring Break in a sample of college students. During the 10 days of Spring Break, 37% of men and 25% of women reported heavy episodic drinking (5/4 drinks for men/women in a row). Although these rates are not much different from non–Spring Break periods (Wechsler, Lee, Kuo, & Lee, 2000), 6% of men and 12% of women reported having sex without a condom. Among students who drank, about one out of three had a hangover and one out of eight reported passing out. Of those who had sex, only one in five students worried about pregnancy. This study also found that about half of the students had prior discussions with friends about Spring Break behaviors, regardless of whether they went on Spring Break trips with friends. Moreover, the formation of these understandings was associated with their health behaviors and experiences, including high-risk drinking, sex without a condom, and alcohol-related negative consequences. This study also noted gender differences such that men were more likely than women to have specific understandings with their friends to get drunk and to have sex with someone new. Men were also more likely than women to have had prior discussions with friends about using condoms. Encouraging friends to have discussions about risks prior to an event may prove to be a valuable intervention technique, but more research in this area is needed.

Research conducted by Shah, Smolensky, Burau, Cech, and Lai (2007) suggested that peaks in STIs between the months of March and May could be associated with Spring Break. Furthermore, research has suggested that attitudes toward these behaviors during Spring Break may be a contributing factor. Findings from an American Medical Association (2006) survey conducted with female college students and graduates demonstrated the perceptions surrounding drinking and sexual behavior during Spring Break. The majority (83%) of respondents agreed that Spring Break trips involve more or heavier drinking than found on college campuses. In relation to sexual risk, just over half (57%) thought that being promiscuous is a way of fitting in during Spring Break and most (74%) stated that Spring Break trips are associated with increased sexual activity. Additionally, findings showed that 59% of the females had sexual intercourse with more than one partner and that 60% of their friends had admitted to having unprotected sex, more often than not, with previously unknown partners.

Although the above research clearly indicates that Spring Break is a window of risk for both high-risk drinking and sexual behavior, little research has examined preventative interventions focused on these risk behaviors during Spring Break. For example, colleges often have Spring Break alcohol education programming, so formal interventions in the published research regarding reducing risk during Spring Break are rare

(Cronin, 1996; Neighbors et al., 2007). One study conducted by Snyder and Misera (2008) examined student perceptions of a Safe Spring Break event. Findings indicated that 89.9% of students learned something new at the event, and 84.5% reported the information would be helpful while on Spring Break. Students also reported that the event was effective at increasing their knowledge regarding specific health behaviors surrounding Spring Break. However, for this study students were not followed longitudinally to evaluate the efficacy of the Safe Spring Break event on Spring Break health behaviors.

In summary, Spring Break represents a window of risk associated with extreme drinking and elevated sexual risk behavior. Young adults who travel for Spring Break are at even greater risk for heavy drinking and related consequences, including risky sexual encounters. Though research has established that Spring Break represents a period of high risk for both drinking and risky sex, targeted interventions have not as of yet been developed for use on college campuses for students going on Spring Break trips. Preventive interventions targeting Spring Break drinking and sexual behavior among young adults are clearly needed.

Other Drinking Events

Several other events have been examined as potential high-risk drinking occasions (Neighbors et al., 2011). Some specific events such as New Year's, Spring Break, and July 4 are more strongly associated with heavier drinking than other specific events such as the Super Bowl, St. Patrick's Day, and Mardi Gras (Neighbors et al., 2011). For example, the proportion of people drinking on Cinco de Mayo was not found to be significantly different from typical weekend drinking, but of those who did consume alcohol on Cinco de Mayo, BACs were estimated to be higher than typical weekend alcohol consumption (Neighbors et al., 2011). Similarly, relative to a typical weekend, fewer individuals drank on Fat Tuesday, Super Bowl Sunday, and President's Day, but of those who did consume alcohol, eBACs were similar to typical weekend drinking (Neighbors et al., 2011). Other drinking events were either associated with greater proportions of drinkers (e.g., Valentine's Day) or higher eBAC (e.g., Cinco de Mayo) but not both. These findings indicate that elevated drinking levels occurred for the majority of events, however the prevalence and the quantity that was consumed varied by the event.

Event Specific Prevention

Event Specific Prevention (ESP) is a logical product of the identification of specific windows of risk. ESP strategies are based on the assumptions that timing and content of intervention strategies are important in targeting windows of risk. Foreknowledge of the timing of an event should provide a distinct advantage for reducing risk during

Table 3.1 Event-Specific Prevention Typology for a 21st Birthday

Prevention	Examples
Knowledge, attitudes, skills, self-efficacy, behavioral intentions	◆ Communicate dangers of 21 shots ◆ Give example of alcohol-free 21 birthday
Environmental change Alcohol-free options Normative environment Alcohol availability Alcohol marketing and promotion Policy development and enforcement	◆ Require servers to attend training for serving those turning 21. ◆ Prohibit bars from giving free shots on 21st birthdays ◆ Prohibit bars from admitting or serving students on midnight of their 21st birthday ◆ Restrict advertising promoting excessive drinking on 21st birthdays
Health protection	◆ Implement a safe ride program for those who decide to drink on their 21st birthday ◆ Recruit friends to watch out for 21st birthday celebrants
Intervention and treatment	◆ Birthday cards including BAC information ◆ Personalized feedback interventions prior to turning 21

this time. If we know in advance when students are going to be especially likely to engage in behavior that may be harmful to them, we should focus our efforts accordingly. Secondly, the contexts of specific events and windows may expose students to different kinds of risks, which may provide direction for intervention content. For example, although this has not been investigated directly, students may be at relatively greater risk for alcohol poisoning on 21st birthdays; for physical assault at football games; and for alcohol-related sexual consequences such as rape, unwanted pregnancy, and STDs during Spring Break. This second assumption illustrates the need to better understand the context of drinking during this window of risk to prevent alcohol-related problems.

Much of the work to date has focused on individual approaches to ESP and is included in reviews of specific events below. A broader perspective of ESP is detailed in Neighbors et al. (2007) and presents an extension of DeJong and Langford's (2002) prevention typology, which describes prevention activities at multiple levels, including individual, group, institution, community, and society (see Table 3.1, for example). The broader perspective also suggests that at each level, intervention strategies may have a range of foci including prevention, environmental change, heath protection, and intervention and treatment. The ESP extension applies DeJong and Langford's more general model to specific events.

Prevention personnel on college campuses have an implicit understanding of the need for ESP, as demonstrated by their implementation of programming for specific events. Unfortunately, these efforts often have no empirically supported basis. Neighbors et al. (2007) provides a framework for thinking comprehensively about ESP from multiple levels. Examples of prevention strategies include education, attitude change, and behavioral interventions around 21st birthdays. Examples of environmental change strategies include provision of alcohol-free alternatives, limiting access, social norms marketing, and policy/law enforcement around football games. An example of health promotion/harm reduction might include offering designated driver and safe rider programs during orientation week. Intervention and treatment options might include provision of Web-based assessment and feedback regarding intentions to drink during specific windows of risk. See Neighbors et al. (2007) for more comprehensive examples.

CONTEXTS ASSOCIATED WITH HIGH-RISK DRINKING

In addition to specific definable discrete events with predetermined dates, several contextual variables have been identified as being associated with excessive drinking. We focus on several of these including weekends and academic breaks, sporting events, pregaming, drinking games, and private or themed parties.

Weekends and Academic Breaks

A number of studies have examined temporal and contextual variability in the frequency and quantity of drinking patterns among college students (e.g., Beets, Flay, Vuchinich, Li, Acock, & Snyder, 2009; Del Boca et al., 2004; Goldman, Greenbaum, Darkes, Brandon, & Del Boca, 2011; Greenbaum et al., 2005; Neal & Fromme, 2007; Neighbors et al., 2011; Tremblay et al., 2010). One of the patterns that has been consistently documented is variation in drinking as a function of the day of week. Frequency and quantity of drinking are lowest from Sunday to Wednesday and higher on Friday and Saturday, with Thursday in the middle (Del Boca et al., 2004; Neal & Fromme, 2007). Recent work has begun to highlight the importance of distinguishing frequency from quantity (Goldman et al., 2011; Neighbors et al., 2011). Examination of the mean number of drinks consumed in a sample of college students on Saturday versus Monday confounds prevalence with quantity, and thus, further research is needed to understand factors that distinguish frequency and quantity of alcohol consumption.

For the purposes of illustration we consider the pattern of weekly drinking in a sample of 1,124 students whose alcohol consumption was assessed with a 90-day timeline follow-back (TLFB; L. Sobell & M. Sobell, 2000) more than three months prior to their 21st birthday. More information on this sample is available in Neighbors et al. (2011). It is important to note that the pattern of weekly drinking and means by day of week in this sample are roughly comparable to those reported in other studies (e.g., Del Boca et al, 2004; Tremblay et al., 2010). Thus, it seems unlikely that the observations we make about this data set are unique to this sample.

Figure 3.1 provides an examination of the mean number of drinks on each day of the week with standard errors. Figure 3.2 presents the proportion of any drinking that occurred on each day. Figure 3.3 presents the average number of drinks consumed on days where any alcohol was consumed by our sample of 1,124 students. Figure 3.3 suggests students drink the same number of drinks on Thursday, Friday, and Saturday, if they drink on those days. It is true that more drinks are consumed by college students on Friday and Saturday than Sunday through Wednesday, with Thursday being in the middle. But this is almost entirely because few students drink any alcohol on Sunday through Wednesday. When students do drink on those days, their drinking is lower than on Thursday, Friday, or Saturday, but not by much. Recent research has also suggested that elevated drinking on Thursday is due to heavy drinkers being more likely to drink on Thursday rather than reflecting differences in quantity consumed on Thursday for most students (Cleveland, Lanza, Ray, Turrisi, & Mallett, in press).

In considering weekly drinking, we might consider the weekends to be windows of risk, but we recognize that this risk is one based largely on prevalence. Blackouts, vomiting, unwanted sexual experiences, and so on, are more prevalent on the weekends because there are more students drinking, and hence, more students drinking in extreme amounts. This pattern may hold in considering some specific holidays or other events and not others.

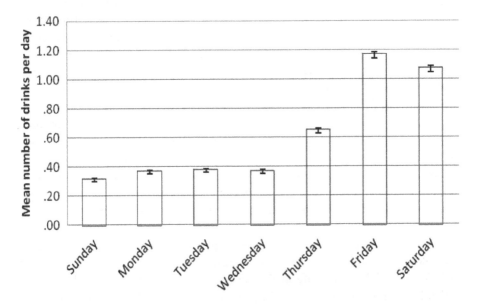

Figure 3.1 The Mean Number of Drinks on Each Day

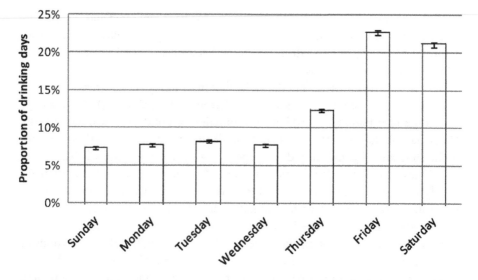

Figure 3.2   The Proportion of Any Drinking That Occurred on Each Day

Academic breaks. Del Boca and colleagues (2004) published a seminal paper showing the above described pattern of drinking by day of week among college students but also a pattern of drinking across weeks. Drinking was significantly higher during weeks that included holidays (i.e., Halloween, Thanksgiving, and New Year's)

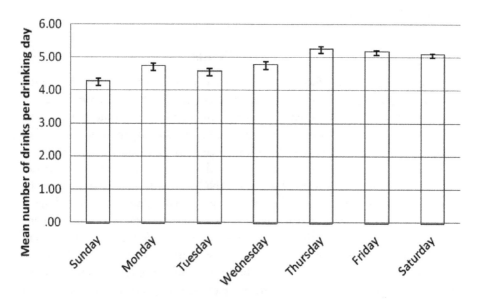

Figure 3.3   The Average Number of Drinks Consumed on Days When Any Alcohol Was Consumed

or academic breaks (Spring Break). This pattern has been replicated and extended by others (Beets et al., 2009; Tremblay et al., 2010). Tremblay and colleagues (2010) additionally noted higher mean drinks during other academic breaks and lower mean drinking during exam periods.

Research has also shown that the variability in drinking across weeks in the academic year is not uniform across students. Greenbaum et al. (2005) identified five trajectories of variability in drinking as a function of holidays or windows of risk. About half of their sample consisted of students who drank relatively little most of the time and slightly more during the weeks of Thanksgiving, Christmas and New Year's, and Spring Break (aka windows of risk). About 10% drank relatively heavily most of the time and more during the identified windows of risk. About 20% had a heavy drinking pattern initially and decreased over the academic year, whereas about 8% started relatively light and increased over the academic year. In both the latter cases, drinking was somewhat higher during the identified windows of risk. Perhaps the most interesting pattern was the 9% who were generally light drinking but drank a lot during windows of risk. These students revealed a pattern of drinking that suggests that, for some, heavy drinking is generally not acceptable; however, it is less unacceptable at certain times. Research has also begun to consider relative risk among windows of risk (Neighbors et al., 2011). In sum, the identification of predictable patterns of drinking and specific events and windows of risk have suggested the need for more precise interventions, directly targeting windows of risk, in addition to more traditional empirically supported interventions (e.g., Dimeff et al., 1999).

Sporting Events

Sporting events, especially football games, are a context in which excessive drinking occurs among college students (e.g., Glassman et al., 2010; Neal & Fromme, 2007; Neighbors et al., 2006). As noted earlier, the distinction between contexts and events is somewhat artificial. This is apparent in considering specific sporting events. For example, Neal, Sugarman, Hustad, Caska, and Carey (2005) found that large increases in alcohol consumption were observed during the football semi-finals and finals of the National Collegiate Athletic Association (NCAA), with more than 60% of the students reporting drinking alcohol on each game day. Glassman and colleagues (2010) revealed that college students who typically consume alcohol on football game days drink on average 7.20 drinks and experience consequences such as blacking out, driving while drinking, vomiting, hangovers, and alcohol-related injuries. Additionally, college football games lead to a significant increase in arrests related to drinking, with a 13% increase in arrests for driving while under the influence, a 41% increase in arrests for disorderly conduct, and a 76% increase in arrests for violating liquor laws (Rees & Schnepel, 2009).

Person and situational characteristics have been identified as risk factors for increased drinking on game days. College students who identify themselves as sports fans endorse higher drinking levels compared to other students (Nelson & Wechsler, 2001), and many college students view game days as an opportunity for heavy drinking to celebrate victors as well as to enhance group cohesion with fellow students (Rabow & Duncan-Schill, 1995). Neal and Fromme (2007) evaluated whether average alcohol consumption and social involvement predicted higher drinking and higher probability of behavioral risks on game days, and found that greater average drinking and greater social involvement predicted an increase in alcohol consumption on game days. Moreover, alcohol consumption during games was differentially associated with behavioral risks, depending on whether the game was a home game or an away game, whether the game took place during the semester or over a semester break, the individual's gender, and the individual's level of social involvement (Neal & Fromme, 2007). Analyses of alcohol quantity at the individual level revealed that in comparison to average amount consumed for women, home games were related to a 0.97 average increase in drinking, nongame Saturdays with a 0.91 average increase in drinking, and away games with a 1.19 average increase in drinking (Neal & Fromme, 2007). Concurrent analyses revealed that for men, home games were related to a 1.93 average increase in drinking, nongame Saturdays with a 0.84 average increase in drinking, and away games with a 1.74 average increase in drinking (Neal & Fromme, 2007). For men, away games and home games were associated with greater increases in alcohol consumption relative to their typical consumption; however, this was not significant for women (Neal & Fromme, 2007).

Tailgating

A specific subcontext of sporting events is *tailgating*, which is the practice of partying prior to a sporting event (Vicary & Karshin, 2002), and which has also been linked with extreme drinking. Studies show that students overestimate the typical amount of alcohol consumed by tailgaters (Neighbors et al., 2006), and perceived tailgating norms are associated with heavier drinking and greater alcohol-related consequences resulting from drinking during tailgating, even after accounting for typical drinking behavior (Neighbors et al., 2006). Tailgating parties at college football games are, therefore, one specific context during which heavy alcohol consumption typically occurs.

Pregaming

Pregaming is a related context during which potentially heavy alcohol consumption can occur. Pregaming derives its name from an association with tailgating, and refers to the practice of partying prior to a sporting event (Vicary & Karshin, 2002); however, the term has come to reflect the consumption of alcohol prior to a primary social gathering or event (Borsari et al., 2007). The purpose of pregaming is to get *buzzed* before attending the event, and may be influenced by the cost or difficulty of obtaining alcohol (e.g., at a school event; Borsari et al., 2007). DeJong and DeRicco (2007) conducted focus groups where students reported that pregaming occurred in small, private contexts such as dorm rooms, and can therefore be more difficult to detect. A common motive for pregaming reported by the students in the focus groups was to reduce social anxiety (DeJong & DeRicco, 2007). Thus, pregaming represents a drinking context whereby the drinker consumes a large amount of alcohol, often in a private location, with the goal of becoming intoxicated prior to going out for the night at a secondary location.

Pedersen, LaBrie, and Kilmer (2009) specific reasons for engaging in pregaming among college age students. Pregaming quantity and frequency was not found to vary as a function of legal drinking age. The specific reasons most endorsed for pregaming among college age students were arriving at an event already "buzzed," making the event more interesting, and saving on money (Pedersen et al., 2009). Males and females were found to have similar reasons for pregaming, however males seem to pregame as a means to increase sexual and social facilitation with peers of the opposite gender (Pedersen et al., 2009).

Parties

Among the more diffuse contexts associated with heavy drinking among college student are parties. Parties may take the form of other contexts (e.g., tailgating parties) or events (New Year's Eve parties). In a study examining drinking behavior between private (parties) and public (bars) drinking environments for underage and legal drinkers, drinking was found to be correlated with contextual variables including having many people intoxicated (e.g., a "party atmosphere"), a perceived or real "wet" environment, playing drinking games, and the availability of illicit drugs (Clapp, Reed, Holmes, Lange, & Voas, 2006). Other environmental predictors of drinking heavily, which may be related to parties, include drinking with friends and drinking hard liquor and beer (Clapp & Shillington, 2001). The only protective factor against heavy episodic drinking found was whether the event was a date (Clapp & Shillington, 2001). Specific contexts such as themed parties (e.g., the Toga party), which have been suggested by anecdotal evidence to be common in U.S. college settings, have been shown to be correlated with heavy drinking and are consistent with contextual environments often sought by heavy drinkers (Clapp et al., 2008). Themed parties have also been shown to be large, sexualized social events where alcohol is readily available (Clapp et al., 2008). These may be high-risk drinking contexts for females especially, as research indicates that females tend to begin drinking earlier in the day in preparation of the social event, and drinking more than men while at the event (Clapp et al., 2008). A number of specific drinking activities occurs in the context of parties but have received limited attention. Doing shots of alcohol is a common practice at parties, particularly in the context of drinking games and pregaming, discussed below. Keg stands (doing a handstand on the rim of a keg while drinking from the tap) are also common occurrences at parties, particularly fraternity parties. Both of these activities, and other similar activities, contribute to large amounts of alcohol consumed in short time periods, leading to elevated BACs. Generally speaking, drinking settings and environmental factors are variables that contribute to the amount of alcohol that is consumed (Clapp, Reed, Holmes, Lange, & Voas, 2006).

Drinking Games

Evidence of drinking games date back to ancient Greece (Garland, 1982) and there are currently more than 500 hundred drinking games that are popular on college campuses (Borsari, Bergen-Cico, & Carey, 2003). Drinking games fall into six major categories: (1) drinking games that require motor skills involving the performance of motor tasks, and failure to adequately do the task results in being required to drink alcohol; (2) drinking games that require verbal skills involving the repetition of long sequences of difficult phrases or nonsense words that increase in difficulty as the player becomes more intoxicated, and making a mistake requires that the player drink alcohol; (3) gambling games that are based on chance and often the stakes are a predetermined amount of alcohol that the losing player has to drink; (4) media games that are more passive than other drinking games, requiring players to drink at a particular cue from a movie or song; (5) team games that pit teams against each other with perhaps the most popular college drinking game being Beer Pong; and (6) consumption games that do not have much strategy and are designed to make the participant consume as much alcohol as possible in the shortest period of time (Borsari & Carey 2006).

Moreover, four common reasons for participating in drinking games have been identified: (1) getting rapidly intoxicated, particularly for those players who do not enjoy the taste of alcohol (Newman, Crawford, & Nellis, 1991); (2) rapidly intoxicating others, which can be accomplished by teaming up and/or assigning drinks to other players (Newman et al., 1991); (3) creating an environment in which students can interact; students have consistently mentioned the social advantages of participating (Rabow & Duncan-Schill, 1994; Newman et al., 1991; West, 2001); and (4) simulating a competitive environment complete with spectators, winners, and losers (Borsari, 2004). Thus, there is a wide selection of drinking games students engage in for a number of different reasons. Research has shown that students report a variety of motives for playing drinking games such as sexual manipulation, fun and celebration, competition and thrills, and conformity (Johnson, Hamilton, & Sheets, 1999; Johnson & Sheets, 2004). Males and females differentially endorse motives, and these were shown to predict specific consequences (Johnson & Sheets, 2004).

Overall, the competition and thrills motive accounted for the largest proportion of variance compared to other identified motives such as conformity or novelty (Johnson & Sheets, 2004).

Research indicates that drinking game participation is relatively common among young adults and is often initiated prior to college attendance (Borsari et al., 2003; Kenney, Hummer, & LaBrie, 2010; Pedersen, 1990). Borsari and colleagues (2003) examined drinking game participation among high school graduates who participated in a college-orientation program prior to matriculation and found that many college-bound students are familiar with drinking games, particularly students who start drinking at an earlier age. Furthermore, results indicate that other drug use such as marijuana is associated with participating in drinking games.

Historically, male undergraduate students are heavier drinkers than females (e.g., Wechsler et al., 2000), and participation in drinking games has long been thought of as a male-dominated activity (e.g., Engs, Diebold, & Hanson, 1996). However, recent research indicates that men and women participate in drinking games at relatively equal rates. Pedersen and LaBrie (2006) examined frequency of drinking game participation among students and found that male and female college students regularly engaged in drinking games, and participation in drinking games was associated with heavy alcohol consumption levels (Pedersen & LaBrie, 2006). Women were found to participate in drinking games at rates that were equivalent to men (Pedersen & Labrie, 2006), and women's alcohol consumption levels paralleled that of men, which is consistent with other reports (e.g., Wechsler, Lee, Nelson, & Kuo, 2002). Moreover, for both men and women, those who participated in drinking games were almost one and a half times more likely to binge drink on typical drinking days than on drinking game days (Pedersen & LaBrie, 2006).

Although participation in drinking games appear to be similar between genders (Pedersen & LaBrie, 2006), females who engage in drinking game activity may be at greater risk for negative consequences such as not using protection during sexual activities, heightened sexual risk, and driving under the influence (NIAAA, 1999). Thus, the extreme alcohol consumption behavior associated with drinking games may increase intoxication levels for females to dangerous levels that may not be reached on typical drinking days that do not involve drinking games (Pedersen & LaBrie, 2006). The implications are that high levels of intoxication can be reached over short periods of time, particularly for females, and that females are at greater risk for negative consequences following drinking games, especially sexual assault (Borsari et al., 2003).

Previous research has examined the link between drinking game participation and pregaming drinking contexts. Evidence suggests that drinking games and pregaming are distinct from each other, but drinking games sometimes occur during pregaming

(Borsari et al., 2007). Borsari and colleagues (2007) also examined the intersection between drinking games, pregaming, and intoxication level on the night of an alcohol violation and found that for their participants, pregaming was significantly associated with intoxication and elevated eBACs, whereas drinking game participation was not (Borsari et al., 2007). In addition, Pederson and LaBrie (2008) found that college students overestimate drinking game participation and pregaming drinking behavior, and perceived behavior was more strongly associated with actual behavior for pregaming than for drinking game participation. Thus, the pregaming context is an important factor to consider in drinking reduction efforts targeting specific events.

Recently (i.e., 2010–2011), a Simulated Drinking Game Procedure (SDGP) using an alcohol-free laboratory protocol has been used to study drinking game behavior (Cameron, Leon, & Correia, 2011; Correia & Cameron, 2010). Participants played drinking games such as Beer Pong (Cameron et al., 2011; Correia & Cameron, 2010), Memory (Cameron et al., 2011), or Three Man (Cameron et al., 2011). In all cases water was used instead of alcohol, and the researchers measured the number of drinks that would be consumed if the participants followed the rules of each game. Researchers then used participant weight and number of drinks to estimate the peak BAC a participant would have achieved if he or she had consumed actual alcohol (Cameron et al., 2011; Correia & Cameron, 2010). Findings indicate that gender, game parameters (variations on "house rules"), and game type (motor skills games, gambling/chance games, or cognitive skills games) impact estimated BAC (Cameron et al., 2011; Correia & Cameron, 2010).

Context Specific Prevention

Relatively little empirical work has focused on context specific prevention. We are not aware of any peer-reviewed studies that have evaluated prevention strategies specifically designed for parties, drinking games, pregaming, or other high-risk contexts. However, existing interventions have incorporated these contexts in discussions about drinking with students. In group-based interventions and individual interventions, students are often asked to describe the contexts in which they engage in heavy drinking. Strategies for reducing drinking in specific contexts have been incorporated into feedback and conversations with students about how they might reduce negative consequences. For example, students are often provided with suggestions that can help them moderate their alcohol consumption in high risk contexts by avoiding drinking games; monitoring their beverage at all times; drinking nonalcoholic beverages in red Solo cups that prevent others from knowing or questioning their beverage choice; alternating alcoholic drinks with water; pacing; limit setting, and so on. Context-specific prevention is currently underdeveloped but seems well worthy of concentrated focus.

CONCLUSIONS

In this chapter, we have attempted to focus the view on excessive college drinking through a somewhat novel lens. Consideration of specific events and contexts associated with extreme drinking among college students has practical implications. Specific events can be anticipated and allow for precise timing and content of prevention resources and strategies. Specific events may also provide opportunities to study extreme drinking and behaviors that cannot be simulated in laboratory settings. In comparison to events, contexts as defined here, are not tied to specific dates but may occur during the course of specific events. Contexts consist of common themes that have emerged and become a part of the college drinking experience. Understanding the nature of these contexts is critical for understanding the culture of college drinking. Efforts to change behaviors are most likely to be effective when accompanied by a comprehensive understanding of the contexts in which those behaviors occur. Understanding contexts provides for greater understanding of specific risks associated with each context and sheds light on motivations for understanding excessive drinking, which can be used in the development of specific intervention strategies directly targeting proximal environmental, interpersonal, and intrapersonal factors associated with drinking. The specific content of events and contexts associated with excessive drinking are culturally specific and likely to change over time, but their pervasive influence and accessibility make them well worthy of additional attention in the etiology and prevention of college drinking.

REFERENCES

American Medical Association. (2006). Sex and intoxication more common among women on spring break according to AMA poll. Available at http://www.alcoholpolicymd.com/pdf/ SpringBreakPollingRelease.pdf

Apostolopoulos, Y. Y., Sönmez, S. S., & Yu, C. H. (2002). HIV-risk behaviours of American spring break vacationers: A case of situational disinhibition? *International Journal of STD & AIDS, 13,* 733–743.

Beets, M. W., Flay, B. R., Vuchinich, S., Li, K., Acock, A., & Snyder, F. J. (2009). Longitudinal patterns of binge drinking among first year college students with a history of tobacco use. *Drug and Alcohol Dependence, 103,* 1–8.

Borsari, B. (2004). Drinking games in the college environment: A review. *Journal of Alcohol & Drug Education, 48,* 29–51.

Borsari, B., Bergen-Cico, D., & Carey, K. B. (2003). Self-reported drinking-game participation of incoming college students. *Journal of American College Health, 51,* 149–154.

Borsari, B., Boyle, K. E., Hustad, J. T. P., Barnett, N. P., Tevyaw, T. O., & Kahler, C. W. (2007). Drinking before drinking: Pregaming and drinking games in mandated students. *Addictive Behaviors, 32,* 2694–2705.

Borsari, B., & Carey, K. B. (2006). How the quality of peer relationships influences college alcohol use. *Drug and Alcohol Review, 25,* 361–370.

B.R.A.D. Foundation. (2008). Schools participating in the B.R.A.D. birthday card program. Available at http://brad21.org/participating_schools.html

Brister, H. A., Wetherill, R. R., & Fromme, K. (2010). Anticipated versus actual alcohol consumption during 21st birthday celebrations. *Journal of Studies on Alcohol and Drugs, 71,* 180–183.

Cameron, J. M., Leon, M. R., & Correia, C. J. (2011). Extension of the simulated drinking game procedure to multiple drinking games. *Experimental and Clinical Psychopharmacology, 19,* 295–302.

Clapp, J. D., Ketchie, J. M., Reed, M. B., Shillington, A. M., Lange, J. E., & Holmes, M. R. (2008). Three exploratory studies of college theme parties. *Drug and Alcohol Review, 27,* 509–518.

Clapp, J. D., Reed, M. B., Holmes, M. R., Lange, J. E., & Voas, R. B. (2006). Drunk in public, drunk in private: The relationship between college students, drinking environments, and alcohol consumption. *American Journal of Drug and Alcohol Abuse, 32,* 275–285.

Clapp, J. D., & Shillington, A. M. (2001). Environmental predictors of heavy episodic drinking. *American Journal of Drug and Alcohol Abuse, 27,* 301–313.

Cleveland, M. J., Lanza, S. T., Ray, A. E., Turrisi, R., & Mallet, K. A. (in press). *Transitions in first-year college student drinking behaviors: Does pre-college drinking moderate the effects of parent- and peer-based intervention components.*

Cooper, M. L. (2002) Alcohol use and risky sexual behavior among college students and youth: Evaluating the evidence. *Journal of Studies on Alcohol, Suppl 14,* 101–117.

Correia, C. J., & Cameron, J. M. (2010). Development of a simulated drinking game procedure to study risky alcohol use. *Experimental and Clinical Psychopharmacology, 18,* 322–328.

Cronin, C. (1996). Harm reduction for alcohol-use-related problems among college students. *Substance Use & Misuse, 31,* 2029–2037.

Day-Cameron, J. M, Muse, L., Hauenstein, J., Simmons, L., & Correia, C. J. (2009). Alcohol use by undergraduate students on their 21st birthday: Predictors of actual consumption, anticipated consumption, and normative beliefs. *Psychology of Addictive Behaviors, 23,* 695–701.

DeJong, W., & DeRicco, B. (2007). *Pre-gaming: An exploratory study of strategic drinking by college students in Pennsylvania.* Unpublished report.

DeJong, W., & Langford, L. M. (2002). A typology for campus-based alcohol prevention: Moving toward environmental management strategies. *Journal of Studies on Alcohol, Suppl 14,* 140–147.

Del Boca, F. K., Darkes, J., Greenbaum, P. E., & Goldman, M. S. (2004). Up close and personal: Temporal variability in the drinking of individual college students during their first year. *Journal of Consulting & Clinical Psychology, 72,* 155–164.

Dimeff, L. A., Baer, J. S., Kivlahan, D. R., & Marlatt, G. A. (1999). *Brief alcohol screening and intervention for college students.* New York, NY: Guilford Press.

Engs, R. C., Diebold, B. A., & Hanson, D. J. (1996). The drinking patterns and problems of a national sample of college students, 1994. *Journal of Alcohol and Drug Education, 41,* 13–33.

Foster, D. W., Rodriguez, L. M. Neighbors, C., DiBello, A., & Chen, C. (2011). The magic number 21: Transitions in drinking. *The Addiction Newsletter, 18* (3), 17–19.

Garland, H. (1982). Goal levels and task performance: A compelling replication of some compelling results. *Journal of Applied Psychology, 67,* 245–248.

Glassman, T. J., Dodd, V. J., Sheu, J., Rienzo, B. A., & Wagenaar, A. C. (2010). Extreme ritualistic alcohol consumption among college students on game day. *Journal of American College Health, 58,* 413–423.

Goldman, M. S., Greenbaum, P. E., Darkes, J., Brandon, K. O., & Del Boca, F. K. (2011). How many versus how much: 52 weeks of alcohol consumption in emerging adults. *Psychology of Addictive Behaviors, 25,* 16–27.

Greenbaum, P. E., Del Boca, F. K., Darkes, J., Wang, C. P., & Goldman, M. S. (2005). Variation in the drinking trajectories of freshmen college students. *Journal of Consulting & Clinical Psychology, 73,* 229–238.

Grekin, E. R., Sher, K. J., & Krull, J. L. (2007). College spring break and alcohol use: Effects of spring break activity. *Journal of Studies on Alcohol & Drugs, 68*(5), 681–688.

Hembroff, L., Atkin, C., Martell, D., McCue, C., & Greenamyer, J. (2007). Evaluation results of 21st birthday card program targeting high-risk drinking. *Journal of American College Health, 56,* 325–333.

Hingson, R., Heeren, T., Winter, M., & Wechsler, H. (2005). Magnitude of alcohol-related mortality and morbidity among U.S. college students ages 18–24: Changes from 1998 to 2001. *Annual Review of Public Health, 26,* 259–279.

Johnson, T. J., Hamilton, S., & Sheets, V. L. (1999). College students' self-reported reasons for playing drinking games. *Addictive Behaviors, 24*(2), 279–286.

Johnson, T. J., & Sheets, V. L. (2004). Measuring college students' motives for playing drinking games. *Psychology of Addictive Behaviors, 18*(2), 91–99.

Josiam, B., Hobson, J., Dietrich, U., & Smeaton, G. (1998). An analysis of the sexual, alcohol and drug related behavioural patterns of students on spring break. *Tourism Management, 19*, 501–513.

Kenney, S. R., Hummer, J. F., & LaBrie, J. W. (2010). An examination of prepartying and drinking game playing during high school and their impact on alcohol-related risk upon entrance into college. *Journal of Youth and Adolescence, 39*, 999–1011.

LaBrie, J. W., Migliuri, S., & Cail, J. (2009). A night to remember: A harm-reduction birthday card intervention reduces high-risk drinking during 21st birthday celebrations. *Journal of American College Health, 57*, 659–663.

Lee, C. M., Lewis, M. A., & Neighbors, C. (2009). Preliminary examination of spring break alcohol use and related consequences. *Psychology of Addictive Behaviors, 23*, 689–694.

Lee, C. M., Maggs, J. L., & Rankin, L. A. (2006). Spring break trips as a risk factor for heavy alcohol use among first-year college students. *Journal of Studies on Alcohol, 67*, 911–916.

Lewis, M. A., Lindgren, K. P., Fossos, N., Neighbors, C., & Oster-Aaland, L. (2009). Examining the relationship between typical drinking behavior and 21st birthday drinking behavior among college students: Implications for event-specific prevention. *Addiction, 104*, 760–767.

Lewis, M. A., Neighbors, C., Lee, C. M., & Oster-Aaland, L. (2008). 21st birthday celebratory drinking: Evaluation of a personalized normative feedback card intervention. *Psychology of Addictive Behaviors, 22*, 176–185.

Marlatt, G. A., Baer, J. S., Kivlahan, D. R., Dimeff, L. A., Larimer, M. E., Quigley, L. A., … Williams, E. (1998). Screening and brief intervention for high-risk college student drinkers: results from a 2-year follow-up assessment. *Journal of Consulting and Clinical Psychology, 66*, 604–615.

Maticka-Tyndale, E., & Herold, E. S. (1997). The scripting of sexual behaviour: Canadian university students on spring break in Florida. *Canadian Journal of Human Sexuality, 6*, 317–328.

National Institute on Alcohol Abuse and Alcoholism. (1999). Are women more vulnerable to alcohol effects? *Alcohol Alert* (Vol. 46). Rockville, MD: U.S. Department of Health and Human Services.

Neal, D. J., & Fromme, K. (2007). Hook 'em horns and heavy drinking: Alcohol use and collegiate sports. *Addictive Behaviors, 32*, 2681–2693.

Neal, D. J., Sugarman, D. E., Hustad, J. T. P., Caska, C. M., & Carey, K. B. (2005). It's all fun and games . . . or is it? collegiate sporting events and celebratory drinking. *Journal of Studies on Alcohol, 66*(2), 291–294.

Neighbors, C., Atkins, D. C., Lewis, M. A., Lee, C. M., Kaysen, D., Mittmann, A., Fossos, N., & Rodriguez, L. M. (2011). Event specific drinking among college students. *Psychology of Addictive Behaviors, 25*, 702–707.

Neighbors, C., Lee, C. M., Atkins, D., Lewis, M. A., Kaysen, D., Mittmann, A., . . . Larimer, M. E. (in press). *A randomized controlled trial for 21st birthday drinking among college students. Journal of Consulting and Clinical Psychology.*

Neighbors, C., Lee, C. M., Lewis, M. A., Fossos, N., & Walter, T. (2009). Internet-based personalized feedback to reduce 21st birthday drinking: A randomized controlled trial of an Event Specific Prevention Intervention. *Journal of Consulting and Clinical Psychology, 77*, 51–63.

Neighbors, C., Lewis, M. A., Atkins, D. C., Jensen, M. M., Walter, T., Fossos, N., . . . Larimer, M. E. (2010). Efficacy of web-based personalized normative feedback: A two-year randomized controlled trial. *Journal of Consulting and Clinical Psychology, 78*, 898–911.

Neighbors, C., Oster-Aaland, L., Bergstrom, R. L., & Lewis, M. A. (2006). Event- and context-specific normative misperceptions and high-risk drinking: 21st birthday celebrations and football tailgating. *Journal of Studies on Alcohol, 67*, 282–289.

Neighbors, C., Spieker, C. J., Oster-Aaland, L., Lewis, M. A., & Bergstrom, R. L. (2005). Celebration intoxication: An evaluation of 21st birthday alcohol consumption. *Journal of American College Health, 54*, 76–80.

Neighbors, C., Walters, S. T., Lee, C. M., Vader, A. M., Vehige, T., Szigethy, T., & DeJong, W. (2007). Event-specific prevention: Addressing college student drinking during known windows of risk. *Addictive Behaviors, 32*, 2667–2680.

Nelson, T. F., & Wechsler, H. (2001). Alcohol and college athletes. *Medicine & Science in Sports & Exercise, 33*, 43–47.

Newman, I. M., Crawford, J. K., & Nellis, M. J. (1991). The role and function of drinking games in a university community. *Journal of American College Health, 39*, 171–175.

Patrick, M. E., Morgan, N., Maggs, J. L., & Lefkowitz, E. S. (2010). "I got your back": Friends' understandings regarding college student spring break behavior. *Journal of Youth and Adolescence, 40*, 108–120.

Patrick, M. E., Neighbors, C., & Lee, C. M. (2012). A hierarchy of 21st birthday drinking norms. *Journal of American College Health, 53*, 922–930.

Pedersen, E. R., & LaBrie, J. (2006). Drinking game participation among college students: Gender and ethnic implications. *Addictive Behaviors, 31*, 2105–2115.

Pedersen, E. R., & LaBrie, J. (2007). Partying before the party: Examining prepartying behavior among college students. *Journal of American College Health, 56*, 237–245.

Pedersen, E. R., Labrie, J. W., & Kilmer, J. (2009). Before you slip into the night, you'll want something to drink: Exploring the reasons for prepartying behavior among college student drinkers. *Issues in Mental Health Nursing, 30*, 354–363.

Pedersen, W. (1990). Drinking games adolescents play. *British Journal of Addiction, 85*, 1483–1490.

Rabow J., & Duncan-Schill, M. (1994). Drinking among college students. *Journal of Alcohol and Drug Education, 40*, 52–64.

Ragsdale, K., Difranceisco, W., & Pinkerton, S. D. (2006). Where the boys are: Sexual expectations and behaviour among young women on holiday. *Culture, Health & Sexuality, 8*, 85–98.

Rees, D. I., & Schnepel, K. T. (2009). College football games and crime. *Journal of Sports Economics, 10*, 68–87.

Rutledge, P. C., Park, A., & Sher, K. J. (2008). 21st birthday drinking: Extremely extreme. *Journal of Consulting & Clinical Psychology, 76*, 511–516.

Shah, A. P., Smolensky, M. H., Burau, K. D., Cech, I. M., & Lai, D. (2007). Recent change in the annual pattern of sexually transmitted diseases in the United States. *Chronobiology International, 24*, 947–960.

Smeaton, G. L., Josiam, B. M., & Dietrich, U. C. (1998). College students' binge drinking at a beach-front destination during spring break. *Journal of American College Health, 46*, 247–254.

Smith, B. H., Bogle, K. E., Talbott, L., Gant, R., & Castillo, H. (2006). A randomized study of four cards designed to prevent problems during college students' 21st birthday celebrations. *Journal of Studies on Alcohol, 67*, 607–615.

Snyder, S. L., & Misera, L. (2008). College students' perceptions of a safe spring break event: An event specific prevention program. *Californian Journal of Health Promotion, 6*, 84–92.

Sobell, L. C., & Sobel, M. E. (2000). Alcohol timeline followback (TLFB). In *Handbook of Psychiatric Measures* (pp. 477–479). Washington, DC: American Psychiatric Association.

Sönmez, S., Apostolopoulos, Y., Yu, C., Yang, S., Mattila, A., & Yu, L. C. (2006). Binge drinking and casual sex on spring break. *Annals of Tourism Research, 33*, 895–917.

Tremblay, P. F., Graham, K., Wells, S., Harris, R., Pulford, R., & Roberts, S. E. (2010). When do first-year college students drink most during the academic year? An internet-based study of daily and weekly drinking. *Journal of American College Health, 58*, 401–411.

Turner, J. C., & Shu, J. (2004). Serious health consequences associated with alcohol use among college students: Demographic and clinical characteristics of patients seen in an emergency department. *Journal of Studies on Alcohol, 65*, 179–183.

Vicary, J. R., & Karshin, C. M. (2002). College alcohol abuse: A review of the problems, issues, and prevention approaches. *Journal of Primary Prevention, 22*, 299–331.

Wechsler, H., Lee, J. E., Kuo, M., & Lee, H. (2000). College binge drinking in the 1990s: A continuing problem: Results of the Harvard School of Public Health 1999 college alcohol study. *Journal of American College Health, 48*, 199–210.

Wechsler, H., Lee, J. E., Nelson, T. F., & Kuo, M. (2002). Underage college students' drinking behavior, access to alcohol, and the influence of deterrence policies. *Journal of American College Health, 50*, 223–236.

Weinhardt, L. S., & Carey, M. P. (2000). Does alcohol lead to sexual risk behavior? Findings from event-level research. *Annual Review of Sex Research, 11*, 125–157.

West, L. A. (2001). Negotiating masculinities in American drinking subcultures. *Journal of Men's Studies, 9*, 371–392.

Wetherill, R. R., & Fromme, K. (2009). Subjective responses to alcohol prime event-specific alcohol consumption and predict blackouts and hangover. *Journal of Studies on Alcohol & Drugs, 70*, 593–600.

4

Theories of College Student Drinking

Stephen A. Maisto, Todd M. Bishop, and Eliza J. Hart

The publication of this book is a statement about the continuing broad interest in and concern about alcohol consumption and related negative consequences among college students. This long-standing concern, at least since the five decades or so when colleges relinquished much of their "in loco parentis" (the legal responsibility of an organization or a person to assume some functions of parents) status toward undergraduate students (Gonzalez, 1988), naturally seeks an explanation and a possible solution. That is where the topic of this chapter, theories of college student drinking, comes in. The chapter is organized in the following way. It begins with a brief discussion of "theory" and its role in science. The next section summarizes the main data that theories of college student drinking (TCSD) are designed to explain the prevalence of alcohol use, especially heavier alcohol use among college undergraduates, and alcohol-related negative consequences. The chapter then proceeds with a summary and analysis of major theories that have been developed or applied to help to understand or to guide the development of interventions for college student drinking. This review and analysis form the basis for concluding recommendations regarding the use of theory to guide future research and interventions in this area.

THEORIES OF COLLEGE STUDENT DRINKING AND THEIR ROLE

Nonscientists, scientists, and philosophers of science have opined and debated about "theory" for centuries. As might be expected, there have been considerable differences recorded regarding the definition of theory (and related terms like *hypothesis* and *model*), but it may not be too difficult to arrive at an agreement among a reasonable group of people about what theory is designed to do, or what function it performs. In this regard, fundamentally, theories in science are created as ways to help organize, explain, and ultimately to predict phenomena (Dennis & Kintsch, 2007; Kantowitz, Roediger, & Elmes, 2005). In this chapter, the essential phenomena of interest are the prevalence of alcohol use, heavy alcohol use, and alcohol-related negative consequences among college students. Consistent with the substantial amount of interest in this topic in the United States, a number of methodologically strong studies have been done to provide the data of interest.

PREVALENCE OF COLLEGE STUDENT DRINKING AND ALCOHOL-RELATED NEGATIVE CONSEQUENCES

An outstanding database on drinking among college undergraduates in the United States has accumulated. In particular, there have been several national surveys completed that have provided a clear view of drinking among college undergraduates. Because the excellent chapter in this volume by Hingson describes these data in detail, there is no need to discuss them here. However, in summary, the data on drinking among college students in the United States have been remarkably stable across the past 30 years: The data show a high and stable prevalence of alcohol use in the last year, as well as a high and stable prevalence of episodic "heavy" drinking and alcohol-related negative consequences. The data also show variability among college students, with stable levels of nonheavy use of alcohol as well as abstinence from alcohol (Nelson, Xuan, Lee, Weitzman, & Wechsler, 2009; O'Malley & Johnston, 2002). Indeed, variability in drinking among college students should not be underestimated. Over the past three decades national surveys and other studies have shown that the prevalence of different drinking patterns and alcohol-related negative consequences varies according to a number of person and environmental variables. Keeping such findings in mind is useful for avoiding the common tendency to think of "college student drinking" as a single entity.

MAJOR THEORIES OF AND APPLIED TO COLLEGE STUDENT DRINKING

The summary of recent major findings on the prevalence of alcohol consumption and alcohol-related negative consequences among college students reaffirms that there is a problem of primarily underage and sometimes harmful alcohol use among college students in the United States, and that the general pattern of use has shown little change over decades of time. The high volume of research on college student drinking that has accordingly appeared since about 1980 has been generated in an attempt to explain the college student alcohol use/consequences data, primarily toward the end of developing more powerful prevention and treatment interventions that target college student drinking (Turrisi, Padilla, & Wiersma, 2000; Wagner & Ingersoll, 2009).

Concurrent with this generation of research, a number of theoretical models have been created to explain and ultimately predict drinking among college students and associated negative consequences, or more general health behavior theories have been applied to achieve the same end. A brief description of several of the better known and frequently applied of these theories follows, along with a representative review of empirical studies that have been published whose aims were to provide a test of the theories. The purpose of the review of empirical studies is to describe a sample of the research that has been done, rather than to provide an exhaustive review of the empirical literature on drinking among college students. The theories were selected for review in the following way. A literature search was conducted by use of PubMed, PsycARTICLES, and PsycINFO, as well as by use of the reference sections of articles that were identified. For the database searches, the following key words/phrases were used: College Drinking; Alcohol AND College Students; College Drinking AND Theory; Alcohol AND College AND Drinking; and Alcohol AND College AND Theory. The theories chosen were those that appeared most frequently in the sources identified and that were judged to have generated a significant amount of research.

THEORIES OF DRINKING AMONG COLLEGE STUDENTS

Alcohol myopia theory. The alcohol myopia theory is a three-part model that asserts that acute alcohol consumption impairs cognitive processing, such that individuals experience a reduction in capacity to attend to internal and external cues (Steele & Josephs, 1990). The three-part model refers to this narrowing of attention as *alcohol myopia*, claiming that individuals' perceptions and cognitive processing may be altered to a degree that they are only able to focus on the most salient cues in their surroundings. The first part of the model suggests that alcohol reduces inhibitions and leads to "drunken excess," resulting in more extreme behaviors when individuals drink. The occurrence of such behavior depends largely on situational cues, with the argument that alcohol causes people to focus on the most salient social cues and to disregard more peripheral social cues. The myopia forms when an individual reacts to the most salient cue without considering any of the potential negative consequences. In the second part of the model, Steele and Josephs argue that when confronted with a situation that questions individuals' important talents or abilities, alcohol inflates their self-confidence by blocking their access to self-evaluative thoughts. In turn, as individuals begin to drink more frequently, this reinforcing effect of alcohol can subsequently lead to alcohol problems. The last part of the model, the attention-allocation model, depends primarily on what activities individuals are engaged in while drinking. On the one hand, it postulates that apart from offspring of alcoholics and highly self-conscious individuals, alcohol reduces stress for all people if any distraction is present. Because alcohol myopia causes individuals to focus only on the most salient stimuli or activity in their immediate environment, this may lead individuals to disregard less meaningful negative emotions (Josephs & Steele, 1990; Steele & Josephs, 1990). Steele and Josephs suggest that the distraction individuals obtain from drinking may act in a way that protects them from feeling distressed, which is highly consistent with the tension reduction model of alcohol use and the development of addiction. A competing component of this model claims that alcohol increases stress for individuals who drink without any distractions present, because the absence of distractions or activity causes people to pay more attention to their negative thoughts (Steele & Josephs, 1990).

The findings of a number of studies testing alcohol myopia among college students are consistent with Steele and Josephs' (1990) theory. In a study investigating the effect of alcohol myopia on two groups of college women—sorority pledges and nonsorority pledges—the drinking patterns of both groups of women fit the alcohol myopia model. In this regard, there was a positive relationship between alcohol consumption and experiencing both positive and negative experiences from drinking. Although slightly higher negative consequences of drinking were reported in the sorority pledge group, overall both groups demonstrated a positive association between alcohol consumption and negative and positive drinking experiences. Women who reported very minimal drinking also reported fewer alcohol-related negative consequences. These findings suggest that interventions to reduce drinking on college campuses may not be effective if they emphasize the negative consequences of drinking, because drinkers are already aware of potential risks. However, they suggest that interventions that focus more on evaluating the immediate situations that encourage drinking and how many drinks individuals consume at one time may be more beneficial. At the same time, this approach focuses on self-monitoring, which may be difficult for individuals to engage in once they have already started drinking. One possible solution would be to put more responsibility into the hands of social organizations that provide alcohol, encouraging leaders of these organizations to implement drink limits (Elias, Bell, Eade, Winsky, Shondrock, Treland, & Fiel 1996).

Some of the studies and reviews examining the effect of alcohol myopia on college students point to an association between alcohol myopia and increased sexual risk (Griffin, Umstattd, & Usdan, 2010; MacDonald, Fong, Zanna, & Martineau, 2000; MacDonald, MacDonald, Zanna, & Fong, 2000). MacDonald et al. (2000) conducted a large study of sexually active, college men who were not in a relationship and were asked to visit a laboratory for one session. They were randomized to an alcohol or placebo condition and watched a video of a male and an attractive female kissing on a couch. The video ended with the two discussing that neither one of them had condoms, but that both of them were "clean" and the female was taking birth control pills. They asked each other what they wanted to do and the video ended abruptly. Participants watching the video filled out a series of questionnaires, including answering the question of whether they would want to engage in unprotected sex with the female in the video. Results indicated that participants who were randomized to the alcohol condition and who reported high levels of sexual arousal were more likely to report a stronger desire to engage in unprotected sex than men who were randomized to a placebo condition and reported lower sexual arousal. These findings were interpreted as showing that in the alcohol and high-arousal condition the most salient cue was having unprotected sex. This was the only condition in which men reported a stronger desire to engage in unprotected sex, demonstrating that in the absence of alcohol or high sexual arousal, sexual risk taking is decreased. These results suggest that underscoring the potential negative effects of unprotected sex on college campuses so that they are more salient may be an effective prevention strategy (MacDonald et al., 2000). In four additional studies, MacDonald et al. (2000) found that the only alcohol condition that elicited a decision not to engage in unprotected sex involved the presence of a strong inhibitory cue—a hand stamp prior to entering a bar that said "AIDS KILLS." This supports the alcohol myopia theory in that when intoxicated, individuals are likely to restrict their attention to the most salient cues.

In additional studies, alcohol myopia theory has been used to explain aggression in young adult men, suggesting that alcohol both increases and decreases aggression, depending on the situational cues that are most salient (Giancola & Corman, 2007; Giancola, Josephs, Parrott, & Duke, 2010). Giancola and Corman (2007) tested the attention-allocation model in regards to alcohol related aggression in young men who were social drinkers. The study involved competing against a confederate in a simple computer task designed to assess who could release the space bar the fastest over a series of trials. If the participant won the trial, he would get to administer a shock to his opponent, choosing the degree of shock on a scale of 0 to 10. Alternatively, if the participant lost the trial, he would receive a shock. Participants were randomly assigned to one of four independent groups formed by the factorial combination of beverage received (alcohol or placebo) and task condition (engage or not engage in a moderate working memory distractor task). Participants were told that if they performed well on the working memory task, then they would receive a monetary bonus at the end of the study. Results indicated that there was a significant beverage by distraction interaction, showing that individuals in the alcohol condition, who did not engage in the distractor task, had the highest aggression scores. As an extension of this study, Giancola and Corman (2007) modified this design to include mild, moderate, and strong working memory distraction tasks. Results from this study also revealed a significant interaction between beverage and distraction, indicating that the distractor task only worked to attenuate aggression in the alcohol group if it was moderate in difficulty. Conclusions were that a mild distractor task may not be distracting enough to decrease aggression and a strong distractor task may elicit more stress and frustration, resulting in higher aggression. In the strong distractor task condition, men may have also given up on the task and shifted their focus to only administering the shocks. Implications for this study suggest that activating working memory in regards to social behavior may reduce alcohol-induced aggression in young men.

Giancola and colleagues (2010) reviewed alcohol myopia theory in regards to various types of risky behavior, including aggression. A proposed suggestion to reduce alcohol-related aggression included implementing salient, frequent, and antiviolence cues. Examples of such cues included painting "jail bars" on mirrors in bars, showing that anyone who chooses to fight, will be sent to jail. Escorting a belligerent individual into another room that has popular games and prizes and relaxation equipment such as massage chairs was another suggested cue. Other techniques aimed to reduce violence include increasing people's mindfulness and self-awareness. Examples of cues aimed to do this included playing videos on some of the televisions in bars, demonstrating the consequences of getting in a fight, signs in bars indicating that fighting will lead to jail time, having bouncers wear shirts that show the relationship between fighting and jail, and setting off the fire alarm when a fight breaks out. These suggestions are helpful from a public health perspective, but will not solve most domestic violence problems. Thus, Giancola and colleagues suggest other violence prevention methods in domestic settings. These also include increasing mindfulness, but other suggestions involve working with a therapist and wearing a wristband that symbolizes a personal nonaggressive cue.

Behavioral economics theory. Generally speaking, behavioral economics is the application of economic principles to human behavior. Researchers have used economic concepts since the 1960s to explain or predict drinking behavior (Babor, Mendelson, Greenberg, & Kuehnle, 1978; Bickel, DeGrandpre, & Higgins, 1993; MacKillop et al., 2010; Mello, McNamee, & Mendelson, 1968; Murphy & MacKillop, 2006). Vuchinich and Tucker (1983) termed the concepts of behavioral economics as the "behavioral theories of choice" and used this model to explain substance use and abuse. They described this theory as an account of how individuals distribute their behavior among a group of available activities, with all of the available activities comprising the proximal environment. Correia (2004) argued that many of the principles of behavioral economics have been borrowed from consumer demand theory, which is the study of how individuals allocate their behavior among a set of available reinforcers. Correia identified four variables that influence consumer demand: income, price, the availability of alternative activities, and reinforcement delay. These variables have given rise to several key models and concepts of behavioral economics that are applied most consistently to addictive behaviors: delay discounting models (Bickel & Marsch, 2001), relative reinforcing efficacy (Babor et al., 1978; Correia & Carey, 1999; Murphy & MacKillop, 2006), and elasticity of demand (Bickel, Madden, & Petry, 1998).

Babor et al. (1978) conducted one of the first studies examining the relationship between cost and alcohol consumption in men. Results indicated that for both social and heavy drinkers, alcohol purchasing and subsequent consumption increased significantly for individuals randomized to a "happy hour" condition. In this condition, the cost of alcohol was decreased for a 3-hour period of the day as opposed to being held at a fixed price in the control condition.

Since Babor's experimental tests of economic principles with drinking behavior, considerable progress has been made toward advancing the behavioral economics approach. One such development is the idea of delay discounting. According to the concept of delay discounting, a delayed reinforcer is worth less than an immediate reinforcer and is highly related to impulsivity and loss of control, behaviors that are typically associated with addiction (Bickel & Marsch, 2001). A study examining delay reward discounting in college students found that heavy drinking students devalue delayed rewards much more than do lighter drinkers, suggesting that college students who engage in heavier drinking may be may be more likely to engage in activities that provide immediate rewards and make more impulsive decisions (Vuchinich & Simpson, 1998). Heavy drinkers may devalue or discount the long-term rewards associated with academic, career, or health-related activities in favor of the immediate rewards associated with drinking (e.g., intoxication, social interactions). Another relevant empirical finding is that, despite the high prevalence of heavy drinking among college students, demand for alcohol is extremely sensitive to manipulations of both drink price (i.e., students drink more when drinks are free or cheap and sharply decrease consumption as price increases; Murphy & MacKillop, 2006), the presence of next day responsibilities such as morning classes (Skidmore & Murphy, 2011), and negative affect (Rousseau, Irons, & Correia, 2011). This latter set of studies suggests that prevention efforts should prioritize price increases for alcohol in bars near college campuses and also consider increasing morning class offerings (Murphy, Correia, & Barnett, 2007).

Murphy et al. (2007) suggest additional intervention and prevention strategies for college student drinkers in applying behavioral economic principles. One such approach includes using reinforcement surveys to assess students' level of engagement in substance-free activities. The aim of these surveys is to highlight activities that are incompatible with alcohol use and to identify activities that are highly enjoyable, but that are not typically participated in (see Murphy, Barnett, & Colby, 2006, for information on student drinkers' ratings of the enjoyment of specific substance-free activities). Another tactic that Murphy et al. identified is the implementation of contingency management interventions, which could provide reinforcement for engaging in activities that are incompatible with alcohol use.

Developmental theory. There have been a number of excellent reviews examining the relationship between adolescent development and alcohol use (Casey & Jones, 2010; Masten, Faden, Zucker, & Spear, 2009; Schulenberg & Maggs, 2002; Spear, 2000; Spear & Varlinskaya, 2005). Schulenberg and Maggs (2002) identified five developmental models explaining the relationship between life transitions and health risks: overload, developmental mismatch, increased heterogeneity, transition catalyst, and heightened vulnerability to chance events. According to this approach, college students may experience stress "overload" because they face a number of transitions within a short period of time, which may lead to high-risk coping mechanisms, such as alcohol use. The developmental mismatch model suggests that a new college environment may not match individuals' needs. When this mismatch occurs, students seek alternate behaviors to fulfill their needs, which might include heavy drinking. The increased heterogeneity model is an extension of the overload and developmental mismatch models. The model posits that individuals who have existing emotional and psychological difficulties will find the transition to college more stressful than their well-functioning peers. As a result, these individuals often turn to drinking as a way to cope (negative reinforcement). The transition catalyst model also states that drinking acts as positive reinforcement in that it helps students create friendships and relationships. Finally, the heightened vulnerability to chance events model suggests that the transition to college provides an arena for seeking novel behaviors, such as drinking.

Schulenberg and Maggs (2002) identify additional changes that influence college drinking such as physical changes, looking and wanting to look older, normative cognitive changes, the late adolescent's idea that he or she is invincible and invulnerable, age-related changes in alcohol outcome expectancies, identification of adult hypocrisy, changes in personal identity, decreases in parental interactions, new peer relationships, romantic relationships, school transitions, and work transitions.

Brown et al. (2008) reviewed multiple development-related factors that may contribute to alcohol use among individuals in late adolescence: brain development, cognitive development, and social and emotional development. For example, as the brain continues to develop, teens' sleep cycles are often affected, causing them to tire less easily at night. As a result, they begin to lose up to two hours of sleep during a normal weekday. Some adolescents choose to cope with this sleep deprivation by using alcohol. Additionally, history of impulsivity in childhood and earlier adolescence increases vulnerability to engage in risky behaviors such as drinking. In regard to cognitive functioning, individuals who have deficits in decision making and executive functioning may be at greater risk for developing an alcohol use disorder. The emergence into university settings marks a critical part of individuals' lives, which is characterized by finding one's identity and more personal freedom. These factors, combined with perceptions of increased drinking acceptability, can also contribute to a rise in alcohol consumption in the college population.

These behavioral changes are likely the product of developmental brain and hormonal changes that take place during adolescence. Some of these changes act as stressors in adolescents as evidenced by increased activation of the hypothalamo-pituitary-adrenal (HPA) axis. Increased activation of the HPA axis, in turn, stimulates hormone release from the hypothalamus (CRH) and pituitary (adrenocorticotropic hormone [ACTH]). ACTH then affects the adrenals, which release cortisol into the blood stream (Spear, 2000). Due to ethical constraints, human studies involving adolescent and young adult alcohol use are often limited in their scope. Thus, animal studies have been helpful in collectively identifying behavioral changes, drinking patterns, and associated brain changes across the lifespan. Because rodents and nonhuman primates also experience a period of adolescence that is characterized by hormone and brain changes, findings from these studies can often be applied to humans. Animal studies have shown that increases in corticosterone may increase the rewarding effects of substance use in adolescence (Spear, 2000).

Doremus, Brunell, Rajendran, and Spear (2005) conducted a series of studies examining ethanol consumption in adolescent and adult rats in which environment and experimental solutions were some of the variables that were manipulated. When compared to adult rats, adolescent rats drank more of the ethanol solution when given a choice between other solutions (water, sucrose, and saccharin). Of note, the decision to consume the ethanol solution was not due to the caloric content of the solution. These findings validated similar previous findings and are important given that human alcohol use increases during adolescence.

In regard to brain development in adolescents, the increase in novel-seeking behavior and cognitive control results from the signaling between and the maturation of the ventral striatum and prefrontal cortex. There is also research demonstrating that changes in the dopamine system play a part in increased sensitivity to rewards. Alcohol further increases activation of the ventral striatum, which provides even more reinforcement for sensation seeking and risk taking (Casey & Jones, 2010). Recent advances in neuroimaging give empirical support for how adolescent brain development plays an important role in susceptibility to alcohol and drug misuse in humans (Bava & Tapert, 2010; Spear, 2002). Bava and Tapert (2010) suggest that the risk to engage in alcohol and drug use may arise as a function of the limbic system and prefrontal regions of the brain developing at different rates. The limbic system develops more quickly than the prefrontal regions, which causes adolescents to engage in activities that are more emotionally salient, such as drinking, at a time when impulse control from the prefrontal region is less developed. Additionally, heavy alcohol use during adolescence may alter levels of executive functioning, such that heavier drinking adolescents show a decline in attention and information processing, lower IQ scores, and a decreased ability to plan ahead.

Other findings that make adolescents more prone to heavy drinking include their decreased sensitivity to the less-desirable effects of alcohol such as social and motor impairment, sedation, withdrawal, and "hangover effects." On the other hand, adolescents appear to be more sensitive to the rewarding properties of alcohol such as social facilitation (Casey & Jones, 2010; Spear & Varlinskaya, 2005). These findings are important given that adolescence can be a particularly stressful time and that adolescents may be more inclined to drink due to alcohol's rewarding properties (Spear & Varlinskaya, 2010). Because adolescence typically extends into early adulthood, is characterized by biological changes that trigger novelty-seeking behavior, and often includes changes in environment (such as attending college) that reinforce alcohol use, developing programs in high schools or on college campuses that teach drink refusal skills and cognitive control may help to curtail alcohol use in college students (Casey & Jones, 2010).

Expectancy theory. Numerous experimental and correlational studies have shown that individuals commonly believe that acute behavioral and psychological changes following alcohol consumption are attributable to its pharmacological effects and that these beliefs or expectancies affect or are associated with actual drinking behavior (Darkes & Goldman, 1993, 1998; Lau-Barraco & Dunn, 2008; Leigh, 1989). Alcohol expectancies are beliefs that an individual holds regarding the relationship between alcohol consumption and its acute physiological, psychological, and social effects (Goldman, Brown, & Christiansen, 1987). Expectancies are thought to develop through a combination of ways, such as actual drug effects, vicarious learning, classical conditioning (Goldman et al., 1987), cultural influences (Critchlow, 1986; Leigh, 1989), and feedback through drinking experiences (Christiansen, Goldman, & Inn, 1982). Feedback from drinking experiences can either serve to support or undermine preconceived beliefs about alcohol's effects. Therefore, although individuals hold expectancies prior to their first drinking experience, subsequent drinking behavior may reinforce or modify these beliefs (Christiansen et al., 1982).

Research on alcohol expectancies and a majority of the expectancy challenges completed to date have utilized samples of college drinkers whose patterns of alcohol use and related negative consequences cover a wide range of severity. For example, using a sample of female college students and community members with varying levels of alcohol use, Beckman (1979) found that female alcoholics are more likely than female nonalcoholics to endorse beliefs that the consumption of alcohol leads to increases in sexual enjoyment, desire, spontaneity, and frequency (Beckman, 1979). In addition, expectancy challenge studies have demonstrated that alcohol expectancies in college drinkers are modifiable and changes in alcohol expectancies produce associated changes in drinking behavior (Lau-Barraco & Dunn, 1998; Darkes & Goldman, 1998). Indeed, much of the literature and evidence supporting expectancy theory is derived from college student samples.

However, more recent analysis calls some of these associations into question and casts some doubt on the effectiveness of interventions in manipulating alcohol-related expectancies. In a recent meta-analysis, Scott-Sheldon, Demartini, Carey, and Carey (2009) examined the efficacy of interventions in modifying expectancies and norms in samples of college students. After reviewing 54 interventions that were administered to 8,569 college students, the authors reported that interventions changed students' attitudes toward drinking, norms, alcohol knowledge, and intention to consume alcohol, all in a lower-risk direction, but they did not tend to change their alcohol expectancies. This finding is provided with the caveat that only 30% of the interventions studied provided some form of expectancy-related feedback. In their own meta-analysis, Hull and Bond (1986) attempted to distinguish expectancy effects from the physiological consequences of alcohol consumption. They reported that alcohol expectancies had their most profound effects when predicting deviant social behavior such as alcohol consumption or sexual arousal, whereas actual alcohol consumption was more frequently associated with deficits in information processing and motor performance. The above findings, particularly those reported by Scott-Sheldon et al. (2009), suggest that expectancy theory may not explain a substantial enough portion of variance to warrant being considered a stand-alone theory of college drinking and may instead be subsumed into other theories attempting to elucidate patterns of alcohol consumption.

Social learning theory. Social learning theory, in its current manifestation, originated from the writings of Bandura (1977, 1986) and of Akers (1985, 2000). A primary concept of the theory is that humans learn much of their behavior, including deviant behavior, by observing others, including influential peer groups and family. Bandura also introduced the concept of reciprocal determinism, which means that learning context and individual differences shape behavior, which in turn influences future choices/chosen context, again influencing subsequent behavior.

Durkin, Wolf, and Clark (2005) described many of the tenets included in Akers's (1998) expansion of social learning theory. Akers proposed a social structural learning model that included four potential dimensions of social structure within which social learning variables influence behavior. These dimensions include differential social organization (e.g., population density), differential location in the social structure (e.g., gender, social class, race), theoretically defined structural variables (e.g., anomie, social disorganization), and differential social location variables (e.g., family/friend groups, work and other reference groups).

Durkin and colleagues (2005) also provided a synopsis of Akers's (2000) understanding of learning. Differential association, differential reinforcement, and definitions are all key components of learning in the context of social learning theory. Differential association primarily involves the direct interactions with others and exposure to their norms. Differential reinforcement involves the risk/reward balance of participating in a given behavior. Definitions, both general and specific, refer to the meanings attached to certain behaviors.

Social learning theory-based constructs have been shown both to predict drinking behavior and to mediate the effects of demographic variables in studies of college binge drinkers on multiple campuses (Durkin et al., 2005; Labrie et al., 2007). Indeed, in a review of the college drinking literature (Baer, 2002) concluded that social processes may contribute more to differences in drinking behavior than personality features. Labrie and colleagues (2007) measured drinking during transition from high school to college in a sample of female college freshman. At the end of high school the students in this study all drank at similar levels; however, when they were assessed one month into their initial semester of college, significant differences were observed. Participants who stated an intention to pledge a sorority in the coming semester reported an increase in number of drinking days, average number of drinks, binge-drinking episodes, and total drinks. These same effects were not observed in those students who did not intend to pledge a sorority, nor were they observed in college athletes (Labrie et al., 2007). Similarly, Read, Wood, and Capone (2005) followed high school seniors into their sophomore year of college and observed a pattern of alcohol use that was generally consistent with social learning theory tenets, particularly reciprocal determinism, such that alcohol offers and social modeling were influenced by (and in turn, influenced) alcohol use. This finding, however, did not extend to alcohol problems, which they hypothesize had more to do with peer selection effects.

Social learning theory has also been applied in college samples to examine the relationship between living environment, vicarious learning of social norms, and alcohol consumption. For example, Ward and Gryczynski (2007) reported modest support for the hypothesis that family and peer alcohol use norms mediate the relationship between living arrangement and heavy alcohol use.

Tension reduction theory. As Conger (1956) postulated, tension reduction theory is derived from drive theory, such that alcohol works in a way that attenuates states like fear or anxiety, and these consequent decreases in negative emotional states reinforce alcohol use. Cappell and Herman (1972) were the first in the literature to label this idea as the "tension reduction theory" and argued that it has two main components: first, that alcohol reduces tension and second, that individuals drink alcohol because of its tension-reducing properties. Tension reduction theory is related to expectancy theory in that its primary hypothesis is that individuals drink because they believe that alcohol will reduce or eliminate negative emotions (Cooper, Frone, Russell, & Mudar, 1995).

Rutledge and Sher (2001) conducted a longitudinal study of college students in late adolescence and tracked them through young adulthood, during which they examined how tension reduction motives related to heavy drinking. Results indicated that during their first year of college both heavy-drinking men and women reported tension reduction motives of similar degrees. However, during years 2 through 4, tension reduction drinking motives were a greater predictor of heavy drinking among men. During their follow-up at year 7, tension reduction drinking motives for men were even greater predictors of heavy drinking than during the last year of college. Rutledge and Sher (2001) suggest that cultural norms may foster stress-related drinking as more accepted among men than women. These results are similar to results found in Kushner, Sher, Wood, and Wood's (1994) study of tension reduction expectancies, anxiety, and alcohol consumption in college freshmen, as well as in Cooper's (1995) study.

Kushner et al. (1994) conducted a study examining tension reducing alcohol expectancies in a group of college students. Results revealed that individuals with a family history of alcoholism reported higher tension reducing alcohol expectancies. More interestingly, only males showed a significant relationship between beliefs about the anxiety-reducing properties of alcohol and subsequent alcohol consumption.

Health belief model. The health belief model (HBM) was formulated in the 1950s by a team of social psychologists working with the United States Public Health

Service in response to the U.S. population's limited participation in disease prevention programs (Stretcher & Rosenstock, 1997). Primarily a value expectancy theory, the HBM involves the desire either to avoid illness or to become healthy as well as the belief that some specific, health-related action can prevent or heal one's sickness. In addition, expectancies were defined by an individual's estimate of how vulnerable he/she is to illness and the probability of being able to decrease risk through personal action (Strecher & Rosenstock, 1997). "In general, it is now believed that individuals will take action to ward off, to screen for, or to control an ill-health condition if they regard themselves as susceptible to the condition, if they believe it to have potentially serious consequences, if they believe that a course of action available to them would be beneficial in reducing either their susceptibility to or the severity of the condition, and if they believe that the anticipated barriers to (or costs of) taking the action are outweighed by its benefits" (Strecher & Rosenstock, 1997, p. 44).

The HBM has been used to guide many colleges' and universities' approaches to problem alcohol use among students and has led to the development of promising interventions (Gonzalez, 1988; Kleinot & Rogers, 1982; Portnoy, 1980). In addition, some studies have suggested that the frequency with which parents discuss alcohol consumption with students leaving for college is influenced by components of the HBM (Cremeens, Usdan, Brock-Martin, & Martin, 2008; Neifeld Wheeler, 2010). Specifically, the more severe/threatening that parents perceive heavy alcohol consumption to be, the more frequent their reported talks about alcohol with their college bound children (Cremeens, et al., 2008).

Theory of reasoned action/planned behavior. The theory of reasoned action (Ajzen & Fishbein, 1980) assumes that behavior is a direct function of behavioral intentions, which consist of attitudes toward the activity in question and the subjective norms that are held, that is, what an individual believes others think should be done in that situation. Furthermore, attitudes regarding the behavior in question are considered to be a product of the beliefs or expectancies that a person holds about the consequences associated with performing or not performing that behavior and his or her evaluation of these consequences. Therefore, if people hold strong beliefs about the likelihood of positive outcomes occurring after a given behavior, then they will have a positive attitude toward that behavior (Montano & Kasprzyk, 2008).

Individuals are assumed to be rational and to make decisions on the basis of critical examination of possible outcomes and the value that they place on them. The relationship between variables is assumed to be causal, with behavioral and normative beliefs acting through attitudes towards behavior and subjective norms to shape behavioral intentions, and subsequent behavior (Ajzen & Fishbein, 1980).

The theory of planned behavior is an extension of the theory of reasoned action and adds the construct of perceived behavioral control. The addition of perceived behavioral control suggests that individuals will be more likely to engage in a particular behavior when they think that they have the ability to achieve a desired outcome.

Two factors contribute to perceived behavioral control—control beliefs and perceived power. Control beliefs refer to the thoughts an individual has about the resources needed to execute a behavior, and perceived power refers to the impact that those resources have on a particular behavior (Montano & Kasprzyk, 2008).

Research with samples of college students has shown that attitudes toward alcohol and social norms act as significant predictors of subsequent use (Laflin, Moore-Hirschl, Weis, & Hayes, 1994) as well as intention to seek treatment (Codd & Cohen, 2003). Collins and Carey (2007) reported results that support most of the constructs in the theory of planned behavior in the explanation of college drinking. In Collins and Carey's study of college drinkers, both attitudes and drink-refusal efficacy, but not subjective social norms, predicted intention to increase drinking behavior.

Theory of social normative behavior. Many studies have examined the relationship between social norms and drinking behavior in college students (Borsari & Carey, 2003; Real & Rimal, 2007; Rimal, Lapinski, Cook, & Real, 2005) and suggest that college students tend to overestimate the amount of alcohol their peers drink and the social acceptability of drinking (Borsari & Carey, 2003). Rimal and Real (2005) proposed that perceived norms consist of descriptive and injunctive norms. Descriptive norms refer to an individual's idea about the prevalence of a particular behavior, and injunctive norms relate to an individual's thoughts about how others perceive a behavior (i.e., the extent to which they approve of it). The theory of normative social behavior is based on the premise that descriptive norms affect individuals' own behaviors through interactions with three normative processes: injunctive norms, outcome expectations, and group identity.

In their original findings describing the theory of normative social behavior (TSNB), Rimal and Real (2005) demonstrated that the effects of descriptive norms on behavior are moderated by group identity, outcome expectancies, and injunctive norms. Real and Rimal (2007) evaluated the influence of peer communication (how often participants talked with their friends or siblings in the past 2 weeks and normally about alcohol consumption) in relation to the TSNB and found that peer communication was significantly associated with alcohol consumption and predicted intention to drink in the future. Findings from this study suggest that interventions to reduce college drinking may be more effective if they focus on changing the thoughts and behaviors of social groups instead of individuals.

Transtheoretical model of behavior change. Prochaska and DiClemente (1982) introduced the transtheoretical model of behavior change as a theory that explains how individuals progress toward integrating behaviors that lead to health maintenance (Prochaska, DiClemente, & Norcross, 1992; Prochaska, Johnson, & Lee, 2009; Prochaska, Redding, & Evers, 2008). They identified 6 main stages of behavior change: precontemplation, contemplation, preparation, action, maintenance, and termination. In the precontemplation stage, individuals typically have no plan to change their behavior in the near future, which is usually defined as the next six months.

The contemplation stage is characterized by a desire to change within the next six months but is also marked by ambivalence. During this stage, individuals begin to become aware of both the pros and cons of their drinking behavior, which can lead to ambivalence about changing and cause them to be stuck in this stage for a long period of time. The preparation stage is identified by the intention to change behavior in the next month, and sometimes individuals have already taken small steps toward change. In the action stage, individuals have made specific changes in their behavior in the past six months. Maintenance is characterized as the having sustained behavior change and working toward preventing relapse. Lastly, termination is associated with complete self-efficacy to resist engaging in the problem behavior in any given situation (Prochaska, et al., 2008).

Prochaska et al. (2008) identified 10 major "processes of change" that individuals must apply to progress through the stages: consciousness raising, dramatic relief, self-reevaluation, environmental reevaluation, self-liberation, helping relationships, counterconditioning, contingency management, stimulus control, and social liberation. Consciousness raising aims to increase awareness about the consequences of the problem behavior and situations that may increase the likelihood of engagement in the problem behavior. Dramatic relief involves activities such as role-playing and grieving that are aimed at eliciting negative emotions that coincide with the problem behavior. Providing feedback on the problem behavior, interpretations of the problem behavior, and media campaigns are types of interventions that work to increase awareness. The purpose of self-reevaluation is to increase awareness about the individual's self-identity. During this process, individuals are encouraged to view themselves from the perspective of a problem drinker as well as from the perspective of a healthy individual. Environmental reevaluation aims to increase awareness about the effects of the problem behavior on others as well as to demonstrate that the individual can act as a positive role model to others by eliminating the problem behavior. Self-liberation is making the commitment to change and believing that one can change. Helping relationships involve developing a healthy social support system that fosters behavior change. Counterconditioning entails learning new healthy behaviors that can replace the problem behaviors. Contingency management involves increasing rewards for healthy behavior and decreasing rewards for behaviors leading to unhealthy behavior. Stimulus control entails removing cues or triggers that promote the unhealthy behavior and adding cues that facilitate the healthy behavior. Social liberation involves the increase of available resources and social opportunities in the community that are aimed at supporting the healthy behavior. Also central to the transtheoretical model of behavior change is the use of decisional balance, which relates to the pros and cons of changing one's behavior. Typically, individuals who are in the precontemplation stage report more cons in regards to changing their behavior than pros.

Recognizing which stage an individual is in is theoretically important to treatment interventions, as different processes of change are hypothesized to match better with different stages of change. In the precontemplation stage, the change processes that may fit best are consciousness raising, dramatic relief, and environmental reevaluation. In the contemplation stage, self-reevaluation may be the best matches. During the preparation stage, self-liberation may be the most useful process to facilitate change. During the action and maintenance stages, contingency management, helping relationships, counterconditioning, and stimulus control are the change processes that are likely to work best.

A large number of studies examining drinking behaviors in college students have used the transtheoretical model in conjunction with assessments or interventions to measure or enhance motivation to change (Borsari & Carey, 2000; Vik, Culbertson, & Sellers, 2000). For example, Vik et al. (2000) used the Stages of Change Readiness and Eagerness Scale (SOCRATES) to measure readiness to change in college drinkers. They found that the majority of heavy drinkers were in the precontemplation stage. Despite experiencing a great deal of drinking-related negative consequences, these individuals still did not recognize a need to change their behaviors.

The use of brief motivation interviewing (BMI) has become a popular intervention approach to enhancing motivation to change (see Carey, this volume). Borsari and Carey (2000) assessed the efficacy of using mandated BMIs to reduce college drinking in students who violated campus alcohol policies. Compared to the alcohol education group (AE), the BMI group had reported fewer alcohol-related problems at the 3- and 6-month follow-ups. However, the literature involving the relationship between BMIs and subsequent alcohol use is mixed. Another study conducted by Borsari, Murphy, and Carey (2009) found that, although college drinkers reported more readiness to change immediately following a BMI and up to 6 months later, readiness to change did not mediate alcohol consumption or alcohol-related problems. This same study also showed that motivation to change did not differ significantly between individuals who received BMIs with a counseling session and those who received BMIs without a counseling session.

PERSONALITY CORRELATES OF COLLEGE DRINKING

The study of personality has a long history as part of behavioral research, and college drinking is no exception. Since R. J. Jessor and Jessor (1983) examined personality correlates predicting young adults transition to drinking, the relationship between personality variables and college drinking has been the focus of several research studies and reviews (Baer, 2002; Brennan, Walfish, & Aubuchon, 1986). In the college-drinking literature, personality is often studied in the form of traits or dispositions that tend to be stable across situations. Although some researchers have operated within the Big Five framework (e.g., Mezquita, Stewart, & Ruiperez, 2010), others have taken a more specific approach by studying individual personality traits such as sensation seeking (e.g., Cyders, Flory, Rainer, & Smith, 2009). Indeed, how one operationalizes personality can be vitally important, as evidenced by McAdams and Donnellan (2009). Their study showed that more narrow facets of personality were often more strongly correlated with drinking variables than their Big Five counterparts. For example, although immoderation predicted significantly more problems with alcohol, alcohol use, and hangover symptoms, neuroticism, the facet under which immoderation is subsumed, produced a smaller effect in the opposite direction (McAdams & Donnellan, 2009). Although there is a wealth of personality research available, for the purposes of this brief review we have followed Baer's lead and have classified the research foci into three broad categories: impulsivity/disinhibition, extraversion/sociability, and neuroticism/emotionality (Baer, 2002).

Impulsivity and sensation seeking are probably the two personality characteristics that have been shown most frequently to be positively related to level of drinking among college students. Research has consistently shown a positive relationship between impulsivity and drinking variables in college students (Brennan et al., 1986; Hittner & Swickert, 2006; Zuckerman, 2007), and sensation seeking has been shown to be a robust predictor of alcohol-related behavior in college students, whether the variable is consumption level or drinking-related problems (McAdams & Donnellan, 2009). Impulsivity has also been explored as a potential moderator between alcohol consumption and negative outcomes in college students. Neal and Carey (2007) reported that impulsivity moderated the relationship between intoxication and negative consequences at the event level, such that those who were intoxicated on a given day were more likely to report negative consequences if they scored higher on measures of impulsivity.

In addition to impulsivity, extraversion has been identified as a personality facet that is linked to alcohol consumption in college students, with more extraverted students tending to report heavier drinking (Martsh & Miller, 1997; McAdams & Donnellan, 2009). In addition to consumption, the relationship between extraversion and drinking motives has also been studied. In samples of college drinkers, extraversion predicts enhancement drinking motives, whereas there is a negative correlation between extraversion and the drinking motive of coping (Mezquita et al., 2010; Stewart & Devine, 2000). However, the desire to drink in order to cope with either depression or anxiety may be more readily explained via the personality construct of neuroticism.

It has been hypothesized that neuroticism/emotionality and general emotional distress are linked to increased alcohol consumption. Indeed, alcohol and substance use problems are often most prevalent in those with co-occurring mental health conditions (Regier et al., 1990). However, results from studies examining neuroticism and alcohol consumption in college students have been mixed (Brennan et al., 1986). Some data suggest that there is a positive relationship between anxiety and frequency, but not quantity, of alcohol use (Igra & Moos, 1979; Lundin & Sawyer, 1965), whereas other data suggest a positive relationship between anxiety and social consequences of alcohol use (Orford, Waller, & Peto, 1974). Still other researchers have found that heavier drinking students tended to report lower levels of anxiety and neuroticism than did lighter drinking students (Ratliff & Burkhart, 1984; Schwarz, Burkhart, & Green, 1978). More recent research (Rush, Becker, & Curry, 2009) showed that students who engaged in binge drinking and binge eating reported significantly greater levels of neuroticism than their nonbinge drinking comparisons. Additionally, neuroticism has been linked to the drinking motives of coping (Mezquita et al., 2010) and conformity (Stewart & Devine, 2000).

Main points regarding theoretical constructs. Table 4.1 presents a summary of main points in the theoretical models we described. As can be seen in Table 4.1, most of the theories listed were designed to address alcohol use and alcohol-related negative consequences. However, several of the theories (theory of reasoned action/planned behavior, transtheoretical model) were created to explain more general phenomena, such as health-related behavior, and even behavior in general (behavioral economics theory, social learning theory) and have been applied to the problem of drinking among college students. The theories listed in Table 4.1 also vary by their scope. In this regard, theories may be multidimensional (e.g., the developmental theories) or more unidimensional (e.g., tension reduction theory, personality theory, theory of social normative behavior). In addition, several of the theories were designed to explain phenomena at a more molar level, say between current perceptions of drinking norms and average pattern of alcohol consumption and related consequences over some period of time. This contrasts with other of the theories, such as myopia theory, the tension reduction hypothesis, and expectancy and personality theory, which are better suited to testing hypotheses about the determinants and consequences of alcohol use at the event level. The latter theories tend to focus on specific, single-factor mechanisms to explain event-level alcohol use, and the theories designed to explain average trends in alcohol use and related problems tend to include multiple variables, sometimes at different levels of analysis (e.g., person variable such as expectancies and environmental variables such as environmental restrictions on alcohol accessibility) to predict average patterns of alcohol use and related consequences. Neither event level nor molar level of analysis and explanation/prediction is "better" than the other; in fact they may be viewed as complementing each other. Nevertheless, it is a point that is pertinent to having reasonable expectations about the kind of data that a theory can be expected to account for in judging its worth. Another point about the theories listed in Table 4.1 is that they favor a psychological/environmental perspective; a more biological perspective is represented heavily only in the developmental models, which are most like true "biopsychosocial" models.

It is important to point out in describing the theories listed in Table 4.1 that there is a considerable degree of overlap among their major constructs. For example, the construct of social norms plays a major role in the theory of social normative behavior and in the theory of reasoned action/planned behavior. In addition, constructs related to motivation to engage in or to change a behavior such as expectancies

Table 4.1 Summaries of Theories of College Student Drinking

Theory	Illustrative Citations	Major Constructs	Designed to Explain/Predict	Applications
• Alcohol Myopia Theory	• Steele and Josephs (1990)	• Inhibition conflict • Alcohol-related cognitive impairment	• Risky/ "excessive" behavior	• Increase salience of consequences of risky/excessive behavior
• Behavioral Economics	• Babor et al. (1978) • Bickel et al. (2003) • Bickel and Marsch (2001)	• Delay discounting • Relative reinforcing efficacy	• Alcohol consumption • Alcohol-related negative consequences	• Reinforce behavioral alternatives to alcohol/other drug use • Environmental control
• Developmental Theories	• Schulenberg and Maggs (2002) [a]	• Life Transitions, 5 Hypotheses: Overload, Developmental Mismatch, Increased Heterogeneity, Transition Catalyst, Heightened Vulnerability to Chance Events	• Heavy alcohol use as part of a general theory of risky behavior	• Stagger timing of a major transition • Increase individual coping capacities • Provide better match between individual needs and contexts • Counter social networks supportive of problem behavior • Provide alternative (to alcohol use) to meeting social/ sensation-seeking goals • Increase awareness of consequences of risky behavior
• Expectancy Theory	• Darkes and Goldman (1998) • Goldman et al. (1987) • Weinhardt (1999)	• Alcohol outcome expectancies	• Alcohol consumption • Alcohol-related negative consequences	• Expectancy "challenge"

[a] Schulenberg & Maggs (2002)

(continued)

Table 4.1 *(continued)*

Theory	Illustrative Citations	Major Constructs	Designed to Explain/Predict	Applications
♦ Social Learning Theory	♦ Akers (1985, 2000) ♦ Bandura (1977, 1986)	♦ Social structure (social organization, social location) ♦ Differential reinforcement ♦ Differential association ♦ Learned meanings of behavior	♦ Alcohol use and alcohol-related negative consequences, as a part of a general theory of behavior	♦ Increase association with social networks that reinforce moderation/abstinence ♦ Ascribe new meanings to heavy alcohol use and alternative behaviors ♦ Change social structure to encourage moderation/abstinence ♦ Increase skills and self-efficacy to engage in non–substance use alternative behaviors
♦ Tension Reduction Theory	♦ Cappell and Greeley (1987) ♦ Cooper et al. (1995) ♦ Rutledge and Sher (2001)	♦ Drinking motives ♦ Negative emotional state	♦ Alcohol consumption ♦ Alcohol-related negative consequences	♦ Teach nonsubstance use ways of coping with negative affect
♦ Health Belief Model	♦ Gonzalez (1988) [b] ♦ Stretcher and Rosenstock (1997)	♦ Perceived susceptibility[b] ♦ Perceived severity ♦ Perceived benefits ♦ Perceived barriers ♦ Cues to action ♦ Self-efficacy	♦ Change in any behavior (in this case, heavy alcohol use) that is a risk to health	♦ Personalize risk[b] ♦ Specify consequences of heavy alcohol use ♦ Specify action to take and the benefits of change ♦ Identify and help to remove barriers to change ♦ Educate, promote awareness of the problem ♦ Build skills to change behavior ♦ Reduce anxiety about change

[b] Gonzalez (1988)

• Theory of Reasoned Action/ Planned Behavior	• Ajzen and Fishbein (1980) • Montano et al. (1997)	• Attitude • Subjective norm • Behavioral intention • Perceived behavioral control • Motivation to comply • Perceived power • Behavioral beliefs	• Alcohol use and alcohol-related negative consequences as part of a general theory of behavior	• Modify positively biased attitudes about alcohol use and its consequences • Evaluate normative beliefs about alcohol use • Enhance power to modify alcohol use, reduce barriers to change • Modify positively biased behavioral beliefs about alcohol use
• Theory of Social Normative Behavior	• Rimal and Real (2005)	• Perceived norms (descriptive and injunctive) • Alcohol outcome expectancies	• Alcohol use • Alcohol-related negative consequences	• Educate about prevalence of alcohol use on campus • Educate about how others perceive heavy alcohol consumption • Educate about consequences of heavy alcohol use
• Trans-theoretical Model	• Prochaska and DiClemente (1982) • Prochaska et al. (1992)	• Stages of behavior change/ Readiness to change	• Motivation to change a specific problem behavior, in this case heavy alcohol use	• Match intervention to an individual's readiness to change the behavior that the intervention targets
• Personality Theory	• R. J. Jessor and Jessor (1983) • Baer (2002)	• "Big Five" • Impulsivity • Sensation seeking	• Stable person variables that predict alcohol use/ consequences or that moderate effects of other variables on alcohol use, either at the average pattern or event level	• Target primary prevention efforts to people who are high on characteristics that tend to be associated with developing patterns of heavy alcohol use and problems • Tailor interventions to person characteristics that tend to be associated with specific patterns of alcohol use or with specific determinants of such use

(alcohol expectancy theory), readiness to change (transtheoretical model), motivation to comply (theory of reasoned action/planned behavior), and relative reinforcing efficacy (behavioral economics theory) appear frequently. Another example is the construct of negative affect, which may be a centerpiece of a theory or is embedded within it (an example of the latter is the overload and increased heterogeneity hypotheses of the developmental approaches). Similarly, the construct of self-efficacy (or perceived behavioral control) plays a major role in social learning theory, the theory of reasoned action/planned behavior, and the health belief model.

Although this chapter is not primarily concerned with interventions that target alcohol consumption in college students, it is of interest to describe the kinds of interventions that may be or have been derived from the different theoretical models. In this regard, as noted earlier, improving the effectiveness of interventions is the ultimate reason for the research and theory development on drinking among college students that have been generated. Table 4.1 shows that there is considerable emphasis on manipulation or change in the campus environment. This follows from the social/environmental/structural focus that a number of the theories have and is consistent with the level and kind of intervention that colleges and universities would seem most likely to implement, given that they can control the campus environment (albeit not other environments in which students may drink). In this regard, a "population," more "campus public health" approach would seem to be favored from an efficiency and financial point of view. One example of such population-based campaigns is the use of advertising campaigns and public messaging on campus to influence extant norms of acceptable and "reinforced" drinking levels among students. Another example is the degree of availability of alcohol on campus to which students may have access. Interventions also address person factors, most commonly perceptions of normative drinking behavior among peers, expectancies about alcohol's acute effects, and motivation to change patterns of alcohol use. Overall, since about the early 2000s (Clapp, Segars, & Voas, 2002), it seems that the interventions typically used in the college context may be traced to identified theoretical models, and these models often were created to address the (structural) level of intervention in the college context that seems most likely to have the most wide-reaching effects on the student population.

SUMMARY OF THE EMPIRICAL EVIDENCE FOR THEORIES OF DRINKING AMONG COLLEGE STUDENTS

The representative review of empirical studies shows generally strong support for each of the respective theories of drinking among college students that was reviewed. In this regard, it is important to note that not all studies found uniform support for a given theory (e.g., Codd & Cohen, 2003; Darkes & Goldman, 1998; Read et al., 2005) as stated in the respective a priori hypotheses. However, the authors in such cases reported "general" support for a theory with a possible explanation for any finding not predicted or contrary to what would be expected from a theory. No studies that were published showed no empirical support for a theory, that is, no entirely "negative findings" studies and the results discussed as disconfirming evidence for a theory were found. Of course, this is not easy to interpret, given the extreme bias against publishing "negative results" but is worth keeping in mind for our later discussion of proposed directions of research on drinking among college students.

ANALYSIS AND CONCLUSIONS

This review raises several questions about existing theories of college student drinking at different levels. It would seem important to address such questions, because theory often is used to guide research on college student drinking and to guide prevention and treatment interventions. Yet, despite the application of such interventions nationwide for at least the past 35 years (Kraft, 1976), the data reviewed at the beginning of this chapter indicate that the prevalence of underage alcohol use, heavy alcohol use, and alcohol-related negative consequences among college students have not shown significant change over that span of time. It is the case that the empirical findings of stability in levels and consequences of alcohol use among college students may be due in part to use of interventions that simply are information-based and that have little empirical support or are governed more by local traditions rather than by empirical evidence (Clapp et al., 2002). In that context, existing theories of drinking among college students may have little to do with the seeming intractability of the problem of alcohol use and related negative consequences among college students. Nevertheless, especially in the past decade there has been a major increase in the application of theory in the development and evaluation of interventions for drinking among college students. Accordingly, a critical analysis of existing theories might help to advance the field by generating future research and theory-building/modification efforts that ultimately will enhance the power of interventions that target drinking among college students.

To begin with the more basic questions about the structure and content of the theories included in Table 4.1, the degree of overlap among several of the theories suggests that it would be possible to "consolidate" the theories as a way to decrease the feel of scatter that reading the literature on college student drinking gives. For example, in several cases among the theories listed in Table 4.1, a hypothesis or theory is subsumed within another, broader-ranging theory. Examples are the constructs of norms, beliefs/expectancies, and motivation to change as components of the health-belief model or the theory of reasoned action/planned behavior. This suggests that the single construct or single dimension theories might be more efficiently considered as components of the larger theory instead of as separate, "stand-alone" theories or hypotheses, if the broader theory seems to be more powerful and to have more utility. This is not to argue that, for example, basic research on specific determinants (causes) of alcohol consumption at the event level, such as "alcohol myopia," or moderators of such effects, such as sensation seeking and alcohol expectancies, should be abandoned. Such research is essential to advance the understanding of alcohol use at the event and ultimately at the general pattern level. Rather, it is important that theory-builders and researchers are cognizant that drinking among college students is a complex phenomenon and that any attempt at a "complete" explanation of it likely will involve a biopsychosocial approach at multiple levels (e.g., person, context) of analysis.

The question of consolidation leads to the possibility of theory "trimming" and "competing" theories. In this regard, the empirical literature on college student drinking is light on systematic testing of theories both within and across research labs. Such an approach seems essential for deriving a theory or model with maximum predictive or explanatory power (Noar & Zimmerman, 2005). Unfortunately, the literature is more characterized by a series of tests of a given model or theory by its proponents but with little or no emphasis on collecting data that might disconfirm a theory to some degree but that would lead to its modification toward greater utility and power (Ogden, 2003). In the same vein, the empirical literature with few exceptions (e.g., Sun & Longazel, 2008; Turrisi et al., 2000) shows little in the way of testing differential predictions or testing competing hypotheses derived from two or more theories (or even parts of existing theories). The end point of such research would be to provide empirical evidence regarding which theory or theories seem to be of most value to the field. Still another (albeit not airtight, because a number of factors besides the adequacy of a theory could account for the outcome of a study) approach that researchers could take that seems especially relevant to the problem of drinking among college students is that the strength (effect size) of prevention interventions derived from two competing theories could be compared, with the stronger intervention suggesting which is the better theory.

Addressing these several questions about the structure and content of theories of college student drinking certainly poses a difficult research agenda for the field. However, there is an overarching question that would seem important to address first. That question is: What do we want theories of college student drinking to "do" for us? That is, what role do we want them to play? The wide-ranging empirical and theoretical literature suggests that the field is far from a consensus on answers to these questions. Nevertheless, clarity about goals could lead toward more systematic and efficient theory development and modification and therefore ultimately more practical value in guiding interventions.

It has been generally accepted that the range of patterns of alcohol consumption and related phenomena such as alcohol-related negative consequences are best viewed from a multidimensional perspective. Therefore, a biopsychosocial view would seem to be the best approach to the problem, given our current knowledge (Maisto, Connors, & Dearing, 2007). Unfortunately, theories of college student drinking often seem to neglect this basic point, that they are essentially designed to explain a range of patterns of alcohol consumption that are prevalent among predominantly emerging adults who happen to be attending college. The college context/environment seems to have played a disproportionately large role in creating theories of college student drinking or in applying other theories to do the same, as noted earlier. We also noted earlier that this in some ways seems sensible, because campus intervention efforts likely are going to emphasize changes in the campus environment rather than in the person as ways to alleviate problems with college student alcohol use. That is an acceptable strategy if it is recognized that the predictive power of any theory that intentionally has such a limited scope likely will limit the power of any intervention that is derived from it to change overall patterns of alcohol consumption and related negative consequences. As mentioned earlier, the importance of taking a biopsychosocial approach to explain drinking among college students and among emerging adults in general, if that is the goal, is not news to researchers and clinicians who work with this age group. Probably the clearest example of this is the long-standing tradition of taking a developmental approach to predicting and explaining alcohol consumption in emerging adults (see Schulenberg & Maggs, 2002, cited in Table 4.1; also Brown et al., 2009, and Masten et al., 2009).

Almost 60 years ago, Straus and Bacon (1953) recognized the importance of the question of what role we want theories of college student drinking to play. As they wrote in the penultimate paragraph of their classic book, "With the knowledge that there are levels of drinking behavior dominated by sociocultural forces, other levels which can be manipulated by guidance and the tools of reason, and still other levels that may be reached only by emotional and social restructuring of the individual, it is possible, in the first place, to avoid the waste involved in making every approach at all levels or on the wrong level" (p. 202). Keeping this in mind could help researchers and clinicians/interventionists make a significant dent in the stubborn statistics on heavy alcohol consumption and alcohol-related negative consequences among college students in the United States.

WHERE DO THEORIES OF DRINKING AMONG COLLEGE STUDENTS GO FROM HERE?

It turns out that the state of theories of drinking among college students reflects the state of theory of health behavior in general (e.g., Noar & Zimmerman, 2005; Ogden, 2003; Suls & Rothman, 2004). This may seem uncanny, until it is realized that several of the theories that are included in Table 4.1 are ones that are applied in different ways or degrees in research on health behavior in general (e.g., theory of reasoned action/ planned behavior, health belief model, transtheoretical model; Noar & Zimmerman, 2005). Accordingly, it seems that the study of drinking among college students would be advanced considerably by the implementation of methods of theory building and modification (Lynham, 2002; Torraco, 2002), some of which have been discussed in the context of health-related behavior (Noar & Zimmerman, 2005; Ogden, 2003; Painter, Borba, Hynes, Mays, & Glanz, 2008; Schwartz, 1982; Suls & Rothman, 2004). A brief summary of these methods follows.

Theories first should be clear about their "boundaries," or what specifically they are designed to explain or predict. As noted earlier, this varies considerably among the theories that have been applied to drinking among college students, as they have ranged from global theories of behavior or health behavior to theories that are specific to alcohol consumption in college students. Second, theories should be specific about their constructs and their conceptual and operational definitions. In the area of college student drinking, this is a critical point, because among the existing theories there is considerably overlap at least conceptually among the constructs that are included. Third, among existing theories of a given phenomenon, choose the one that is most precise about its constructs and their interrelationships, and apply those same criteria if choosing among existing theories. This allows testing of specific hypotheses that follow from a theory and clarifies the criteria for its confirmation or disconfirmation. If a theory is disconfirmed, it is important to modify or discard the theory if problems with internal validity of the research design do not account for the findings.

Related to the topic of testing theories and their confirmation or disconfirmation, it is important for researchers to keep in mind that multiple methods and research designs may be used for this purpose. Likely because psychologists constitute a large percentage of researchers who are active in this area, a quantitative approach to data collection is most prevalent in the empirical literature. Moreover, probably because of the nature of questions asked and the context (college/university campuses) that is of central concern, cross-sectional and longitudinal survey studies are the most prevalent research designs. (An exception to the trend in research design is the common appearance of experimental designs to test myopia theory and the early basic research on alcohol-related expectancies.) However, other methods, such as qualitative methodology, should be considered as applicable in the study of drinking among college students. Taking a multimethod approach to research design and data-collection methods would be consistent with the multivariable complexity of drinking among college students and would likely accelerate the advancement of knowledge about it (Schubert, 2010).

The fourth step in this process is the emergence of the "best" theory of drinking among college students. "Best" means the theory of a phenomenon that explains or predicts it in the most parsimonious and precise way (Dennis & Kintsch, 2007). There are several ways to determine which theory meets these criteria, but it seems that the preferred way is to conduct full (as compared to tests of one or two constructs that are part of a theory) tests of competing theories, that is, of theories that lead to contrasting hypotheses (Noar & Zimmerman, 2005). We found no evidence in the college student drinking literature of full competing theory testing, and there is extremely little evidence of such research on health behavior in general (Painter et al., 2008).

CONCLUSIONS

As noted earlier, empirical studies of drinking among college students and of interventions designed to modify it have increased substantially in the past two decades. This activity is based on the premise that interventions that are based on empirical findings are more effective than those that are not. Similarly, there is an assumption that theoretical models of drinking among college students that are based on good research will generate the best research and will lead ultimately to the strongest interventions. This chapter has shown that the high volume of research and theory on college student drinking unfortunately has not led to the degree of advancement in intervention strength (based on reported effect sizes) that has been hoped for, and that the research does not have a "cumulative" (and thus a cumulative knowledge base) feel to it but rather seems compartmentalized. There likely are several reasons for this, but one likely is that the process of theory building, research generation from theory, and theory modification as currently reflected in the literature needs considerable adjustment if the promise of advanced knowledge and stronger interventions is to be realized.

In an introduction to a special issue of *Psychological Methods* devoted to the use of multiple data sets toward the end of accelerating the accumulation of knowledge from multiple individual research projects, Curran (2009) quoted Paul Meehl (1978) on theories in psychology that seems applicable here: "It is simply a sad fact that in soft psychology theories rise and decline, come and go, more as a function of baffled boredom than anything else; and the enterprise shows a disturbing absence of that *cumulative* character that is so impressive in disciplines like astronomy, molecular biology, and genetics" (p. 807). Meehl's words currently seem extreme, as psychology in general has done much in the past 33 years to address his concerns. The same is true in the specific study of and intervention for drinking among college students; as mentioned earlier, in recent years interventions aimed at the individual or the environmental levels have been based increasingly on theory and have been shown to have empirical support. Examples include motivational interventions, skills-based interventions, and normative reeducation interventions, especially those involving personal feedback (Larimer & Cronce, 2007). Still, the study and advancement of knowledge about drinking among college students, as is true for many other areas of study in the behavioral and social sciences, would benefit by more systematic attention paid to theory development, and, more importantly, to theory modification and refinement.

REFERENCES

Ajzen, I., & Fishbein, M. (1980). *Understanding attitudes and predicting social behavior.* Englewood Cliffs, NJ: Prentice Hall.

Akers, R. L. (1985). *Deviant behavior: A social learning approach* (3rd ed.). Belmont, CA: Wadsworth.

Akers, R. L. (1998). *Social learning and social structure: A general theory of crime and deviance.* Boston, MA: Northeastern University Press.

Akers, R. L. (2000). *Criminological theories: Introduction, evaluation, and application* (3rd ed.). Los Angeles, CA: Roxbury Publishing.

Babor, T. F., Mendelson, J. H., Greenberg, I., & Kuehnle, J. (1978). Experimental analysis of the "happy hour": Effects of purchase price on alcohol consumption. *Psychopharmacology, 58*(1), 35–41.

Baer, J. S. (2002). Student factors: Understanding individual variation in college drinking. *Journal of Studies on Alcohol,* 40–53.

Bandura, A. (1977). *Social learning theory.* Upper Saddle River, NJ: Prentice Hall.

Bandura, A. (1986). *Social foundations of thought and action: A social cognitive theory.* Upper Saddle River, NJ: Prentice Hall.

Bava, S., & Tapert, S. F. (2010). Adolescent brain development and the risk for alcohol and other drug problems. *Neuropsychology Review, 20*(4), 398–413.

Beckman, L. J. (1979). Reported effects of alcohol on the sexual feelings and behavior of women alcoholics and non-alcoholics. *Journal of Studies on Alcohol, 40*(3), 272–282.

Bickel, W. K., DeGrandpre, R. J., & Higgins, S. T. (1993). Behavioral economics: A novel experimental approach to the study of drug dependence. *Drug and Alcohol Dependence, 33*(2), 173–192.

Bickel, W. K., Madden, G. J., & Petry, N. M. (1998). The price of change: The behavioral economics of drug dependence. *Behavior Therapy, 29*(4), 545–565.

Bickel, W. K., & Marsch, L. A. (2001). Toward a behavioral economic understanding of drug dependence: Delay discounting processes. *Addiction, 96*(1), 73–86.

Borsari, B., & Carey, K. B. (2000). Effects of a brief motivational intervention with college student drinkers. *Journal of Consulting and Clinical Psychology, 68*(4), 728–733.

Borsari, B., & Carey, K. B. (2003). Descriptive and injunctive norms in college drinking: A meta-analytic integration. *Journal of Studies on Alcohol, 64*(3), 331–341.

Borsari, B., Murphy, J. G., & Carey, K. B. (2009). Readiness to change in brief motivational interventions: A requisite condition for drinking reductions? *Addictive Behaviors, 34*(2), 232–235.

Brennan, A. F., Walfish, S., & Aubuchon, P. (1986). Alcohol-use and abuse in college-students .1. A review of individual and personality-correlates. *International Journal of the Addictions, 21*(4–5), 449–474.

Brown, S. A., McGue, M., Maggs, J., Schulenberg, J., Hingson, R., Swartzwelder, S., . . . Murphy, S. (2008). A developmental perspective on alcohol and youths 16 to 20 years of age. *Pediatrics, 121, Suppl 4,* S290–310.

Cappell, H., & Herman, C. P. (1972). Alcohol and tension reduction. A review. *Quarterly Journal of Studies on Alcohol, 33*(1), 33–64.

Casey, B. J., & Jones, R. M. (2010). Neurobiology of the adolescent brain and behavior: Implications for substance use disorders. *Journal of the American Academy of Child and Adolescent Psychiatry, 49*(12), 1189–1201.

Christiansen, B. A., Goldman, M. S., & Inn, A. (1982). Development of alcohol-related expectancies in adolescents: Separating pharmacological from social-learning influences. *Journal of Consulting and Clinical Psychology, 50*(3), 336–344.

Clapp, J. D., Segars, L., & Voas, R. (2002). A conceptual model of the alcohol environment of college students. *Journal of Human Behavior in the Social Environment, 5,* 73–90.

Codd, R. T., & Cohen, B. N. (2003). Predicting college student intention to seek help for alcohol abuse. *Journal of Social and Clinical Psychology, 22*(2), 168–191.

Collins, S. E., & Carey, K. B. (2007). The theory of planned behavior as a model of heavy episodic drinking among college students. *Psychology of Addictive Behaviors: Journal of the Society of Psychologists in Addictive Behaviors, 21*(4), 498–507.

Conger, J. J. (1956). Alcoholism: Theory, problem and challenge. II. Reinforcement theory and the dynamics of alcoholism. *Quarterly Journal of Studies on Alcohol, 17*(2), 296–305.

Cooper, M. L., Frone, M. R., Russell, M., & Mudar, P. (1995). Drinking to regulate positive and negative emotions: A motivational model of alcohol use. *Journal of Personality and Social Psychology, 69*(5), 990–1005.

Correia, C. J. (2004). Behavioral economics: Basic concepts and clinical applications. In W. Cox & E. Klinger (Eds.), *Handbook of Motivational Counseling: Concepts, Approaches, and Assessment* (pp. 49–64). Hoboken, NJ: Wiley.

Correia, C. J., & Carey, K. B. (1999). Applying behavioral theories of choice to substance use in a sample of psychiatric outpatients. *Psychology of Addictive Behaviors, 13*(3), 207–212.

Cremeens, J. L., Usdan, S. L., Brock-Martin, A., & Martin, R. J. (2008). Parent-child communication to reduce heavy alcohol use among first year college students. *College Student Journal, 42*(1), 152–163.

Critchlow, B. (1986). The powers of John Barleycorn: Beliefs about the effects of alcohol on social behavior. *American Psychologist, 41*(7), 751–764.

Curran, P. J. (2009). The seemingly quixotic pursuit of a cumulative psychological science: Introduction to the special issue. *Psychological Methods, 14*(2), 77–80.

Cyders, M. A., Flory, K., Rainer, S., & Smith, G. T. (2009). The role of personality dispositions to risky behavior in predicting first-year college drinking. *Addiction, 104*(2), 193–202.

Darkes, J., & Goldman, M. S. (1993). Expectancy challenge and drinking reduction: Experimental evidence for a mediational process. *Journal of Consulting and Clinical Psychology, 61*(2), 344–353.

Darkes, J., & Goldman, M. S. (1998). Expectancy challenge and drinking reduction: Process and structure in the alcohol expectancy network. *Experimental and Clinical Psychopharmacology, 6*(1), 64–76.

Dennis, S., & Kintsch, W. (2007). Evaluating theories. In R. J. Sternberg, H. L. Roediger III, & D. F. Halpern (Eds.), *Critical thinking in psychology* (pp. 143–159). New York, NY: Cambridge University Press.

Doremus, T. L., Brunell, S. C., Rajendran, P., & Spear, L. P. (2005). Factors influencing elevated ethanol consumption in adolescent relative to adult rats. (Vol. 29, p. 1796). *Alcoholism-Clinical and Experimental Research, 29*(11), 2052–2052.

Durkin, K. F., Wolfe, T. W., & Clark, G. A. (2005). College students and binge drinking: An evaluation of social learning theory. *Sociological Spectrum, 25*(3), 255–272.

Elias, J. W., Bell, R. W., Eade, R., Underwood, T., Winsky, K., Shonrock, M. D., . . . Fiel, R. (1996). Alcohol myopia, expectations, social interests, and sorority pledge status. *Journal of Alcohol and Drug Education, 42*(1), 78–90.

Giancola, P. R., & Corman, M. D. (2007). Alcohol and aggression: A test of the attention-allocation model. *Psychological science, 18*(7), 649–655.

Giancola, P. R., Josephs, R. A., Parrott, D. J., & Duke, A. A. (2010). Alcohol myopia revisited: Clarifying aggression and other acts of disinhibition through a distorted lens. *Perspectives on Psychological Science, 5*(3), 265–278.

Goldman, M. S., Brown, S. A., & Christiansen, B. A. (1987). Expectancy theory: Thinking about drinking. In H. T. Blane & K. E. Leonard (Eds.), Psychological theories of drinking and alcoholism (pp. 181–226). New York: Guilford Press.

Gonzalez, G. M. (1988). Theory and applications of alcohol and drug education as a means of primary prevention on the college campus. *Journal of College Students Psychotherapy, 2*(3–4), 89–113.

Griffin, J. A., Umstattd, M. R., & Usdan, S. L. (2010). Alcohol use and high-risk sexual behavior among collegiate women: A review of research on alcohol myopia theory. *Journal of American College Health, 58*(6), 523–532.

Hittner, J. B., & Swickert, R. (2006). Sensation seeking and alcohol use: A meta-analytic review. *Addictive Behaviors, 31*(8), 1383–1401.

Hull, J. G., & Bond, C. F. (1986). Social and behavioral consequences of alcohol-consumption and expectancy—A metaanalysis. *Psychological Bulletin, 99*(3), 347–360.

Igra, A., & Moos, R. H. (1979). Alcohol-use among college-students—Some competing hypotheses. *Journal of Youth and Adolescence, 8*(4), 393–405.

Jessor, R. J., & Jessor, S. I. (1983). Adolescent development and the onset of drinking. *Digest of Alcoholism Theory & Application, 2*(2), 5–13.

Josephs, R. A., & Steele, C. M. (1990). The two faces of alcohol myopia: Attentional mediation of psychological stress. *Journal of Abnormal Psychology, 99*(2), 115–126.

Kantowitz, B. H., Roediger, H. L., & Elmes, D. G. (2005). *Experimental psychology: Understanding psychological research*. Belmont, CA: Wadsworth/Thomson.

Kleinot, M. C., & Rogers, R. W. (1982). Identifying effective components of alcohol misuse prevention programs. *Journal of Studies on Alcohol, 43*(7), 802–811.

Kraft, D. P. (1976). College students and alcohol: The 50 plus 12 project. *Alcohol Health and Research World, 1*, 10–14.

Kushner, M. G., Sher, K. J., Wood, M. D., & Wood, P. K. (1994). Anxiety and drinking behavior: Moderating effects of tension-reduction alcohol outcome expectancies. *Alcoholism, Clinical and Experimental Research, 18*(4), 852–860.

LaBrie, J. W., Huchting, K., Pedersen, E. R., Hummer, J. F., Shelesky, K., & Tawalbeh, S. (2007). Female college drinking and the social learning theory: An examination of the developmental transition period from high school to college. *Journal of College Student Development, 48*(3), 344–356.

Laflin, M. T., Moore-Hirschl, S., Weis, D. L., & Hayes, B. E. (1994). Use of the theory of reasoned action to predict drug and alcohol use. *International Journal of the Addictions, 29*(7), 927–940.

Larimer, M. E., & Cronce, J. M. (2007). Identification, prevention, and treatment revisited: Individual-focused college drinking prevention strategies 1999–2006. *Addictive Behaviors, 32*(11), 2439–2468.

Lau-Barraco, C., & Dunn, M. E. (2008). Evaluation of a single-session expectancy challenge intervention to reduce alcohol use among college students. *Psychology of Addictive Behaviors: Journal of the Society of Psychologists in Addictive Behaviors, 22*(2), 168–175.

Leigh, B. C. (1989). Confirmatory factor analysis of alcohol expectancy scales. *Journal of Studies on Alcohol, 50*(3), 268–277.

Lundin, R. W., & Sawyer, C. R. (1965). The relationship between test anxiety, drinking patterns and scholastic achievement in a group of undergraduate college men. *Journal of General Psychology, 73*, 143–146.

Lynham, S. A. (2002). Quantitative research and theory building: Dubin's method. *Advances in Developing Human Resources, 4*(3), 242–276.

MacDonald, T. K., Fong, G. T., Zanna, M. P., & Martineau, A. M. (2000). Alcohol myopia and condom use: Can alcohol intoxication be associated with more prudent behavior? *Journal of Personality and Social Psychology, 78*(4), 605–619.

MacDonald, T. K., MacDonald, G., Zanna, M. P., & Fong, G. T. (2000). Alcohol, sexual arousal, and intentions to use condoms in young men: Applying alcohol myopia theory to risky sexual behavior. *Health Psychology: Official Journal of the Division of Health Psychology, American Psychological Association, 19*(3), 290–298.

MacKillop, J., Miranda, R. Jr., Monti, P. M., Ray, L. A., Murphy, J. G., Rohsenow, D. J., . . . Gwaltney, C. J. (2010). Alcohol demand, delayed reward discounting, and craving in relation to drinking and alcohol use disorders. *Journal of Abnormal Psychology, 119*(1), 106–114.

Maisto, S. A., Connors, G. J., & Dearing, R. (2007). *Alcohol use disorders*. Gottigen, Germany: Hogrefe & Huber.

Martsh, C. T., & Miller, W. R. (1997). Extraversion predicts heavy drinking in college students. *Personality and Individual Differences, 23*(1), 153–155.

Masten, A. S., Faden, V. B., Zucker, R. A., & Spear, L. P. (2009). A developmental perspective on underage alcohol use. *Alcohol Research & Health, 32*(1), 3–15.

McAdams, K. K., & Donnellan, M. B. (2009). Facets of personality and drinking in first-year college students. *Personality and Individual Differences, 46*(2), 207–212.

Meehl, P. E. (1978). Theoretical risks and tabular asterisks—Karl, Ronald, and slow progress of soft psychology. *Journal of Consulting and Clinical Psychology, 46*(4), 806–834.

Mello, N. K., McNamee, H. B., & Mendelson, J. H. (1968). Drinking patterns of chronic alcoholics: gambling and motivation for alcohol. *Psychiatric research reports, 24*, 83–118.

Mezquita, L., Stewart, S. H., & Ruiperez, M. A. (2010). Big-five personality domains predict internal drinking motives in young adults. *Personality and Individual Differences, 49*(3), 240–245.

Montano, D. E., & Kasprzyk, D. (2008). The theory of reasoned action, the theory of planned behavior, and the integrated behavioral model. In K. Glanz, B. K. Rimer, & K. Viswanath (Eds.), *Health behavior and health education: Theory, research, and practice* (4th ed., pp. 67–96). San Francisco, CA: Jossey-Bass.

Murphy, J. G., Barnett, N. P., & Colby, S. M. (2006). Alcohol-related and alcohol-free activity participation and enjoyment among college students: A behavioral theories of choice. *Experimental and Clinical Psychopharmacology, 14*(3), 339–349.

Murphy, J. G., & MacKillop, J. (2006). Relative reinforcing efficacy of alcohol among college student drinkers. *Experimental and clinical psychopharmacology, 14*(2), 219–227.

Murphy, J. G., Correia, C. J., & Barnett, N. P. (2007). Behavioral economic approaches to reduce college student drinking. *Addictive Behaviors, 32*, 2573–2585.

Neal, D. J., & Carey, K. B. (2007). Association between alcohol intoxication and alcohol-related problems: An event-level analysis. *Psychology of Addictive Behaviors, 21*(2), 194–204.

Neifeld Wheeler, W. S. (2010). Readiness to act: Use of the health belief model in understanding parental communication about alcohol for incoming college students. *Dissertation Abstracts International Section A: Humanities and Social Sciences, 71*(4-A), 1199.

Nelson, T. F., Xuan, Z., Lee, H., Weitzman, E. R., & Wechsler, H. (2009). Persistence of heavy drinking and ensuing consequences at heavy drinking colleges. *Journal of Studies on Alcohol and Drugs, 70*(5), 726–734.

Noar, S. M., & Zimmerman, R. S. (2005). Health behavior theory and cumulative knowledge regarding health behaviors: Are we moving in the right direction? *Health Education Research, 20*(3), 275–290.

Ogden, J. (2003). Some problems with social cognition models: A pragmatic and conceptual analysis. *Health Psychology, 22*(4), 424–428.

O'Malley, P. M., & Johnston, L. D. (2002). Epidemiology of alcohol and other drug use among American college students. *Journal of Studies on Alcohol. Supplement*(14), 23–39.

Orford, J., Waller, S., & Peto, J. (1974). Drinking behavior and attitudes and their correlates among university-students in England .1. Principal components in drinking domain .2. Personality and social influence .3. Sex-differences. *Quarterly Journal of Studies on Alcohol-Part A, 35*(4), 1316–1374.

Painter, J. E., Borba, C. P. C., Hynes, M., Mays, D., & Glanz, K. (2008). The use of theory in health behavior research from 2000 to 2005: A systematic review. *Annals of Behavioral Medicine, 35*(3), 358–362.

Portnoy, B. (1980). Effects of a controlled-usage alcohol education-program based on the health belief model. *Journal of Drug Education, 10*(3), 181–195.

Prochaska, J. O., & Diclemente, C. C. (1982). Trans-theoretical therapy—Toward a more integrative model of change. *Psychotherapy-Theory Research and Practice, 19*(3), 276–288.

Prochaska, J. O., DiClemente, C. C., & Norcross, J. C. (1992). In search of how people change: Applications to addictive behaviors. *American Psychologist, 47*(9), 1102–1114.

Prochaska, J. O., Johnson, S., & Lee, P. (2009). The transtheoretical model of behavior change. In S. A. Shumaker, J. K. Ockene, & K. A. Riekert (Eds.), *The handbook of health behavior change* (3rd ed., pp. 59–84). New York, NY: Springer.

Prochaska, J. O., Redding, C. A., & Evers, K. E. (2008). The transtheoretical model and stages of change. In K. Glanz, B. K. Rimer, & K. Viswanath (Eds.), *Health Behavior and Health Education* (4th ed., pp 97–121). San Francisco, CA: Jossey-Bass.

Ratliff, K. G., & Burkhart, B. R. (1984). Sex-differences in motivations for and effects of drinking among college-students. *Journal of Studies on Alcohol, 45*(1), 26–32.

Read, J. P., Wood, M. D., & Capone, C. (2005). A prospective investigation of relations between social influences and alcohol involvement during the transition into college. *Journal of Studies on Alcohol, 66*, 23–34.

Real, K., & Rimal, R. N. (2007). Friends talk to friends about drinking: Exploring the role of peer communication in the theory of normative social behavior. *Health Communication, 22*(2), 169–180.

Regier, D. A., Farmer, M. E., Rae, D. S., Lock, B. Z., Keith, S. J., Judd, L. L., & Goodwin, F. K. (1990). Comorbidity of mental disorders with alcohol and other drug abuse: Results from the epidemiological catchment area (ECA) study. *Journal of the American Medical Association, 264*, 2511–2518.

Rimal, R. N., Lapinski, M. K., Cook, R. J., & Real, K. (2005). Moving toward a theory of normative influences: How perceived benefits and similarity moderate the impact of descriptive norms on behaviors. *Journal of Health Communication, 10*(5), 433–450.

Rimal, R. N., & Real, K. (2005). How behaviors are influenced by perceived norms: A test of the theory of normative social behavior. *Communication Research, 32*, 389–414.

Rousseau, G. S., Irons, J. G., & Correia, C. J. (2011). Reinforcing value of alcohol in a drinking to cope paradigm. *Drug and Alcohol Dependence, 118*, 1–4.

Rush, C. C., Becker, S. J., & Curry, J. F. (2009). Personality factors and styles among college students who binge eat and drink. *Psychology of Addictive Behaviors, 23*(1), 140–145.

Rutledge, P. C., & Sher, K. J. (2001). Heavy drinking from the freshman year into early young adulthood: The roles of stress, tension-reduction drinking motives, gender and personality. *Journal of Studies on Alcohol, 62*(4), 457–466.

Schubert, C. (2010). Biopsychosocial research revisited. *Journal of Psychosomatic Research, 68*(4), 389–390.

Schulenberg, J. E., & Maggs, J. L. (2002). A developmental perspective on alcohol use and heavy drinking during adolescence and the transition to young adulthood. *Journal of Studies on Alcohol, 54*–70.

Schwartz, G. E. (1982). Testing the biopsychosocial model—The ultimate challenge facing behavioral medicine. *Journal of Consulting and Clinical Psychology, 50*(6), 1040–1053.

Schwarz, R. M., Burkhart, B. R., & Green, S. B. (1978). Turning on or turning off: Sensation seeking or tension reduction as motivational determinants of alcohol use. *Journal of Consulting and Clinical Psychology, 46*(5), 1144–1145.

Scott-Sheldon, L. A. J., DeMartini, K. S., Carey, K. B., & Carey, M. P. (2009). Alcohol interventions for college students improves antecedents of behavioral change: Results from a meta-analysis of 34 randomized controlled trials. *Journal of Social and Clinical Psychology, 28*(7), 799–823.

Skidmore, J. R., & Murphy, J. G. (2011). The effect of drink price and next-day responsibilities on college student drinking: A behavioral economic analysis. *Psychology of Addictive Behaviors, 25*(1), 57–68.

Spear, L. P. (2000). The adolescent brain and age-related behavioral manifestations. *Neuroscience and Biobehavioral Reviews, 24*(4), 417–463.

Spear, L. P. (2002). The adolescent brain and the college drinker: Biological basis of propensity to use and misuse alcohol. *Journal of Studies on Alcohol, Suppl 14*, 71–81.

Spear, L. P., & Varlinskaya, E. I. (2005). Adolescence. Alcohol sensitivity, tolerance, and intake. *Recent Developments in Alcoholism, 17*, 143–159.

Spear, L. P., & Varlinskaya, E. I. (2010). Sensitivity to ethanol and other hedonic stimuli in an animal model of adolescence: Implications for prevention science? *Developmental Psychobiology, 52*(3), 236–243.

Steele, C. M., & Josephs, R. A. (1990). Alcohol myopia. Its prized and dangerous effects. *American Psychologist, 45*(8), 921–933.

Stewart, S. H., & Devine, H. (2000). Relations between personality and drinking motives in young adults. *Personality and Individual Differences, 29*(3), 495–511.

Straus, R. & Bacon, S. D. (1953). *Drinking in College.* New Haven, CT: Yale University Press.

Stretcher, V., & Rosenstock, I. M. (1997). The health belief model. In K. Glanz, F. M. Lewis, & B. K. Rimer (Eds.), *Health behavior and health education: Theory, research and practice* (2nd ed.). San Francisco, CA: Jossey-Bass.

Suls, J., & Rothman, A. (2004). Evolution of the biopsychosocial model: Prospects and challenges for health psychology. *Health Psychology, 23*(2), 119–125.

Sun, I. Y., & Longazel, J. G. (2008). College students' alcohol-related problems: A test of competing theories. *Journal of Criminal Justice, 36*(6), 554–562.

Torraco, R. J. (2002). Research methods for theory building in applied disciplines: A comparative analysis. *Advances in Developing Human Resources, 4*(3), 355–376.

Turrisi, R., Padilla, K. K., & Wiersma, K. A. (2000). College student drinking: an examination of theoretical models of drinking tendencies in freshmen and upperclassmen. *Journal of Studies on Alcohol, 61*(4), 598–602.

Vik, P. W., Culbertson, K. A., & Sellers, K. (2000). Readiness to change drinking among heavy-drinking college students. *Journal of Studies on Alcohol, 61*(5), 674–680.

Vuchinich, R. E., & Simpson, C. A. (1998). Hyperbolic temporal discounting in social drinkers and problem drinkers. *Experimental and Clinical Psychopharmacology, 6*(3), 292–305.

Vuchinich, R. E., & Tucker, J. A. (1983). Behavioral theories of choice as a framework for studying drinking behavior. *Journal of Abnormal Psychology, 92*(4), 408–416.

Wagner, C. C., & Ingersoll, K. S. (2009). Beyond behavior: Eliciting broader change with motivational interviewing. *Journal of Clinical Psychology, 65*(11), 1180–1194.

Ward, B. W., & Gryczynski, J. (2007). Alcohol use and participation in organized recreational sports among university undergraduates. *Journal of American College Health, 56*(3), 273–280.

Zuckerman, M. (2007). *Sensation seeking and risky behavior.* Washington, DC: American Psychological Association.

PART II
Assessment, Intervention and Prevention Strategies

5

Review of Clinical Assessment Tools

Matthew P. Martens, Brooke J. Arterberry, Jennifer M. Cadigan,
and Ashley E. Smith

It is crucial that researchers and clinicians working to reduce excessive alcohol use and related consequences among college students have confidence that their data collection tools are reliable and accurately reflect the construct that they are intending to measure. For example, a brief intervention efficacious at reducing alcohol-related problems among college students may appear ineffective if the research team used a measure that did not accurately assess such problems (see Cronbach & Meehl, 1955; Smith, 2005). Clinicians attempting to ascertain information about a student's alcohol use must also have confidence in the information they are collecting to make the best possible decisions regarding treatment planning, appropriateness for services, and the need for a higher level of care.

People who work in the area of college student alcohol use have a number of assessment tools at their disposal. The primary purpose of this chapter is to review several of these measures, focusing in particular on screening tools, measures of alcohol use, measures of alcohol-related problems, and formal diagnostic measures. We also address considerations for clinicians interested in conducting unstructured or semi-structured assessments of a college student's drinking habits. First, though, we turn our attention to two important conceptual issues in this area: reliability and validity of self-report measures of alcohol use and categorizing alcohol-related problems among college students.

RELIABILITY AND VALIDITY OF SELF-REPORT

The vast majority of alcohol-related assessments used with college students involve self-report, making the reliability and validity of this type of measure an important question. The issue of whether self-report measures of alcohol use are reliable and valid has been debated for quite some time (e.g., Babor, Steinberg, Anton, & Del Boca, 2000; Midanik, 1988; L. C. Sobell & Sobell, 1978; Stacy, Widaman, Hays, & DiMatteo, 1985; Watson, Tilleskjor, Hoodecheck-Schow, Pucel, & Jacobs, 1984). In general, researchers have concluded that self-report data provides reliable and valid results as long as the individual collecting the data reduces potential sources of bias in the respondent, such as lack of anonymity/confidentiality, confusion regarding assessment instructions, and perceived negative consequences associated with truthful responding (F. K. Del Boca & Darkes, 2003; F. Del Boca & Noll, 2000). Among college students, a recent meta-analysis supported the validity of self-report measures by showing no overall mean differences between self- and collateral-reports of alcohol use (Borsari & Muellerleile, 2009), whereas other research has demonstrated a strong relationship between estimated and actual drinking levels (e.g., estimated versus actual peak blood alcohol concentration; Carey & Hustad, 2002). There are aspects of the college drinking environment that may at times influence the precision of students' self-reports, such as engaging in activities like drinking games or "chugging" contests where calculating the number of standard drinks consumed becomes challenging. Nevertheless, research generally indicates that researchers and clinicians can feel reasonably confident about using self-report measures to assess college student alcohol use, provided they attempt to minimize sources of potential bias.

There are, however, two issues to which researchers and clinicians using self-report measures with college students should pay particular attention. First, college students who are completing self-report alcohol assessments in the context of a university-mandated intervention might underreport their alcohol consumption. One study among students mandated to receive a university intervention asked participants to estimate their alcohol use in the month preceding the infraction at two time-points: prior to the mandated intervention (time one) and one month later after receiving the intervention (time two). Results indicated students reported less drinking prior to the intervention at time one versus time two; it is unclear whether the passage of time or concerns about additional punishment for accurately disclosing alcohol use at time caused underreporting (Walker & Cosden, 2007). Considering that mandated students are an important and high-risk intervention population (Barnett & Read, 2005), researchers and clinicians should pay particular attention to reducing potential sources of bias when collecting self-report data among these students (e.g., repeatedly assuring students that their responses to the questionnaires will have no bearing on their sanction). This could be especially important when assessing individuals under the age of 21 who may be concerned about admitting to illegal behaviors. A second issue involves college students' ability to accurately assess how many standard drinks they have consumed on a particular night (i.e., a standard drink is 12 ounces of beer, 5 ounces of wine, 1.5 ounces of 80-proof liquor; National Institute on Alcohol Abuse and Alcoholism [NIAAA], 2008). Research indicates that college students often "overpour" different types of alcohol when asked to free-pour a standard drink amount (White, Kraus, McCracken, & Swartzwelder, 2003), and estimating the number of standard drinks consumed might be particularly challenging when students are drinking in a situation where a large quantity of a mixed drink has been pre mixed (Barnett, Wei, & Czachowski, 2009). Engaging in activities like drinking games or "chugging" contests can also influence the accuracy of self-reports, given the rapid speed at which drinks are consumed. These findings highlight the importance of educating college students about the definition of a standard drink when conducting assessments using this metric.

CONCEPTUALIZING ALCOHOL-RELATED PROBLEMS AMONG COLLEGE STUDENTS

The issue of whether psychological disorders should be classified as dimensional versus categorical continues to be an important topic of interest among psychologists in general (e.g., Brown & Barlow, 2009; Ruscio, Walters, Marcus, & Caczetow, 2010; Widiger, Livesley, & Clark, 2009). When considering alcohol-related problems, this involves whether such problems should be conceptualized along a single severity continuum or via distinct qualitative/taxonomic categories (i.e., alcohol abuse versus dependence). In general, item-response theory analyses indicate that alcohol-related symptoms exist on a single severity continuum and the categorical distinction between alcohol abuse and dependence, especially the notion that alcohol dependence symptoms are systematically more severe than alcohol abuse symptoms, is not supported (Krueger et al., 2004; Langenbucher et al., 2004; Saha, Chou, & Grant, 2006). These findings also extend to college student drinkers. One study among college students showed that *DSM-IV* abuse and dependence criteria were intermixed along a single severity continuum (Beseler, Taylor, & Leeman, 2010), while other studies of alcohol problems measures specific to adolescents or college students have also supported the existence of a single severity continuum (Kahler, Strong, & Read, 2005; Neal, Corbin, & Fromme, 2006). Thus, the evidence suggests that when conceptualizing alcohol misuse among college students, researchers and clinicians should utilize a dimensional rather than categorical/taxonomic framework (e.g., conceptualizing a student as "low," "medium," or "high" in terms of alcohol-related risks rather than attempting to determine if the student meets a specific diagnostic criteria). Nonetheless, later in this chapter assessment strategies for assigning an alcohol dependence or abuse diagnosis are reviewed due to the frequency with which the *DSM-IV* criteria are used in clinical settings.

SPECIFIC CLINICAL ASSESSMENTS

We now turn our attention to specific assessment domains, including screening measures, measures of alcohol consumption, measures of alcohol-related problems, diagnostic assessments, and measures of other alcohol-related constructs. We review some of the most commonly used measures in each category, focusing on reliability, validity, and clinical utility of the measure. Tables summarizing the measures discussed are also provided.

Screening Assessments

Researchers and clinicians working in the area of college student drinking often need to quickly determine whether a student is engaging in heavy or "at-risk" drinking, which could indicate the need for an intervention. Clinicians tend to use screening assessments to determine if an individual requires a more thorough assessment for alcohol-related problems, while researchers often use these types of assessments as an initial screen for study eligibility. Some of the measures described below may also be used as outcome measures of alcohol use/problems in research studies, but for the purposes of this chapter we are focusing on their use as screening tools (see Table 5.1).

The Alcohol Use Disorders Identification Test (AUDIT). The AUDIT (Saunders, Aasland, Babor, de la Fuente, & Grant, 1993) is one of the most frequently used measures to screen for problematic alcohol use. Originally developed from a

Table 5.1 Screening Assessments

Measure	Description	Scoring Procedures
Alcohol Use Disorders Identification Test (AUDIT)	10 items assessing alcohol use (first 3 items) and alcohol-related problems (remaining items)	Each item scored on 0–4 scale; total score = 0–40. Scores of 8+ are used as cutoff for hazardous drinking
5+/4+ "Binge" drinking criteria	Single-item assessing for binge drinking via number of drinks consumed in one sitting over a specific time frame (usually past two weeks)	5+ alcoholic drinks for males = binge drinking; 4+ alcoholic drinks for females = binge drinking. 3+ occasions in the preceding 2 weeks often considered "frequent" binge drinking
OQ45 Clinical Checklist	45 total items; 3 items assess substance abuse; 2 of which are considered critical items and signified by dotted circle around score	Any score larger than 0 flagged for follow-up by the clinician
CAGE	4 questions involving one's drinking: feeling a need to cut down drinking, being annoyed at others' criticism of one's drinking, feeling guilty about drinking, and needing an "eye-opening" drink in the mornings	Each item scored 0 (No) or 1 (Yes); total score = 0-4. Scores of 2+ used as cutoff for alcohol-related problems

Table 5.1 *(Continued)*

Measure	Description	Scoring Procedures
Michigan Alcoholism Screening Test (MAST)	24 questions assessing for an alcohol use diagnosis	Items are weighted and scored using yes/no format; total score = 0-53. Scores of 5–6 possible problem drinker, 7+ considered a marker for "alcoholic"
Short Michigan Alcoholism Screening Test (SMAST)	13 questions corresponding to alcohol-related problems	Items scored dichotomously, 0 (No) or 1 (Yes); total score = 0-13. Score of 3 indicates possible problem drinking, 4+ potential alcohol abuse

World Health Organization project involving multiple countries, the full AUDIT contains 10 items. The first three items query quantity/frequency of alcohol use and frequency of heavy drinking occasions (6 + drinks), and are sometimes used as their own screening instrument (i.e., the AUDIT-C: Bush, Kivlahan, McDonnell, Fihn, & Bradley, 1998). The remaining items assess other symptoms of problematic alcohol use (e.g., feeling guilty about one's drinking, injuring someone as a result of drinking, withdrawal and other symptoms of dependence). Items are scored such that each item has a minimum score of 0 and a maximum score of 4, with total scores of 8 or higher recommended as a marker of hazardous alcohol use (Babor, Higgins-Biddle, Saunders, & Monteiro, 2001; Saunders et al., 1993).

Several studies with college student samples showed that scores on the AUDIT were associated in the expected direction with theoretically relevant constructs, such as alcohol cravings (Connor, Feeney, Jack, Young, 2010), impulsivity-related traits (MacKillop, Mattson, Anderson MacKillop, Castelda, & Donovick, 2007), personal and social alcohol-related problems (O'Hare, 2005), and drinking game participation (Zamboanga et al., 2007). Other studies have assessed the degree to which the AUDIT accurately assessed high-risk drinking or the existence of alcohol-related disorders among college students in both the US and internationally (Aertgeerts et al., 2000; Fleming, Barry, & McDonald, 1991; Kokotailo et al., 2004). In the most recent of these studies among U.S. college students, Kokotailo and colleagues (2004) used Receiver Operating Characteristic (ROC) analyses and found that the AUDIT identified at-risk drinking (area under the curve = .87) better than either a lifetime (area under the curve = .78) or past-year (area under the curve = .79) alcohol use disorder. A cutoff score of 8+ yielded the highest combined sensitivity (.82) and specificity (.78) for identifying at-risk drinking. Changing the cutoff score by plus or minus two points increased sensitivity and specificity, respectively, to .91. Thus, findings from this study suggest that a cutoff score of 8+ on the full-scale AUDIT may be an accurate overall predictor of at-risk drinking among college students (see also Devos-Comby & Lange, 2008). It is important that these findings be replicated in other samples, though, and it would also be useful for researchers to examine the utility of the AUDIT-C as a screening tool specifically among college students.

5+/4+ drinks ("Binge Drinking"). Perhaps the most commonly used means of identifying college students engaging in risky drinking involves the definition of "heavy episodic" or "binge drinking" established by Wechsler and his colleagues (Wechsler, Davenport, Dowdall, Moeykens, & Castillo, 1994; Wechsler & Nelson, 2001): 5+ drinks for men or 4+ drinks for women in one sitting in the preceding 2 weeks. The 5+/4+ definition of binge drinking was not designed to be a clinical measure, but a simple means of assessing harmful drinking (Wechsler & Nelson, 2001). Substantial evidence suggests the definition meets this objective. Students classified as binge drinkers are considerably more likely than nonbinge drinkers to experience a host of alcohol-related problems, and frequent binge drinkers (3+ binge drinking episodes in the preceding 2 weeks) are more likely than infrequent binge drinkers (1 to 2 binge-drinking episodes in the preceding 2 weeks) to experience such problems (Wechsler et al., 1994; Wechsler & Isaac, 1992; Wechsler, Lee, Kuo, & Lee, 2000). For example, one national study found that frequent binge drinkers were more than 21 times more likely than nonbinge drinkers to report experiencing five or more distinct alcohol-related problems (e.g., doing something later regretted, engaging in unsafe sexual activity, getting injured), whereas infrequent binge drinkers were almost 5 times as likely as nonbinge drinkers to report five or more problems (Wechsler et al., 2000). Research has also shown that students classified as binge drinkers were more likely to experience other health and behavioral problems such as smoking cigarettes and using illicit drugs (Wechsler, Dowdall, Davenport, & Castillo, 1995), and were more likely to report blood alcohol concentration (BAC) levels above the .08 legal limit for intoxication (McMillen, Hillis, & Brown, 2009). Finally, clinical researchers often use the 5+/4+ definition as inclusion criteria in studies designed to assess the efficacy of novel interventions for at-risk college drinkers (e.g., Butler & Correia, 2009; Carey, Carey, Maisto, & Henson, 2006; Neighbors, Larimer, & Lewis, 2004; Schaus, Sole, McCoy, Mullett, & O'Brien, 2009; Walters, Vader, Harris, Field, & Jouriles, 2009).

There are, however, limitations to the 5+/4+ definition of binge drinking, including ambiguity regarding the definition of "one sitting," neglecting individual difference factors associated with alcohol absorption, and confusion regarding what constitutes a single drink. For example, the BAC of a 200-pound man who consumed 5 drinks over the course of 6 hours would be considerably less (approximately .02) than that of a 100-pound woman who consumed three drinks over the course of a single hour (approximately .13), but the former would meet the definition of binge drinking whereas the latter would not. Also, one study found that a higher threshold for binge drinking (e.g., 10+ drinks on an occasion) was a better predictor of subsequent negative alcohol-related outcomes than the 5+/4+ criteria (Jackson, 2008). In 2004 the National Institute on Alcohol Abuse and Alcoholism approved a definition of binge drinking that involved consuming alcohol in a manner that resulted in a

BAC level at or above the legal limit of .08, which typically involved 5+ drinks for men or 4+ drinks for women over approximately 2 hours (NIAAA, 2004). This standard for binge drinking does not seem to be used with much frequency in the literature, though. In sum, there are several ways to operationalize the concept of binge drinking (Courtney & Polich, 2009), and it is possible that the 5+/4+ definition may not be the optimal way to do so. But, the 5+/4+ measure does have value as a brief screen that can be used to identify students who are at risk for experiencing problems as a result of their alcohol use. Additionally, students categorized as frequent binge drinkers via this definition will likely warrant further clinical attention.

Clinical checklists. A type of measure often used in clinical settings to screen for excessive alcohol use is a checklist that assesses an array of mental health–related problems. For example, one of the most commonly used measures in college counseling centers is the Outcome Questionnaire 45 (OQ-45: Lambert et al., 1996). The OQ-45 is a 45-item measure scored on a 5-point scale where individuals indicate the degree to which they have experienced specific mental health-related symptoms. Students presenting for services often complete this measure prior to the initiating treatment, which provides clinicians with information regarding presenting problems. The OQ-45 can then assess changes in presenting symptoms prior to subsequent appointments. Three of the items assess potentially problematic alcohol use (needing a drink to get going in the morning, trouble in school or work due to drinking, being annoyed at others from criticizing one's drinking), so clinicians using the measure at the beginning of treatment with an individual client could determine if he or she initially endorsed problems in that area and evaluate if changes occurred over time. There is substantial evidence that, overall, the OQ-45 is a reliable and valid measure of general symptom presentation among college students and accurately assesses clinical change over time (e.g., Jenks Kettmann et al., 2007; Lambert et al., 1996; Vermeersch et al., 2004). However, little is known about the reliability and validity of the specific alcohol use items on the measure (or such items on other, less standardized clinical checklists). Measures like the OQ-45 can certainly alert clinicians to a student's endorsement of alcohol-related problems and therefore the need for appropriate services, but it is likely such measures also will miss many who are engaging in at-risk drinking practices.

Other screening measures. Other commonly used screening measures in the general adult population that have been used to assess for problematic alcohol use among college students include the CAGE (Ewing, 1984) and the Michigan Alcoholism Screening Test (MAST: Selzer, 1971, or its short version, the SMAST: Selzer, Vinokur, & van Rooijen, 1975). The CAGE contains four questions corresponding to cutting down on drinking (C), feeling annoyed about others asking about their drinking (A), feeling guilty about one's drinking (G), and needing a drink as an "eye opener" in the morning (E). The MAST and SMAST contain questions designed to assess for an alcohol use diagnosis, such as concerns from others about one's drinking, neglecting obligations because of drinking, and getting arrested as a result of drinking. Research on the CAGE among college students suggest the measure is not sensitive in terms of identifying students with alcohol-related problems (Aertgeerts et al., 2000; Clements, 1998; Devos-Comby & Lange, 2008; Heck & Williams, 1995). Similar concerns exist regarding the MAST (Clements, 1998; Devos-Comby & Lange, 2008), and given its focus on symptoms associated with a formal alcohol-related diagnosis it may be limited in identifying college drinkers who are experiencing problems related to their alcohol use, but who fall below a diagnostic threshold.

Summary of screening measures. Researchers and clinicians can choose from several measures designed to assess for hazardous drinking among college students, and should consider their particular needs and possible logistical limitations when selecting a measure to utilize. One-item measures such as the 5+/4+ measure of binge drinking are likely sufficient in some circumstances (e.g., identifying students who are appropriate for a brief preventative intervention), particularly when identifying a possible alcohol use disorder is not a priority. In other situations, a more comprehensive screening tool like the AUDIT may provide more appropriate information (e.g., identifying college students who should be screened for more intensive services). An area warranting further attention from clinical researchers involves reliability and validity analyses on measures that have not yet been extensively examined among college students (e.g., the AUDIT-C, clinical checklists like the OQ-45 items).

Measures of Alcohol Use

There are multiple ways in which clinicians and researchers can ascertain alcohol consumption, ranging from simple single-item measures (e.g., the 5+/4+ measure of binge drinking) to comprehensive in-person interviews. In addition, many different types or patterns of alcohol consumption may be of interest depending on the clinical or research issue at hand, such as frequency of alcohol use, overall quantity of use, or quantity on one's peak drinking occasion. In the college student population, alcohol-related risk often involves heavy drinking that occurs relatively infrequently (e.g., binge drinking once or twice a week), so obtaining information on daily or weekly drinking patterns is often more relevant than simply obtaining information on "typical" drinking or overall summary measures (e.g., number of drinking days per month). Further, regardless of the type of measure used, it is crucial first to educate students on what constitutes a standard "drink" (see NIAAA, 2008). Such education is necessary because students are often unaware of the specifics of this definition, and may thus consider a drink containing multiple shots of alcohol (e.g., a Long Island iced tea, a bowl of "party punch" served at a campus party) as a single drink. In situations where there are popular local drinks that contain more than one standard drink (e.g., a popular bar's specialty cocktail that contains three standard drinks), such information could also be included in a standard drink definition for one's measure.

It is beyond the scope of this chapter to review every possible way in which clinicians and researchers assess for alcohol use, therefore, we will limit our presentation to those measures most commonly used in the college student population (see Table 5.2). It is also important to note that some of the measures we discussed as screening tools (e.g., the AUDIT, 5+/4+ criteria for binge drinking) can also be used to assess for alcohol use. The measures we discuss below, though, are typically not used as screening tools or for categorizing drinking status (e.g., establishing one as a "binge" drinker).

Timeline Followback (TLFB). The TLFB (Sobell, Maisto, Sobell, & Cooper, 1979; L. C. Sobell & Sobell, 1995) is perhaps the most comprehensive self-report tool for assessing an individual's alcohol use. Usually completed in a one-on-one interview

Table 5.2 Alcohol Use Measures

Measure	Description	Scoring Procedures
Timeline Followback (TLFB)	Assesses alcohol intake history over a specific timeframe (e.g., past 60 days) using a customizable calendar	Can be used to calculate multiple alcohol use measures, such as percent drinking days, average number of drinks per week, peak number of drinks on a single occasion, and typical number of drinks on drinking days
Daily Drinking Questionnaire (DDQ)	Calendar-based assessment of alcohol consumption over the course of a week, where individuals are asked to indicate their "typical" drinking over a specified timeframe (e.g., past month)	Can be used to calculate multiple alcohol use measures, including drinking days per week, total drinks per week, typical weekend drinking, and typical drinks per drinking day
Single-item measures	Single-item measures are used to assess for numerous alcohol consumption variables, such as peak number of drinks on a single occasion, number of hours consuming alcohol on a specific occasion (which can be used to estimate BAC), number of drinks consumed the last time one socialized, and overall quantity/ frequency of alcohol use	Scoring procedures generally involve simply recording the response given (e.g., the individual indicates 12 drinks on his or her heaviest drinking occasion in the past 30 days). Standard formulas are used to calculate BAC from estimates of number of drinks consumed over a specific timeframe.
Drinking Styles Questionnaire (DSQ)	Includes items that assess both alcohol consumption and negative alcohol-related consequences	Scores are calculated for a drinking/ drunkenness subscale and alcohol-related problems subscale. Items on the drinking subscale include alcohol quantity, alcohol use frequency, and frequency of drunkenness. Individual items are scored on a Likert scale.

format, the interviewer and respondent utilize a calendar to assess drinking quantity and/or other related variables (e.g., hours spent drinking [used to calculate estimated BAC], perceived intoxication level, drug use) on each day over a specific timeframe (e.g., past 30 days). From these data a host of quantity/frequency measures of alcohol consumption can be calculated, such as drinking days per week, total drinks per week, weekday/weekend drinks per week, highest number of drinks consumed in a day, and days per week exceeding some alcohol use threshold. The calendar can be customized to facilitate recall by highlighting noteworthy dates over the period of assessment. For example, in studies with college students the calendar could highlight events such as local and national holidays, important university events, major sporting events relevant to the university, and other specific dates that would help facilitate recall of drinking behavior (e.g., F. K. Del Boca, Darkes, Greenbaum, & Goldman, 2004; Goldman, Greenbaum, Darkes, Brandon, & Del Boca, 2011; Greenbaum, Del Boca, Darkes, Wang, & Goldman, 2005). The TLFB has been adapted for use among college students in formats outside of the one-on-one interview, including via the web (Lee, Lewis, & Neighbors, 2009; McMillen et al., 2009) and in group settings (J. LaBrie, Pedersen, & Earleywine, 2005; Pedersen & LaBrie, 2006). Studies have supported the reliability and validity of the measure with college students (e.g., Cohen & Vinson, 1995; Pedersen & LaBrie, 2006; Sobell, Sobell, Klajner, Pavin, & Basian, 1986), with recent evidence suggesting that reliability increases with shorter assessment windows (e.g., repeated 7-day assessments versus 30-day assessments: Hoeppner, Stout, Jackson, & Barnett, 2010). The TLFB is often used in clinical trials with college students or as a criterion measure when evaluating the validity of other types of assessments (e.g., Barnett, Murphy, Colby, & Monti, 2007; Bernhardt et al., 2009; Darkes & Goldman, 1993; J. W. LaBrie, Pedersen, & Tawalbeh, 2007; Wood, Capone, LaForge, Erickson, & Brand, 2007).

Although used extensively as a research measure, little is known regarding the degree to which the TLFB is used in clinical settings with college students. We suspect it is used relatively infrequently, due in part to time considerations associated with completing the interview. Yet, clinicians working with college students experiencing problems associated with excessive alcohol use may obtain considerable benefit from using this measure. Besides obtaining an accurate estimate of the student's overall drinking habits, the TLFB provides the clinician with specific information about days, time of year, and specific events that are particular risk factors for the student. For example, in the course of the TLFB the client and clinician might realize that his or her excessive drinking seems to be centered primarily on university sporting events and holidays. Thus, treatment could focus on reducing alcohol use based on the client's idiographic risk profile. Such individualized data are generally not available from less extensive measures of alcohol use. Some evidence exists indicating that the process of completing the TFLB itself might cause college students to reduce their drinking, presumably in response to such a detailed assessment of their drinking habits (Carey et al., 2006).

Therefore, clinicians who utilize a TLFB may be providing an additional intervention to their clients engaging in at-risk drinking behaviors.

Daily Drinking Questionnaire (DDQ). The DDQ (R. L. Collins, Parks, & Marlatt, 1985) is another calendar-based measure of alcohol use. When completing the DDQ individuals are asked to indicate how much they typically drink on each day of the week over a specified timeframe (e.g., past 30 days). Similar to the TLFB, multiple calculations can be made from these data (e.g., drinks per week, drinks per drinking day). The DDQ is often modified to include information on typical hours spent drinking on each day of the week, which allows one to calculate estimated BAC level (e.g., Dimeff, Baer, Kivlahan, & Marlatt, 1999). It can also be modified to assess other information of interest to the researcher or clinician, such as alcohol consumption over one's heaviest drinking week in a specified timeframe. Thus, the DDQ provides a greater degree of precision than a single-item measure assessing quantity or frequency of alcohol use, but not as much precision as a measure like the TLFB.

Perhaps the best evidence for the validity of the DDQ among college students comes from the brief intervention literature, where a host of studies have shown that alcohol use rates based on the measure changed in the hypothesized direction as a result of the treatment (e.g., Butler & Correia, 2009; Larimer et al., 2001, 2007; Lewis & Neighbors, 2007; Marlatt et al., 1998; Murphy et al., 2004; Neighbors et al., 2004). Other studies among college students have shown values from the DDQ were correlated in the expected direction with constructs such as mindfulness (Fernandez, Wood, Stein, & Rossi, 2010), positive beliefs about the role of alcohol in college life (Osberg et al., 2010), use of alcohol-related protective behavioral strategies (Martens, Pedersen, LaBrie, Ferrier, & Cimini, 2007), and drinking motives (Martens, Rocha, Martin, & Serrao, 2008). Finally, research has shown good convergent validity between the DDQ and TLFB, although college students may overreport alcohol consumption on the DDQ relative to the TLFB (R. L. Collins, Kashdan, Koutsky, Morsheimer, & Vetter, 2008; Lozano & Stephens, 2010).

The DDQ presents an attractive alternative to clinicians and researchers who do not have the time to administer a more in-depth measure like the TLFB, but still wish to obtain some degree of detailed alcohol use information. Most college students should be able to complete the measure in less than a minute, and the DDQ will give the clinician or researcher a relatively nuanced picture of the individual's drinking practices. For example, consider one student who typically consumes two drinks per night each day of the week, and another who drinks only on Friday and Saturday night but consumes seven drinks each night. Both students would respond in an identical manner if simply asked "how many drinks do you typically have each week," but have considerably different risk profiles for harmful alcohol-related consequences (the second student would likely be at greater risk). In this scenario the DDQ would provide the clinician or researcher with a clearer understanding of the student's drinking practices and areas in need of intervention.

The DDQ does have limitations in comparison to a measure like the TLFB that captures actual drinking over a specified time period. One limitation is that the DDQ does not account for drinking rates in response to external events that may be somewhat atypical for the individual and therefore provides misleading information to the researcher or clinician. For example, a student who completed the DDQ the week after going on spring break might overreport typical drinking in response to the recent experience, or a student completing the DDQ during finals might underreport typical drinking because he or she has curbed alcohol use for that particular week. A related limitation of the DDQ is that it does not capture irregular occurrences of high-volume drinking occasions that warrant clinical attention. For example, consider a student who only drinks once or twice a month but consumes 10+ drinks on each occasion and experiences negative consequences as a result of these experiences. This student may indicate that he or she "typically" consumes zero drinks each day of the week, thus, his or her at-risk drinking behaviors would not be captured by the DDQ. These limitations notwithstanding, the DDQ can provide clinicians and researchers with a reasonably clear picture of most college students' drinking habits in a short amount of time.

Single-item alcohol use measures. Clinicians and researchers can assess a wide array of drinking-related variables via single-item measures. For example, instead of administering a DDQ or TLFB, one could ask a student to estimate how many times or how much he or she drinks in a typical week, month, or year. Presumably, such a measure would not be as accurate as estimates using more thorough assessment procedures. There are, though, single-item measures of alcohol quantity and/or frequency that clinicians and researchers may wish to use in instances when more detailed assessments are not possible, or to complement measures such as the DDQ. One commonly used measure that may have particular value is peak alcohol consumption over a specified timeframe (such as past 30 days), which can be used by the clinician or researchers to estimate peak BAC. Estimated BAC can be calculated from a straightforward formula[1] that accounts for gender, body weight, drinks consumed, and number of hours spent drinking (Matthews & Miller, 1979). Peak BAC may be a particularly useful measure for clinicians for at least two reasons. First, it may help identify students whose drinking is putting them at imminent risk for very serious consequences like significant injury or death (e.g., BAC $\geq$ .25). Such students could be referred by the clinician for appropriate clinical services. Second, it is fairly straightforward to link different BAC levels to specific alcohol-related risks, such as driving while intoxicated (BAC $\geq$ .08) and impaired coordination/ risk of blackouts (BAC $\geq$ .15) (for examples of BAC-specific feedback, see Dimeff et al., 1999; "How much is too much," 2009). Such BAC-specific risks are commonly

---

[1] The formula is [(number of standard drinks/2) * (Gender Constant * Body Weight in lbs)]-(.016 * hours spent drinking). The gender constant is 9.0 for women and 7.5 for men.

included in college student alcohol intervention studies (e.g., Butler & Correia, 2009; Larimer et al., 2007; Marlatt et al., 1998; Murphy, Denhardt, Skidmore, Martens, & McDevit-Murphy, 2010). If a measure of peak BAC were combined with something like the DDQ, the clinician could obtain information from the student about his or her typical alcohol consumption and riskiest drinking occasion over a specified timeframe, the combination of which might better facilitate an appropriate intervention. Similarly, the combination would allow the clinical researcher to assess intervention effects on both drinking quantity in general (e.g., average drinks per week derived from the DDQ) and high-risk drinking (e.g., peak BAC). It should be remembered, however, that estimating BAC has limitations, primarily due to the assumptions included in the calculations (e.g., that alcohol was consumed at a consistent pace), and possible errors in measurement or in self report (e.g., body weight, drink measurement).

Other examples of single-item measures that may be clinically useful include number of drinks the last time one socialized or "partied" (American College Health Association, 2009) and binge- or heavy-drinking episodes in the preceding month or 2 weeks (described earlier in the chapter). In addition, other measures existing in the literature include multiple single-item measures of alcohol consumption. For example, the Drinking Styles Questionnaire (Smith, McCarthy, & Goldman, 1995) uses graded responses to assess typical drinking quantity, typical frequency, typical frequency of drunkenness, proportion of times drinking leads to drunkenness, and peak drinks on one occasion.

Probably the most important concern with using single-item measures involves their reliability and validity in comparison to more extensive assessments like the TLFB. However, several studies have suggested single-item measures are reasonably reliable and valid at assessing alcohol-related behaviors. For example, in a large epidemiological study of the general U.S. adult population, cutoff scores from single-item measures of peak number of drinks on one day and frequency of 5+/4+ drinking days had high sensitivity and specificity in identifying alcohol use disorders (Dawson, Pulay, & Grant, 2010). Research specific to college students has also supported the use of single-item measures. One recent study examined the reliability and validity of two single-item measures assessing days per week using alcohol and typical number of drinks per drinking occasion (Dollinger & Malmquist, 2009). Test-retest reliability of the two measures across 11 weeks was excellent ($r = .84–.85$), and the single-item measures were correlated with 14-day daily log measures of alcohol consumption ($r = .46–.72$). Other studies have shown that retrospective self-report BAC was strongly correlated with BAC derived from an in vivo breath test (Carey & Hustad, 2002) and single-item measures of alcohol use have been shown to be correlated in the expected direction with alcohol-related risks (e.g., Neal & Carey, 2007; Neal & Fromme, 2007; Turner, Bauerle, & Shu, 2004). Taken together, these findings support the validity of single-item measures of alcohol consumption among college students, though their clinical utility is likely lower than the TLFB or DDQ.

Summary of alcohol use measures. Clinicians and researchers have many options when assessing alcohol consumption among their clients or research participants, ranging from simple single-item measures to comprehensive interviews assessing daily alcohol consumption. Each type of measure has logistical and/or psychometric limitations that need to be considered when deciding which type of assessment would best suit one's purpose. At a minimum, we recommend clinicians and researchers obtain basic information on typical weekly/monthly patterns (e.g., administer the DDQ) and high-quantity drinking (e.g., peak alcohol consumption over the past 30 days). A more detailed assessment of a student's alcohol use is best obtained through a measure like the TLFB, ideally delivered in an interview-based format.

Measures of Alcohol-Related Problems

The next portion of the chapter describes five commonly used measures of alcohol-related problems associated with excessive and/or frequent alcohol consumption among college students (see Table 5.3). This section does not address measures that include alcohol-related problems but are often used for screening purposes (e.g., the AUDIT, CAGE, or MAST), nor does it address measures explicitly designed to assign an alcohol diagnosis.

The Rutgers Alcohol Problem Index (RAPI). Originally designed to assess alcohol-related problems among younger adolescents, the RAPI (White & Labouvie, 1989) is nonetheless an extensively used measure of alcohol-related problems in the college student population (Devos-Comby & Lange, 2008). The RAPI consists of 23 items typically scored on a 5-point scale where the respondent indicates the number of times he or she has experienced the problem (*never* to *more than 10 times*) in a particular timeframe (e.g., past month, past year). The RAPI has been frequently used as an outcomes measure in clinical trials among college students (e.g., Borsari & Carey, 2000; Carey et al., 2006; Carey, Henson, Carey, & Maisto, 2009; Larimer et al., 2001, 2007; Marlatt et al., 1998; Neighbors et al., 2004) and as a criterion variable in scale validation projects (e.g., Bonar et al., 2011; S. E. Collins, Logan, & Neighbors, 2010; Martens et al., 2007; Osberg et al., 2010). In general, results have shown alcohol problems scores derived from the measure are internally consistent and correlated in the expected direction with theoretically relevant constructs like alcohol consumption (see Devos-Comby & Lange, 2008).

The extensive use of the RAPI among college students has been criticized because the measure was not explicitly designed to be used with that population and therefore does not contain some specific problems salient among college students (e.g., regretted sexual behavior and driving while intoxicated: Devos-Comby & Lange, 2008). Further, the validity of the measure among college students has only

Table 5.3   Alcohol Problems Measures

Measure	Description	Scoring Procedures
Rutgers Alcohol Problems Index (RAPI)	23 items; respondent indicates the number of times he or she has experienced the problem in a particular timeframe (e.g., past month, past year)	Each item scored on 5-point scale (0 = *never*; 4 = *10 or more times*)
Young Adult Alcohol Problems Screening Test (YAAPST)	36 items assessing lifetime problems, number of problems over a certain time frame, and severity of past-year problems	On more frequently endorsed items (e.g., having a headache after drinking) response options range from *never* to *40 or more times*, less frequently endorsed items scored in yes/no format
Young Adult Alcohol Consequences Questionnaire (YAACQ)	48 items assessing problems across eight different subdomains (Social/Interpersonal Consequences, Impaired Control, Self-Perception, Self-Care, Risk Behaviors, Academic/Occupational concerns, Physical Dependence, Blackout Drinking)	Each item scored in a yes/no format
Brief Young Adult Alcohol Consequences Questionnaire (BYAACQ)	24 items from the original YAACQ	Each item scored in a yes/no format
College Alcohol Problems Scale (CAPS)	8 items organized onto two subscales: Personal Problems and Social Problems	Each item scored on a 6-point scale: (1 = *never*; 6 = *10 or more times*)

been explicitly examined in a handful of studies. In applying item response theory (IRT)-based models to a dichotomously scored RAPI (i.e., indicating if the problem has been experienced via a simple yes/no format), one study found that a reduced 18-item measure was invariant between men and women and between respondents' senior year in high school and first year in college (Neal et al., 2006). This study also found the items were skewed toward the more severe end of an alcohol problem continuum, suggesting that the measure may be best used among a more severe drinking population. A second IRT study among college students, this time using the traditional continuously scored version of the measure, found removing 7 of the 23 items reduced gender bias on the measure while yielding almost identical correlations as the full measure with alcohol consumption and a different measure of alcohol-related problems (Earleywine, LaBrie, & Pedersen, 2008). A third study among college students used both exploratory and confirmatory factor analysis on a dichotomously scored version of the RAPI to determine if the items could be organized into meaningful subfactors (Martens, Neighbors, Dams-O'Connor, Lee, & Larimer, 2007). Results from this study supported the existence of 3 factors: abuse/dependence symptoms (e.g., withdrawal), personal consequences (e.g., neglecting responsibilities), and social consequences (e.g., fighting with a friend). However, few subsequent studies among college students have utilized these subscales, so additional psychometric data is lacking (for an exception, see Groeschel, Wester, & Sedivy, 2010). Together these findings suggest that researchers need to continue to explore the reliability and validity of the RAPI as a means of accurately assessing alcohol-related problems among college students, as there is inconsistent evidence regarding the ideal scoring procedures and item inclusion/organization.

The Young Adult Alcohol Problems Screening Test (YAAPST). The YAAPST was designed explicitly for the college student population (Hurlbut & Sher, 1992). The original measure contains 27 items assessed as a unidimensional measure of alcohol-related problems, with response options varying across items depending upon its specific content. A 36-item version of the measure also exists that has been used in studies with college students (e.g., Palfai & Wood, 2001; Wood, Read, Palfai, & Stevenson, 2001). Research has generally supported the reliability and validity of the YAAPST, in the form of satisfactory internal consistence, test-retest reliability, and correlations with relevant constructs like alcohol use, alcohol cravings, and alcohol-related expectancies (Hurlbut & Sher, 1992; Kahler, Strong, Read, Palfai, & Wood, 2004; McEvoy, Stritzke, French, Lang, & Ketterman, 2004; Palfai & Wood, 2001; Shields et al., 2008; Wood et al., 2001).

Three aspects of the YAAPST may make it a particularly useful measure in a clinical context. First, unlike other measures providing only a single index for each problem (e.g., number of times experienced in the past year), for each item on the YAAPST respondents indicate whether they ever experienced the problem and if they experienced the problem in the past year (which could be easily modified to any timeframe). Respondents also indicate the severity of the past-year problem in terms of the number of times it occurred. Thus, one can obtain scores on the YAAPST that reflect number of lifetime problems, number of problems over a certain timeframe, and severity of past-year problems, giving the clinician a wide array of data to use in an intervention setting. Second, the developers of the YAAPST recognized that some alcohol-related problems occur more frequently than others and created response options accordingly. On more frequently endorsed items (e.g., having a headache after drinking), the response options range from *never* to *40 or more times*, whereas less frequently endorsed items (e.g., feeling dependent on alcohol) are endorsed in a yes/no format. These variable response options provide more precision to clinicians who are interested in gauging the frequency of relatively common problems, while maintaining a simpler response format for infrequently endorsed items. Finally, one study utilizing IRT analyses confirmed the YAAPST assessed a wide range of alcohol problem severity (Kahler et al., 2004). Items range from problems experienced by the majority of students who reported drinking in the past year (e.g., memory loss, sick or vomiting after drinking) to items endorsed by less than 1% of the sample (e.g., suspended from school, seeking professional help). The YAAPST is not used as frequently in the college drinking literature as other alcohol problems assessments (Devos-Comby & Lange, 2008), but is an attractive option for clinicians and researchers interested in obtaining a relatively detailed assessment of a college student's alcohol-related problems.

The Young Adult Alcohol Consequences Questionnaire/Brief Young Adult Alcohol Consequences Questionnaire (YAACQ/B-YAACQ). Two relatively new instruments also designed specifically for college students are the YAACQ (Read, Kahler, Strong, & Colder, 2006) and the B-YAACQ (Kahler et al., 2005). The 48-item YAACQ was developed by including items from two existing questionnaires—the YAAPST and the Drinkers Inventory of Consequences (Miller, Tonigan, & Longabaugh, 1995)—as well as items developed by the scale authors. Responses on the measure are scored in a yes/no format in terms of whether or not the problem has been experienced over a specified timeframe. The B-YAACQ utilizes the same yes/no format, but includes only 24 of the original items. The YAACQ is perhaps the most comprehensive measure of alcohol-related problems among college students (Devos-Comby & Lange, 2008) encompassing problems across eight different subdomains (Social/Interpersonal Consequences, Impaired Control, Self-Perception, Self-Care, Risk Behaviors, Academic/Occupational concerns, Physical Dependence, Blackout Drinking: Read et al., 2006). In contrast, the B-YAACQ was developed utilizing IRT analyses designed to assess alcohol problems on a unidimensional problem severity continuum (Kahler et al., 2005). Research has supported the factor structure of the YAACQ and the unidimensionality of the B-YAACQ, and shown that scores on the measures are internally consistent, have satisfactory test-retest reliability, and correlate in the expected direction with relevant constructs (Kahler et al., 2005; Kahler, Hustad, Barnett, Strong, & Borsari, 2008; Read et al., 2006; Read, Merrill, Kahler, & Strong, 2007).

For clinicians and researchers interested in obtaining information about problems across different behavioral domains and who are willing to use a longer measure, the YAACQ would be a preferable option. For those interested in obtaining a single summary of the number of different types of problems the individual has experienced, the B-YAACQ would be an appropriate choice. These measures have an advantage over the RAPI due to their development specifically for the college student population, but have been utilized in far fewer studies than the RAPI. Further, the yes/no response format of the measure does not provide as much clinical information as that provided by the YAAPST, but the measure is simpler and more efficient to score (especially the B-YAACQ).

The College Alcohol Problems Scale (CAPS). A final measure designed to specifically assess for alcohol-related problems among college students is the CAPS (Maddock, LaForge, Rossi, & O'Hare, 2001; O'Hare, 1997). Although there are slightly different versions of the measure, the strongest validity data exists for an 8-item version (e.g., Maddock et al., 2001; Talbott, Umstattd, Usdan, Martin, & Geiger, 2009). Scores on the CAPS are organized onto two subscales: Personal Problems and Social Problems. Factor analytic studies have supported the distinctiveness of the two subscales, and scores on the measure have been shown to be correlated in the expected direction with alcohol use and other relevant constructs (Earleywine et al., 2008; Maddock et al., 2001; Martens, LaBrie, Hummer, & Pedersen, 2008; McGee, Williams, & Kypri, 2010; Skeel, Pilarski, Pytlak, & Neudecker, 2008; Talbott et al., 2009). The CAPS is an attractive measure for researchers who wish to use a brief measure of alcohol-related problems designed specifically for college students, but the measure's value as a clinical tool may be limited. The small number of items limits the scope of information available to clinicians regarding a student's alcohol-related problems, and the degree to which the measure assesses a wide range of problems on a severity continuum is unknown. It is possible the measure could have value as a brief screening tool, but we are unaware of any studies that have investigated whether or not the measure can be used to accurately identify "at-risk" college student drinkers. Therefore, while the measure has value as a brief research measure, its clinical utility is somewhat limited.

Summary of alcohol-related problems measures. Similar to assessing alcohol use, clinicians and researchers have several options when deciding how to assess alcohol-related problems among their clients or research participants. We believe that each of the measures reviewed in this section can be appropriately used to assess alcohol-related problems among college students; clinicians and researchers need to use their best judgment in light of the research evidence on each measure in selecting which scale(s) best meets their specific needs.

Diagnosing Alcohol Use Disorders (AUD) Among College Students

This section of the chapter focuses on assessment strategies used to assign a diagnosis of a *DSM-IV* AUD (alcohol dependence or abuse) among college students (see Table 5.4). It is important to note that these measures differ from measures discussed earlier in the chapter (e.g., the AUDIT, CAGE, MAST), which are used to screen for the likelihood of a diagnosis but do not comprehensively address AUD symptom criteria. The format of this section will differ slightly from previous sections in that the emphasis will not be on different types of specific diagnostic measures. The reason for this is because assigning a *DSM-IV* AUD diagnosis requires one to examine a uniform set of criteria, so different measures purporting to assess for the existence of a disorder will nonetheless be assessing the same criteria. Diagnostic criteria

Table 5.4 Diagnostic Assessments

Measure	Description	Scoring Procedures
Alcohol Use Disorder and Associated Disabilities Interview Schedule—*Diagnostic and Statistical Manual of Mental Disorders—*Fourth Edition (AUDADIS-IV)	Diagnostic interview for alcohol and drug use disorders, as well as mood, anxiety, and personality disorders. Also assesses alcohol consumption, drug use, tobacco use, and family history of substance use, depression, and antisocial personality disorder	Diagnoses are assigned based on *DSM-IV* criteria; measures of consumption/drug use are based on interview responses. No skip-outs on the measure allows for determining "subclinical" problems (e.g., experiencing one or two alcohol dependence symptoms). Yields both past-year and lifetime diagnoses
Semi-Structure Assessment for the Genetics of Alcoholism (SSAGA)	Diagnostic interview for alcohol abuse/dependence and related psychiatric disorders (e.g., major depression, panic disorder, bulimia). Also assesses tobacco use, psychosis, and suicidal behavior	Diagnoses are based on *DSM*-IIIR criteria and other classification systems (e.g., ICD-10). Uses skip-out questions for each diagnostic category
Self-report checklists	Self-report statements that correspond to diagnostic criteria (e.g., "I have experienced legal problems as a result of my alcohol use; I often drink alcohol in larger amounts or over a longer period than I intended")	Items are generally scored via yes/no format; yes responses are used to identify a diagnosis

for alcohol dependence includes experiencing at least three of the following seven symptoms over a 12-month period: (1) tolerance, (2) withdrawal, (3) drinking more or drinking longer than intended, (4) unsuccessful efforts at or a persistent desire to reduce drinking, (5) spending a great deal of time using alcohol, trying to obtain alcohol, or recovering from alcohol's effects, (6) giving up or reducing important social, recreational, or occupation activities because of alcohol, and (7) using alcohol despite physical or psychological problems associated with its use (American Psychiatric Association, 2000). Diagnostic criteria for alcohol abuse includes experiencing at least one of the following over a 12-month period: (a) failing to fulfill work, school, or home obligations due to alcohol use, (b) recurrently using alcohol in hazardous situations (like driving a car while impaired), (c) legal problems associated with alcohol use, and (d) using alcohol despite social or interpersonal problems associated with its use (American Psychiatric Association, 2000). An individual cannot meet criteria for alcohol abuse if he or she has ever met criteria for alcohol dependence. A diagnosis is usually assigned after some type of clinical interview with the individual, but self-report checklists have also been utilized in the research literature. We should note that as of this chapter's writing, there are proposed revisions for the *DSM-5* involving the creation of a single disorder for all substances including a severity specifier. Thus, the categorical distinction between alcohol abuse and dependence would no longer be part of the clinical lexicon (American Psychiatric Association, 2010). We anticipate, though, the material discussed below in regard to assigning *DSM-IV* diagnoses will also apply to assigning a diagnosis under the new criteria.

Interview-based assessments. The most valid means of assessing for the presence of an AUD is through a structured or semi-structured clinical interview where each of the diagnostic criteria is assessed. There have been several large studies that have used these interviews to examine prevalence of AUDs in the college student population. For example, the National Epidemiologic Survey on Alcohol and Related Conditions (NESARC) utilized the Alcohol Use Disorder and Associated Disabilities Interview Schedule-Diagnostic and *Statistical Manual of Mental Disorders*–Fourth Edition (AUDADIS-IV: Grant, Dawson, & Hasin, 2001) to examine the prevalence of alcohol use disorders among 43,309 U.S. adults above the age of 18 (Grant, Moore, Shepard, & Kaplan, 2003). The AUDADIS-IV is a structured interview that includes multiple questions in an effort to determine if the respondent meets each diagnostic criteria for either alcohol abuse or dependence. The reliability and validity of the AUDADIS-IV or earlier versions of the measure have been well established (e.g., Grant et al., 2003a; Grant, Harford, Dawson, Chou, & Pickering, 1995; Hasin, Carpenter, McCloud, Smith, & Grant, 1997). Dawson, Grant, Stinson, and Chou (2004) examined the prevalence of AUDs among a subsample (*n* = 8,666) of college-age subjects (18 to 29 years of age) in the NE-SARC study. They found that 18.7% of college students met past-year diagnostic criteria for either alcohol abuse or dependence, and those in college were more likely to meet diagnostic criteria for alcohol dependence than those not in college (10.9% vs. 8.4%). Another example of a clinical interview used to assess for the presence of an AUD in college students is the Semi-Structured Assessment for the Genetics of Alcoholism (SSAGA: Bucholz et al., 1994). A study using the SSAGA to determine the diagnostic rates of AUDs among 19- to 21-year-old women found that 9% of college students met criteria for past-year dependence and 6% met past-year criteria for past-year abuse (Slutske et al., 2004). These percentages were similar to those reported for college women in the NESARC study (Dawson et al., 2004), and suggest concordance between the interviews. Although studies examining the validity of structured or semi-structured interviews for AUDs specifically among college students are lacking, it is likely such interviews remain the most reliable and valid means of assessing for the presence or absence of such a disorder. Some structured interview items are publicly available (e.g., Chen, Yi, Dawson, Stinson,

& Grant, 2010), making it easier for clinicians and researchers to use them to assess for AUDs among college students.

Self-report assessments. Studies among college students have also used simple self-report checklists to assess for the presence of an AUD. In the largest such study, Knight and colleagues (2002) utilized a self-report checklist adapted from the SSAGA (Bucholz et al., 1994) among a sample of 14,138 undergraduate students at U.S. colleges. The authors reported 6.3% of the students met past-year diagnostic criteria for alcohol dependence and 31.6% met diagnostic criteria for alcohol abuse. In another study among college students at a single university that utilized this checklist (n = 2,270), Simons, Carey, and Wills (2009) found that 11% of the sample who reported using alcohol (92% of the total sample) met past 6-month diagnostic criteria for alcohol dependence and 47% reported at least one symptom of alcohol abuse (although the percentage of students meeting diagnostic criteria for abuse would be lower because some students reporting at least one symptom of abuse also presumably met diagnostic criteria for dependence). These findings suggest that prevalence rates for alcohol dependence calculated via structured interviews and self-report checklists are relatively similar, but the percentage of college students meeting diagnostic criteria for alcohol abuse is much higher when self-report checklists are used. If we assume structured diagnostic interviews are the "gold standard" for assigning a diagnosis, then it appears that self-report diagnostic checklists may over-diagnose alcohol abuse in college students.

Other Measures of Alcohol-Related Constructs

There are scores of measures assessing various constructs relevant to alcohol consumption among college students, including perceived drinking among other studies (i.e., social norms: Baer, Stacy, & Larimer, 1991) motivations for drinking (e.g., Cooper, 1994), expectancies regarding the use of alcohol (e.g., Fromme, Stroot, & Kaplan, 1993), readiness to change one's drinking, (e.g., Rollnick, Heather, Gold, & Hall, 1992), use of protective behavioral strategies designed to reduce heavy alcohol use and related harms (e.g., Martens et al., 2005), family history of alcoholism (e.g., Sher & Descutner, 1986), perceived alcohol use among other students (e.g., Baer et al., 1991), drinking refusal self-efficacy (Oei, Hasking, & Young, 2005), and alcohol-related disinhibition (Leeman, Toll, & Volpicelli, 2007). There are a number of ways these types of assessments could be utilized in clinical work with college students. For example, several studies have shown that providing personalized normative feedback, or how one's own alcohol use and perceptions of other students' use compares to actual student norms, is an efficacious intervention (e.g., Lewis & Neighbors, 2007; Lewis, Neighbors, Oster-Aaland, Kirkeby, & Larimer, 2007; Neighbors et al., 2004; Neighbors, Lee, Lewis, Fossos, & Walters, 2009). National norms for alcohol consumption among college students in general are publically available (e.g., The Core Institute, 2008), thus, it would be relatively easy for a clinician to ask the student to complete measures like the Drinking Norms Rating Form (Baer et al., 1991) and an alcohol consumption questionnaire (e.g, the DDQ) and provide the student social norms feedback. Other possibilities could involve obtaining information about a students' alcohol-related expectancies and discussing with him or her the reality of those expectancies (see Darkes & Goldman, 1993, 1998) or examining the degree to which a student endorses different types of drinking motives and adjusting one's clinical work accordingly (e.g., a student who drink primarily for social reasons may require a different type of intervention than one who drinks primarily to cope with negative affect). Another possibility could involve assessing the use of protective behavioral or drinking control strategies (Sugarman & Carey, 2007) in an effort to facilitate cognitive-behavioral or motivational enhancement-based interventions that could increase the use of such strategies.

Informal/Semi-Structured Assessments

In many settings, clinicians do not use structured or validated measures to assess behavior, instead relying on informal or semi-structured idiographic assessments. Although concerns exist regarding the reliability and validity of such assessments (Groth-Marnat, 2003), they are a common part of the clinical lexicon and can yield information unique to an individual client that can facilitate appropriate services. For example, in many college counseling centers, clinicians will conduct an initial intake assessment where they ask about problems or symptoms experienced in a number of areas (e.g., interpersonal difficulties, negative affect, academic work). We believe including alcohol use and problem questions in such assessments is imperative. As part of an informal assessment clinicians should attempt to obtain a clear picture of a student's alcohol use patterns by asking more than just a question about general use (e.g., typical number of days drinking per week). Determining such general drinking patterns is important, but given the episodic nature of college student drinking clinicians should also ask questions about possible high-risk instances, such as drinking while intoxicated, blacking out, or becoming ill as a result of drinking. If a student indicates some problems associated with alcohol use, it may also be important to ask additional questions about drinking behavior (e.g., Wulfert, Greenway, & Dougher, 1996). For example, the clinician may want to determine if the student's drinking varies by beverage type (e.g., he or she does not drink excessively when consuming beer but does do so when consuming shots of liquor) or external settings (e.g., he or she drinks less at bars than at parties) as well as assessing motives for using alcohol. It would also be important to assess for the use of co-occurring substances when addressing alcohol use. By nature, informal and/or semi-structured assessments are somewhat idiosyncratic to the clinician utilizing them, but we believe it is important that (a) alcohol use and related risks be included in such assessments with college students and (b) for students reporting potential problems with alcohol use, clinicians follow up with questions designed to provide a clear picture of an individual's unique profile in regards to their behavior.

FUTURE DIRECTIONS/SUMMARY

We believe there are a number of research areas that are important for advancing the use of clinical assessment measures of college student drinking. The list below is by no means exhaustive, yet represents several important domains with potential to improve clinical assessment (and thereby clinical treatment) in this area:

1. **Translational research.** It is important that researchers conduct more studies examining the reliability, validity, and clinical utility of commonly used assessment measures in settings where campus alcohol-related services are provided, such as counseling centers, health centers, wellness centers, and services provided to judicially mandated students. (e.g., university counseling centers, university health centers, wellness centers). For example, although the OQ-45 is a commonly used problems checklist in college counseling centers, little is known about the degree to which it identifies and assesses outcomes for students with alcohol-related issues.

2. **Clinical applications of alcohol-related constructs.** It is unknown the degree to which assessing many alcohol-related constructs (e.g., drinking motives, alcohol expectancies, family risk of alcoholism) can positively impact clinical practice. Such constructs have been included in many widely disseminated brief personalized feedback-based interventions (e.g., BASICS), but the degree to which many of the factors actually contribute to intervention success is unknown. Some studies have shown changes in constructs like social norms (e.g., Neighbors et al., 2004) and protective behavioral strategies (e.g., Barnett et al., 2007; Larimer et al., 2007) mediated the efficacy of brief alcohol interventions. Determining if and how other alcohol-related constructs positively impact drinking changes could be an important means of enhancing the effectiveness of interventions within this population.

3. **Ecological momentary assessment (EMA).** EMA involves collecting data in "real-world" environments and assesses current or very recent behaviors (Trull & Ebner-Priemer, 2009). Such data can be collected via several different means, including handheld electronic devices, cellular telephones, and daily web-based diaries. Gathering such data has several important benefits for alcohol researchers and clinicians, including increased assessment accuracy, ability to better examine situational cues associated with alcohol use, and detailed idiographic data that could be utilized in a clinical context (Shiffman, 2010). For example, a clinician could provide a homework assignment to a

client involving self-monitoring of his or her alcohol intake, which could be accomplished via an EMA-based assessment tool downloaded onto the client's cell phone. Research on the use of EMA in the area of college student drinking is in its infancy, and research on its application in the clinical realm is nonexistent. However, technological advances have the potential to make a tremendous impact on research and clinical work in the area.

4. **New diagnostic criteria.** As mentioned previously in this chapter, the proposed revision to the *DSM* system involves a single alcohol use disorder that includes a moderate and severe specifier (American Psychiatric Association, 2010). Switching from the abuse/dependence distinction will be more consistent with evidence suggesting alcohol-related diagnostic symptoms exist along a single continuum. Nonetheless, the release of a new diagnostic system will require additional research on topics such as how well screening measures assess for the likelihood of an AUD and the reliability and validity of measures designed to assign a formal alcohol use disorder diagnosis.

Researchers and clinicians interested in screening for at-risk drinking, assessing alcohol consumption and related problems, and evaluating for the presence of an AUD among the college student population have a number of options at their disposal. The primary purpose of this chapter was to review many of these measures, address the strengths and limitations of each, and provide some recommendations regarding their use. No single measure in a particular domain can be recommended in all instances, and professionals working in the area of alcohol prevention among college students will have to determine what types of assessments meet their particular needs. This chapter helps professionals make more informed choices. In addition, we hope the knowledge base on this topic continues to expand and therefore improve the clinical services provided to college students who engage in at-risk drinking.

REFERENCES

Aertgeerts, B., Buntinx, F., Bande-Knops, J., Vandermeulen, C., Roelants, M., Ansoms, S., & Feverey, J. (2000). The value of CAGE, CUGE, and AUDIT in screening for alcohol abuse and dependence among college freshmen. *Alcoholism: Clinical and Experimental Research, 24,* 53–57.

American College Health Association. (2009). American College Health Association-National College Health Assessment Spring 2008 reference group data report (abridged). *Journal of American College Health, 57,* 477–488.

American Psychiatric Association. (2000). *Diagnostic and statistical manual of mental disorders* (Revised 4th ed.). Washington, DC: Author.

American Psychiatric Association. (2010). *DSM-5 development: R oo alcohol use disorder.* Retrieved from http://www.dsm5.org/ProposedRevision/Pages/proposedrevision.aspx?rid=452

Babor, T. F., Higgins-Biddle, J. C., Saunders, J. B., & Monteiro, M. G. (2001). *The alcohol use disorders identification test: Guidelines for use in primary care, second edition* (WHO Publication No. WHO/MSD/MSB/01.6a). Retrieved from World Health Organization website http://whqlibdoc.who.int/hq/2001/WHO_MSD_MSB_01.6a.pdf

Babor, T. F., Steinberg, K., Anton, R., & Del Boca, F. K. (2000). Talk is cheap: Measuring drinking outcomes in clinical trials. *Journal of Studies on Alcohol, 61,* 55–63.

Baer, J. S., Stacy, A., & Larimer, M. (1991). Biases in the perception of drinking norms among college students. *Journal of Studies on Alcohol, 54,* 54–60.

Barnett, N. P., Murphy, J. G., Colby, S. M., & Monti, P. M. (2007). Efficacy of counselor vs. computer-delivered intervention with mandated college students. *Addictive Behaviors, 32,* 2529–2548.

Barnett, N. P., & Read, J. P. (2005). Mandatory alcohol intervention for alcohol-abusing college students: A systematic review. *Journal of Substance Abuse Treatment, 29,* 147–158.

Barnett, N. P., Wei, J., & Czachowski, C. (2009). Measured alcohol content in college party mixed drinks. *Psychology of Addictive Behaviors, 23,* 152–156.

Bernhardt, J. M., Usdan, S., Mays, D., Martin, R., Cremeens, J., & Arriola, K. J. (2009). Alcohol assessment among college students using wireless mobile technology. *Journal of Studies on Alcohol and Drugs, 70,* 771–775.

Beseler, C. L., Taylor, L. A., & Leeman, R. F. (2010). An item-response theory analysis of *DSM-IV* alcohol-use disorder criteria and "binge" drinking in undergraduates. *Journal of Studies on Alcohol and Drugs, 71,* 418–423.

Bonar, E. E., Rosenberg, H., Hoffmann, E., Kraus, S. W., Kryszak, E., Young, K. M., Bannon, E. E. (2011). Measuring university students' self-efficacy to use drinking self-control strategies. *Psychology of Addictive Behaviors, 25,* 155–161.

Borsari, B., & Carey, K. B. (2000). Effects of a brief motivational intervention with college student drinkers. *Journal of Consulting and Clinical Psychology, 68,* 728–733.

Borsari, B., & Muellerleile, P. (2009). Collateral reports in the college setting: A meta-analytic integration. *Alcoholism: Clinical and Experimental Research, 33,* 826–838.

Brown, T. A., & Barlow, D. H. (2009). A proposal for a dimensional classification system based on the shared features of the DSM-IV anxiety and mood disorders: Implications for assessment and treatment. *Psychological Assessment, 21,* 256–271.

Bucholz, K. K., Cadoret, R., Cloninger, R. C., Dinwiddie, S. H., Hesselbrock, V. M., Nurnberger, J. I., . . . Schuckit, M. A. (1994). A new, semi-structured psychiatric interview for use in genetic linkage studies: A report on the reliability of the SSAGA. *Journal of Studies on Alcohol, 55,* 149–158.

Bush, K., Kivlahan, D. R., McDonell, M. B., Fihn, S. D., & Bradley, K. A. (1998). The AUDIT alcohol consumption questions (AUDIT-C): An effective brief screening test for problem drinking. *Archives of Internal Medicine, 158,* 1789–1795.

Butler, L. H., & Correia, C. J. (2009). Brief alcohol intervention with college student drinkers: Face-to-face versus computerized feedback. *Psychology of Addictive Behaviors, 23,* 163–167.

Carey, K. B., Carey, M. P., Maisto, S. A., & Henson, J. M. (2006). Brief motivational interventions for heavy college drinkers: A randomized controlled trial. *Journal of Consulting and Clinical Psychology, 74,* 943–954.

Carey, K. B., Henson, J. M., Carey, M. P., & Maisto, S. A. (2009). Computer versus in-person intervention for students violating campus alcohol policy. *Journal of Consulting and Clinical Psychology, 77,* 74–87.

Carey, K. B., & Hustad, J. T. P. (2002). Are retrospectively reconstructed blood alcohol concentrations accurate? Preliminary results from a field study. *Journal of Studies on Alcohol, 63,* 762–766.

Chen, C. M., Yi, H., Dawson, D. A., Stinson, F. S., & Grant, B. F. (2010). *Alcohol use and alcohol use disorders in the United States: Main findings from the 2004–2005 Wave 2 national epidemiologic survey of alcohol and related conditions (NESARC).* (NIH Publication No. 10–7677). Bethesda, MD: National Institute on Alcohol Abuse and Alcoholism.

Clements, R. (1998). A critical evaluation of several alcohol screening instruments using the CIDI-SAM as a screening measure. *Alcoholism: Clinical and Experimental Research, 22,* 985–993.

Cohen, B. B., & Vinson, D. C. (1995). Retrospective self-report of alcohol consumption: Test-retest reliability by telephone. *Alcoholism: Clinical and Experimental Research, 19,* 1156–1161.

Collins, R. L., Kashdan, T. B., Koutsky, J. R., Morsheimer, E. T., & Vetter, C. J. (2008). A self-administered timeline followback to measure variations in underage drinkers' alcohol intake and binge drinking. *Addictive Behaviors, 33,* 196–200.

Collins, R. L., Parks, G. A., & Marlatt, G. A. (1985). Social determinants of alcohol consumption: The effects of social interaction and model status on the self-administration of alcohol. *Journal of Consulting and Clinical Psychology, 53*, 189–200.

Collins, S. E., Logan, D. E., & Neighbors, C. (2010). Which came first: The readiness or the change? Longitudinal relationships between readiness to change and drinking among college drinkers. *Addiction, 105*, 1899–1909.

Connor, J. P., Feeney, G. F. X., Jack, A., & Young, R. M. (2010). The obsessive compulsive drinking scale is a valid measure of alcohol cravings in young adults. *Alcoholism: Clinical and Experimental Research, 34*, 2155–2161.

Cooper, M. L. (1994). Reasons for drinking among adolescents: Development and validation or a four-dimensional measure of drinking motives. *Psychological Assessment, 6*, 117–128.

The Core Institute (2008). *2008 annual data. Core alcohol and drug survey long form-form 194. Executive summary.* Available at http://www.core.siuc.edu/pdfs/report08.pdf

Courtney, K. E., & Polich, J. (2009). Binge drinking in young adults: Data, definitions, and determinants. *Psychological Bulletin, 135*, 142–156.

Cronbach, L. J., & Meehl, P. E. (1955). Construct validity in psychological tests. *Psychological Bulletin, 52*, 281–302.

Darkes, J., & Goldman, M. S. (1993). Expectancy challenge and drinking reduction: Experimental evidence for a meditational process. *Journal of Consulting and Clinical Psychology, 61*, 344–353.

Darkes, J., & Goldman, M. S. (1998). Expectancy challenge and drinking reduction: process and structure in the alcohol expectancy network. *Experimental and Clinical Psychopharmacology, 6*, 64–76.

Dawson, D. A., Grant, B. F., Stinson, F. S., & Chou, P. S. (2004). Another look at heavy episodic drinking and alcohol use disorders among college and noncollege youth. *Journal of Studies on Alcohol, 65*, 477–488.

Dawson, D. A., Pulay, A. J., & Grant, B. F. (2010). A comparison of two single-item screeners for hazardous drinking and alcohol use disorder. *Alcoholism: Clinical and Experimental Research, 34*, 364–374.

Del Boca, F. K., & Darkes, J. (2003). The validity of self-reports of alcohol consumption: State of the science and challenges for research. *Addiction, 98*, S1–S12.

Del Boca, F. K., Darkes, J., Greenbaum, P. E., & Goldman, M. S. (2004). Up close and personal: Temporal variability in the drinking of individual college students during their first year. *Journal of Consulting and Clinical Psychology, 72*, 155–164.

Del Boca, F., & Noll, J. A. (2000). Truth or consequences: The validity of self-report data in health services research on addictions. *Addiction, 95*, S347–S360.

Devos-Comby, L., & Lange, J. E. (2008). Standardized measures of alcohol-related problems: A review of their use among college students. *Psychology of Addictive Behaviors, 22*, 349–361.

Dimeff, L. A., Baer, J. S., Kivlahan, D. R., & Marlatt, G. A. (1999). *Brief alcohol screening and intervention for college students: A harm reduction approach.* New York, NY: Guilford Press.

Dollinger, S. J., & Malmquist, D. (2009). Reliability and validity of single-item self reports: With special relevance to college students' alcohol use, religiosity, study, and social life. *Journal of General Psychology, 136*, 231–241.

Earleywine, M., LaBrie, J. W., & Pedersen, E. R. (2008). A brief Rutgers alcohol problem index with less potential for bias. *Addictive Behaviors, 33*, 1249–1253.

Ewing, J. A. (1984). Detecting alcoholism: The CAGE questionnaire. *JAMA, 252*, 1905–1907.

Fernandez, A. C., Wood, M. D., Stein, L. A. R., & Rossi, J. S. (2010). Measuring mindfulness and examining its relationship with alcohol use and negative consequences. *Psychology of Addictive Behaviors, 24*, 608–616.

Fleming, M. F., Barry, K. L., & MacDonald, R. (1991). The alcohol use disorders identification test (AUDIT) in a college sample. *International Journal of the Addictions, 26*, 1173–1185.

Fromme, K., Stroot, E., & Kaplan, D. (1993). Comprehensive effects of alcohol: Development and psychometric assessment of a new expectancy questionnaire. *Psychological Assessment, 5*, 19–26.

Goldman, M. S., Greenbaum, P. E., Darkes, J., Obremski Brandon, K., & Del Boca, F. (2011). How many versus how much: 52 weeks of alcohol consumption in emerging adults. *Psychology of Addictive Behaviors, 25*, 16–27.

Grant, B. F., Dawson, D. A., & Hasin, D. S. (2001). *The alcohol use disorder and associated disabilities interview schedule–DSM-IV version.* Bethesda, MD: National Institute on Alcohol Abuse and Alcoholism.

Grant, B. F., Dawson, D. A., Stinson, F. S., Chou, S. P., Kay, W., & Pickering, R. P. (2003a). The Alcohol Use Disorder and Associated Disabilities Interview Schedule-IV (AUDADIS-IV): Reliability of alcohol consumption, tobacco use, family history of depression and psychiatric diagnostic modules in a general population sample. *Drug and Alcohol Dependence, 71,* 7–16.

Grant, B. F., Harford, T. C., Dawson, D. A., Chou, P. S., & Pickering, R. P. (1995). The alcohol use disorder and associated disabilities interview schedule (AUDADIS): Reliability of alcohol and drug modules in a general population sample. *Drug and Alcohol Dependence, 39,* 37–44.

Grant, B. F., Moore, T. C., Shepard, J., & Kaplan, K. (2003b). *Source and accuracy statement: Wave 1 of the 2001–2002 national epidemiologic survey on alcohol and related conditions (NESARC).* Bethesda, MD: National Institute on Alcohol Abuse and Alcoholism.

Greenbaum, P. E., Del Boca, F. K., Darkes, J., Wang, C., & Goldman, M. S. (2005). Variation in drinking trajectories of freshmen college students. *Journal of Consulting and Clinical Psychology, 73,* 229–238.

Groeschel, B. L., Wester, S. R., & Sedivy, S. K. (2010). Gender role conflict, alcohol, and help seeking among college men. *Psychology of Men and Masculinity, 11,* 123–129.

Groth-Marnat, G. (2003). *Handbook of psychological assessment* (4th ed.). Hoboken, NJ: Wiley.

Hasin, D., Carpenter, K. M., McCloud, S., Smith, M., & Grant, B. F. (1997). The alcohol use disorder and associated disabilities interview schedule (AUDADIS): Reliability of alcohol and drug modules in a clinical sample. *Drug and Alcohol Dependence, 44,* 133–141.

Heck, E. J., & Williams, M. D. (1995). Using the CAGE to screen for drinking-related problems in college students. *Journal of Studies on Alcohol, 56,* 282–286.

Hoeppner, B. B., Stout, R. L., Jackson, K. M., & Barnett, N. P. (2010). How good is fine-grained timeline follow-back data? Comparing 30-day TLFB and repeated 7-day TLFB alcohol consumption reports on the person and daily level. *Addictive Behaviors, 35,* 1138–1143.

How much is too much? (2009, May). *The Police Notebook.* Retrieved from www.ou.edu/oupd/bac.htm

Hurlbut, S. C., & Sher, K. J. (1992). Assessing alcohol problems in college students. Journal of American *College Health, 41,* 49–58.

Jackson, K. M. (2008). Heavy episodic drinking: Determining the predictive utility of five or more drinks. *Psychology of Addictive Behaviors, 22,* 68–77.

Jenks Kettmann, J. D., Schoen, E. G., Moel, J. E., Cochran, S. V., Greenberg, S. T., & Corkery, J. M. (2007). Increasing severity of psychopathology at counseling centers: A new look. *Professional Psychology: Research and Practice, 38,* 523–529.

Kahler, C. W., Hustad, J., Barnett, N. P., Strong, D. R., & Borsari, B. (2008). Validation of the 30-day version of the Brief Young Adult Alcohol Consequences Questionnaire for use in longitudinal studies. *Journal of Studies on Alcohol and Drugs, 69,* 611–615.

Kahler, C. W., Strong, D. R., & Read, J. P. (2005). Toward efficient and comprehensive measurement of the alcohol problems continuum in college students: The brief young adult alcohol consequences questionnaire. *Alcoholism: Clinical and Experimental Research, 29,* 1180–1189.

Kahler, C. W., Strong, D. R., Read, J. P., Palfai, T. P., & Wood, M. D. (2004). Mapping the continuum of alcohol problems in college students: A Rasch model analysis. *Psychology of Addictive Behaviors, 18,* 322–333.

Knight, J. R., Wechsler, H., Kuo, M., Seibring, M., Weitzman, E. R., & Schuckit, M. A. (2002). Alcohol abuse and dependence among U.S. college students. *Journal of Studies on Alcohol, 63,* 263–270.

Kokotailo, P. K., Egan, J., Gangnon, R., Brown, D., Mundt, M., & Fleming, M. (2004). Validity of the alcohol use disorders identification test in college students. *Alcoholism: Clinical and Experimental Research, 28,* 914–920.

Krueger, R. F., Nichol, P. E., Hicks, B. M., Markon, K. E., Patrick, C. J., Iacono, W. G., & McGue, M. (2004). Using latent trait modeling to conceptualize an alcohol problems continuum. *Psychological Assessment, 16,* 107–119.

LaBrie, J., Pedersen, E., & Earleywine, M. (2005). A group administered timeline followback assessment of alcohol use. *Journal of Studies on Alcohol, 66,* 693–697.

LaBrie, J. W., Pedersen, E. R., & Tawalbeh, S. (2007). Classifying risky-drinking college students: Another look at the two-week drinker type categorization. *Journal of Studies on Alcohol and Drugs, 68,* 86–90.

Lambert, M. J., Burlingame, G. M., Umphress, V., Hansen, N. B., Vermeersch, D. A., Clouse, G. C., & Yanchar, S. C. (1996). The reliability and validity of the outcome questionnaire. *Clinical Psychology and Psychotherapy, 3,* 249–258.

Langenbucher, J. W., Labouvie, E., Martin, C. S., Sanjuan, P. M., Bavly, L., Kirisci, L., & Chung, T. (2004). An application of item response theory analysis to alcohol, cannabis, and cocaine criteria in DSM-IV. *Journal of Abnormal Psychology, 113,* 72–80.

Larimer, M. E., Lee, C. M., Kilmer, J. R., Fabiano, P. M., Stark, C. B., Geisner, I. M., . . . Neighbors, C. (2007). Personalized mailed feedback for college drinking prevention: A randomized clinical trial. *Journal of Consulting and Clinical Psychology, 75,* 285–293.

Larimer, M. E., Turner, A. P., Anderson, B. K., Fader, J. S., Kilmer, J. R., Palmer, R. S., . . . Cronce, J. M. (2001). Evaluating a brief alcohol intervention for fraternities. *Journal of Studies on Alcohol, 62,* 370–380.

Lee, C. M., Lewis, M. A., & Neighbors, C. (2009). Preliminary examination of spring break alcohol use and related consequences. *Psychology of Addictive Behaviors, 23,* 689–694.

Leeman, R. F., Toll, B. A., & Volpicelli, J. R. (2007). The drinking induced disinhibition scale (DIDS): A measure of three types of disinhibiting effects. *Addictive Behaviors, 32,* 1200–1219.

Lewis, M. A., & Neighbors, C. (2007). Optimizing personalized normative feedback: The use of gender-specific referents. *Journal of Studies on Alcohol and Drugs, 68,* 228–237.

Lewis, M. A., Neighbors, C., Oster-Aaland, L., Kirkeby, B. S., & Larimer, M. E. (2007). Indicated prevention for incoming freshmen: Personalized normative feedback and high-risk drinking. *Addictive Behaviors, 32,* 2495–2508.

Lozano, B. E., & Stephens, R. (2010). Comparison of participatively set and assigned goals in the reduction of alcohol use. *Psychology of Addictive Behaviors, 24,* 581–591.

MacKillop, J. Mattson, R. E., Anderson MacKillop, E. J., Castelda, B. A., & Donovick, P. J. (2007). Multidimensional assessment of impulsivity in undergraduate hazardous drinkers and controls. *Journal of Studies on Alcohol and Drugs, 68,* 785–788.

Maddock, J. E., Laforge, R. G., Rossi, J. S., & O'Hare, T. M. (2001). The college alcohol problems scale. *Addictive Behaviors, 26,* 385–398.

Marlatt, G. A., Baer, J. S., Kivlahan, D. R., Dimeff, L. A., Larimer, M. E., Quigley, L. A., et al. (1998). Screening and brief intervention for high-risk college student drinkers: Results from a 2-year follow-up assessment. *Journal of Consulting and Clinical Psychology, 66,* 604–615.

Martens, M. P., Ferrier, A. G., Sheehy, M. J., Corbett, K., Anderson, D. A., & Simmons, A. (2005). Development of the protective behavioral strategies survey. *Journal of Studies on Alcohol, 66,* 698–705.

Martens, M. P., LaBrie, J. W., Hummer, J. F., & Pedersen, E. R. (2008). Understanding sport-related drinking motives in college athletes: Psychometric analyses of the athlete drinking scale. *Addictive Behaviors, 33,* 974–977.

Martens, M. P., Neighbors, C., Dams-O'Connor, K., Lee, C. M., & Larimer, M. E. (2007). The factor structure of a dichotomously scored Rutgers alcohol problems index. *Journal of Studies on Alcohol and Drugs, 68,* 597–606.

Martens, M. P., Pedersen, E. R., LaBrie, J. W., Ferrier, A. G., & Cimini, M. D. (2007). Measuring alcohol-related protective behavioral strategies among college students: Further examination of the protective behavioral strategies scale. *Psychology of Addictive Behaviors, 21,* 307–315.

Martens, M. P., Rocha, T. L., Martin, J. L., & Serrao, H. F. (2008). Drinking motives and college students: Further examination of a four-factor model. *Journal of Counseling Psychology, 55,* 289–295.

Matthews, D. B., & Miller, W. R. (1979). Estimating blood alcohol concentration: Two computer programs and their applications in therapy and research. *Addictive Behaviors, 4,* 55–60.

McEvoy, P. M., Stritzke, W. G. K., French, D. J., Lang, A. R., & Ketterman, R. L. (2004). Comparison of three models of alcohol craving in young adults: A cross validation. *Addiction, 99,* 482–497.

McGee, R., Williams, S., & Kypri, K. (2010). College students' readiness to reduce binge drinking: Criterion validity of a brief measure. *Drug and Alcohol Dependence, 109,* 236–238.

McMillen, B. A., Hillis, S. M., & Brown, J. M. (2009). College students' responses to a 5/4 drinking question and maximum blood alcohol concentration calculated from a timeline followback questionnaire. *Journal of Studies on Alcohol and Drugs, 70*, 601–605.

Midanik, L. T. (1988). Validity of self-reported alcohol use: A literature review and assessment. *British Journal of Addiction, 83*, 1019–1029.

Miller, W. R., Tonigan, J. S. & Longabaugh, R. (1995). *The Drinker Inventory of Consequences (DrInC): An Instrument for Assessing Adverse Consequences of Alcohol Abuse.* Project MATCH Monograph Series, Vol. 4. DHHS Publication No. 95-3911. Rockville, MD: National Institute on Alcohol Abuse and Alcoholism.

Murphy, J. G., Benson, T. A., Vuchinich, R. E., Deskins, M. M., Eakin, D., Flood, A. M., . . . Torrealday, O. (2004). A comparison of personalized feedback for college student drinkers with and without a motivational interview. *Journal of Studies on Alcohol, 65*, 200–203.

Murphy, J. G., Dennhardt, A. A., Skidmore, J. R., Martens, M. P., & McDevitt-Murphy, M. E. (2010). Computerized versus motivational interviewing alcohol interventions: Impact on discrepancy, motivation, and drinking. *Psychology of Addictive Behaviors, 24*, 628–639.

National Institute on Alcohol Abuse and Alcoholism. (2004, Winter). NIAAA council approves definition of binge drinking. *NIAAA Newsletter.* Retrieved from NIH website http://pubs.niaaa.nih.gov/publications/Newsletter/winter2004/Newsletter_Number3.pdf

National Institute on Alcohol Abuse and Alcoholism. (2008). *Tips for cutting down on drinking* (NIH Publication No. 07-3769). Retrieved from http://pubs.niaaa.nih.gov/publications/tips/tips.pdf

Neal, D. J., & Carey, K. B. (2007). Association between alcohol intoxication and alcohol-related problems: An event-level analysis. *Psychology of Addictive Behaviors, 21*, 194–204.

Neal, D. J., Corbin, W. R., & Fromme, K. (2006). Measurement of alcohol-related consequences among high school and college students: Application of item response models to the Rutgers alcohol problem index. *Psychological Assessment, 18*, 402–414.

Neal, D. J., & Fromme, K. (2007). Event-level intoxication of and behavioral risks during the first year of college. *Journal of Consulting and Clinical Psychology, 75*, 294–306.

Neighbors, C., Larimer, M. E., & Lewis, M. A. (2004). Targeting misperceptions of descriptive drinking norms: Efficacy of a computer-delivered personalized normative feedback intervention. *Journal of Consulting and Clinical Psychology, 72*, 434–447.

Neighbors, C., Lee, C. M., Lewis, M. A., Fossos, N., & Walter, T. (2009). Internet-based personalized feedback to reduce 21st-birthday drinking: A randomized controlled trial of an event-specific preventive intervention. *Journal of Consulting and Clinical Psychology, 77*, 51–63.

Oei, T. P. S., Hasking, P. A., & Young, R. M. (2005). Drinking refusal self-efficacy questionnaire-revised (DRSEQ-R): A new factor structure with confirmatory factor analysis. *Drug and Alcohol Dependence, 78*, 297–307.

O'Hare, T. (1997). Measuring problem drinking in first time offenders: Development and validation of the college alcohol problems scale (CAPS). *Journal of Substance Abuse Treatment, 14*, 383–387.

O'Hare, T. (2005). Comparing the AUDIT and 3 drinking indices as predictors of personal and social drinking problems in freshman first offenders. *Journal of Alcohol and Drug Education, 49*(3), 37–61.

Osberg, T. M., Atkins, L., Bucholz, L., Shirshova, V., Swiantek, A., Whitley, J., . . . Oquendo, N. (2010). Development and validation of the college life alcohol salience scale: A measure of beliefs about the role of alcohol in college life. *Psychology of Addictive Behaviors, 24*, 1–12.

Palfai, T., & Wood, M. D. (2001). Positive alcohol expectancies and drinking behavior: The influence of expectancy strength and memory accessibility. *Psychology of Addictive Behaviors, 15*, 60–67.

Pedersen, E. R., & LaBrie, J. (2006). A within-subjects validation of a group-administered timeline followback for alcohol use. *Journal of Studies on Alcohol, 67*, 332–335.

Read, J. P., Kahler, C. W., & Strong, D. R. (2006). Development and preliminary validation of the Young Adult Alcohol Consequences Questionnaire. *Journal of Studies on Alcohol, 67*, 169–177.

Read, J. P., Merrill, J. E., Kahler, C. W., & Strong, D. R. (2007). Predicting functional outcomes among college drinkers: Reliability and predictive validity of the Young Adult Alcohol Consequences Questionnaire. *Addictive Behaviors, 32*, 2597–2610.

Rollnick, S., Heather, N., Gold, R., & Hall, W. (1992). Development of a short "readiness to change" questionnaire for use in brief, opportunistic interventions among excessive drinkers. *British Journal of Addiction, 87*, 743–754.

Ruscio, J., Walters, G. D., Marcus, D. K., & Kaczetow, W. (2010). Comparing the relative fit of categorical and dimensional latent variable models using consistency tests. *Psychological Assessment, 22*, 5–21.

Saha, T. D., Chou, S. P., & Grant, B. F. (2006). Toward an alcohol use disorder continuum using item response theory: Results from the national epidemiologic survey on alcohol and related conditions. *Psychological Medicine, 36*, 931–941.

Saunders, J. B., Aasland, O. G., Babor, T. F., de la Fuente, J. R., & Grant, M. (1993). Development of the alcohol use disorders identification test (AUDIT): WHO collaborative project on early detection of persons with harmful alcohol consumption-II. *Addiction, 88*, 791–804.

Schaus, J. F., Sole, M. L., McCoy, T. P., Mullett, N., & O'Brien, M. C. (2009). Alcohol screening and brief intervention in a college student health center: A randomized controlled trial. *Journal of Studies on Alcohol and Drugs, 16*, S131–S141.

Selzer, M. L. (1971). The Michigan alcoholism screening test: The quest for a new diagnostic instrument. *American Journal of Psychiatry, 127*, 1653–1658.

Selzer, M. L., Vinokur, A., & van Rooijen, L. (1975). A self-administered short Michigan alcoholism screening test (SMAST). *Journal of Studies on Alcohol, 36*, 117–126.

Sher, K. J., & Descutner, C. (1986). Reports of paternal alcoholism: Reliability across siblings. *Addictive Behaviors, 11*, 25–30.

Shields, A. L., Campfield, D. C., Miller, C. S., Howell, R. T., Wallace, K., & Weiss, R. D. (2008). Score reliability of adolescent alcohol screening measures: A meta-analytic inquiry. *Journal of Child and Adolescent Substance Use, 17*(4), 75–97.

Shiffman, S. (2009). Ecological momentary assessment (EMA) in studies of substance use. *Psychological Assessment, 21*, 463–475.

Simons, J. S., Carey, K. B., & Wills, T. A. (2009). Alcohol abuse and dependence symptoms: A multidimensional model of common and specific etiology. *Psychology of Addictive Behaviors, 23*, 415–427.

Skeel, R. L., Pilarski, C., Pytlak, K., & Neudecker, J. (2008). Personality and performance-based measures in the prediction of alcohol use. *Psychology of Addictive Behaviors, 22*, 402–409.

Slutske, W. S., Hunt-Carter, E. E., Nabors-Oberg, R. E., Sher, K. J., Bucholz, K. K., Madden, P. A. F. . . . Heath, A. C. (2004). Do college students drink more than their non-college attending peers? Evidence from a population-based longitudinal female twin study. *Journal of Abnormal Psychology, 113*, 530–540.

Smith, G. T. (2005). On construct validity: Issues of method and measurement. *Psychological Assessment, 17*, 396–408.

Smith, G. T., McCarthy, D. M., & Goldman, M. S. (1995). Self-reported drinking and alcohol-related problems among early adolescents: Dimensionality and validity over 24 months. *Journal of Studies on Alcohol, 56*, 383–394.

Sobell, L. C., Maisto, S. A., Sobell, M. B., & Cooper, A. M. (1979). Reliability of abusers' self-reports of drinking behaviour. *Behaviour Research and Therapy, 17*, 157–160.

Sobell, L. C., & Sobell, M. B. (1978). Validity of self-reports in three populations of alcoholics. *Journal of Consulting and Clinical Psychology, 46*, 901–907.

Sobell, L. C., & Sobell, M. B. (1995). *Timeline Followback (TLFB) user's manual.* Toronto, Canada: Addiction Research Foundation.

Sobell, M. B., Sobell, L. C., Klajner, F., Pavin, D., & Basian, E. (1986). The reliability of a timeline method for assessing normal drinker college students' recent drinking history: Utility for alcohol research. *Addictive Behaviors, 11*, 149–161.

Stacy, A. W., Widaman, K. F., Hays, R., & DiMatteo, M. R. (1985). Validity of self-reports of alcohol and other drug use: A multitrait-multimethod assessment. *Journal of Personality and Social Psychology, 49*, 219–232.

Sugarman, D. E., & Carey, K. B. (2007). The relationship between drinking control strategies and college student alcohol use. *Psychology of Addictive Behaviors, 21*, 338–345.

Talbott, L. L., Umstattd, M. R., Usdan, S. L., Martin, R. J., & Geiger, B. F. (2009). Validation of the college alcohol problems scale-revised (CAPS-r) for use with non-adjudicated first-year students. *Addictive Behaviors, 34,* 471–473.

Trull, T. J., & Ebner-Priemer, U. W. (2009). Using experience sampling methods/ecological momentary assessment (ESM/EMA) in clinical assessment and clinical research: Introduction to the special section. *Psychological Assessment, 21,* 457–462.

Turner, J. C., Bauerle, J., & Shu, J. (2004). Estimated blood alcohol concentration correlation with self-reported negative consequences among college students using alcohol. *Journal of Studies on Alcohol, 65,* 741–749.

Vermeersch, D. A., Whipple, J. L., Lambert, M. J., Hawkins, E. J., Burchfield, C. M., & Okishi, J. C. (2004). Outcome questionnaire: Is it sensitive to changes in counseling center clients. *Journal of Counseling Psychology, 51,* 38–49.

Walker, S., & Cosden, M. (2007). Reliability of college student self-reported drinking behavior. *Journal of Substance Abuse Treatment, 33,* 405–409.

Walters, S. T., Vader, A. M., Harris, T. R., Field, C. A., & Jouriles, E. N. (2009). Dismantling motivational interviewing and feedback for college drinkers: A randomized clinical trial. *Journal of Consulting and Clinical Psychology, 77,* 64–73.

Watson, C. G., Tilleskjor, C., Hoodecheck-Schow, B. A., Pucel, J., & Jacobs, L. (1984). Do alcoholics give valid self-reports? *Journal of Studies on Alcohol, 45,* 344–348.

Wechsler, H., Davenport, A., Dowdall, G., Moeykens, B., & Castillo, S. (1994). Health and behavioral consequences of binge drinking in college. *Journal of the American Medical Association, 272,* 1672–1677.

Wechsler, H., Dowdall, G. W., Davenport, A., & Castillo, S. (1995). Correlates of college student binge drinking. *American Journal of Public Health, 85,* 921–926.

Wechsler, H., & Isaac, N. (1992). 'Binge' drinkers at Massachusetts colleges. *Journal of the American Medical Association, 267,* 2929–2931.

Wechsler, H., Lee, J. E., Kuo, M., & Lee, H. (2000). College binge drinking in the 1990s: A continuing problem. *Journal of American College Health, 48,* 199–210.

Wechsler, H., & Nelson, T. F. (2001). Binge drinking and the American college student: What's five drinks? *Psychology of Addictive Behaviors, 15,* 287–291.

White, A. M., Kraus, C. L., McCracken, L. A., & Swartzwelder, H. S. (2003). Do college students drink more than they think? Use of a free-pour paradigm to determine how college students define standard drinks. *Alcoholism: Clinical and Experimental Research, 27,* 1750–1756.

White, H. R., & Labouvie, E. W. (1989). Towards the assessment of adolescent problem drinking. *Journal of Studies on Alcohol, 50,* 30–37.

Widiger, T. A., Livesley, W. J., & Clark, L. (2009). An integrative dimensional classification of personality disorder. *Psychological Assessment, 21,* 243–255.

Wood, M. D., Capone, C., LaForge, R., Erickson, D. J., & Brand, N. H. (2007). Brief motivational intervention and expectancy challenge with heavy drinking college students: A randomized factorial study. *Addictive Behaviors, 32,* 2509–2528.

Wood, M. D., Read, J. P., Palfai, T. P., & Stevenson, J. F. (2001). Social influence processes and college student drinking: The meditational role of alcohol outcome expectancies. *Journal of Studies on Alcohol, 62,* 32–43.

Wulfert, E., Greenway, D. E., & Dougher, M. J. (1996). A logical functional analysis of reinforcement-based disorders: Alcoholism and pedophilia. *Journal of Consulting and Clinical Psychology, 64,* 1140–1151.

Zamboanga, B. L., Horton, N. J., Tyler, K. M. B., O'Riordan, S. S., Calvert, B. D., & McCollum, E. C. (2007). The utility of the AUDIT in screening for drinking game involvement among female college students. *Journal of Adolescent Health, 40,* 359–361.

6

Applying Harm-Reduction Strategies on College Campuses

Jason R. Kilmer and Diane E. Logan

Harm-reduction approaches seek to both reduce the harms associated with risky behaviors and improve individual quality of life through compassionate and pragmatic means (Collins et al., 2011). This definition is intentionally broad as it covers myriad techniques, targeted behaviors, and intervention levels, though it shares the common goals of reducing some form of harm and increasing life satisfaction. Harm reduction grew out of the understanding that some individuals will continue to engage in problematic behaviors even when they experience unwanted consequences, and that abstinence is not universally identified as the only desirable outcome. The evolution of this approach has not been without controversy—for many, this represents quite a paradigm shift (and necessitates thinking differently about what successful intervention outcomes might look like). However, particularly as it relates to college student drinking, the overwhelming body of evidence identifies this as an empirically supported, efficacious strategy.

A historical perspective of harm-reduction notes a greater acceptance and tolerance of harm-reduction approaches in Europe (specifically, Great Britain and

This chapter is dedicated to the memory of Alan Marlatt—our advisor, mentor, and friend. At a time when alcohol-prevention programs were focused exclusively on abstinence-only outcomes and often utilized ineffective and confrontational scare tactics, Alan championed a harm-reduction approach that focused on reducing risks and harms to the individual and his or her community, and on meeting people where they were in terms of their readiness to change. It is hard to separate his humane, compassionate, sensitive style from any discussion of the harm reduction approach. Alan is sorely missed, yet his work carries on through his former students and the numerous researchers and practitioners who have utilized and extended his groundbreaking work.

the Netherlands) as well as Canada compared with the United States (see Collins et al., 2011, for an overview). Harm-reduction strategies, while seeing abstinence as the most risk-free and harm-free outcome, view any steps toward reduced risk as steps in the right direction. Consequently, harm-reduction strategies can include everything from individually focused approaches to changes in policy. The first harm-reduction approaches consisted of legislation regarding drug distribution, regulation, and substitution. Such policy legislation targets multiple behaviors (e.g., legal and illegal drug use, alcohol and tobacco use, gambling, overeating) with varying levels of strictness and enforcement (e.g. restrictions on prescriptions based on medical diagnoses, illegal categorization of some substances, restricted alcohol and tobacco sales due to age or location, restrictions on casino locations, recommendations on healthy eating and exercise). Political debates continue on the necessity and scope of such legislation; some examples in the United States are movements to decriminalize marijuana, add pictures warning of tobacco use risk to cigarette packaging, and policies that restrict fat and salt additives in food. The common theme in all of these examples of legislation is to minimize the negative impact and promote satisfaction at an individual, community, and/or societal level.

Examples of original harm-reduction interventions also included needle exchange programs and safe injection sites, both of which have demonstrated positive outcomes but continue to face a great deal of controversy today. These programs seek to meet individuals where they are compassionately and pragmatically, valuing human rights and individual choice while seeking to minimize consequences on individual (e.g., accidental overdose), community (e.g., HIV infection), and societal (e.g., public health care costs) levels while providing medical oversight, sterilized instruments, and community outreach including counseling and rehabilitation offerings. These substance use programs have also been extended to alcohol use through "wet housing" programs, which provide living arrangements without the requirement of abstinence from alcohol (e.g., Larimer et al., 2009). The continued controversy, in spite of the success of these programs at reducing morbidity and mortality rates, stems in part from the classification of problematic (and addictive) behaviors under a disease model with an assumption that "curing" the disease can only occur through complete abstinence (see Larimer et al., 2011, for an overview of alcohol and the disease model). Additionally, controversy can also be fueled by perspectives that see harm-reduction efforts as "enabling" a person struggling with substance use or inadvertently encouraging use through reducing natural consequences. Financial concerns also incite the debate, particularly in tough economic times, when harm-reduction programs compete with other social services designed to sustain and improve lives. Independent of the current state of controversy, a harm-reduction approach considers problematic behaviors from a contextual perspective, acknowledges positive outcomes of controlled or moderate drinking/use, and considers any steps toward reduced risk to be acceptable. This is not to say that harm reduction does not support abstinence as an outcome—to the contrary, abstinence would provide the greatest reduction in harm by eliminating the behavior. The divergence comes from the acceptance of reductions in use and harm and increases in life satisfaction as successful alternative outcomes for individuals who are not interested in or who are unable to achieve complete and continuous abstinence.

In this chapter, we explore the relationship between harm reduction and alcohol use by college students, including factors associated with alcohol-related harm, examples of specific harm-reduction techniques, and further opportunities for the application of harm-reduction approaches to reducing the problems associated with college drinking.

COLLEGE STUDENT ALCOHOL USE AND RELATED CONSEQUENCES

College students demonstrate a wide range of drinking patterns and consequences. The decision to drink can be associated with a range of unwanted consequences or harms; these consequences on their own can sometimes be distressing for students (e.g., getting in a fight with a friend, blacking out and not remembering part of an evening), yet any delayed social, academic, or personal impact that follows (e.g., any "fallout" based on impact to social circles, loss of friends several days beyond the actual incident) can be problematic as well (Leigh & Lee, 2008). In some cases, however, outcomes related to drinking may not be seen by a student as "negative" and are instead seen as expected or routine, more neutral, or even positive effects (Leigh & Lee, 2008; Logan, Henry, Vaughn, Luk, & King, 2012; Mallett, Bachrach, & Turrisi, 2008). With a reference group of 30,093 students from 39 campuses assessed during the fall of 2010, the American College Health Association's National College Health Assessment helps to provide a glimpse into the type of alcohol-related consequences students are experiencing (ACHA, 2011). Within the 30 days prior to completing the survey, 15.2% of students said that they drove after drinking any alcohol at all, and 2.5% drove after having five or more drinks. Overall, the most frequently endorsed consequence was doing something they later regretted (experienced by 23.3% of total respondents, and endorsed by about one-third of those who reported any drinking). One in five (21.3%) students reported forgetting where they were or what they did (or "blacking out"). Students also reported as consequences of drinking that they had unprotected sex (11.6%), physically injured themselves (10.9%), got in trouble with the police (3.1%), physically injured another person (1.9%), had sex with someone without giving their consent (1.5%) or without getting the other person's consent (0.4%), and seriously considered suicide (1.3%) (ACHA, 2011). It is clear that alcohol misuse can be associated with range of health and mental health problems.

HARM-REDUCTION APPROACHES

Fortunately, a range of strategies exist in the realms of prevention and intervention that result in reductions in drinking and related consequences. Those with the greatest empirical support in reducing drinking and related consequences (e.g., the Alcohol Skills Training Program [ASTP] and the Brief Alcohol Screening and Intervention for College Students [BASICS] program) utilize a harm-reduction approach (Larimer & Cronce, 2002, 2007; Cronce & Larimer, 2011). At the time these strategies were developed, they represented quite a departure from the traditional abstinence-only programs that were available to drinkers in general and specifically college students. Far from carrying a "just say no" message, programs such as ASTP and BASICS actively acknowledge that drinking might occur (even by those under the legal drinking age), and focus on reducing the harms associated with drinking. These programs meet the compassionate (individual-focused and nonassumptive) and pragmatic (effective and realistic) definition of a harm-reduction approach, and seek to both minimize consequences (fewer blackouts, less vomiting) and maximize life success (improved grades, better social interactions).

As described earlier, these harm-reduction approaches are not anti-abstinence; in fact, the most harm-free or risk-free outcome following a harm-reduction intervention *is* abstinence. Instead, ASTP, BASICS, and other programs using a harm-reduction philosophy acknowledge that any steps toward reduced risk are steps in the right direction. Adopting this philosophy can involve rethinking what might be considered a "successful" outcome following an intervention beyond an outcome like drinks per occasion. For example, a 180-pound male student who consumes five drinks in an hour will have an estimated blood alcohol content (BAC) of .088%, and is at risk for experiencing nausea, impaired motor coordination, and compromised decision making (in addition to being over the legal limit for BAC). If this student reduces his rate of drinking by allowing more time to elapse between drinks or alternating alcoholic and nonalcoholic drinks, and now consumes these five drinks over three hours, his BAC will be .056%. This change in the timing of drinking—without any reduction in drinking quantity—would likely result in safer experience both for this person and perhaps the people around him. This is an example of a harm-reduction strategy that could be included in intervention approaches.

Harm-reduction approaches may be especially appropriate for the college population due to characteristics associated with the developmental stages associated with what is described as *emerging adulthood* (Arnett, 2000). During this transitional time, students enjoy increasing responsibility while maintaining the safety net afforded by reliance on others for guidance and assistance (including parents as well as campus programs and departments). Students identify as more independent, though they do not assume the full responsibility or label of *adulthood*. Abstinence-only programs are likely to be seen as too extreme or unrealistic for the social norms of campus. Education-only programs can be less effective as these emerging adults may resist being told what to do or not respond to generic messages that do not take into account their particular drinking pattern and social and personal characteristics. Further, most interventions are developed for participants with an established maladaptive drinking pattern, while college students may still be in the early stages of a fairly unpredictable drinking trajectory and do not view their alcohol use as a problem (Vik, Culbertson, & Sellers, 2000).

A true harm-reduction approach is careful not to send a mixed message—it is made clear that if a student is under 21, it is illegal to drink, but that this fact does not preclude the possibility of using strategies to minimize harm, should an underage individual decide to drink. It is also made clear that driving after any drinking is also illegal and dangerous. For those students who are interested in abstinence, skills and strategies for achieving and maintaining abstinence are reviewed. However, if a student makes the choice to drink, a harm-reduction message emphasizes ways to do so in a less dangerous or less risky way (not necessarily in a "safe" way, which might imply no risks to the student). The key to increasing a student's willingness to utilize harm-reduction strategies appears to be eliciting personally relevant reasons to change, which, in many programs with college students, is facilitated by the use of motivational interviewing and personalized feedback (W. R. Miller & Rollnick, 2002).

Motivational interviewing is a nonjudgmental, nonconfrontational clinical approach that can be utilized to prompt contemplation of change in those who had previously not been considering change, and, for those who are ambivalent about changing, to explore and resolve that ambivalence. One of the basic principles of motivational interviewing involves developing a sense of discrepancy or cognitive dissonance between values and goals that are important to the individual and ways in which the status quo could be in conflict with these values and goals. For example, a student's goal might be to achieve a certain grade point average so that financial aid is maintained and not jeopardized; the reality might be that due to drinking, this student has inconsistently attended class (due to how he or she feels the morning after drinking) and has chosen to go out and drink with friends over study time. If the student recognizes the impact to a goal or value, and then determines he or she would like to see this impact lessened, the student's motivation to change will likely be enhanced. During discussions with students, it is often the case that a "hook" will surface that serves as the goal, value, or topic that prompts consideration of a change in one's drinking behavior. Some examples of common hooks, including decision making, aggression, tolerance, and time spent intoxicated are discussed further in the next session.

Harm-reduction programs have been successfully implemented with groups (e.g., ASTP) and individuals (e.g., BASICS). When delivered in a group setting, the emphasis is on encouraging participants to consider what they would like to see happen (and, similarly, not happen) while drinking. The discussion will often include information on the role that expectancies play in alcohol's social effects (relaying findings from balanced-placebo studies that show that students who expect alcohol but receive none nevertheless show the social effects of alcohol, while their peers who expect nonalcoholic drinks but actually receive alcohol show no changes in social effects and, instead, attribute the physical effects they are feeling to being tired, warm, or clumsy). Groups such as ASTP also include open-ended questions that are intended to elicit examples of the consequences or unwanted effects students would like to see reduced, followed by a discussion of strategies that could be implemented to reduce the likelihood of those unintended consequences, and may or may not incorporate personalized feedback (Kivlahan, Marlatt, Fromme, Coppel, & Williams, 1990; E. Miller, Kilmer, Kim, Weingardt, & Marlatt, 2001). When delivered to individuals, interventions can be delivered in a variety of settings and through a range of methods; when in an individually focused intervention like BASICS, the presentation of personalized graphic feedback is included (Marlatt et al., 1998; Dimeff, Baer, Kivlahan, & Marlatt, 1999).

In BASICS, students complete an alcohol screening that collects information on a range of variables assessing drinking and related behaviors or consequences, and the data from this assessment is used to generate personalized graphic feedback. The student meets with a BASICS facilitator who utilizes motivational interviewing strategies as the feedback is reviewed with the student (for more information on brief interventions like, this see chapter 9). Although these individual feedback strategies can be effectively delivered in a variety of ways including computerized or mailed feedback, in-person interventions may provide the best opportunity to meet the student where he or she is, and to understand the student's unique risks, reasons for drinking, and potentially reasons for wanting to change drinking. Additionally, the in-person intervention could provide the most dynamic opportunity to explore and highlight areas of importance to the student to find the proverbial "hook" or reason for change, and could be used to support the student's self-efficacy by identifying strategies acceptable to the student to implement less risky behaviors. The student's selection of a goal for behavior change (which may include but isn't necessarily abstinence), a key component of BASICS, is absolutely consistent with the harm-reduction approach. Further, this emphasis on meeting the student where he or she is in terms of their readiness to change, what the student sees as important in his or her life, and even what role alcohol plays for the student is consistent with harm-reduction principles. What makes BASICS a clear example of a harm-reduction strategy involves the emphasis on strategies that do not necessarily involve abstinence but that reduce unwanted harms or consequences. Instead, the student who has decided to make a change in his or her drinking as a function of reviewing the personalized feedback could try to change behaviors surrounding the drinking context (e.g., avoiding or altering his or her approach to drinking games, not accepting a drink when the contents are unknown), change what he or she drinks (e.g., drinking the same number of standard drinks, but drinking those that are less potent and concentrated), or change the rate of drinking (e.g., slowing down, pacing drinking, or alternating alcoholic with nonalcoholic drinks). The student is approached from a collaborative, compassionate perspective while supporting autonomy and self-efficacy in any decisions to minimize or alter use. The pragmatism of the intervention stems from not demanding abstinence when this goal is seen as unrealistic for the student, and accepting that underage and/or problematic drinking may continue to occur particularly given the social and contextual factors that maintain consumption, but acknowledging that reduction of harm and increase of satisfaction is still a viable and attainable outcome.

INFORMATION ON FACTORS CONTRIBUTING TO HARM THAT CAN BE INCLUDED IN HARM-REDUCTION INTERVENTIONS

It has been demonstrated that information-only prevention programs tend to increase knowledge but may not result in behavior change (Larimer & Cronce, 2002, 2007). However, providing information in the context of motivational enhancement interventions can often be helpful. For example, explaining alcohol-related phenomena that can contribute to student experiences could result in a student making connections between his or her current behavior and ways in which changes in drinking could result in changes in these experiences or consequences. We briefly summarize some of the areas in which information (delivered in the context of a discussion of what the student has experienced and sees as problematic) could be used during a harm-reduction intervention. These considerations may be overlooked during an abstinence-only program as discussions of varying effects while under the influence of alcohol might not be explored, whereas harm reduction provides the ideal opportunity to discuss risks and benefits along the spectrum between abstinence and continued heavy, unregulated drinking.

Alcohol myopia. Steele and Josephs (1990) describe alcohol myopia (which, in optical terms, refers to near-sightedness) as a phenomenon in which alcohol results in a "myopic" focus on certain cues, including concrete cues in the environment and cues that are related to what a person is immediately feeling. In any given situation, inhibiting cues or factors are present (e.g., worrying about saying or doing something that one later regrets) as are impelling cues or factors (e.g., finding something as funny or seeing something as a great idea at the time). Alcohol myopia theory suggests that when under the influence of alcohol, impelling cues are most salient and tend to be focused on at the expense of inhibiting cues (M. A. Lewis, Rees, Logan, Kaysen, & Kilmer, 2010; Steele & Josephs, 1990). Given that the most frequently endorsed consequence by college students is doing something they later regretted, providing information about alcohol myopia (particularly if a person sees consequences as unwanted) could serve to prompt contemplation of change or result in connections being made between the BACs a student is typically achieving and the consequences he or she is experiencing as a result.

Aggression. As campuses continue to emphasize the importance of violence prevention efforts, considering the role that alcohol can play is certainly relevant. One contributing factor to aggression could be alcohol myopia—a person is more likely to attend to an impelling cue (e.g., "that person bumped into me on purpose — I should shove him back") and is less likely to attend to inhibiting cues (e.g., "I'm the one that ran into him, and it's not that big a deal" or "if I hit this person, there will be consequences"). However, it appears more complicated than this, because a person's beliefs and expectancies about alcohol cannot be considered separately from the situation. Lang, Goeckner, Adesso, and Marlatt (1975) demonstrated that men who believed they were drinking alcohol (even when they weren't) behaved more aggressively than men who expected a nonalcoholic drink (and nevertheless received alcohol) regardless of whether they were provoked or not. A person dealing with the consequences of recurrent alcohol-related aggressive actions may want to see the harm from these reduced, and this is another case where a motivational discussion concerning the role of alcohol in increasing aggression could prompt movement toward change.

Tolerance. For some students, the primary harm they are trying to avoid could be an alcohol poisoning or concern of being addicted or developing a "problem." They may view other physical consequences such as blacking out, passing out, vomiting, or other consequences as "normal" or not that worrisome. Students may even see tolerance as desirable if their sense is that they can "hold" their liquor, allowing them to party longer, while others are "lightweights." However, tolerance is a factor associated with dependence, and could be related to other harms a student sees as unwanted (e.g., the financial and caloric impact of needing more alcohol to achieve a desired effect). When the harm a student hopes to avoid is, in fact, an extreme outcome like an alcohol poisoning, the emphasis is still on examining strategies that will reduce the likelihood of this outcome occurring. This could involve setting drink limits that will be up to and not exceeding blood alcohol levels where a risk of death could be a possibility. Alternatively, this could involve being aware of other factors associated with an overdose and planning accordingly. For example, Siegel and Ramos (2002) describe the role that learning plays in the development of tolerance, and explained that through classical conditioning, familiar cues could become conditioned stimuli that elicit an anticipatory response in the body opposite of the direction a substance acts. In studies with college students, these cues can even include taste, such that a student demonstrates greater tolerance to a familiar tasting beverage (meaning that they are in the presence of a familiar tasting cue) than to a novel tasting beverage of the same potency (Siegel, 2005). The harm-reduction implications related to this tolerance research would therefore include being aware of instances or episodes in which typical cues are absent, and to then drink less in these settings or in the absence of typical cues. This research, when presented to students within a harm-reduction framework, can also help eliminate cognitive dissonance between what the science tells us about subjective effects at varying blood alcohol levels and the student's actual experience. Abstinence-only interventions would not consider instruction on maintaining a lower blood alcohol level or focus on the self-awareness required to stop or alternate beverages to maintain the positive effects while minimizing potential consequences. This intervention approach gives us an opportunity to increase critical thinking and planning in college student clients as well as to minimize harm in novel situations.

Time. Time can be quite valuable to college students, and is often overlooked as a potential hook for motivation to change. Although students often have some understanding of how many hours they drink on how many different days, they are often unaware of the time required to completely metabolize alcohol. In addition to the hours spent "partying," there is a secondary consideration of the time it takes for one's blood alcohol level to return to .00%. In other words, a student may be actively drinking from 10 p.m. until 2 a.m. (4 hours), but may retain a positive BAC for a significant number of hours later. If that student achieved a BAC of .08%, the alcohol would remain in the system for approximately 5 hours. At .16%, 10 additional hours would be impacted, and at .24%, in addition to an increased likelihood of blacking out and/or passing out, that student would carry a positive blood alcohol level for 15 additional hours. In the previous example in which the student stopped drinking at 2 a.m., this student would still have detectable alcohol in her system until 5 p.m., would be in excess of the .08% legal driving limit until noon, and would not have reached a safe driving level (.00%) until dinnertime. For the student who feels strongly about avoiding drinking and driving, this information could generate concern and a subsequent desire to reduce drinking.

The slow rate of oxidation has significant potential impacts for the student beyond driving as well. In short, a 4-hour drinking occasion just became 20 hours of being possibly compromised by alcohol. There is increased stress placed on the liver when the body is processing alcohol for that many consecutive hours. The cognitive abilities required to complete homework or attend classes are compromised, as are motor coordination and reaction time. Decision making would also be impaired until well into the afternoon, which has additional implications for any chosen activities. Further, the student's quality of sleep during the night would have been compromised given the presence of alcohol, with a particular impact on rapid eye movement (REM) sleep being suppressed (Roehrs & Roth, 2001). The most clearly documented impact following this disruption of sleep cycles is daytime fatigue and sleepiness; noteworthy is that students identify sleep difficulties as the second most endorsed contributor to academic problems (17.8% of students) behind only stress (25.4% of students)

(ACHA, 2011). If a "hook" for a student is trying to improve his or her grades or if a student sees fatigue and tiredness as his or her primary challenge, the relationship to alcohol consumption could be examined, as could ways in which changes in alcohol use could result in changes in these unwanted outcomes.

Harm reduction and the proverbial "hook." Once we've found a hook, whether it be decision making, aggression, tolerance, time (including time spent intoxicated or time directed to alcohol consumption at the expense of time allocated to other valued activities), or calories (or for that matter, financial cost, embarrassment, academic failure, etc.), a harm-reduction approach will attempt to minimize the unwanted effects on the student. Many of these consequences can be minimized or eliminated entirely if one goes up to but does not exceed a moderate BAC of .06% (this limit can be set by a student through use of a personalized blood alcohol chart, and will be impacted by the student's birth sex, weight, number of drinks consumed, and time spent drinking). This level has been identified as the "Point of Diminishing Returns" (Dimeff et al., 1999), where one more drink is not likely to increase the euphoric experiences but is likely to intensify the dysphoric effects. This information about the biphasic effect of alcohol helps to puts students' experiences in a context (e.g., a student understands why drinking more to reclaim a lost buzz does not result in getting the same buzz back, and instead results in feeling tired or sick), and a decision might be made to select a moderate (and presumably less harmful) drinking limit to maximize the positives and minimize the depressant effects. Further, by choosing to go up to but not exceed this .06% BAC, many of the "hook" consequences described previously would be minimized or avoided entirely, including little to no effect on decision making and greatly fewer hours spent oxidizing the alcohol. Granted, a student might still see a higher BAC as more pleasurable and might be drinking to achieve intoxication effects (e.g., Murphy, Barnett, & Colby, 2006)—if the student nevertheless acknowledges that there are some unwanted effects associated with drinking in that way and would like to reduce these, sets a new limit that is lower than a previously attained BAC (even if still above .06%), which will result in reduced harms, then any steps toward reduced risk are steps in the right direction. For example, particularly when personalized charts are not available, a student might choose to avoid "binge" drinking (defined as 4/5 drinks for men/women) by setting a limit below that level.

HARM-REDUCTION STRATEGIES

Once we have elicited personally relevant reasons for changing and identified realistic goals, harm-reduction strategies can then include protective behavioral strategies (PBS), or cognitive-behavioral strategies that can reduce alcohol consumption and/or consequences. These strategies can target different aspects of drinking (e.g., decreased consumption vs. fewer harms), and can occur before, during, or after drinking. For some students, the decision to make changes related to their drinking with the hope of reducing, minimizing, or avoiding harms could be accompanied by the need to learn new strategies or behaviors. These are often strategies that would never get discussed in a prevention or intervention program focusing on an abstinence-only outcome; it is acknowledged that drinking might very well occur, and the emphasis is on approaching drinking in a less dangerous or less risky way.

The assessment of protective behavioral strategies (PBS) can be done to get a sense of what behaviors are already being utilized by a student and what strategies might be attractive to the student. There are two primary scales of PBS: the Protective Behavioral Strategies Scale (PBSS; Martens et al., 2005; Martens, Pedersen, LaBrie, Ferrier, & Cimini, 2007c) and the Strategy Questionnaire (Sugarman & Carey, 2007) that can be used to assess behaviors a student is already engaging in or, for purposes of discussion during an intervention, could consider implementing. These measures group strategies under three separate categories each: the PBSS measures strategies under Stopping/Limiting Drinking, Manner of Drinking, and Serious Negative

Table 6.1 Protective Behavioral Strategies (PBS) Relevant to Harm-Reduction interventions With College Student Drinkers

Protective Behavioral Strategies Scale

Stopping/Limiting Drinking

- Determine not to exceed a set number of drinks
- Alternate alcoholic and nonalcoholic drinks
- Have a friend let you know when you have had enough to drink
- Leave the bar/party at a predetermined time
- Stopping drinking at a predetermined time
- Drink water while drinking alcohol
- Put extra ice in your drink

Manner of Drinking

- Avoid drinking games
- Avoid drinking shots of liquor
- Avoid mixing different types of liquor
- Drink slowly rather than gulping or chugging
- Avoid trying to "keep up" or "out-drink" others

Avoiding Serious Negative Consequences

- Use a designated driver
- Make sure you go home with a friend
- Know where your drink has been at all times

(Martens et al., 2005; Martens et al., 2007c)

Table 6.1   *(continued)*

Strategy Questionnaire

Selective Avoidance

+ Avoid situations where heavy drinking is likely

+ Alternate alcohol and nonalcoholic drinks

+ Refuse drinks

+ Avoid risky situations/behaviors including doing shots, funneling or "shotgunning" beers, drinking games, and "pregaming" or drinking before going out

Strategies While Drinking

+ Drink slowly

+ Drink less-concentrated beverages

+ Keep track of drinks

+ Space drinks out

+ Limit drinking to certain days of the week

+ Limit cash and avoid carrying credit/ATM cards while drinking

+ Eat before and while drinking

+ Engage in other activities to space drinks out

+ Be aware of internal cues of intoxication

Alternatives

+ Participate in activities that don't involve alcohol

+ Practice social skills without alcohol

+ Find other ways to reduce stress

+ Be prepared with coping strategies in high-risk situations

(Sugarman & Carey, 2007)

Consequences, while the Strategy Questionnaire focuses on Selective Avoidance, Strategies while Drinking, and Alternatives (see Table 6.1 for a complete list of strategies and categories).

Theoretically, these strategies are entirely consistent with harm-reduction approaches. The sheer number of strategies in the table (which, although inclusive, is by no means exhaustive) demonstrates the fluidity required to meet students where they are in terms of drinking. For some students, consuming fewer drinks per occasion would not be desirable but drinking on fewer days per week or ensuring a safe ride home might be possibilities. Other students may want to participate in the same number of events but restrict the number of drinks or attend without drinking at all. Students seeking abstinence would also choose strategies consistent with their goals, including alternatives and refusal skills. Although an abstinence-only intervention would ignore the majority of these strategies, harm-reduction approaches offer choices.

Are these choices and alternatives effective? Research typically demonstrates that greater use of strategies is associated with less harm. In particular, methods involving Stopping/Limiting Drinking, Manner of Drinking, and Serious Negative Consequences have been associated with less heavy episodic drinking, fewer drinks per week, and fewer alcohol-related consequences (Martens et al., 2005, 2007a). Selective Avoidance and Alternatives were also associated with less drinking, though Strategies while Drinking was actually positively correlated with drinking in one study (Sugarman & Carey, 2007). A follow-up study found that globally increasing strategy use did not translate into decreased drinking as measured by number of drinks, average BAC, or heaviest BAC (Sugarman & Carey, 2009), though students wanting to decrease their consumption increased their use of Selective Avoidance but not Strategies while Drinking or Alternatives. In addition to direct effects on drinking, studies have also evaluated PBS as a mediator of outcomes. Barnett, Murphy, Colby, and Monti (2007) found that PBS influenced the volume of drinks (though not the frequency of drinking) among mandated students receiving an in-person intervention that included a focus on PBS, whereas there was no effect for students receiving a computer-delivered intervention. Martens, Ferrier, and Cimini (2007b) found the use of strategies mediated alcohol use and consequences but only for students drinking for positive motives (social and enhancement) with no effect for negative motives (conformity and coping). Taken together, these studies illustrate the potential impact of behavioral strategies on reducing consumption and associated harm, as well as the need for further evaluation of the complex relationship between specific strategies and other predictors of use and problems (e.g., motives, intervention delivery).

In addition to exploring the effectiveness and classification of strategies, we also need to evaluate the prevalence of these strategies among college students. The reference group from the American College Health Association's National College Health Assessment allows for an examination of the frequency with which students utilize eleven different strategies that could serve to reduce harm experienced during a drinking occasion. Fortunately, several of these strategies are already being employed by students who make the choice to drink. Excluding students who answered "Not applicable/Don't drink" to each of the items, and examining the prevalence of students using each strategy "most of the time" or "always," it appears most students who drink are already frequently staying with the same group of friends the entire time they drink (which, presumably, reduces the likelihood of getting into a questionable or dangerous scenario) (84.4%), using a designated driver (83.2%), eating before and or during drinking (which slows the rate of absorption of alcohol into the blood stream) (76.6%), keeping track of how many drinks they consumed (66%), and sticking with one kind of alcohol when drinking (50%).

However, six other strategies appear to be employed much less often, or used "most of the time" or "always" by less than half of the respondents who consume alcohol. Limit-setting strategies appear to be used less frequently whether they are based on internal cues (determining, in advance, not to exceed a set number of drinks, 41.5%) or external cues (having a friend let them know when they've had enough, 38.8%). Consumption during drinking games often results in a rapid pace of consuming a considerable amount of alcohol, and avoiding drinking games was only endorsed by 37.4% of respondents. Altering drinking behaviors with an outcome of slowing consumption also appeared to be utilized less frequently, with only 31.6% pacing their drinks to one or fewer per hour, and 28.7% alternating between alcoholic and nonalcoholic drinks. Finally, the least frequently endorsed strategy, choosing not to drink alcohol (27.1%), suggests that abstinence is not a realistic or widely accepted goal for the majority of this population, though it also highlights that one in four respondents actually do choose to avoid all alcohol-related harms by not drinking in some instances.

Taken together, these studies have important implications for harm-reduction prevention and intervention work. First, there are myriad strategies available and we do not need to assume a one-size-fits-all attitude when presenting these options to students. Some students may not be willing to alter their behaviors when drinking but may be willing to go out less, while others may want to go out frequently but reduce one or two drinks in those situations. Second, many students are already using some of these strategies, which gives us the opportunity to support their self-efficacy as they are succeeding in implementation, discuss their motives in using these strategies (i.e., examine which harms are they already trying to avoid), and discuss new/ alternative strategies as additions in a toolbox of options for avoiding alcohol-related harms. Third, education about and even implementation of strategies does not necessarily translate to reductions in alcohol use, highlighting the importance of identifying reasons for change and specific behavioral plans for reducing drinks and/or limiting consequences. Finally, it is important to keep in mind that these strategies can be effective both for those who make the choice to drink (by promoting moderation techniques) and those who don't (by supporting abstinence strategies).

POLICY AS A FORM OF HARM REDUCTION

Many policies focus on community or societal harm reduction, and seek to minimize consequences through restrictions on obtaining or consuming alcohol, as well as activities performed after consumption (such as setting a blood alcohol level limit for operating a vehicle). For example, legislation setting the minimum legal drinking age at 21, banning drink specials, banning pooling of funds for purchase of kegs, and limiting the location of bars nears college campuses seeks to reduce harms associated with college and/or underage drinking, including individual consequences experienced by the drinker and community concerns such as traffic accidents and fatalities. Other harm-reduction approaches can take the form of policy by reducing or lowering barriers on access to services or assistance, or by offering programs that, on their own, can reduce harms. Consequently, although harm-reduction strategies might be explicitly discussed during individually focused brief interventions, campus-wide policy efforts also may have a harm-reduction impact. Among the most visible of these on some college campuses are amnesty policies that protect students from repercussions on campus if and when help is sought for a classmate. These policies are based on the premise that when a student needs medical attention due to alcohol use, his or her peers are reluctant to call for help for fear of getting themselves, the endangered student, or others in attendance in some sort of trouble with the institution (Oster-Aaland & Eighmy, 2007). Thus, by advertising to students that such an amnesty policy exists, and by educating students on the signs of an alcohol poisoning (and when to call for help), the hope is that harm can be reduced by connecting students with care when indicated. Although the percentage of students worrying about getting the person they are calling about in trouble seems to go down after such amnesty policies are adopted (D. K. Lewis & Marchell, 2006), policies requiring treatment after an incident necessitating medical care can have the opposite effect where students say they would be less likely to seek help for a peer (Colby, Raymond, & Colby, 2000). It is important to note that both of these policies fall under the guise of harm reduction with considerably different outcomes. Additional research is needed to examine the impact of such policies (including any unintended repercussions) and to understand any other factors associated with help seeking for alcohol-related emergencies (Oster-Aaland & Eighmy, 2007).

Other policies and programs have also been designed with reducing harm in mind, including campus-sponsored "safe rides" programs, which provide free or low-cost transportation from venues where students are likely to be drinking to their residences (thereby eliminating or reducing the risk that driving after drinking would take place) (DeJong, 1995; DeJong & Langford, 2002). Such approaches require more comprehensive evaluation, particularly if they result in the unintended impact of increasing risky drinking (National Institute on Alcohol Abuse and Alcoholism, 2002).

OPPORTUNITIES FOR APPLICATION

There are myriad opportunities for applying harm-reduction strategies on college campuses, focused on meeting students where they are in terms of their drinking. At the most global level, harm-reduction strategies can be offered through a universal prevention approach (e.g., see Larimer et al., 2007, for a review of a mailed feedback and tips intervention). Efforts like these reach abstainers and heavy drinkers alike, with the goal of reducing current (or future) harms for themselves and their peers. Students are also accessible through targeted interventions based on interests and group memberships, including residence hall–specific activities and programs for Greeks or athletes. In these situations, details can be tailored to meet the common interests of the group and promote peer support in implementing behavior change.

Opportunities for individual efforts can also occur in a variety of ways. For example, several researchers (e.g., Fleming et al., 2010; Schaus, Sole, McCoy, Mullett, & O'Brien, 2009) have demonstrated that brief interventions can be successfully delivered in campus health centers even when substance use is not directly related to a student's initial visit. Other students may be identified only after coming to the attention of campus administrators due to violation of a campus alcohol policy such as underage drinking or public intoxication. These "mandated" students afford unique challenges as they tend to be more defensive than their volunteer counterparts to discussions about their drinking (Palmer et al., 2010), but many have already identified one unwanted consequence of their drinking (i.e., getting caught) and may be more open to discussions of strategies to maintain changes they have already made (Barnett et al., 2006). Regardless, harm-reduction interventions, which emphasize the opportunity to meet these individuals where they are, particularly if they are not treatment-seeking, are a good fit.

There can be some misunderstanding on campuses about the intent of harm-reduction approaches, and some might question why anything other than an abstinence-only option is available. It seems that these often emotional arguments can best be responded to with a shift toward more empirical discussions that emphasize what the science shows about "what works" on the college campus. There is clear value in continuing to research approaches that will impact student health, including research that allows for the dissemination of accepted techniques, refines effective strategies, and defines which interventions work best for which students. It is possible that some education to administration, staff, and faculty will be needed—Nelson, Toomey, Lenk, Erickson, and Winters (2010) showed that one in five college administrators were unaware of the "Call to Action" task force report released by the National Institute on Alcohol Abuse and Alcoholism (NIAAA) in 2002, which reviewed strategies with demonstrated effectiveness in reducing drinking, consequences, or both (NIAAA, 2002), including mentions of BASICS by name.

FUTURE DIRECTIONS

As campuses continue to examine ways to best support the health and well-being of their students, it is clear that, as a field, we have a growing number of options for impacting alcohol use and related consequences. It is also clear, however, that alcohol use can co-occur with a range of other issues, including anxiety, depression, self-injury, and other drug use (see review in Kilmer & Bailie, 2012). Understanding the context in which harm-reduction strategies are implemented (and the impact they can have) is of importance, particularly for those in divisions of student life or student affairs. For example, many offices are uniquely equipped to identify students who could benefit from an intervention because of "frontline" staff who might see when a student is struggling. Their own buy-in and belief in any harm-reduction programs on campus could be important in how the program is described to a student, and their own skill in making a referral in a nonthreatening, nonjudgmental way could set the stage for a more successful intervention once the student makes it to the level of the provider.

It is clear that brief interventions like BASICS can be implemented in health and counseling centers on college campuses following a brief screening (e.g., Martens et al., 2007a), and considering ways to improve screening to reduce the likelihood of students "slipping through the cracks" is an important future direction. For example, although 20.6% of college students meet criteria for a past-year alcohol use disorder, only 3.9% of full-time students with an alcohol use disorder receive counseling or services of any kind (Wu, Pilowsky, Schlenger, & Hasin, 2007). This suggests that opportunities to identify students at risk for alcohol abuse or dependence could result in referral to brief interventions that could reduce harm or consequences experienced by that student. In fact, Hingson (2010) has suggested that if more student health services implement screening and brief interventions for every routine visit, this would increase exposure to empirically supported interventions and possibly achieve benefits across campus.

Related to health and counseling centers, with a dramatic increase in the number of students on college campuses being prescribed anti depressants and other prescription medications (Schwartz, 2006), future studies of harm-reduction interventions could consider risks related to drug interactions, factors impacting medication effectiveness, and clinical guidelines for practitioners delivering interventions. Other directions might include evaluating extensions of brief interventions with a harm-reduction focus (already proven to work with alcohol) to other substances in the college setting (e.g., marijuana, nicotine). For example, ongoing work by our colleagues has focused on evaluating brief individual, in-person interventions for marijuana use utilizing personalized feedback consistent with BASICS protocols. Other studies have targeted brief interventions to include additional concerns, like depression (Geisner, Neighbors, & Larimer, 2006). Further, with recent research providing guidance for how to best serve students sanctioned or mandated to intervention after alcohol-related violations, it is clear that research is needed to identify effective approaches for students sanctioned for marijuana and additional substances other than alcohol. Additionally, it is possible that targeting frequent heavy drinking through outreach and screening could ultimately impact other health or mental health domains. For example, Serras, Saules, Cranford, and Eisenberg (2010) evaluated self-injury behavior among undergraduate and graduate students, and found that 14.3% of students hurt themselves without the intent of killing themselves in the past year. Although a number of factors were associated with increased odds of self-injury behaviors, of note was that frequent "binge drinking" (at least three "binge drinking" occasions in the past 2 weeks) was a significant predictor of self-injury. The authors conclude that campus prevention efforts could be best directed at more frequent "binge drinkers" and those who use illicit drugs, given the potential for co-occurring threats to health and other harms (Serras et al., 2010).

Any one strategy or approach employed by a university or college to respond to harmful alcohol use will not be sufficient, and a variety of complementary individually focused and environmental approaches are likely necessary. Increasingly, as schools face financial and budgetary realities, there is consideration of which prevention program or strategy to select; the most successful efforts include environmental approaches in addition to individually focused strategies (see Fairlie, Erickson, and Wood, this volume). Because the approaches with the most success in reducing alcohol use and related consequences utilize a harm-reduction approach, it is clear that the cutting edge research undertaken in the mid-1980s and early 1990s on programs like the Alcohol Skills Training Program and BASICS was extraordinarily important in establishing a foundation for the program development, implementation, and evaluation taking place today. Whether working at a college or university in a research capacity, in applied work with students, or in a position that bridges both, the use of similar techniques related to identifying a "hook" and meeting others on campus where they are (including administrators, clinicians, and researchers) will preserve and improve the quality and scope of harm-reduction approaches.

REFERENCES

American College Health Association. (2011). *American college health association-national college health assessment II: Reference group data report fall 2010*. Linthicum, MD: American College Health Association.

Arnett, J. J. (2000). Emerging adulthood: A theory of development from the late teens through the twenties. *American Psychologist, 55*, 469–480.

Barnett, N. P., Murphy, J. G., Colby, S. M., & Monti, P. M. (2007). Efficacy of counselor vs. computer-delivered intervention with mandated college students. *Addictive Behaviors, 32*(11), 2529–2548.

Barnett, N. P., O'Leary Tevyaw, T., Fromme, K., Borsari, B., Carey, K. B., Corbin, W. R., . . . Monti, P. M. (2004). Brief alcohol interventions with mandated or adjudicated college students. *Alcoholism: Clinical and Experimental Research, 28*, 966–975.

Colby, J. C., Raymond, G. A., & Colby, S. M. (2000). Evaluation of a college policy mandating treatment for students with substantiated drinking problems. *Journal of College Student Development, 41*(4), 395–404.

Collins, S. E., Clifasefi, S. L., Logan, D. E., Samples, L., Somers, J., & Marlatt, G. A. (2011). Harm reduction: Current status, historical highlights, and basic principles. In G. A. Marlatt, M. E. Larimer, & K. Witkiewitz (Eds.), *Harm reduction: Pragmatic strategies for managing high-risk behaviors* (2nd ed., pp. 3–35). New York, NY: Guilford Press.

Cronce, J. M., & Larimer, M. E. (2011). Individual-focused approaches to the prevention of college student drinking. *Alcohol Research & Health, 34*, 210–221.

DeJong, W. (1995). *Preventing alcohol-related problems on campus: Impaired driving: A guide for program coordinators*. Newton, MA: Higher Education Center for Alcohol and Other Drug Prevention.

DeJong, W., & Langford, L. M. (2002). A typology for campus-based alcohol prevention: Moving toward environmental management strategies. *Journal of Studies on Alcohol, Suppl 14*, 140–147.

Dimeff, L. A., Baer, J. S., Kivlahan, D. R., & Marlatt, G. A. (1999). *Brief alcohol screening and intervention for college students (BASICS)*. New York, NY: Guilford Press.

Fleming, M. F., Balousek, S. L., Grossberg, P. M., Mundt, M. P., Brown, D., Wiegel, J. R., . . . Saewyc, E. M. (2010). Brief physician advice for heavy drinking college students: A randomized controlled trial in college health clinics. *Journal of Studies on Alcohol and Drugs, 71*, 23–31.

Geisner, I. M., Neighbors, C., & Larimer, M. E. (2006). A randomized clinical trial of a brief, mailed intervention for symptoms of depression. *Journal of Consulting and Clinical Psychology, 74*, 393–399.

Hingson, R. W. (2010). Commentary on Nelson, Toomey, Lenk, et al. (2010): "Implementation of NIAAA college drinking task force recommendations: How are colleges doing 6 years later?" *Alcoholism: Clinical and Experimental Research, 34*, 1694–1698.

Kilmer, J. R., & Bailie, S. K. (2012). The impact of college student substance use: Working with students on campus. In H. E. White & D. L. Rabiner (Eds.), *Substance use in college students* (pp. 235–252), New York, NY: Guilford Press.

Kivlahan, D. R., Marlatt, G. A., Fromme, K., Coppel, D. B., & Williams, E. (1990). Secondary prevention with college drinkers: Evaluation of an alcohol skills training program. *Journal of Consulting and Clinical Psychology, 58*, 805–810.

Lang, A. R., Goeckner, D. J., Adesso, V. J., & Marlatt, G. A. (1975). Effects of alcohol on aggression in male social drinkers. *Journal of Abnormal Psychology, 84*, 508–518.

Larimer, M. E., & Cronce, J. M. (2002). Identification, prevention, and treatment: A review of individual-focused strategies to reduce problematic alcohol consumption by college students. *Journal of Studies on Alcohol, Suppl 14*, 148–163.

Larimer, M. E., & Cronce, J. M. (2007). Identification, prevention, and treatment revisited: Individual-focused college drinking prevention strategies 1999–2006. *Addictive Behaviors, 32*, 2439–2468.

Larimer, M. E., Lee, C. M., Kilmer, J. R., Fabiano, P. M., Stark, C. B., Geisner, I. M., . . . Neighbors, C. (2007). Personalized mailed feedback for college drinking prevention: A randomized clinical trial. *Journal of Consulting and Clinical Psychology, 75*, 285–293.

Larimer, M. E., Dillworth, T., Neighbors, C., Lewis, M. A., Montoya, H. D., & Logan, D. E. (2011). Harm reduction for alcohol use. In G. A. Marlatt, M. E. Larimer, & K. Witkiewitz (Eds.), *Harm reduction: Pragmatic strategies for managing high-risk behaviors* (2nd ed., pp. 63–106). New York, NY: Guilford Press.

Larimer, M. E., Malone, D. K., Garner, M. D., Atkins, D. C., Burlingham, B., Lonczak, H. S., . . . Marlatt, G. A. (2009). Health care and public service use and costs before and after provision of housing for chronically homeless persons with severe alcohol problems. *Journal of the American Medical Association, 301*, 1349–1357.

Leigh, B., & Lee, C. (2008). What motivates extreme drinking? In M. Martinic & F. Measham (Eds.), *Swimming with crocodiles: The culture of extreme drinking* (pp. 53–78). New York, NY: Routledge/ Taylor & Francis.

Lewis, D. K., & Marchell, T. C. (2006). Safety first: A medical amnesty approach to alcohol poisoning at a U.S. university. *International Journal of Drug Policy, 17*, 329–338.

Lewis, M. A., Rees, M., Logan, D. E., Kaysen, D. L., & Kilmer, J. R. (2010). Use of drinking protective behavioral strategies in relation to sex-related alcohol negative consequences: The mediating role of alcohol consumption. *Psychology of Addictive Behaviors, 24*, 229–238.

Logan, D. E., Henry, T., Vaughn, M., Luk, J. W., & King, K. M. (2012). Rose-colored beer goggles: The relation between experiencing alcohol consequences and perceived likelihood and valence. *Psychology of Addictive Behaviors, 26, 311–317*.

Mallett, K., Bachrach, R., & Turrisi, R. (2008). Are all negative consequences truly negative? Assessing variations among college students' perceptions of alcohol related consequences. *Addictive Behaviors, 33*, 1375–1381.

Marlatt, G. A., Baer, J. S., Kivlahan, D. R., Dimeff, L. A., Larimer, M. E., Quigley, L. A.,... Williams, E. (1998). Screening and brief intervention for high-risk college student drinkers: Results from a two-year follow-up assessment. *Journal of Consulting and Clinical Psychology, 66*(4), 604–615.

Martens, M. P., Cimini, M. D., Barr, A. R., Rivero, E. M., Vellis, P. A., Desemone, G. A., & Horner, K. J. (2007a). Implementing a screening and brief intervention for high-risk drinking in university-based health and mental health care settings: Reductions in alcohol use and correlates of success. *Addictive Behaviors, 32,* 2563–2572.

Martens, M. P., Ferrier, A. G., & Cimini, M. D. (2007b). Do protective behavioral strategies mediate the relationship between drinking motives and alcohol use in college students? *Journal of Studies on Alcohol and Drugs, 68,* 106–114.

Martens, M. P., Ferrier, A., Sheehy, M. J., Corbett, K., Anderson, D. A., & Simmons, A. (2005). Development of the protective behavioral strategies survey. *Journal of Studies on Alcohol, 66,* 698–705.

Martens, M. P., Pedersen, E. R., LaBrie, J. W., Ferrier, A. G., & Cimini, M. D. (2007c). Measuring alcohol-related protective behavioral strategies among college students: Further examination of the protective behavioral strategies scale. *Psychology of Addictive Behaviors, 21,* 307–315.

Miller, E., Kilmer, J. R., Kim, E. L., Weingardt, K. R., & Marlatt, G. A. (2001). Alcohol skills training for college students. In P. M. Monti, S. M. Colby, & T. A. O'Leary (Eds.), *Adolescents, alcohol and substance abuse: Reaching teens through brief intervention* (pp. 183–215). New York, NY: Guilford Press.

Miller, W. R., & Rollnick, S. (2002). *Motivational interviewing: Preparing people for change* (2nd ed.). New York, NY: Guilford Press.

Murphy, J. G., Barnett, N. P., & Colby, S. M. (2006). Alcohol-related and alcohol-free activity participation and enjoyment among college students: A behavioral theories of choice analysis. *Experimental and Clinical Psychopharmacology, 14,* 339–349.

National Institute on Alcohol Abuse and Alcoholism. (2002). *A call to action: Changing the culture of drinking at U.S. colleges.* NIH Publication No. 02–5010.

Nelson, T. F., Toomey, T. L., Lenk, K. M., Erickson, D. J., & Winters, K. C. (2010). Implementation of NIAAA college drinking task force recommendations: How are colleges doing 6 years later? *Alcoholism: Clinical and Experimental Research, 34,* 1687–1693.

Oster-Aaland, L., & Eighmy, M. A. (2007). Medical amnesty policies: Research is needed. *NASPA Journal, 44,* 715–727.

Palmer, R. S., Kilmer, J. R., Ball, S. A., & Larimer, M. E. (2010). Intervention defensiveness as a moderator of drinking outcome among heavy-drinking mandated college students. *Addictive Behaviors, 35,* 1157–1160.

Roehrs, T., & Roth, T. (2001). Sleep, sleepiness, and alcohol use. *Alcohol, Research, & Health, 25,* 101–109.

Schaus, J., Sole, M., McCoy, T. P., Mullett, N., & O'Brien, M. C. (2009). Alcohol screening and brief intervention in a college student health center: A randomized controlled trial. *Journal of Studies on Alcohol and Drugs, Suppl 16,* 131–141.

Schwartz, A. J. (2006). Are college students more disturbed today? Stability in the acuity and qualitative character of psychopathology of college counseling center clients: 1992–1993 through 2001–2002. *Journal of American College Health, 54,* 327–337.

Serras, A., Saules, K. K., Cranford, J. A., & Eisenberg, D. (2010). Self-injury, substance use, and associated risk factors in a multi-campus probability sample of college students. *Psychology of Addictive Behaviors, 24,* 119–128.

Siegel, S., & Ramos, B. M. C. (2002). Applying laboratory research: Drug anticipation and the treatment of drug addiction. *Experimental and Clinical Psychopharmacology, 10,* 162–183.

Siegel, S. (2005). Drug tolerance, drug addiction, and drug anticipation. *Current Directions in Psychological Science, 14,* 296–300.

Steele, C. M., & Josephs, R. A. (1990). Alcohol myopia: Its prized and dangerous effects. *American Psychologist, 45,* 921–933.

Sugarman, D. E., & Carey, K. B. (2007). The relationship between drinking control strategies and college student alcohol use. *Psychology of Addictive Behaviors, 21,* 338–345.

Sugarman, D. E., & Carey, K. B. (2009). Drink less or drink slower: The effects of instruction in alcohol consumption and drinking control strategy use. *Psychology of Addictive Behaviors, 23,* 577–585.

Vik, P. W., Culbertson, K. A., & Sellers, K. (2000). Readiness to change drinking among heavy-drinking college students. *Journal of Studies on Alcohol, 61,* 674–680.

Wu, L., Pilowsky, D. J., Schlenger, W. E., & Hasin, D. (2007). Alcohol use disorders and the use of treatment services among college-age young adults. *Psychiatric Services, 58,* 192–200.

7

Campus and Community Interventions to Reduce Alcohol Use, Abuse, and Consequences

Anne M. Fairlie, Darin J. Erickson, and Mark D. Wood

OVERVIEW AND INTRODUCTION

Given the long-standing and seemingly intractable impact of alcohol abuse among college students, there is growing recognition that substantial progress can only be achieved through the thoughtful integration of a complementary array of individual and environmental intervention approaches. As reviewed in Chapter 6 and Chapters 8–12, individual-level approaches typically seek to reduce alcohol abuse and negative consequences by altering alcohol-related cognitions, motivations, or other factors *internal* to the individual. Alternatively, and we think critically, this chapter focuses on approaches that typically target factors *external* to the individual, attempting to achieve reductions in alcohol use, abuse, and consequences by altering aspects of the environment, which can effect an individual's alcohol-related behavior.

Emerging empirical evidence suggests that environmental strategies can appreciably reduce alcohol use and problems on college campuses and their surrounding communities (DeJong & Langford, 2002; Task Force of the National Advisory Council on Alcohol Abuse and Alcoholism, 2002; Toomey, Lenk, & Wagenaar, 2007; Toomey & Wagenaar, 2002). Environmental interventions are delivered at the campus, community, state, or national level rather than the individual level. As detailed in the following sections, the target population for environmental interventions varies across strategies, ranging from the minimum legal drinking age (MLDA) law, which impacts the general population, to university-specific regulations that restrict access to alcohol on a particular campus. Other examples of environmental strategies include imposing restrictions on alcohol access by requiring beer keg registration, increasing and publicizing enforcement efforts related to alcohol-impaired driving or identification checks, and increasing alcohol excise taxes. Environmental strategies associated with mandating training for responsible beverage service apply to both on- and off-premise establishments, where alcohol consumption occurs at the site of sale for on-premise (e.g., bars) but not off-premise (e.g., liquor stores) establishments (DeJong & Langford, 2002; Toomey et al., 2007).

Historical Background

The environmental approach for reducing campus drinking problems is derived from prior community-based efforts with adults (e.g., Hingson et al., 1996; Holder et al., 1997) and adolescents (e.g., Perry et al., 1996) that targeted aspects of the physical, social, economic, and legal environments that affect alcohol consumption. With explicit recognition of the clear need to improve and expand the scope of campus prevention efforts, in 1999 the National Institute on Alcohol Abuse and Alcoholism (NIAAA) established a task force to review the literature on evidence-based strategies for reducing college student drinking and its harmful consequences. The Task Force of the National Advisory Council on Alcohol Abuse and Alcoholism (2002) issued a report for college and university officials that encouraged the incorporation of evidence-based strategies into alcohol prevention and intervention efforts.

The Task Force report characterized the prevention strategies according to a 4-tier system, which was based on the available scientific evidence at the time regarding their effectiveness in reducing alcohol use and problems. Tier 1 strategies consisted of intervention approaches that had been shown to be effective among college students and consisted entirely of interventions delivered at the individual-level for high-risk drinkers. Tier 2 strategies were those with demonstrated efficacy in the general population that could be implemented and evaluated in the college population. Several environmental approaches to reduce alcohol use and its consequences were included in the Tier 2 strategies, including enforcing the MLDA, restrictions on alcohol outlet density, increased prices and excise taxes, and responsible beverage service training. Tier 3 strategies were comprised of environmental approaches that had strong theoretical support but had yet to be rigorously evaluated, including social norms marketing campaigns and the adoption of campus-based policies that may reduce high-risk alcohol use, such as implementing alcohol-free, expanded late-night student activities. Tier 4 strategies consisted of intervention approaches that have been shown to be ineffective.

Two reports have provided a thorough summary of the research on environmental strategies, including policies to decrease social and commercial access to alcohol and to regulate the manner in which alcohol is distributed (Toomey et al., 2007; Toomey & Wagenaar, 2002). The more recent of these reviews concluded that a sufficient body of research had accumulated to support the application of environmental policies and strategies in college populations. The authors also noted that while existing research suggested that a multistrategy approach is most optimal, the empirical knowledge base could not yet yield recommendations for particular combinations of environmental approaches. Building on these and other reviews, this chapter summarizes the current evidence pertaining to environmental strategies and their effectiveness among college students. First, we present the current evidence on the effectiveness of specific environmental strategies. We then provide an overview of several multicomponent environmental interventions targeting college student drinking. Third, we discuss considerations and provide recommendations for college and university officials interested in implementing environmental strategies. We conclude by addressing barriers that college and university officials may face in implementing environmental approaches on campus and in surrounding communities.

CURRENT EVIDENCE ON ENVIRONMENTAL STRATEGIES

A variety of environmental strategies for reducing alcohol use and consequences have been empirically evaluated. This review describes environmental strategies that have been used in the general population with a special focus on college students.

MLDA and Alcohol Access

The impact and enforcement of the MLDA is one of the most well-evaluated alcohol policies (Wagenaar & Toomey, 2002). Current MLDA laws, which are consistent across all 50 states, specify that it is illegal to sell or provide alcohol to individuals under age 21. Many studies have found that lowering the drinking age during the 1970s was associated with increased consumption and traffic crash deaths among 18- to 20-year-olds. Subsequent raising of the drinking age to 21 led to decreased consumption and traffic crashes that extended downward into the adolescent population (McCartt, Hellinga, & Kirley, 2010; Voas, Tippetts, & Fell, 2003; Wagenaar & Toomey, 2002).

Despite the effectiveness of the age-21 MLDA, underage youth and young adults continue to drink alcohol and experience alcohol-related harms. Among youth, the prevalence of high-risk drinking (i.e., 5+ drinks in a row during the previous 2 weeks) steadily increases from 7.8% among 8th graders to 25.2% among 12th graders (Johnston, O'Malley, Bachman, & Schulenberg, 2010a). Among full-time college students, the prevalence of this pattern of high-risk drinking is 31.3% for women and 45.3% for men (Johnston, O'Malley, Bachman, & Schulenberg, 2010b).

One reason for the continued high level of alcohol use by youth is that the age-21 MLDA laws—which restrict the purchase, possession, and consumption of alcohol as well as the provision and sale of alcohol to underage individuals—are often not well enforced. In one study, Wagenaar and Wolfson (1995) found that few states were actively enforcing MLDA laws in the early 1990s. When enforcement did occur, it was typically directed toward underage youth, whereas little enforcement was focused on adults who illegally provided or sold alcohol to minors. As a result of low enforcement, youth have had relatively easy access to alcohol and often then become a source of alcohol for other underage youth.

Underage individuals can obtain alcohol from a variety of social and commercial sources (Fabian, Toomey, Lenk, & Erickson, 2008; Wechsler, Lee, Nelson, & Kuo, 2002). Social sources are any individuals, over or under the age of 21, who provide alcohol to underage persons. For underage college students, social access to alcohol can occur at a number of venues including parties, homes or residences, in or around licensed alcohol establishments, and in public areas. Commercial sources are licensed alcohol establishments that illegally sell alcohol to underage persons. Underage individuals who are able to purchase large quantities of alcohol (e.g., a beer keg) may then readily provide alcohol to other underage individuals.

The use of a fake ID has been identified as one of the most common methods of obtaining alcohol (Fabian et al., 2008). In a U.S. national sample, the prevalence of fake ID ownership was 7.7% for incoming first-year students (Nguyen, Walters, Rinker, Wyatt, & DeJong, 2011), but then increases dramatically during the college years. Martinez, Rutledge, and Sher (2007) found that 32% of students had obtained fake IDs by the end of their second year at one large state university, and fake ID ownership strongly predicted heavy drinking and signs of alcohol dependence, even after controlling statistically for other risk factors such as prior drinking and fraternity or sorority involvement. Martinez and Sher (2010) examined methods of fake ID obtainment and found that the most common methods were being given a fake ID by a nonrelative (45%) and purchasing a fake ID (36%).

As discussed later under recommendations, active enforcement of existing policies is needed to reduce both social and commercial access to alcohol among underage college students. Next we highlight a number of community and campus-based strategies that affect illegal access to alcohol as well as high-risk drinking among college students.

Price

Consistent with behavioral economic theory (Murphy, Correia, & Barnett, 2007), a large body of research across diverse populations strongly supports that alcohol price is inversely related to alcohol consumption and related problems (Wagenaar, Salois, & Komro, 2009). Furthermore, among college students, higher beer price is associated with fewer incidences of trouble with police or college authorities, property damage, arguments/fights, and sexual assault (Chaloupka, Grossman, & Saffer, 2002). There is also evidence that the effect of price on alcohol consumption is stronger among groups with less disposable income, like college students (Kuo, Wechsler, Greenberg, & Lee, 2003). Recent "micro-level" research provides convergent evidence of this association. Using a hypothetical alcohol purchase task with 207 college students, Skidmore and Murphy (2011) found that mean levels of hypothetical alcohol consumption were associated with drink pricing, such that higher drinks prices were associated with lower hypothetical consumption. When examining the association between price and level of intoxication among 804 bar patrons near a university, O'Mara et al. (2009) found that a 10% increase in the cost per gram of alcohol (equivalent to $1.40 per drink) was associated with a substantial reduction (30%) in the risk of intoxication (BAC $\geq$ .08%). Additional research suggests that the effect of price on alcohol consumption may vary by characteristics of the drinker, with heavy drinking college students being less sensitive to increases in price than lighter drinking students (Murphy & MacKillop, 2006).

The price of alcohol can also be increased through the implementation of policies affecting alcohol promotions, including policies that restrict happy hours or other price promotions (e.g., bottomless cups, ladies' night) in alcohol establishments. Research suggests that drink promotions are quite common around college campuses, with more than 60% of off-premise outlets offering some type of price promotions and more than 70% of on-premise establishments offering weekend beer specials (Kuo et al., 2003). Further, these drink promotions are associated with heavier self-reported alcohol use. Other research shows that states with comprehensive laws targeting underage drinking and restrictions on volume sales (e.g., happy hours), in combination with greater enforcement, had lower rates of alcohol-impaired driving among college students (Wechsler, Lee, Nelson, & Lee, 2003).

Another well-supported way to influence the price of alcohol is through tax policy. Federal taxes vary by the type of alcohol (beer, wine or spirits) and the percentage by volume of alcohol content (i.e., the strength of the alcohol). In addition, the degree to which alcohol is taxed through state-specific policies varies greatly across states. Moreover, certain states, such as New Hampshire and Massachusetts, do not impose a sales tax for alcohol. Typically, state or federal alcohol taxes are not adjusted for inflation so that, without periodic adjustments, the inflation-adjusted price of alcohol decreases over time.

In sum, many studies have shown that higher alcohol prices are associated with lower rates of alcohol use and some alcohol-related problems (see Wagenaar et al., 2009, for a meta-analytic review), including those that disproportionally affect younger drinkers (e.g., violence, unintentional injury, traffic crashes). Accordingly, the CDC's Community Guide Task Force recently recommended increasing the unit price of alcohol by raising taxes (Elder et al., 2010).

Alcohol Outlet Density

Just as price affects the availability of alcohol (through economic means), alcohol outlet density also affects the availability of alcohol. A number of studies have examined the association between the density of alcohol establishments, alcohol consumption, and a variety of alcohol-related consequences. These studies vary greatly in how alcohol outlet density is measured (e.g., population versus areal density), the size of the geographic area (e.g., city, Zip code, neighborhood), study design (e.g., ecological, hierarchical, longitudinal), and the statistical model employed. Even with this variability, these studies have consistently found that a higher alcohol outlet density is associated with higher alcohol consumption (Gruenewald, Madden, & Janes, 1992; Scribner, Cohen, & Fisher, 2000) and a higher number of associated consequences, including alcohol-impaired driving (Stout, Sloan, Liang, & Davies, 2000; Treno, Grube, & Martin, 2003), traffic crashes (Gruenewald & Johnson, 2010; Treno, Johnson, Remer, & Gruenewald, 2007), injuries (Gruenewald, Freisthler, Remer, Lascala, Treno, & Ponicki, 2010) and crime (Britt, Carlin, Toomey, & Wagenaar, 2005; Toomey et al., 2012). These positive associations have also been shown specifically among college students and around college campuses (Kypri, Bell, Hay, & Baxter, 2008; Scribner et al., 2008, 2010; Weitzman, Folkman, Folkman, & Wechsler, 2003; Williams, Chapoupka, & Wechsler, 2005). Although not specific to college populations, the CDC Community Guide, which is based on a systematic literature review, recommends limiting the density of alcohol establishments to prevent excessive alcohol use and related problems (Campbell et al., 2009).

Compliance Checks

Compliance checks are a law enforcement tool where an underage (or, more rarely, obviously intoxicated) person attempts to purchase alcohol under supervision of a law enforcement agent; if alcohol is sold, the server and/or the owner may face penalties. Several studies have assessed specific effects of compliance checks on alcohol sales to youth. Preusser, Williams, and Weinstein (1994) observed a decrease from 59% to 26% in the proportion of underage alcohol sales following three waves of compliance checks at off-premise alcohol establishments. Similarly, Grube (1997) found a substantial decrease from 45% to 16% in the proportion of underage sales at off-premise establishments in intervention communities conducting compliance checks, compared with a much smaller decrease (47% to 35%) in sales in comparison communities. In one community, following quarterly police compliance checks at off-premise establishments along with accompanying media coverage and increased penalties, Barry and colleagues (2004) found that sales to underage youth decreased from 28% to 10%. Wagenaar, Toomey, and Erickson (2005) found an immediate 17% reduction in the likelihood of sales to underage youth in on-premise and off-premise establishments that had been checked by law enforcement. However, within three months, these effects decayed to an 8.2% long-term reduction in on-premise establishments, while no long-term effects were observed among off-premise establishments.

The research indicates that it is important to conduct compliance checks at alcohol establishments and to conduct the checks frequently (i.e., several times per year) to maintain a reduction in the likelihood of alcohol sales to underage youth. The Centers for Disease Control and Prevention (CDC) Community Guide recommends use of enhanced enforcement programs (i.e., compliance checks) as an effective strategy to reduce underage purchasing (Elder et al., 2007). To date, research has not examined the effectiveness of compliance checks in noncollege communities as compared to communities that are proximal to a university or college where a greater proportion of underage persons may attempt to purchase alcohol. Proximity to a university is likely to be an important determinant of underage sales, as server behavior may vary depending on the proportion of total sales to a younger clientele.

Responsible Beverage Service

To help reduce illegal sales to underage or intoxicated students, alcohol servers, managers, and owners of retail establishments selling alcohol, whether on or near campus, can be required to attend training on how to responsibly serve alcohol. As of January 1, 2010, 36 states have laws regarding responsible beverage service (RBS) training, with a substantial amount of variability as to whether the training is voluntary or mandatory and who is trained. Statewide RBS training laws vary greatly, with stronger laws specifying the required program content (e.g., ensuring skill-building components), penalties for noncompliance with the policy, and the inclusion of active monitoring. Oregon has one of the strongest responsible beverage service laws in the United States, and researchers have found that traffic crash deaths decreased following Oregon's enactment of a responsible beverage service law (Holder & Wagenaar, 1994).

The evidence for the effectiveness of server training to prevent underage sales is somewhat mixed. A few early research studies showed that server training at alcohol establishments might decrease the likelihood of alcohol sales to underage youth and improve server behaviors (Gliksman, McKenzie, Single, & Douglas, 1993; Grube, 1997), but other studies have found that server training programs did not decrease alcohol sales to underage youth (Howard-Pitney, Johnson, Altman, & Hopkins, 1991; Lang, Stockwell, Rydon, & Beele, 1998; McKnight, 1991). What studies have consistently shown, however, is that the support of management is critical, as managers can create an environment that facilitates servers (e.g., supporting and rewarding responsible server behavior, implementing supportive policies). Recent work on manager training has shown promise, although studies suggest that training programs alone are not sufficient to prevent sales to youth (Toomey et al., 2001; Wagenaar et al., 2005).

Research on the effectiveness of responsible beverage service programs and policies for preventing sales to intoxicated patrons is also mixed. For instance, a recent randomized trial of a manager training program showed a reduction in sales to obviously intoxicated patrons, although this immediate effect had dissipated within three months of the training (Toomey et al., 2008b). Many programs have only changed servers' knowledge and attitudes or altered behaviors nonspecific to alcohol service (e.g., offering food). In summary, research has shown that not all responsible beverage service–training programs are equal, and the most effective training programs include a focus on policy development for managers and skill-building techniques for alcohol servers. Although research indicates that training programs may not by themselves reduce alcohol sales to underage or intoxicated individuals, the effectiveness of training programs may be enhanced when they are accompanied by media campaigns that publicize law enforcement efforts associated with responsible beverage service (Lang et al., 1998; Wagenaar et al., 2005).

Keg Registration

One of the primary concerns with beer kegs (bulk containers of alcohol, often eight gallons or larger) is that they are purchased by youth or adults who then make alcohol illegally available to a large number of underage youth in settings that foster heavy drinking. Effective deterrence is contingent on the belief that there is a strong likelihood that a provider would be caught and penalized. Beer keg registration laws address this by requiring that all beer kegs have a unique identifier and that retailers collect the purchaser's name and address. This enables law enforcement to identify and hold responsible the person who purchased the keg if it is found to be a source of alcohol for underage youth. As of January 1, 2010, 31 states have keg registration laws, with variability in terms of the definition of a keg, whether it is illegal to destroy the label, what purchaser information is collected, and whether a deposit is required. Although keg registration is new and has not yet been fully evaluated, initial results appear promising. Ringwalt and Paschall (2011) recently showed that strict state-level keg registration laws are associated with lower alcohol consumption and less frequent alcohol-impaired driving among teens.

Policies also can be implemented to reduce the flow of alcohol at parties held on and off campus. Presently, the research evaluating these policy recommendations is limited. Beer kegs are banned on the majority of college campuses in the United States, and studies suggest that these bans, in combination with other policies, may decrease alcohol-related problems. One study found that allowing self-service of alcohol at parties may lead to more drinking among college students (Geller & Kalsher, 1990). Another study found that serving students low-alcohol content beer may lead to lower blood alcohol content (BAC) levels than serving regular alcohol content beer, even though the students consumed the same number of drinks (Geller, Kalsher, & Clarke, 1991). Available evidence suggests that banning beer kegs, requiring the availability of low-alcohol content drinks, and banning self-service of alcohol may lead to decreased consumption and related problems. Alternatively, it may be the case that banning kegs would lead to increased consumption of inexpensive liquor, which could increase individuals' intoxication levels. Therefore, policies restricting the purchase or consumption of a particular type of alcohol may lead to altered consumption patterns associated with alternative alcoholic beverages, particularly among certain subgroups of the population such as college students. Accordingly, these potential iatrogenic effects should be considered in future evaluations.

Campus Alcohol Bans

Colleges and universities have established policies that ban alcohol from the entire campus (i.e., a dry campus) or parts of the campus, whereby persons of legal age can consume alcohol only in certain places (e.g., in residence halls). A U.S. national survey by Wechsler, Seibring, Liu, and Ahl (2004) found that approximately a third of 4-year institutions did not permit alcohol use on campus regardless of age. Research has shown that students who attend a college that bans alcohol from the entire campus were more likely to abstain from alcohol, less likely to be heavy episodic drinkers, and less likely to experience negative secondhand effects from drinking by other students (Wechsler, Lee, Gledhill-Hoyt, & Nelson, 2001a). Although part of this association is likely due to selection effects (e.g., nondrinkers opting into more restrictive environments), lower rates of heavy episodic drinking at schools with alcohol bans have been found regardless of whether students engaged in heavy episodic drinking in high school, suggesting that alcohol bans can, at least to some extent, influence the occurrence of heavy drinking in college regardless of previous drinking experience. At colleges that allow alcohol on campus, students who live in alcohol- and tobacco-free residences have been shown to be less likely to use alcohol and experience secondhand effects from other students' drinking, with stronger associations among students who did not engage in heavy episodic drinking in high school (Wechsler, Lee, Nelson, & Lee, 2001b). However, for alcohol-, but not tobacco-free residences, students' heavy drinking did not differ from that of students in housing where no such restrictions were imposed. Research has also shown that students who live in residential learning communities (RLCs), where individuals have a common interest in a particular academic theme, reported less alcohol consumption and experienced fewer alcohol-related consequences than students who did not live in RLCs (Boyd et al., 2008; McCabe et al., 2007). Moreover, compared to non-RLC students, the students in RLCs had lower drinking rates prior to college and exhibited a less pronounced increase in maximum drinks from precollege to the first college semester (McCabe et al., 2007).

Although Wechsler and colleagues (2001a) found a lower likelihood of heavy episodic drinking at schools with an alcohol ban, among students who consumed alcohol in the past 30 days, no differences were found between students at schools with a ban and those without a ban on drinking 10 or more times in a month and being intoxicated three or more times in the past 30 days. Accordingly, the need for preventive interventions and the types of interventions, such as harm reduction approaches, may be similar across campuses regardless of the presence of a campus-based alcohol ban.

Importantly, the effects of campus-based alcohol policies on consumption and related harms may vary depending on community and environmental factors (e.g., alcohol outlet density, price promotions). Campus-based alcohol policies also may fuel perceptions that university administrators are simply moving alcohol problems from the campus to nearby communities (Wood et al., 2009), which suggests potential for the use of complementary on-campus and community-based prevention efforts. More research is needed to determine the joint effects of campus-based alcohol restrictions and community-based environmental strategies on student drinking and related harms.

Class Schedules

Thursday nights have been considered, at least anecdotally, heavy drinking nights for college students. The low number of Friday morning classes may be a contributing factor, with drink specials and promotions of campus-area bars and restaurants potentially reinforcing this effect. Although the effect of Friday classes on Thursday night drinking has long been theorized, few studies have been conducted in this area (Paschall, Kypri, & Saltz, 2006; Wood, Sher, & Rutledge, 2007). Research suggests that students who do not schedule a class on Friday are more likely to drink heavily on Thursday night than students with an early Friday morning class, and this effect was found to be more pronounced among men (Wood et al., 2007). It is worth noting that bi-directional effects could be responsible for these findings—having a lighter Friday class schedule increases Thursday night drinking *and* heavy drinking students are less likely to sign up for Friday classes. Skidmore and Murphy (2011), using a hypothetical alcohol purchase task, manipulated next-day responsibilities and observed that having a test the next day was associated with lower hypothetical consumption, suggesting the potential utility of increasing Friday responsibilities (e.g., test administration on Fridays) for reducing Thursday night drinking. As a result of the increased attention on the role of class schedules in student drinking behavior, some colleges have begun to institute policies that increase the offering of classes on Friday morning. Additional research is needed, especially intervention research where class schedule is varied experimentally, to determine whether these policies reduce student drinking behavior on Thursday nights.

Alcohol-Free and Alternative Activities

Alcohol-free activities and venues are commonly used to minimize heavy drinking among students and have long been highlighted as a way to reduce alcohol consumption (DeJong et al., 1998; Vicary & Karshin, 2002; Wechsler et al., 2002). The Task Force (2002) identified "implementing alcohol-free, expanded late night activities" as a Tier 3 strategy. In a recent survey of 22 colleges, Ringwalt, Paschall, and Gitelman (2011) found that, among 48 prevention strategies, creating and promoting new alcohol-free events and settings was the lone strategy endorsed by all colleges. To date, however, there has been little research to evaluate the effectiveness of alcohol-free activities and venues to reduce student alcohol use and associated problems. Noted concerns include program costs and limited reach in terms of both the frequency of these events as well as the number of students who attend them (Toomey, Lenk, Nelson, & Jones, in press). An additional concern is that alcohol-free events may increase the likelihood of drinking *before* the event (e.g., "pregaming") (DeJong, DeRicco, & Schneider, 2010).

Wei, Barnett, and Clark (2010) recently conducted the first study to use an event-focused approach to compare alcohol consumption at alcohol-free and alcohol-serving campus events. They examined the attendance of more than 500 students across 59 campus parties in relation to the students' typical alcohol use as well as their event-night alcohol use, intoxication, and pregaming behavior. The investigators found that rates of attendance at alcohol-serving parties were twice as high as those at alcohol-free parties (90% versus 44% of the sample). Students who had attended an alcohol-free party reported significantly fewer alcohol-related problems than those who had not attended an alcohol-free party. Among students who had attended both alcohol-serving and alcohol-free parties, students drank significantly more in terms of frequency and quantity on nights they had attended alcohol-serving parties compared to alcohol-free parties. Of interest, although more drinks were consumed before the alcohol-free parties than the alcohol-serving parties, this greater number of drinks did not appear to enhance risk. Specifically, when attending alcohol-free parties, students attained average estimated BACs that were nearly half of that obtained when attending alcohol-serving parties, suggesting the potential utility of alcohol-free programming.

In sum, it appears that although alcohol-free events can promote less risky drinking, they appear to be less appealing in terms of student attendance. As noted by Wei et al. (2010), future research investigating factors that enhance the appeal of alcohol-free events are needed.

Social Norms Marketing Campaigns

Over the past two decades, social norms marketing (SNM) has been, arguably, the most commonly used and widely publicized campus-based approach aimed at reducing collegiate alcohol abuse, prompting Keeling (2000, p. 53), in a special journal issue on social norms research, to identify it as "de rigueur in campus health promotion." The impetus for SNM came from Perkins and Berkowitz (1986), who proposed correcting ubiquitous student misperceptions about others' drinking as a simple and efficient means of reducing heavy episodic drinking.

Initial support was provided in a 5-year quasi-experimental design (Haines & Spear, 1996). SNM was introduced in Year 3, with survey data revealing significant drops (18.5%) in normative perceptions of heavy episodic drinking as well as self-reported heavy episodic drinking (9%) by Year 5, contrasted with relatively stable national trends in heavy episodic drinking from the Monitoring the Future Study (Johnston, O'Malley, & Bachman, 1993). Supportive results were also observed in numerous additional small-scale quasi-experimental or single-group pretest–posttest designs (Perkins, 2002). Citing a lack of evidence from randomized trials, the NIAAA Task Force on College Drinking designated SNM as a Tier 3 intervention due to strong theoretical support but a lack of rigorous empirical evidence.

Subsequently, the most methodologically rigorous SNM study to date, a multisite randomized trial of SNM, observed modest intervention effects in its initial investigation (DeJong et al., 2006) with a failure to replicate in the second investigation (DeJong et al., 2009b). Subsequent analysis on the moderating effect of alcohol outlet density suggests that the SNM interventions used in this study were less effective when implemented on campuses in "wetter" communities (e.g., higher on-premise alcohol outlet density in the community) (Scribner et al., 2011). Another recent study by Turner, Perkins, and Bauerle (2008) evaluated an SNM campaign that initially targeted first-year students and was adapted incrementally over six years to target the undergraduate student body as a whole. Using cross-sectional annual surveys, results showed significant increases across survey years in the likelihood of *not* experiencing alcohol-related consequences. Furthermore, among first-year students, recall of campaign messages was significantly related to reductions in consequences. Although the use of a single site facilitated the ability to saturate the campus with SNM messages, the nonrandomized, single-site/no-comparison design substantially limits the interpretation of these findings.

Despite widespread popularity, practical and conceptual appeal, and relatively cost-efficient implementation, overall support for SNM interventions in reducing alcohol use and consequences remains modest (see Toomey et al., 2007, for a similar conclusion). Strong inferences regarding the efficacy of this approach have been substantially hampered by a continued overreliance on substandard designs. Given the current state of knowledge, we recommend caution in adopting SNM campaigns, particularly as a stand-alone intervention. Multisite randomized trials, on a scale smaller than that of DeJong and colleagues' study, that combine needed methodological rigor with the ability to strongly implement the intervention would provide needed resolution on this approach. Research examining the effectiveness of SNM as compared to and in conjunction with other environmental approaches, such as increased enforcement on or near campuses is also needed.

Multicomponent Environmental Interventions

Potential approaches and considerations. Thus far we have focused on the isolated effects of environmental strategies on college student alcohol use and related harms. It is also important to simultaneously test multipronged environmental interventions to determine whether a more comprehensive approach results in even greater reductions in alcohol use and related harms.

Multicomponent environmental interventions can include any combination of environmental strategies, and as a result they typically involve numerous campus and community sectors, depending on the types of strategies being implemented. For instance, evaluating the effectiveness of roadside DUI checkpoints or police party patrols cannot occur without input and cooperation with local law enforcement, and it is widely recognized that publicizing such initiatives is also critical for maximizing effectiveness. Typically, multicomponent interventions involve collaboration between the campus (e.g., campus substance use prevention members, student affairs office) and local (e.g., local law enforcement, on- and off-premise alcohol retail establishments, neighborhood organizations) communities, and may also include the involvement of stakeholders, such as undergraduate students and concerned citizens from the community. Therefore, the delivery of multicomponent interventions is complicated by the need to organize a group of campus and community members around a common goal or set of goals and decisions about the intervention strategies to be implemented in order to achieve the stated goals.

Studies evaluating the effectiveness of multicomponent interventions have varied in the degree to which the campus and community members have been able to choose which alcohol-related issues to focus on and which strategies to implement. For example, Wagoner, Rhodes, Lentz, and Wolfson (2010) allowed the campus community partnerships to select from a list of most promising strategies, whereas Saltz and colleagues (Nygaard & Saltz, 2010; Saltz, Paschall, McGaffigan, & Nygaard, 2010) used a more directive approach for intervention delivery in the planning and implementation phases.

Empirically tested multicomponent intervention trials. Past reviews suggest that multicomponent environmental approaches are promising tools for reducing alcohol use and problems among college students (Toomey et al., 2007). Notably, the "A Matter of Degree Program" was a multicomponent intervention targeting college student alcohol use (Weitzman, Nelson, Lee, & Wechsler, 2004). The specific intervention components varied across schools, with the most commonly targeted activities addressing alcohol availability (e.g., keg registration, RBS training), legal sanctions (e.g., police enforcement at parties), and the sociocultural context (e.g., alcohol-free programming). Although campuses were not randomly assigned to condition, the study benefited from the inclusion of 10 intervention campuses and 32 comparison campuses. The 10 intervention campuses did not significantly differ from the comparison campuses on the alcohol consumption outcomes, and limited effects were observed for alcohol-related problems. However, the five sites with the highest levels of implementation did exhibit declines in alcohol consumption and alcohol-related problems in contrast to predominantly increasing or stable trends at the comparison sites (Weitzman et al., 2004).

Although college students were not a specific target, the Communities Mobilizing for Change on Alcohol (CMCA) project evaluated the effects of a 15-community randomized trial among 18- to 20-year-olds, high school students, and alcohol establishments (Wagenaar et al., 2000a; Wagenaar, Murray, & Toomey, 2000b). The intervention targeted alcohol sales to underage individuals, alcohol availability through social sources, and community norms associated with underage drinking, and the authors reported an overall intervention effect across alcohol outcomes for 18- to 20-year-olds and significant intervention effects for this age group on the provision of alcohol to an underage person.

College students were also targeted in a test of a multicomponent intervention designed to reduce driving under the influence (DUI) (Clapp et al., 2005). Using a quasi-experimental design, one university served as the comparison school and a second university served as the intervention school, with seven surveys administered across the 3-year study period at both campuses. Intervention components included increased law enforcement (i.e., DUI checkpoints, DUI patrols), as well as local and campus media coverage on DUI and those enforcement activities. Self-reported DUI rates were significantly lower at the intervention school compared to relatively stable rates at the comparison school; comparisons of alcohol use rates between the schools were not reported. This study suggests that environmental strategies may be effective for reducing alcohol-impaired driving among college students.

Several multicomponent environmental interventions have been empirically tested among college student populations since the publication of the most recent review by Toomey and colleagues (2007). Two recent studies were conducted to investigate the effects of multicomponent environmental interventions as part of the Rapid Response to College Drinking Problems initiative (Saltz, Welker, Paschall, Feeney, & Fabiano, 2009; Wood et al., 2009). The Rapid Response initiative was developed in response to the Task Force (2002) report to bring together alcohol research scientists and college and university officials and advance the science on college drinking prevention through the evaluation of targeted research projects (DeJong, Larimer, Wood, & Hartman, 2009a).

Saltz and colleagues (2009) evaluated a multicomponent intervention called Neighborhoods Engaging with Students (NEST) that used alcohol control strategies and an education campaign. A quasi-experimental design was used with one university serving as the comparison site and two universities serving as the intervention sites without randomization to condition. The interventions differed somewhat across the two sites, since the second intervention site was initially recruited as a comparison site but received separate funding for a similar intervention and was retained instead as an intervention site. The three key components of NEST were enforcement activities (e.g., increased party patrols and increased compliance checks within 2 miles of campus), neighborhood engagement strategies (e.g., education regarding responsibilities when living in a community, neighborhood forums), and late-night activities on campus that targeted underage, first-year students. At each school, students were surveyed at baseline and then one year later using random cross-sectional samples of undergraduate students. The students at the two intervention schools, in contrast to those at the comparison school, reported significant reductions in the likelihood of any heavy drinking (five or more consecutive drinks in the past 2 weeks) and in the frequency of heavy drinking. No significant intervention effects were observed for the number of drinks consumed when students last partied or socialized, the number of times drunk at off-campus parties, or the number of consequences experienced.

The Common Ground project evaluated a multicomponent environmental approach using a nonrandomized design with one intervention campus and one comparison campus (Wood et al., 2009). Phase 1 of the intervention publicized student support of alcohol control policies. Phase 2 of the intervention consisted of increased local law enforcement efforts, a responsible beverage service program with local retailers, and an on-campus media campaign. The media campaign publicized local enforcement efforts, university policies, alcohol-related state laws, and chapter reform efforts among fraternity and sorority members. The campus-community coalition was involved in prevention efforts at the intervention campus, but a direct approach was ultimately implemented by research staff to more readily engage local police and alcohol retailers in targeted intervention efforts. A series of random-sample cross-sectional surveys were conducted at the intervention campus (four annual surveys) and the comparison campus (three annual surveys). Wood and colleagues reported a linear increase in awareness of formal alcohol control efforts, perceived likelihood of consequences for alcohol-impaired driving, and perceived likelihood of responsible alcohol service. Larger effect sizes were observed at the intervention campus compared to smaller or opposite effects observed at the comparison campus. Local police report data showed a 27% decrease in student-specific arrests and citations at the intervention campus. However, no significant differences were found across survey years on self-reported alcohol use behaviors or alcohol-impaired driving at either the intervention or comparison campuses. Of note, DUI checkpoints (i.e., sobriety checkpoints) are considered unconstitutional in the state where this study was conducted, therefore, rendering it impossible to include them as part of the environmental intervention. Given demonstrated effectiveness of other studies that have included DUI checkpoints (Clapp et al., 2005), Wood et al. speculated that DUI checkpoints may be an important component of environmental interventions targeting drinking and driving in the college population.

The Safer California Universities study used a community-based approach with campus liaisons to target heavy alcohol use at off-campus settings including fraternity and sorority houses (Nygaard & Saltz, 2010; Saltz et al., 2010). Fourteen public universities were matched on baseline alcohol data, and half of the universities were randomly assigned to receive the intervention. The intervention consisted of enforcement activities (i.e., DUI checkpoints, compliance checks, party patrols) and publicity for those efforts (e.g., Web site, newspaper articles, email). At each intervention campus, one or two campus liaisons were responsible for coordinating task force members and implementing the intervention activities (Nygaard & Saltz, 2010). Four surveys were conducted annually with random cross-sectional samples of undergraduate students. Students were asked about attendance at and drinking in six targeted settings: fraternity or sorority (Greek) party, residence hall party, campus event (e.g., football game), off-campus party, bar/restaurant, and an outdoor setting (e.g., public park). Relative to the comparison schools, students at the intervention schools showed significant reductions in reports of getting drunk the last time they went to an off-campus party and a bar/restaurant as well as the last time they went to any of the six settings. However, no intervention effects were observed for the risk of intoxication at a Greek party, a dorm party, a campus event, or outdoors. A similar pattern of findings was observed for the risk of being intoxicated at least once during the semester at each of the six settings and the proportion of occasions that students reported getting drunk at each of the six settings. Secondary analyses suggested that intervention effects were stronger at universities with a higher level of program implementation.

Glassman and colleagues provide a case study report of a social marketing intervention that included a media campaign focusing on the social consequences of excessive alcohol consumption (e.g., embarrassment, social rejection), increased police enforcement, and the offering of alcohol-free activities (Glassman, Dodd, Miller, & Braun, 2010). The authors reported a downward trend for heavy episodic drinking and alcohol-impaired driving over the 3.5-year study period. It should be noted that the case study has several important limitations (e.g., inclusion of a single university, low-response rate, limited outcome analyses) that limit the ability to draw firm conclusions. Nevertheless, it does constitute a recent example of a multicomponent intervention that implemented environmental strategies.

One concern about multicomponent environmental interventions for college student populations is that the rigor of the research designs varies. For instance, although some studies used random assignment to conditions (e.g., Saltz et al., 2010), most did not (e.g., Glassman et al., 2010; Saltz et al., 2009; Weitzman et al., 2004; Wood et al., 2009). The methodological limitations of the studies thus limit the ability to draw causal inferences about intervention effects. Furthermore, although it is common to include intervention components that address alcohol availability and policy enforcement and then publicize those efforts with a media campaign, the inclusion of multiple environmental strategies makes it difficult to identify the effectiveness of any given strategy or subset of strategies. Available evidence does suggest that level of implementation has a substantial impact on intervention effectiveness, with greater program implementation producing more favorable results.

Social capital. Social capital is one potential avenue of research that may be particularly informative in the context of multicomponent environmental interventions to reduce college student alcohol use. Social capital is a conceptual category, rather than a singular construct, that encompasses social networks, civic participation, and norms of reciprocity (Putnam, 2004; Szreter & Woolcock, 2004). There is debate on the definition and types of social capital (i.e., bonding, bridging, linking) and whether the construct should be measured at the individual- or society-level (Putnam, 2004; Szreter & Woolcock, 2004). Social capital has been hypothesized to affect health and health behaviors via a variety of mechanisms, such as social support, communication patterns, and social identity (Putnam, 2004).

To date, a limited number of studies have examined social capital in the context of college student alcohol use (Theall et al., 2009; Weitzman & Chen, 2005; Weitzman & Kawachi, 2000). In these studies, social capital was operationalized as volunteer- ism or participation in various organizations (e.g., fraternity or sorority membership, religious group). Weitzman and colleagues (Weitzman & Chen, 2005; Weitzman & Kawachi, 2000) observed a negative association between campus-level social capital, in the form of volunteerism, and alcohol-related outcomes, whereas Theall et al. (2009) observed a negative association between individual-level, but not campus-level, social capital and alcohol-related outcomes.

A more in-depth understanding of the *culture* of college student drinking may be necessary to successfully integrate social capital within environmental preventive interventions, especially given the real social benefits associated with drinking and the critical importance of social-developmental competencies in emerging adulthood. For example, it may be valuable to incorporate research on the development of social capital within the study of college students' reasons or motives for drinking given the role of social and facilitative motives in alcohol consumption (LaBrie, Hummer, & Pedersen, 2007; Lee, Geisner, Lewis, Neighbors, & Larimer, 2007). In addition, it is possible that research on the development of social capital among college populations will lead to new ideas for environmental intervention strategies. Campus-level social capital, defined as volunteerism, has been positively associated with light drinking, but negatively associated with heavy episodic drinking, suggesting that social capital may relate to contextual or social aspects of drinking (Weitzman & Kawachi, 2000). Interventions that increase opportunities for social bonding, camaraderie, and dating in the context of alcohol-free activities may be more broadly appealing to students, and increase social capital, which, in turn, may result in reductions in alcohol abuse and consequences.

RECOMMENDATIONS AND CONSIDERATIONS FOR CAMPUS AND COMMUNITY ADMINISTRATORS

In this section, practical guidelines are provided for college and university officials interested in implementing environmental strategies in order to assist in the process of selection and implementation.

Identification of Campus-Specific Needs

Administrators and prevention specialists should identify key on-campus personnel who can be involved in addressing alcohol-related concerns. Individuals from a variety of campus departments (e.g., president, student affairs, substance abuse services, health services, residence life, counseling center, faculty with related interests) can mobilize as a formal group. Campus officials should then reach out to key individuals in the community, including law enforcement, owners or managers of alcohol establishments, administrators at other local colleges, and community or school-based prevention specialists. Many universities already have a campus-community coalition or task force that can focus toward a common set of agreed-upon goals.

Campus and community administrators should become knowledgeable about the extent of alcohol use behaviors and alcohol-related harms among students and in the local community [see Busteed (2002) for a number of "benchmark indicators"]. Administrators may have access to data on student alcohol-related behaviors as part of surveys conducted through student affairs or elsewhere. It is important to also track general trends in alcohol-related medical transports, on-campus substance-related infractions, and local police reports involving students in order to consider how to best direct university resources and assist students (DeJong, 2008; DeJong & Langford, 2006). As described by Neighbors and colleagues (2007), administrators and staff can monitor and target particular events (e.g., sports events, spring break, "Greek week" among fraternity and sorority members) or time periods (e.g., move-in period prior to the beginning of classes). One strategy that may reduce pregaming is altering the floor checking schedules of the resident assistants prior to major campus or nearby community events.

Other factors to consider include the number of alcohol establishments in the surrounding communities. Given the association between alcohol outlet density and alcohol use and problems, university staff can work with local municipalities to limit alcohol availability through licensing regulation. In addition, university staff can assist in targeting off-campus neighborhoods that have issues related to student parties (e.g., alcohol-impaired driving, noise, litter) in cooperation with local law enforcement and groups such as realtors, neighborhood associations and municipal governments (DeJong & Vehige, 2008). It is worth emphasizing that colleges and universities with alcohol bans should still carefully consider which alcohol-related behaviors are important targets for environmental strategies, since drinking and related harms remain a concern despite the existence of such policies (Wechsler et al., 2001a).

Selection and Implementation of Environmental Strategies

Ideally, campus and community officials would work collaboratively in selecting alcohol-related behaviors to be targeted as well as the intervention strategies to be implemented (Wagenaar et al., 1999). As highlighted in the preceding section, the process of selecting environmental strategies for reducing alcohol-related harms should be informed by the results of a needs assessment for the particular campus (DeJong, 2009; Hingson & Howland, 2002). For example, colleges or universities may offer a disproportionally low number of classes on Friday mornings. Accordingly, it may be beneficial for faculty and staff from student and academic affairs to more equally distribute the academic workload across the entire week with particular emphasis on required courses, which would make it more difficult for students to "opt-out" of taking these classes. Faculty and staff also may be encouraged to administer tests, quizzes, or other evaluative assignments during morning classes, such that attendance is expected for the completion of certain class requirements. Furthermore, the adoption of responsible beverage service policies and training or related alcohol control policies would be particularly relevant for campuses that allow alcohol service at campus events (e.g., to prevent pregaming or tailgating at sport venues), have an on-premise alcohol establishment, or have experienced problems with alcohol retailers in campus communities. Mindful of the association between price and alcohol consumption, campuses can also implement policies to ban campus advertisements of community-based price promotions and work with local municipalities and alcohol retailers to regulate and promote similar policies and practices off campus.

Responsible Beverage Service Recommendations

Campus and community administrators can become involved in advocating for the adoption of a stricter state law regarding responsible beverage service training. As support from management has been identified as a critical component of successful responsible beverage service, universities can work with the local hospitality industry to help managers convey such support to frontline staff and to provide positive publicity to participating businesses. These strategies can be extended to include compliance checks at on- and off-premise establishments. Owner and manager training should cover how to develop, communicate, and enforce policies around selling alcohol responsibly. Training of alcohol servers/sellers should focus on how to check age identification and how to refuse alcohol service to those who are underage. Establishments that have monitoring systems to ensure alcohol sales laws are being followed are less likely to sell alcohol to underage individuals (Wolfson et al., 1996). Several research studies have found that younger servers (e.g., less than 30 years old) are more likely to sell alcohol to an underage person (Forster, Murray, Wolfson & Wagenaar, 1995), although other studies have not found this association (Toomey, Komro, Oakes, & Lenk, 2008c).

Similar to preventing alcohol sales to underage patrons, states, communities, and colleges can require RBS training for servers and managers of alcohol establishments to prevent patrons from becoming highly intoxicated. The need for responsible beverage service training is clearly indicated by studies showing that alcohol servers at the majority of alcohol establishments, community festivals, and professional stadiums will serve alcohol to customers who are obviously intoxicated (Lenk, Toomey, & Erickson, 2006; Toomey, Erickson, Lenk, & Kilian, 2008a; Toomey, Erickson, Patrek, Fletcher, & Wagenaar, 2005; Toomey et al., 2004). Alcohol servers can be trained to slow service of alcohol, promote alcohol-free beverages and food, and cut off service to patrons who are already intoxicated. To encourage responsible alcohol service, managers need to be trained and incentivized to create a work environment that has clear expectations for responsible alcohol service (e.g., by setting and implementing establishment policies, backing up and rewarding servers' responsible serving behavior). Managers can also set establishment policies that directly affect alcohol use—for example, policies to serve only standard-size drinks rather than oversize drink glasses and pitchers or to set prices per drink rather than entry fees that cover the cost of drinks. RBS recommendations for on-campus events may also include the availability of low alcohol content beverages and nonalcoholic alternatives, the availability of individual-level education regarding social hosting (available to all students), and the establishment of RBS requirements (e.g., trained bartenders, nondrinking party managers) for any group holding an alcohol-service party.

As reviewed earlier, lax and inconsistent enforcement of MLDA has been documented (Wagenaar & Wolfson, 1995). In addition to the responsible beverage service recommendations suggested above, the ability to detect fake identification cards can have substantial impact in preventing sales and service to underage individuals. College and university administrators can work with local police departments and owners/managers to promulgate training of personnel in on- and off-premise establishments in the detection of false IDs. Increasingly, the use of bar codes on licenses facilitates the use of portable age-verification scanners, which can be purchased by universities or police departments and deployed at retail establishments. As with all environmental approaches, publicizing the initiative along with the penalties for use of a fake ID could appreciably augment its effectiveness.

In summary, we recommend a broadly inclusive action-oriented collective that includes key campus and community representatives. Leadership or explicit support from high-level university administrators (e.g., president, vice president for student affairs) is also critically important for conveying the message that the university seeks to partner with the local community and not merely push alcohol problems outside the campus borders.

Two points made earlier also bear reiteration here. First, results of multipronged environmental interventions suggest that intervention effects may be enhanced by targeting particular outcomes (e.g., alcohol-impaired driving, MLDA enforcement) rather than attempting to focus on a broader array of outcomes. Second, and of equal importance, level of implementation impacts effectiveness. These factors coupled with limited prevention resources firmly underscore the importance of careful consideration of benchmark and problem indicators as detailed above to inform the selection of both environmental and individual-level initiatives. In addition to the campus-level environmental interventions described here, computerized and event specific (e.g., 21st birthday) individual interventions can often be feasibly administered to the entire study body (Chapter 10, this volume). Although formal evaluation of intervention effectiveness may not be possible, continued monitoring of benchmark and problem indicators related to targeted outcomes can be used to sustain support for initiatives, provide evidence for institutionalization, or signal when a change in focus or strategies is needed.

ADDRESSING BARRIERS TO ENVIRONMENTAL PREVENTION EFFORTS

Information on the state of the evidence for college drinking interventions provided by the Task Force (2002) report and updates (Toomey et al., 2007) should assist college and university officials in selecting evidence-based strategies for implementation on their campuses. Recently, Nelson, Toomey, Lenk, Erickson, and Winters (2010) conducted a survey of 351 colleges and universities to determine the extent to which the Tier 1 and Tier 2 intervention strategies recommended by the Task Force had been implemented. They found that a striking proportion of the schools had not implemented the recommended environmentally focused intervention strategies. For instance, 86% of the schools reported that they had not collaborated with advocacy groups or other authorities about increasing the price of alcohol. Approximately 75% of the schools had not collaborated with advocacy groups or other authorities about instituting mandatory responsible beverage service training. Almost half (47%) of the schools had not collaborated with local law enforcement about compliance checks for alcohol establishments. As emphasized by Nelson and colleagues, it is crucial that future work seek to understand the barriers that may prevent greater adoption of environmental strategies. These barriers include lack of resources, most notably money and time/personnel, difficulties in creating and sustaining collaborations between university personnel and key individuals from outside the university (e.g., police, owners and managers of alcohol establishments, community leaders), and deciding which alcohol-related issues to target as well as which environmental strategies to implement.

Barriers due to lack of money and time/personnel require diligent and creative solutions, particularly in difficult economic times when university and external funds are stretched thin. University administrators may be able to reapportion part of student fees toward prevention efforts and should also consider implementing a fine system for alcohol violations, which can be directed toward these ends (Cohen & Rogers, 1997). Time and personnel barriers can be addressed by faculty and student involvement. Graduate and undergraduate student involvement in supervised research can enable prevention staff to expand their efforts while affording students a valuable professional experience. Faculty involvement in supervision can be incentivized by tangible administrative recognition of these activities as valued teaching and service contributions (e.g., considerations in teaching load determinations) (Ryan & DeJong, 1998).

We recognize from firsthand experience the difficulties inherent in creating and sustaining a broad yet functional campus and community collaborative (DeJong, 2010; Wood et al., 2009). There are no magic bullets to easily overcome divisive and potentially acrimonious perspectives on what constitutes the most pressing issues and where the responsibility for "fixing" them lies. Nonetheless, through balanced organizational structure and consistent focus on superordinate goals, demonstrable progress can be made. We refer readers to the successful examples that we have reviewed here as well as to other published guidelines for building organizational capacity (DeJong, 2010; DeJong & Langford, 2006; Florin, Mitchell, & Stevenson, 1993; Florin, Mitchell, Stevenson, & Klein, 2000; Zimmerman & DeJong, 2003) and for creating and sustaining campus-community coalitions (DeJong, 2010; Zimmerman, 2004).

Faculty researchers may be able to assist college and university administrators in determining the factors that improve the process of implementing environmental strategies. Importantly, despite its demonstrated importance, "implementation per se has been largely ignored by the research community, despite its centrality to conducting effectiveness studies" (Saltz et al., 2010, p. 499). Accordingly, greater attention to the implementation process will likely aid both college administrators and the research community. By detailing the process of implementation, college and university administrators may gain insight into how to effectively administer such strategies at their own institutions. As noted, it is widely recognized that the effectiveness of most environmental approaches is augmented by communication campaigns that publicize the initiatives. Nonetheless, the effectiveness of on-campus media campaigns, including those that publicize alcohol policies and enforcement, may subside over time as the novelty of the message wears off (Saltz et al., 2009). Accordingly, delivery of certain intervention strategies, such as long-running media campaigns, should account for the presence of a new incoming freshman class each academic year.

CONCLUSIONS

As reviewed here, environmental strategies encompass an array of both effective and promising approaches for reducing alcohol use and related harms among college students. As underscored by the NIAAA Task Force report (2002), there is a need for a comprehensive approach to reducing student drinking that addresses individuals, including high-risk drinkers, the student population as a whole, and the campus and surrounding community. Accordingly, the environmental strategies described in this chapter should be used in conjunction with other individual-level strategies (e.g., online alcohol education, motivational interviewing for mandated students), since no single intervention is sufficient to address the harms associated with college student alcohol use.

REFERENCES

Barry, R., Edwards, E., Pelletier, A., Brewer, R., Naimi, T., Redmond, A., & Ramsey, L. (2004). Enhanced enforcement of laws to prevent alcohol sales to underage persons – New Hampshire, 1999 – 2004. *Morbidity and Mortality Weekly Report, 53*(21), 452–454.

Boyd, C. J., McCabe, S. E., Cranford, J. A., Morales, M., Lange, J. E., Reed, M. B., . . . Scott, M. S. (2008). Heavy episodic drinking and its consequences: The protective effects of same-sex, residential living-learning communities for undergraduate women. *Addictive Behaviors, 33*(8), 987–993. doi: 10.1016/j.addbeh.2008.03.005

Britt, H., Carlin, B. P., Toomey, T. L., & Wagenaar, A. C. (2005). Neighborhood-level spatial analysis of the relationship between alcohol outlet density and criminal violence. *Environmental and Ecological Statistics, 12,* 411–426.

Busteed, B. H. (2002). Taking measure of campus alcohol abuse. *Trusteeship,* Nov/December, 8–12.

Campbell, C. A., Hahn, R. A., Elder, R., Brewer, R., Chattopadhyay, S., Fielding, J.,...Task Force on Community Preventive Services. (2009). The effectiveness of limiting alcohol outlet density as a means of reducing excessive alcohol consumption and alcohol-related harms. *American Journal of Preventive Medicine, 37*(6), 556–569.

Chaloupka, F. J., Grossman, M., & Saffer, H. (2002). The effects of price on alcohol consumption and alcohol-related problems. *Alcohol Research & Health, 26*(1), 22–34.

Clapp, J. D., Johnson, M., Voas, R. B., Lange, J. E., Shillington, A., & Russell, C. (2005). Reducing DUI among college students: Results of an environmental prevention trial. *Addiction, 100,* 327–334.

Cohen, F., & Rogers, D. (1997). Effects of alcohol policy change. *Journal of Alcohol and Drug Education, 42,* 69–82.

DeJong, W. (2008). *Methods for assessing college student use of alcohol and other drugs.* Washington, DC: U.S. Department of Education, Higher Education Center for Alcohol and Other Drug Abuse and Violence Prevention. Available at www.higheredcenter.org/files/product/methods.pdf

DeJong, W. (2009). *Problem analysis: The first step in prevention planning.* Washington, DC: U.S. Department of Education, Higher Education Center for Alcohol and Other Drug Abuse and Violence Prevention. Available at www.higheredcenter.org/files/product/problem-analysis.pdf

DeJong, W. (2010). *Building an infrastructure for AODV prevention: Coalitions and statewide initiatives.* U.S. Department of Education, Office of Safe and Drug-Free Schools, Higher Education Center for Alcohol and Other Drug Abuse and Violence Prevention, Washington, D.C. Available at www. higheredcenter.org/files/product/building-an-infrastructure-for-aodv-prevention.pdf

DeJong, W., DeRicco, B., & Schneider, S. K. (2010). Pregaming: An exploratory study of strategic drinking by college students in Pennsylvania. *Journal of American College Health, 58,* 307–316.

DeJong, W., & Langford, L. M. (2002). A typology for campus-based alcohol prevention: Moving toward environmental management strategies. *Journal of Studies on Alcohol, Suppl 14,* 140–147.

DeJong, W., & Langford, L. M. (2006). *Evaluating environmental management approaches to alcohol and other drug abuse prevention.* U.S. Department of Education, Office of Safe and Drug-Free Schools, Higher Education Center for Alcohol and Other Drug Abuse and Violence Prevention, Washington, D.C. Available at www.higheredcenter.org/files/product/evaluating.pdf

DeJong, W., Larimer, M. E., Wood, M. D., & Hartman, R. (2009a). NIAAA's rapid response to college drinking problems initiative: Reinforcing the use of evidence-based approaches in college alcohol prevention. *Journal of Studies on Alcohol and Drugs, Suppl 16,* 5–11.

DeJong, W., Schneider, S. K., Towvim, L. G., Murphy, M. J., Doerr, E. E., Simonsen, N. R., . . . Scribner, R. A. (2006). A multisite randomized trial of social norms marketing campaigns to reduce college student drinking. *Journal of Studies on Alcohol, 67*(6), 868–879.

DeJong, W., Schneider, S. K., Towvim, L. G., Murphy, M. J., Doerr, E. E., Simonsen, N. R.,... Scribner, R. A. (2009b). A multisite randomized trial of social norms marketing campaigns to reduce college student drinking: A replication failure. *Substance Abuse, 30*(2), 127–140. doi: 10.1080/08897070902802059

DeJong, W., & Vehige, T. (2008). *The off-campus environment: Approaches for reducing alcohol and other drug problems.* Washington, DC: U.S. Department of Education, Higher Education Center for

Alcohol and Other Drug Abuse and Violence Prevention. Available at: www.higheredcenter.org/files/product/off-campus.pdf

DeJong, W., Vince-Whitman, C., Colthurst, T., Cretella, M., Gilbreath, M., Rosati, M., & Zweig, K. (1998). *Environmental management: A comprehensive strategy for reducing alcohol and other drug use on college campuses.* Newton, MA: Higher Education Center for Alcohol and Other Drug Prevention, Department of Education. Available at www.higheredcenter.org/files/product/enviro-mgnt.pdf

Elder, R. W., Lawrence, B., Ferguson, A., Naimi, T. S., Brewer, R. D., Chattopadhyay, S. K., . . . Task Force on Community Preventive Services. (2010). The effectiveness of tax policy interventions for reducing excessive alcohol consumption and related harms. *American Journal of Preventive Medicine, 38*(2), 217–229.

Elder, R. W., Lawrence, B., Janes, G., Brewer, R. D., Toomey, T. L., Hingson, R. W., . . . Fielding, J. (2007). *Enhanced enforcement of laws prohibiting sale of alcohol to minors: Systematic review of effectiveness for reducing sales and underage drinking* (pp. 181–188). Transportation Research E-Circular, Issue E-C123.. Available at http://onlinepubs.trb.org/onlinepubs/circulars/ec123.pdf

Fabian, L. E. A., Toomey, T. L., Lenk, K. M., & Erickson, D. J. (2008). Where do underage college students get alcohol? *Journal of Drug Education, 38*(1), 15–26.

Florin, P., Mitchell, R., & Stevenson, J. (1993). Identifying training and technical assistance needs in community coalitions: A developmental approach. *Health Education Research: Theory and Practice, 8*, 417–432.

Florin, P., Mitchell, R., Stevenson, J., & Klein, I. (2000). Predicting intermediate outcomes for prevention coalitions: A developmental perspective. *Evaluation and Program Planning, 23*(3), 341–346. doi: 10.1016/S0149-7189(00)00022-7

Forster, J. L., Murray, D. M., Wolfson, M., & Wagenaar, A. C. (1995). Commercial availability of alcohol to young people: Results of alcohol purchase attempts. *Preventive Medicine, 24*, 342–347.

Geller, E. S., & Kalsher, M. J. (1990). Environmental determinants of party drinking: Bartenders vs. self-service. *Environment and Behavior, 22*, 74–90.

Geller, E. S., Kalsher, M. J., & Clarke, S. W. (1991). Beer versus mixed-drink consumption at fraternity parties: A time and place for low-alcohol alternatives. *Journal of Studies on Alcohol, 52*, 197–204.

Glassman, T. J., Dodd, V., Miller, E. M., & Braun, R. E. (2010). Preventing high-risk drinking among college students: A social marketing case study. *Social Marketing Quarterly, 16*(4), 92–110. doi: 10.1080/15245004.2010.522764

Gliksman, L., McKenzie, D., Single, E., & Douglas, R. (1993). The role of alcohol providers in prevention: An evaluation of a server intervention programme. *Addiction, 88*(9), 1195–1203. doi: 10.1111/j.1360-0443.1993.tb02142.x

Grube, J. W. (1997). Preventing sales of alcohol to minors: Results from a community trial. *Addiction, 92, Suppl 2*, S251–S260.

Gruenewald, P. J., Freisthler, B., Remer, L., Lascala, E. A., Treno, A. J., & Ponicki, W. R. (2010). Ecological associations of alcohol outlets with underage and young adult injuries. *Alcoholism: Clinical and Experimental Research, 34*(3), 519–527.

Gruenewald, P. J., & Johnson, F. W. (2010). Drinking, driving, and crashing: A traffic-flow model of alcohol-related motor vehicle accidents. *Journal of Studies on Alcohol and Drugs, 71*(2), 237–248.

Gruenewald, P. J., Madden, P., & Janes, K. (1992). Alcohol availability and the formal power and resources of state alcohol beverage control agencies, *Alcoholism: Clinical and Experimental Research, 16*(3), 591–597.

Haines, M., & Spear, S. F. (1996). Changing the perception of the norm: A strategy to decrease binge drinking among college students. *Journal of American College Health, 45*, 134–140.

Hingson, R. W., & Howland, J. (2002). Comprehensive community interventions to promote health: Implications for college-age drinking problems. *Journal of Studies on Alcohol, Suppl 14*, 226–240.

Hingson, R., McGovern, T., Howland, J., Hereen, T., Winter, M., & Zakocs, R. (1996). Reducing alcohol-impaired driving in Massachusetts: The saving lives program. *American Journal of Public Health, 86*, 791–797.

Holder, H. D., Saltz, R. F., Grube, J. W., Treno, A. J., Reynolds, R. I., Voas, R. B, & Gruenewald, P. J. (1997). Summing up: Lessons from a comprehensive community prevention trial. *Addiction, 92,* Suppl 2, S293–S301.

Holder, H. D., & Wagenaar, A. C. (1994). Mandated server training and reduced alcohol-involved traffic crashes: A time series analysis of the Oregon experience. *Accident Analysis and Prevention, 26*(1), 89–97. doi: 10.1016/0001-4575(94)90071-X

Howard-Pitney, B., Johnson, M. D., Altman, D. G., & Hopkins, R. (1991). Responsible alcohol service: A study of server, manager, and environmental impact. *American Journal of Public Health, 81*(2), 197–199. doi: 10.2105/AJPH.81.2.197

Johnston, L. D., O'Malley, P. M. & Bachman, J. G. (1993). *National survey results on drug use from the Monitoring the Future Study: 1975–1992* (Vol. 2). Rockville, MD: National Institute on Drug Abuse, U.S. Department of Health and Human Services.

Johnston, L. D., O'Malley, P. M., Bachman, J. G., & Schulenberg, J. E. (2010a). *Monitoring the Future national survey results on drug use, 1975–2009: Volume I, Secondary school students* (NIH Publication No. 10–7584). Bethesda, MD: National Institute on Drug Abuse.

Johnston, L. D., O'Malley, P. M., Bachman, J. G., & Schulenberg, J. E. (2010b). *Monitoring the Future national survey results on drug use, 1975–2009: Volume II, College students and adults ages 19–50* (NIH Publication No. 10–7585). Bethesda, MD: National Institute on Drug Abuse.

Keeling, R. P. (2000). Social norms research in college health. *Journal of American College Health, 49,* 53–56.

Kuo, M., Wechsler, H., Greenberg, P., & Lee, H. (2003). The marketing of alcohol to college students: The role of low prices and special promotions. *American Journal of Preventive Medicine, 25*(3), 204–211. doi: 10.1016/S0749-3797(03)00200-9

Kypri, K., Bell, M. L., Hay, G. C., & Baxter, J. (2008). Alcohol outlet density and university student drinking: A national study. *Addiction, 103*(7), 1131–1138.

LaBrie, J. W., Hummer, J. F., & Pedersen, E. R. (2007). Reasons for drinking in the college student context: The differential role and risk of the social motivator. *Journal of Studies on Alcohol and Drugs, 68*(3), 393–398.

Lang, E., Stockwell, T., Rydon, P., & Beele, A. (1998). Can training bar staff in responsible serving practices reduce alcohol-related harm? *Drug and Alcohol Review, 17,* 39–50. doi: 10.1080/09595239800187581

Lee, C. M., Geisner, I. M., Lewis, M. A., Neighbors, C., & Larimer, M. E. (2007). Social motives and the interaction between descriptive and injunctive norms in college student drinking. *Journal of Studies on Alcohol and Drugs, 68*(5), 714–721.

Lenk, K. M., Toomey, T. L., & Erickson, D. J. (2006). Propensity of alcohol establishments to sell to obviously intoxicated patrons. *Alcoholism: Clinical and Experimental Research, 30*(7), 1194–1199.

Martinez, J. A., Rutledge, P. C., & Sher, K. J. (2007). Fake ID ownership and heavy drinking in underage college students: Prospective findings. *Psychology of Addictive Behaviors, 21,* 226–232.

Martinez, J. A., & Sher, K. J. (2010). Methods of "fake ID" obtainment and use in underage college students. *Addictive Behaviors, 35,* 738–740.

McCabe, S. E., Boyd, C. J., Cranford, J. A., Slayden, J., Lange, J. E., Reed, M. B., . . . Scott, M. S. (2007). Alcohol involvement and participation in residential learning communities among first-year college students. *Journal of Studies on Alcohol and Drugs, 68*(5), 722–726.

McCartt, A. T., Hellinga, L. A., & Kirley, B. B. (2010). The effects of minimum legal drinking age 21 laws on alcohol-related driving in the United States. *Journal of Safety Research, 41*(2), 173–181.

McKnight, A. J. (1991). Factors influencing the effectiveness of server-intervention education. *Journal of Studies on Alcohol, 52*(5), 389–397.

Murphy, J. G., Correia, C. J., & Barnett, N. P. (2007). Behavioral economic approaches to reduce college drinking. *Addictive Behaviors, 32,* 2573–2585.

Murphy, J. G., & MacKillop, J. (2006). Relative reinforcing efficacy of alcohol among college student drinkers. *Experimental and Clinical Psychopharmacology, 14,* 219–227. doi: 10.1037/1064-1297.14.2.219

Neighbors, C., Walters, S. T., Lee, C. M., Vader, A. M., Vehige, T., Szigethy, T., & DeJong, W. (2007). Event-specific prevention: Addressing college student drinking during known windows of risk. *Addictive Behaviors, 32,* 2667–2680. doi: 10.1016/j.addbeh.2007.05.010

Nelson, T. F., Toomey, T. L., Lenk, K. M., Erickson, D. J., & Winters, K. C. (2010). Implementation of NIAAA college drinking task force recommendations: How are colleges doing 6 years later? *Alcoholism: Clinical and Experimental Research, 34*(10), 1687–1693. doi: 10.1111/j.1530–0277.2010.01268.x

Nguyen, N., Walters, S. T., Rinker, D. V., Wyatt, T. M., & DeJong, W. (2011). Fake ID ownership in a US sample of incoming college students. *Addictive Behaviors, 36,* 759 – 761.

Nygaard, P., & Saltz, R. (2010). Communication between researchers and practitioners: Findings from a qualitative evaluation of a large-scale college intervention. *Substance Use & Misuse, 45,* 77–97. doi: 10.3109/10826080902864985

O'Mara, R. J., Thombs, D. L., Wagenaar, A., C., Rossheim, M. E., Merves, M. L., Hou, W.,... Goldberger, B. A. (2009). Alcohol price and intoxication in college bars. *Alcoholism: Clinical and Experimental Research, 33,* 1973–1980.

Paschall, M. J., Kypri, K., & Saltz, R. F. (2006). Friday class and heavy alcohol use in a sample of New Zealand college students. *Journal of Studies on Alcohol, 67*(5), 764–769.

Perkins, H. W. (2002). Social norms and the prevention of alcohol misuse in collegiate contexts. *Journal of Studies on Alcohol, Suppl 14,* 164–172.

Perkins, H. W., & Berkowitz, A. D. (1986). Perceiving the community norms of alcohol use among students: Some research implications for campus alcohol education programming. *International Journal of the Addictions, 21*(9–10), 961–976.

Perry, C. L., Williams, C. L., Veblen-Mortenson, S., Toomey, T. L., Komro, K. A., Anstine, P. S., . . . Wolfson, M. (1996). Project Northland: Outcomes of a community-wide alcohol use prevention program during early adolescence. *American Journal of Public Health, 86,* 956–965.

Preusser, D. F., Williams, A. F., & Weinstein, H. B. (1994). Policing underage alcohol sales. *Journal of Safety Research, 25,* 127–133.

Putnam, R. D. (2004). Commentary: "Health by association": Some comments. *International Journal of Epidemiology, 33,* 667–671. doi: 10.1093/ije/dyh204

Ringwalt, C. L., & Paschall, M. J. (2011). The utility of keg registration laws: A cross-sectional study. *Journal of Adolescent Health, 48,* 106–108. doi: 10.1016/j.jadohealth.2010.05.012

Ringwalt, C. L., Paschall, M. J., & Gitelman, A. M. (2011). Alcohol prevention strategies on college campuses and student alcohol abuse and related problems. *Journal of Drug Education, 41*(1), 99–118. doi: 10.2190/DE.41.1.f

Ryan, B., & DeJong, W. (1998). *Making the link: Faculty and prevention.* Washington, DC: U.S. Department of Education, Higher Education Center for Alcohol and Other Drug Prevention. Available at www.higheredcenter.org/files/product/faculty-prevention.pdf

Saltz, R. F., Paschall, M. J., McGaffigan, R. P., & Nygaard, P. M. O. (2010). Alcohol risk management in college settings: The safer California universities randomized trial. *American Journal of Preventive Medicine, 39*(6), 491–499. doi: 10.1016/j.amepre.2010.08.020

Saltz, R. F., Welker, L. R., Paschall, M. J., Feeney, M. A., & Fabiano, P. M. (2009). Evaluating a comprehensive campus-community prevention intervention to reduce alcohol-related problems in a college population. *Journal of Studies on Alcohol and Drugs, Suppl 16,* 21–27.

Scribner, R. A., Cohen, D. A., & Fisher, W. (2000). Evidence of structural effect for alcohol outlet density: A multilevel analysis. *Alcoholism: Clinical and Experimental Research, 24*(2), 188–195. doi: 10.1111/j.1530–0277.2000.tb04590.x

Scribner, R. A., Mason, K. E., Simonsen, N. R., Theall, K., Chotalia, J., Johnson, S., . . . DeJong, W. (2010). An ecologic analysis of alcohol outlet density and campus-reported violence at 32 U.S. colleges. *Journal of Studies on Alcohol and Drugs, 71,* 184–191.

Scribner, R. A., Mason, K., Theall, K., Simonsen, N., Schneider, S. K., Towvim, L. G., & DeJong, W. (2008). The contextual role of alcohol outlet density in college drinking. *Journal of Studies on Alcohol and Drugs, 69*(1), 112–120.

Scribner, R. A., Theall, K. P., Mason, K., Simonsen, N., Schneider, S. K., Towvim, L. G., & DeJong, W. (2011). Alcohol prevention on college campuses: The moderating effect of the alcohol environment on the effectiveness of social norms marketing campaigns. *Journal of Studies on Alcohol and Drugs, 72*(2), 232–239.

Skidmore, J. R., & Murphy, J. G. (2011). The effect of drink price and next day responsibilities on college student drinking: A behavioral economic analysis. *Psychology of Addictive Behaviors, 25*, 57–68. doi: 10–1037/a0021118.

Stout, E. M., Sloan, F. A., Liang, L., & Davies, H. H. (2000). Reducing harmful alcohol-related behaviors: Effective regulatory methods. *Journal of Studies on Alcohol, 61*(3), 402–412.

Szreter, S., & Woolcock, M. (2004). Health by association? Social capital, social theory, and the political economy of public health. *International Journal of Epidemiology, 33*, 650–667. doi: 10.1093/ije/dyh013

Task Force of the National Advisory Council on Alcohol Abuse and Alcoholism. (2002). *A call to action: Changing the culture of drinking at U.S. colleges*, NIH Publication No. 02–5010, Bethesda, MD: National Institute on Alcohol Abuse and Alcoholism.

Theall, K., DeJong, W., Scribner, R., Mason, K., Schneider, S. K., & Simonsen, N. (2009). Social capital in the college setting: The impact of participation in campus activities on drinking and alcohol-related harms. *Journal of American College Health, 58*(1), 15–23.

Toomey, T. L., Erickson, D. J., Carlin, B. P., Quick, H. S., Harwood, E. M., Lenk, K. M., & Ecklund, A. M. (2012). Is the density of alcohol establishments related to non-violent crime? *Journal of Studies on Alcohol and Drugs, 73*, 21–25.

Toomey, T. L., Erickson, D. J., Lenk, K. M., & Kilian, G. (2008a). Likelihood of illegal alcohol sales at professional sport stadiums. *Alcoholism: Clinical & Experimental Research, 32*(11), 1859–1854.

Toomey, T. L., Erickson, D. J., Lenk, K. M., Kilian, G. R., Perry, C. L., & Wagenaar, A. C. (2008b). A randomized trial to evaluate a management training program to prevent illegal alcohol sales. *Addiction, 103*(3), 405–413.

Toomey, T. L., Erickson, D. J., Patrek, W., Fletcher, L. A., & Wagenaar, A. C. (2005). Illegal alcohol sales and use of alcohol control policies at community festivals. *Public Health Reports, 120*(2), 165–173.

Toomey, T. L., Komro, K. A., Oakes, J. M., & Lenk, K. M. (2008c). Propensity for illegal alcohol sales to underage youth in Chicago. *Journal of Community Health, 33*(3), 134–138.

Toomey, T. L., Lenk, K. M., Nelson, T. F., & Jones, A. M. (in press). Impact of alcohol policies on college student health (including alcohol access restrictions, policy enforcement, amnesty policies). In *Encyclopedia of Addictive Behaviors*.

Toomey, T. L., Lenk, K. M., & Wagenaar, A. C. (2007). Environmental policies to reduce college drinking: An update of research findings. *Journal of Studies on Alcohol and Drugs, 68*, 208–219.

Toomey, T. L., & Wagenaar, A.C. (2002). Environmental policies to reduce college drinking: Options and research findings. *Journal of Studies on Alcohol, Suppl. No. 14*, 193–205.

Toomey, T. L., Wagenaar, A. C., Erickson, D. J., Fletcher, L. A., Patrek, W., & Lenk, K. M. (2004). Illegal alcohol sales to obviously intoxicated patrons at licensed establishments. *Alcoholism: Clinical and Experimental Research, 8*(5), 769–774.

Toomey, T. L., Wagenaar, A. C., Gehan, J. P., Kilian, G., Murray, D. M., & Perry, C. L. (2001). Project ARM: Alcohol risk management to prevent sales to underage and intoxicated patrons. *Health Education and Behavior, 28*, 186–199.

Treno, A. J., Grube, J. W., & Martin, S. E. (2003). Alcohol availability as a predictor of youth drinking and driving: A hierarchical analysis of survey and archival data. *Alcoholism: Clinical and Experimental Research, 27*(5), 835–840. doi: 10.1097/01.ALC.0000067979.85714.22

Treno, A. J., Johnson, F. W., Remer, L. G., & Gruenewald, P. J. (2007). The impact of outlet densities on alcohol-related crashes: A spatial panel approach. *Accident Analysis and Prevention, 39*(5), 894–901. doi: 10.1016/j.aap.2006.12.011

Turner, J., Perkins, H. W., & Bauerle, J. (2008). Declining negative consequences related to alcohol misuse among students exposed to a social norms marketing intervention on a college campus. *Journal of American College Health, 57*(1), 85–94.

Vicary, J. R., & Karshin, C. M. (2002). College alcohol abuse: A review of the problems, issues, and prevention approaches. *Journal of Primary Prevention, 22*(3), 299–331. doi: 10.1023/A:1013621821924

Voas, R. B., Tippetts, A. S., & Fell, J. C. (2003). Assessing the effectiveness of minimum legal drinking age and zero tolerance laws in the United States. *Accident Analysis and Prevention, 35*(4), 579–587.

Wagenaar, A. C., Gehan, J. P., Jones-Webb, R., Toomey, T. L., Forster, J. L., Wolfson, M., & Murray, D. (1999). Communities mobilizing for change on alcohol: Lessons and results from a 15-community randomized trial. *Journal of Community Prevention, 27*, 315–326.

Wagenaar, A. C., Murray, D. M., Gehan, J. P., Wolfson, M., Forster, J. L., Toomey, T. L., . . . Jones-Webb, R. (2000a). Communities mobilizing for change on alcohol: Outcomes from a randomized community trial. *Journal of Studies on Alcohol, 61*, 85–94.

Wagenaar, A. C., Murray, D. M., & Toomey, T. L. (2000b). Communities mobilizing for change on alcohol (CMCA): Effects of a randomized trial on arrests and traffic crashes. *Addiction, 95*, 209–217.

Wagenaar, A. C., Salois, M. J., & Komro, K. A. (2009). Effects of beverage alcohol price and tax levels on drinking: A meta-analysis of 1003 estimates from 112 studies. *Addiction, 104*, 179–190. doi: 10.1111/j.1360–0443.2008.02438.x

Wagenaar, A. C., & Toomey, T. L. (2002). Effects of minimum drinking age laws: Review and analyses of the literature from 1960 to 2000. *Journal of Studies on Alcohol, Suppl 14*, 206–225.

Wagenaar, A. C., Toomey, T. L., & Erickson, D. J. (2005). Preventing youth access to alcohol: Outcomes from a multi-community time-series trial. *Addiction, 100*(3), 335–345.

Wagenaar, A. C., & Wolfson, M. (1995). Deterring sales and provision of alcohol to minors: A study of enforcement in 295 counties in four states. *Public Health Reports, 110*(4), 419–427.

Wagoner, K. G., Rhodes, S. D., Lentz, A. W., & Wolfson, M. (2010). Community organizing goes to college: A practice-based model to implement environmental strategies to reduce high-risk drinking on college campuses. *Health Promotion Practice, 11*(6), 817–827. doi: 10.1177/1524839909353726

Wechsler, H., Lee, J. E., Gledhill-Hoyt, J., & Nelson, T. F. (2001a). Alcohol use and problems at colleges banning alcohol: Results of a national survey. *Journal of Studies on Alcohol, 62*, 133–141.

Wechsler, H., Lee, J. E., Nelson, T. F., & Kuo, M. (2002). Underage college students' drinking behavior, access to alcohol, and the influence of deterrence policies. *Journal of American College Health, 50*(5), 223–236.

Wechsler, H., Lee, J. E., Nelson, T. F., & Lee, H. (2001b). Drinking levels, alcohol problems and secondhand effects in substance-free college residences: Results of a national study. *Journal of Studies on Alcohol, 62*(1), 23–31.

Wechsler, H., Lee, J. E., Nelson, T. F., & Lee, H. (2003). Drinking and driving among college students: The influence of alcohol-control policies. *American Journal of Preventive Medicine, 25*(3), 212–218. doi: 10.1016/S0749–3797(03)00199–5

Wechsler, H., Seibring, M., Liu, I-C., & Ahl, M. (2004). Colleges respond to student binge drinking: Reducing student demand or limiting access. *Journal of American College Health, 52*(4), 159–168.

Wei, J., Barnett, N. P., & Clark, M. (2010). Attendance at alcohol-free and alcohol-service parties and alcohol consumption among college students. *Addictive Behaviors, 35*(6), 572–579. doi: 10.1016/j.addbeh.2010.01.008

Weitzman, E. R., & Chen, Y. Y. (2005). Risk modifying effect of social capital on measures of heavy alcohol consumption, alcohol abuse, harms, and secondhand effects: National survey findings. *Journal of Epidemiology and Community Health, 59*(4), 303–309. doi: 10.1136/jech.2004.024711

Weitzman, E. R., Folkman, A., Folkman, M. P., & Wechsler, H. (2003). The relationship of alcohol outlet density to heavy and frequent drinking and drinking-related problems among college students at eight universities. *Health & Place, 9*, 1–6.

Weitzman, E. R., & Kawachi, I. (2000). Giving means receiving: The protective effect of social capital on binge drinking on college campuses. *American Journal of Public Health, 90*(12), 1936–1939.

Weitzman, E. R., Nelson, T. F., Lee, H., & Wechsler, H. (2004). Reducing drinking and related harms in college: Evaluation of the 'A Matter of Degree' program. *American Journal of Preventive Medicine, 27*, 187–196.

Williams, J., Chaloupka, F. J., & Wechsler, H. (2005). Are there differential effects of price and policy on college students' drinking intensity? *Contemporary Economic Policy, 23*, 78–90. doi: 10.1093/cep/byi007

Wolfson, M., Toomey, T. L., Murray, D. M., Forster, J. L., Short, B. J., & Wagenaar, A. C. (1996). Alcohol outlet policies and practices concerning sales to underage people. *Addiction, 91*, 589–602.

Wood, M. D., DeJong, W., Fairlie, A. M., Lawson, D., Lavigne, A. M., & Cohen, F. (2009). Common Ground: An investigation of environmental management alcohol prevention initiatives in a college community. *Journal of Studies on Alcohol and Drugs, Suppl 16*, 96–105.

Wood, P. K., Sher, K. J., & Rutledge, P. C. (2007). College student alcohol consumption, day of the week, and class schedule. *Alcoholism: Clinical and Experimental Research, 31*(7), 1195–1207. doi: 10.1111/j.1530–0277.2007.00402.x

Zimmerman, R. (2004). *Campus and community coalitions in AOD prevention.* Washington CD: U.S. Department of Education, Higher Education Center for Alcohol, Drug Abuse, and Violence Prevention.

Zimmerman, R., & DeJong, W. (2003). *Safe lanes on campus: A guide for preventing impaired driving and underage drinking.* Washington, DC: U.S. Department of Education, Higher Education Center for Alcohol, Drug Abuse, and Violence Prevention. Available at www.ed.gov/admins/lead/safety/safelanes.pdf

8

Stepped Care in the College Setting

Brian Borsari

THE PROBLEM: ALCOHOL USE IN COLLEGE

Over the past 20 years, heavy episodic (or "binge") drinking has become recognized as the most important health hazard for college students (National Institute on Alcohol Abuse and Alcoholism [NIAAA], 2002). Ongoing debate over the term binge drinking (see Carey, 2001) led the NIAAA to redefine binge drinking as consuming five or more drinks (four or more for women) in approximately two hours (NIAAA, 2004, p. 3). This definition corresponds with a blood alcohol level (BAL) of 0.08 or higher, which is distinct from risky drinking (which corresponds to a BAL ranging from 0.05 to 0.08). Roughly 40% of college students, including close to half of men, drink in this manner at least once every 2 weeks, a trend that has remained consistent for more than a decade (Johnston, O'Malley, Bachman, & Schulenberg, 2010). Binge drinking often results in negative consequences, including damage to self, others, and property, and more than 1,400 students die each year due to alcohol-related injuries (Hingson, Zha, & Weitzman, 2009). Students who share the college environment with heavy drinkers are also adversely affected. Compared to students at low drinking level schools, those at high drinking level schools are close to 4 times as likely to suffer at least one problem due to the excessive drinking of others, ranging from having their studies interrupted to sexual assault (Wechsler, Lee, Hall, Wagenaar, & Lee, 2002).

The work in this chapter was supported by National Institute on Alcohol Abuse and Alcoholism Grants R01 AA015518 and R01 AA017874 to B. Borsari. The author would like to thank Johnn T. P. Hustad and Nadine Mastroleo for their helpful suggestions regarding the structure and content of the chapter. The contents of this chapter do not represent the views of the Department of Veterans Affairs or the United States Government.

Close to 90% of schools provide counseling and treatment for alcohol use (Wechsler, Seibring, Liu, & Ahl, 2004). However, most colleges and universities also have implemented standard educational programs in order to reduce student drinking. For example, between 1993 and 2001, schools significantly increased the number and intensity of educational programs (e.g., lectures, meetings), multisession educational groups, and special college courses addressing alcohol use (Wechsler, Lee, Kuo et al., 2002). Although research on the effectiveness of these programs has been beset by methodological limitations such as lack of randomization, high attrition, lack of control or comparison groups, nonequivalent control groups, short follow-ups, and convenience samples, available data suggest that these group programs have not demonstrated consistent or long-standing reductions in alcohol use (Hingson et al., 1997; Larimer & Cronce, 2007; NIAAA, 2002; Wechsler, Lee, Nelson, & Kuo, 2002). Therefore, education alone is unlikely to produce the desired behavioral change when delivered without additional intervention. Given the disappointing results of traditional alcohol programs, more targeted, systematic approaches may be needed to assist students in recognizing and reducing hazardous drinking behaviors. Further, findings suggest that college students represent a heterogeneous population for which a "one size fits all" treatment approach may be inappropriate. Instead, an approach that tailors treatment may be more clinically effective, efficient, and cost-effective.

This chapter describes stepped care as an approach that may permit college alcohol programs to allocate their resources more efficiently and effectively. A caveat is of note: Although there have been advances in environmental strategies to address college drinking over the past decade (see Saltz, 2011), and these would make a suitable first (least intensive) step of treatment, the stepped care approach discussed in this chapter is for students who continue to drink heavily despite these efforts. This population likely consists of two types of college students—those who present for treatment to address their drinking, and those who are referred to campus administration for violating campus alcohol policies (also known as mandated students). As the majority of college students do not see their alcohol use as a problem, and even fewer present for treatment (see Buscemi et al., 2010; Knight et al., 2002), stepped care is discussed primarily in the context of providing a variety of treatments for mandated students. That said, there is nothing preventing the implementation of stepped care with the general student population.

"ONE SIZE DOES NOT FIT ALL"

The prevalence of high-risk drinking on college campuses has also led to increased enforcement of alcohol policies (Hoover, 2003; Porter, 2006). This has created a steady increase in the number of mandated students. Tens of thousands of college students receive campus alcohol violations and mandatory alcohol interventions each year, and in a 2000 survey more than 84% of schools reported having a program for students referred for alcohol violations (Anderson & Gadaleto, 2001). Mandated students are at higher risk for alcohol-related problems compared to nonsanctioned students (e.g., Fromme & Corbin, 2004), and this situation has resulted in many campus alcohol programs having large numbers of mandated students requiring assessment and/or treatment.

To a large extent, individual campus alcohol policies determine the characteristics of the mandated student population. For example, a campus that is "dry," (i.e., prohibits all alcohol) will have a higher proportion of violations for alcohol possession than a "wet" campus that permits alcohol possession by students of legal drinking age. Furthermore, policy enforcement differs across campuses, such that students who receive discipline or sanctions may be a select group on some campuses (e.g., only those who are arrested or transported to the emergency room for intoxication). Campuses with well-publicized "medical amnesty" policies that eliminate or reduce sanctions for students involved in alcohol-related medical emergencies (see Lewis & Marchell, 2006) may have a higher proportion of intoxication cases. For example, in one study of mandated students more than 80% of participants were students who had been taken to the local emergency department of a local hospital for intoxication (Barnett, Murphy, Colby, & Monti, 2007). In contrast, in another study only 6% of the sample of 64 mandated students were referred for hospitalization for alcohol use (Borsari & Carey, 2005). In sum, there may be important policy-driven campus differences in drinking profiles among alcohol violators, and research with larger samples is needed.

A study using data from four different mandated student trials that were conducted at four diverse colleges discovered three profiles that are indicative of the heterogeneity of the mandated student population (Barnett et al., 2008). Each profile had a meaningful number of students, indicating that the profiles occur with some degree of frequency across the campuses. The cluster that we labeled "Why Me?" was characterized by below-average levels of prior alcohol use and problems, drinking in the referral incident, and feelings of responsibility. In addition, the majority of cases in this cluster across both samples (92%) had received possession or presence (i.e., being in the presence of alcohol) violations on their campus. Individuals in this cluster were relatively low-risk students who had an incident that was low in severity compared to medical incidents or more complex alcohol-related infractions. In contrast, the "So What?" profile showed above-average levels of prior alcohol use and problems, moderate levels of drinking in the incident and responsibility, and low levels of perceived incident aversiveness. Although the majority of these cases also had possession or presence violations (80%), this cluster was distinct in that it had a higher proportion of male students and had significantly higher alcohol and drug use than the other two clusters. The "Bad Incident" group was characterized by low prior alcohol use and low-to-moderate prior alcohol problems, but high levels of aversiveness, responsibility, and incident drinking. Members of this cluster were more likely to be first-year students, and a high proportion (70%) had been medically evaluated for intoxication as the precipitating incident. Although there were a high proportion of medical incidents in this category, there were also many behavioral infractions; in fact, of all of the behavioral infractions, 53% of them occurred in this "Bad Incident" group. Thus, the "Bad Incident" group was not as clearly characterized by the type of incident as the other clusters. In sum, this study and subsequent research with mandated students (e.g., Mastroleo, Murphy, Colby, Monti, & Barnett, 2011; Wray, Simons, & Dvorak, 2011) indicate that mandated students are a heterogeneous population that may benefit from a variety of interventions of differing intensity.

STEPPED CARE—THEORY AND PRACTICE

The term *stepped care* describes the way different interventions are linked together and to the clinical guidelines used to make referrals (see Figure 8.1). In stepped care, also known as an adaptive intervention or dynamic treatment regime (Murphy, 2005; Murphy, Lynch, Oslin, McKay, & TenHave, 2007), assignment to different steps of care can be based on individual characteristics, past treatment failure, clinical judgment, and/or established research-based guidelines (Murphy, 2005; Murphy et al., 2007)

Treatment dose is based on decision rules linking the characteristics of the individual to the different levels of program components (Collins, Murphy, & Bierman, 2004). Stepped care approaches are becoming increasingly common in the treatment of psychological disorders (O'Donohue & Draper, 2011), and are particularly appealing because individual characteristics are considered when selecting the least restrictive, intrusive, and costly treatment that has a good chance of being successful. Individuals not responding to the initial level of care (called *nonresponders*) are then provided more intensive treatments.

Stepped care has several advantages if properly implemented (Collins et al., 2004; Collins, Murphy, Nair, & Strecher, 2005; O'Donohue & Draper, 2011; M. B. Sobell & Sobell, 2000). First, it can reduce the negative effects of inappropriately assigned treatment. Occasionally, concern is raised regarding an individual receiving treatment that is not intensive enough (M. B. Sobell & Sobell, 2000). However, comprehensive pretreatment screening and continued monitoring inherent in a properly implemented stepped care helps ensure the assignment of appropriate treatment, as individuals who respond poorly to one level of treatment are quickly referred to a more intensive treatment. Second, stepped care can conserve resources by assigning individuals only the amount of care that they require. Third, the gradual intensification of treatment for nonresponders increases the amount of contact with treatment providers, providing opportunities to implement treatment recommendations and identify areas of difficulty. Fourth, individualized treatments are likely to be better received than generic approaches, thus increasing compliance and satisfaction with care. Finally, the implementation of objective and appropriate decision rules permit the treatment of a wide range of symptom severity.

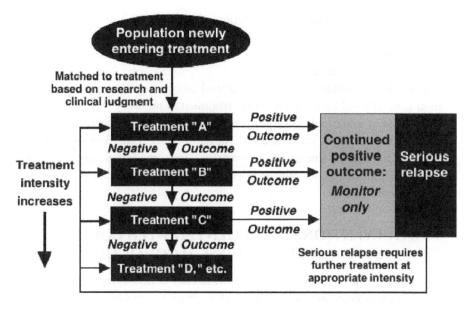

Figure 8.1   Stepped-Care Model of Treatment
Source: From M. B. Sobell and Sobell (2000, p. 574). Used with permission of the authors.

WHAT GOES WHEN?

In stepped care, the decision to assign an individual to different levels of treatment is based on the individual's response on a *tailoring variable* (Collins et al., 2004). Any measureable behavior or trait can be used as a tailoring variable; ideally, a tailoring variable should be clearly associated with an expected response to treatment. An example of a tailoring variable in the mandated student population would be recidivism. Specifically, one would expect students who responded to intervention would not receive another alcohol-related infraction. In contrast, those students who received a subsequent infraction could be viewed as not responding to the administered intervention. Therefore, recidivism would be a tailoring variable with two levels (yes/no).

The implementation of appropriate *decision rules* is also a key component of the stepped care approach. Without them, inappropriate assignment occurs, lessening the effectiveness of all levels of treatment. Good decision rules have three characteristics (Collins et al., 2004). First, they are based on an accurate model of the relationship between tailoring variables, treatment dosage, and outcome. Second, they are objective and operationalize the treatment to be provided at a certain value (or values) of the tailoring variable. Third, they are comprehensive, addressing any contingency that is likely to occur. This ensures that the majority of individuals will be systematically and appropriately referred to different levels of care. A decision rule incorporating the example of the tailoring variable mentioned previously could be: A mandated student who receives a subsequent infraction will receive a 2-hour individual brief motivational intervention unless she or he requests individual treatment and/or meets *DSM-IV* criteria for alcohol dependence and then she or he will be referred to the counseling center for treatment.

In sum, it is advisable to implement stepped care by providing a minimal intervention first, followed by a more intensive treatment, if necessary. The heterogeneity of alcohol use in mandated college students make them an appropriate population for stepped care, as many students may have significantly reduced or stopped their alcohol use prior to presenting for intervention. Thus, the initial application of a stepped care approach should evaluate brief, feasible interventions that have empirical evidence of efficacy.

INTERVENTIONS IMPLEMENTED WITH COLLEGE STUDENTS TO ADDRESS ALCOHOL USE

Over the past 15 years there has been a surge of interest in developing, implementing, and evaluating interventions for college student drinkers (see Carey, Scott-Sheldon, Carey, & DeMartini, 2007; Cronce & Larimer, 2011; Larimer & Cronce, 2002, 2007; Scott-Sheldon, Carey, Elliott, Bolles, & Carey, 2009). As a reaction to high levels of alcohol use and associated negative consequences among college students, various interventions aimed at reducing harm and high-risk drinking behaviors have been developed (see Chapters 12 and 13 of this volume for reviews of intervention approaches). Although far from a comprehensive review, common evidence-based intervention options that might be included as part of a stepped care approach are briefly reviewed below, ordered from the least to most intensive. Furthermore, to place these interventions in the context of stepped care, one can conceptualize interventions such as mailed feedback or brief advice may be best suited for initial steps of treatment, while BMIs and group interventions may be best suited for subsequent steps (see Table 8.1).

Mailed feedback. Mailed feedback has emerged as a cost- and time-efficient technique to inform students of their personal risks associated with alcohol use. Specifically, students complete an assessment and then receive mailed personalized feedback. This feedback often consists of a detailed description of their personal drinking habits, alcohol-related expectancies, drinking norms, alcohol-related consequences, and tips to reduce drinking. This information is hypothesized to make the students' drinking more salient by providing numbers and graphs detailing personal use, thus increasing the discrepancy between current behaviors and personal and social standards. This discrepancy may then result in drinking reductions.

Providing mailed personalized feedback to college students has resulted in reduced drinking and alcohol-related problems (Agostinelli, Brown, & Miller, 1995). Mailed feedback has also been used in conjunction with other interventions. For example, students who received mailed personalized feedback reported lower levels of alcohol

Table 8.1   Interventions With Empirical Support That Could Be Included in Stepped Care Model.

Modality	Length	Content	Mandated/ Volunteer	Recommended Step
Mailed feedback	15–30 minutes to read	Personal alcohol use seedback Alcohol-related consequences Alcohol education Perceived norms Strategies for reduced drinking	Volunteer	First
Brief advice	5–30 minutes	Alcohol information Advice to cut down drinking	Both	First
Computer-delivered alcohol interventions	15 minutes–4 hours	Personal alcohol use Alcohol-related consequences Alcohol education Perceived norms Tips for reduced drinking Drink refusal skills	Both	First or second
Brief motivational interventions	One to three 45- to 60-minute sessions	Personal alcohol use Alcohol-related consequences Alcohol education Perceived norms Tips for reduced drinking Decisional balance Drink refusal skills	Both	Second
Group intervention	1 session	Personal alcohol use Alcohol-related consequences Alcohol education Perceived norms Tips for reduced drinking Drink refusal skills	Both	Second or third
Group intervention	2–8 sessions	Personal alcohol use Alcohol-related consequences Alcohol education Role plays Perceived norms Tips for reduced drinking Drink refusal skills	Both	Third or fourth

use compared to a no-treatment control and reported similar reductions compared to students who had received a 2-hour motivational and educational session in addition to mailed feedback (Walters, Bennett, & Miller, 2000). However, these studies used a relatively brief follow-up period (6 to 8 weeks). Research does indicate that alcohol reductions following the reception of mailed feedback may fade with time. Specifically, Collins, Carey, and Sliwinski (2002) found that students mailed personalized feedback reduced their alcohol use compared to an assessment-only control at 6-week follow-up; however, group differences were no longer significant at the 6-month follow-up. In sum, mailed feedback may facilitate changes in alcohol use and problems in college students; however, this approach may be obsolete given advances in technology and the emergence of computer-delivered alcohol interventions.

Brief advice. Brief advice, also known as a *minimal intervention* or *simple advice*, has been defined as "the shortest or least intense activity that has a therapeutic or preventive effect" (Babor, 1994, p. 1128). Consisting of one contact with the individual, brief advice prescribes a certain change but does not always specify a personalized way to achieve this objective (see Chapter 18 in Miller & Rollnick, 2002). In adults, feedback regarding the risks associated with alcohol use and problems has been related to behavior change in alcohol use, with as little as 5- to 15-minute brief advice sessions incorporating such feedback have been found to be effective in reducing alcohol use in adults (Bien, Miller, & Tonigan, 1993; Moyer, Finney, Swearingen, & Vergun, 2002; Wilk, Jensen, & Havighurst, 1997).

A series of studies indicates that brief advice may facilitate reductions in alcohol use and associated problems in college students. One study recruiting college students presenting to a university emergency room indicated that between 75 and 87% of students screened for alcohol problems agreed to receive a 5- to 25-minute open-ended counseling session. During the session, counselors discussed personal alcohol use and problems and also gave students a brochure addressing risks associated with alcohol use and strategies to reduce alcohol-related risk. At 3-month follow-up, students demonstrated significant reductions in alcohol use, problems, and dependence symptoms, and more than 77% viewed the minimal intervention as somewhat or very helpful (Helmkamp et al., 2003). Two recent studies used brief advice as a control condition in trials evaluating more intensive motivational interventions for high-risk college students in college health clinics. One study provided a general health booklet and two follow-up phone calls (Fleming et al., 2010) and the other provided students with a booklet addressing alcohol use and standard treatment at the clinic (Schaus, Sole, McCoy, Mullett, & O'Brien, 2009). Participants who received the brief advice control condition in both trials reported significant reductions in alcohol use and problems, at times equivalent to those exhibited by the participants receiving the more intensive treatment. Therefore, the brief advice may have been responsible for the observed reductions in use and problems; however, regression to the mean or a natural progression out of risky drinking are possible confounds (Fleming et al., 2010). That said, this research indicates that brief advice addressing risks associated with drinking and providing tips to reduce alcohol use may be an appropriate and effective intervention for some college students.

Computer-delivered alcohol interventions (CDAIs). Since 2000, advances including increased access to the Internet and faster Internet connections have resulted in greater incorporation of electronic methods of communication (email, streaming video, interactive programs) into interventions (see Walters, Wright, & Shegog, 2006, for review). Computer-delivered alcohol interventions (CDAIs), delivered via the web or by other means such as CD-ROM, are a promising approach in the college setting as they may reduce risky drinking given their broad reach and also reduce the administrative burden on college counseling centers (Zisserson, Palfai, & Saitz, 2007). Indeed, meta-analysis indicate that CDAIs have evidence of efficacy (Carey et al., 2009).

Several empirically supported multicomponent CDAIs exist and these interventions often include a combination of strategies to reduce alcohol use (e.g., alcohol education, alcohol norms clarification, alcohol expectancy challenges, decisional balance, and harm reduction strategies). CDAIs that have received empirical support for facilitating reductions in alcohol use and/or problems include AlcoholEdu for College (Hustad, Barnett, Borsari, & Jackson, 2010; Paschall, Antin, Ringwalt, & Saltz, 2011), Alcohol 101 (Carey, Carey, Henson, Maisto, & DeMartini, 2011) e-CHUG (Walters, Vader, & Harris, 2007), College Alc (Paschal, Bersamin, Fearnow-Kenney, Wyrick, & Currey, 2006), the College Drinker's Check-up (Hester, Delaney, & Campbell, 2011), and MyStudentBody (Chiauzzi, Green, Lord, Thum, & Goldstein, 2005). AlcoholEdu for College, College Alc, and MyStudentBody target incoming and first-year college students, while the College Drinker's Check-up targets heavy drinking college students. The amount of time to complete the range of currently implemented CDAIs varies widely. For example, the completion time for AlcoholEdu is approximately 2 to 3 hours, College Alc lasts approximately one hour, the College Drinker's Check-up takes approximately 45 minutes, and MyStudentBody can be completed in approximately one to three hours. Therefore, several wide-ranging, cost-effective and empirically supported CDAIs exist that are plausible candidates for first or second steps in stepped care interventions.

Brief motivational interventions. Brief motivational interventions (BMIs) are brief interventions that incorporate motivational interviewing (MI), defined as a "client-centered, directive method for enhancing intrinsic motivation to change by exploring and resolving ambivalence" (Miller & Rollnick, 2002, p. 25). MI combines both style (e.g., empathy) and technique (e.g., reflective listening) to create an atmosphere of collaboration during the session. BASICS (Brief Intervention and Screening for College Students; Dimeff, Baer, Kivlahan, & Marlatt, 1999), a specific BMI developed for use with college students, uses individualized personal feedback sessions to enhance students' motivation to change high-risk drinking behaviors and reduce alcohol-related consequences. Originally tested with voluntary students using professional counselors, efficacy studies have shown this brief, individual motivational feedback intervention significantly reduced alcohol consumption and negative consequences with effects remaining through 2- and 4-year follow-ups (Baer, Kivlahan, Blume, McKnight, & Marlatt, 2001; Marlatt et al., 1998). Since this original efficacy study, a number of adapted BMIs have been tested with both voluntary and mandated samples, leading Larimer and Cronce (2002, 2007) to conclude that BMIs appear to be more effective for reducing alcohol use in college students than education, values clarification (determining how alcohol use influences personal values and goals) and normative education (providing accurate information regarding peer alcohol use and approval of drinking). More recent research suggests that BMIs are effective with mandated students who continue to exhibit heavy episodic drinking after the referral incident (see case example, this chapter). Therefore, given their flexibility and efficacy, BMIs may be an important component in stepped care programs for mandated college students.

Single-session group interventions. Single-session group interventions have also resulted in reductions in alcohol use and problems. These group interventions are typically designed to provide basic information about alcohol and other drugs, allow students to evaluate the personal risks associated with their drinking, and provide healthier options to alcohol use. Although there is considerable variability in the length and content of these single session groups, they have been associated with reductions in alcohol use and/or alcohol-related problems in mandated (LaBrie, Thompson, Huchting, Lac, & Buckley, 2007; LaChance, Ewing, Bryan, & Hutchison, 2009; Walters, Gruenewald, Miller, & Bennett, 2001) and volunteer college students (LaBrie et al., 2009; LaBrie, Pedersen, Lamb, & Quinlan, 2007; Michael, Curtin, Kirkley, Jones, & Harris, 2006).

Multisession group interventions. As a more involved and intensive level of stepped care, multisession skills training programs can be implemented for groups of mandated students. Two group interventions have been developed and empirically evaluated for college students, the Alcohol Skills Training Program (ASTP; Miller, Kilmer, Kim, Weingardt, & Marlatt, 2001) and the Lifestyles Management Class (LMC; Fromme & Corbin, 2004).

The ASTP was developed as a secondary prevention for college student drinkers (Fromme, Marlatt, Baer, & Kivlahan, 1994). This intervention provides information regarding the risks associated with alcohol use to drinkers and nondrinkers alike, and skills are provided to help the students reduce or stop their alcohol use. The ASTP uses motivational interviewing techniques, endorses harm reduction, and incorporates the stages of change model (see Norcross, Krebs, & Prochaska, 2011). Originally designed to be implemented in eight 90-minute weekly sessions (Kivlahan, Marlatt, Fromme, & Coppel, 1990), the ASTP was later reduced to six 90-minute weekly sessions (Baer et al., 1992). Research evaluating the ASTP with college students has consistently found post-intervention reductions in alcohol use and problems, even as much as one and two years following the intervention. Further refinement of the ASTP has resulted in ten conceptually distinct components that can be delivered during two 90-minute sessions (see Miller et al., 2001, for a detailed description). This approach can also be delivered individually. That said, the multi-session ASTP was found to have equivalent outcomes to a single-session BMI (Baer et al., 1992). Therefore, the ASTP may be preferable when it is desirable to implement multiple sessions or when the intervention must be administered in group format.

The Lifestyles Management Class (LMC) is another group intervention that was developed for college students. The LMC consists of two 2-hour group sessions during which the group leaders maintain a nonjudgmental atmosphere and work to include all group members in discussions in order to increase students' knowledge about their alcohol use and increase motivation to reduce heavy alcohol use (Fromme & Corbin, 2004). Students are also encouraged to adopt healthy lifestyle choices by acquiring skills in behavioral self-management of time, alcohol use, and stress. In addition, the stage of change model is presented, along with exploration of barriers to behavioral change. Blood alcohol levels, tolerance, and gender differences in alcohol use are discussed, along with considerations about the legal consequences of alcohol use. During the LMC, students are encouraged to discuss the misperception of peer norms. Accurate statistics about college drinking are provided to the students and compared to their own perceptions using personalized graphic feedback. Alcohol myopia is also addressed, emphasizing the relationship between alcohol use and sexual behavior. Harm-reduction skills are provided, encouraging the students to maintain balance in their lifestyles and exercise self-management. Recent research (Fromme & Corbin, 2004) with the LMC indicates that is effective in reducing drinking and driving with both college students screened from the student body population as well as mandated students. In addition, the LMC can be administered with equal effectiveness by professional and peer interventionists, an important consideration for future dissemination in college alcohol programs.

In sum, many interventions of different length and intensity have been developed to address college student drinking. However, it is worth mentioning that there does not appear to be a simple dose–response relation with college alcohol interventions. That is, simply providing the most intensive interventions available, even if resources were available to do so, would not reduce alcohol use and problems to low-risk levels for all students. In contrast, recent reviews indicate that effect sizes of all of these interventions relative to control conditions are generally small to moderate. For example, many students who receive a BMI continue to drink heavily and experience alcohol-related problems (Carey et al., 2007; Moreira, Smith, & Foxcroft, 2009). Although interventions that include motivational interviewing (MI) and feedback may be slightly more effective than feedback only, including computerized feedback interventions (Carey et al., 2009; Mun, White, & Morgan, 2009; Walterset al., 2007), providing relatively longer MI sessions (i.e., 10 vs. 50 minutes; Kulesza,

Apperson, Larimer, & Copeland, 2010), or providing booster sessions (Barnett et al., 2007) does not appear to improve outcomes. However, Walters and colleagues (2009) demonstrated that the combination of personalized feedback and motivational interviewing was more effective than either ingredient in isolation. All of these studies did not use stepped care models (participants were not assigned to successive treatments based on nonresponse or a severity indicator). The question then arises: What intervention should be administered and when to reduce risky alcohol use in college students in the most efficacious and efficient manner? Stepped care provides a framework in which to address this issue, and a recent study examined the implementation of this approach with mandated college students.

CASE EXAMPLE OF STEPPED CARE
IN THE COLLEGE SETTING

Project ASSISST (**ASS**essment and **I**ntervention for **S**anctioned **S**tudents) implemented stepped care with mandated college students at a university in the Northeast United States . This project was a large-scale implementation of the first formal attempt to implement stepped care with mandated students (see Borsari, O'Leary Tevyaw, Barnett, Kahler, & Monti, 2007). As can be seen in Figure 8.2, there were two steps of intervention—Brief Advice (BA) and a Brief Motivational Intervention (BMI).

All participants received Step 1, which consisted of a baseline assessment and brief advice. Six weeks later, all students returned for a subsequent assessment. The *tailoring variables* were heavy drinking episodes (defined as four or more drinks on one occasion for women, five or more for men; NIAAA, 2004) and negative alcohol-related consequences (measured by the Brief Young Adult Alcohol Consequences Questionnaire, or B-YAACQ; Kahler, Strong, & Read, 2005). The *decision rule* was that students who reported four or more binge episodes and/or experienced five or more alcohol-related problems in the past month were eligible to receive Step 2, a 45- to 60-minute brief motivational intervention. As this was clinical trial, students who remained at risk using the decision rule were randomized to (a) Step 2 or (b) an assessment-only control (AO).

Participants were 67% male, 96% Caucasian, and 68% freshman with a mean age of 18.68 (*SD* = 0.78). They were cited for possession of alcohol (78.18%), being in the presence of alcohol (12.14%), alcohol-related behavior (9.30%), and alcohol-related medical complications (0.38%). All 598 participants completed a 45-minute baseline assessment immediately prior to receiving the Step 1 brief advice. Six weeks after the baseline assessment and brief advice, 581 of 598 (97%) participants completed a follow-up web assessment. Of the 582 participants who completed the 6-week assessment, two students withdrew, and it was discovered at the end of the project that 16 students had been misclassified and were removed from the sample. Of the 564 remaining students, 102 (20%) participants were identified as low risk and did not meet inclusion

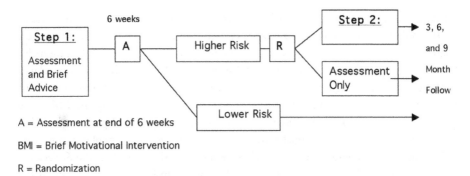

Figure 8.2 Project ASSISST (Assessment and Intervention for Sanctioned Students)

criteria for the Step 2 intervention (i.e., continued heavy drinking behaviors). Of the 462 (80%) who were deemed high risk and were randomized to receive a BMI or assessment only (AO), 57 students had completed their 6-week assessment over the summer break and were also removed from the current analyses. Of the remaining 405 participants, 43 (10%) met the Step 2 criterion for risky drinking (four or more binge episodes in past 6 weeks), 87 (22%) met the Step 2 criterion for minimum YAACQ score (5 or more endorsed items on the YAACQ), and 275 (68%) met both Step 2 criteria. Of these participants, 211 were randomly assigned to receive a BMI and 194 were assigned to assessment-only. Urn randomization (Stout, Wirtz, Carbonari, & Del Boca, 1994), using gender and race as blocking variables, was used to randomly assign these participants to the BMI or an assessment-only control.

Regarding changes in drinking, Generalized Estimating Equation (GEE) models were used to examine the effect of BMI compared to the assessment-only group. The models predicting number of heavy drinking days and peak Blood Alcohol Content (pBAC) did not indicate differences between the two groups over time. In contrast, the main effect of BMI on the number of problems endorsed on the B-YAACQ was significant, indicating a 17% reduction in the incidence rate of problems in BMI compared to AO. Furthermore, the BMI × time interaction was nonsignificant, indicating that the differential effect of BMI persisted over time.

There also appeared to be group differences in recidivism as well. At each follow-up, participants were asked whether they had received another infraction for violation of school alcohol policy since their previous assessment. Not surprisingly, the low-risk group had low rates of recidivism throughout the follow-ups. In the high-risk students, those who received a BMI reported significantly fewer infractions over the course of the 9-month follow-up than the participants in the assessment-only group (37 vs. 60 infractions over the 9-month follow-up).

Project ASSISST was the first large-scale evaluation of stepped care with mandated college students. This project contributes to the growing literature on reducing risky drinking in mandated students in several ways. First and foremost, the study demonstrates that the stepped care approach is feasible and effective in reducing alcohol-related problems in mandated students. Students who continued to drink at high-risk levels following a peer-delivered brief advice session did reduce their alcohol-related consequences following a more intensive brief motivational intervention, reductions that were maintained at nine months. Second, individuals receiving the BMI were also less likely to receive subsequent referrals for violating alcohol policy, which has clear implications for the administrative and counseling resources of college campuses. Third, the students who were identified as being low-risk drinkers at the 6-week assessment continued to report low levels of alcohol use and problems throughout the study. This study suggests that administering a more intensive BMI to the low-risk students would not have been an efficient allocation of resources. Granted, the findings must be considered in light of limitations such as the lack of collateral reports, a primarily Caucasian sample, and possible assessment reactivity on outcomes. That said, these findings support the implementation of stepped care in the college setting, as well as highlighting some considerations that should be taken into account.

CONSIDERATIONS FOR IMPLEMENTING A STEPPED CARE PROGRAM

Stepped care is a promising approach for treating mandated students, and there are many interventions that can be incorporated in a comprehensive program of care. Although program planners can be creative when developing a stepped care program for treating college students, certain considerations should be addressed to avoid problems that will threaten the effectiveness of the entire endeavor.

First, it is important to include interventions that have empirical evidence supporting their implementation and are credible and well tolerated by students. Otherwise, the participants will simply proceed to the next level of treatment or, worse yet, drop out of treatment. Although each step of treatment will not be 100% efficacious, implementing unproved or, worse yet, iatrogenic treatments will throw the systematic assignment of stepped treatment into disarray.

Second, as just mentioned, care should be taken when determining which tailoring variables to use. It is important that tailoring variables correspond with the desired treatment outcome. For example, in a program designed to reduce alcohol use in mandated students, appropriate tailoring variables could address alcohol use (e.g., exhibiting heavy episodic drinking in the past 2 weeks), problems experienced as a result of drinking (e.g., hangovers, blackouts), or recidivism (subsequent violation of campus alcohol policies). The type of tailoring variable must also be considered. Specifically, if the tailoring variable is dichotomous, the decision to assign to more intensive treatment is relatively straightforward: If recidivism is a tailoring variable, students who violate alcohol policy receive more intensive treatment. In contrast, a more sophisticated approach for deciding on an intervention would be to use the individual's response to the violation as a tailoring variable. For example, in the Barnett et al. 2008 study, those in the "Bad Incident" cluster reported high levels of personal responsibility for the incident. Therefore, these students may be more interested in avoiding subsequent consequences from drinking, and may be more open to interventions that provide specific protective behavioral strategies or suggestions on how to make or maintain reductions in their alcohol use. In contrast, students with low feelings of responsibility for the incidents (those in the "Why Me?" and "So What?" groups) might find it difficult to find meaning in the violation (which tended to more minor such as alcohol possession or being in the presence of alcohol). Instead, students in these two groups may benefit from interventions that utilize motivational interviewing (Miller & Rollnick, 2002) to explore ambivalence about alcohol use, whereas providing advice or specific strategies to reduce drinking may not be well received.

Sophisticated tailoring variables such as personal responsibility for the event may help link students with more appropriate and potentially effective steps of treatment. However, if the tailoring variable is continuous, cut-off scores or thresholds need to be determined to accurately identify those requiring more intensive treatment. If cutoffs are too low, many students will require more treatment, straining the resources of the program. Cutoffs that are too high will fail to identify the students that require a more intensive step of treatment. Project ASSISST inadvertently demonstrated the difficulty in striking a balance between practicality and comprehensive delivery of interventions. Specifically, the selection of tailoring variables and decision rules for this study highlights a central issue in the implementation of stepped care: identifying who is eligible for the next step of care. At the time of the development of this project, previous research with a convenience sample of nonmandated students indicated that 44% of college students reported binge drinking 1- to 2 times per week (Wechsler, Lee, Kuo, et al., 2002) and 78% of students endorsed 5 or more items on the B-YAACQ (Kahler et al., 2005). We assumed that mandated students receiving Step 1 in our study would continue to drink slightly above average levels, so we conservatively estimated that 50% of our participants would be eligible for and complete Step 2 following a brief advice session (Step 1). This estimate turned out to be very conservative—in reality, more than 80% of the students were deemed to be high-risk drinkers and eligible for the Step 2 intervention. The resources of the project, and the randomization of approximately half of the participants to an assessment-only group, permitted the retention of these tailoring variables and decision rule throughout the project. In contrast, a college counseling center with fewer resources may not have been able to accommodate all of the students identified as risky drinkers following a brief advice session. Therefore, each institution should take into account resources when establishing a stepped care model. Perhaps other tailoring variables and decision rules may reduce the referrals to the next, more intensive step of care (e.g., students receiving another referral are assigned to receive a BMI). However, a reduction in referrals would also reduce the services to the many students who continue to drink in a risky fashion without being referred for another violation of campus policy.

Third, the method of assessing tailoring variables is an important consideration, as intentional misrepresentation may occur if students are aware of what self-reported behaviors will be used to indicate further treatment. Overall, college students do not appear to significantly misrepresent their alcohol use (Borsari & Muellerleile, 2009). However, if using self-report data as a tailoring variable, it is important to keep the values that indicate further treatment as private as possible to reduce situational demand characteristics. In contrast, objective variables (e.g., recidivism) could be used to determine treatment level and response in mandated students. Such objective measures do not involve any self-report, thus lowering the possibility of intentional bias or obfuscation. That said, a limitation of using recidivism is that the likelihood of receiving a violation may vary greatly across settings and due to different enforcement practices and may not represent risky drinking at all (e.g., students being cited for being in the presence of alcohol).

Finally, once the tailoring variables and the interventions to be used in the stepped care program have been determined, decision rules addressing as many contingencies as possible must be established to ensure that all students receive appropriate care. The more comprehensive these decision rules, the less likely inappropriate and inconsistent treatment assignments will occur. For example, certain referral sources might want their clients to get a more intensive level of care during the initial encounter. That said, there are some indicators of severity (e.g., daily heavy drinking, risk of withdrawal, significant drug use, consistently reaching very high intoxication levels, regular drinking and driving) that may prompt immediate referral to more intensive treatment such as multisession groups or individual counseling. Therefore, it is especially important to establish guidelines regarding immediate referral to more intensive treatment for students displaying serious problems that are unlikely to respond to less intensive interventions (e.g., alcohol abuse or dependence). Detailed decision rules not only improve the consistency of treatment, but also make replication of results much easier (Collins et al., 2004).

FUTURE DIRECTIONS

There has been a remarkable amount of research over the past 15 years on a wide range of interventions for college students. That said, there is a need for continued research on precisely how, and for whom, these interventions work. Mechanisms of behavior change (MOBC) are defined as processes or events that lead to therapeutic improvement (Kazdin, 2007). MOBC have not received much research attention in the past few decades, although appreciation of its importance is increasing (see Apodaca & Longabaugh, 2009). A better understanding of MOBC will facilitate the refinement of existing interventions, as emphasis is placed on the components of treatment that are known to bring about desired changes and ineffective components are removed or revised. In addition, understanding of MOBC informs the study of factors that moderate treatment efficacy: Once MOBC are identified, individual differences in MOBC can be considered during treatment assignment. Therefore, improved understanding of MOBC is particularly relevant in stepped care, which seeks to assign the most effective yet least intensive treatment to the individual.

Second, continued research on improving the efficacy and effectiveness of interventions, administered alone or in combination, is needed. For example, a recent study examined how to improve the effectiveness of computer delivered interventions (Jouriles et al., 2010). Specifically, the authors randomized students to either spend 20 minutes reading computer-delivered feedback about their alcohol use or to spend that time reading and writing down as much of the feedback as they could recall. The latter group not only retained information better but also demonstrated reductions in personal alcohol use, which were mediated by increased memory for the feedback information. Such continued evaluation of the efficacy and effectiveness of treatments will improve interventions that are administered at each step. Regarding stepped care, there have been a number of developments in the theory of stepped care over the past decade (see Murphy et al., 2007) as well as advancements in the analysis of the data these multistepped trials generate. Stepped care approaches addressing cancer and depression can be complex, and rather than comparing the different treatments offered at each step, new parametric models can compare all possible treatment combinations across all steps of the stepped care approach (see Miyahara & Wahed, 2010; Wahed, 2010). Incorporation of such methodological advances will only enhance the efficacy of stepped care in the college setting.

Third, and perhaps most importantly, researchers and clinicians would benefit from a better understanding of what can compel college students to recognize the risks inherent in their alcohol use and to seek any level of treatment. Research has consistently demonstrated that most college student drinkers rarely see themselves as having a problem with drinking (Knight et al., 2002; Vik, Culbertson, & Sellers, 2000). A recent study examined correlates of help seeking in a sample of 197 heavy drinkers (Buscemi et al., 2010). Findings indicate that 18% of the students had sought help from their drinking from friends, family, the Internet, or reading a pamphlet on alcohol use, and that the interventions discussed in this chapter were rarely, if ever, used (less than 3% of the students). Students who did seek help were more likely to report depression, alcohol problems, and a discrepancy between their alcohol use and that of their friends. That said, the vast majority of heavy drinkers in the sample had not sought any type of assistance, even those who reported alcohol-related problems and a discrepancy between their current and ideal level of drinking.

The disconnect between students reporting heavy alcohol use and consequences and a lack of engagement in treatment has been a problem for years. More than 15 years ago, more than 2,400 college students were asked about their interest in five different steps of a comprehensive stepped care approach to limiting alcohol use (Black & Coster, 1996). These 5 steps of care were (1) pamphlets and brochures; (2) single-group session from a health care assistant; (3) take home work including audio and video materials; (4) intensive series of group sessions; and (5) multiple individual counseling sessions with a health care professional. Results indicated overall lack of interest in all of the alcohol interventions; "respondents are most interested in interventions that require less time and effort and the least interested in interventions that are considered 'traditional' and more intensive. . . . generally, however, respondents lacked interest in any intervention" (Black & Coster, 1996, p. 104). This viewpoint can be accommodated by stepped care, as the approach recommends that briefer interventions should be administered unless there is a lack of a response, in which more intensive steps may be implemented. In this way, stepped care aligns with the Institute of Medicine's (1990) recommendation that no one treatment will work for everyone and that individual considerations should be taken into account (e.g., severity of alcohol use and problems, personal preferences for treatment modality). Therefore, fostering motivation for receiving interventions addressing alcohol use in the general college student population is an important area of future research (see Palmer, Kilmer, & Larimer, 2006). Together, such efforts will make stepped care much more relevant and useful in the college setting.

Finally, it must be acknowledged that there are costs associated with the continued monitoring of the tailoring variables that are an integral part of the stepped care approach. Of course, the type and intensity of monitoring depends solely on the tailoring variables (e.g., alcohol use vs. recidivism) and the decision rules (a student drinking more than 20 drinks per week receives Step 2 vs. a student who receives another alcohol citation receives Step 2). However, a recent pilot study provides compelling evidence that a stepped care approach can have significant savings (Drummond et al., 2009). In this study conducted in the United Kingdom, more than 1,700 men in primary care practices were screened using the Alcohol Use Disorders Identification Test (AUDIT; Saunders, Aasland, Babor, de la Fuente, & Grant, 1993). Those with a score of 8 or more were randomly assigned to receive stepped care ($n = 54$) or a control condition consisting of a 5-minute directive advice session and an informational booklet from the nurse ($n = 58$). The stepped care condition had three steps of treatment: (1) one 40-minute motivational interviewing session with a trained nurse; (2) four 50-minute sessions of motivational enhancement therapy (Miller, 1995); and (3) referral to community alcohol treatment. In this project, the tailoring variable was units of alcohol consumed in the past month, and the decision rule was that patients who had consumed 21 or more units in one week or 10 or more units on any one day were eligible for the next step of treatment. In practice, all 58 individuals in the control group received a minimal intervention. Of the 54 individuals assigned to stepped care, 52 individuals received Step 1, 17 individual received Step 2, and 1 individual received Step 3. As was expected, providing a Step 1 intervention (the 40-minute MI session) was more expensive than the control intervention ($340 versus $34 per session). Over the 6-month follow-up period, however, examination of costs associated with health care, social services, the criminal justice system, and alcohol-related accidents revealed that stepped care provided a savings of more than $15,000 compared to the control condition. Extrapolating these results to the 11.5 million college students in the United States indicates that the amount of resources required to implement stepped care, although considerable, will cost considerably less than providing students with interventions that are not needed or, worse, ineffective. That said, additional research is needed that considers the economics costs and benefits of implementing stepped care versus standard approaches to administering interventions to address drinking in the college setting.

CONCLUSION

Stepped care is a promising approach for providing a variety of interventions to a heterogeneous population of college students. Research conducted to date, though limited in scope, provides support for the feasibility and efficacy of stepped care in the college setting. That said, the continued development and refinement of interventions of varying intensity that reduce risky alcohol use in college students must be done to improve the flexibility and effectiveness of stepped care. It will also be vital to increase the student's motivation to engage any of the interventions provided in the context of stepped care. Through such continued efforts, stepped care can provide effective, appropriate, and cost-effective treatment to college students who require additional help in reducing their risky alcohol use.

REFERENCES

Agostinelli, G., Brown, J. M., & Miller, W. R. (1995). Effects of normative feedback on consumption among heavy drinking college students. *Journal of Drug Education, 25*(1), 31–40.

Anderson, D. S., & Gadaleto, A. (2001). *Results of the 2000 college alcohol survey: Comparison with 1997 results and baseline year.* Fairfax, VA: Center for the Advancement of Public Health, George Mason University.

Apodaca, T. R., & Longabaugh, R. (2009). Mechanisms of change in motivational interviewing: A review and preliminary evaluation of the evidence. *Addiction, 104*(5), 705–715.

Babor, T. F. (1994). Avoiding the horrid and beastly sin of drunkenness—Does dissuasion make a difference? *Journal of Consulting and Clinical Psychology, 62*(6), 1127–1140.

Baer, J. S., Kivlahan, D. R., Blume, A. W., McKnight, P., & Marlatt, G. A. (2001). Brief intervention for heavy-drinking college students: 4-year follow-up and natural history. *American Journal of Public Health, 91*(8), 1310.

Baer, J. S., Marlatt, G. A., Kivlahan, D. R., Fromme, K., Larimer, M. E., & Williams, E. (1992). An experimental test of three methods of alcohol risk reduction with young adults. *Journal of Consulting and Clinical Psychology, 60*(6), 974–979.

Barnett, N. P., Borsari, B., Hustad, J. T. P., O'Leary Tevyaw, T., Colby, S. M., Kahler, C. W., & Monti, P. M. (2008). Profiles of college students mandated to alcohol interventions. *Journal of Studies on Alcohol and Drugs, 69,* 684–694.

Barnett, N. P., Murphy, J. G., Colby, S. M., & Monti, P. M. (2007). Efficacy of counselor vs. computer-delivered intervention with mandated college students. *Addictive Behaviors, 32*(11), 2529–2548.

Bien, T. H., Miller, W. R., & Tonigan, J. S. (1993). Brief interventions for alcohol problems: A review. *Addiction, 88*(3), 315.

Black, D. R., & Coster, D. C. (1996). Interest in a stepped approach model (SAM): Identification of recruitment strategies for university alcohol programs. *Health Education Quarterly, 23*(1), 98–114.

Borsari, B., & Carey, K. B. (2005). Two brief alcohol interventions for mandated college students. *Psychology of Addictive Behaviors, 19*(3), 296–302.

Borsari, B., & Muellerleile, P. (2009). Collateral reports in the college setting: A meta-analytic integration. *Alcoholism: Clinical and Experimental Research, 33*(5), 826–838.

Borsari, B., O'Leary Tevyaw, T., Barnett, N. P., Kahler, C. W., & Monti, P. M. (2007). Stepped care for mandated college students: A pilot study. *American Journal on Addictions, 16*, 131–137.

Buscemi, J., Murphy, J. G., Martens, M. P., McDevitt-Murphy, M. E., Dennhardt, A. A., & Skidmore, J. R. (2010). Help-seeking for alcohol-related problems in college students: correlates and preferred resources. *Psychology of Addictive Behaviors, 24*(4), 571–580.

Carey, K. B. (2001). Understanding binge drinking: Introduction to the special issue. *Psychology of Addictive Behaviors, 15*(4), 283–286.

Carey, K. B., Carey, M. P., Henson, J. M., Maisto, S. A., & DeMartini, K. S. (2011). Brief alcohol interventions for mandated college students: Comparison of face-to-face counseling and computer-delivered interventions. *Addiction, 106*(3), 528–537.

Carey, K. B., Scott-Sheldon, L. A. J., Carey, M. P., & DeMartini, K. S. (2007). Individual-level interventions to reduce college student drinking: A meta-analytic review. *Addictive Behaviors, 32*(11), 2469–2494.

Carey, K. B., Scott-Sheldon, L. A. J., Elliott, J. C., Bolles, J. R., & Carey, M. P. (2009). Computer delivered interventions to reduce college student drinking: A meta-analysis. *Addiction, 104*(11), 1807–1819.

Chiauzzi, E., Green, T. C., Lord, S., Thum, C., & Goldstein, M. (2005). My student body: A high-risk drinking prevention web site for college students. *Journal of American College Health, 53*(6), 263–274.

Collins, L. M., Murphy, S. A., & Bierman, K. L. (2004). A conceptual framework for adaptive preventive interventions. *Prevention Science, 5*(3), 185–196.

Collins, L. M., Murphy, S. A., Nair, V. N., & Strecher, V. J. (2005). A strategy for optimizing and evaluating behavioral interventions. *Annals of Behavioral Medicine, 30*(1), 65–73.

Collins, S. E., Carey, K. B., & Sliwinski, M. J. (2002). Mailed personalized normative feedback as a brief intervention for at-risk college drinkers. *Journal of Studies on Alcohol, 63*(5), 559–567.

Cronce, J. M., & Larimer, M. E. (2011). Individual-focused approaches to the prevention of college drinking. *Alcohol, Research & Health, 34*, 210–221.

Dimeff, L. A., Baer, J. S., Kivlahan, D. R., & Marlatt, G. A. (1999). *Brief alcohol screening and intervention for college students (BASICS): A harm reduction approach.* New York, NY: Guilford Press.

Drummond, C., Coulton, S., James, D., Godfrey, C., Parrott, S., Baxter, J., . . . Peters, T. (2009). Effectiveness and cost-effectiveness of a stepped care intervention for alcohol use disorders in primary care: pilot study. *British Journal of Psychiatry, 195*(5), 448–456.

Fleming, M. F., Balousek, S. L., Grossberg, P. M., Mundt, M. P., Brown, D., Wiegel, J. R., . . . Saewyc, E. M. (2010). Brief physician advice for heavy drinking college students: A randomized controlled trial in college health clinics. *Journal of Studies on Alcohol and Drugs, 71*(1), 23–31.

Fromme, K., & Corbin, W. (2004). Prevention of heavy drinking and associated negative consequences among mandated and voluntary college students. *Journal of Consulting and Clinical Psychology, 72*(6), 1038.

Fromme, K., Marlatt, G. A., Baer, J. S., & Kivlahan, D. R. (1994). The alcohol skills training program: A group intervention for young adult drinkers. *Journal of Substance Abuse Treatment, 11*(2), 143–154.

Helmkamp, J. C., Hungerford, D. W., Williams, J. M., Manley, W. G., Furbee, P. M., Horn, K. A., & Pollock, D. A. (2003). Screening and brief intervention for alcohol problems among college students treated in a university hospital emergency department. *Journal of American College Health, 52*(1), 7.

Hester, R. K., Delaney, H. D., & Campbell, W. (2011). The college drinker's check-up: Outcomes of two randomized clinical trials of a computer-delivered intervention. *Psychology of Addictive Behaviors.*

Hingson, R. W., Berson, J., Dowley, K., Plant, M., Single, E., & Stockwell, T. (1997). Interventions to reduce college student drinking and related health and social problems. In M. Plant, E. Single, & T. Stockwell (Eds.), *Alcohol: Minimising the harm: What works?* (pp. 143–170). London, England: Free Association Books.

Hingson, R. W., Zha, W. X., & Weitzman, E. R. (2009). Magnitude of and trends in alcohol-related mortality and morbidity among us college students ages 18–24, 1998–2005. *Journal of Studies on Alcohol and Drugs*, 12–20.

Hoover, E. (2003). Drug and alcohol arrests increased on campuses in 2001. *Chronicle of Higher Education, 49*.

Hustad, J. T., Barnett, N. P., Borsari, B., & Jackson, K. M. (2010). Web-based alcohol prevention for incoming college students: A randomized controlled trial. *Addictive Behaviors, 35*(3), 183–189.

Institute of Medicine. (1990). *Broadening the base of treatment for alcohol problems*. Washington, DC: National Academy Press.

Johnston, L. D., O'Malley, P. M., Bachman, J. G., & Schulenberg, J. E. (2010). *Monitoring the Future national survey results on drug use, 1975–2009: Volume II, College students and adults ages 19–50*. Bethesda, MD: National Institute on Drug Abuse.

Jouriles, E. N., Brown, A. S., Rosenfield, D., McDonald, R., Croft, K., Leahy, M. M., & Walters, S. T. (2010). Improving the effectiveness of computer-delivered personalized drinking feedback interventions for college students. *Psychology of Addictive Behaviors, 24*(4), 592–599.

Kahler, C. W., Strong, D. R., & Read, J. P. (2005). Toward efficient and comprehensive measurement of the alcohol problems continuum in college students: The brief young adult alcohol consequences questionnaire. *Alcoholism, Clinical and Experimental Research, 29*(7), 1180–1189.

Kazdin, A. E. (2007). Mediators and mechanisms of change in psychotherapy research. *Annual Review of Clinical Psychology, 3*, 1–27.

Kivlahan, D. R., Marlatt, G. A., Fromme, K., & Coppel, D. B. (1990). Secondary prevention with college drinkers: Evaluation of an alcohol skills training program. *Journal of Consulting and Clinical Psychology, 58*(6), 805.

Knight, J. R., Wechsler, H., Kuo, M., Seibring, M., Weitzman, E. R., & Schuckit, M. A. (2002). Alcohol abuse and dependence among U.S. college students. *Journal of Studies on Alcohol, 63*(3), 263–270.

Kulesza, M., Apperson, M., Larimer, M. E., & Copeland, A. L. (2010). Brief alcohol intervention for college drinkers: How brief is? *Addictive Behaviors, 35*(7), 730–733.

LaBrie, J. W., Huchting, K. K., Lac, A., Tawalbeh, S., Thompson, A. D., & Larimer, M. E. (2009). Preventing risky drinking in first-year college women: Further validation of a female-specific motivational-enhancement group intervention. *Journal of Studies on Alcohol and Drugs, Suppl 16*, 77–85.

LaBrie, J. W., Pedersen, E. R., Lamb, T. F., & Quinlan, T. (2007). A campus-based motivational enhancement group intervention reduces problematic drinking in freshmen male college students. *Addictive Behaviors, 32*(5), 889–901.

LaBrie, J. W., Thompson, A. D., Huchting, K., Lac, A., & Buckley, K. (2007). A group motivational interviewing intervention reduces drinking and alcohol-related negative consequences in adjudicated college women. *Addictive Behaviors, 32*(11), 2549–2562.

LaChance, H., Ewing, S. W. F., Bryan, A. D., & Hutchison, K. E. (2009). What makes group MET Work? A randomized controlled trial of college student drinkers in mandated alcohol diversion. *Psychology of Addictive Behaviors, 23*(4), 598–612.

Larimer, M. E., & Cronce, J. M. (2002). Identification, prevention and treatment: A review of individual-focused strategies to reduce problematic alcohol consumption by college students. *Journal of Studies on Alcohol, Suppl 14*, 148–163.

Larimer, M. E., & Cronce, J. M. (2007). Identification, prevention, and treatment revisited: individual-focused college drinking prevention strategies 1999–2006. *Addictive Behaviors, 32*, 2439–2468.

Lewis, D. K., & Marchell, T. C. (2006). Safety first: A medical amnesty approach to alcohol poisoning at a U.S. University. *International Journal of Drug Policy, 17*, 329–338.

Marlatt, G. A., Baer, J. S., Kivlahan, D. R., Dimeff, L. A., Larimer, M. E., Quigley, L. A., . . . Williams, E. (1998). Screening and brief intervention for high-risk college student drinkers: Results from a 2-year follow-up assessment. *Journal of Consulting and Clinical Psychology, 66*(4), 604–615.

Mastroleo, N. R., Murphy, J. G., Colby, S. M., Monti, P. M., & Barnett, N. P. (2011). Incident-specific and individual-level moderators of brief intervention effects with mandated college students. *Psychology of Addictive Behaviors, 25*(4), 616–624.

Michael, K. D., Curtin, L., Kirkley, D. E., Jones, D. L., & Harris, R. (2006). Group-based motivational interviewing for alcohol use among college students: An exploratory study. *Professional Psychology-Research and Practice, 37*(6), 629–634.

Miller, E. T., Kilmer, J. R., Kim, E. L., Weingardt, K. R., & Marlatt, G. A. (2001). Alcohol skills training for adolescents. In S. M. C. P. M. Monti, & T. O'Leary Tevyaw (Eds.), *Adolescents, alcohol, and substance abuse: Reaching teens through brief interventions* (pp. 183–215). New York, NY: Guilford Press.

Miller, W. R. (1995). *Motivational enhancement therapy manual: A clinical research guide for therapists treating individuals with alcohol abuse and dependence, Volume 2.* New York, NY: DIANE.

Miller, W. R., & Rollnick, S. (2002). *Motivational interviewing: Preparing people for change* (2nd ed.). New York, NY: Guilford Press.

Miyahara, S., & Wahed, A. S. (2010). Weighted Kaplan-Meier estimators for two-stage treatment regimes. *Statistics in Medicine, 29*(25), 2581–2591.

Moreira, M. T., Smith, L. A., & Foxcroft, D. (2009). Social norms interventions to reduce alcohol misuse in university or college students. *Cochrane Database of Systematic Reviews, 3*, CD006748.

Moyer, A., Finney, J. W., Swearingen, C. E., & Vergun, P. (2002). Brief interventions for alcohol problems: A meta-analytic review of controlled investigations in treatment-seeking and non-treatment-seeking populations. *Addiction, 97*(3), 279–292.

Mun, E. Y., White, H. R., & Morgan, T. J. (2009). Individual and situational factors that influence the efficacy of personalized feedback substance use interventions for mandated college students. *Journal of Consulting and Clinical Psychology, 77*(1), 88–102.

Murphy, S. A. (2005). An experimental design for the development of adaptive treatment strategies. *Experimental Design, 12*(1), 28.

Murphy, S. A., Lynch, K. G., Oslin, D., McKay, J. R., & TenHave, T. (2007). Developing adaptive treatment strategies in substance abuse research. *Drug and Alcohol Dependence, 88, Suppl 2*, S24–S30.

NIAAA. (2002). *A call to action: Changing the culture of drinking at US colleges.* Bethesda, MD: National Institutes on Alcohol Abuse and Alcoholism.

NIAAA. (2004). NIAAA council approves definition of binge drinking. *NIAAA Newsletter, 3*, 3.

Norcross, J. C., Krebs, P. M., & Prochaska, J. O. (2011). Stages of change. *Journal of Clinical Psychology, 67*(2), 143–154.

O'Donohue, W. T., & Draper, C. (Eds.). (2011). *Stepped care and eHealth: Practical applications to behavioral disorders.* New York, NY: Springer.

Palmer, R. S., Kilmer, J. R., & Larimer, M. E. (2006). If you feed them, will they come? The use of social marketing to increase interest in attending a college alcohol program. *Journal of American College Health, 55*(1), 47–52.

Paschal, M. J., Bersamin, M., Fearnow-Kenney, M., Wyrick, D., & Currey, D. (2006). Short-term evaluation of a web-based college alcohol misuse and harm prevention course (college alc). *Journal of Alcohol and Drug Education, 50*(3), 49–65.

Paschall, M. J., Antin, T., Ringwalt, C. L., & Saltz, R. F. (2011). Evaluation of an Internet-based alcohol misuse prevention course for college freshmen: Findings of a randomized multi-campus trial. *American Journal of Preventive Medicine, 41*(3), 300–308.

Porter, J. (2006, October 27). Alcohol arrests amongst college students continue to increase. *Chronicle of Higher Education.*

Saltz, R. F. (2011). Environmental approaches to prevention in college settings. *Alcohol Research and Health, 34*, 204–209.

Saunders, J. B., Aasland, O. G., Babor, T. F., de la Fuente, J. R., & Grant, M. (1993). Development of the alcohol use disorders identification test (AUDIT): WHO Collaborative project on early detection of persons with harmful alcohol consumption–II. *Addiction, 88*(6), 791–804.

Schaus, J. F., Sole, M. L., McCoy, T. P., Mullett, N., & O'Brien, M. C. (2009). Alcohol screening and brief intervention in a college student health center: A randomized controlled trial. *Journal on Studies of Alcohol and Drugs, Suppl 16*, 131–141.

Scott-Sheldon, L. A. J., Carey, K. B., Elliott, J. C., Bolles, J. R., & Carey, M. P. (2009). Computer-delivered interventions to reduce college student drinking: A meta-analysis. *Addiction, 104*(11), 1807–1819.

Sobell, M. B., & Sobell, L. C. (2000). Stepped care as a heuristic approach to the treatment of alcohol problems. *Journal of Consulting and Clinical Psychology, 68*(4), 573–579.

Stout, R. L., Wirtz, P. W., Carbonari, J. P., & Del Boca, F. K. (1994). Ensuring balanced distribution of prognostic factors in treatment outcome reserach. *Journal of Studies on Alcohol, Suppl 12*, 70–75.

Vik, P. W., Culbertson, K. A., & Sellers, K. (2000). Readiness to change drinking among heavy-drinking college students. *Journal of Studies on Alcohol, 61*(5), 674–680.

Wahed, A. S. (2010). Inference for two-stage adaptive treatment strategies using mixture distributions. *Journal of the Royal Statistical Society: Series C: Applied Statistics, 59*, 1–18.

Walters, S. T., Bennett, M. E., & Miller, J. H. (2000). Reducing alcohol use in college students: A controlled trial of two brief interventions. *Journal of Drug Education, 30*(3), 361–372.

Walters, S. T., Gruenewald, D. A., Miller, J. H., & Bennett, M. E. (2001). Early findings from a disciplinary program to reduce problem drinking by college students. *Journal of Substance Abuse Treatment, 20*(1), 89–91.

Walters, S. T., Vader, A. M., & Harris, T. R. (2007). A controlled trial of web-based feedback for heavy drinking college students. *Prevention Science, 8*, 83–88.

Walters, S. T., Vader, A. M., Harris, T. R., Field, C. A., & Jouriles, E. N. (2009). Dismantling motivational interviewing and feedback for college drinkers: a randomized clinical trial. *J Consult Clin Psychol, 77*(1), 64–73.

Walters, S. T., Wright, J. A., & Shegog, R. (2006). A review of computer and Internet-based interventions for smoking behavior. *Addictive Behaviors, 31*(2), 264–277.

Wechsler, H., Lee, J. E., Hall, J., Wagenaar, A. C., & Lee, H. (2002). Secondhand effects of student alcohol use reported by neighbors of colleges: The role of alcohol outlets. *Social Science and Medicine, 55*, 425–435.

Wechsler, H., Lee, J. E., Kuo, M., Seibring, M., Nelson, T. F., & Lee, H. (2002). Trends in college binge drinking during a period of increased prevention efforts. Findings from 4 Harvard school of public health college alcohol study surveys: 1993–2001. *Journal of American College Health, 50*, 203–217.

Wechsler, H., Lee, J. E., Nelson, T. F., & Kuo, M. (2002). Underage college students' drinking behavior, access to alcohol, and the influence of deterrence policies. Findings from the Harvard school of public health college alcohol study. *Journal of American College Health, 50*(5), 223–236.

Wechsler, H., Seibring, M., Liu, I. C., & Ahl, M. (2004). Colleges respond to student binge drinking: Reducing student demand or limiting access. *Journal of American College Health, 52*(4), 159–168.

Wilk, A. I., Jensen, N. M., & Havighurst, T. C. (1997). Meta-analysis of randomized control trials addressing brief interventions in heavy alcohol drinkers. *Journal of General Internal Medicine, 12*(5), 274–283.

Wray, T. B., Simons, J. S., & Dvorak, R. D. (2011). Alcohol-related infractions among college students: Associations with subsequent drinking as a function of sensitivity to punishment. *Psychology of Addictive Behaviors, 25*(2), 352–357.

Zisserson, R. N., Palfai, T., & Saitz, R. (2007). "No-contact" interventions for unhealthy college drinking: Efficacy of alternatives to person-delivered intervention approaches. *Substance Abuse, 28*(4), 119–131.

9

Brief Motivational Interventions

Kate B. Carey

The brief motivational intervention (BMI) is a brief interaction that provides personalized feedback and uses motivational enhancement strategies to promote alcohol risk reduction. The term BMI has been used sometimes in the literature to refer to brief interventions that may be delivered by computer or other media when they are characterized by personalized feedback designed to enhance motivation for change. However, the focus of this chapter will be the face-to-face format of BMIs, which empirical evidence has shown to be consistently efficacious in reducing drinking and its consequences among at-risk college drinkers.

BMIs are brief because they may last from 10 minutes to about an hour (e.g., Kulesza, Apperson, Larimer, & Copeland, 2010). A common format consists of an initial assessment of current drinking and related risks, followed by a feedback session (Dimeff, Baer, Kivlahan, & Marlatt, 1999). Alternative approaches may involve concurrent assessment of a more limited number of consumption and related variables during the BMI (Terry, 2011). The assessment phase allows the interventionist to develop personalized feedback on the individual's consumption and consequences and sometimes other dimensions of alcohol-related risk. Normative comparisons may be presented to help the drinker contextualize their drinking behavior. BMIs generally employ a motivational interviewing (MI) style (Miller & Rollnick, 2002), an approach designed to help persons who are ambivalent about change to identify and resolve the sources of ambivalence. In this context, the use of MI promotes a nonconfrontational and collaborative discussion that serves to mobilize and enhance the drinker's personal reasons for change. BMIs used in college settings generally encourage participants to consider harm reduction goals, consistent with a public health intervention model (Marlatt, 2002).

BMIs are typically employed as an indicated prevention strategy with higher-risk drinkers such as those who have been screened for at-risk or problematic drinking patterns or those who have been mandated to an intervention because of an alcohol-related incident. However, BMIs also have been used productively with a wide range of drinkers, including as a selective prevention strategy when at-risk groups (not individuals) are targeted (Turrisi et al., 2009) and as a universal prevention strategy for freshmen (Wood et al., 2010). When the participant is a light drinker, the focus tends to be harm prevention and affirmation of skills for making safe choices in risky drinking environments. When the participant is a heavier drinking student with alcohol-related problems, discussions focus on harm reduction and may be supplemented with referrals to more intensive intervention (e.g., Babor et al., 2007). In cases when elevated risk involves symptoms of alcohol dependence, BMI should be supplemented with a more thorough diagnostic assessment and, if indicated, more intensive treatment. The choice of BMI as an intervention strategy generally assumes that participant possesses the skills to implement change goals. Thus, a BMI is ideal for a wide range of drinkers whose primary barrier to change is problem recognition and motivation for change.

ORIGINS

BMIs tailored for college drinkers trace their roots to the Drinker's Check-Up (Miller, Sovereign, & Krege, 1988), a brief, feedback-based intervention targeted to nondependent problem drinkers who were not seeking treatment. William Miller and colleagues developed a low-threshold "check-up" akin to a medical check-up and advertised for participants through print ads. Like the familiar medical consultation, the Drinker's Check-Up consisted of assessment, feedback, and goal setting in an integrated intervention. It incorporated elements of brief interventions considered to be effective, summarized by the acronym FRAMES: providing personalized Feedback, emphasizing individual Responsibility for change, offering clear Advice for change, providing a Menu of options, use of Empathetic style and support of personal Self-efficacy (Miller & Sanchez, 1994). The brief consultation opportunity marketed as a "check-up" and not alcohol treatment attracted self-referrals from drinkers in the community; controlled evaluations revealed that after two-sessions (an alcohol assessment and a feedback session) participants significantly reduced drinking and consequences (Miller, Benefield, & Tonigan, 1993; Miller et al., 1988). The Drinker's Check-Up was subsequently adapted for other populations of drinkers. When offered as a motivational induction session before treatment, it enhanced treatment attendance and engagement (Walitzer, Dermen, & Connors, 1999). Also, a version of a Drinker's Check-Up tailored to college students was described as one component of a comprehensive alcohol prevention program (Miller, Toscova, Miller, & Sanchez, 2000).

Parallel developments were taking place at the University of Washington, the site of a series of controlled studies of alcohol prevention programs for heavy drinking college students. An unexpected finding shaped subsequent intervention development. Specifically, Baer and colleagues (1992) reported equivalent outcomes for a group alcohol skills training class (ASTP) consisting of six 90-minute sessions, and a 1-hour motivational interview. The briefer intervention provided personalized feedback and advice, consistent with FRAMES and the Drinkers Check-Up, and included some of the informational content tailored to college drinkers contained in the longer ASTP. Subsequent research from the Washington group evaluated a similarly brief intervention that took an explicitly harm reduction approach with at-risk freshman students (Marlatt et al., 1998). Significant reductions in drinking and alcohol consequences were observed up to 4 years later in students who received the brief intervention as freshmen relative to no-treatment controls (Baer, Kivlahan, Blume, McKnight, & Marlatt, 2001). Furthermore, the brief intervention effect was robust across gender, family history of alcoholism, and residence (Marlatt et al., 1998). This brief feedback-based intervention tailored to college drinkers was manualized and is now known as BASICS (Brief Alcohol Screening and Intervention for College Students) (Dimeff et al., 1999).

EVOLUTION AND DIVERSIFICATION OF BMIs

The publication of the BASICS manual promoted dissemination of BMIs in college settings, and served as a springboard for adaptations. Variations emerged on several dimensions, including the (a) predominance and nature of personalized feedback, (b) the kind of normative comparisons provided, (c) the amount of alcohol education offered, (d) the extent of personalized goal setting incorporated into the intervention, and (e) the nature of the interventionist. It is clear that BMIs are continuously evolving as they are tailored to specific types of students and college environments.

One dimension on which BMIs vary is the relative emphasis on MI style (e.g., Walters & Baer, 2006) versus personalized feedback (e.g., Dimeff et al., 1999). Personalized feedback alone is effective in prompting drinking reduction in general population and student samples (Riper et al., 2009; Walters & Neighbors, 2005), and is generally considered a core component of BMIs. However, the amount of personalized feedback provided in BMIs ranges from minimal to extensive, relative to MI-style discussion of the topics raised by the feedback. Examples of this variability across successful BMIs follow.

Feedback data may be derived from various sources. The original BASICS supplemented information gathered on self-report questionnaires with a period of self-monitoring of drinking behavior prior to the feedback session (Dimeff et al., 1999; Marlatt et al., 1998). However, many subsequent applications obtain assessment data exclusively from initial surveys (e.g., Carey, Carey, Maisto, & Henson, 2006; McNally, Palfai, & Kahler, 2005; Wood, Capone, Laforge, Erickson, & Brand, 2007). Information used for personalized feedback may also be obtained within the session, when prior assessment data are lacking or deemed inaccurate.

BMIs also vary in terms of the specific types of feedback provided. In fact, the BASICS manual encourages programs to develop their own assessment packages to use as sources of feedback. Thus, a common core of personalized feedback includes recent consumption (e.g., drinks per week, recent peak drinking), average and peak BAC values, alcohol-related consequences, other risk behaviors (e.g., drinking and driving, risky sexual behavior), and perceived norms. Additional feedback elements incorporated in some BMIs include alcohol-related expectancies (Borsari & Carey, 2005; Larimer et al., 2001; White et al., 2006), time spent on drinking versus other activities (Butler & Correia, 2009; Murphy, Dennhardt, Skidmore, Martens, & McDevitt-Murphy, 2010), money spent on alcohol and/or calories attributable to alcohol intake (Murphy et al., 2010; Wood et al., 2007), energy expenditure needed to burn off alcohol calories (Turrisi et al., 2009), and protective behavioral strategies employed (Barnett et al., 2007; Turrisi et al., 2009). Some BMIs also include feedback on personal risk factors such as family history of alcohol problems (White et al., 2006; Wood et al., 2007), AUDIT score (Barnett, Murphy, Colby, & Monti, 2007; Walters, Vader, Harris, Field, & Jouriles, 2009), drug use (Murphy et al., 2010; White et al., 2006), or depression scores (White et al., 2006). Targeting type of feedback to the concerns of specific student groups (e.g., athletes) enhances the chance that it is viewed as relevant and engaging. Personalized feedback can serve dual motivational purposes: to provoke a heightened awareness of current behavior and potentially generate a sense of discrepancy between current behavior and an implicit set of standards.

An additional source of variability within BMIs is the nature of the normative comparisons. Comparison of student consumption with peer drinking (or perception of peer drinking) has also been referred to as normative correction or personalized normative feedback. This comparison serves to create a sense of discrepancy, a key motivational principle of MI (Miller & Rollnick, 2002), and is thought to be particularly effective with adolescents and young adults because of their developmental focus on peer relationships (Brown, 2004). Normative comparisons may create two sources of discrepancy: between self-other (i.e., "your typical drinks per week places you in the 87th percentile of college students nationwide") and between perceptions of other's behavior and their actual behavior (i.e., "you estimated that college women typically consume 12 drinks a week, when the norm for women on your campus is 5 drinks a week"). Inclusion of normative comparisons is a core component of BMIs because it appears to be an active ingredient of the intervention. Research has demonstrated that changes in perceived norms mediate the efficacy of BMI across multiple samples (Borsari & Carey, 2000; Carey, Henson, Carey, & Maisto, 2010; Doumas, McKinley, & Book, 2009; Doumas, Workman, Smith, & Navarro, 2011; Wood et al., 2007).

Given the key role normative information plays in BMIs, questions have been raised as to the appropriate normative comparison group. Recent research highlights the value of providing gender-specific norms; for female students with a strong gender identity, using female norms results in greater reductions in drinking (Lewis & Neighbors, 2007). Some BMIs provide both gender-specific national norms and local campus norms to increase the personal relevance of the normative comparisons on consumption (e.g., Carey, Carey, Henson, Maisto, & DeMartini, 2011; Carey,

Henson, Carey, & Maisto, 2009). Norms for groups that are at least one step closer to the student than the "typical college student" (i.e., similar on gender, ethnicity, and/or residential status) are uniquely predictive of drinking behavior (Larimer et al., 2009) and thus may be the optimal choice for normative feedback. Thus, there may be value in selecting normative feedback from relevant affiliation groups if perceived personal relevance results in greater attention and processing of the corrective normative feedback, and adjustments in perceived norms are considered proximal determinants of drinking behavior. Other examples reported in the literature include providing norms specific to members of Greek organizations (Larimer et al., 2001) and student athletes (LaBrie, Hummer, Huchting, & Neighbors, 2009).

It is worth noting that choice of normative reference group will have implications for the degree of similarity between estimated and actual norms, and students' own use relative to actual peer norms. The closer the comparison group, the more like the student the actual norms will be, and the more accurate will be the students' estimates. Thus, the largest discrepancies between estimated and actual norms will be observed for more distal groups (e.g., college students nationwide) whereas smaller discrepancies will be obtained when feedback is given for reference groups closer to the student. Given that normative feedback is designed (in part) to highlight a discrepancy between perceived and actual norms, common wisdom suggests that the optimal reference group is relevant and moderately proximal but not too close to ensure that there is room for downward adjustment.

BMIs provide both structured and unstructured opportunities to enhance knowledge about alcohol and drinking. Experience reveals gaps in knowledge on topics such as standard drink size and blood alcohol concentration (BAC) estimation, gender differences, and behavioral effects; effects of alcohol on the brain; tolerance; causes of blackouts; what is meant by alcohol poisoning; effects of alcohol on sleep; impacts of alcohol on physical fitness; and methods of drinking to avoid excessive intoxication. Often student interest is high when these topics are presented in an engaging way that respects their autonomy. Descriptions of BMIs available in the literature reveal that many include a core of alcohol educational content such as BAC and safer drinking strategies. The core may be tailored to student characteristics; as an example, Turrisi and colleagues (2009) presented information relevant to athletes on the effects of alcohol on athletic performance and injury recovery. Interventionists may be prepared to offer additional information as windows of opportunity and curiosity present themselves.

Additional components of BMIs that are included in some protocols include discussions of harm reduction (Borsari & Carey, 2005; Carey et al., 2011; Carey, Carey, et al., 2006; Carey et al., 2009), explicit discussion of setting goals for safer drinking (Barnett et al., 2007; Carey et al., 2011; Carey, Carey, et al., 2006; Carey et al., 2009; McNally et al., 2005; Murphy et al., 2010), and presenting a menu of behavioral tips for safer drinking (e.g., Carey, Carey, et al., 2006; Murphy et al., 2004; Turrisi et al., 2009).

Goal setting itself has motivational effects, consistent with theories of self-regulation (Miller & Brown, 1991). Together these components provide opportunities for the student to verbalize a commitment to change, known to be predictive of behavior change outside of the session (Amrhein, Miller, Yahne, Palmer, & Fulcher, 2003; Apodaca & Longabaugh, 2009). Recent studies have incorporated additional components based in behavioral theories of choice, such as discussion of college and career goals, and how they relate to decisions about substance use (Murphy et al., 2010), and discussion of enjoyable social activities that don't involve drinking (Carey et al., 2011). Incorporation of these elements recognizes that drinking behavior of college students occurs in a context where multiple options for allocating time exist, and developmental goals may compete at any given time (e.g., having a rich social life and getting good grades). Enhancing the salience of alternatives to the drinking culture may serve to encourage students to make decisions more consistent with their goals and values.

Finally, the person who delivers the BMI varies. Whereas initially BMIs were delivered by trained counselors (often graduate students in clinical/counseling psychology), student peers have also been trained to deliver these interventions. Whether BMIs are equally effective when delivered by professionals or peers has received minimal attention. The few direct comparisons conducted with college alcohol interventions reveal no distinct advantage of trained counselors (Fromme & Corbin, 2004; Larimer et al., 2001). However, when studies using peer counselors to deliver BMIs have evaluated adherence to MI principles, they have reported suboptimal ratings of MI skill, despite high student satisfaction with the intervention (Cimini et al., 2009; Turrisi et al., 2009). Thus, there appears to be little difference in the efficacy of peer versus professional counselors, even though there are differences in the ability to deliver the intervention using sound MI style. Of potential relevance is a meta-analysis on the potential mechanisms of change in MI (Apodaca & Longabaugh, 2009). Inadequate evidence was found to document the direct impact of MI-consistent behaviors on outcomes (i.e., reflective listening, affirming), but MI-inconsistent behaviors (e.g., confronting and directing) on the part of the therapist were associated with worse outcomes. Thus, it is not yet known whether type of interventionist matters to outcomes, as long as she or he avoids MI-inconsistent behaviors.

BMIs have evolved into a family of interventions with a common core of content and style, but with considerable variations on both. Although the focus of this chapter is interventions delivered in-person, BMIs for college drinkers have also been adapted for administration by computer (Hester, Squires, & Delaney, 2005) and in groups (LaBrie et al., 2008; LaBrie et al., 2009). It is also worth noting that BMIs tailored to college students have developed in parallel with the broader use of brief alcohol interventions in health care settings. Screening and brief intervention models have been manualized for use in primary care (Babor & Higgins-Biddle, 2001; National Institute on Alcohol Abuse and Alcoholism, 2005), emergency care (Higgins-Biddle,

Hungerford, & Cates-Wessel, 2009) and public health settings (American Public Health Association, 2008).

EMPIRICAL SUPPORT FOR BMIs

Face-to-face BMIs are consistently efficacious in reducing drinking and its consequences among at-risk college drinkers. Risk reduction associated with participation in a BMI has been demonstrated in a variety of student subgroups: heavy drinking volunteers (e.g., Borsari & Carey, 2000; Carey, Carey, et al., 2006; Marlatt et al., 1998; Wood et al., 2007), mandated students (e.g., Barnett et al., 2007; Carey et al., 2011; Carey et al., 2009; White, Mun, Pugh, & Morgan, 2007), students screened for at risk drinking at health centers (Fleming et al., 2010; Schaus, Sole, McCoy, Mullett, & O'Brien, 2009), and freshman athletes (Turrisi et al., 2009). Furthermore, when reported, client satisfaction ratings favor BMI over alternate, less personalized interventions (Butler & Correia, 2009; Carey et al., 2009; Murphy et al., 2001). This growing body of research allows more confident conclusions to be drawn about the efficacy of BMIs in college settings.

Early studies established that students who participated in BMIs showed significantly better outcomes than students who received assessment-only or no-treatment conditions (e.g., Borsari & Carey, 2000; Marlatt et al., 1998). Based on these initial controlled evaluations, BMIs emerged as one of three interventions designed for college students known to be efficacious (Larimer & Cronce, 2002; Task Force of the National Advisory Council on Alcohol Abuse and Alcoholism, 2002). A subsequent narrative review confirmed additional empirical support for motivational interventions incorporating personalized normative feedback, across a wider range of student groups (Larimer & Cronce, 2007) and remarked that these components appear to be efficacious whether feedback is delivered in-person or via computer or mail.

Quantitative reviews also provide evidence that the individual components of BMIs are associated with better outcomes on alcohol consumption and consequences in college samples. A meta-analysis on individual-level alcohol interventions for college students revealed effect sizes across outcome measures ranging from small to medium (Carey, Scott-Sheldon, Carey, & DeMartini, 2007). Factors related to intervention were examined for their ability to explain variability in effect size estimates. Stronger effects were observed when an intervention was delivered in-person, to an individual (vs. group), using motivational interviewing, and providing personalized normative feedback. A recently completed meta-analysis examining face-to-face versus computer-delivered alcohol interventions for college drinkers reveals stronger effects for face-to-face interventions at both short- and long-term follow-ups (Carey et al., 2012). The face-to-face interventions tend to produce significant effects across a wider range of alcohol outcome variables.

As mentioned, studies designed to demonstrate the efficacy of BMIs relative to no intervention have yielded consistently favorable results. Relatively few studies compare BMI to active comparison conditions. In these more rigorous tests of efficacy, BMIs do not always differ significantly from other alcohol-focused interventions, such as personalized feedback alone (Murphy et al., 2004) or multicomponent computer-delivered interventions (Barnett et al., 2007; Carey et al., 2011). However, when differential effects between active interventions are found they favor BMI (e.g., Borsari & Carey, 2005; Carey et al., 2011; Doumas et al., 2011; Murphy et al., 2010).

Recent research has addressed more sophisticated questions about BMI efficacy. Walters et al. (2009) used a dismantling design to demonstrate that an intervention consisting of MI plus personalized feedback produced better outcomes than the individual components (feedback-only or MI-only). Three recent comparative efficacy studies compared BMI to other empirically supported face-to-face interventions. Wood et al. (2007) evaluated the separate and combined effects of BMI and an expectancy challenge intervention with student volunteers who were screened for risky drinking. Wood and colleagues found that both interventions reduced drinking in the short term and the BMI produced reductions in problems as well. Relative to the expectancy challenge, the BMI effects maintained better at the final follow-up. Wood and colleagues found no added benefit for participating in both of the interventions. Two separate studies evaluated the separate and combined effects of BMI and a parent handbook intervention. In the first, Turrisi and colleagues (2009) targeted first-year athletes, and found that the combined group was most efficacious in reducing consumption and consequences over the first year, but unlike the parent intervention, the BMI alone reduced weekend drinking and peak consumption. The second study evaluated BMI and a parent intervention separately and in combination as a universal prevention strategy for incoming freshmen (Wood et al., 2010). Participation in BMI (either alone or in combination) prevented the onset of heavy episodic drinking and negative consequences to a greater extent than either the parent intervention or assessment only. The combination of the two interventions had an additive effect only on the likelihood of experiencing negative consequences. In summary, the positive effects of BMI have held up when compared to active alternative interventions, and some evidence suggests that efficacy is enhanced when the individually focused BMI is combined with an alcohol abuse prevention intervention that involves parents.

Moderator analyses can identify for whom and under what conditions does an intervention produce the better or worse outcomes. As a general rule, BMIs are equally effective for both male and female students (Carey et al., 2009; Carey et al., 2011; Marlatt et al., 1998), a consistent finding that reflects the ease with which BMIs can be tailored to individual students. Murphy et al. (2001) reported that heavier drinkers assigned to BASICS improved more than those assigned to education or assessment only. Influenced by this finding, subsequent studies of BMIs generally screen students for heavy drinking (e.g., meeting criteria for a binge episode at least once a month) or target at-risk groups (such as mandated students or athletes). Neither family history of alcohol problems (Marlatt et al., 1998) nor an elevated AUDIT score (Carey et al., 2009) interacted with BMI outcomes in at-risk drinkers. Whereas a wide range of students will benefit from participating in a BMI, recent studies have identified student characteristics that predict relatively poor response to alternative interventions relative to BMI. Specifically, women (Carey et al., 2009; Carey et al., 2011) and African American students (Murphy et al., 2010) respond significantly better to a BMI than to computer-delivered interventions.

Differential efficacy favoring BMIs is emerging for an important subgroup of students—those who are mandated to take an intervention after having violated campus alcohol policy. The process of being sanctioned for an alcohol-related event has been associated with modest reductions in consumption (e.g., Carey et al., 2009; Hustad et al., 2011; Morgan, White, & Mun, 2008), raising the difficulty for detecting differential outcomes among active interventions. Nonetheless, mounting evidence indicates that mandated students respond more positively to BMIs relative to alternative active interventions. BMIs have compared favorably to computer-delivered interventions (Carey et al., 2009; Carey et al., 2011, Doumas et al., 2011), to written personalized feedback (White et al., 2007), to individual alcohol education sessions (Borsari & Carey, 2005), and to treatment-as-usual (including computer-delivered and group modalities; Amaro et al., 2009). To date, no alternative intervention has resulted in more risk reduction than BMI with mandated students. Given current evidence, BMIs appear to be the intervention of choice for mandated students.

In sum, the empirical evidence supports continued use of BMIs as an intervention option for college alcohol abuse prevention. They are well-received by multiple student subgroups and may be better received than popular computer-delivered prevention programs by some students. Furthermore, BMIs have been adapted for universal, selective, and indicated prevention goals. Future research will continue to identify optimal settings and targets for their use, as well as active ingredients through components analysis. Preliminary evidence suggests that combining individually focused BMIs with interventions involving parents might enhance outcomes for students transitioning to college.

SUGGESTIONS FOR CONDUCTING A BRIEF MOTIVATIONAL INTERVENTION

The following sections offer concrete suggestions for preparing for and implementing BMIs for college drinkers. Sample dialog is provided to illustrate how the components are delivered in a motivational style.

Preparation

Planning to implement BMIs for college alcohol prevention will include at least three components. First, it is helpful for the persons who will implement the program to be familiar with motivational interviewing so that the content can be delivered in ways that emphasize collaboration, promote autonomy, and avoid resistance. Second, to provide personalized feedback with normative comparisons, appropriate sets of drinking norms need to be identified. Third, the desired feedback components of the BMI need to be identified and a feedback form template developed. Each of these preparatory steps are discussed in turn.

MI style. MI is characterized by a client-centered yet directive counseling style that enhances motivation for change by helping individuals clarify and resolve ambivalence about behavior change (Miller & Rollnick, 2002). Not just a set of therapeutic techniques, good MI reflects a certain spirit or set of assumptions about the client and the role of the counselor. For example, one assumes that every student has potential for changing his or her drinking behavior, but not that every student has a "problem" with alcohol. In fact, the term *problem* should rarely be used unless raised by the student, as it may engender reactance from young adults who believe that heavy drinking is a normal part of the college experience. In MI, the counselor is a guide rather than an expert, and seeks to establish a collaborative stance. This approach emphasizes student autonomy and personal agency, conditions associated with successful health behavior change (Sheldon, Joiner, & Williams, 2003). Thus, one assumes that the reasons for and methods of change will be derived from a student's idiosyncratic concerns, goals, and preferences. In the context of a BMI, it is usually better to support a student-generated plan, as long as it is consistent with harm reduction, than to try to persuade the student to pursue a plan that the counselor may see as preferable.

The techniques of MI serve to engage the student in active exploration and problem solving, developing discrepancy between the status quo of risky drinking and student's goals and values, and supporting self-efficacy for making changes within the student's social environment. MI style is well suited to young adults who are establishing their independence and autonomy from authority figures, yet who are also still developing their self-regulation skills with regard to health risk behaviors such as drinking. Experience suggests that MI adds considerable value when working with students who start the intervention with a level of resistance or wariness; implementing principles such as expressing empathy and rolling with resistance, coupled with techniques such reflective listening, can create an interaction in which initially resistant students become engaged in the intervention. The use of MI may explain why BMIs produce risk reduction and high levels of satisfaction even among mandated students.

Interventionists who wish to cultivate their MI skills have several resources available to them. The Miller and Rollnick (2002) book is a good start for an introduction to the theory and techniques, and Rosengren's (2009) workbook on building motivational interviewing skills contains useful exercises for shaping MI style. The Motivational Interviewing Network of Trainers (MINT) maintains a website (www.motivationalinterviewing.org/) where training opportunities are posted, with a searchable list of trainers. Another helpful site affiliated with MINT contains videos, books, and other resources for students of MI (http://motivationalinterview.net/).

Obtain appropriate norms for normative feedback. Many universities and colleges administer the CORE survey, or the National College Health Assessment (NCHA) to learn about their students and help them to plan and/or evaluate prevention programming. These are good sources of local norms for drinks per week, as both collect such data. Gender-specific percentiles can be generated by tabulating drinks per week separately for each gender and then creating user-friendly tables for interventionists to use to match a given student's drinks per week with the appropriate percentile rank. Local norms may also be available for heavy drinking frequency, alcohol-related problems, and other variables of interest. Institutions interested in initiating their own local survey assessment for the purpose of generating representative norms can find guidelines for conducting surveys online (e.g., DeJong, 2008) or from their social science departments.

Information on student drinking patterns aggregated across campuses can be obtained from the online reports published by the American College Health Association (e.g., American College Health Association, 2010; Wechsler, Molnar, Davenport, & Baer, 1999) and the Core Institute (www.core.siuc.edu/results.html). User-friendly but somewhat dated tables for determining gender-specific percentiles for binge drinking (Wechsler et al., 1999) and drinks per week (Meilman, Presley, & Cashin, 1997) have been derived from national college databases. Finally, Chan and colleagues (Chan, Neighbors, Gilson, Larimer, & Marlatt, 2007) provide norms tables for adults from the National Epidemiologic Survey on Alcohol and Related Conditions. Gender- and age-specific percentiles can be obtained for drinks per week, whereas means are presented for drinks per typical occasion. Relevant reference groups are individuals aged 18 to 20 or 21 to 25, and include individuals both attending and not attending college.

Personalized feedback form. Prior to implementing a BMI, one must decide what specific feedback will be delivered, and how the feedback will be presented to the student. Several models for personalized feedback forms are publicly available (Dimeff et al., 1999; Walters & Baer, 2006). A sample feedback form for a female student, containing a composite data for illustrative purposes, appears in Figure 9.1. The feedback form serves two important functions. It helps to structure the session and, because the student is encouraged to take it home, it also serves as a reminder and future reference. Feedback forms tend to be structured similarly because they start with consumption feedback and end with goal setting and/or tips for safer drinking, with other forms of feedback and didactic elements in the middle. The rationale for this sequencing is that the most descriptive, least threatening feedback elements are presented first (i.e., consumption); potentially more sensitive feedback elements (i.e., consequences) appear farther into the intervention after rapport and a nonjudgmental tone has been established. Elements that involve thinking about change (i.e., goal setting and/or protective behavioral strategies) are best placed at the end of the session after opportunities have emerged for the student to express some concerns and change talk.

Implementing the BMI

A BMI is implemented in two phases. The first involves conducting a preliminary assessment, which may take the form of a self-report survey, a structured interview, and/or self-monitoring of alcohol consumption for a 1- to 2-week period. Schedule sufficient time to harvest the data provided by the student to populate the personalized feedback form.

The second phase is the feedback session, which can vary in structure and content as discussed. This section will follow the elements represented on the personalized feedback form contained in Figure 9.1, consistent with the interventions described by Carey and colleagues (Carey et al., 2011; Carey, Carey, et al., 2006; Carey et al., 2009). This BMI was adapted from BASICS, tailored to the students with whom we have worked. We supplement the feedback form with handouts to elaborate on specific topics. This BMI structure is but one option and, as discussed previously, BMIs structured in different ways have proven efficacious. This section selectively highlights common issues and opportunities that emerge in some sections, based on our experience. The samples of dialog that are used to illustrate points of implementation are adapted from BMIs conducted with mandated students.

Session Structure
+ Orientation to session.
+ Consumption feedback: average and peak, heavy drinking, normative comparisons when available.
+ BAC information: factors affecting BAC, relationship of BAC to behavior, BAC and the brain (handout), personalized feedback on average and peak BAC.
+ Tolerance: definition, personalized feedback.
+ Drinking games.
+ Biphasic curve (handout).
+ Perceived norms: student estimates of same gender drinking, normative comparisons.
+ Alcohol-related consequences.
+ Risky behaviors related to drinking: drinking and driving, sexual situations later regretted.

- Harm-reduction discussion (handout) and goal setting.
- Tips for safer drinking.
- Fun things to do that do not involve drinking.

Orientation to session. A brief orientation to the session is useful to help to set the tone for collaborative interaction. Mandated students, in particular, may expect the alcohol intervention to be punitive. In contrast, the interventionist conveys principles consistent with the MI spirit (Miller & Rollnick, 2002), such as empathy, respect, autonomy support, and collaboration. An illustration follows.

Introducing the BMI session

I: What we are going to do for the next hour is have a conversation about your experiences with alcohol. And I'm going to provide some information. Some of it may be familiar to you already, but some of it will probably be new. What we have found is that more-informed drinkers tend to make wiser choices when it comes to their drinking. So hopefully some of this conversation will be interesting to you and what you do with it after today is up to you. Okay?

S: Okay.

I: And you should know that I am not going to tell you what to do about your drinking. Obviously, you know yourself best, so you know what works for you.

S: That's fine.

I: I've prepared a guide to structure our discussion today. It is all based on the questionnaires that you filled out last week. Any questions before we get started?

S: No, not really. Sounds good so far.

Consumption feedback. During the first section, when consumption feedback is presented, we have found it helpful to focus on two goals: (1) establishing a shared sense of accuracy regarding the feedback, and (2) engaging the student in the discussion by using active listening strategies. Given the patterning of college drinking, providing feedback on average drinking (e.g., drinks per week) and then some measure of peak or heavy drinking (e.g., maximum consumed on one occasion) is useful to capture occasional extremes that can lead to negative consequences. Students are reminded that the source of the numbers is their own self-report, but even so, some are surprised to see the numbers in summary form. They may struggle to integrate the feedback with their own self-image or their knowledge of peer drinking behavior. Simple reflections and rolling with resistance are useful techniques at this early stage of the intervention, to allow the student time to think through the implications of the feedback, as illustrated below.

Personalized Feedback for ID# XXXX

*Your Drinking Patterns*_____

According to the information you provided for the past month:

- You drank alcohol: _16_ times
- Average number of drinks per week: _18_ drinks
- Maximum number of drinks in a single day: _12_ drinks
- Number of drinks during the heaviest week of drinking: _21_ drinks

*Your Drinking Compared to the National and Local College Average*_____

In an average week,

- You drank more than _96_ % of college women nationwide.
- You drank more than _88_ % of female students on this campus.

*Heavier Drinking Days*_____

Heavier drinking days are considered to be 4 or more drinks for women and 5 or more drinks for men. After many scientific studies, **this was the drinking level that showed significantly higher risk for alcohol-related negative events** such as car accidents, fighting, and unprotected or unplanned sex.

- You reported _6_ heavier drinking days in the last month.
- This frequency is higher than _79_ % of female students on this campus.

*Level of Intoxication*_____

One way to look at your drinking patterns is by examining the amount of alcohol circulating in your blood when drinking, or blood alcohol content (BAC). A high BAC means you are more intoxicated compared to a lower BAC. Your BAC is affected by many factors, including

- gender
- body weight
- number of drinks
- time over which drinks are consumed

For the *average social drinker*, the effect of alcohol is a function of BAC:

.02	• Nontolerant drinkers begin to feel some effect (approximately one drink)
.04	• Most people begin to feel relaxed • Greater talkativeness • Less self-conscious • Attention and reaction times start to be impaired
.06	• Social judgment is impaired • Lowered inhibitions

Figure 9.1 Implementing the BMI: Phase 2, The Feedback Session

.08	• Impairment of fine muscle coordination (e.g., driving skills) • People do things they would not do when sober • Increased risk of nausea
.10	• Legal intoxication in all states • Slurred speech • Noticeable deterioration of reaction time and muscle control
.15	• Balance and movement are impaired • Vomiting may occur as a protective reaction
.20	• Memory blackout is likely, causing loss of recall for events occurring while intoxicated
.25	• Severe motor disturbances • Sensory perceptions greatly impaired • Semi-stupor
.30	any people lose consciousness • Risk of death

*Your BAC Feedback*_____

• In the past month, you typically drank _5_ drinks over _4_ hour(s).
  This would make your **average BAC** about _.07_
• On your heaviest drinking occasion in that month, you drank _12_ drinks over _6_ hour(s).
  This would make your **highest BAC** about _.24_
• The legal driving limit in this state is a BAC of **.08%**.

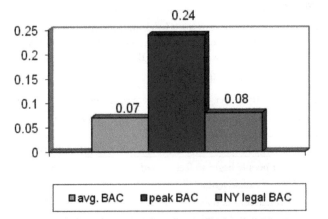

If you are reaching these BAC levels without feeling the effects shown on the chart, you have developed higher tolerance to alcohol. **Developing a tolerance overrides your body's way of telling you that you have had too much to drink.** Because you have to drink more to get the same effect, tolerance can make drinking more expensive and less enjoyable at lower BACs.

Figure 9.1 *(continued)*

Tolerance levels	
>.18	very high
.121 – .18	high
.061 – .12	medium
.00 – .06	low

←your average BAC

*Drinking Games*_____

You did report playing drinking games in the past month. **Because people often drink more and faster during drinking games than they would normally, BACs can rise faster and higher than expected.**

Article IV.

*Perceptions of Others Drinking*_____

During the survey, we asked you to report what you thought the average college woman drank in a typical week. The following chart compares your estimation to the actual number of drinks college women report consuming in a typical week, based on random surveys conducted within the last 5 years.

	Your Estimation (females on this campus)	Actual number (females on this campus)	Actual number (female students across US)
Average drinks/week for a female student	23	9	4

You overestimated your female students' drinking on this campus by _14_ drinks per week. You are not alone. Most college students think that their classmates drink much more than they really do. However, **people who perceive the norm to be higher than it really is may end up drinking more to match an inflated perception.**

*Article V. Alcohol-Related Consequences*_____
According to the information you provided:

in the past month
I have had a hangover (headache, sick stomach) the morning after I had been drinking
The quality of my work or schoolwork has suffered because of my drinking
I have felt bad about myself because of my drinking
When drinking, I have done impulsive things I later regretted
My drinking has created problems between myself and my boyfriend/girlfriend, parents, or other near relatives
I have found that I needed larger amounts of alcohol to feel any effect, or that I could no longer get high or drunk on the same amount that used to get me high or drunk

Figure 9.1   *(continued)*

Risky Behavior Related to Drinking

You reported:

I have not driven a car when I knew I had too much to drink.
My drinking has gotten me into sexual situations I regretted.

My plan for harm prevention

The chance of harm coming to you as a result of drinking decreases with lower BACs and safer drinking practices.

Tips for Safer Drinking

- Eat before drinking.
- If you choose to drink, sip instead of chug.
- Keep track of how much you drink.
- Set a drinking limit before entering a social drinking situation (e.g., BAC <.06).
- Take more time between drink refills.
- Alternate alcoholic drinks with non alcoholic beverages.
- Avoid drinking games.
- Experiment with drinking less and refusing drinks.
- Choose drinks with less alcohol content.
- Use the buddy system at parties; go with friends who can look after each other's safety.
- Don't leave your drink unattended.
- Call a cab for a ride home.
- Use a designated driver.

Fun Things to Do Besides Drinking

End time	:

Figure 9.1 *(continued)*

Feedback on Drinking Patterns

I: Okay. Well, let's get started then. Looking at first section, it summarizes your drinking patterns. We had asked about the month prior to the sanction, ending with and including the event itself. And in that month you had mentioned that you drank alcohol about eight times. How does that look?

S: Yeah, it's right, probably.

I: So that seems about accurate?

S: Yeah.

I: Okay. You had also indicated that the average number of drinks you have per week is about six.

S: Oh, per week, yeah, yeah, probably. That was like my first month of college, so ...

I: So things are different now, then?

S: Yeah, I don't drink that, I mean I don't drink that much anymore but I probably drink the same amount, but maybe only one night, but I don't drink two nights a week, you know what I mean?

I: I see. So, that seems about right for this particular month.

S: Yeah.

I: But maybe now you're not going out quite as much. Is that what you're saying? Okay. So then, thinking back to this particular period, what was a typical drinking occasion like for you?

. . .

I: All right. Getting back to the form, you had mentioned that the maximum number of drinks you had in a single day for that month was probably around five drinks. Does that particular day stand out at all?

S: No, I, a lot of that's just kind of like guessing. I mean I don't really get like hammered. I'm more of like a social drinker and I drink because, not like to fit in or like peer pressure but I just kind of drink because like everyone else is. I mean, I get tipsy and that's fine but I don't get like forgetting my name kind of thing.

I: So this was a more just kind of social occasion where maybe you felt a little tipsy but it doesn't really stand out as atypical.

S: Nope.

I: Okay. And then finally, you had mentioned that you had had about eight drinks during your heaviest week of drinking which is really just a couple more than a typical week. Does that week stand out at all?

S: Mm mm.

I: Okay. Well just kind of looking over these numbers, I'm curious what your reactions are to seeing your drinking summarized like this.

S: I don't know, I feel like these are really high numbers but then I guess like if it's during the weekend, it's not that bad, but I don't know.

I: Well, taking that six drinks, it looks like you drank more than 75% of college women nationwide. And I know you had just said a moment ago that . . .

S: Seems really high.

I: That seems very high to you.

S: But I mean I guess well I don't know, I just feel like a lot more people drink a lot more than that. But maybe it's like, like one person who drinks 15 drinks but other people. ... You know what I'm saying. But, I don't know, maybe 'cause I'm a big girl I can drink. I don't know, but I guess.

I: So where would you've expected to see yourself if you were going to guess?

S: Probably 50. Like I feel like I'm right in the middle.

I: So this is a little bit higher than where you expected to see yourself. But it sounds like that you do sort of recognize that there is a whole spectrum of drinkers really. You mentioned you know, you know there are people who really aren't even going out, maybe people are doing other things. Yup, and this is really just showing you that there is a whole range from people who aren't drinking at all, all the way out to people who are drinking heavily. And you're falling above the midpoint, in the middle of the upper half of college women.

BAC and tolerance. In our experience most students possess inaccurate or incomplete knowledge of the principles of alcohol absorption, metabolism, and adaptation underlying these topics. Common misunderstandings include failure to take into account gender differences in BAC beyond body size, and the assumption that if one develops tolerance then one does not reach high BACs. Students may also misunderstand standard drink sizes used to calculate BACs. Additional queries regarding blackouts and alcohol poisoning tend to emerge during these sections. Direct questions can always be answered to the best of the interventionist's ability and, in the absence of a student-generated question, the interventionist may offer some content information/clarification with permission, consistent with MI. Whenever presenting alcohol information that is not personalized, interventionists are advised to maintain a conversational rather than a didactic style, regularly soliciting reactions, asking students for examples from their own experience, and checking in when nonverbal cues suggest confusion or uncertainty.

Perceived norms. By the time perceived norms are introduced, the student has usually made the observation that, "but it seems like everybody I know drinks like I do." These comments reflect the reality that drinking is a social behavior among college students, and individuals tend to socialize with others who have similar drinking habits. Exposure to lighter drinkers is less frequent when a student is immersed in a heavy drinking social group, leading to a potentially skewed impression of "typical" drinking. Invariably, students overestimate peer drinking (even when asked about same-gender students on their campus). This can open up productive discussions of how one develops his or her sense of peer drinking norms, and the potential implications of believing in exaggerated norms. Discussing the source of normative perceptions serves to raise questions about the accuracy of these perceptions (how do you really know how much others are drinking at a party, especially the majority who are not loud about it?), potentially weakening their influence (Prentice, 2008). Also, because both theory (Perkins, 2003) and research (Carey, Borsari, Carey, & Maisto, 2006) suggest that people may increase their drinking to approach a perceived norm, it may be valuable to discuss this risk explicitly.

Perceived Norms

I: We can now talk about perceptions of other people's drinking, what you notice going on around you, also called perceived drinking norms. You know people have a tendency to form their ideas about what they think is normal or typical by observing what's going on around them. So we asked you what you thought the average college woman here drank in the course of a week. And you had felt that the typical (Student's University) female probably drank around 23 drinks in a week. And actually the number is significantly lower— it's nine. So it looks like you overestimated by about 14 drinks. What went into your estimation?

S: I guess it's maybe not 30 but seems like higher than nine. But I guess I wasn't really thinking about the people who just don't drink at all, or . . . I would of thought it was a lot higher.

I: Why would you think it would be a lot higher?

S: 'Cause I feel like people here drink to get drunk. Like not many people kind of drink the way I do. We just kind of like drink to get relaxed and then going back and like hanging out or doing whatever. Instead of going and playing beer pong and like getting drunk at frat parties kind of thing, so I feel like I don't know, a lot people I see go out and get wasted.

I: So it sounds like just kind of looking around you, you're noticing that your mentality when it comes to drinking is maybe different than what it appears a lot of people's are and that you feel like you're noticing a lot people who are really getting extremely intoxicated and you recognize yourself as sort of different from that. And you are not alone—a lot of people tend to overestimate that number.

S: Really? That makes me feel a little better.

I: Mhm. And it makes sense because you know the people who are getting extremely intoxicated are just more noticeable than people who you know aren't out at all drinking, people who maybe are just having one or two or people just hanging out. And you know something to think about is that people sometimes have a tendency to adjust their own habits around what they think normal is. So if people have this idea of normal that's actually inflated, you could end up upping your own habits to match this number that's not even right.

S: That makes sense.

Alcohol-related consequences. From the student's perspective, being presented with a list of consequences can be a potentially uncomfortable experience. We tend to introduce this information softly by saying, "These are the not-so-good effects of alcohol that you endorsed on the questionnaire; take a look over this list and tell me which of these stand out to you." Such permission to focus on the most salient relieves the student of the need to talk about all of them, and the self-selection provides an opportunity to find out why that consequence was particularly troublesome. Typically, if the interventionist listens well and maintains a nonjudgmental empathetic stance, students will address most if not all of the listed consequences. This section provides ample opportunities to elicit and reflect on change talk. MI techniques such as amplified and double-sided reflections are often appropriate here. When negative affect or embarrassment is associated with an event, asking for elaboration and/ or reflecting on affect can be useful. Providing a summary at the end of this section may focus the student on the accumulating impact of his or her drinking behaviors (cf. crystallization of discontent) (Baumeister, 1996) and sets the stage for discussion of harm reduction later in the intervention.

Harm reduction and goal setting. We discuss the notion of harm reduction (Marlatt & Witkiewitz, 2002) explicitly to challenge assumptions made by students that if they don't drink as they do now then the only alternative is not to drink at all. Many find abstinence socially and personally untenable. Thus, the image of a continuum of drinking patterns, with few at the heavy end and many at the lighter end, opens up the option for moving down the continuum of consumption to experience fewer consequences. This shared conceptual framework allows the interventionist to ask, "Given that you said you would like to avoid embarrassing situations and blacking out, what are your thoughts about what you would like to do to avoid these in the future?" Consistent with principles of goal setting, the student's goal(s) may need to be shaped to be more specific, measurable, and realistic (Doran, 1981). We recommend writing down the goal(s) to serve as a reminder after the session. Students who are not ready to commit to a specific goal can be encouraged to think of goal setting as a resource they can use in the future.

Tips for safer drinking. Research reveals that most college drinkers are employing some strategies to help them drink safely, also known as *protective behavioral strategies* (Martens et al., 2004; Sugarman & Carey, 2007). Thus when introducing tips for safer drinking it is wise to acknowledge that the student may already be using some of these strategies and ask which the student has found helpful. Then she or he can be prompted to identify others to be tried, especially in service of the self-identified change goal.

Tips for Safer Drinking

I: Just looking at these tips, these are different things that other people have mentioned have been helpful for them to keep their drinking safer. And we've touched on some of them already—using a designated driver and things like that. Sounds like we just talked a little bit about maybe the buddy system sort of thing, avoiding the drinking games. What others do you think would work particularly well for you?

S: I already use the buddy system. I think all these things are things I already do.

I: Okay. So looking it over you feel like a good chunk of these are things that you're already doing …

S: Well aside from the BAC thing, but I guess I can do that now.

I: Mhm. How do you think that would be for you to try to set a drinking limit?

S: I think, I mean I'm not sure anything would change, but I guess I'd just be more conscious of how much I'm drinking. I would set myself a goal at a .06 and then get my little card out.

I: Okay, so maybe just in addition to the couple of other things that you had mentioned, just maybe you could try using the BAC card to keep under a set limit, is that what you're saying?

Summary. At the end of the BMI, after all the content has been discussed, it can be useful to offer a selective summary of the change talk elicited in the session. Aim to use the student's words whenever possible in these summaries. The interventionist may highlight some of the discrepancies produced by the feedback, and/or reiterate the consequences or risks that were perceived as negative. Change plans may be reviewed and self-efficacy supported. Inviting the student to provide feedback is a good way to help the student process the experience, and to provide affirmations for the student's effort and intentions to take steps toward healthier drinking. The following is an example of a session summary.

Intervention Summary

I: Well great, we talked a bit about different things that had occurred as a result of your drinking and different realms where alcohol had affected your life. You have come up with some good ideas for things that you can do and continue to do to really keep your drinking safe, to keep it at a level where you feel comfortable. At this point we've finished what I had planned for today. What are some of your reactions to what we covered?

S: I'm still like really shocked at how many, I really thought that more college people drank, or more college girls drank more. And I'm still shocked that I'm in the top like 25% but it makes sense when you, when I think about everything I guess. I still think that when I made my guess I just didn't really realize like how far off I was.

I: So some things are still a little bit surprising to you.

S: Mhm. But it all makes sense. And a lot of it I kind of already knew, so.

I: Okay. So some surprises, some stuff that you already knew. Overall it seems to sort of make sense logically.

S: Mhm.

I: Okay. Well thank you so much for taking the time to talk with me. I know that this is personal and sensitive material, so I again I really appreciate your openness. And as I said at the beginning, you know yourself best, you know what kinds of things work with you and you know what kinds of behaviors you want to be involved in so what you do with this is totally up to you.

S: Okay.

CONCLUSIONS

The BMI is a useful addition to the toolbox for college alcohol abuse prevention for several reasons. A relatively low-threshold intervention, it is brief, it offers a level of privacy that group interventions cannot, and it does not require admission of a problem or concern. It is personally tailored to each student and, not surprisingly, most students find it interesting and informative. The face-to-face administration and use of MI style are particularly advantageous for students who may not engage fully in a less personalized program, such as heavier drinkers, mandated students, or those who have already been exposed to another intervention (cf. Borsari chapter, this volume). One can speculate that the level of engagement achieved with personalized materials presented by a skilled counselor optimizes opportunities for deeper, elaborated processing in ways that group-based or computer-delivered interventions may not. Its flexible structure allows it to be targeted to specific risk groups and tailored on dimensions deemed important in a given context (e.g., health care, mental health, judicial affairs).

The growing evidence base for BMI efficacy supports continued dissemination efforts. One challenge for prevention professionals is to advocate for implementation of empirically supported alcohol interventions on their campuses, even in times of limited resources. Another is to identify settings for BMIs and other evidence-based strategies that will expand the reach of prevention programming to at-risk drinkers, such as contacts in health and counseling centers, residence halls, athletic programs, and judicial affairs, and through specific events such as freshman orientation, health fairs, and National Alcohol Screening Day.

Future challenges for evaluation researchers include identifying active ingredients (beyond normative feedback) so that the BMI might be streamlined to its essential elements, and determining when BMIs might be preferred and when alternative intervention do just as well, in order to inform resource allocation on campuses. Also important are continued efforts to improve BMI efficacy by modifying content and adding complementary intervention components so as to enhance initial outcomes and maintain risk reduction gains over time.

REFERENCES

American College Health Association. (2010). *American college health association-national college health assessment II: Reference group data report spring 2010.* Linthieum, MD: American College Health Association.

American Public Health Association. (2008). Alcohol screening and brief intervention: A guide for public health practitioners. Retrieved from www.adp.ca.gov/SBI/pdfs/Alcohol_SBI_Manual.pdf

Amaro, H., Ahl, M., Matsumoto, A., Prado, G., Mule, C., Kemmemer, A.,... Mantella, P. (2009). Trial of the university assistance program for alcohol use among mandated students. *Journal of Studies on Alcohol and Drugs, Suppl 16*, 45–56.

Amrhein, P. C., Miller, W. R., Yahne, C. E., Palmer, M., & Fulcher, L. (2003). Client commitment language during motivational interviewing predicts drug use outcomes. *Journal of Consulting and Clinical Psychology, 71*(5), 862–878.

Apodaca, T. R., & Longabaugh, R. (2009). Mechanisms of change in motivational interviewing: A review and preliminary evaluation of the evidence. *Addiction, 104*(5), 705–715. doi: 10.1111/j.1360–0443.2009.02527.x

Babor, T. F., & Higgins-Biddle, J. C. (2001). *Brief intervention for hazardous and harmful drinking: A manual for use in primary care.* Geneva, Switzerland: World Health Organization.

Babor, T. F., McRee, B. G., Kassebaum, P. A., Grimaldi, P. L., Ahmed, K., & Bray, J. (2007). Screening, brief intervention, and referral to treatment (SBIRT): Toward a public health approach to the management of substance abuse. *Substance Abuse, 28*(3), 7–30.

Baer, J. S., Kivlahan, D. R., Blume, A. W., McKnight, P., & Marlatt, G. A. (2001). Brief intervention for heavy-drinking college students: 4-year follow-up and natural history. *American Journal of Public Health, 91*(8), 1310–1316.

Baer, J. S., Marlatt, G. A., Kivlahan, D. R., Fromme, K., Larimer, M. E., & Williams, E. (1992). An experimental test of three methods of alcohol risk reduction with young adults. *Journal of Consulting and Clinical Psychology, 64,* 974–979.

Barnett, N. P., Murphy, J. G., Colby, S. M., & Monti, P. M. (2007). Efficacy and mediation of counselor vs. computer delivered interventions with mandated college students. *Addictive Behaviors, 32,* 2529–2548.

Baumeister, R. F. (1996). The crystallization of discontent in the process of major life change. In T. F. Heatherton & J. L. Weinberger (Eds.), *Can personality change?* (pp. 281–297). Washington, DC: APA.

Borsari, B., & Carey, K. B. (2000). Effects of a brief motivational intervention with college student drinkers. *Journal of Consulting and Clinical Psychology, 68*(4), 728–733.

Borsari, B., & Carey, K. B. (2005). Two brief alcohol interventions for mandated college students. *Psychology of Addictive Behaviors, 19*(3), 296–302.

Brown, B. B. (2004). Adolescents' relationships with peers. In R. M. Lerner & L. Steinberg (Eds.), *Handbook of adolescent psychology* (2nd ed., pp. 363–394). Hoboken, NJ: Wiley.

Butler, L. H., & Correia, C. J. (2009). Brief alcohol intervention with college student drinkers: Face-to-face versus computerized feedback. [Randomized Controlled Trial]. *Psychology of Addictive Behaviors, 23*(1), 163–167. doi: 10.1037/a0014892

Carey, K. B., Borsari, B., Carey, M. P., & Maisto, S. A. (2006). Patterns and importance of self-other differences in college drinking norms. *Psycholology of Addictive Behaviors, 20*(4), 385–393.

Carey, K. B., Carey, M. P., Henson, J. M., Maisto, S. A., & DeMartini, K. S. (2011). Brief alcohol interventions for mandated college students: Comparison of face-to-face counseling and computer-delivered interventions. *Addiction, 106*(3), 528–537. doi: 10.1111/j.1360–0443.2010.03193.x

Carey, K. B., Carey, M. P., Maisto, S. A., & Henson, J. M. (2006). Brief motivational interventions for heavy college drinkers: A randomized controlled trial. *Journal of Consulting and Clinical Psychology, 74,* 943–954.

Carey, K. B., Henson, J. M., Carey, M. P., & Maisto, S. A. (2009). Computer versus in-person intervention for students violating campus alcohol policy. *Journal of Consulting and Clinical Psychology, 77*(1), 74–87. doi: 2009–00563–016 [pii] 10.1037/a0014281

Carey, K. B., Henson, J. M., Carey, M. P., & Maisto, S. A. (2010). Perceived norms mediate effects of a brief motivational intervention for sanctioned college drinkers. *Clinical Psychology: Science & Practice, 17,* 59–72.

Carey, K. B., Scott-Sheldon, L., Carey, M. P., & DeMartini, K. (2007). Individual-level interventions to reduce college student drinking: A meta-analytic review. *Addictive Behaviors, 32,* 2469–2494.

Carey, K. B., Scott-Sheldon, L.A.J., Elliott, J. C., Garey, L., & Carey, M. P. (2012). *Face-to-face versus computer-delivered alcohol interventions for college drinkers: A meta-analytic review, 1998 to 2010.* Unpublished manuscript (under review).

Chan, K. K., Neighbors, C., Gilson, M., Larimer, M. E., & Marlatt, G. A. (2007). Epidemiological trends in drinking by age and gender: Providing normative feedback to adults. *Addictive Behaviors, 32*(5), 967–976. doi: 10.1016/j.addbeh.2006.07.003

Cimini, M. D., Martens, M. P., Larimer, M. E., Kilmer, J. R., Neighbors, C., & Monserrat, J. M. (2009). Assessing the effectiveness of peer-facilitated interventions addressing high-risk drinking among judicially mandated college students. *Journal of Studies on Alcohol and Drugs, Suppl 16*), 57–66.

DeJong, W. (2008). Methods for assessing college student use of alcohol and other drugs. Retrieved from http://www.higheredcenter.org/files/product/methods.pdf

Dimeff, L. A., Baer, J. S., Kivlahan, D. R., & Marlatt, G. A. (1999). *Brief alcohol screening and intervention for college students (BASICS): A harm reduction approach.* New York, NY: Guilford Press.

Doran, G. T. (1981). There's a S.M.A.R.T. way to write management's goals and objectives. *Management Review, 70*(11), 35–36.

Doumas, D. M., McKinley, L. L., & Book, P. (2009). Evaluation of two web-based alcohol interventions for mandated college students. *Journal of Substance Abuse Treatment, 36*(1), 65–74. doi: S0740–5472(08)00084–6 [pii] 10.1016/j.jsat.2008.05.009

Doumas, D. M., Workman, C., Smith, D., & Navarro, A. (2011). Reducing high-risk drinking in mandated college students: Evaluation of two personalized normative feedback interventions. *Journal of Substance Abuse Treatment, 40*(4), 376–385. doi: 10.1016/j.jsat.2010.12.006

Fleming, M. F., Balousek, S. L., Grossberg, P. M., Mundt, M. P., Brown, D., Wiegel, J. R., . . . Saewyc, E. M. (2010). Brief physician advice for heavy drinking college students: A randomized controlled trial in college health clinics. *Journal of Studies on Alcohol and Drugs, 71*(1), 23–31.

Fromme, K., & Corbin, W. (2004). Prevention of heavy drinking and associated negative consequences among mandated and voluntary students. *Journal of Consulting & Clinical Psychology, 72*, 1038–1049.

Hester, R. K., Squires, D. D., & Delaney, H. D. (2005). The drinker's check-up: 12-month outcomes of a controlled clinical trial of a stand-alone software program for problem drinkers. *Journal of Substance Abuse Treatment, 28*(2), 159–169.

Higgins-Biddle, J. C., Hungerford, D. W., & Cates-Wessel, K. (2009). Screening and brief interventions (SBI) for unhealthy alcohol use: A step-by-step implementation guide for trauma centers. *CDC* Retrieved from http://www.cdc.gov/InjuryResponse/alcohol-screening/pdf/SBI-Implementation-Guide-a.pdf

Hustad, J. T. P., Short, E. A., Borsari, B., Barnett, N. P., Tevyaw, T. O., & Kahler, C. W. (2011). College alcohol citations result in modest reductions in student drinking. *Journal of Substance Abuse Treatment, 40*, 281–286.

Kulesza, M., Apperson, M., Larimer, M., & Copeland, A. (2010). Brief alcohol intervention for college drinkers: How brief is brief? *Addictive Behaviors, 35*(7), 730–733.

LaBrie, J. W., Huchting, K., Tawalbeh, S., Pedersen, E. R., Thompson, A. D., Shelesky, K., . . . Neighbors, C. (2008). A randomized motivational enhancement prevention group reduces drinking and alcohol consequences in first-year college women. *Psychology of Addictive Behaviors, 22*(1), 149–155. doi: 10.1037/0893-164X.22.1.149

LaBrie, J. W., Hummer, J. F., Huchting, K. K., & Neighbors, C. (2009). A brief live interactive normative group intervention using wireless keypads to reduce drinking and alcohol consequences in college student athletes. *Drug and Alcohol Review, 28*(1), 40–47. doi: 10.1111/j.1465-3362.2008.00012.x

Larimer, M. E., & Cronce, J. M. (2002). Identification, prevention and treatment: a review of individual-focused strategies to reduce problematic alcohol consumption by college students. *Journal of Studies on Alcohol, Suppl 14*, 148–163.

Larimer, M. E., & Cronce, J. M. (2007). Identification, prevention, and treatment revisited: individual-focused college drinking prevention strategies 1999–2006. *Addictive Behaviors, 32*(11), 2439–2468. doi: S0306-4603(07)00147-5 [pii] 10.1016/j.addbeh.2007.05.006

Larimer, M. E., Kaysen, D. L., Lee, C. M., Kilmer, J. R., Lewis, M. A., Dillworth, T., . . . Neighbors, C. (2009). Evaluating level of specificity of normative referents in relation to personal drinking behavior. *Journal of Studies on Alcohol and Drugs, Suppl 16*, 115–121.

Larimer, M. E., Turner, A. P., Anderson, B. K., Fader, J. S., Kilmer, J. R., Palmer, R. S., & Cronce, J. M. (2001). Evaluating a brief alcohol intervention with fraternities. *Journal of Studies on Alcohol, 62*(3), 370–380.

Lewis, M. A., & Neighbors, C. (2007). Optimizing personalized normative feedback: The use of gender-specific referents. *Journal of Studies on Alcohol and Drugs, 68*(2), 228–237.

Marlatt, G. A., Baer, J. S., Kivlahan, D. R., Dimeff, L. A., Larimer, M. E., Quigley, L. A., . . . Williams, E. (1998). Screening and brief intervention for high-risk college student drinkers: Results from a 2-year follow-up assessment. *Journal of Consulting and Clinical Psychology, 66*, 604–615.

Marlatt, G.A. (2002). *Harm reduction: Pragmatic strategies for managing righ-risk behaviors.* New York, NY: Guilford Press.

Marlatt, G. A., & Witkiewitz, K. (2002). Harm reduction approaches to alcohol use: Health promotion, prevention, and treatment. *Addictive Behaviors, 27*(6), 867–886.

Martens, M. P., Taylor, K. K., Damann, K. M., Page, J. C., Mowry, E. S., & Cimini, M. D. (2004). Protective behavioral strategies when drinking alcohol and the relationaship to negative alcohol-related conseuqences in college students. *Psychology of Addictive Behaviors, 18*(4), 390–393.

McNally, A. M., Palfai, T. P., & Kahler, C. W. (2005). Motivational interventions for heavy drinking college students: Examining the role of discrepancy-related psychological processes. *Psychology of Addictive Behaviors, 19*(1), 79–87.

Meilman, P. W., Presley, C. A., & Cashin, J. R. (1997). Average weekly alcohol consumption: Drinking percentiles for American college students. *Journal of American College Health, 45*(5), 201–204. doi: 10.1080/07448481.1997.9936885

Miller, W. R., Benefield, R. G., & Tonigan, J. S. (1993). Enhancing motivation for change in problem drinking: A controlled comparison of two therapist styles. *Journal of Consulting and Clinical Psychology, 61*(3), 455–461.

Miller, W. R., & Brown, J. M. (1991). Self-regulation as a conceptual basis for the prevention and treatment of addictive behaviors. In N. Heather, W. R. Miller & J. Greely (Eds.), *Self-control and the addictive behaviours* (pp. 3–79). Sydney, Australia: Maxwell Macmillan.

Miller, W. R., & Rollnick, S. (2002). *Motivational interviewing: Preparing people for change* (2nd ed.). New York, NY: Guilford Press.

Miller, W. R., & Sanchez, V. C. (1994). Motivating young adults for treatment and lifestyle change. In G. S. Howards & P. E. Nathan (Eds.), *Alcohol use and misuse by young adults* (pp. 15–24). Notre Dame, IN: University of Notre Dame Press.

Miller, W. R., Sovereign, G. A., & Krege, B. (1988). Motivational interviewing with problem drinkers: II. The drinker's check up as a preventative intervention. *Behavioral Psychotherapy, 16*, 251–268.

Miller, W. R., Toscova, R. T., Miller, J. H., & Sanchez, V. (2000). A theory-based motivational approach for reducing alcohol/drug problems in college. *Health Education & Behavior, 27*(6), 744–759.

Morgan, T. J., White, H. R., & Mun, E. Y. (2008). Changes in drinking before a mandated brief intervention with college students. *Journal of Studies on Alcohol and Drugs, 69*, 286–290.

Murphy, J. G., Benson, T. A., Vuchinich, R. E., Deskins, M. M., Eakin, D., Flood, A. M., . . . Torrealday, O. (2004). A comparison of personalized feedback for college student drinkers delivered with and without a motivational interview. *Journal of Studies on Alcohol, 65*(2), 200–203.

Murphy, J. G., Dennhardt, A. A., Skidmore, J. R., Martens, M. P., & McDevitt-Murphy, M. E. (2010). Computerized versus motivational interviewing alcohol interventions: Impact on discrepancy, motivation, and drinking. *Psychology of Addictive Behaviors, 24*(4), 628–639. doi: 10.1037/a0021347

Murphy, J. G., Duchnick, J. J., Vuchinich, R. E., Davison, J. W., Karg, R. S., Olson, A. M., . . . Coffey, T. T. (2001). Relative efficacy of a brief motivational intervention for college student drinkers. *Psychology of Addictive Behaviors, 15*(4), 373–379.

National Institute on Alcohol Abuse and Alcoholism. (2005). Helping patients who drink too much: A clinician's guide. Retrieved from www.niaaa.nih.gov/Publications/EducationTrainingMaterials/Documents/guide.pdf

Perkins, H. W. (Ed.). (2003). *The social norms approach to preventing school and college age substance abuse.* San Francisco, CA: Jossey-Bass.

Prentice, D. A. (2008). Mobilizing and weakening peer influence as mechanisms for change behavior: Implications for alcohol intervention programs. In M. J. Prinstein & K. A. Dodge (Eds.), *Understanding peer influence in children and adolescents.* New York, NY: Guilford Press.

Riper, H., van Straten, A., Keuken, M., Smit, F., Schippers, G., & Cuijpers, P. (2009). Curbing problem drinking with personalized-feedback interventions: A meta-analysis. *American Journal of Preventive Medicine, 36*(3), 247–255. doi: 10.1016/j.amepre.2008.10.016

Rosengren, D. B. (2009). *Building motivational interviewing skills: A practitioner workbook.* New York, NY: Guilford Press.

Schaus, J. F., Sole, M. L., McCoy, T. P., Mullett, N., & O'Brien, M. C. (2009). Alcohol screening and brief intervention in a college student health center: A randomized controlled trial. *Journal of Studies on Alcohol and Drugs, Suppl 16*, 131–141.

Sheldon, K. M., Joiner, T., & Williams, D. M. (2003). *Motivating health: Applying self-determination in the clinic.* New Haven, CT: Yale University Press.

Sugarman, D. E., & Carey, K. B. (2007). The relationship between drinking control strategies and college student alcohol use. *Psychology of Addictive Behaviors, 21*(3), 338–345.

Task Force of the National Advisory Council on Alcohol Abuse and Alcoholism. (2002). A call to action: Changing the culture of drinking at U.S. colleges. In National Institute on Alcohol Abuse and Alcoholism (Ed.), *NIH Publication No. 02.5010.*

Terry, D. L. (2011). *Screening and brief intervention for hazardous alcohol use: A pilot study in a college counseling center.* Dissertation. Syracuse University.

Turrisi, R., Larimer, M. E., Mallett, K. A., Kilmer, J. R., Ray, A. E., Mastroleo, N. R., . . . Montoya, H. (2009). A randomized clinical trial evaluating a combined alcohol intervention for high-risk college students. *Journal of Studies on Alcohol and Drugs, 70*(4), 555–567.

Walitzer, K. S., Dermen, K. H., & Connors, G. J. (1999). Strategies for preparing clients for treatment. A review. *Behavior Modification, 23*(1), 129–151.

Walters, S. T., & Baer, J. S. (2006). *Talking with college students about alcohol: Motivational strategies for reducing abuse.* New York, NY: Guilford Press.

Walters, S. T., & Neighbors, C. (2005). Feedback interventions for college alcohol misuse: What, why, and for whom? *Addictive Behaviors, 30,* 1168–1182.

Walters, S. T., Vader, A. M., Harris, T. R., Field, C. A., & Jouriles, E. N. (2009). Dismantling motivational interviewing and feedback for college drinkers: A randomized clinical trial. *Journal of Consulting and Clinical Psychology, 77*(1), 64–73. doi: 2009–00563–015 [pii] 10.1037/a0014472

Wechsler, H., Molnar, B. E., Davenport, A. E., & Baer, J. S. (1999). College alcohol use: A full or empty glass? *Journal of American College Health, 47*(6), 247–252. doi: 10.1080/ 07448489909595655

White, H. R., Morgan, T. J., Pugh, L. A., Celinska, K., Labouvie, E. W., & Pandina, R. J. (2006). Evaluating two brief substance-use interventions for mandated college students. *Journal of Studies on Alcohol, 67*(2), 309–317.

White, H. R., Mun, E. Y., Pugh, L., & Morgan, T. J. (2007). Long-term effects of brief substance use interventions for mandated college students: Sleeper effects of an in-person personal feedback intervention. *Alcoholism: Clinical & Experimental Research, 31*(8), 1380–1391.

Wood, M. D., Capone, C., Laforge, R., Erickson, D. J., & Brand, N. H. (2007). Brief motivational intervention and alcohol expectancy challenge with heavy drinking college students: A randomized factorial study. *Addictive Behaviors, 32*(11), 2509–2528. doi: S0306–4603(07)00189-X [pii] 10.1016/ j.addbeh.2007.06.018

Wood, M. D., Fairlie, A. M., Fernandez, A. C., Borsari, B., Capone, C., Laforge, R., & Carmona-Barros, R. (2010). Brief motivational and parent interventions for college students: A randomized factorial study. *Journal of Consulting and Clinical Psychology, 78*(3), 349–361.

10

Computerized Interventions

William Campbell and Reid K. Hester

INTRODUCTION

In this chapter we review the ways that computers are used to deliver interventions to prevent and/or reduce heavy drinking in college drinkers. We present research findings on the methods and mechanisms that have been investigated, as well as summaries of the latest "stand-alone" programs currently available. We discuss settings and applications for computer delivered interventions (CDIs), because they vary widely and may greatly influence the success of their implementation. Finally, we consider possible future directions that CDIs for heavy drinking college drinkers may take.

In contrast with the expensive, time-intensive nature of some face-to-face interventions, CDIs can provide cost-effective, individual-focused solutions to a campus and community-wide problem. CDIs also offer many appealing user-friendly features. Once set up, they are convenient to administer, they afford consistent presentation of intervention components, and typically provide resources for managing and analyzing institution-wide data that is generated as students interact with them. Most CDIs are adaptable to the needs and qualities of the institution employing them. CDIs may also enhance certain aspects of clinical interventions. For example, CDIs can deliver interventions to people who might not otherwise seek treatment (Cunningham & Van Mierlo, 2009), and, given the privacy they offer, may afford greater validity of self-report (Elliot, Carey, & Bolles, 2008). Finally, with their combination of broad reach and tailored individualization, CDIs fulfill the National Institute on Alcohol Abuse and Alcoholism's (NIAAA) Task Force on College Drinking 3-in-1 conception of successful interventions, as they can simultaneously impact individual students and the student body as a whole, and can improve relations with the greater college community when they target university organizations (e.g. athletes, Greek organizations) that interact with the local public (NIAAA, 2007).

Most, but not all of the CDIs presented here are considered brief motivational interventions (BMIs). Researchers originally developed BMIs for alcohol misuse that were administered in a face-to-face format. A growing body of research, however, makes it clear that computers lend themselves well to delivering BMIs for alcohol misuse in general and for college students in particular (for reviews see Bewick et al., 2008; Cunningham & Van Mierlo, 2009; Elliot et al., 2008; Hallet, Maycock, Kypri, Howat, & McManus, 2009; S. Walters, Miller & Chiauzzi, 2005). A recent meta-analysis of CDIs for college students found "qualified support for the efficacy of CDIs to reduce alcohol use and problems in college students" (Carey, Scott-Sheldon, Elliott, Bolles, & Carey, 2009, p. 1812). Common findings associate CDIs with immediate reductions in problematic drinking, and slower developing but long-term reductions in alcohol related problems. Improvements tend to vary across outcomes, depending on a variety of factors, as discussed later. Still, average effect sizes, when compared to assessment-only controls, though relatively small ($d.$ = 0.09-0.28), are similar to those found in CDIs for the general population (Carey et al., 2010). The good news is that researchers who develop CDIs for college alcohol misuse are steadily acquiring more insight into which therapeutic mechanisms work best, as well as an understanding of other the factors that influence their effectiveness.

CDI MECHANISMS

CDIs typically use many of the same therapeutic mechanisms that have traditionally been used in brief motivational interventions with heavy drinking college students. The most common of them may be grouped into the categories of assessment, personalized feedback, education and resource referral, skills-building exercises, and self-evaluation exercises. It is worth considering each of these categories individually because they are each impacted differently by the computer interface. Also, some of these mechanisms can be (and have been) used both as individual interventions in their own right as well as supplements to broader, multifaceted therapeutic programs. Finally, it is useful to understand how they interact as the components of the various stand-alone interventions considered in the next section. For that reason, this section also discusses the nonspecific CDI factors of program style and structure.

Assessment. In a clinical context, computers offer the same efficient functionality that they do in any administrative role. With regard to the delivery of an intervention, this translates into a convenient and reliable means for acquiring, analyzing, and storing intake assessment information. But even in this role, there are important implications that administrators should consider when using computers to deliver interventions to address college drinking. Researchers have found, for example, that computers, due to the confidentiality they provide, influence how students respond to assessment questions. (Cunningham, 2009; Gerbert et al., 1999; Turner et al., 1998; White, Mun, & Morgan, 2008). White et al. (2008) found that students who were given follow-up interviews over the phone at 7 months reported one less drinking *occasion* per week (on average) than did those who reported their information on a computer in an administrative office. It is unclear whether this reduction actually represents an average of one occasion per student or can be accounted for by the heavier drinkers who significantly underreported their total drinking (White et al., 2008), but in-person underreporting is a concern when accurate assessment of population data is needed. Such a tendency to underreport can be minimized with computer assessment, especially in students who feel they may have something to lose (such as an athletic scholarship), whether the assessment is used as the prelude to face-to-face therapy, or as the first module of a CDI.

Moreover, there has been renewed interest among alcohol researchers in investigating assessment reactivity as a useful clinical tool. The finding that assessment itself may entail therapeutic benefit either as a prelude (e.g., Bien, Miller, & Tonigan, 1993) or an adjunct to treatment (Finn & Tonsager, 1997) isn't new, but the interest now is in understanding the impact that assessment has as an intervention in its own right (Hester, Delaney, & Campbell, 2012; Kypri, Langley, Saungers, & Cashell-Smith, 2006; McCambridge & Day, 2008; S. T. Walters, Vader, Harris, & Jouriles, 2009). A recent clinical trial of a new CDI found that simply completing a drinking assessment in a clinical setting, without feedback, leads to significant reductions in drinking among college students (Hester et al., 2012). Though more research on assessment reactivity is required, it is clear that it has the potential to significantly influence harmful alcohol use. Perhaps more importantly, when properly employed, assessment has the potential to set the stage for and enhance the subsequent therapeutic intervention(s).

Personalized feedback. Personalized feedback, presented in the context of an alcohol intervention for college drinkers, typically provides information about quantity and frequency of use, effects of blood alcohol content (BAC), personal risk factors, and other pertinent information from the individual student's assessment that ties their behavior to its consequences. Personalized feedback has long been a staple of effective BMIs (e.g.,the Brief Alcohol Screening and Intervention for College Students, BASICS; Dimeff, Baer, Kivlahan, & Marlatt, 1999), and CDIs have the advantage over face-to-face interventions in that they offer immediate and error-free calculation of summary items, and thereby reliably present accurate and appropriate feedback. Personalized normative feedback (PNF) is also one of the most researched and validated aspects of CDIs for college students (Bewick et al., 2008; Cunningham et al., 2010; Lewis & Neighbors, 2006; Neighbors, Larimer, & Lewis, 2004). Research has shown that the impact of the feedback is enhanced through the use of university-specific and gender-based normative comparisons (Hagman, Clifford, & Noel, 2007; Larimer & Cronce, 2007; Moreira, Smith, & Foxcroft, 2009; Perkins, 2002; S. T. Walters, Vader, & Harris, 2007).

In addition to serving as an intervention in its own right, CDIs may extend the function of feedback by tailoring the program's material for the student using it. This may be accomplished either by programming that selects content contingent upon assessment results (e.g., a branching paradigm that provides information about symptoms of tolerance and dependence when a heavier drinker is using the program), or simply by directing the student to information elsewhere on the site that is pertinent to their personal circumstances. Finally, CDIs that allow for repeated assessments over time can provide feedback about how an individual's behavior is changing or staying the same. Such feedback either may enhance the maintenance of a change or, lacking that, may signal to students that they need more help in changing their drinking.

Education and resource referral. The most common function that CDIs perform in the treatment of college student alcohol misuse is to provide educational material about the facts, risks, and harms associated with drinking, as well as information about where to get help. Common educational topics include alcohol's effects on the body, risks associated with alcohol use, harm-reduction behaviors, interactions between alcohol and other drugs, and information about campus policies and local DUI laws. This information is typically presented in a variety of formats: didactic text, interactive exercises and games, and narrative elements, such as branching video vignettes of common social situations that college drinkers may find themselves in, wherein key choice points are presented with both good and bad outcomes. Unfortunately, no matter how engaging the presentation, research consistently finds that alcohol knowledge and resource information alone are not effective at altering alcohol consumption or related high-risk behaviors among college students (e.g., Croom et al., 2009; Donohue, Allen, Maurer, Ozols, & DeStefano, 2004). Though perhaps not surprising, this finding is disappointing, because nothing could be theoretically simpler than the broad dissemination of beneficial health-related information via computer.

Alcohol-related information may be more beneficial to students who have already initiated self-directed behavior change (Carey, Henson, Carey, & Maisto, 2009). Such "teachable moments" (Barnett, Monti, & Wood, 2001) need not be generated just by circumstances in the student's life. Consistent with motivational interviewing (Miller & Rollnick, 2002), some CDIs use PNF to enhance discrepancies between students' stated values and actual outcomes to increase their motivation to change. Once in a state of such self-awareness, information about the hazards of drinking may be more effectively presented to students.

Skills-building exercises. There have to date been relatively few skills building exercises deployed in CDIs. One common exercise involves teaching students to calculate their own BAC as they drink. They first teach students the definition of a standard drink and provide information about the effect of eating or consuming nonalcoholic beverages on BAC. Students enter their gender and weight and observe the effect of consuming various drinks over time. Another exercise attempts to educate students about drink-refusal skills, sometimes by suggesting responses (e.g., "I would, but I have a test tomorrow") and other times by playing branching video vignettes that show the consequences of student actors giving various responses.

Self-evaluation exercises. Some CDIs ask students to think more deeply about their drinking. Decisional balance exercises typically ask students to consider the "good things" and "not so good things" about their drinking. The list of good things is usually short and the rewards short term while the not so good things is often longer and consequences more long term. This contrast can help move heavy drinking students from not thinking about their drinking to considering whether the good things are worth the not so good things. Another exercise that typically follows personalized normative feedback asks students to consider changes that they might make in their drinking, and to make a behavior change plan. A third exercise asks students about their values and how drinking fits in with them.

Structure and tone. Generally speaking, there are two ways a CDI may be structured (Cunningham, 2009). One approach is fairly directive (i.e., College Drinker's Check-Up; eCheckup to go), and guides the user through a series of exercises that are completed in succession. The other approach makes the entire content of the program available to users who decide on their own how they would like to proceed through the material (i.e., Alcohol 101 +; MyStudentBody). The former method seeks to generate a particular experience (e.g., assessment, feedback, realization), whereas the latter capitalizes on the notion that individuals will have their own, self-directed sense of what they need from an intervention. The structured approach may work better for one-time interventions, while sites to which students return repeatedly would seem to benefit from less-structured access, but there is no evidence that supports one method over the other (Cunningham, 2009).

Therapeutic style. All of the treatment components mentioned earlier act on the mechanisms of change traditionally considered to be relevant to behavior change; they inform, educate, and evoke discrepant awareness in the student while supporting the student in exploring alternative behaviors. The obvious difference is that a computer, and not a person, is delivering the therapy, and that means "common factors" (e.g., empathy, positive regard, rapport) of counselor-based interventions are not at play. Many researchers hold that these factors involve important motivating variables that are necessary for lasting behavior change (Miller, 2000; Rogers, 1957). Though in this domain computers may be at a clinical disadvantage, it is an empirical question how much empathy is needed to motivate people to change their heavy drinking. As with face-to-face therapy, the "tone" with which the program presents the intervention, and responds to the student's engagement, will impact its effectiveness at motivating students to change their drinking. To varying degrees, CDIs present material in an empathic and nonjudgmental tone that encourages the student to explore the material. Moreover, when feedback is personalized, a student may feel that his or her problems have been accurately perceived and communicated (a key component of accurate empathy; Truax & Carkhuff, 1967). Finally, when programs branch into different modules based on the student's responses, or provide pop-up windows that anticipate common emotional reactions to feedback, they can support the student's exploration of behavior change.

COMMERCIALLY AVAILABLE CDIs: PROGRAM DESCRIPTIONS

In this section, we present descriptions of, and the evidence for, various stand-alone CDIs that have been developed specifically for college drinkers. These CDIs typically offer user-friendly features (for both administrator and user), and vary both in strategies used and the evidence for their effectiveness. We do not include here descriptions of other CDIs for alcohol misuse that are available to the general public (e.g., Drinker'sCheck-up.com, CheckYourDrinking.net), though these are occasionally deployed in university settings. Although designed as stand-alone interventions, the programs described here may also be used as components of more comprehensive campus-wide programs.

Alcohol 101 Plus. Alcohol 101 Plus is an educational, interactive, harm-reduction program developed by the Century Council, a nonprofit consortium of prominent alcohol distillers. It has a "virtual campus" layout from which users navigate through its various components according to their interests. Given its unstructured format, the amount of time it takes to view the site may depend primarily on the interest of the student visiting the site, but most of the site's content may be viewed in 30 to 60 minutes. Its primary intent is to educate students about negative outcomes relative to alcohol misuse, teach harm-reduction strategies, provide resources, and inform students about healthy alternatives to drinking. Though it may be used with the general student population, it particularly targets four groups—first-year students, Greeks, athletes and mandated students—to address issues specific to them. The program contains several short video vignettes, some that include branching "video decision scenarios" in which students may select either the "take a drink" or "refuse to drink" option and then watch as the video plays out the consequences of the choice. There are games that test the student's knowledge about alcohol and the body, expectancy effects of alcohol, and consequences of getting arrested for driving under the influence, and a virtual bar that teaches students the effect of various drinking patterns on someone of their own weight and gender. Easily accessible on the Internet, Alcohol 101 Plus may also be administered in a classroom setting along with available group leader materials.

Empirical support for Alcohol 101. Researchers evaluating Alcohol 101 (the version prior to Alcohol 101 Plus) found that it helps students develop more realistic expectancies about the effects of alcohol and likewise promotes the intention to practice harm reduction behaviors (Reis & Riley, 2002; Sharmer, 2001). However, even though it has

Table 10.1 Commercially Available Programs

Program Name	Developer and Contact Information	Purpose	Completion Time	Design and Components	Administrative Features	Cost
Alcohol 101 Plus	Century Council alcohol101plus.org	Prevention: Educational	30–60 minutes	Interactive, multimedia	n/a	Free
MyStudentBody	Inflexxion, Inc. mystudentbody.com	Prevention: Educational	90–120 minutes	Interactive, multimedia, personalized, self-assessment, pre- and posttests	Real-time data feedback; annual report; may be tailored to specific populations	Pricing unavailable; based on student population
eCheckup to Go eCheckuptogo	San Diego St. Univ. Research Foundation echeckuptogo.com	Prevention and individual intervention	30 minutes	Drinking assessment and personalized normative feedback; multiple use for long-term tracking, expectancy	Real-time data access; summary and analysis reports available on demand	$975 annual fee
AlcoholEdu	EverFi outsidetheclassroom.com	Primary prevention: Educational	2–3 hours	Interactive, multimedia, personalized goal planner, BAC calculator, pre- and posttests	Annual student drinking and nondrinking data summaries and trend analysis	Price based on student population; ex. 2,500–3,500 freshmen = $29,900 per year
College Alc	EverFi outsidetheclassroom.com	Primary prevention: Educational	60–90 minutes	Interactive, some multimedia, BAC calculator, pre- and posttests, workbook for sanctioned students	Annual student drinking data summary	Price based on student population; ex. 2,500–3,500 freshmen = $15,000 per year

Name / Provider	Type	Duration	Assessment	Customization	Cost
Alcohol Innerview EverFi outsidetheclassroom.com	Assessment and harm reduction for sanctioned students	20–30 minutes	Behavior and drinking assessment and feedback	n/a	Free
College Drinker's Check-up (CDCU) Research Division, Behavior Therapy Associates, LLP collegedrinkerscheckup.com	Prevention and individual intervention	35–45 minutes	Drinking assessment and personalized normative feedback, decisional balance exercise, behavior change exercise	Appearance and referral resources customizable	$2,500 for <15,000 students; $4,500 for >15,000: One-time fee, no annual license fee
Alcohol-Wise 3rd Millenium Classrooms 3rdmilclassrooms.com	Education, primary prevention, individual intervention	1–2 hours	Includes eCheckuptogo, pre- and posttests, BAC calculator, personalized interactions	Manage student use, automatic completion notification	$7 per student or $12,000 per year
Under the Influence 3rd Millenium Classrooms 3rdmilclassrooms.com	Assessment and education for sanctioned students	2–3 hours	Includes eCheckuptogo, pre- and posttests, BAC calculator, personalized interactions	Manage student use, automatic completion notification	$35 per student or $3,000 per year
Alcohol Response-Ability The Bacchus Network bacchusnetwork.org	Assessment and education for sanctioned students	(4) 1-hour sessions	Pre- and posttests	Content customizable when purchased in bulk	$35 per student

been shown that the program can influence these proposed mechanisms of drinking behavior, it has not shown efficacy in changing drinking behavior itself. In a study that compared Alc 101 to a cognitive-behavioral (CBT) drink-refusal skills training intervention, Alc 101 outperformed CBT in both increasing awareness about the harms of alcohol and the intent to reduce that harm, but CBT actually produced a greater reduction in drinking (Donohue et al., 2004). Researchers found that students mandated to treatment by their university who received the Alc 101 program had a lower number of drinking days but a higher average number of drinks per occasion at a 12-month follow-up assessment compared to a counselor administered BMI (Barnett, Murphy, Colby, & Monti, 2007). When compared to an expectancy challenge, Alc 101 produced no significant effects among students on drinks per week or frequency of heavy drinking episodes (Lau-Barraco & Dunn, 2008). Investigators who compared Alc 101 Plus to a counselor-administered BMI for mandated students found that the drinking behavior of those who received the CDI returned to presanction levels at 12-month follow-up, and that the modest reduction that did occur within that timeframe was most likely the result of a reaction to the sanction itself (Carey, Henson, et al., 2009). Finally, Murphy, Dennhardt, Skidmore, Martens, and McDevitt-Murphy (2010) found that a counselor-administered BASICS intervention enhanced motivation to change and discrepancy more than Alcohol 101 Plus, and was rated more favorably by students. One-month follow-up outcomes indicated larger drinking reduction effect sizes in the BASICS condition, but no statistically significant group differences. Overall, outcome research on Alcohol 101 would not suggest that it is effective in reducing drinking in heavy drinking students.

MyStudentBody. MyStudentBody, developed by Inflexxion Inc., employs a motivational, self-assessment approach to alcohol misuse modeled on the BASICS intervention (Dimeff et al., 1999). The program is explored over multiple sessions that take a total of 90- to 120 minutes to complete. Content is designed to help students examine their beliefs and behaviors, and to consider the possible consequences of their actions through the use of interactive tools, peer stories, and other didactic components. As part of the personalized feedback generated from the assessment, the program suggests specific material in the site for students to consider. The program also serves as a general wellness resource, addressing other topics related to sexual activity, nutrition and the deleterious effects of stress on healthy functioning. Content may be tailored for specific populations of new students, athletes, Greeks, and students mandated to treatment due to policy violations. The program also offers other administrator capabilities. MyStudentBody provides access to aggregate data about students' use of the site and self-reported health risks. It also tracks individual students' progress and completion of alcohol and drug courses, allows administrators to analyze the efficacy of the program relative to their goals, and provides feedback designed to help address the specific needs of their institution. MyStudentBody also offers a component designed to improve communication between students and their parents.

Empirical support for MyStudentBody. In the first randomized clinical trial of a CDI, Chiauzzi and colleagues found that heavy-drinking students who received the MyStudentBody intervention significantly reduced their alcohol consumption and alcohol related problems more than students who received access to a comparable education-only website (Chiauzzi, Green, Lord, Thum, & Goldstein, 2005). The program had similar effects on students regardless of their level of motivation to change their drinking when they entered the study. Over time though, the students in the comparison condition matched the reductions of students in the CDI. Students accessed the MyStudentBody program from their home computers (or in school computer centers) and were far more likely to recommend the intervention to their friends than were those students presented with the same material in the less engaging format. The experimental subjects, foreshadowing many tests of CDIs to follow, reported subjectively that they considered it an appealing means for addressing alcohol problems.

eCheckuptoGo. The eCheckuptogo program for college drinkers, developed by researchers at San Diego State University, delivers a brief motivational intervention through an assessment and personalized normative feedback. The program presents a single, self-guided, concise (approximately 20 minutes) intervention that follows the feedback with tailored information about the user's drinking and related risk factors. It uses text, illustrations and three short educational videos. The eCheckuptogo program may be retaken on multiple occasions so that students can track changes in their use and risk behavior. Should administrators wish students to spend more time reflecting on their feedback, an additional "Personal Reflections" component may be added to the program. This component, which derives questions from each user's unique profile, invites the student to consider more carefully the social norms and personal choices that influence his or her drinking behavior. As with other programs, the eCheckuptogo may be implemented across a variety of settings and with diverse populations such as first-year students, mandated students, Greeks and athletes.

Empirical support for eCheckuptogo. The eCheckuptogo program has been evaluated both as an intervention for heavy drinkers (S. T. Walters et al., 2007) and as a primary prevention program for incoming freshmen (Doumas & Andersen, 2009). S. T. Walters and colleagues (2007) found that the eCheckuptogo program accelerated declines among heavy drinkers in both peak BAC and drinks per week, relative to controls, although those students not receiving the eCheckuptogo had similar levels of reduced drinking at the 4-month follow-up. On the other hand, Doumas and Andersen (2009) found that first-year heavy drinkers who were given the eCheckuptogo program by a research assistant during a class in their spring semester reduced both their drinking and their alcohol related problems relative to heavy drinking controls, who reported increases both in drinking and alcohol related problems. Murphy et al. (2010) compared eCheckuptogo to an assessment-only control group and a counselor-administered BASICS intervention. Both interventions were associated with increases in motivation and normative discrepancy, but BASICS increased the students' self-ideal discrepancy more than eCheckuptogo and was rated more favorably by students. One-month follow-up outcomes indicated larger drinking-reduction effect sizes in the BASICS condition, and that BASICS, but not eCheckuptogo was associated with statistically significant reductions in weekly and binge drinking relative to the assessment-only control group.

Alcohol-Wise. Alcohol-Wise is a prevention program designed by 3rd Millennium Classrooms specifically for first-year college students. This program enhances the eCheckuptogo assessment and feedback protocol with various didactic presentations in an effort to increase both the salience and retention of the curriculum. To that end, the program also generates risk scores for students (based on their responses to a pretest and eCheckuptogo) to characterize the severity of their drinking related issues. Alcohol-Wise also includes attitudes and behavior surveys, harm reduction exercises and tests of alcohol related knowledge. Customizable features include information about local resources, text relative to the student's risk score and up to 10 questions that may be designed to gather data of interest for the participating institution. Running a little more than an hour to administer, it includes a 30-day follow-up component, and also offers add-on sessions for sexual awareness and social responsibility, as well as an optional supplemental module for Greek students. The program includes features that allow administrators to monitor and prompt student compliance. There are no reported empirical data pertaining to the effectiveness of this program.

Under the Influence. Under the Influence, also created by 3rd Millenium, is designed as an intervention for sanctioned students. Taking about 3 hours to complete, it contains the same content as Alcohol-Wise but also includes information about the more severe effects and risks of alcohol consumption on health, legal issues and long-term consequences such as tolerance and withdrawal. Under the Influence also has a section that relates alcohol use to other psychological problems that occur at higher rates among those with more problematic use patterns. Under the Influence has not been subjected to any empirical analysis that has been published.

AlcoholEdu. AlcoholEdu is the most comprehensive of three products developed by EverFi (formerly Outside the Classroom) to address the problem of harmful alcohol use among college students (the other two are College Alc and Alcohol Innerview). AlcoholEdu is a population-level program that is designed to be administered to all incoming first-year students and, by providing a common knowledge base to the entire student body over time, seeks to alter the drinking culture of the college that uses it. Taking about two to three hours total to complete across primary and follow-up sessions, the program employs a multimedia format (blogs, IM chats, and videos), interactive exercises, surveys, goal-setting exercises and tests of program-related material. It also tailors a portion of its content to the students' level of consumption, and high-risk drinkers receive normative feedback relative to national statistics in order to correct any misconceptions they may have about their use. There are related programs that have been developed specifically for mandated students (AlcoholEdu for

Sanctions), Greek students (GreekLifeEdu), and a module designed specifically for parents. The program also delivers email to students throughout the year to reconnect them to their plan so that they can monitor their progress. The program's appearance and some content may be customized to the needs and resources of the institution. Administrators get feedback on their students' use patterns, comparisons to national norms, and other data about their behaviors, as well as assistance from the program's developers with implementation, technical issues and data analysis.

College Alc. College Alc is an online alcohol education-prevention program also intended for use with an entire incoming class of first-year students. Similar to AlcoholEdu but without the full array of multimedia offerings or administrative support, College Alc is offered as a more affordable option for institutions with budgetary constraints. There are five lessons that take about 60 to 90 minutes to complete, and are designed to correct students' understanding of alcohol's effects and the normative use of their peers, to help them understand the physiological effects of alcohol, and to inform them about risks pertaining to alcohol expectancies and use. Lessons also provide information related to drinking and driving, unsafe sex, and violence, and teach harm-reduction strategies germane to alcohol poisoning, overdose, and dependency. The program contains a pre- and posttest, as well as optional pre- and postbehavioral surveys. College Alc also offers a workbook specifically for mandated students.

Alcohol Innerview. Although both AlcoholEdu and College Alc are longer, multisession interventions, Alcohol Innerview offers a comprehensive assessment and personalized normative feedback program in a single 20- to 30-minute session. Alcohol Innerview can be used either as a BMI in its own right, or as a supplement to another intervention program. In addition to the feedback, it informs students about their personal risk factors and other possible negative consequences of their behavior. It then provides the student with some harm reduction strategies.

Empirical support for AlcoholEdu, College Alc, and Alcohol Innerview. When administered to incoming first-year students, early research into the efficacy of AlcoholEdu found that although it increased students' knowledge of alcohol effects and related risks, it did not increase protective behaviors nor did it reduce risk-related behaviors, high-risk drinking or alcohol related harm (Croom et al., 2009). Subsequent investigations have shown that a revised version of the program demonstrated a modest impact both on drinking and alcohol-related consequences (Hustad, Barnett, Borsari, & Jackson, 2010; Lovecchio, Wyatt, & DeJong, 2010). Further, a 2010 randomized clinical trial compared 15 universities that implemented AlcoholEdu to 15 that did not. One study reported that incoming first-year students who received the intervention initially reduced their heavy drinking and frequency of drinking, but these effects did not persist, especially among students who failed to complete the entire program (Paschall, Antin, Ringwalt and Saltz, 2011a); a related study found a similar initial decrease and later regression in alcohol-related problems (Paschall, Antin, Ringwalt and Saltz, 2011b).

Two studies have investigated the efficacy of College Alc. One study found no reductions in any drinking or related behaviors, and a modest impact on alcohol related attitudes (Paschall, Bersamin, Fearnow-Kenney, Wyrick, & Currey, 2006). Another study, using the same sample, found that students who drank before they enrolled in college did reduce their heavy drinking and alcohol-related problems at follow-up, but nondrinkers using the program exhibited the opposite results. From this follow-up investigators conjectured that the program may be more beneficial to drinkers than to nondrinkers (Bersamin, Paschall, Fearnow-Kenney, & Wyrick, 2007), but others cite methodological issues with the study (Hustad et al, 2010). Alcohol Innerview has not been empirically investigated.

Evidence when comparing Alcohol Edu and eCheckuptogo. One research group conducted a study to compare whether a comprehensive program such as AlcoholEdu was more effective as a primary prevention for incoming students than the much briefer (and less expensive) eCheckuptogo program. Incoming student-users of both programs reported less alcohol use at the one-month follow-up than did the assessment-only control group. Likewise, students using both programs decreased their alcohol-related consequences, while for students in the control group, alcohol associated harms increased at follow-up. Researchers found that AlcoholEdu was slightly more effective than eCheckuptogo at reducing negative consequences associated with drinking, most likely due to its more extensive harm-reduction educational materials (Hustad et al., 2010).

The College Drinker's Check-up (CDCU). The CDCU was adapted by researchers at Behavior Therapy Associates from the Drinker's Check-up, a CDI originally developed for heavy drinking adults (Hester, Squires, & Delaney, 2005) that was adapted, in turn, from the original face-to-face protocol of the same name (Miller, Sovereign, & Krege, 1988). The CDCU is designed to be administered in one, relatively brief (approximately 35-minute) session. It begins with a screen for heavy drinking, and those who screen positive are invited to use the rest of the program. Students then proceed to a module that includes a decisional balance exercise, a comprehensive assessment of drinking and drug use, alcohol-related problems, and risk factors for future alcohol-related problems. A module then provides personalized drinking quantity, frequency and alcohol-related problems feedback based on gender- and university-specific norms. A final module returns to the initial decisional balance exercise and prompts users to consider the "good things" and the "not so good things" about their drinking as it further develops discrepancy between their drinking behavior and their goals as a student. The program then asks students about their readiness to change their drinking. It takes this readiness into account when ultimately helping the user to develop a plan to reduce their drinking and subsequent risk for alcohol-related problems.

Empirical support for the CDCU. Our research team evaluated the CDCU in a clinical setting (research division offices at a private behavioral therapy practice located some distance from the university) with 18- to 24-year-old heavy drinking students. The first randomized clinical trial compared students receiving the CDCU program to an assessment-only control group. Both groups significantly reduced both their consumption and alcohol-related problems at one month, and continued to reduce drinking and reports of adverse consequences at 12-month follow-up. Students receiving the CDCU showed greater improvement across outcome measures (Hester et al., 2011).

The significant reductions in the assessment-only control group in this first study suggested that this group had demonstrated assessment reactivity. To rule out the influence of assessment reactivity, we conducted a second randomized clinical trial comparing the CDCU group to a *delayed* assessment control group. In this study, all of the differences in drinking outcomes at the one-month follow-up favored the CDCU group with an average effect size of $d = .82$, a large-effect size. Comparing the two studies, the results support the notion that the assessment, feedback, and additional motivational elements in the CDCU produced the reductions in drinking and related negative consequences, and not the effect of the clinical setting, or factors related to being a subject in a clinical trial (Hester et al., 2011).

Alcohol Response-Ability. Alcohol Response-Ability is a 4-part interactive educational program developed by the BACCHUS and GAMMA Peer Education Network specifically for students who run afoul of their school's alcohol policy. Each part of the text-based program takes an hour to complete. The first informs the student about the physiological and behavioral effects of alcohol. The next section assesses the student's alcohol use, identifies risk factors, and warns the students of consequences that will occur if he or she fails to change their behavior. The third section seeks to promote a sense of personal responsibility in the student by exploring the various decisions he or she makes on a typical night of drinking, thereby encouraging the development of harm reduction behaviors. The final section (which may be customized by the participating institution with a bulk registration purchase) presents the student with further resources to support behavior change, and includes a posttest to ensure that course materials have been mastered, as well as indicating to the administrator that the program has been completed. To date, Alcohol Response-Ability has not been subjected to any empirical research.

EVIDENCE FOR USING CDIs WITH SPECIFIC POPULATIONS

Athletes. Two studies have evaluated the benefits of offering CDIs for college athletes. Doumas and Haustveit (2008) found that heavy-drinking first-year athletes accessing a web-based personalized feedback program (CheckYourDrinking.net) for 15 minutes reduced their drinking significantly more than athletes who spent 15 minutes surfing a web-based education program. Martens and colleagues (2010) extended these results by comparing three conditions: feedback targeted specifically to athletes, feedback based on general college norms, and an athlete-oriented education-only control condition. Students entered their information on a website and were later sent a link to a separate web page, either containing their feedback results or information about the effects of alcohol on athletic performance. They found that heavy-drinking athletes in the targeted condition reduced their peak BAC at 6 months more than did athletes in the other two conditions. Interestingly, outcomes for athletes receiving feedback based on general college norms were no different than those who received the computer-delivered information about alcohol's effect on their performance; a finding that may support the efficacy of tailored educational CDIs (Martens, Kilmer, Beck, & Zamboanga, 2010).

Mandated students. Many of the stand-alone programs reviewed earlier have been developed for use with students mandated to treatment due to violations of their school's alcohol policies, but only one has actually been evaluated for use with that population. Alcohol 101 (the precursor to Alcohol 101 Plus) has been correlated with increases in both more realistic alcohol expectancies and intent to practice harm reduction behaviors (Reis & Riley, 2002; Sharmer, 2001). However, the program has produced nonsignificant effects on the actual drinking behavior of students mandated to treatment, whether compared to CBT (Donohue et al., 2004) or BMIs (Barnett et al., 2007; Carey et al., 2009). Results evaluating the effectiveness of personalized normative feedback programs (PNF) with mandated students have been mixed. Though one study found that students in a computer-delivered PNF condition reduced the amount, frequency and intensity of their drinking at one month (Doumas, McKinley, and Book, 2009), another study using a computer generated PNF program attributed students' changes in drinking behavior to the sanction itself (White et al., 2008). This analysis was corroborated by the Carey et al., 2009, study, which likewise concluded that CDIs (as with other interventions for mandated students) may work best in support of students who have already decided to change their drinking, while more problematic drinkers probably require more intensive intervention to capitalize on the "teachable moment" that the sanction provides.

COMMERCIALLY AVAILABLE CDIs: SUMMARY OF EMPIRICAL FINDINGS

Considering the number of programs available, and their wide dissemination, there exists in these interventions a relative paucity of efficacy research (Carey et al., 2010). Research that has been conducted generally finds that significant effects, when they occur, are among heavy drinkers, and often do not persist. Low-risk drinkers tend not to change their drinking in response to CDIs. The effect usually seen is an accelerated reduction in drinking. That is, over time, heavy-drinking students in the control groups also tend to reduce their drinking albeit more slowly, and eventually "catch up" with students who received the intervention. Importantly, Carey and colleagues concluded that CDIs for alcohol misuse generally perform as well as other (counselor delivered) interventions for college students, reducing risk "across the full range of available measures of alcohol use quantity, frequency and problems" (2009, p. 1813). Finally, the feasibility research done on CDIs typically finds that high numbers of students who use them find them informative, engaging, and worthy of being recommended to a friend.

Overall, CDIs for college drinking have been found to be effective at reducing the quantity, frequency and severity of hazardous alcohol use (Carey et al., 2009). However, there is significant heterogeneity in the results of CDIs. Although some have shown little to no evidence of effectiveness (e.g., Alcohol 101), others have not been evaluated at all. On the other hand, some programs have demonstrated large effect sizes and reductions in drinking that persist out to 12 months (e.g., CDCU). We recommend that college administrators who are considering implementing CDIs look closely at the outcome data.

FACTORS RELEVANT TO THE IMPLEMENTATION OF CDIs

Researchers who address the problem of college alcohol misuse generally acknowledge the great potential, if not the actual effectiveness, that CDIs bring to bear on this serious public health concern. Their ability to combine broad reach, accessibility, and individualization with empirically validated treatments presents an unprecedented opportunity to simultaneously impact both population prevention and individual interventions (Carey et al., 2010; Cunningham & Van Mierlo, 2009; Elliot, Carey, & Bolles, 2009; Larimer & Cronce, 2007). However, the development and investigation of CDIs is still in its nascent stages, and many general questions about implementation await further empirical investigation. What follows here are some general issues and specific recommendations that administrators should take into account when they consider utilizing CDIs at their institutions.

One important issue among developers of computer-delivered behavioral health interventions involves how to assess and influence engagement with program material. Researchers have noted that users often engage the intervention to less of a degree than they hoped for (Eysenbach, 2005). To increase engagement, it is important to consider factors involving both the CDI itself as well as factors external to it. According to the health communication theory behind tailored feedback, intervention content will be attended to more closely and retained better if it is individualized to the user, but engagement will also be influenced by factors associated with message presentation (Rimer & Kreuter, 2006). Both the aesthetic appeal of the intervention as well as its structure have been found to be more important to engagement than its putative authoritativeness (Danaher & Seely, 2009; Stanford, Tauber, Fogg, & Marable, 2002).

With regard to context of implementation, it is not always clear how a CDI's efficacy will translate into real-world settings (Cunningham, 2009). The effectiveness of a given CDI may depend on the manner and setting in which it is used. In the media-rich world of the typical college student, one obvious appeal of CDIs is that they can be implemented in a preferred environment of student activity (e.g., dorm room). However, it can be difficult to compete with the entertainment value of much of the material available on the Internet. Administrators should consider that a CDI's intended impact might easily be lost amidst the ocean of other Internet-delivered data that students wade through on a daily basis. Thus, for example, a program that is evaluated in a classroom or laboratory setting may not achieve the same results when a student uses it in a dorm. Likewise, some prevention material may be sufficiently presented in a first-year seminar, while an intervention for mandated students might most effectively be presented in a student health clinic.

Administrators might also consider supplemental ways to enhance retention of program material. A recent study required students completing a CDI to spend 20 minutes either rereading or writing down their feedback. Results demonstrated that students who process computer-delivered feedback more fully not only retained it better, but also reduced their drinking more than students who did not process the feedback (Jouriles et al., 2010).

Secondly, since computers today may be used at any step an institution's behavioral health program, we recommend that administrators be aware of the factors that influence their impact at each step. As discussed earlier, the use of computers may influence the accuracy of intake assessment data. By providing immediate feedback, computers may make a single session with a counselor more effective. Though capable of presenting information in a variety of engaging formats, there is no guarantee that such a presentation induces significant engagement with the material. Skills-building exercises, while easily transferred to computer formats, may likewise not impact the student as fully as the same exercise done face-to-face with a counselor or in a classroom.

Research into the interactions between CDI components and contexts of use is still in its beginning stages (Ritterbrand, Thorndike, Cox, Kovatchev, & Gonder-Frederick, 2009). Given these considerations, we have four recommendations:

1. Administrators should take advantage of CDIs potential to deliver the NIAAA's Task Force on College Drinking 3-in-1 conception of successful interventions. They should choose CDIs that assess both drinking and alcohol-related problems, provide personalized normative feedback using gender and university specific norms, and offer further exercises to capitalize on the "teachable

moment" this feedback creates for the student. The campus-wide distribution of such a program becomes a de facto prevention program, helping the entire student body to become more aware of their own and each others' healthy and hazardous drinking behavior.

2. Strategically deployed, computers can also serve as the foundation for a stepped-care approach (Borsari, Tevyaw, Barnett, Kahler, & Monti, 2007; M. Sobell & L. Sobell, 2000) to a campus-wide intervention and prevention program. By combining the dissemination of educational material (such as harm reduction strategies and referrals for resources) with assessment and personalized normative feedback, a program utilizing CDIs can be used to identify students who might benefit further from face-to-face counseling.

3. Administrators should seek out CDIs that get the student to interact with it in some personalized way. Personalized normative feedback, apart from being one of the most effective interventions for college alcohol misuse, promotes personal involvement with the program in just this way. Moreover, it appeals to students' curiosity about their peers' behavior. Decisional balance and goal-setting exercises can also encourage personal involvement in the program. If these features are lacking, consider programs that include tests to assure comprehension of program content.

4. Considering that CDIs may be more effective in some settings than others (Cunningham, 2009), consider the context in which CDIs are deployed. Although administrators may reasonably expect some benefit from CDIs made generally available to their students over the Internet, we recommend considering the potential costs and benefits of having students receive the intervention in more controlled settings such as classrooms, administrative offices or clinical settings. Controlling the context of the intervention may improve engagement and thereby significantly increase course completion and therapeutic impact, especially among populations that may exhibit less motivation to do so, such as mandated students.

FUTURE DIRECTIONS

Though few areas in alcohol abuse research and treatment are advancing as rapidly (and in as many directions) as the field of CDIs, it is possible to imagine what the next decade may hold. We see six paths of future directions.

1. CDIs will continue to improve in their ability to deliver interventions. Specifically, their effectiveness at producing tailored feedback will improve. Researchers are already envisioning programs that provide feedback based not only on alcohol related behaviors and social norms, nor even just typologies that arise from maladaptive pattern of abuse, but also with regard to cognitive ability,

cognitive style, personality variables, cultural variables, and perhaps even to patterns of responding to the tasks that the program presents to the student. Improved tailoring will thus improve not only drinking related feedback, but also how the program selects content with which the user interacts.

2. There are several recognized mediators of drinking-related behavior change, such as self-efficacy and drinking expectancies, for which CDIs have only been lightly developed (S. T. Walters & Neighbors, 2011). CDIs will also make advances as programs are developed for empirically validated interventions that have yet to find their way into computer applications, such as behavioral economics (Murphy, Correia, & Barnett, 2007).

3. S. T. Walters and Neighbors have also noted that one untapped mine of potential for CDIs exists in the development of interventions that mimic or capitalize on Internet-driven social networks. Taking this idea further, so called serious game developers have been exploring how multiplayer online games can be used to creatively solve problems in business and research settings (McGonigal, 2010). It seems only a matter of time before some enterprising young gamer comes up a with a university-wide game, perhaps based on behavioral economic principles, that promotes low-risk drinking and perhaps even uses in-game feedback to shape risk-reducing behavioral repertoires.

4. Another direction is the use of cell phone text messaging to promote low-risk drinking and prosocial activities. For example, CDI administrators could offer discount tickets to on-campus dances, movies, plays, recitals, and so on, as a reward for going through the CDI. Subsequent texting to these students throughout the semester could encourage them to participate in fun activities that are not associated with heavy drinking.

5. CDIs will start to be implemented on smartphones and tablets as "apps." Smartphones and tablets are proliferating and people are using them in lieu of desktop and laptop computers. This presents an opportunity to develop applications that have an ongoing interaction with heavy-drinking students. For example, David Gustafson and colleagues are developing apps for smartphones that tap into users' social networks in support of recovery from alcohol dependence (Gustafson et al., 2011). It is entirely feasible that others will start developing apps that encourage protective behaviors when drinking and drinking in less risky ways.

6. Another avenue is that of biosensors such as alcohol monitors interacting with apps or cell phones to provide immediate feedback to students about their level of drinking and consequent risks (Barnett, Tidey, Murphy, Swift, & Colby, 2011). Once a generation of researchers arises that understands how these functions may be situated seamlessly in the contexts in which behaviors occur, it is only a matter of time before they start to examine their potential effectiveness in reducing heavy drinking and its alcohol-related risks in college students.

REFERENCES

Barnett, N. P., Monti, P. M., & Wood, M. (2001). Motivational interviewing for alcohol-involved adolescents in the emergency room. In E. F. Wagner & H. P. Waldron (Eds.), *Innovations in adolescent substance abuse interventions* (pp. 143–168). Amsterdam, The Netherlands: Pergamon/Elsevier.

Barnett, N. P., Murphy, J. G., Colby, S. M., & Monti, P. M. (2007). Efficacy of counselor vs. computer-delivered intervention with mandated college students. *Addictive Behaviors, 32,* 2529–2548.

Barnett, N. P., Tidey, J., Murphy, G. G., Swift, R., & Colby, S. M. (2011). Contingency management for alcohol use reduction: A pilot study using a transdermal alcohol sensor. *Drug and Alcohol Dependence, 118,* 391–399.

Bersamin, M., Paschall, M. J., Fearnow-Kenney, M., & Wyrick, D. (2007). Effectiveness of a web-based alcohol misuse and harm prevention course (College Alc) among high- and low-risk students. *Journal of American College Health, 55,* 247–254.

Bewick, B. M., Trusler, K., Barkham, M., Hill, A. J., Cahill, J., & Mulhern, B. (2008). The effectiveness of web-based interventions designed to decrease alcohol consumption—A systematic review. *Preventive Medicine, 47,* 17–26.

Bien, T. H., Miller, W. R., & Tonigan, J. S. (1993). Brief interventions for alcohol problems: A review. *Addiction, 88,* 315–336.

Borsari, B., Tevyaw, T., Barnett, N. P., Kahler, C. W., & Monti, P. M. (2007). Stepped care for mandated college students: A pilot study. *American Journal on Addictions, 16,* 131–137.

Carey, K. B., Henson, J. M., Carey, M. P., & Maisto, S.A. (2009). Computer versus in-person interventions for students violating campus alcohol policy. *Journal of Consulting and Clinical Psychology, 77,* 74–87.

Carey, K. B., Scott-Sheldon, L. A. J., Elliot, J. C., Bolles, J. R., & Carey, M. P. (2009). Computer-delivered interventions to reduce college student drinking: A meta-analysis. *Addiction, 104,* 1807–1819.

Chiauzzi, E., Green, T. Lord, S. Thum, & Goldstein, M. (2005). My Student Body: A high risk drinking prevention website for college students. *Journal of American College Health, 53,* 263–274.

Croom, K., Lewis, D., Marchell, T., Lesser, M. L., Reyna, V. F., Kubicki-Bedford, L.,… Staiano-Coico, L. (2009). Impact of an online education course on behavior and harm for incoming first-year college students: Short-term evaluation of a randomized trial. *Journal of American College Health, 57,* 445–454.

Cunningham, J. A. (2009). Internet evidence-based treatments. In P. Miller (Ed.), *Evidence based addiction treatment* (pp. 379–398). Amsterdam, The Netherlands. Elsevier.

Cunningham, J. A., & Van Mierlo, T. (2009). Methodological issues in the evaluation of internet-based interventions for problem drinking. *Drug and Alcohol Review, 28,* 12–17.

Cunningham, J. A., Wild, T. C., Cordingley, J., Van Mierlo, T., & Humphreys, K. (2010). Twelve-month follow-up results from a randomized controlled trial of a brief personalized feedback intervention for problem drinkers. *Alcohol and Alcoholism, 45,* 258–262.

Danaher, B. G., & Seely, J. R. (2009). Methodological issues in research on web-based behavioral interventions. *Annals of Behavioral Medicine, 38,* 28–39.

Dimeff, L. A., Baer, J. S., Kivlahan D. R., & Marlatt, G. A. (1999). *Brief alcohol screening and intervention for college students.* New York, NY: Guilford Press.

Donohue, B., Allen, D. N., Maurer, A., Ozols, J., & DeStefano, G. (2004). A controlled evaluation of two prevention programs in reducing alcohol use among college students at low and high risk for alcohol related problems. *Alcohol Prevention,* 13–33.

Doumas, D. M., & Andersen, L. L. (2009). Reducing alcohol use in first-year university students: Evaluation of a web-based personalized feedback program. *Journal of College Counseling, 12,* 18–32.

Doumas, D. M., McKinley, L. L. and Book, P. (2009) Evaluation of two web-based alcohol interventions for mandated college students. *Journal of Substance Abuse Treatment, 36,* 65–74.

Doumas, D. M., & Haustveit, T. (2008). Reducing heavy drinking in intercollegiate athletes: Evaluation of a web-based personalized feedback program. *Sports Psychologist, 22,* 212–228.

Elliot, J. C., Carey, K. B., & Bolles, J. R. (2008). Computer-based interventions for college drinking: A qualitative review. *Addictive Behaviors, 33,* 994–1005.

Eysenbach, G. (2005). The law of attrition. *Journal of Medical Internet Research, 7*(1), e11.

Finn, S. E., & Tonsager, M.,E. (1997). Information gathering and therapeutic models of assessment: Complimentary paradigms. *Psychological Assessment, 9*, 374–385.

Gerbert, B., Bronstone, A., Pantilat, S., McPhee, S., Allerton M., & Moe, J. (1999). When asked patients tell: Disclosure of sensitive health-risk behaviors. *Medical Care, 37*, 104–111.

Gustafson D., Boyle, M. G., Shaw B., Isham A., McTavish F., Richards S.,… Johnson K. (2011). E-health solutions for patients with alcohol problem. *Alcohol Research and Health, 33*, 320–327.

Hagman, B. T., Clifford, P. R., & Noel, N.E. (2007). Social norms theory-based interventions: Testing the feasibility of a purported mechanism of action. *Journal of American College Health, 56*, 293–298.

Hallett, J., Maycock, B., Kypri, K., Howat, P., & McManus, A. (2009). Development of a web-based alcohol intervention for university students: Processes and challenges. *Drug and Alcohol Review, 28*, 31–39.

Hester, R. K., Squires, D. D., & Delaney, H. D. (2005). The computer-based drinker's check-up: 12 month outcomes of a controlled clinical trial with problem drinkers. *Journal of Substance Abuse Treatment, 28*, 159–169.

Hester, R. K., Delaney, H. D., & Campbell, W. (2012). The college drinker's check-up: Outcomes of two randomized clinical trials of a computer-delivered intervention. *Psychology of Addictive Behaviors 26*, 1-12.

Hustad, J. T. P., Barnett, N. P., Borsari, B., & Jackson, K. M. (2010). Web-based alcohol prevention for incoming college students: A randomized controlled trial. *Addictive Behaviors, 35*, 183–189.

Jouriles, E. N., Brown, A. S., Rosenfield, D., McDonald, R., Croft, K., Leahy, M. M., & Walters, S. T. (2010). Improving the effectiveness of computer-delivered personalized drinking feedback interventions for college students. *Psychology of Addictive Behaviors, 24*, 592–599.

Kypri, K., Langley, J. D., Saungers, J. B., & Cashell-Smith, M. L. (2006). Assessment may conceal therapeutic benefit: Findings from a randomized controlled trial for hazardous drinking. *Addiction, 102*, 62–70.

Larimer, M. E., & Cronce, J. M. (2007). Identification, prevention and treatment revisited: Individual-focused college prevention strategies 1999–2006. *Addictive Behaviors, 32*, 2439–2468.

Lau-Barraco, C., & Dunn, M. E. (2008). Evaluation of a single-session expectancy challenge intervention to reduce alcohol use among college students. *Psychology of Addictive Behaviors, 22*, 168–175.

Lewis, M. A., & Neighbors, C. (2006). Who is the typical college student? Implications for personalized normative feedback interventions. *Addictive Behaviors, 31*, 2120–2126.

Lovecchio, C. P., Wyatt, T. M., & DeJong, W. (2010). Reductions in drinking and alcohol-related harms reported by first-year college students taking an online alcohol education course: A randomized trial. *Journal of Health Communication, 15*, 805–819.

Martens, M. P., Kilmer, J. R., Beck, N. C., & Zamboanga, B. L. (2010). The efficacy of a targeted personalized drinking feedback intervention among intercollegiate athletes: A randomized controlled trial. *Psychology of Addictive Behaviors, 24*, 660–669.

McCambridge, J., & Day, M. (2008). Randomized controlled trial of the effects of completing the alcohol use disorders identification test questionnaire on self-reported hazardous drinking. *Addiction, 103*, 241–248.

McGonigal, J. (2011). *Reality is broken.* New York, NY: Penguin Press.

Miller, W. R. (2000). Rediscovering fire: Small interventions, large effects. *Psychology of Addictive Behaviors, 14*, 6–18.

Miller W. R., & Rollnick, S. (2002). *Motivational interviewing.* New York, NY: Guilford Press.

Miller, W. R., Sovereign, R. G., & Krege, B. (1988). Motivational interviewing with problem drinkers: II. The drinker's check-up as a preventative intervention. *Behavioral Psychotherapy, 16*, 251–268.

Moreira, M. T., Smith, L. A., & Foxcroft, D. (2009). Social norms interventions to reduce alcohol misuse in university or college students (Review). *Cochrane Database of Systematic Reviews, 3*, CD006748.

Murphy, J. G., Correia, C. J., & Barnett, N. P. (2007). Behavioral economic approaches to reduce college student drinking. *Addictive Behaviors, 32*, 2573–2585.

Murphy, J. G., Dennhardt, A. A., Skidmore, J. R., Martens, M. P., & McDevitt-Murphy, M. E. (2010). Computerized versus motivational interviewing alcohol interventions: Impact on discrepancy motivation and drinking. *Psychology of Addictive Behaviors, 24*, 628–639.

National Institutes of Health. (2007). *What colleges need to know now: An update on college drinking research.* Bethesda, MD: National Institutes of Health, DHHS (NIH publication no. 07–5010).

Neighbors, C., Larimer, M. E., & Lewis, M. A. (2004). Targeting misperceptions of descriptive drinking norms: Efficacy of a computer delivered personalized normative feedback intervention. *Journal of Consulting and Clinical Psychology, 72*, 434–447.

Paschall, M. J., Antin, T., Ringwalt, C. L., & Saltz, R. F. (2011a). Evaluation of an internet-based alcohol misuse prevention course for college freshmen: Findings of a randomized multi-campus trial. *American Journal of Preventive Medicine, 41*, 300–308.

Paschall M. J., Antin, T., Ringwalt, C. L., & Saltz, R. F. (2011b). Effects of AlcoholEdu for college on alcohol-related problems among freshmen: A randomized multicampus trial. *Journal of Studies on Alcohol and Drugs, 72*, 642–650.

Paschall, M. J., Bersamin, M., Fearnow-Kenney, M., Wyrick, D., & Currey, D. (2006). Short-term evaluation of a web-based college alcohol misuse and harm prevention course (College Alc). *Journal of Alcohol and Drug Education, 50*, 49–65.

Perkins, H. W. (2002). Social norms and the prevention of alcohol misuse in collegiate contexts. *Journal of Studies on Alcohol, S14*, 164–172.

Reis, J., & Riley, W. (2002). Assessment of a computer-supported alcohol education intervention program. *Health Education, 102*, 124–132.

Rimer, B. K., & Kreuter, M. W. (2006). Advancing tailored health communication: A persuasion and message effects perspective. *Journal of Communication, 56*, S184–S201.

Ritterbrand, L. M., Thorndike, F. P., Cox, D. J., Kovatchev, B. P., & Gonder-Frederick, L.A. (2009). A behavior change model for internet interventions. *Annals of Behavioral Medicine, 38*, 18–27.

Rogers, C. R. (1957). The necessary and sufficient conditions of therapeutic personality change. *Journal of Consulting and Clinical Psychology, 21*, 95–103.

Sharmer, L. (2001). Evaluation of alcohol education programs on attitude, knowledge and self-reported behavior of college students. *Evaluation and the Health Professions, 24*, 336–358.

Sobell, M. B., & Sobell, L. C. (2000). Stepped care as a heuristic approach to the treatment of alcohol problems. *Journal of Consulting and Clinical Psychology, 68*, 573–579.

Stanford, J., Tauber, E. R., Fogg B. J., & Marable, L. (2002). Experts vs. online consumers: A comparative credibility study of health and finance web sites. *Consumer Reports Webwatch.* Retrieved from www. consumerwebwatch.org/pdfs/expert-vsonline-consumers.pdf.

Truax, C. B., & Carkhuff, R. (1967). *Toward effective counseling and psychotherapy.* New Brunswick, NJ: Aldine.

Turner, C. F., Ku, L., Rogers, S. M., Lindberg, L. D., Pleck, J. H., & Sonenstein, F. L. (1998). Adolescent sexual behavior, drug use and violence: Increased reporting with computer survey technology. *Science, 280*, 867–874.

Walters, S. Miller, E., & Chiauzzi, E. (2005.) Getting wired for wellness: e-interventions for addressing college drinking. *Journal of Substance Abuse Treatment, 29*, 139–145.

Walters, S. T., Vader, A. M., & Harris, T. R. (2007). A controlled trial of web-based feedback for heavy drinking college students. *Prevention Science, 8*, 83–88.

Walters, S. T., Vader, A. M., Harris, R. T., & Jouriles, E. N. (2009). Reactivity to alcohol assessment measures: An experimental test. *Addiction, 104*, 1305–1310.

Walters, S. T., & Neighbors, C. (2011) College prevention: A view of past (and future) web-based approaches. *Alcohol Research and Health, 34*, 222–224.

White, H. R., Mun, E. Y., & Morgan, T. J. (2008). Do brief personalized feedback interventions work for mandated students or is it just getting caught that works? *Psychology of Addictive Behaviors, 22*, 107–116.

11

Treating Comorbid Disorders

Rachel L. Bachrach and Jennifer P. Read

Though the field of psychology long has studied college students simply as a sample of convenience, a now sizeable literature underscores the study of psychological phenomena in this population as a valuable goal in its own right. Indeed, the age of onset for many serious psychological disorders falls within the developmental periods of late adolescence and emerging adulthood, years that for many overlap with college attendance (R. Kessler et al., 2005). These "emerging adult" years can be broadly characterized as an *age of instability* (Arnett, 2000, 2005) with hallmark features including an increase in independence and autonomy, a decrease in adult supervision, and a shift in both quantity and quality of peer relationships (Shaver, Furman, & Buhrmester, 1985). These factors can create an environment of unique challenges for students as they learn to navigate new roles, freedoms, and responsibilities.

For college students, this navigation often occurs in an environmental context where heavy drinking is common. In addition to well-documented and fairly widespread heavy episodic drinking and associated consequences (Hingson, Heeren, Winter, & Wechsler, 2005; Hingson, Zha, & Weitzman, 2009; O'Malley & Johnston, 2002; Wechsler, Lee, Kuo, & Lee, 2000; Wechsler & Nelson, 2008), a substantial portion of U.S. college students meet *DSM-IV*-TR defined criteria for alcohol dependence, with past-year prevalence rates estimated at 6% to 12% (Blanco et al., 2008; Knight et al., 2002). Past-year prevalence rates of alcohol abuse are even higher, with as many as a third of students meeting criteria for this diagnosis (Dawson, Grant, Stinson, & Chou, 2005; Knight et al., 2002; Slutske, 2005).

Though college students have been described by some as an elite or protected group with respect to mental health (Henrich, Heine, & Norenzayan, 2010), this perception has not been well supported in the empirical literature. More young adults are attending college than ever before; approximately 50% of high school seniors will enroll in college (U.S. Census Bureau, 2007). Thus, today's college students represent a broader swatch of the population than they once did. This broader representation is reflected in the fact that rates of psychological disorders among college students are similar to those of their noncollege attending peers (e.g., Blanco et al., 2008). Among these are major depression and anxiety disorders (Hunt & Eisenberg, 2010), including posttraumatic stress disorder (PTSD; Read, Ouimette, White, Colder, & Farrow, 2011; Smyth, Heron, Wonderlich, Crosby, & Thompson, 2008; Twamley, Hami, & Stein, 2004), as well as eating disorders (Hoyt & Ross, 2003) and attention-deficit/hyperactivity disorder (ADHD; Garnier-Dykstra, Pinchevsky, Caldeira, Vincent, & Arria, 2010).

Epidemiological studies with older adult samples show clearly that problem alcohol involvement commonly presents concurrent with other psychological dysfunction (i.e., comorbidity; R. C. Kessler et al., 1996; Regier et al., 1990; Ross, Glaser, & Germanson, 1988; Swendsen & Merikangas, 2000). Moreover, a robust literature shows that co-occurring substance use and other psychological disorders are linked to worse outcomes across multiple domains relative to substance misuse alone (e.g., Cornelius et al., 2004; Goldsmith & Garlapati, 2004; McCarthy, Tomlinson, Anderson, Marlatt, & Brown, 2005). As both psychopathology and widespread heavy drinking have been documented in college students, consideration of co-occurrence between the two, and implications of such comorbidity is warranted. Yet the extent to which problem drinking in college students co-occurs with other psychological conditions has not been well studied, and there is a notable paucity of treatment options to address comorbidity in this population.

In this chapter, we discuss the comorbidity between alcohol misuse and psychological disorders in the college population, and we review assessment and treatment implications for students, highlighting gaps in the literature and areas for future inquiry. It should be noted that the vast majority of alcohol research within the college student population has not assessed *DSM-IV*-defined alcohol use disorders per se, but rather has focused on "problem drinking," which can include both heavy episodic (or "binge") drinking as well as other hazardous drinking outcomes (e.g., Wechsler et al., 2000). Thus, most of the research that we present in this chapter examines the link between problem alcohol use and psychopathology. In this chapter we focus primarily on co-occurring "Axis I" disorders. We begin with a brief overview of the phenomenon of comorbidity and its implications for diagnosis and intervention.

WHAT IS COMORBIDITY AND WHY DOES IT OCCUR?

Comorbidity is present when two or more disorders or other pathological processes occur at the same time. In the field of psychology, comorbidity is so common as to be as much the rule as the exception (First, 2005; Nathan & Langenbucher, 1999; Widiger & Clark, 2000; Widiger & Samuel, 2005). The reason for this pervasive comorbidity has been the subject of much debate, one that may be of nosological as well as clinical relevance. Below we outline briefly some of the explanations for high rates of comorbidity that have been posited.

Symptom overlap. Many psychological disorders share symptomatology. As such, it is possible for an individual to meet criteria for two (or more) diagnoses due simply to an overlap in symptom presentation and not necessarily because of "true comorbidity" (i.e., distinct underlying pathology; First, 2005). In such cases, comorbidity is spurious, and does not necessarily represent a meaningful clinical status. Alcohol and other substance use disorders are some of the most commonly represented in co-occurrences with mental disorders (Grant et al., 2004; R. C. Kessler et al., 1996; Regier et al., 1990), and it has been argued that some of the co-occurrences can be accounted for by the fact that several of the diagnostic symptoms are highly similar to symptoms of other disorders such as anxiety or depression. For example, some of the more mild withdrawal effects from alcohol (e.g., fatigue, irritability, dysphoria, impaired sleep, feeling on edge) overlap directly with the symptoms of major depression and generalized anxiety. Yet several large-scale epidemiological studies have taken this into account when assessing prevalence rates of comorbid mental and substance disorders (i.e., rule-out substance-induced psychological disorders; e.g., Dawson et al., 2005), and still have observed high rates of co-occurrence. Thus, comorbidity rates between alcohol use disorders (AUDs) and mental disorders likely are not solely a function of *DSM* nosology.

Trait vulnerabilities. Other perspectives on comorbidity focus on the role of individual-level characteristics, or traits, which may function as a shared pathway to multiple phenotypic symptom expressions. One such perspective, the trait vulnerability hypothesis, asserts that certain temperamental features predispose one to both risky alcohol use and mental illness (e.g., Clark, 2005; Krueger et al., 2002). These trait vulnerabilities may begin with heritable characteristics to which individuals are biologically predisposed. For example, Krueger (1999) put forth a two-factor model of internalizing versus externalizing pathology, with depressive and anxiety disorders falling within the internalizing factor (negative emotionality) and substance dependence and antisocial behavior falling within the externalizing factor (disinhibition, impulsivity). Importantly, Krueger observed a positive correlation between the internalizing and externalizing factors. This hints at a possible mechanistic association between internalizing types of pathology (e.g., depression, posttraumatic stress disorder [PTSD], generalized anxiety disorder [GAD]) and externalizing pathology (e.g., substance misuse), which might help to explain this relatively common co-occurrence. More recently, Kotov et al. (2011) expanded this model by including a broader range of Axis I and Axis II disorders, and again identified core underlying dimensions (i.e., internalizing, externalizing, thought disorder, somatoform, and antagonism) that may account for comorbidity.

A variant of this shared vulnerability hypothesis is the "scar hypothesis" (Beevers, Rohde, Stice, & Nolen-Hoeksema, 2007; Lewinsohn, Steinmetz, Larson, & Franklin,

1981). The scar hypothesis asserts that mental illness will leave its "mark" on an individual, rendering him or her vulnerable to future psychopathology (in this case, alcohol problems). In this sense, it is not the disorder itself that causes an increased risk for problem alcohol use, but the effect of the original primary mental disorder on trait predispositions. For example, a history of depression or anxiety may render someone more vulnerable to future heavy drinking as they may be more likely to experience episodic shifts in mood that lead to drinking, or may be more vigilant in guarding against negative mood, and thus quicker to seeking relief from drinking when the threat of negative mood or even stressful life events present themselves. Also, life experiences such as trauma and its resulting psychological effects can pose further risk for "scarring" effects, and as such, are risk factors for a broad variety of deleterious psychological outcomes, including heavy alcohol and drug use (Breslau, Davis, & Schultz, 2003; Smyth et al., 2008, Wonderlich et al., 2001). As such, those with a trauma history may be at risk for not just one, but multiple problem outcomes.

Moreover, someone with a primary AUD may be vulnerable to experiencing negative mood due to both the physiological effects of alcohol as well as the social and societal consequences of alcohol misuse (e.g., isolation, financial problems, academic failure). Thus, this pattern can be bidirectional.

Environmental vulnerabilities. Environmental factors such as socioeconomic status, family/parent characteristics, peer influences, and ethnicity also influence the co-occurrence of problem alcohol use and psychopathology (Bulik & Sullivan, 1993; Saraceno, Munafó, Heron, Craddock, & van den Bree, 2009). Uniquely relevant to college students is the college environment, which has been shown to be an important determinant of both psychological stress and risky drinking behaviors. Theorists have suggested that the transition from adolescence to the college milieu (e.g., academic pressure, increased financial responsibility, and more reliance on peers than parental monitoring/guidance) may contribute to hazardous alcohol consumption (see J. E. Schulenberg & Zarrett, 2006). For example, students who drank in high school as a means to cope with stress might find the transition to college particularly difficult. It is possible that these students might be more sensitive to stress, and thus find college independence and academic pressure daunting. As they have used alcohol in the past to cope with stress, they might again turn to alcohol to cope with new stressors, which then could make them vulnerable to developing mood or anxiety symptoms (which might not have developed if better coping resources were available). As such, students with preexisting vulnerabilities (e.g., genetic, trait, socio-demographic) might be most at risk to perceiving the transition to the college environment as stressful, and thus, turn to alcohol as an easily accessible way of controlling their mood and worry.

Causal process. Some theories posit a direct and causal relationship between problem drinking and co-occurring psychological dysfunction. Among these are *self-medication* and *high-risk* theories. Derived from related theories such as Tension Reduction and Stress Dampening (Greeley & Oei, 1999; Sher, 1987), self-medication theory posits that individuals learn to rely on alcohol to cope with or to manage aversive psychological symptoms (e.g., anxiety, sadness, depression; Baker, Piper, McCarthy, Majeskie, & Fiore, 2004; Khantzian, 2003; Lang, Patrick, & Stritzke, 1999; Stewart, 1996). Alcohol use is negatively reinforced by the alleviation of negative affective states (stress, dysphoria) following its ingestion. Empirical support for longitudinal models of self-medication theory is mixed but does offer at least some evidence of support for this conceptualization (Deykin Levy, & Wells, 1987; R. C. Kessler et al., 1996; Kushner, Sher, & Erickson, 1999; McFarlane et al., 2009; Miller, Vogt, Mozley, Kaloupek, & Keane, 2006; Najdowski & Ullman, 2009; Ouimette, Coolheart, Funderburk, & Brown, 2007; Read, Merrill, Griffin, Bachrach, & Khan, 2012).

Others have proposed that the harmful consequences of risky alcohol use increases the likelihood that one will develop psychopathology. Termed the *high-risk hypothesis*, this model theorizes that deleterious alcohol use puts one at risk for severe substance-related physiological impairment and psychosocial consequences (e.g., sleep disturbance, hangover, blackouts, physical and sexual assaults, academic failure), which might increase one's risk for developing psychological disorders (e.g., Chilcoat & Breslau, 1998). This hypothesis may be particularly relevant for college students, as they consistently report a higher range of negative consequences and other risky behavior associated with alcohol use than their noncollege peers (Fromme, Corbin, & Kruse, 2008; O'Malley & Johnston, 2002; Substance Abuse and Mental Health Services Administration [SAMHSA], 2003, 2008).

COMORBIDITY OF ALCOHOL USE AND MENTAL HEALTH SYMPTOMS

Whatever the cause, alcohol problems that co-occur with other psychological distress symptoms have the potential to compromise successful adaptation to and functioning in college, and to derail progress toward independent adulthood. Yet the problem of comorbidity in college students has been vastly understudied. In what is to our knowledge the only large-scale epidemiological study of comorbidity in college students, Dawson et al. (2005) found that students with past-year alcohol dependence were twice as likely to report a comorbid mood or anxiety disorder compared to lifetime abstainers. Moreover, other data show that a notable number of young adults meet criteria for multiple co-occurring substance use disorders (Barrett, Darredeau, & Pihl, 2006; Grekin, Sher, & Wood, 2006; Newman et al., 1996; Palmer et al., 2009). As both alcohol and illicit drug use peaks in emerging adults, students engaging in both of these behaviors deleteriously might also be at risk for developing serious psychological problems.

In numerous smaller-scale studies, problem drinking has been linked to general psychological distress broadly (Geisner, Larimer, & Neighbors, 2004) and specifically to a number of individual psychological disorders. For example, depression is among the most common of the mental disorders and has been linked to problem drinking (though not necessarily to consumption itself) in college students (Geisner et al., 2004; Nagoshi, 1999; Patock-Peckham, Huchinson, Cheong, & Nagoshi, 1998). Deykin et al. (1987) showed that students with a history of alcohol abuse are 4 times more likely to have a history of major depression than their nonabusing college peers. More recently, Dennhardt and Murphy (2011) showed that, after controlling for drinking levels, depression was associated with alcohol problems among both African-American and Anglo-Caucasian students. Moreover, data show that depression confers risk not only for alcohol problems during college, but also for continued heavy drinking after college (Nagoshi, 1999; Patock-Peckham et al., 1998).

Glass and Flory (2012) found students with ADHD to be more likely to have alcohol-related problems, despite not actually drinking more. Ross and Tisdall (1994) reported that AUDs were significantly related to mania, panic and GAD in their treatment-seeking sample of college students. In a non–treatment-seeking college sample, Kushner et al. (1999) found significant concurrent and prospective relationships between AUDs and anxiety disorders (e.g., GAD, panic, agoraphobia, social phobia). More recently, Goldsmith, Tran, Smith, and Howe (2009) found a significant relationship between self-reported GAD and problem drinking as measured by the Alcohol Use Disorders Identification Test. Read, Colder, et al. (2012) also found PTSD to predict alcohol problems over the first year of college. Lastly, at least two studies have linked disordered eating to alcohol problems in college students (Anderson, Simmons, Martens, Ferrier, & Sheehy, 2006; Dunn, Larimer, & Neighbors, 2002).

In addition, at least one study (Dawson et al., 2005) suggests that college students may be at elevated risk for alcohol comorbidity relative to other noncollege populations. Together this literature highlights a need for screening and identification of both alcohol behavior and associated comorbid conditions, as alcohol consequences may be a red flag for other pathology, and psychological distress might be a warning sign for problem drinking.

PROBLEMATIC OUTCOMES OF COMORBID ALCOHOL USE AND MENTAL HEALTH SYMPTOMS

The fact that there has been so little research examining co-occurring psychological disorders in college students is unfortunate, as comorbidity is associated with myriad deleterious outcomes. Individuals with comorbid diagnoses evidence greater clinical impairment prior to treatment, lower compliance in treatment, and greater likelihood of symptom reoccurrence post-treatment (e.g., R. A. Brown & Ramsey, 2000; P. J. Brown, Recupero, & Stout, 1995; Burns & Teesson, 2002; Foa & Williams, 2010; Goldsmith & Garlapati, 2004; Manwani et al., 2007; Newman et al., 1996). For college students, co-occurring alcohol and other psychological distress could impair functioning (e.g., academic, occupational, and interpersonal problems; Breslau, Lane, Sampson, & Kessler, 2008; Hunt & Eisenberg, 2010; Kessler, Foster, Saunders, & Stang, 1995; Kitzrow, 2003; Tanner et al., 2007) both during the college years and beyond.

Comorbidity may also have specific implications for the drinking trajectories of young adults. For example, data show that problem drinking that co-occurs with other psychological distress may be less likely to resolve over time (see Mueser, Noordsy, Drake, & Fox, 2003). This could have implications for the postcollege years; though some young adults "mature out" of heavy drinking (Johnston, O'Malley, Bachman, & Schulenberg, 2009), others do not (e.g., Bennett, McCrady, Johnson, & Pandina, 1999; O'Neill, Para, & Sher, 2001; J. Schulenberg, O'Malley, Bachman, Wadsworth, & Johnston, 1996). These individuals whose heavy drinking persists are at risk for continued and even greater alcohol problems in middle-late adulthood (Chen & Kandel, 1995; Jackson, Sher, Gotham, & Wood, 2001; McCabe et al., 2005, 2007). Given the literature that suggests worse substance outcomes for those with persistent co-occurring psychological dysfunction, it is possible that co-occurring psychopathology confers risk for nonresolution of problem drinking in the transition out of college, or may be an explanatory factor in differentiating those students who continue to drink problematically and those who do not. To date, such questions have not been examined.

As the third leading cause of death among emerging adults (Centers for Disease Control, 2007), suicide is another risk for heavy-drinking college students with comorbid psychopathology. Problem drinking has been identified as a risk factor for suicide, both in the general adult and college student populations (Gonzalez, Bradizza, & Collins, 2009; Powell et al., 2001; Schaeffer, Jeglic, & Stanley, 2008). When under the influence of alcohol, individuals are more likely to act impulsively and without inhibition. Thus, depression in the context of heavy drinking confers particular risk for suicide (Cornelius et al., 1995). In light of the general prevalence of both depression and heavy drinking in college students (Wechsler et al., 2000; Zivan, Eisenberg, Gollust, & Golberstein, 2009), proactive assessment for this risk is warranted. College-based health or counseling centers may benefit from the implementation of routine screening of not only suicidal risk but substance misuse for all clinic visitors. Students identified as being at risk could be provided with referrals and resources, or could be targeted for both suicide and alcohol-based prevention programs.

ASSESSMENT OF COMORBID ALCOHOL AND PSYCHOLOGICAL DISORDERS

Given the numerous harmful effects that may follow from co-occurring problem drinking and other distress, proactive assessment and early identification are needed. We already have noted the importance of early detection, which can be achieved through simple screening measures either during college matriculation (universal method) or at counseling or health clinics on campus (indicated method). In addition to screening, several other approaches also are available. Structured clinical interviews are the gold standard of assessment, and many such interviews have been developed for the detection of psychological disorders, including substance use disorders (e.g., The Structured Clinical Interview for DSM Disorders; First, Spitzer, Gibbon, & Williams, 1996). Among these, the Mini International Neuropsychiatric Interview (MINI; Sheehan et al., 1998) may be most practical for the needs of many campus-based clinicians as the MINI is a brief (approximately 15 minutes), easy-to-administer structured clinical interview assessing common Axis I disorders (e.g., GAD, Major Depressive Episode, AUDs, Social Phobia). As such, the MINI provides a quick overview of individual psychological functioning, which may be valuable in detecting co-occurring distress. It can also be used as a baseline for eventual tracking of treatment progress. Unlike other structured clinical interviews, the MINI does not require extensive training, and is not time consuming to administer.

As noted, many college students drink in ways that are problematic, but that fall below diagnostic thresholds and therefore may not be detected in a diagnostic interview. To identify this kind of drinking as it may occur concomitant to other psychological distress, a number of brief self-report assessments are available, including the Young Adult Alcohol Consequences Questionnaire (YAACQ; Read, Kahler, Strong, & Colder, 2006), the Rutgers Alcohol Problem Inventory (RAPI; White & Labouvie, 1989) and the Young Adult Alcohol Problems Screening Test (YAAPST; Hurlbut & Sher, 1992). All of these measures provide brief and comprehensive assessment of the ways in which alcohol is negatively affecting a student's well-being (see also Martens et al., this volume, for more information on alcohol problem assessment).

A number of other factors relevant to problem drinking in college can also be assessed. These include assessing perceptions of peer alcohol use (i.e., descriptive norms), risk factors for developing an AUD (such as parental alcohol history), alcohol expectancies (beliefs about the effects of alcohol), and protective behaviors that might reduce heavy drinking or its consequences.

Functional assessment can be highly valuable in the evaluation of comorbid symptom presentations (see Mueser et al. 2003), as it allows the clinician to gather detailed information on what role alcohol use plays in the student's daily life. This would include the history and pattern of one's alcohol use (e.g., when, where, amounts) as well as antecedents (e.g., expectancies, motivations, affect) and consequences of consumption. With this approach the clinician should obtain a background of the student's other presenting problems (depression, anxiety, ADHD, etc.) and seek to establish links between these symptoms and the student's alcohol use patterns. A timeline follow-back procedure (Sobell & Sobell, 1992) might be useful at this stage to gain a fine-grained analysis of the student's alcohol involvement and temporal associations between drinking and other symptoms. This functional assessment can then be used to generate hypotheses regarding factors maintaining the problematic alcohol use, and also can aid in treatment planning. For example, if the student's alcohol consumption can be linked through functional assessment to worry or anxiety, then the clinician may consider incorporating emotion regulation techniques into the intervention approach.

TREATMENT OF COMORBID ALCOHOL AND PSYCHOLOGICAL DISORDERS: MODELS FROM THE NONCOLLEGE LITERATURE

Reviews by the National Institute of Mental Health, National Institute on Alcohol Abuse and Alcoholism, and the National Institute on Drug Abuse have concluded that integrated treatments for clients presenting with both alcohol and psychological problems are the most cost-effective and beneficial (see Drake, Mercer-McFadden, Mueser, McHugo, & Bond, 1998; Petrakis, Gonzalez, Rosenheck, & Krystal, 2002; U.S. Department of Health and Human Services, 2010). As such, treatment for comorbid alcohol and other psychological distress likely will have the greatest impact if it is integrated. Integrated treatments by definition are comprised of a variety of components, some of which include a focus on harm reduction rather than total abstinence, case management, individual/group/family therapy, relapse prevention, and may include a motivational enhancement component (Drake et al., 1998).

What do these integrated treatments look like? Examples of such treatments, developed for noncollege populations, are plentiful. Many are cognitive-behavioral based (e.g., R. A. Brown & Ramsey, 2000; Kemp, Harris, Vurel, & Sitharthan, 2007; Kushner et al., 2006; Najavits, 2002; Schadé et al., 2005). Besides cognitive restructuring and activities scheduling, common components of treatment include relaxation training, social skills-assertiveness training, and relapse prevention/treatment maintenance. Although cognitive-behavioral therapy (CBT) interventions are the most well studied, treatment selection ultimately must be based on appropriateness for the presenting problems, empirical support, and feasibility within the college environment.

Outcome studies show some promising results for these integrated treatments, suggesting that they increase the likelihood of abstinence, reduce relapse, and decrease anxiety/depressive symptoms at follow-up (e.g., Kay-Lambkin, Baker, Lewin, & Carr, 2009; Kemp et al., 2007; Schadé et al., 2005). However, findings for integrated treatments with comorbid severe mental illness (e.g., schizophrenia, bipolar disorder) have been more equivocal (Bride, MacMaster, & Webb-Robbins, 2006). This is an important factor to take into account when considering treatment interventions for college students, as there likely are limits to what services a college campus can realistically provide for the student whose alcohol problems co-occur with certain types of significant and impairing psychopathology.

FUTURE DIRECTIONS IN RESEARCH AND TREATMENT

Though some integrated treatments for problem drinking and co-occurring psychological disorders have been developed (e.g., Mueser et al., 2003; Najavits, 2002), the need for treatments specific to the college population has been profoundly overlooked. Effective treatments for comorbidity clearly are needed, but should not simply be lifted summarily from existing interventions validated in older adult populations. Drinking—even problem drinking—in college students is a phenomenon that reflects the unique culture of the college social ethos. Accordingly, context-appropriate integrated interventions that can be implemented within the unique environment of the college context will likely be most successful.

To our knowledge, only one study has assessed the efficacy of an integrated treatment for young adults (aged 17 to 25; Kemp et al., 2007). These individuals presented to a community mental health clinic with co-occurring psychotic and substance abuse diagnoses and received 4 to 6 sessions of brief CBT. Compared to treatment as usual, the CBT group exhibited greater reductions in substance and alcohol use, as well as improvement in self-efficacy. Clearly, more research with a broader range of presenting problems is needed. Below we outline some suggestions for next steps and future directions on treatment development and testing for co-occurring alcohol and other psychological disorders in college students.

Who? In contrast to more reactive models of intervention, where treatment is provided only to those who self-identify as having a problem and are seeking services at their own initiation, integrated interventions for co-occurring alcohol and other problems in college will need to be more proactive. Recent data show that problem drinkers in college may not self-identify as being in need of treatment (Barnett et al., 2008; Epler, Sher, Loomis, & O'Malley, 2009; Knight et al., 2002; Wu, Pilowsky, Schlenger, & Hasin, 2007) and are not likely to seek out psychological services independently (Blanco et al., 2008; Buscemi, Murphy, Martens, McDevitt-Murphy, Dennhardt, & Skinner, 2010; Eisenberg, Golberstein, & Gollust, 2007; Kushner et al., 1999; Wu et al., 2007). As such, despite the ubiquity of heavy drinking and alcohol-related consequences, treatment seeking for alcohol problems in college is rare.

The same is true for other types of psychological dysfunction. For example, Eisenberg et al. (2007) found that of those students who screened positive for depression, GAD, or panic, in most cases the majority did not seek treatment. This may be because, compared to the general population, college students view themselves as less vulnerable when facing psychological problems (e.g., Turner & Quinn, 1999). In another study, Cranford, Eisenberg, and Serras (2009) found that students who reported co-occurring frequent heavy episodic drinking and mood/anxiety disorders perceived a greater need for help (therapy/counseling/medication) compared to those students who drank heavily but did not meet mood/anxiety criteria. Yet only about 38% of these students actually received treatment.

In light of this literature, it seems that traditional models of waiting for the client to come to treatment will not be adequate for college students. Instead, programs that use screening and outreach, with clearly delineated pathways of care, will be more effective in delivering help to those students who may benefit from it. The field already has a strong example of such a proactive approach in the drinking intervention literature. In fact, interventions that aim to reduce problem drinking in individuals who do not self-identify as needing alcohol treatment is the modal and indeed recommended approach to drinking intervention on college campuses in the United States (Borsari, Tevyaw, Barnett, Kahler, & Monti, 2007; Epler et al., 2009; Fromme & Corbin, 2004; Knight et al., 2002).

A few examples of more outreach-based interventions for alcohol comorbidity can be found in the literature. For example, Reynolds, MacPherson, Tull, Baruch, and Lejuez (2011) attempted to address co-occurring disorders (depression and alcohol problems) in college students through a universal, behavioral activation (BA)–based intervention program for students attending orientation. Initially developed to treat depression, BA is based in behavioral theory, and posits that exposure to daily activities that are value-consistent and that bring happiness will increase rewarding emotional experiences. These experiences may "simultaneously reduce negative affect and improve positive affect through overt behavior change" (Reynolds et al., 2001, p. 556). Findings showed that, compared to controls, students reported reductions in alcohol-related problems but not alcohol use or depressed mood. Samples were small in this study and students were not selected into this program based on depression scores, which might have obscured program effects.

Geisner, Neighbors, Lee, and Larimer (2007) mailed personalized alcohol feedback to students elevated on depressed mood. Besides information on normative misperceptions, this included information on the role of alcohol in the maintenance of depression, strategies for how to cope with depression and tips for how to moderate drinking. Students who corrected their normative perceptions of alcohol involvement reduced both their alcohol use and related consequences at one-month follow-up.

In addition, campus counseling centers and health clinics typically are among the first places college students experiencing serious mental health problems will present for treatment (Robbins, May, & Corzzini, 1985; Stone & Archer, 1990). Proactive assessment, identification, and referral resources should be made available at these locations for the efficient treatment of students in need.

What? A number of efficacious interventions for reducing harmful alcohol behavior in college students have been developed and tested (see Carey, chapter 9 in this volume; Larimer & Cronce, 2007). Many of the most widely used and empirically supported are those grounded in either cognitive-behavioral theory or approaches that promote skills building (e.g., brief motivational interventions [BMI], Borsari & Carey, 2000; Brief Alcohol Screening and Intervention for College Students [BASICS], Dimeff, Baer, Kivlahan, & Marlatt, 1999). These interventions, because of their flexibility, show much potential to be extended and combined with CBT-based treatments for Axis I disorders, as data suggest that successful treatment is most likely one that targets both phenomena together (e.g., Back, 2010). For example, it would be helpful for students with comorbid depression and AUD to understand the link between their mood and drinking behavior. Through CBT, students would learn to identify and rate moods, link moods with drinking situations, and learn how their negative cognitions might be a precipitant to their moods and drinking behavior. Though typically geared to drinking, BMI or BASICS-based interventions could readily incorporate screening for depression or anxiety and provide feedback and motivational enhancement pertaining to the use of alcohol to modulate mood. This approach has been used successfully in college-based interventions for other present-ing problems (i.e., depression; see Geisner, Neighbors, & Larimer, 2006).

There are some intra- and interpersonal skills that are important to address as well. Assertiveness skills are among these, given the ample amount of social drinking situ-ations college students are faced with (e.g., how to refuse a drink at a Greek event). Moreover, for students with anxiety disorders such as social phobia or PTSD who drink primarily to manage social interactions, both social skills and relaxation training may help to minimize the likelihood that these students will drink to cope with their anxiety before attending social functions on campus. As data show that postinterven-tion drinking decrements can also be accompanied by reports of diminished reinforce-ment from social alternatives (Murphy, Correia, Colby, & Vuchinich, 2005), social skills training could also help to build skills around forging gratifying interpersonal relationships that do not rely on heavy drinking.

When? The college calendar year is temporally punctuated (semester breaks, summer vacations) in ways that schedules of most other populations are not. Student drinking tends to vary according to this unique schedule (e.g., increasing during spring break, decreasing during finals; Del Boca, Darkes, Greenbaum, & Goldman, 2004; Neighbors et al., 2011) thus, successful treatments for co-occurring problem drinking and other disorders must be able to bend to the exigencies of college academia. As noted, brief interventions have shown efficacy in reducing problem drinking among college students (see Larimer & Cronce, 2007) and be-cause of their brevity and in many cases multicomponent structure, may be well suited for adaptation to address co-occurring conditions in the college environ-ment. Moreover, the incorporation of web and other technology in the delivery of these treatments can accommodate changing schedules, exam periods, and semester breaks (see the following).

How? In addition to a greater focus on early detection and outreach, the mode of intervention is an important consideration. Treatments also must be accessible and *visible*. As noted recently by Epler et al. (2009), "It is particularly important to reach out and educate college students about the availability of treatment options given the high rates of hazardous drinking and drinking problems in this population" (p. 27).

The kind of proactive approach advocated above likely will increase visibility and accessibility of treatment options (e.g., during primary care visits; see Fleming et al., 2010). In addition, several other steps can be taken. Kitzrow (2003) suggests using freshman orientation (e.g., Reynolds et al., 2011), residence halls, and Greek houses as venues for highlighting mental health services currently being offered on campus. Moreover, access to campus mental health care must be made clear in terms of location, price, and expertise (Mowbray et al., 2006). The use of free campus newspapers, chalking, bulletin boards, email, and campus radio affords college ample opportunities for free or modest advertising costs of psychological services.

Additionally, campuses could hold screening days for depression, anxiety, eating disorders, and alcohol use whereby students could walk into campus counseling centers and/or psychological clinics for a free and anonymous brief individual meeting to assess risk for these disorders. These screening days could be timed to correspond to national events sponsored by Screening for Mental Health (www.mentalhealthscreening.org), which include National Alcohol Screening Day (NASD), National Depression Screening Day (NDSD), and National Eating Disorder Screening Program (NEDSP). Regarding NASD, the event attracts a significant number of college students engaging in high-risk drinking (Greenfield et al., 2003; Wallenstein, Pigeon, Kopans, Jacobs, & Aseltine, 2007). Research highlighting the correlation between alcohol-related problems and disordered eating among students attending NEDSP also highlights the need for screening events to address both targeted and comorbid disorders (Heidelberg & Correia, 2009). Finally, there is evidence to suggest that empirically supported interventions can be effectively incorporated into screening events (Benson, Ambrose, Mulfinger, & Correia, 2004; Henslee et al., 2006).

The past decade represents a period of a rapidly changing technological landscape. Almost monthly, new Internet-capable social network applications and devices are introduced (e.g., Facebook, Twitter). In no population is this change more evident than with college students, as data show that college students are among the first to adopt such new technologies (Caruso & Salaway, 2008). Indeed, so comfortable with Internet technologies are these young adults that they have been termed by some as the "Net Generation." Interventions that maximize the outreach and interactive potential of the Internet and other technology are likely to be well received by heavy-drinking college students (see Buscemi et al., 2010). Judd and Kennedy (2010) point to specific trends in college Internet use, which may inform the development of interventions for comorbidity in college students. In their 5-year study, these investigators observed a movement away from traditional email, and toward social networking (e.g., chat rooms, Facebook, message boards). Indeed, use of social networking technology increased from 50% to 65% in just 5 years. Given the importance of social influences of alcohol use in college (Borsari & Carey, 2001, 2003), this type of technology in particular offers great potential for this population.

SUMMARY AND CONCLUSIONS

The problem of heavy and problematic drinking in college students has been widely researched. Yet the extent to which such drinking co-occurs with other psychological symptom presentations has not. A large literature suggests worse drinking and other outcomes for individuals whose alcohol involvement co-occurs with other psychological distress, and such co-occurrence has the potential to derail successful adaptation to and functioning in college and beyond. Examination of co-occurring alcohol and other psychological distress—its prevalence, causes, associated outcomes, and interventions—is needed.

Here we have outlined what is to date the limited body of research literature on the topic of alcohol misuse as it co-occurs with other psychological distress, with a particular emphasis on treatment. As we have noted, this is an important area, and one that is rife with opportunities for future research and intervention development. It is our hope that in the future, researchers, college counselors, wellness professionals, and campus administrators will endeavor to tackle some of the currently unresolved issues, and to integrate what already is known about treatment of comorbid alcohol and psychological distress to best serve the mental health needs of college students.

REFERENCES

Anderson, D. A., Simmons, A. M., Martens, M. P., Ferrier, A. G., & Sheehy, M. J. (2006). The relationship between disordered eating behaviors and drinking motives in college-age women. *Eating Behaviors, 7*, 419–422.

Arnett, J. J. (2000). A theory of development from the late teens through the twenties. *American Psychologist, 55*, 469–480.

Arnett, J. J. (2005). The developmental context of substance use in emerging adulthood. *Journal of Drug Issues, 35*, 235–253.

Back, S. E. (2010). Toward an improved model of treating co-occurring PTSD and substance use disorders. *The American Journal of Psychiatry, 167*, 11–13.

Baker, T. B., Piper, M. E., McCarthy, D. E., Majeskie, M. R., & Fiore, M.C. (2004). Addiction motivation reformulated: An affective processing model of negative reinforcement. *Psychological Review, 111*, 33–51.

Barnett, N. P., Borsari, B., Hustad, J. T., Tevyaw, T. O. Colby, S. M., Kahler, C. W., & Monti, P. M. (2008). Profiles of college students mandated to alcohol intervention. *Journal of Studies on Alcohol and Drugs, 69*, 684–694.

Barrett, S. P., Darredeau, C., & Pihl, R. O. (2006). Patterns of simultaneous polysubstance use in drug using university students. *Human Psychopharmacology: Clinical and Experimental, 21*, 255–263.

Beevers, C. G., Rohde, P., Stice, E., & Nolen-Hoeksema, S. (2007). Recovery from major depressive disorder among female adolescents: A prospective test of the scar hypothesis. *Journal of Consulting and Clinical Psychology, 75*, 888–900.

Bennett, M. E., McCrady, B. S., Johnson, V., & Pandina, R. J. (1999). Problem drinking from young adulthood to adulthood: Patterns, predictors and outcomes. *Journal of Studies on Alcohol, 60*, 605–614.

Benson, T. A., Ambrose, C. A., Mulfinger, A. M. M., & Correia, C. J. (2004). Integrating mailed personalized feedback and alcohol screening events: A feasibility study. *Journal of Drug Education, 34*, 327–334.

Blanco, C., Okuda, M., Wright, C., Hasin, D. S., Grant, B. F., Liu, S., & Olfson, M. (2008). Mental health of college students and their non-college-attending peers: Results from the national epidemiologic study on alcohol and related conditions. *Archives of General Psychiatry, 65*, 1429–1437.

Borsari, B., & Carey, K. B. (2000). Effects of a brief motivational intervention with college student drinkers. *Journal of Consulting and Clinical Psychology, 68*, 728–733.

Borsari, B., & Carey, K.B. (2001). Peer influences on college drinking: A review of the research. *Journal of Substance Abuse, 13/14*, 391–424.

Borsari, B., & Carey, K. B. (2003). Descriptive and injunctive norms in college drinking: A meta-analytic integration. *Journal of Studies on Alcohol, 64*, 331–341.

Borsari, B., Tevyaw, T., Barnett, N. P., Kahler, C. W., & Monti, P. M. (2007). Stepped care for mandated college students: A pilot study. *American Journal on Addictions, 16*, 131–137.

Breslau, N., Davis, G. C., & Schultz, L. R. (2003). Posttraumatic stress disorder and the incidence of nicotine, alcohol, and other drug disorders in persons who have experienced trauma. *Archives of General Psychiatry, 60*, 289–294.

Breslau, J., Lane, M., Sampson, N., & Kessler, R. C. (2008). Mental disorders and subsequent educational attainment in a US national sample. *Journal of Psychiatric Research, 42*, 708–716.

Bride, B. E., MacMaster, S. A., & Webb-Robbins, L. (2006). Is integrated treatment of co-occurring disorders more effective than nonintegrated treatment? *Best Practices in Mental Health, 2*, 43–57.

Brown, P. J., Recupero, P. R., & Stout, R. (1995). PTSD substance abuse comorbidity and treatment utilization. *Addictive Behaviors, 20*, 251–254.

Brown, R. A., & Ramsey, S. E. (2000). Addressing comorbid depressive symptomatology in alcohol treatment. *Professional Psychology: Research and Practice, 31*, 418–422.

Bulik, C. M., & Sullivan, P. F. (1993). Comorbidity of bulimia and substance abuse: Perceptions of family of origin. *International Journal of Eating Disorders, 13*, 49–56.

Burns, L., & Teesson, M. (2002). Alcohol use disorders comorbid with anxiety, depression and drug use disorders: Findings from the Australian national survey of mental health and well being. *Drug and Alcohol Dependence, 68*, 299–307.

Buscemi, J., Murphy, J. G., Martens, M. P., McDevitt-Murphy, M. E., Dennhardt, A. A., & Skidmore, J. R. (2010). Help-seeking for alcohol-related problems in college students: Correlates and preferred resources. *Psychology of Addictive Behaviors, 24*, 571–580.

Carey, K. B. (2012). Brief motivational interventions. In C. Correia, J. Murphy, & N. Barnett (Eds.), *College student alcohol abuse: A guide to assessment, intervention, and prevention.* Hoboken, NJ: Wiley

Caruso, J. B., & Salaway, G. (2008). *The ECAR study of undergraduate students and information technology, 2008.* (Research Study Vol. 8). Retrieved from http://net.educause.edu/ir/library/pdf/ERS0808/RS/ ERS0808w.pdf

Centers for Disease Control. (2007). *10 Leading causes of death by age group, United States—2007.* Retrieved from http://www.cdc.gov/injury/wisqars/pdf/Death_by_Age_2007-a.pdf

Chen, K., & Kandel, D. B. (1995). The natural history of drug use from adolescence to the mid-thirties in a general population sample. *American Journal of Public Health, 85*, 41–47.

Chilcoat, H. D., & Breslau, N. (1998). Investigations of causal pathways between PTSD and drug use disorders. *Addictive Behaviors, 23*, 827–840.

Clark, L. (2005). Temperament as a unifying basis for personality and psychopathology. *Journal of Abnormal Psychology, 114*, 505–521.

Cornelius, J. R., Maisto, S. A., Martin, C. S., Bukstein, O. G., Salloum, I. M., Daley, D. C., . . . Clark, D. B. (2004). Major depression associated with earlier alcohol relapse in treated teens with AUD. *Addictive Behaviors, 29*, 1035–1038.

Cornelius, J. R., Salloum, I. M., Mezzich, J., Cornelius, M. D., Fabrega, H., Ehler, J. G., . . . Mann, J. J. (1995). Disproportionate suicidality in patients with comorbid major depression and alcoholism. *American Journal of Psychiatry, 152*, 358–364.

Cranford, J. A., Eisenberg, D., & Serras, A. M. (2009). Substance use behaviors, mental health problems, and use of mental health services in a probability sample of college students. *Addictive Behaviors, 34*, 134–145.

Dawson, D. A., Grant, B. F., Stinson, F. S., & Chou, P. S. (2005). Psychopathology associated with drinking and alcohol use disorders in the college and general adult populations. *Drug and Alcohol Dependence, 77*, 139–150.

Del Boca, F. K., Darkes, J., Greenbaum, P. E., & Goldman, M. S. (2004). Up close and personal: Temporal variability in the drinking of individual college students during their first year. *Journal of Consulting and Clinical Psychology, 72*, 155–164.

Deykin, E. Y., Levy, J. C., & Wells, V. (1987). Adolescent depression, alcohol and drug abuse. *American Journal of Public Health, 77*, 178–182.

Dimeff, L. A., Baer, J. S., Kivlahan, D. R., & Marlatt, G. A. (1999). *Brief alcohol screening and intervention for college students (BASICS): A harm reduction approach.* New York, NY: Guilford Press.

Dennhardt, A. A., & Murphy, J. G. (2011). Associations between depression, distress tolerance, delay discounting and alcohol related problems in Caucasian and African American college students. *Psychology of Addictive Behaviors, 25*, 595–604.

Drake, R. E., Mercer-McFadden, C., Mueser, K. T., McHugo, G. J., & Bond, G. R. (1998). Review of integrated mental health and substance abuse treatment for patients with dual disorders. *Schizophrenia Bulletin, 24*, 589–608.

Dunn, E. C., Larimer, M. E., & Neighbors, C. (2002). Alcohol and drug-related negative consequences in college students with bulimia nervosa and binge eating disorder. *International Journal of Eating Disorders, 32*, 171–178.

Eisenberg, D., Golberstein., & Gollust, S. E. (2007). Help-seeking and access to mental health care in a university student population. *Medical Care, 45*, 594–601.

Epler, A. J., Sher, K. J., Loomis, T. B., & O'Malley, S. S. (2009). College student receptiveness to various alcohol treatment options. *Journal of American College Health, 58*, 26–32.

First, M. B. (2005). Mutually exclusive versus co-occurring diagnostic categories: The challenge of diagnostic comorbidity. *Psychopathology, 38*, 206–210.

First, M. B., Spitzer, R. L, Gibbon M., & Williams, J. B. W. (1996). *Structured clinical interview for DSM-IV Axis I disorders, Clinician Version (SCID-CV).* Washington, DC: American Psychiatric Press.

Fleming, M. F., Balousek, S. L., Grossberg, P. M., Mundt, M. P., Brown, D., Wiegel, J. R., . . . Saewyc, E. M. (2010). Brief physician advice for heavy drinking college students: A randomized controlled trial in college health clinics. *Journal of Studies on Alcohol and Drugs, 71*, 23–31.

Foa, E. B., & Williams, M. T. (2010). Methodology of a randomized double-blind clinical trial for co-morbid posttraumatic-stress disorder and alcohol dependence. *Mental Health and Substance Use: Dual Diagnosis, 3*, 131–147.

Fromme, K., & Corbin, W. (2004). Prevention of heavy drinking and associated negative consequences among mandated and voluntary college students. *Journal of Consulting and Clinical Psychology, 72*, 1038–1049.

Fromme, K., Corbin, W. R., & Kruse, M. I. (2008). Behavioral risks during the transition from high school to college. *Developmental Psychology, 44*, 1497–1504.

Garnier-Dykstra, L. M., Pinchevsky, G. M., Caldeira, K. M., Vincent, K. B., & Arria, A. M. (2010). Self-reported adult attention-deficit/hyperactivity disorder symptoms among college students. *Journal of American College Health, 59*, 133–136.

Geisner, I. M., Larimer, M. E., & Neighbors, C. (2004). The relationship among alcohol use, related problems, and symptoms of psychological distress: Gender as a moderator in a college sample. *Addictive Behaviors, 29*, 843–848.

Geisner, I., Neighbors, C., & Larimer, M. E. (2006). A randomized clinical trial of a brief, mailed intervention for symptoms of depression. *Journal of Consulting and Clinical Psychology, 74*, 393–399.

Geisner, I., Neighbors, C., Lee, C. M., & Larimer, M. E. (2007). Evaluating personal alcohol feedback as a selective prevention for college students with depressed mood. *Addictive Behaviors, 32*, 2776–2787.

Glass, K., & Flory, K. (2012). Are symptoms of ADHD related to substance use among college students? *Psychology of Addictive Behaviors, 26*, 124–132.

Goldsmith, A. A., Tran, G. Q., Smith, J. P., & Howe, S. R. (2009). Alcohol expectancies and drinking motives in college drinkers: Mediating effects on the relationship between generalized anxiety and heavy drinking in negative-affect situations. *Addictive Behaviors, 34*, 505–513.

Goldsmith, R. J., & Garlapati, V. (2004). Behavioral interventions for dual-diagnosis patients. *Psychiatric Clinics of North America, 27*, 709–725.

Gonzalez, V. M., Bradizza, C. M., & Collins, L. R. (2009). Drinking to cope as a statistical mediator in the relationship between suicidal ideation and alcohol outcomes among underage college drinkers. *Psychology of Addictive Behaviors, 23,* 443–451.

Grant, B. F., Stinson, F. S., Hasin, D. S., Dawson, D. A., Chou, S. P., Dufour, M. C., . . . Kaplan, K. (2004). Prevalence and co-occurrence of substance use disorders and independent mood and anxiety disorders: results from the national epidemiologic survey on alcohol and related conditions (NESARC). *Archives of General Psychiatry, 61,* 807–816.

Greeley, J., & Oei, T. (1999). Alcohol and tension reduction. In K. E. Leonard & H. T. Blane (Eds.), *Psychological theories of drinking and alcoholism* (pp. 14–53). New York, NY: Guilford Press.

Greenfield, S. F., Keliher, A., Sugerman, D., Kozloff, R., Reizes, J. M., Kopans, B., & Jacobs, D. (2003). Who comes to voluntary, community-based alcohol screening? Results of the first national alcohol screening day, 1999. *American Journal of Psychiatry, 160,* 1677–1683.

Grekin, E. R., Sher, K. J., & Wood, P. K. (2006). Personality and substance dependence symptoms: Modeling substance-specific traits. *Psychology of Addictive Behaviors, 20,* 415–424.

Heidelberg, N. F., & Correia, C. J. (2009). Dieting behavior and alcohol use behavior among national eating disorders screening program participants. *Journal of Alcohol and Drug Education, 53,* 53–64.

Henrich, J., Heine, S. J., & Norenzayan, A. (2010). The weirdest people in the world? *Behavioral and Brain Sciences, 33,* 61–135.

Henslee, A. M., Irons, J. G., Day, J. M., Butler, L., Benson, T. A., & Correia, C. J. (2006). Using national alcohol screening day to deliver personalized feedback: A pilot study. *Journal of Drug Education, 36,* 271–278.

Hingson, R. W., Heeren, T., Winter, M., & Wechsler, H. (2005). Magnitude of alcohol-related mortality and morbidity among U.S. college students ages 18–24: Changes from 1998 to 2001. *Annual Review of Public Health, 26,* 259–279.

Hingson, R. W., Zha, W., & Weitzman, E. R. (2009). Magnitude of and trends in alcohol-related mortality and morbidity among U.S. college students ages 18–24, 1998–2005. *Journal of Studies on Alcohol and Drugs, 70*(Suppl 16), 12–20.

Hoyt, W. D., & Ross, S. D. (2003). Clinical and subclinical eating disorders in counseling center clients: A prevalence study. *Journal of College Student Psychotherapy, 17,* 39–54.

Hunt, J., & Eisenberg, D. (2010). Mental health problems and help-seeking behavior among college students. *Journal of Adolescent Health, 46,* 3–10.

Hurlbut, S. C., & Sher, K. J. (1992). Assessing alcohol problems in college students. *Journal of American College Health, 41,* 49–58.

Jackson, K. M., Sher, K. J., Gotham, H. J., & Wood, P. K. (2001). Transitioning into and out of large-effect drinking in young adulthood. *Journal of Abnormal Psychology, 110,* 378–391.

Johnston, L. D., O'Malley, P. M., Bachman, J. G., & Schulenberg, J. E. (2009). *Monitoring the Future national survey results on drug use, 1975-2008. Volume II: College students and adults ages 19-50* (NIH Publication No. 09-7403). Bethesda, MD: National Institute on Drug Abuse.

Judd, T., & Kennedy, G. (2010). A five-year study of on-campus internet use by undergraduate biomedical students. *Computers & Education, 55,* 1564–1571.

Kay-Lambkin, F. J., Baker, A. L., Lewin, T. J., & Carr, V. J. (2009). Computer-based psychological treatment for comorbid depression and problematic alcohol and/or cannabis use: A randomized controlled trial of clinical efficacy. *Addiction, 104,* 378–388.

Kemp, R., Harris, A., Vurel, E., & Sitharthan, T. (2007). Stop using stuff: Trial of a drug and alcohol intervention for young people with comorbid mental illness and drug and alcohol problems. *Australasian Psychiatry, 15,* 490–493.

Kessler, R., Berglund, P., Demler, O., Jin, R., Merikangas, K. R., & Walters, E. F. (2005). Lifetime prevalence and age-of-onset distributions of *DSM-IV* disorders in the national comorbidity survey replication. *Archives of General Psychiatry, 62,* 593–602.

Kessler, R. C., Foster, C. L., Saunders, W. B., & Stang, P. E. (1995). Social consequences of psychiatric disorders, I: Educational attainment. *American Journal of Psychiatry, 152,* 1026–1032.

Kessler, R. C., Nelson, C. B., McGonagle, K. A., Edlund, M. J., Frank, R. G., & Leaf, P. J. (1996). The epidemiology of co-occurring addictive and mental disorders: Implications for prevention and service utilization. *American Journal of Orthopsychiatry, 66,* 17–31.

Khantzian, E. J. (2003). The self-medication hypothesis revisited: The dually diagnosed patient. *Primary Psychiatry, 10*, 47–48, 53–54.

Kitzrow, M. A. (2003). The mental health needs of today's college students: Challenges and recommendations. *NASPA, 41*, 167–181.

Knight, J. R., Wechsler, H., Kuo, M., Seibring, M., Weitzman, E. R., & Schuckit, M. A. (2002). Alcohol abuse and dependence among U.S. college students. *Journal of Studies on Alcohol, 63*, 263–270.

Kotov, R., Ruggero, C. J., Krueger, R. F., Watson, D., Yuan, Q., & Zimmerman, M. (2011). New dimensions in the quantitative classification of mental illness. *Archives of General Psychiatry, 68*, 1003–1011.

Krueger, R. F. (1999). The structure of common mental disorders. *Archives of General Psychiatry, 56*, 921–926.

Krueger, R. F., Hicks, B. M., Patrick, C. J., Carlson, S. R., Iacono, W. G., & McGue, M. (2002). Etiologic connections among substance dependence, antisocial behavior and personality: Modeling the externalizing spectrum. *Journal of Abnormal Psychology, 111*, 411–424.

Kushner, M. G., Donahue, C., Sletten, S., Thuras, P., Abrams, K., Peterson, J., & Frye, B. (2006). Cognitive behavioral treatment of comorbid anxiety disorder in alcoholism treatment patients: Presentation of a prototype program and future directions. *Journal of Mental Health, 15*, 697–707.

Kushner, M. G., Sher, K. J., & Erickson, D. J. (1999). Prospective analysis of the relation between *DSM-III* anxiety disorders and alcohol use disorders. *American Journal of Psychiatry, 156*, 723–732.

Lang, A. R., Patrick, C. J., & Stritzke, W. G. K. (1999). Alcohol and emotional response: A multidimensional-multilevel analysis. In K. E. Leonard & H. T. Blane (Eds.), *Psychological theories of drinking and alcoholism,* (2nd ed., pp. 328–371). New York, NY: Guilford Press.

Larimer, M. E., & Cronce, J. M. (2007). Identification, prevention, and treatment revisited: Individual-focused college drinking prevention strategies 1999–2006. *Addictive Behaviors, 32*, 2439–2468.

Lewinsohn, P. M., Steinmetz, J. L., Larson, D. W., & Franklin, J. (1981). Depression-related cognitions: Antecedent or consequence? *Journal of Abnormal Psychology, 90*, 213–219.

Manwani, S. G., Szilagyi, K. A., Zablotsky, B., Hennen, J., Griffin, M. L., & Weiss, R. D. (2007). Adherence to pharmacotherapy in bipolar disorder patients with and without co-occurring substance use disorders. *Journal of Clinical Psychiatry, 68*, 1172–1176.

McCabe, S. E., Knight, J. R., Teter, C. J., & Wechsler, H. (2005). Non-medical use of prescription stimulants among U.S. college students: Prevalence and correlates from a national survey. *Addiction, 99*, 96–106.

McCabe, S. E., West, B. T., & Wechsler, H. (2007). Trends and college-level characteristics associated with the non-medical use of prescription drugs among U.S. college students from 1993–2001. *Addiction, 102*, 455–465

Martens, M. (2012). *Review of clinical assessment tools.* In C. Correia, J. Murphy, & N. Barnett (Eds.), *College student alcohol abuse: A guide to assessment, intervention, and prevention.* Hoboken, NJ: Wiley.

McCarthy, D. M., Tomlinson, K. L., Anderson, K. G., Marlatt, G. A., & Brown, S. A. (2005). Relapse in alcohol- and drug-disordered adolescents with comorbid psychopathology: Changes in psychiatric symptoms. *Psychology of Addictive Behaviors, 19*, 28–34.

McFarlane, A. C., Browne, D., Bryant, R. A., O'Donnell, M., Silove, D., Creamer, M., & Horsley, K. (2009). A longitudinal analysis of alcohol consumption and the risk of posttraumatic symptoms. *Journal of Affective Disorders, 118*, 166–172.

Miller, M. W., Vogt, D. S., Mozley, S. L., Kaloupek, D. G., & Keane, T. M. (2006). PTSD and substance-related problems: The mediating roles of disconstraint and negative emotionality. *Journal of Abnormal Psychology, 115*, 369–379.

Mowbray, C. T., Megivern, D., Mandiberg, J. M., Strauss, S., Stein, C. H., Collins, K., . . . Lett, R. (2006). Campus mental health services: Recommendations for change. *American Journal of Orthopsychiatry, 76*, 226–237.

Mueser, K. T., Noordsy, D. L., Drake, R. E., & Fox, L. (2003). *Integrated treatment for dual disorders: A guide to effective practice.* New York, NY: Guildford Press.

Murphy, J. G., Correia, C. J., Colby, S. M., & Vuchinich, R. E. (2005). Using behavioral theories of choice to predict drinking outcomes following a brief intervention. *Experimental and Clinical Psychopharmacology, 13*, 93–107.

Nagoshi, C. T. (1999). Perceived control of drinking and other predictors of alcohol use and problems in a college student sample. *Addiction Research, 7*, 291–306.

Najavits, L. M. (2002). *Seeking safety: A treatment manual for PTSD and substance abuse.* New York, NY: Guilford Press.

Najdowski, C. J., & Ullman, S. E. (2009). Prospective effects of sexual victimization on PTSD and problem drinking. *Addictive Behaviors, 43*, 965–968.

Nathan, P. E., & Langenbucher, J. W. (1999). Psychopathology: Description and classification. *Annual Review of Psychology, 50*, 79–107.

Neighbors, C. Atkins, D. C., Lewis, M. A., Lee, C. M., Kaysen, D., Mittmann, A. . . . Rodriguez, L. M. (2011). Event-specific drinking among college students. *Psychology of Addictive Behaviors.* doi: 10.1037/a0024051

Newman, D. L., Moffitt, T. E., Caspi, A, Magdol, L., Silva, P. A., & Stanton, W. R. (1996). Psychiatric disorder in a birth cohort of young adults: Prevalence, comordbitiy, clinical significance, and new case incidence from ages 11 to 21. *Journal of Consulting and Clinical Psychology, 64*, 552–562.

O'Malley, P. M., & Johnston, L. D. (2002). Epidemiology of alcohol and other drug use among American college students. *Journal of Studies on Alcohol, 63*(Suppl 14), 23–39.

O'Neill, S. E., Para, G. R., & Sher, K. J. (2001). Clinical relevance of heavy drinking during the college years: Cross-sectional and prospective perspectives. *Psychology of Addictive Behaviors, 15*, 350–359.

Ouimette, P., Coolhart, D., Funderburk, J., & Brown, P.J. (2007). Precipitants of first substance use in recently abstinent substance use disordered patients with PTSD. *Addictive Behaviors, 32*, 1719–1727.

Palmer, R. H. C., Young, S. E., Hopfer, C. J., Corley, R. P., Stallings, M. C., Crowley, T. J., & Hewitt, J. K. (2009). Developmental epidemiology of drug use and abuse in adolescence and young adulthood: Evidence of generalized risk. *Drug and Alcohol Dependence, 102*, 78–87.

Patock-Peckham, J. A., Huchinson, G. T., Cheong, J., & Nagoshi, C. T. (1998). Effect of religion and religiosity on alcohol use in a college student sample. *Drug and Alcohol Dependence, 49*, 81–88.

Petrakis, I. L., Gonzalez, G., Rosenheck, R., & Krystal, J. H. (2002). Comorbidity of alcoholism and psychiatric disorders. *Alcohol Research and Health, 26*, 81–89.

Powell, K., Kresnow, J., Mercy, J., Potter, L., Swann, A., Frankowski, R., & . . . Bayer, T. L. (2001). Alcohol consumption and nearly lethal suicide attempts. *Suicide and Life-Threatening Behavior, 32*, 30–41.

Read, J. P., Colder, C. R., Merrill, J. E., Ouimette, P., White, J., & Swartout, A. (2012). Trauma and posttraumatic stress symptoms predict alcohol and other drug consequence trajectories in the first year of college. *Journal of Consulting and Clinical Psychology.* Advance online publication. doi: 10.1037/a0028210

Read, J. P., Kahler, C. W., Strong, D. R., & Colder, C. R. (2006). Development and preliminary validation of the young adult alcohol consequences questionnaire. *Journal of Studies on Alcohol, 67*, 169–177.

Read, J. P., Merrill, J. E., Griffin, M. J., Bachrach, R. L., & Khan, S. (2012). *Posttraumatic stress and alcohol problems: Self-medication or trait vulnerability.* Manuscript submitted for publication.

Read, J. P., Ouimette, P., White, J., Colder, C., & Farrow, S. (2011). Rates of *DSM–IV*-TR trauma exposure and posttraumatic stress disorder among newly matriculated college students. *Psychological trauma: Theory, research, practice, and policy, 3*, 148–156.

Regier, D. A., Farmer, M. E., Rae, D. S., Locke, B. Z., Keith, S. J., Judd, L. L., & Goodwin, F. K. (1990). Comorbidity of mental disorders with alcohol and other drug abuse: Results from the epidemiologic catchment area (ECA) study. *Journal of the American Medical Association, 264*, 2511–2518.

Reynolds, E. K., MacPherson, L., Tull, M. T., Baruch, D. E., & Lejuez, C. W. (2011). Integration of the brief behavioral activation treatment for depression (BATD) into a college orientation program: Depression and alcohol outcomes. *Journal of Counseling Psychology, 58*, 555–564.

Robbins, S. B., May, T. M., & Corazzini, J. G. (1985). Perceptions of client needs and counseling center staff roles and functions. *Journal of Counseling Psychology, 32*, 641–644.

Ross, H. E., Glaser, F. B., & Germanson, T. (1988). The prevalence of psychiatric disorders in patients with alcohol and other drug problems. *Archives of General Psychiatry, 45*, 1023–1031.

Ross, H. E., & Tisdall, G. W. (1994). Alcohol use and abuse in a university psychiatric health service: Prevalence and patterns of comorbidity with other psychiatric problems. *Journal of Alcohol and Drug Education, 39*, 63–74.

Saraceno, L., Munafó, M., Heron, J., Craddock, N., & van den Bree, M. M. (2009). Genetic and non-genetic influences on the development of co-occurring alcohol problem use and internalizing symptomatology in adolescence: A review. *Addiction, 104,* 1100–1121.

Schadé, A., Marquenie, L. A., van Balkon, A. J., Koeter, M. W., de Beurs, E., van den Brink, W., & van Dyck, R. (2005). The effectiveness of anxiety treatment on alcohol-dependent patients with a comorbid phobic disorder: A randomized controlled trial. *Alcoholism: Clinical and Experimental Research, 29,* 794–800.

Schaeffer, M., Jeglic, E. L., & Stanley, B. (2008). The relationship between suicidal behavior, ideation, and binge drinking among college students. *Archives of Suicide Research, 12,* 124–132.

Schulenberg, J., O'Malley, P. M., Bachman, J. G., Wadsworth, K. N., & Johnston, L. D. (1996). Getting drunk and growing up: Trajectories of frequent binge drinking during the transition to young adulthood. *Journal of Studies on Alcohol, 57,* 289–304.

Schulenberg, J. E., & Zarrett, N. R. (2006). Mental health during emerging adulthood: Continuity and discontinuity in courses, causes, and functions. In J. J. Arnett & J. L. Tanner (Eds.), *Emerging adults in America: Coming of age in the 21st century* (pp. 135–172). Washington, DC: American Psychological Association.

Shaver, P., Furman, W., & Buhrmester, D. (1985). Transition to college: Network changes, social skills, and loneliness. In S. Duck, D. Perlman, S. Duck, & D. Perlman (Eds.), *Understanding personal relationships: An interdisciplinary approach* (pp. 193–219). Thousand Oaks, CA: Sage.

Sheehan, D. V., Lecrubier, Y., Sheehan, K., Amorim, P., Janavs, J., Weiller, E., . . . Dunbar, G. C. (1998). The mini-international neuropsychiatric interview (M.I.N.I.): The development and validation of a structured diagnostic psychiatric interview for *DSM-IV* and ICD-10. *Journal of Clinical Psychiatry, 59*(Suppl 20), 22–33.

Sher, K. J. (1987). Stress response dampening. In H. T. Blane & K. E. Leonard (Eds.), *Psychological theories of drinking and alcoholism* (pp. 227–271). New York, NY: Guilford Press.

Slutske, W. S. (2005). Alcohol use disorders among US college students and their non-college-attending peers. *Archives of General Psychiatry, 62,* 321–327.

Smyth, J. M., Heron, K. E., Wonderlich, S. A., Crosby, R. D., & Thompson, K. M. (2008). The influence of reported trauma and adverse events on eating disturbance in young adults. *International Journal of Eating Disorders, 41,* 195–202.

Sobell, L. C., & Sobell, M. B. (1992). Timeline follow-back: A technique for assessing self-reported ethanol consumption. In J. Allen & R. Z. Litten (Eds.), *Measuring alcohol consumption: Psychosocial and biological methods* (pp. 41–72). Totowa, NJ: Humana Press.

Stewart, S. H. (1996). Alcohol abuse in individuals exposed to trauma: A critical review. *Psychological Bulletin, 120,* 83–112.

Stone, G. L., & Archer, J. (1990). College and university counseling centers in the 1990s: Challenges and limits. *Counseling Psychologist, 18,* 539–607.

Substance Abuse and Mental Health Services Administration. (2003). *Alcohol use and risks among young adults by college enrollment status.* Retrieved from www.oas.samhsa.gov/2k3/College/college.pdf

Substance Abuse and Mental Health Services Administration. (2008). *Results from the 2007 national survey on drug use and health: National findings* (DHHS Publication No. SMA 08–4343). Retrieved from http://oas.samhsa.gov/nsduh/2k7nsduh/2k7Results.pdf

Swendsen, J. D., & Merikangas, K. R. (2000). The comorbidity of depression and substance use disorders. *Clinical Psychology Review, 20,* 173–189.

Tanner, J. L., Reinherz, H. Z., Beardslee, W. R., Fitzmaurice, G. M., Leis, J. A., & Berger, S. R. (2007). Change in prevalence of psychiatric disorders from ages 21 to 30 in a community sample. *Journal of Nervous and Mental Disease, 195,* 298–306.

Turner, A. L., & Quinn, K. F. (1999). College students' perceptions of the value of psychological services: A comparison with APA's public education research. *Professional Psychology: Research and Practice, 30,* 368–371.

Twamley, E. W., Hami, S., & Stein, M. B. (2004). Neuropsychological function in college students with and without posttraumatic stress disorder. *Psychiatry Research, 126,* 265–274.

U.S. Census Bureau. (2007). *Educational Attainment in the United States: 2007.* Retrieved from www. census.gov/prod/2009pubs/p20-560.pdf

U.S. Department of Health and Human Services, National Institutes of Health, National Institute on Drug Abuse. (2010). *Comorbidity: Addiction and other mental illnesses* (NIH Publication No. 10-5771). Retrieved from www.drugabuse.gov/pdf/rrcomorbidity.pdf

Wallenstein, G. V., Pigeon, S., Kopans, B., Jacobs, D. G., & Aseltine, R. (2007). Results of national alcohol screening day: College demographics, clinical characteristics, and comparison with online screening. *Journal of American College Health, 55,* 341–350.

Wechsler, H., Lee, J. E., Kuo, M., & Lee, H. (2000). College binge drinking in the 1990s: A continuing problem: Results of the Harvard School of Public Health 1999 college alcohol study. *Journal of American College Health, 48,* 199–210.

Wechsler, H., & Nelson, T. F. (2008). What we have learned from the Harvard School of Public Health college alcohol study: Focusing attention on college student alcohol consumption and the environmental conditions that promote it. *Journal of Studies on Alcohol and Drugs, 69,* 481–490.

White, H. R., & Labouvie, E. W. (1989). Towards the assessment of adolescent problem drinking. *Journal of Studies on Alcohol, 50,* 30–37.

Widiger, T. A., & Clark, L. (2000). Toward *DSM-V* and the classification of psychopathology. *Psychological Bulletin, 126,* 946–963.

Widiger, T. A., & Samuel, D. B. (2005). Diagnostic categories or dimensions? A question for the diagnostic and statistical manual of mental disorders—Fifth edition. *Journal of Abnormal Psychology, 114,* 494–504.

Wonderlich, S. A., Crosby, R. D., Mitchell, J. E., Thompson, K. M., Redlin, J., Demuth, G., Smyth, J., & Haseltine, B. (2001). Eating disturbance and sexual trauma in childhood and adulthood. *International Journal of Eating Disorders, 30,* 401–412.

Wu, L., Pilowsky, D. J., Schlenger, W. E., & Hasin, D. (2007). Alcohol use disorders and the use of treatment services among college-age young adults. *Psychiatric Services, 58,* 192–200.

Zivan, K., Eisenberg, D., Gollust, S. E., & Golberstein, E. (2009). Persistence of mental health problems and needs in a college student population. *Journal of Affective Disorders, 117,* 180–185.

12

Treating Drug Abuse

Meredith A. Terlecki, Anthony H. Ecker, Amy L. Copeland, and Julia D. Buckner

More than one third of college students endorsed current (past year) illicit drug use (Johnston, O'Malley, Bachman, & Schulenberg, 2010) and nearly 30% endorsed tobacco smoking (Rigotti, Lee, & Wechsler, 2000). Drug use among college students adversely impacts mental health with nearly half of college students meeting diagnostic criteria for an alcohol or cannabis use disorder (Caldeira et al., 2009). Despite the high rates of substance use disorders (SUD) among college students, the vast majority of students with a SUD do not seek treatment (Caldeira et al., 2009). Thus, it is important for universities and communities to develop strategies to intervene effectively with students who abuse drugs.

Although psychosocial treatments for tobacco and illicit drug use have received growing empirical attention in recent years among adolescent and noncollege young adult samples, considerably less work has focused on treatments for college students. Most of the extant research on treatment for illicit SUD concerns psychosocial treatments of cannabis use disorders, presumably because cannabis remains the most commonly used illicit drug among students (Johnston et al., 2010). This chapter reviews the extant literature on drug treatments for college students to both provide a comprehensive summary of best practice treatments for this population as well as to inform future directions for much needed work in this important, yet understudied, area.

EDUCATION BASED DRUG PREVENTION

Campus-based educational classes are the most common approaches to addressing problematic alcohol and other drug (AOD) use on college campuses, with most campuses officially sponsoring AOD prevention programs (West & Graham, 2005). The structure and content of such classes vary by campus, although most provide information on alcohol/drug-related harm, risk factors related to alcohol/drug use, normative feedback (i.e., correcting misperceptions of peer AOD), and harm-reduction strategies in a 1- to 3-hour group meeting. Although educational classes are related to increased awareness of problematic AOD-use (Walters & Bennett, 2000), increased knowledge has not been found to correlate with reduced AOD use or related problems (for review see Larimer & Cronce, 2007). Further, programs target alcohol and nicotine use more aggressively than illicit drug use, which may explain why administrator perceptions of student drug use remained unchanged despite prevention efforts (Licciardone, 2003). Lack of evidence that AOD education programs meaningfully reduce college drug use indicates a need for different approaches in preventing student drug use.

EDUCATION-BASED DRUG TREATMENT FOR MANDATED STUDENTS

The lack of compelling data supporting education-based drug programs is concerning because students who violate campus AOD policy are typically mandated to campus-based AOD education classes (Barnett & Read, 2005). In some respects, the campus judicial process has become a point of intervention for students who misuse AOD. Because AOD education classes appear to be the least effective method for decreasing AOD use (Barnett & Read, 2005; Walters, Bennett, & Noto, 2000), mandated students may continue to engage in risky drug use after attending these programs.

BRIEF MOTIVATIONAL INTERVENTIONS (BMI)

BMIs are directive, client-centered psychotherapies that utilize motivational interviewing (MI) techniques (Miller & Rollnick, 2002) to explore and resolve ambivalence to change problematic behaviors (e.g., drug use). BMI is a promising approach for use with college student drug users given its nonconfrontational and nonjudgmental style (Larimer & Cronce, 2007), which may appeal to students who are resistant to the idea of treatment and/or likely to disengage from an education-based lecture about the consequences of risky drug use (Barnett & Read, 2005; Larimer & Cronce, 2007). Unfortunately, few studies have tested the utility of BMI for college drug use; thus, its efficacy for reducing college drug use and use-related problems is unclear. Later we provide a review of the few studies evaluating BMIs with college students and other relevant populations (e.g., college-aged young adults, adolescents).

BRIEF ALCOHOL SCREENING AND INTERVENTION FOR COLLEGE STUDENTS (BASICS)

BMIs for college students tend to be based on the BASICS protocol (Dimeff, Baer, Kivlahan, & Marlatt, 1999), an empirically supported treatment for college student alcohol use (U.S. Department of Health and Human Services [USDHHS], 2002). The purpose of BASICS is to raise awareness of risky drinking behaviors and to develop a discrepancy between current and desired alcohol use, with the overarching goal of decreased use. BMIs were developed to target heavy and problem drinking (not alcohol dependence). The following BASICS components are discussed in a 45- to 60-minute open-ended conversation: (1) student's alcohol use compared to campus norms; (2) drinking-related problems (e.g., missing classes due to hangover); (3) risks and benefits of use; (4) alcohol outcome expectancies; and (5) strategies to reduce use (if such strategies are requested). A personalized normative feedback (PNF) form is typically presented to students and used as a tool for sparking discussion about the student's drinking patterns and highlighting relevant drinking-related risk factors to enhance motivation to change drinking behaviors. PNF forms include a graphic display of the student's drinking patterns relative to campus norms and psychoeducational material about alcohol-related health risks.

BASICS has been adapted to address other substances. Adapted BASICS protocols typically include supplementary drug information for the treatment of both alcohol and drug use. Despite compelling evidence in support of BASICS-type BMI for reducing college alcohol use (for review, see Larimer & Cronce, 2007), surprisingly no known outcome studies have evaluated the efficacy of an adapted BASICS-type BMI that exclusively targets college drug use.

Only two published studies evaluated BASICS-type BMI for the treatment of both drug and alcohol use among college students. White and colleagues (2006) evaluated a BASICS-type counselor-guided BMI with PNF compared to a PNF only condition in a randomized controlled trial (RCT) among college students referred for an AOD campus policy violation (11.0% had a drug [cannabis] violation). The BMI included two sessions. In the first, participants met in small groups with a counselor for 60 minutes to complete baseline measures. In the second, participants met with the same counselor for 30 minutes to review the PNF form. The PNF consisted of: normative feedback; estimations of peak blood alcohol content (BAC) levels; discussion of risky alcohol- and drug-related risky behaviors (e.g., unprotected sex after using AOD); personal risk factors for AOD use (e.g., depression, family history of alcoholism); estimates on the average amount of money spent on cigarettes (but not alcohol or drugs); psychoeducation on alcohol tolerance; negative consequences related to smoking cigarettes; BAC levels and health-risks related to alcohol intoxication; and strategies to reduce risky AOD-related behaviors (e.g., using designated driver). The intervention was delivered by counselors trained in MI under the supervision of a clinical psychologist.

At 3-month follow-up, students in both conditions reported decreased substance use (alcohol, cigarette, and cannabis use) and alcohol- and drug-related problems (White et al., 2006). In fact, one third of students who endorsed baseline cannabis use reported cannabis abstinence at 3 months regardless of condition. Yet, at 15-month follow-up, participants in both conditions reported significantly *greater* frequency of cannabis use and cigarette smoking relative to baseline levels, although drug-related problems remained stable. This finding raises concerns over the long-term efficacy of either treatment approach for reducing cannabis use and cigarette smoking among mandated students. Additionally, given that only 11% of the sample was mandated to treatment as a result of a cannabis policy violation (although approximately one fourth of the sample endorsed cannabis use), it remains unknown how students mandated for cannabis treatment specifically would respond to BASICS-type BMI.

Amaro and colleagues (2010) evaluated a BASICS-type BMI for decreasing college AOD use. The sample consisted of students who self-referred to the university health center for medical or mental health services. Participants were also recruited via advertisements on campus. BMI was conducted by nurses who received weekly supervision by a clinical psychologist. The intervention consisted of two 45- 60-minute sessions using PNF containing both alcohol and drug use information. Data were collected in the first session and used to produce the feedback component, which was reviewed in the second session. The alcohol use feedback components included discussion of the participant's drinking patterns, normative feedback, psychoeducation on alcohol-related health effects, alcohol risk factors, and the "readiness ruler," which was used to assess motivation to change. The drug use feedback components were identical to alcohol components. At baseline, 98.4% of the sample reported current (past 6 months) alcohol use (with 67.2% reporting weekly binge drinking), 56.1% reported current illicit drug use (mostly cannabis), and 19.6% reported current illegal use of prescription drugs. At 6 months post-BMI, students reported significant within-groups reductions in alcohol and drug use. The largest decrease was observed in weekly binge drinking episodes, which decreased by nearly 17%, with smaller decreases observed for alcohol use, illicit drug use, and prescription drug use. There was a significant decrease in number of alcohol-related problems (but not of drug-related problems). Importantly, those reporting the highest levels of alcohol or drug use at baseline demonstrated the greatest reductions in use. Yet the clinical significance of observed reductions in use is questionable given that use of alcohol and drugs decreased by only 2.7% (for prescription drugs) to just more than 5% for alcohol and illicit drugs. Further, more than 90% of students continued to use alcohol and more than half continued to use illicit drugs. Students reported a mean of nearly eight alcohol-related problems at follow-up. It is also noteworthy that analyses were conducted only on those students who completed baseline and follow-up assessments. Because authors did not report attrition rates, it is unknown whether the heaviest drinking or drug-using students failed to complete treatment or respond to the 6-month follow-up assessment. Further, no comparison group was utilized and the slight decreases in use observed may be attributable to other factors. Despite these limitations, this study demonstrates the feasibility of employing a BASICS-type BMI program on campus within a university health system and suggests such programs may be useful in decreasing frequency of use and some use-related problems, especially among heavier users.

An innovative tobacco smoking cessation program developed for college student smokers is the Students Using Computerized Coaching to Effectively Stop Smoking (SUCCESS; Prokhorov et al., 2007). Project SUCCESS randomly assigned college students to: (1) a motivational intervention that included an in-person motivational counseling plus health feedback and an interactive Internet-based program with personalized newsletters tailored to students level of motivation to quit or (2) a standard care condition that was comprised of brief (5–10 minutes) counseling plus bibliotherapy. At 10-month follow-up (Prokhorov et al., 2008), the two conditions did not significantly differ on self-reported quit rates, with only 26% of the motivational group and 29% of the control group reporting quitting. Biological measures suggested a slightly higher quit rate (17%) among those in the motivational group compared to controls (10%), although both groups demonstrated low rates of quitting. Motivation was related to outcomes. Specifically, among students in the preparation stage of change, quit rates were higher among those in the motivational group (32%) than the control group (11%), suggesting this type of intervention may be more effective with those students already taking steps to reduce or quit smoking.

BMI FOR DRUG USE AMONG YOUNG ADULTS

BMIs have been developed and evaluated for reducing AOD use among nontreatment-seeking young adults. Among United Kingdom Further Education students (equivalent to U.S. junior colleges or trades schools), students aged 16 to 20 reporting at least weekly drug use for the past 3 months (nearly half reported near daily cannabis use) were recruited to undergo an RCT consisting of either BMI or standardized drug education class (McCambridge & Strang, 2004). The BMI was a single 60-minute session comprised of an open-ended, MI-based conversation about basic drug education, student's substance use, nondrug-related values and goals, risky behaviors, and actual and potential consequences of drug use (normative feedback was not provided). The overarching goal of the session was to encourage change in AOD use.

Three months after the intervention session, significant differences were observed between the BMI and drug education conditions for cannabis use, cigarette smoking, and alcohol use (McCambridge & Strang, 2004). Specifically, BMI participants' cannabis use declined 66% (16% of participants discontinued cannabis use), cigarette smoking decreased by 12%, and alcohol use decreased by 39%. Control participants reported a 27% *increase* in cannabis use, a 12% *increase* in cigarette smoking, and a 12% *increase* in alcohol use. No significant between-groups differences were observed for noncannabis drug use. It is noteworthy that at 3-month follow-up, substance use was still quite high; BMI participants reported using cannabis on average more than 5 times per week and smoking an average of 25 tobacco cigarettes per week. At 12-months posttreatment (McCambridge & Strang, 2005), weekly frequency of cannabis use, cigarette smoking, and alcohol use were not significantly different between the BMI and control conditions. Participants reported using cannabis an average of 9 to 12 times per week and smoking 28 to 34 tobacco cigarettes per week. Importantly, significant findings at 3-month follow-up were no longer significant at 12-month follow-up, raising concerns over the long-term efficacy of this BMI for drug use among young adults. It is also noteworthy that older students (i.e., age 18 to 19) were less likely to complete follow-up assessments, so data regarding outcomes from this age cohort may be somewhat biased. These data suggest that BMI can be used to decrease cannabis use in the short term, but students continue to use cannabis at high rates (daily) in the long term.

The efficacy of BMI for reducing drug use was also among young adults 16 to 22 (60% full-time secondary and higher education students in the United Kingdom) (Marsden et al., 2006). Social services workers recruited participants who reported primary past-month use of stimulant drugs (i.e., ecstasy, cocaine, or crack-cocaine) on at least four occasions. Participants were randomized to a 45- to 60-minute single-session BMI or a control condition that received psychoeducation about the health risks related to stimulant use. The BMI included a discussion of the participant's lifestyle and interests, drug use habits, perceptions about costs and benefits of their drug use, problems experienced due to drug use, and plans for behavior change (no normative feedback was provided). Participants in both conditions received psychoeducation regarding health risks related to alcohol and stimulant use. Contrary to expectation, no significant between-groups differences were observed for frequency of any drug at 6-month follow-up, with both conditions reporting significantly fewer days using ecstasy, cocaine, crack, and cannabis. Yet, it is also unclear how clinically meaningful the within-groups reductions for ecstasy, cocaine, and crack were, given that use only decreased in the BMI condition by 10.6, 3.9, and 4.8 days of the past 90 days.

Stein, Hagerty, Herman, Phipps, and Anderson (2011) evaluated a two-session BMI for cannabis use with nontreatment seeking cannabis-using women (18- to 24 years old, 69.9% with college experience or a college degree, 40% with baseline cannabis dependence). In the first MI session, therapists assessed the participants' substance use, provided feedback about participants' substance use patterns and cannabis problems, and encouraged participants to develop a "change plan" to reduce cannabis use or to change any health behavior (e.g., increase exercise). One month later, the "change plan" was reviewed and the therapist provided strategies (e.g., identifying high-risk situations) to help participants meet their goals. MI participants reduced cannabis use by 6.6 days per month, whereas the assessment-only control group showed a 2-day reduction in cannabis use; yet, these findings were only significant at the 3-month follow-up assessment (not the 1- and 6-month follow-up assessments). The intervention had no effect on cannabis problem severity over time. Importantly, women with higher baseline motivation to quit cannabis in the BMI condition were significantly less likely to use cannabis at each follow-up. Thus, this BMI may be effective for those with higher motivation to reduce cannabis use at treatment entry.

Other BMI protocols specific to cannabis use have demonstrated some utility in reducing drug use in noncollege populations, such as the Marijuana Check-Up (Stephens, Roffman, Fearer, Williams, & Burke, 2007) and the Teen Marijuana Check-Up (Walker, Roffman, Stephens, Wakana, & Berghuis, 2006). Both protocols are based on the Brief Drinker Check-Up (Miller, Benefield, & Tonigan, 1993), an empirically supported BMI for treating heavy drinking and alcohol problems in adults (Miller et al., 1993). The adult Marijuana Check-Up is a single 90-minute session and the Teen Marijuana Check-Up is similar to the adult version, presented over two 30- to 60-minute sessions. In both versions, therapists review a PNF with the participant, explore the participant's self-efficacy for reducing use, and conduct a cost/benefit analysis for reducing use. The intervention was designed to appeal to nontreatment-seeking individuals experiencing cannabis-related problems who are ambivalent about reducing use. Adults[1] (aged 18 to 57) who completed the Marijuana Check-Up reported less frequent cannabis use at a 12-month follow-up. Yet, use only decreased from an average of 5.76 days per week to 4.65 days at follow-up. Among teens (age 14 to 19), the Check-Up was related to decreased cannabis use at 3-month follow-up (Martin & Copeland, 2008; Walker et al., 2006). However, cannabis use remained high (60% of days in the Martin and Copeland sample, nearly half the days in the Walker et al. sample). Thus, this intervention seems insufficient to reduce cannabis use and related problems as a stand-alone treatment, which is not surprising given it was not designed as such. Yet, this intervention may represent a starting point for beginning to reduce drug use among ambivalent users who may be reluctant to seek longer, more formal treatment.

Secondary reductions in drug use among students undergoing BMI for alcohol use. Several studies have observed secondary reductions in cannabis use among students who underwent BASICS (i.e., BMI for alcohol use that did not address drug use). For instance, incoming college first-year students were randomized to one of four alcohol interventions: (1) BASICS; (2) parent intervention; (3) combined BASICS plus parent intervention; and (4) assessment-only control (Grossbard et al., 2010). In the interventions with parental involvement, parents were mailed a handbook containing descriptive information on college student drinking, strategies for communicating with their college-bound teens, and suggestions for teaching teens to reduce the influence of peer pressure. Parents were asked to read the handbook and address alcohol-related topics with their teens prior to college entry. BASICS included a 45- to 60-minute review of the participant's PNF. Trained peer facilitators provided information on the participant's alcohol use, normative drinking information, alcohol expectancies, negative consequences of alcohol use, and protective behaviors to reduce alcohol-related risk. Students in BASICS conditions received the intervention when they arrived on campus to begin college. Unexpectedly, no condition produced

---

[1] No higher education information was presented in this study.

reductions in alcohol, other illicit drug (noncannabis), or nicotine use 10-months follow-up. Participants in BASICS-only, parent-only, and control conditions reported increased cannabis use at 10 months, whereas combined participants reported stable cannabis use over time. The combined intervention reported significantly less cannabis use relative to BASICS-only and control conditions. Overall, study findings suggest that most students will increase cannabis use during the first year of college, but parental involvement before a BMI may be useful to help prevent students' cannabis use from increasing during this time.

Counter to Grossbard et al.'s (2010) finding that BASICS (without parental involvement) did not reduce cannabis use among college students, secondary reductions in cannabis use were observed after a single session MI-based alcohol intervention (that did not include discussions of drug use) with young adults (aged 18 to 24; 36.7% college students) recruited in an emergency room (Magill, Barnett, Apodaca, Rohsenow, & Monti, 2009). Participants (half of whom presented for alcohol-related medical treatment) were randomized to receive either a single session of MI with PNF or a PNF-only condition. More than half of the participants endorsed current (past month) cannabis use at baseline. At 6-month follow-up, participants reported significantly less frequent cannabis use in both conditions, but no differences between conditions. At 12-month follow-up, only participants in the BMI condition reported using cannabis less frequently than they used at baseline, decreasing their use from a mean of 16 days per month to 9 days per month. Participants in the Magill et al. (2009) study used cannabis more frequently at baseline than those in the Grossbard et al. (2010) study, suggesting that among heavier cannabis users, exploring and resolving ambivalence about reducing use of one substance (in this case alcohol) may generalize to other substances.

In sum, there is some evidence supporting existing BMIs for reducing heavy or risky drug use among college students (White et al., 2006; White, Mun, Pugh, & Morgan, 2007) and college-age young adults (Marsden et al., 2006; McCambridge & Strang, 2004, 2005) especially in the short term. Some data suggest that BMIs for college drug use may be most effective at reducing drug use among those with higher motivation to quit drug use at treatment entry (Magill et al., 2009; Stein et al., 2011). Because brief treatments are theoretically appealing and generally considered to be cost-effective for treating alcohol use (Neighbors, Barnett, Rohsenow, Colby, & Monti, 2010), additional research evaluating their utility for reducing college drug use is warranted. In particular, given that available BMIs were generally not related to clinically meaningful long-term reductions in drug use, work is necessary to test methods to improve long-term outcomes. Given that current BMIs for drug use have been based on BMIs for alcohol use, the development of BMI protocols tailored specifically to college drug use may be an important next step in this line of work as adaptations of BMIs for alcohol use might not be sufficient for treating drug use. Also, more research is necessary to determine the optimal dose of BMI for college drug use. Given that drug use rates remain high following one and two session BMIs, it may be necessary to evaluate the utility of longer BMIs (e.g., three or four sessions) and/or the incorporation of cognitive-behavioral techniques to arm students with coping skills that may help them better reduce their drug use. Furthermore, effective drug use treatment for adults and non college young adults may not generalize to college drug use, again suggesting that specific interventions warrant development and investigation.

WEB-BASED INTERVENTIONS

Although the provision of PNF alone (delivered via written packet) leads to short-term reductions in drug use among college students (White et al., 2006), there is evidence of increases in cannabis use 15 months following PNF alone (White et al., 2007). Thus, it has been posited that PNF delivered via the Internet may be more efficacious than that delivered via a written packet (e.g., White et al., 2006). Yet, despite the appeal of Web-based PNF interventions, they have not received much empirical attention. In the only published study of the utility of Web-based PNF on college illicit drug use, incoming first-year students reporting current (past 3 months) cannabis use were randomized to an online PNF intervention or assessment-only control prior to college entry (Lee, Neighbors, Kilmer, & Larimer, 2010). Unfortunately, no significant within- or between-groups differences in cannabis use frequency were observed at a 3-month follow-up, and participants in both conditions continued to use cannabis on approximately nine occasions in the past 90 days. At 6-month follow-up, frequency of use increased to more than 11 occasions in the past 90 days in both groups. Because the observed treatment effects appear to dissipate over time, future research might address ways to maintain treatment gains among those who appear to benefit from the intervention. For example, given that counselor-delivered personalized feedback for alcohol use appears more effective than Web-based feedback alone among college students (Walters, Vader, Harris, Field, & Jouriles, 2009), future work may benefit from examining the utility of combining Web-based intervention with counselor contact to reduce college drug use.

Notably, authors identified two factors that appear to play an important role in whether Web-based PNF may be efficacious: history of family drug use problems and student motivation to change drug use (Lee et al., 2010). Family drug use problems moderated the relation between condition and outcomes, such that in the PNF condition, students who endorsed a positive family history of drug use also reported lower cannabis use at follow-up relative. Among those without a family history there were no differences between conditions. Also, higher motivation to change at baseline was related to better treatment outcomes. Together, these data suggest Web-based PNF interventions may be helpful for those students motivated to change their cannabis use due to their own problematic cannabis experiences or due to witnessing the negative consequences of use experienced by family members.

A promising Web-based PNF intervention known as the THC Online Knowledge Experience (e-Toke; www.echeckuptogo.com) is currently under investigation. e-Toke focuses specifically on cannabis use. It was developed by modifying the electronic Check Up To Go (e-Chug; www.echeckuptogo.com), a Web-based interface shown to be efficacious for reducing college student drinking quantity and negative consequences (Hustad, Barnett, Borsari, & Jackson, 2010). e-Toke allows students to report cannabis use via an online assessment system, which then produces an electronic PNF form. No outcome data have not yet been published. More information about the intervention can be found at www.echeckuptogo.com.

More work has been conducted evaluating the efficacy of Web-based interventions for college student smoking. Yet, in a recent review of Web-based tobacco smoking cessation interventions for adults, college students, and adolescents, there was insufficient evidence to support their use for college student smokers given that only one study with college students met their RCT inclusion criteria (Hutton et al., 2011). In that RCT (An et al., 2008), college student smokers were randomized to a Web-based smoking cessation intervention or control group. Intervention participants were asked to visit the Web site once per week to report weekly use of cigarettes (and other health-related information including alcohol use and stress levels) and take an interactive online quiz containing information on smoking-related health problems and nicotine dependence. Participants also received tailored weekly emails from peer support staff encouraging quit attempts. Control participants received an email containing links to an online smoking cessation resource. At 30-week follow-up, intervention participants self-reported significantly greater current (past 30-day) nicotine abstinence (41% abstinent) than controls (23% abstinent). Yet, conditions did not significantly differ at a 6-month follow-up, suggesting that Web-based interventions may not have long-term impact on reducing college smoking.

In sum, despite the appeal of Web-based interventions for college drug use, there is little empirical support, particularly for long-term outcomes. Web-based BMIs are cost effective and can be made easily available to students (Walters, Hester, Chiauzzi, & Miller, 2005), which may support reductions in drug use among students unlikely to voluntarily seek treatment. Thus, development and evaluation of Web-based interventions that produce meaningful and sustained reductions in college drug use will be an important area of future work.

INTERVENTIONS THAT WARRANT EVALUATION FOR TREATING COLLEGE DRUG USE

Given the lack of empirically supported interventions for the prevention and/or treatment of college drug use, additional research is necessary to examine the potential utility of other treatments found to be efficacious in other populations. The following treatments have some empirical support for treating drug use in adult, adolescent, and noncollege young adult populations (i.e., these treatments have not yet been examined specifically among college students): cognitive-behavioral therapy (CBT), motivation enhancement therapy (MET), contingency management (CM), and drug counseling (DC).

Cognitive-behavioral therapy (CBT). CBT is an effective psychosocial treatment for SUDs among adults broadly (i.e., not necessarily college students or college-aged adults) (for review see, Magill & Ray, 2009). The focus of CBT is to help the clients gain awareness of drug use cues and teach them to respond to triggers without using drugs. CBT for SUD lasts an average of 18 sessions (Magill & Ray, 2009). Most CBTs for SUD involve skills training (e.g., drug refusal skills), relapse prevention, and restructuring of unhelpful drug-related cognitions (e.g., "I can only relax if I smoke cannabis"). Among adults in the Magill and Ray (2009) review, treatment outcomes (e.g., less frequent use, greater drug free urinalyses) endure about 6 to 9 months posttreatment, but dissipate by 12 months. Given a large body of research supporting the short-term efficacy of CBT for SUD among adults (Magill & Ray, 2009), it is assumed that CBT would garner the same impact among college students. However, this assumption has not been explicitly tested. It is possible that some college students may have less severe drug use and/or less motivation to change drug use behaviors which may result in poorer CBT outcomes.

Motivational enhancement therapy (MET). MET was originally developed for alcohol use disorders (Miller, Zweben, DiClemente, & Rychtarik, 1992). It combines psychoeducational feedback with MI skills to explore and resolve ambivalence about changing substance use. Although we know of no studies explicitly examining the utility of MET for college drug use, the addition of MET to CBT can motivate clients to enter and adhere to treatment (McKee et al., 2007). MET + CBT involves 1 to 4 initial motivation building sessions of MET followed by a skills-based CBT protocol (The Marijuana Treatment Project Research Group [MTPRG], 2004). Among adults with cannabis dependence (M_{age} = 36 years; $M_{education}$ = 14 years), 9 sessions of CBT + MET led to greater reductions in cannabis use frequency than two sessions of MET-only or delayed treatment (MTPRG, 2004). However, at 4-month follow-up, the CBT + MET condition reported using cannabis 36% of the past 90 days and the MET only condition reported using cannabis 57% of the past 90 days. Among college-age young adults (aged 18 to 25; 18% with some college experience) with cannabis dependence, those receiving 8 sessions of MET + CBT attended more sessions and reported greater cannabis abstinence at 6-month follow-up than did patients in DC (Carroll et al., 2006). However, between-groups differences only approached significance and both groups showed low abstinence rates at follow-up (31% in MET + CBT; 21% in drug counseling). In sum, MET may help engage ambivalent users in CBT leading to reduced use, but further work is necessary to help patients further reduce their use.

Contingency management (CM). CM involves the provision of positive reinforcement (e.g., vouchers for goods, prizes) to reward a desired behavior (e.g., substance abstinence, therapy attendance) to increase its occurrence (Higgins, Budney, Bickel, & Foerg, 1994; Petry, Martin, Cooney, & Kranzler, 2000). Among adults (not necessarily college students), CM is an efficacious stand-alone treatment for reducing drug use and increasing therapy attendance (for review see Stitzer & Petry, 2006). CM has also been evaluated as an auxiliary component in CBT and MET for cannabis use, which has shown to facilitate treatment retention and drug abstinence (for review see Budney, Moore, Sigmon, & Higgins, 2006). The addition of CM to MET + CBT, MET, and DC increased treatment retention and cannabis abstinence for both CBT + MET and DC protocols among cannabis-using adults (Carroll et al., 2006). Similarly, among probation-referred young adult (ages 18 to 25) cannabis users, the addition of CM to court-mandated MET improved treatment attendance and retention, although attendance did not necessarily translate to better outcomes (Sinha, Easton, Renee-Aubin, & Carroll, 2003).

Although we know of no published studies examining the utility of CM for illicit drug use among college students, CM protocols for nicotine treatment among college students have been evaluated and demonstrate some promise. Correia and Benson (2006) tested whether contingent monetary rewards (i.e., rewards contingent on providing an expired breath CO sample reading less than 8 parts per million [ppm]) would increase nicotine abstinence among college student smokers. Participants were randomly assigned to either a low- or high-reinforcement condition in an ABA design (e.g., baseline 1, intervention, baseline 2) with each phase lasting 1 week. Noncontingent monetary reinforcement ($4 for attending each session) was given during the baseline phases regardless of participant's expired breath CO reading. In the low-reinforcement condition, participants received $1 for the initial negative CO sample and consecutive abstinent readings earned participants and extra $.50 per reading. In the high-reinforcement condition, reinforcements were double those of the low-reinforcement condition. During the intervention phase, students submitted significantly more negative CO readings relative to the baseline weeks. The high-reward condition led to significantly greater nicotine abstinence than did the low-reward condition, suggesting higher reinforcement conditions may promote initial nicotine abstinence among college student cigarette smokers.

A similar ABA design (baseline 1, intervention, baseline 2) demonstrated that one large reinforcement provided after a 1-week period of abstinence helped initiate nicotine abstinence among college smokers (Irons & Correia, 2008). Students were paid one lump sum ($65) for submitting a nicotine-free urinalysis and an expired breath CO sample that was lower than 4ppm. Participants were given 1 week to establish abstinence. The week of brief abstinence was related to significantly greater nicotine abstinence (i.e., hours elapsed since last cigarette) (baseline 1: $M = 0.14$; intervention: $M = 69.00$; baseline 2; $M = 12.67$) and reduced number of cigarettes smoked per day (baseline 1: $M = 11.50$; intervention: $M = 3.40$; baseline 2; $M = 6.50$).

Given these encouraging results, it theoretically follows that adding CM to CBT or MI may produce better outcomes, as CM may serve as an external reinforcer for compliance with treatment protocols thereby increasing the likelihood students will attend treatment, adhere to protocols, practice skills, and so on. Unfortunately, little work has examined this question and the available data are not promising. In one such study, contingent (reinforcement was provided for nicotine-negative biomeasures) and noncontingent reward (reinforcement was provided regardless of nicotine level) conditions for tobacco cessation treatment were crossed with motivational enhancement versus relaxation in a 2 x 2 experimental design (Tevyaw et al., 2009). Students receiving contingent monetary reward had significantly higher continuous abstinence rates during the program, but there were no between-group differences between reinforcement conditions in abstinence rates at 6 months posttreatment. Despite these discouraging findings, it is noteworthy that students receiving the motivational enhancement plus CM showed significant pre- to posttreatment increased interest in cessation. Thus, CM may be useful to augment other treatment modalities among particular types of patients (e.g., those with lower internal motivation to change at treatment presentation).

The feasibility of implementing a CM program for college students may be limited by concerns about CM such as patient/provider contact frequency, cost, and ethical concerns (see Petry, 2010). Future work will be necessary to determine whether CM (alone or in conjunction with other treatments) meaningfully reduces drug use among college students. Future work evaluating the clinical and cost-effectiveness of CM with college samples is also warranted. To strive to make CM affordable for campus-based service providers, it may be worthwhile to evaluate whether vouchers for campus-based services (e.g., dining services or sports tickets) would be sufficient reinforcement to reduce drug use (e.g., cannabis) among college students.

Drug counseling (DC). DC is an abstinence-based intervention that emphasizes the client's need to recognize symptoms of drug addiction as problematic and to change the "people, places, and things" related to drug use (Mercer & Woody, 1999). In support of manualized DC, the combination of group- and individual-manualized DC decreased addictions severity ratings among cocaine dependent adults (aged 18 to 60; $M_{education}$ = 13 years) relative to group DC only and supportive therapy (Crits-Christoph et al., 1999). Yet, individual DC alone appears to be the least effective therapeutic approach to both engage treatment mandated young adult drug users in treatment and reduce drug use (Carroll et al., 2006). Further, it is not clear whether effective drug counseling protocols are consistently employed on college campuses and/or offered by appropriately trained staff (Juhnke et al., 2002; Stone & Vespia, 2000). To illustrate, 99% of college administrators report that students can receive AOD treatment at the student counseling center and 85% of colleges have a dedicated alcohol/substance specialist available for students; however, only 49% of schools engage in outcome monitoring of campus AOD services (Anderson & Galadeto, 2006). Further, it is noteworthy that there is currently considerable variability in the availability and nature of DC services on campus.

COMMUNITY DRUG TREATMENT REFERRALS

Community treatment referrals (including individual outpatient, intensive outpatient, or 12-step groups) are often utilized for mandated college student drug users after first-line campus-based AOD education efforts have failed (i.e., multiple drug policy campus violations; Juhnke et al., 2002) or if appropriate treatment is not available on campus (Freeman, 2001). This is concerning as, in one study, 42% of college students referred off-campus for psychotherapy by a campus provider did not meet with the off-campus provider (Owen, Devdas, & Rodolfa, 2007). Thus, the provision of referral options alone may not effectively facilitate off-campus treatment, leaving the at-risk student without appropriate treatment or follow-up care.

Juhnke et al. (2002) have provided some guidelines to inform decisions regarding when to address college drug use on campus versus when to refer to community treatment providers. Their recommendations specifically concern students who are mandated for treatment for AOD policy violations. They recommend establishing a cohesive treatment network among judicial officials and campus counseling services to offer appropriate assessment and treatment for students who violate AOD policies. Campus-based treatments would be warranted for students who do not meet diagnostic criteria for substance dependence, but who might be experiencing problematic use including having difficulty managing academic demands due to use, recurrent social or interpersonal problems, or multiple legal problems. They require educational class attendance for minor AOD policy violations only (e.g., underage alcohol possession). Residual offenders and drug policy violators would be required to undergo a clinical psychological assessment by a trained substance use counselor on campus. The assessment results would allow the counselor (not the judicial officer) to make clinically informed AOD treatment recommendations. These recommendations merit further evaluation for both feasibility and effectiveness at reducing AOD use.

Of note, campus drug counselors often require students to attend community 12-step programs such as narcotics anonymous (NA) as part of drug-related disciplinary sanctions (Sias & Goodwin, 2007). This practice is concerning because no specific treatment outcome studies have examined whether such programs are efficacious for college drug use. Rather, campus administrators are encouraged to select off-campus providers that offer empirically supported drug assessment and treatment services. Such treatments would include MET or BMI given that students (especially mandated students) may be difficult to engage in treatment as well as CM for those students who may benefit from external motivators to help them attend sessions and abstain from use. Treatment may also include CBT to teach students skills to manage their drug use. Ideally, off-campus providers should be located within walking distance of campus and offer extended hours so students can seek treatment without missing classes.

There are several circumstances under which community treatment referrals are warranted. Few university health care centers are able to provide medically supervised substance use detoxification, in-patient programming, or intensive outpatient treatment (IOP) (Keller, Bennett, McCrady, & Paulus, 1994). Thus, students with substance dependence, especially those experiencing physiological withdrawal, may be best served in a chemical detoxification unit or IOP treatment center. For example, benzodiazepines are related to dangerous withdrawal symptoms, and medical attention should be provided to aid in benzodiazepine cessation efforts.

In recognizing that this high-risk group of college students often must decide between pursuing higher education goals or receiving full-time AOD treatment, select specialized undergraduate universities with recovery-focused programming (e.g., recovery support groups, peer support meetings, and educational groups) are being developed (Harris-Wilkes, 2010), although the efficacy of such programs for improving academic performance or improving long-term drug abstinence has not been tested. Given the time-intensive nature of many outpatient and inpatient drug use treatment programs, college students need support and guidance while undergoing detoxification and/or IOP treatment. For instance, college administrators are encouraged to seek out IOP programs in the community that offer flexible hours for treatment (e.g., meetings on evenings, weekends) so that students are better able to remain in school and attend classes (if they so choose) while attending IOP sessions. In light of data suggesting that parental involvement can be useful in helping students decrease substance use (Grossbard et al., 2010) it may be useful to refer students to in-patient detox and/or IOP programs that include some family involvement. It is recommended that campus officials remain engaged in the referral process if possible. Regular follow-up meetings with the student and the student's treatment provider may help the student manage academic and treatment related demands.

CONSIDERATIONS AND RECOMMENDATIONS WHEN WORKING WITH COLLEGE STUDENTS

College students have some unique treatment needs for which specific interventions or intervention components may need to be developed. Data suggest college students experiencing drug-related problems are reluctant to voluntarily seek drug treatment (e.g., Buckner, Ecker, & Cohen, 2010). This finding signifies a serious need for methods for identifying high-risk students and encouraging them to consider changing their drug use and/or attending drug use treatment. As such, universities are faced with the challenge of developing and implementing effective drug screening and motivation enhancement approaches in addition to providing students with effective treatment for drug misuse. Given the proliferation of Internet use, one means by which universities can screen students is via Web-based problems. Yet the research on Web-based interventions for drug use is in its infancy. Thus, in light of data suggesting that Web-based interventions may be useful at decreasing cannabis use among college students with significant family histories of drug use and/or those motivated to change their drug use (Lee et al., 2010), universities interested in utilizing Web-based interventions may consider targeting these students for such interventions.

Unfortunately, most students will not be identified by campus officials until a serious AOD campus policy violation has occurred. Given that mandated students represent a high-risk group of AOD users, the provision of effective AOD treatment is critical in addition to helping the student navigate sanction-related consequences. For instance, students who are cited with an AOD policy violation risk suspension, expulsion, loss of student aid, and loss of campus employment. Those who are involved in their community legal system experience the typical stressors of the criminal justice system. Addressing these difficulties in treatment and helping the student fulfill the imposed sanction requirements may prove useful and help facilitate continued college enrollment postcitation. It may also be helpful for college administrators to work with students to problem-solve ways in which students can continue to meet their academic requirements should they remain enrolled while undergoing treatment (e.g., medical-excused absences if students must miss assignments for treatment sessions). Administrators can work with students to determine when it is appropriate for them to take a medical leave of absence from school while receiving treatment and aid the application process for such leaves.

Additionally, the evaluation of existing AOD-related programming is warranted by campus officials to determine whether programming reduces AOD use and related harm. Further, integration between student mental health services and judicial affairs proceedings could provide more cohesive treatment for AOD policy offenders, including the development of empirically supported treatment recommendations for AOD policy offenders, and clinician symptom monitoring of students who are referred for AOD individual treatment.

Techniques geared toward addressing treatment nonengagement are needed, as young adults are unlikely to attend treatment (Sinha, Easton, Renee-Aubin et al., 2003). Also, the educational demands of young adults in drug treatment may prohibit attendance for particular indicated treatments. For example, students might not be able to attend IOP programs, as they would compromise class attendance and coursework completion to meet treatment attendance requirements. Mason and Luckey (2003) discuss additional concerns of young adults engaged in substance use treatment, which may also generalize to college students, including that young adults in treatment are more likely to live with someone who currently uses substances than older adults. Thus, the living environment of college students may present environmental triggers for drugs, which may compromise treatment gains and increase risk for relapse.

Emerging data also suggest that some college students have co-occurring psychopathology that may play an etiological and/or maintaining role in their drug use and use-related problems. To illustrate, negative emotional states such as depression (e.g., Buckner, Keough, & Schmidt, 2007) and social anxiety (e.g., Buckner, Mallott, Schmidt, & Taylor, 2006; Buckner & Schmidt, 2008, 2009) appear especially related to cannabis-related problems among college students. Socially anxious students appear especially vulnerable to using cannabis to avoid social scrutiny by cannabis-using peers and to manage negative emotional states (Buckner, Bonn-Miller, Zvolensky, & Schmidt, 2007). Yet using cannabis to manage negative emotional states mediated the relation between social anxiety and cannabis problems. In fact, voluntary and mandated students undergoing BASICS for alcohol had poorer outcomes if they suffered from elevated social anxiety at baseline (Terlecki, Buckner, Larimer, & Copeland, 2011), suggesting students with chronically elevated negative affect may benefit from interventions aimed at helping these students learn more adaptive means by which to manage negative emotional states. Further, these data suggest that it is important to assess students' psychological functioning when making treatment recommendations and decisions, as many students using and abusing substances may be suffering from untreated psychological problems that could be directly or indirectly related to students' drug use.

CONCLUDING REMARKS

As college students experience a wide range of levels of substance use and use-related problems, there may not be a one-size-fits-all approach for treating drug use in this population. Unfortunately, little research has examined the utility of the various drug treatments available for college students, making recommendations regarding best practices necessarily tentative. The current literature is limited to combined alcohol and drug treatments for college students (Amaro et al., 2010; White et al., 2006; White et al., 2007) or BMIs for drugs among general samples of college-age young adults (Marsden et al., 2006; McCambridge & Strang, 2004, 2005; Sinha, Easton, & Kemp, 2003; Stein et al., 2011). Thus, future work is necessary to determine how college students will respond to BMIs designed to target drug use. Treatment approaches for college student drug use may need to be more than extensions of existing brief treatments for college alcohol use and different from drug use treatments for adults and noncollege populations. Future work could benefit from the development of interventions specifically geared toward the thoughts, feelings, and behaviors related to college student drug use. Notably, drug use severity and motivational levels may moderate treatment outcomes. There is also a lack of information regarding treatment outcomes for students mandated to drug treatment. In addition, given that short-term gains do not tend to persist, it is necessary to evaluate the efficacy of booster sessions to maintain decreases in college drug use.

Developing a more cohesive campus and community relationship has been vital to ameliorating problematic college drinking (Bergen-Cico, Urtz, & Baretto, 2004; Gebhardt, Kaphingst, & DeJong, 2000) and may prove useful in treating college drug use. Such cohesive approaches utilize traditional AOD prevention strategies (e.g., AOD education at first-year student orientation, social norms marketing) coupled with strategies to extend regulation of college student AOD use off campus. Such strategies may include posting notices near student housing detailing the consequences of an AOD policy violation (e.g., loss of student aid) and working cooperatively with off-campus landlords, encouraging them to abide by AOD-use laws (i.e., reporting suspected or known college drug use). Further, campus and community police can work together to send a strong AOD law enforcement message. For example, community police can patrol off-campus college student housing, monitor illegal AOD use activity, and strictly enforce AOD use laws among students. Further, community police can report to campus officials about students caught engaging in illegal AOD use so that the university can be involved in follow-up care and/or disciplinary action (Gebhardt et al., 2000). Further, we know of no universal drug treatment guidelines for college students. Development of such guidelines may help campus officials determine appropriate drug treatment options for college students.

Unfortunately, the most commonly used methods of preventing drug use on college campus (i.e., drug education, DC) may not be the most effective. Although BMIs, CBT, MET + CBT, and CM for drug use have demonstrated utility in other populations, the few studies conducted with college students or college-aged peers suggest they may produce short-term (but not long-term) reductions in college drug use. The lack of empirically supported treatments for college students leaves students vulnerable to continued drug-related harm while enrolled in school, which may threaten their physical health and their ability to remain in school and fully benefit from their academic experience. Thus, based on the current literature, the choice treatment for college student drug use remains undetermined. However, the provision of in-person PNF and/or health feedback on the risks of drugs appears to have some effect on reducing drug use, especially among those students motivated to reduce use (although these findings may not generalize to tobacco use).

There are many avenues for future work in this area. For instance, it has been suggested that college drug treatments may be particularly beneficial if integrated within the college curriculum (Krohn & Goetz, 2005), although some universities may have reservations about issuing credit for such purposes. For tobacco use, these programs should include both pharmacological [e.g., Zyban, Chantix; nicotine replacement therapies (NTRs)] in combination with behavioral counseling to yield the highest success rates (Fiore et al., 2008). One such program that has been proposed offers tobacco-smoking cessation as a 2-credit course, in an effort to enhance motivation to participate among students interested in quitting smoking. The program protocol includes education regarding the adverse health effects of smoking and pharmacological cessation aids available, skills training in problem-solving and stress relief, and social support mentoring for outside of the classroom (the Goetz Plan; Krohn & Goetz, 2005). Research testing these exciting programs will be an important step in this line of work.

Additionally, future research could test whether longer or "less brief" BMIs are necessary to produce meaningful reductions in drug use among college students, given that the standard BMI framework was not related to clinically meaningful long-term reductions in student drug use. Additional work could also benefit from examining ways to engage parents in student drug treatment given data suggesting parental involvement may improve outcomes (Grossbard et al., 2010). Future work may also benefit from testing the utility of personalized drug treatments that are tailored to the individual needs and concerns of the student. For instance, it may be that students low in problem recognition may benefit from several sessions of MI to explore and resolve ambivalence about behavioral change whereas students high in internal motivation to change drug use may benefit from fewer sessions of MI combined with CBT to teach them skills to help them achieve and maintain their treatment goals. Research is also necessary to determine the best ways to incorporate CM into drug treatment given that it is capable of producing initial periods of smoking abstinence (Correia & Benson, 2006; Irons & Correia, 2008). Future work could also examine whether establishing cohesive treatment planning with campus officials, campus mental health providers, and preselected community treatment referrals proves useful to targeting drug use on campus.

REFERENCES

Amaro, H., Reed, E., Rowe, E., Picci, J., Mantella, P., & Prado, G. (2010). Brief screening and intervention for alcohol and drug use in a college student health clinic: Feasibility, implementation, and outcomes. *Journal of American College Health, 58*, 357–364. doi: 10.1080/07448480903501764

An, L. C., Klatt, C., Perry, C. L., Lein, E. B., Hennrikus, D. J., Pallonen, U. E.,... Ehlinger, E. P. (2008). The RealU online cessation intervention for college smokers: A randomized controlled trial. *Preventive Medicine, 47*, 194–199. doi: 10.1016/j.ypmed.2008.04.011

Anderson, D. S., & Galadeto, A. F. (2006). Results of the 2006 college alcohol survey: Comparison with 2003 results, 1994 results and baseline year. Fairfax, VA: Center for the Advancement of Public Health, George Mason University.

Barnett, N. P., & Read, J. P. (2005). Mandatory alcohol intervention for alcohol-abusing college students: A systematic review. *Journal of Substance Abuse Treatment, 29*, 147–158. doi: 10.1016/j.jsat.2005.05.007

Bergen-Cico, D., Urtz, A., & Baretto, C. (2004). Longitudinal assessment of the effectiveness of environmental management and enforcement strategies on college student substance abuse behaviors. *NASPA Journal, 41*, 235–262.

Buckner, J. D., Bonn-Miller, M. O., Zvolensky, M. J., & Schmidt, N. B. (2007). Marijuana use motives and social anxiety among marijuana-using young adults. *Addictive Behaviors, 32*, 2238–2252. doi: 10.1016/j.addbeh.2007.04.004

Buckner, J. D., Ecker, A. H., & Cohen, A. S. (2010). Mental health problems and interest in marijuana treatment among marijuana-using college students. *Addictive Behaviors, 35*, 826–833. doi: 10.1016/j.addbeh.2010.04.001

Buckner, J. D., Keough, M. E., & Schmidt, N. B. (2007). Problematic alcohol and cannabis use among young adults: The roles of depression and discomfort and distress tolerance. *Addictive Behaviors, 32*, 1957–1963. doi: 10.1016/j.addbeh.2006.12.019

Buckner, J. D., Mallott, M. A., Schmidt, N. B., & Taylor, J. (2006). Peer influence and gender differences in problematic cannabis use among individuals with social anxiety. *Journal of Anxiety Disorders, 20*, 1087–1102. doi: 10.1016/j.janxdis.2006.03.002

Buckner, J. D., & Schmidt, N. B. (2008). Marijuana effect expectancies: Relations to social anxiety and marijuana use problems. *Addictive Behaviors, 33,* 1477–1483. doi: 10.1016/j.addbeh.2008.06.017

Buckner, J. D., & Schmidt, N. B. (2009). Social anxiety disorder and marijuana use problems: The mediating role of marijuana effect expectancies. *Depression and Anxiety, 26,* 864–870. doi: 10.1002/da.20567

Budney, A. J., Moore, B. A., Sigmon, S. C., & Higgins, S. T. (2006). Contingency management interventions for cannabis dependence. In R. A. Roffman & R. S. Stephens (Eds.), *Cannabis dependence: Its nature, consequences, and treatment* (pp. 155–179). Cambridge, United Kingdom: Cambridge University Press.

Caldeira, K. M., Kasperski, S. J., Sharma, E., Vincent, K. B., O'Grady, K. E., Wish, E. D., & Arria, A. M. (2009). College students rarely seek help despite serious substance use problems. *Journal of Substance Abuse Treatment, 37,* 368–378. doi: 10.1016/j.jsat.2009.04.005

Carroll, K. M., Easton, C. J., Nich, C., Hunkele, K. A., Neavins, T. M., Sinha, R.,... Rounsaville, B. J. (2006). The use of contingency management and motivational/skills-building therapy to treat young adults with marijuana dependence. *Journal of Consulting and Clinical Psychology, 74,* 955–966. doi: 10.1037/0022–006x.74.5.955

Correia, C. J., & Benson, T. A. (2006). The use of contingency management to reduce cigarette smoking among college students. *Experimental and Clinical Psychopharmacology, 14,* 171–179. doi: 10.1037/1064–1297.14.2.171

Crits-Christoph, P., Siqueland, L., Blaine, J., Frank, A., Luborsky, L., Onken, L. S.,... Beck, A. T. (1999). Psychosocial treatments for cocaine dependence: National institute on drug abuse collaborative cocaine treatment study. *Archives of General Psychiatry, 56,* 493–502. doi: 10.1001/archpsyc.56.6.493

Dimeff, L. A., Baer, J. S., Kivlahan, D., & Marlatt, G. A. (1999). *Brief alcohol screening and intervention for college students (BASICS): A harm reduction approach.* New York, NY: Guilford Press.

Fiore, M., Jaen, C. R., Baker, T. B., Bailey, W. C., Bennett, G., & Benowitz, N. L. (2008). A clinical practice guideline for treating tobacco use and dependence: 2008 update: A U.S. public health service report. *American Journal of Preventive Medicine, 35,* 158–176. doi: 10.1016/j.amepre.2008.04.009

Freeman, M. S. (2001). Innovative alcohol education program for college and university judicial sanctions. *Journal of College Counseling, 4,* 179.

Gebhardt, T. L., Kaphingst, K., & DeJong, W. (2000). A campus-community coalition to control alcohol-related problems off campus: An environmental management case study. *Journal of American College Health, 48,* 211. doi: 10.1080/07448480009599306

Grossbard, J. R., Mastroleo, N. R., Kilmer, J. R., Lee, C. M., Turrisi, R., Larimer, M. E., & Ray, A. (2010). Substance use patterns among first-year college students: Secondary effects of a combined alcohol intervention. *Journal of Substance Abuse Treatment, 39,* 384–390. doi: 10.1016/j.jsat.2010.07.001

Harris-Wilkes, K. (2010). College campuses becoming active site for array of recovery support services. *Alcoholism & Drug Abuse Weekly, 22,* 1–7.

Higgins, S. T., Budney, A. J., Bickel, W. K., & Foerg, F. E. (1994). Incentives improve outcome in outpatient behavioral treatment of cocaine dependence. *Archives of General Psychiatry, 51,* 568–576. doi: 10.1001/archpsyc.1994.03950070060011

Hustad, J. T. P., Barnett, N. P., Borsari, B., & Jackson, K. M. (2010). Web-based alcohol prevention for incoming college students: A randomized controlled trial. *Addictive Behaviors, 35,* 183–189. doi: 10.1016/j.addbeh.2009.10.012

Hutton, H. E., Wilson, L. M., Apelberg, B. J., Avila Tang, E., Odelola, O., Bass, E. B., & Chander, G. (2011). A systematic review of randomized controlled trials: Web-based interventions for smoking cessation among adolescents, college students, and adults. *Nicotine & Tobacco Research, 13,* 227–238. doi: 10.1093/ntr/ntq252

Irons, J. G., & Correia, C. J. (2008). A brief abstinence test for college student smokers: A feasibility study. *Experimental and Clinical Psychopharmacology, 16,* 223–229. doi: 10.1037/1064–1297.16.3.223

Johnston, L. D., O'Malley, P. M., Bachman, J. G., & Schulenberg, J. E. (2010). *Monitoring the future national survey results on drug use 1975–2009. Volume II: College students and adults ages 19–50.* (NIH Publication No. 10-7585). Bethesda, MD.

Juhnke, G. A., Huffman, S. B., Nilsen, K. B., Adams, J. R., Dew, B. J., Jordan, J. P., . . . Schroat, D. A. (2002). Establishing an alcohol and other drug assessment and intervention program within an on-site counselor education research and training clinic. *Journal of Addictions & Offender Counseling, 22*, 83.

Keller, D. S., Bennett, M. E., McCrady, B. S., & Paulus, M. D. (1994). Treating college substance abusers: The New Jersey collegiate substance abuse program. *Journal of Substance Abuse Treatment, 11*, 569–581. doi: 10.1016/0740-5472(94)90009-4

Krohn, F. B., & Goetz, K. M. (2005). The Goetz plan: A practical smoking cessation program for college students. *College Student Journal, 39*, 260–268.

Larimer, M. E., & Cronce, J. M. (2007). Identification, prevention, and treatment revisited: Individual-focused college drinking prevention strategies 1999–2006. *Addictive Behaviors, 32*, 2439–2468. doi: 10.1016/j.addbeh.2007.05.006

Lee, C. M., Neighbors, C., Kilmer, J. R., & Larimer, M. E. (2010). A brief, Web-based personalized feedback selective intervention for college student marijuana use: A randomized clinical trial. *Psychology of Addictive Behaviors, 24*, 265–273. doi: 10.1037/a0018859

Licciardone, J. C. (2003). Outcomes of a federally funded program for alcohol and other drug prevention in higher education. *American Journal of Drug and Alcohol Abuse, 29*, 803–827. doi: 10.1081/ADA-120026262

Magill, M., Barnett, N. P., Apodaca, T. R., Rohsenow, D. J., & Monti, P. M. (2009). The role of marijuana use in brief motivational intervention with young adult drinkers treated in an emergency department. *Journal of Studies on Alcohol and Drugs, 70*, 409–413.

Magill, M., & Ray, L. A. (2009). Cognitive-behavioral treatment with adult alcohol and illicit drug users: A meta-analysis of randomized controlled trials. *Journal of Studies on Alcohol and Drugs, 70*, 516–527.

Marijuana Treatment Project Research Group. (2004). Brief treatments for cannabis dependence: Findings from a randomized multisite trial. *Journal of Consulting and Clinical Psychology, 72*, 455–466. doi: 10.1037/0022-006X.72.3.455

Marsden, J., Stillwell, G., Barlow, H., Boys, A., Taylor, C., Hunt, N., & Farrell, M. (2006). An evaluation of a brief motivational intervention among young ecstasy and cocaine users: No effect on substance and alcohol use outcomes. *Addiction, 101*, 1014–1026. doi: 10.1111/j.1360-0443.2006.01290.x

Martin, G., & Copeland, J. (2008). The adolescent cannabis check-up: Randomized trial of a brief intervention for young cannabis users. *Journal of Substance Abuse Treatment, 34*, 407–414. doi: 10.1016/j.jsat.2007.07.004

Mason, M. J., & Luckey, B. (2003). Young adults in alcohol-other drug treatment: An understudied population. *Alcoholism Treatment Quarterly, 21*, 17–32.

McCambridge, J., & Strang, J. (2004). The efficacy of single-session motivational interviewing in reducing drug consumption and perceptions of drug-related risk and harm among young people: Results from a multi-site cluster randomized trial. *Addiction, 99*, 39–52. doi: 10.1111/j.1360-0443.2004.00564.x

McCambridge, J., & Strang, J. (2005). Deterioration over time in effect of motivational interviewing in reducing drug consumption and related risk among young people. *Addiction, 100*, 470–478. doi: 10.1111/j.1360-0443.2005.01013.x

McKee, S. A., Carroll, K. M., Sinha, R., Robinson, J. E., Nich, C., Cavallo, D., & O'Malley, S. (2007). Enhancing brief cognitive-behavioral therapy with motivational enhancement techniques in cocaine users. *Drug and Alcohol Dependence, 91*, 97–101. doi: 10.1016/j.drugalcdep.2007.05.006

Mercer, D., & Woody, G. (1999). *Individual drug counseling.* Retrieved from http://archives.drugabuse.gov/PDF/Manual3.pdf

Miller, W. R., Benefield, R., & Tonigan, J. (1993). Enhancing motivation for change in problem drinking: A controlled comparison of two therapist styles. *Journal of Consulting and Clinical Psychology, 61*, 455–461. doi: 10.1037/0022-006X.61.3.455

Miller, W. R., & Rollnick, S. (2002). *Motivational interviewing: Preparing people for change* (2nd ed.). New York, NY: Guilford Press.

Miller, W. R., Zweben, A., DiClemente, C. C., & Rychtarik, R. G. (Eds.). (1992). *Motivational enhancement therapy manual: A clinical research guide for therapists treating individuals with alcohol abuse and dependence.* Department of Health and Human Services Publication No. ADM92-1894. Washington, DC: U.S. Government Printing Office.

Neighbors, C. J., Barnett, N. P., Rohsenow, D. J., Colby, S. M., & Monti, P. M. (2010). Cost-effectiveness of a motivational intervention for alcohol-involved youth in a hospital emergency department. *Journal of Studies on Alcohol and Drugs, 71*, 384–394.

Owen, J., Devdas, L., & Rodolfa, E. (2007). University counseling center off-campus referrals: An exploratory investigation. *Journal of College Student Psychotherapy, 22*, 13–29. doi: 10.1300/J035v22n02–03

Petry, N. M. (2010). Contingency management treatments: Controversies and challenges. *Addiction, 105*, 1507–1509. doi: 10.1111/j.1360–0443.2009.02879.x

Petry, N. M., Martin, B., Cooney, J. L., & Kranzler, H. R. (2000). Give them prizes and they will come: Contingency management for treatment of alcohol dependence. *Journal of Consulting and Clinical Psychology, 68*, 250–257. doi: 10.1037/0022–006x.68.2.250

Prokhorov, A. V., Fouladi, R. T., De Moor, C., Warneke, C. L., Luca, M., Jones, M. M.,... Gritz, E. R. (2007). Computer-assisted, counselor-delivered smoking cessation counseling for community college students: Intervention approach and sample characteristics. *Journal of Child & Adolescent Substance Abuse, 16*, 35–62.

Prokhorov, A. V., Yost, T., Mullin-Jones, M., de Moor, C., Ford, K. H., Marani, S.,... Emmons, K. M. (2008). Look at your health: Outcomes associated with a computer-assisted smoking cessation counseling intervention for community college students. *Addictive Behaviors, 33*, 757–771.

Rigotti, N. A., Lee, J. E., & Wechsler, H. (2000). US college students' use of tobacco products. *JAMA: The Journal of the American Medical Association, 284*, 699–705. doi: 10.1001/jama.284.6.699

Sias, S. M., & Goodwin, L. R. (2007). Students' reactions to attending 12-step meetings: Implications for counselor education. *Journal of Addictions & Offender Counseling, 27*, 113–156.

Sinha, R., Easton, C., & Kemp, K. (2003). Substance abuse treatment characteristics of probation-referred young adults in a community-based outpatient program. *American Journal of Drug & Alcohol Abuse, 29*, 585–597. doi: 10.1081/ada-120023460

Sinha, R., Easton, C., Renee-Aubin, L., & Carroll, K. M. (2003). Engaging young probation-referred marijuana-abusing individuals in treatment: A pilot trial. *American Journal on Addictions, 12*, 314–323. doi: 10.1080/10550490390226905

Stein, M. D., Hagerty, C. E., Herman, D. S., Phipps, M. G., & Anderson, B. J. (2011). A brief marijuana intervention for non-treatment-seeking young adult women. *Journal of Substance Abuse Treatment, 40*, 189–198. doi: 10.1016/j.jsat.2010.11.001

Stephens, R. S., Roffman, R. A., Fearer, S. A., Williams, C., & Burke, R. S. (2007). The marijuana check-up: Promoting change in ambivalent marijuana users. *Addiction, 102*, 947–957. doi: 10.1111/j.1360–0443.2007.01821.x

Stitzer, M., & Petry, N. (2006). Contingency management for treatment of substance abuse. *Annual Review of Clinical Psychology, 2*, 411–434. doi: 10.1146/annurev.clinpsy.2.022305.095219

Stone, G. L., & Vespia, K. M. (2000). How good is mental health care on college campuses? *Journal of Counseling Psychology, 47*, 498–510. doi: 10.1037/0022–0167.47.4.498

Terlecki, M. A., Buckner, J. D., Larimer, M. E., & Copeland, A. L. (2011). The role of social anxiety in a brief alcohol intervention for heavy-drinking college students. *Journal of Cognitive Psychotherapy, 25*, 7–21. doi: 10.1891/0889–8391.25.1.7

Tevyaw, T. O. L., Colby, S. M., Tidey, J. W., Kahler, C. W., Rohsenow, D. J., Barnett, N. P.,... .Monti, P. M. (2009). Contingency management and motivational enhancement: A randomized clinical trial for college student smokers. *Nicotine & Tobacco Research, 11*, 739–749. doi: 10.1093/ntr/ntp058

USDHHS. (2002). *A call to action: Changing the culture of drinking at U.S. colleges. Task force of the National Advisory Council on Alcohol Abuse and Alcoholism, National Institute on Alcohol Abuse and Alcoholism, National Institutes of Health.* (NIH Publication No. 02–5010). Bethesda, MD: NIH.

Walker, D. D., Roffman, R. A., Stephens, R. S., Wakana, K., & Berghuis, J. (2006). Motivational enhancement therapy for adolescent marijuana users: A preliminary randomized controlled trial. *Journal of Consulting and Clinical Psychology, 74*, 628–632. doi: 10.1037/0022–006X.74.3.628

Walters, S. T., & Bennett, M. E. (2000). Addressing drinking among college students: A review of the empirical literature. *Alcoholism Treatment Quarterly, 18*, 61–77. doi: 10.1300/J020v18n01_04

Walters, S. T., Bennett, M. E., & Noto, J. V. (2000). Drinking on campus: What do we know about reducing alcohol use among college students? *Journal of Substance Abuse Treatment, 19*, 223–228. doi: 10.1016/s0740–5472(00)00101-x

Walters, S. T., Hester, R. K., Chiauzzi, E., & Miller, E. (2005). Demon rum: High-tech solutions to an age-old problem. *Alcoholism: Clinical and Experimental Research, 29,* 270–277. doi: 10.1097/01. alc.0000153543.03339.81

Walters, S. T., Vader, A. M., Harris, R. T., Field, C. A., & Jouriles, E. N. (2009). Dismantling motivational intervewing and feedback for college drinkers: A randomized controlled trial. *Journal of Consulting and Clinical Psychology, 77,* 64–73. doi: 10.1037/a0014472

West, S. L., & Graham, C. W. (2005). A survey of substance abuse prevention efforts at Virginia's colleges and universities. *Journal of American College Health, 54,* 185–191. doi: 10.3200/JACH.54.3.185–192

White, H. R., Morgan, T. J., Pugh, L. A., Celinska, K., Labouvie, E. W., & Pandina, R. J. (2006). Evaluating two brief substance-use interventions for mandated college students. *Journal of Studies on Alcohol, 67,* 309–317.

White, H. R., Mun, E. Y., Pugh, L., & Morgan, T. J. (2007). Long-term effects of brief substance use interventions for mandated college students: Sleeper effects of an in-person personal feedback intervention. *Alcoholism: Clinical & Experimental Research, 31,* 1380–1391. doi: 10.1111/j.1530–0277.2007.00435.x

13

The Role of Training and Supervision in Delivering Empirically Supported Treatments for College Student Drinkers

Nadine R. Mastroleo and Erica Eaton Short

The roles that training and supervision play in the implementation and dissemination of effective prevention and intervention efforts to reduce alcohol use and associated consequences is critical to meeting the goals of researchers, practitioners, and university administrators. As hazardous drinking among college students remains a significant health concern (Dimeff, Baer, Kivlahan, & Marlatt, 1999; Hingson, Zha, & Weitzman, 2009; O'Malley & Johnston, 2002; Turrisi, Mallett, Mastroleo, & Larimer, 2006), a range of intervention approaches have been tested to reduce heavy drinking and associated harm in college students (for reviews, see Larimer & Cronce, 2002, 2007). Despite the evidence base and the increase in the numbers and types of educational interventions for college students, detailed descriptions of the training and supervision of treatment providers is often excluded from manualized treatments and resources (see Dimeff et al., 1999, for example). This is true for both group- and individually based interventions, each of which have shown efficacy in reducing alcohol use and associated harm with high-risk college students (see Larimer & Cronce, 2002, 2007). Manuals have included the necessary components for implementing the intervention, yet guidelines on ways in which to train and offer continued supervision to practitioners is lacking. The goal of this chapter is to offer guidelines, based on best practices, on ways in which training and supervision can be implemented to ensure fidelity to intervention protocol. Using information from procedures identified in efficacy trials and considering available university resources, this chapter describes: (1) the training methods often used for brief alcohol interventions, (2) the range of professionals who may deliver brief alcohol interventions, (3) how intervention training may differ based upon the targeted student population, and (4) specific training and supervision techniques that are designed to maximize treatment fidelity (i.e., the accuracy with which the intervention is implemented).

INTERVENTION APPROACHES WITH COLLEGE STUDENT DRINKERS

Universities have a variety of empirically supported intervention options from which to choose (see Carey, this volume). A number of institutions use individual- or group counseling approaches to intervene with high-risk students (e.g., first-year students, mandated students). Both one-on-one and group interventions often include a meeting with a treatment provider who may be a professional counselor, health services or student affairs staff member, or undergraduate peer counselor. The range of experiences and training of the treatment provider vary, and no empirical research to date has examined the relationship between counselor characteristics and successful intervention skill acquisition. Most professional counselors and student affairs staff members hold, at minimum, a master's degree (e.g., Counseling, Educational Leadership, Higher Education, Psychology, Public Health). Undergraduate peer counselors are typically fellow students with an interest in health education, psychology, or counseling, but without formal training in counseling or health education. Yet, each group has been successful in intervening and reducing drinking with college students (e.g., Barnett, Murphy, Colby, & Monti, 2007; Borsari & Carey, 2005; Carey, Henson, Carey & Maisto, 2009; Marlatt et al., 1998; Mastroleo, Turrisi, Carney, Ray, & Larimer, 2010; White, Mun, Pugh, & Morgan, 2007). Regardless of the treatment provider's background, a general knowledge of alcohol and its effects on the body, ways to reduce harm associated with alcohol use, specific laws and rules surrounding alcohol use on campus and in the surrounding community, and good interpersonal and communication skills may contribute to successful intervention outcomes. The skills for conducting group interventions also require the treatment provider to manage group dynamics, including dominant group member personalities. Although there is no identified formula that guarantees a successful intervention approach, having a background in working with college students and some general alcohol content and counseling skills combined with effective training and supervision should support the success of intervention approaches.

Professional- and peer-led group and individual approaches have been tested in an effort to reduce alcohol use and associated negative consequences in college students. The majority of these interventions have incorporated Motivational Interviewing (MI; W. R. Miller & Rollnick, 2002) strategies to enhance college students' readiness to change and support shifts to less harmful drinking behaviors.

Mandated and voluntary students who have received professionally led, one-on-one individual brief motivational interventions (BMI) have consistently shown lower alcohol consumption and alcohol-related problems relative to no-treatment or attention-control conditions (e.g., Borsari & Carey, 2005; Carey et al., 2009; Marlatt et al., 1998; White et al., 2007). However, group interventions have resulted in mixed findings related to drinking and alcohol-related consequences (Fromme & Corbin, 2004; LaBrie, Lamb, Pedersen, & Quinlan 2006; LaChance, Feldstein Ewing, Bryan, & Hutchinson, 2009; Palmer, 2004). One group-based model that has been associated with reduced weekly drinking and estimated peak BAC is the Alcohol Skills Training Program (ASTP; Baer et al., 1992; Kivlahan, Marlatt, Fromme, Coppel, & Williams, 1990). Of note is that in a number of the research trials examining professionally led interventions, many of the treatment providers were graduate students in clinical psychology or a closely related field, often with only a few years of clinical training. Although these are typically highly competitive graduate programs that select students who are bright and possess strong interpersonal skills, this supports the notion that these approaches can be successfully implemented with counselors with limited (i.e., 1 to 2 years) formal clinical training/experience.

Individual peer-led interventions have also been tested, mostly targeting voluntary college students. This cost-effective approach has the potential to increase dissemination, is commonly used for health promotion on college campuses, and has generally been regarded as an effective strategy (D'Andrea & Salovey, 1998; Ender & Winston, 1984; Hatcher, 1995). Research on alcohol interventions indicates trained peer counselors (college undergraduates) may be equal or more effective than professional providers in implementing these interventions (Larimer et al., 2001; Larimer & Cronce, 2002). Fromme and Corbin (2004) and Bergen-Cico (2000) note that college students relate better to peers than to older adults, that peer-delivered programs have a stronger influence on students' attitudes and behavior, and that using upperclass students (juniors or seniors) to deliver substance abuse programs may be effective for first-year students. However, prior to 1998 (with the exception of Klepp, Halper, & Perry's 1986 study), the use of peers to provide individual skills-based or motivational enhancement interventions for alcohol reduction had not been thoroughly evaluated (Klepp, Halper, & Perry, 1986; Larimer et al., 2001; Larimer & Cronce, 2002, 2007; Mastroleo et al., 2010; E. T. Miller & Marlatt, 1998; Turrisi et al., 2009).

Peer-led brief alcohol interventions. Larimer and colleagues (2001) used peer providers to deliver the Brief Alcohol Screening and Intervention for College Students (BASICS; Dimeff et al., 1999) in individual sessions to first-year members of Greek social organizations, and compared them to a professionall led BASICS and an assessment-only control condition. Fraternity members in the treatment groups showed reductions in drinks per week (15.5 to 12) and peak blood alcohol concentration (pBAC) (.12% to .08%), while the control group showed an increase in drinks per week (14.5 to 17) and no change in pBAC over time. Further, fraternity members who received a BASICS session from a peer provider showed significantly larger decreases in typical pBAC than those who had professional providers. In sum, peer providers were as, or more, effective than professional providers in reducing drinking behaviors in this first comparison study of peers to professionals in an alcohol intervention (Larimer et al., 2001). Fromme and Corbin (2004) used a similar design to evaluate peer versus professional providers of a skills-based group intervention and found no differences in responsiveness to peers versus professional interventionists. Finally, in two separate randomized controlled trials, Mastroleo et al. (2010) and Turrisi et al. (2009) found reductions in drinking behaviors when using peer counselors as BASICS interventionists with samples of first-semester students during their transition to college. Taken together, these findings suggest that peer providers are acceptable and potentially preferable for implementing brief interventions with college student drinkers.

Given the success of the above identified approaches, the dissemination of BASICS and group-based intervention programs has reached a large number of university campuses. However, in practice, training and supervision practices commonly found in research settings are not typically transferred to college settings, and an important next step is to develop and disseminate protocols for training counselors.

APPROACHES TO COUNSELOR TRAINING AND SUPERVISION

The methods utilized in the training and supervision of counselors varies widely. Of particular note is the discrepancy between empirically validated training and supervision protocol and the reality of common practice approaches.

Evidence-Based Application Approach

In each of the past research studies examining the efficacy of peer- and professionally led brief interventions, specific implementation approaches were followed to ensure intervention fidelity (evidence-based application approach, EAA; as identified in Mastroleo et al., 2010). For example, Larimer et al. (2001) examined a professional versus peer-led BASICS (Dimeff et al., 1999) intervention with high-risk (Greek social organization members) college students and described the intervention training as 8 to 12 hours of didactic training over 2 days incorporating alcohol information, accurate normative information, drinking reduction techniques, and MI principles. Initial training was followed with one or two supervised interviews. Before beginning the study, all counselors met competency requirements for intervention fidelity, and ongoing, group supervision was provided throughout the trial. Interventions conducted by counselors trained using this EAA resulted in reduced drinking outcomes with heavy drinking, high-risk college students (e.g., Larimer et al., 2001). Similar methods were used in Turrisi et al. (2009) where all peer counselors met MI threshold competency levels according to the MITI 2.0 (Moyers, Martin, Manuel, Hendrickson, & Miller, 2005; minimal scores of 5 for MI Spirit and Empathy) prior to BASICS implementation.

Other studies have implemented an adapted BASICS session using professional level counselors as intervention agents (e.g., Barnett et al., 2007; Borsari & Carey, 2005; Borsari et al., under review; Carey et al., 2009; Martens et al., 2007; Wood, Capone, Laforge, Erickson, & Brand, 2007). Studies consistently included master's and doctoral level counselors and advanced clinical psychology graduate students who were specifically trained in MI, alcohol content information, and intervention protocol. Following initial trainings, counselors conducted, on average, two role plays in which individual feedback from clinical supervisors was offered in order to enhance MI and intervention skill demonstration. These training procedures match identified methods for training and improving MI skills for substance use counseling (e.g., W. R. Miller, Yahne, Moyers, Martinez, & Pirritano, 2004) and have resulted in consistently high-fidelity score ratings of counselor implementation. For example, Barnett et al. (2007) reported a mean score of 2.04 out of 3 (representing meeting expectations of intervention component delivery) while also identifying a mean MITI 2.0 score (Moyers et al., 2005) greater than 6 for MI Spirit and Empathy (on a 7-point scale). Borsari and colleagues (2011) found similar results with average counselor MISC (Motivational Interviewing Skills Code; W. R. Miller et al., 2003) scores over 5 (where 5 represents threshold competency). Although empirical research studies have identified successful training approaches, the time demands, limited financial resources, and structure needed to reproduce these procedures is potentially difficult for universities to implement identical procedures.

Common Practice Approaches

A national survey conducted by Mastroleo and colleagues (2008) examined the training and supervision approaches used to implement individual peer-based alcohol intervention approaches in a naturalistic setting. Although some research studies have identified initial training time ranging from 12 to 40 hours (e.g., Barnett et al., 2007; Larimer et al., 2001; Turrisi et al., 2009), in practice the model training time for peer counselors was 10 hours with one third of programs conducting trainings over one weekend. Just over one half of the programs surveyed (56.8%) reported using some form of supervision and of these, the majority used peer counselor self-reports (rather than audio or videotaping). Only 41% used weekly and 11% used monthly or semester/quarterly meetings to explore peer counselor concerns and examine delivery progress. Further, less than 30% of university peer-based alcohol intervention programs evaluated counselor competency prior to, or during, the intervention. Of the programs implementing counselor competency evaluations, 92% used subjective evaluation procedures such as counselor self-report (Mastroleo, Mallett, Ray, & Turrisi, 2008). It seems that in practice, manualized interventions are being incorporated into college alcohol prevention efforts, yet training and supervision varies widely and competency evaluation of peer counselors is not consistent with what has been proven effective in research studies.

Counselor Skills Impact on Drinking Behaviors

In working with college students, clinicians' goals revolve around increasing contemplation and intrinsic motivation to change drinking and/or to implement harm-reduction practices intended to reduce future alcohol-related problems. This method is done by using open-ended questions, reflections, summaries, and expression of empathy as major therapeutic components (W. R. Miller & Rollnick, 2002). Counselor skills and interactions with clients are one of many intervention components, which are thought to impact treatment response. For example, when sessions are conducted in a manner that is confrontational, results have found *clients drink more* (W. R. Miller et al., 1993). Recent studies with professional counselors found that MI-Consistent (MICO; e.g., complex reflections, affirm, emphasize control) behaviors are associated with fewer drinks per week (Moyers, Martin, Houck, Christopher, & Tonigan, 2009). However, when counselors used more MI-Inconsistent behaviors (MIIN; e.g., direct, confront, warn), it resulted in worse drinking outcomes (Karno & Longabaugh, 2004, 2005; W. R. Miller & Downs, 1993).

In a study examining the use of MI skills on drinking outcomes, Tollison, Lee et al. (2008) examined relationships between MI microskill behavior counts (open/closed ended question, simple/complex reflections) (see Table 13.1 for microskill definitions), readiness to change drinking behaviors, and postintervention drinking behaviors with supervised peer counselors implementing a BASICS intervention. Results indicated a higher rate of closed questions from peer counselors was associated with less contemplation to change drinking behaviors in participants postintervention. Also, use of a greater number of simple reflections was associated with increased drinking at three months, but when simple reflections were balanced by complex reflections, the effect on drinking was attenuated. A replication found similar results (Tollison, Mastroleo et al., 2008). In sum, when examining peer-delivered BMIs with voluntary, high-risk college students, the use of higher-level MI skills (e.g., complex reflections) predicted better drinking outcomes (Tollison, Lee et al., 2008). Taken together, these studies highlight the importance of competent delivery of MI skills and the potential importance of training and supervision of counselors to appropriately deliver MI skills during BMIs to impact client drinking reductions.

Table 13.1 MI Microskills Definitions

	Definition
Questions	
Open	Used to encourage conversation through opportunities for clients to explain and expand on thoughts, feelings, experiences related to a topic. Used to encourage client to talk without feeling defensive. Questions may start with the following stems: *How, Tell me more, What, In what way.*
Closed	Question can be answered with yes/no or one word phrase answers. Caution in using this form of question; limits the client in expressing thoughts, feelings. Does not often encourage conversation. However, can be used effectively to help move session along, gain clarification on a specific area, or gain permission for moving forward with session. Questions may start with the following stems: *Where, Are you, Do you want to, Is this.*
Simple reflections	
Repeat	Simply repeating the speaker's words, adding little or no meaning to what the client said (e.g., Client: *"Drinking makes it so much easier for me to talk to new people"*; Counselor: *"So when you drink you find it easier to talk to new people."*)
Rephrase	Repeats speaker's words but replaces/substitutes some words with synonyms (e.g., Client: *"Drinking makes it so much easier for me to talk to new people"*; Counselor: *"Drinking makes you more comfortable when you meet and talk to new people."*)
Complex reflections	
Paraphrase	Reflects what is said but also infers meaning, hypothesis testing-amplifying change talk (e.g., Client: *"Drinking makes it so much easier for me to talk to new people"*; Counselor: *"You're more social and less nervous around new people when you drink."*)
Double-sided reflections	A type of paraphrasing but reflects both sides of ambivalence described by the speaker (e.g., Series of Client Statements: *"I really like to drink when I am with my friends"*; *"Drinking makes it so much easier for me to talk to new people"*; *"I wake up really sluggish and tired after a night of drinking"*; *"Waking up with a hangover really ruins the rest of my day."* Counselor: *"On the one hand, drinking with your friends seems to make it easier to talk to new people; and on the other hand, after a night of drinking you wake up tired and hung over, which is something you don't like feeling."*)
Metaphor	A figure of speech in which a word or phrase literally denoting one kind of object or idea is used in place of another to suggest a likeness or analogy between them (e.g., Client: *"I really want to go out and be with my friends but all they ever do is drink and I don't want to be around that."* Counselor: *"You're really stuck between a rock and a hard place."*)

Table 13.1   *(continued)*

	Definition
Reflection of feeling	Emphasizes the emotional component of what is said—takes into account body language and inflection/tone in voice of client while making statements (e.g., Client: *"When drunk students come home from a night out, I am constantly being woken up by their noise!"* [Client makes statement with arms folded and in a sharp, cutting tone] Counselor: *"You're angry with the students who come home and disturb your sleep."*)
Summary	Pulls together information from speaker statements; captures the highlights in a succinct statement (e.g., Series of Client statements during session: *"I really like to drink when I am with my friends"; "Drinking makes it so much easier for me to talk to new people"; "I wake up really sluggish and tired after a night of drinking"; "Waking up with a hangover really ruins the rest of my day"; "I know drinking causes me to be more lazy and not get as much done during my day"; "I have enjoyed the mornings when I wake up that I don't feel tired or hungover"; "I rarely get a good night's sleep on the weekends either because of my own or someone else's drinking."*
	Counselor: *"You've talked about some positive things related to drinking such as it being easier to talk to new people and having fun with your friends and you have also noted that on many occasions either your own drinking or someone else's causes you to not get as much sleep as you might like and sometimes ends up with you feeling hungover and tired."*)

Originally published in Mastroleo et al., 2009.

WHAT DOES COUNSELOR TRAINING LOOK LIKE?

As previously identified, training can be implemented in a variety of formats. The flexibility in format allows universities to adapt content and training to best meet the needs of their staff and resources. It is important to incorporate a training format, style, content, and time frame that most closely match the needs of individual counselors and programs (Keeling & Engstrom, 1993). A wide variety of protocols exist to train counselors to effectively implement program procedures (e.g., one-day trainings, weekend training, semester based trainings). Although no studies have systematically tested training model approaches, past research has identified that a one-time training protocol with no follow-up is not effective in teaching the skills essential to implement an intervention with fidelity (W. R. Miller et al., 2004). Despite the lack of research examining varying training methods and the ability to meet program objectives and desired client outcomes, organized training manuals have been developed to aid in administering intervention programs within a university structure (e.g., Dimeff et al., 1999; Hatcher, Walsh, Reynolds, & Sullivan, 1995b; E. T. Miller, Kilmer, Kim, Weingardt, & Marlatt, 2001). Regardless of how much time is spent in trainings, a number of essential training components are necessary to ensure treatment providers (professional or peer) are prepared to conduct drinking interventions with college students.

Didactic Training

Initial training (in which the background and essential components of the intervention model are described) is often didactic in nature. Common components of this aspect of training are the elements of MI (W. R. Miller & Rollnick, 2002), the stages of change model (Prochaska & DiClemente, 1982), and psychoeducation on intervention components (alcohol content and the way in which alcohol works in the body; see Table 13.2 for Alcohol Content Information).

Further, programs typically teach basic clinical techniques including listening and helping skills. The amount of time spent on each area varies, as do total hours in training and methods of teaching content. These trainings are typically conducted in small groups, prior to or at the start of the academic year, where interaction between the trainer and participants is strongly encouraged. In addition, video or audiotaped examples of the intervention may be used to more clearly demonstrate the way in which sessions are implemented. It is often helpful to show examples of the intervention, especially for new trainees, to more clearly synthesize the manner in which the didactic training links to the actual implementation of the intervention (e.g., Motivational Interviewing: Professional Training Series, 1998; APA Harm Reduction with High School Students, 2005; see Table 13.3). This is true for both individual and group based interventions.

Table 13.2 Alcohol Component and Content Area for Brief Interventions With College Students

Content/Component Area
Pros/cons of drinking
Drinking patterns
Heavy drinking
Blood alcohol levels
Biphasic effects of alcohol
Beliefs about peer alcohol use (e.g., normative feedback)
Beliefs about alcohol (expectancies)
Alcohol consequences
Role of alcohol and sex
Alcohol dependence
Alcohol tolerance
Family history of alcohol dependence
Dietary effects of alcohol use
Financial costs of alcohol consumption
Protective behaviors

For more information on content and training see Dimeff et al., 1999.

Table 13.3 Additional MI Intervention, Training, and Supervision Resources

Skill Area	Resource
Motivational interviewing skills	www.motivationalinterviewing.org/ www.motivationalinterview.org/clinicians/Side_bar/skills_maintenence.html
	Miller, W. R., & Rollnick, S. (2002). *Motivational interviewing: Preparing people to change addictive behavior* (2nd ed.). New York, NY: Guilford Press.
MI skill and delivery supervision	www.motivationalinterview.org/Documents/MIA-STEP.pdf
Intervention fidelity	Mastroleo, N. R., Mallett, K. A., Turrisi, R., & Ray, A. E. (2009). Psychometric properties of the peer proficiency assessment (PEPA): A tool for evaluation of undergraduate peer counselors' motivational interviewing fidelity. *Addictive Behaviors, 34,* 717–722.
	Miller, W. R., Moyers, T. B., Ernst, D., & Amrhein, P. (2003). *Manual for the motivational interviewing skills code (MISC)* Version 2.0. Retrieved from www.motivationalinterview.org/training/MISC2.pdf
	Moyers, T. B., Martin, T., Manuel, J. K., Hendrickson, S. M. L., & Miller, W. R. (2005). Assessing competence in the use of motivational interviewing. [Electronic; Print]. *Journal of Substance Abuse Treatment, 28*(1), 19–26.
	MITI manual: http://casaa.unm.edu/download/miti.pdf
Basic counseling skills resources	Guindon, M. H. (2011). *A counseling primer: An introduction to the profession.* New York, NY: Routledge.
	Ivey, A. E., & Ivey, M. B. (2008). *Essentials of intentional interviewing: Counseling in a multicultural world.* Belmont, CA: Thomson Brooks/Cole.
Alcohol component and content	Dimeff, L. A., Baer, J. S., Kivlahan, D. R., & Marlatt, G. A. (1999). *Brief alcohol screening and intervention for college students: A harm reduction approach.* New York, NY: Guilford Press. www.collegedrinkingprevention.gov/ www.collegedrinkingprevention.gov/ NIAAACollegeMaterials/TaskForce/TaskForce_TOC.aspx
Brief alcohol screening and intervention for college students (BASICS)	http://nrepp.samhsa.gov/ViewIntervention.aspx?id=124 http://depts.washington.edu/abrc/basics.htm
	Dimeff, L. A., Baer, J. S., Kivlahan, D. R., & Marlatt, G. A. (1999). *Brief alcohol screening and intervention for college students: A harm reduction approach.* New York, NY: Guilford Press.
Video resources	*Motivational Interviewing: Professional Training Series,* 1998 American Psychological Association. (2005). *Harm Reduction with High School Students.*

One program suggested using 70 hours of academic training plus additional time in practical training areas for an alcohol/drug and other health peer counseling program (Edelstein & Gonyer, 1993). Other programs describe spending 8 to 12 hours of didactic training with one or two supervision sessions (Larimer et al., 2001; Turrisi et al., 2009), 16-hours over 2 days with continued supervision (Mastroleo et al., 2010; Mastroleo et al., under review), 30 to 40 hours over a 2-week period (Barnett et al., 2007; Borsari & Carey, 2005; Borsari et al., in press; Pyle & Snyder, 1971; Wood et al., 2007), 30 hours during a 2-credit semester training course (Allen, 1993), and a 4-day training workshop prior to the beginning of the academic year (Pitts, 1996). Although variation in time and format are duly noted, content and the integration of skill development are the most important components of a counselor training program (Keeling & Engstrom, 1993).

Content of training almost always includes training counselors in the use of active listening, empathic responses, genuineness in sessions, positive regard for clients, relationship building skills, nonverbal behavior training, role-playing, communication skills, job-specific training, and the integration of skills (e.g., Allen, 1993; Barnett et al., 2007; Borsari et al., under review; Hatcher, 1995a; Mastroleo et al., 2010; Pitts, 1996; Wood et al., 2007; see Table 13.3 for counseling skill-building materials). Identification of these skills has been pulled from literature related to the microcounseling skills approach and their perceived effective use in counseling (Ivey, 1971). Specific training for each element is integrated as decided by program directors and trainers based on individual needs for each program. Keeling and Engstrom (1993) support this method as they describe the importance of developing a specific training protocol to best match the needs of each individual group of counselors. Although the training protocol may change based on the needs of a group of counselors, providing training on basic counseling and listening skills is essential and is conducted within the majority of intervention training programs. As such, when training undergraduate peer counselors more time and attention will likely be needed to help develop individual counseling skills. In contrast, when working with professional counselors or advanced graduate students, less time on counseling skills will be necessary. All interventionists (peer, professional, student affairs staff), however, will likely need specific training on alcohol content and the finer points of the specific intervention. A good number of brief alcohol interventions cover a wide range of alcohol-based education components (see Table 13.2), so specific training and exposure to these content areas is essential to intervention delivery with fidelity.

Counselor training for individual interventions. In each of the previously discussed research studies, training and supervision of peer and professional interventionists was standardized and produced counselors able to deliver the prescribed treatment with fidelity. Specifically, most studies described the intensive training and supervision counselors completed prior to intervention implementation, including individual one-on-one supervision meetings to improve MI skills, ongoing weekly group supervision meetings to discuss client cases and concerns, and review of audio-recorded sessions with both written and verbal feedback about the intervention sessions. Past studies implementing peer-led BASICS conducted a minimum of two role plays while being required to meet adherence criteria on MI fidelity evaluations (e.g., score of 5 or higher on Empathy and MI Spirit ratings on MITI 2.0; Moyers et al., 2005) prior to working with clients (e.g., Larimer et al., 2001; Turrisi et al., 2009). This approach highlights the importance placed on systematically preparing peer counselors to conduct interventions.

Counselor training for group interventions. Training interventionists to implement a group intervention is similar to trainings developed for individual intervention delivery. Specifically, training begins with instructing the interventionist in MI skills and the specific intervention protocol. Once the interventionist is informed of the theoretical background and establishes the skill set necessary to implement the protocol, training is transitioned to using these skills within a group setting. Special attention is aimed at preparing interventionists to effectively manage groups while adhering to the treatment protocol. Techniques include initiating group discussion with an open-ended question, actively listening to the group members' responses, and reflecting (when appropriate) to direct the discussion back to the group. In groups, it is particularly easy for the interventionist to gravitate toward the "instructing" trap, and to not include group members in the discussion. This psychoeducation approach is less powerful than actively engaging group members in the discussion (W. R. Miller & Rollnick, 2002; Walters & Baer, 2006). Therefore, interventionists are instructed to have individual interactions with group members and to encourage group members to share experiences while adding to the overall discussion. Furthermore, interventionists are trained to use summary statements when possible to synthesize and reflect the various contributions of group members. As with training for individual sessions, conducting role plays until the group counselors are comfortable and proficient and maintaining consistent individual and group supervision to discuss clinical and procedural issues are both crucial for successful interventions (e.g., see E. T. Miller et al., 2001 for ASTP implementation model). A recent example of a standardized method for training and supervising is Palmer et al. (2010), who trained peer counselors in MI and ASTP content over 12 hours, after which the counselors were supervised on delivery of the manualized ASTP intervention (Palmer, Kilmer, Ball, & Larimer, 2010).

Counselor Skill Acquisition

Several studies have examined the mechanisms of MI skill acquisition and retention with professional and peer counselors. W. R. Miller et al. (2004) conducted a randomized trial comparing five training conditions (clinical workshop only, workshop + feedback (WF), workshop + individual coaching sessions (WC), workshop + feedback + coaching (WFC), and self-training control). Results indicated that only the conditions that included feedback and/or coaching helped counselors exceed the proficiency standard for MI-adherent behaviors 4 months after baseline. Clinicians in the WF, WC, and WFC demonstrated higher skill proficiency in ratio of reflections to questions and in percentage of complex reflections; skills that have been previously identified as vital to the appropriate implementation of MI. Similarly, Schoener et al. (2006) found that training followed by supervision aided community mental health therapists in improving MISC scores on empathy, MI spirit, reflective listening, reducing closed-ended questions, and advising without permission. Baer et al. (2004) examined professional counselors following a 2-day training workshop on retention of MI skills after 2 months. With no ongoing supervision posttraining, less than 50% of trainees achieved and sustained MI proficiency standards, and there was an overall decline in MI proficiency at follow-up compared to the initial postworkshop assessment. These studies suggest workshops presented by trained experts followed by continued clinical supervision may be the best method for disseminating MI skills to practitioners (Martino, Ball, Nich, Frankforter, & Carroll, 2008).

Two recent studies examined the effect of supervision on peer counselors' abilities to acquire necessary MI skills and subsequent delivery of a BASICS intervention with voluntary and mandated college students (Mastroleo et al., 2010; Mastroleo et al., under review). Both studies used identical training methods: peer counselors received 12 hours of MI and BASICS training focusing on use of MI skills, alcohol content, and the BASICS intervention. The training was followed by completion of two role-plays, after which one group received individual, in-person supervision of MI skills. Using session audiotapes, both groups were evaluated on MI skill demonstration (e.g., open/closed questions, simple/complex reflections). In one study delivering BASICS to voluntary first-year students, peer counselors randomized to the supervision condition who were initially deficient in MI skills acquired the necessary skills to adequately deliver a BASICS intervention with fidelity (Mastroleo et al., 2010). In the second study delivering BASICS to mandated college students, standard supervision (group only) was compared to enhanced supervision (group + individual). Results identified differential effects of supervision on MI skills outcomes. Specifically, the enhanced supervision condition resulted in a significantly higher percent of complex reflections (36% vs. 27% for control). Similarly, there was a higher ratio of reflections to questions for enhanced supervision peer counselors .42 (vs. .33 for standard). However, differences for MI Spirit were nonsignificant (MI Spirit: enhanced supervision M = 2.89(.617); standard M = 2.67(.686); Mastroleo et al., under review). These findings support the importance of including individual supervision as a vital training component with peer counselors, especially those deficient in MI skills following initial training.

Training Exercises

To more clearly tie didactic content to intervention implementation, a series of training exercises may be used to target specific skill acquisition. As identified by the

Motivational Interviewing Page (www.motivationalinterview.org/index.html), practicing skills throughout the course of training is essential for proper use of MI skills and likely also plays an important role in delivering specific intervention components. Although a description of the various exercises used to help counselors develop the skills necessary to deliver an intervention is beyond the scope of this chapter, it is important for trainers to implement exercises in a way that builds on informational content, while also supporting the development of a skill set (for more information see Table 13.3). Initially, the focus is on mastering basic skills (e.g., rapport building, counseling microskills) needed for intervention delivery. As trainees acquire these skills, the focus will move toward advanced level skills (e.g., complex reflections, rolling with resistance, group dynamics management). The progression of exercises is fundamental to skill acquisition, as appropriately challenging trainees over the course of the skill building process, without potentially discouraging individuals early, is an important balance a trainer must find.

Practice, Practice, Practice

The final steps in preparing counselors to conduct interventions (either group or individual) with college students is to practice the skills through the use of role-plays and practice intervention sessions. Past research has shown substantial improvements posttraining after conducting two to three role-play sessions regardless of delivery by a peer or professional counselor (e.g., Borsari et al., under review; Larimer et al., 2001; Mastroleo et al., 2010; Mastroleo et al., under review). In fact, the majority of empirically based research studies testing college-based interventions use supervised role-plays as the capstone exercise before permitting counselors to meet with students. Although there is no empirically supported prescribed number of practice sessions a counselor should conduct prior to entering the field, a number of research studies noted a minimum of two role-plays prior to intervention implementation. By completing full-session role-plays, the counselor has the opportunity to implement all aspects of the intervention allowing for practice of skills delivery and content information, while also becoming more familiar and comfortable with the intervention approach. The clinical supervisor should review the session (either audio or video recorded) to ensure that skills are appropriately utilized. In addition, as individual components may be more challenging for a counselor to deliver, completing additional role-play segments may enhance the delivery of specific sections. As each protocol is unique, helping counselors feel confident and comfortable with the individual intervention is essential. Much of the final training involved with delivering an intervention with fidelity relies on the role of supervision and skill coaching to successfully help counselors truly adopt the skills needed to complete interventions (Conant, Sloane, & Zimmer, 1993; Mastroleo et al., under review; W. R. Miller et al., 2004).

COUNSELOR SUPERVISION

A long history of general psychotherapy literature has explored the role of counselor supervision in the effort to improve counseling skills and client outcomes (Frayn, 1991; Freud, 1986; for reviews see Goodyear & Bernard, 1998; Leddick & Bernard, 1980). Within this context, supervision has been defined as, "an intervention provided by a more senior member of a profession to a more junior member or members of that same profession" (Bernard & Goodyear, 2004, p. 8). Clinical supervision provides counselor trainees a bridge between academic and clinical experiences by blending learned theory and skills with practice (Williams, 1995). Beutler (1988) noted the importance of systematic feedback and reflection on counseling skills, typically offered through supervision. Hill, Charles, and Reed (1981) and Wiley and Ray (1986) identified the importance of receiving intentional, clear feedback as is available through supervision, and noted that research data confirms that unsupervised counseling experience does not improve trainees clinical progress. When considering dissemination of manualized treatments (e.g., BMIs with college students), Carroll (2002) noted the importance of ensuring interventions are implemented as intended. Further, Holloway and Neufeldt (1995) state that expert feedback is needed to assist in the counselor's implementation until the trainee is able to incorporate the principles that govern timing, judgment, and delivery within the context of the session. Bernard and Goodyear (2004) advise that supervision must accompany practice if counselor trainees (peer and professional) are to acquire the required conceptual ability and necessary practice skills.

Although mechanisms of counseling skill acquisition in brief alcohol interventions have rarely been examined, past studies have explored relationships between counselor self-efficacy, skill demonstration, and the role supervision plays in enhancing both (Larson et al., 1992; Mitchell, 2008). Mitchell (2008) identified nonsignificant correlations between style, frequency, and time spent discussing clinical cases in supervision and counselor self-efficacy, while Larson et al. (1992) found improvements in counselor self-efficacy strongly correlated with improvements in counselor skills over time. Working collaboratively with the counselor to identify areas of strength and challenge is important to improve skills while maintaining and enhancing counselor self-efficacy. Therefore, it would seem supervision, as an intervention, may aid in improving counselor self-efficacy, thereby improving client satisfaction and outcomes. However, the small number of studies and the mixed findings on the role of counselor self-efficacy for acquisition of counseling microskills warrants further investigation.

Among the variety of programs, the way in which supervision is carried out has varied. Some programs offer individual weekly meetings to revisit training topics, discuss ongoing cases, concerns, and client progress; others use small group meetings; and still others note no specific continued supervision or tracking of counselor abilities (e.g., Murasky & Sevig, 1995; Pitts, 1996; Turrisi et al., 2009).

Larimer et al. (2001), Barnett et al. (2007), and Wood et al. (2007) noted using ongoing supervision throughout the intervention implementation period.

Peer Counselor Supervision

When considering the use of peer counselors as intervention agents, the early integration of supervision is an important component of a quality program. Hatcher and colleagues (1995b) describe the process of incorporating supervision into the overall program model through an initial conversation surrounding feelings toward authority figures, what the peers like and expect from a supervisor, and distortions that can take place in a supervisory relationship. The authors go on to note the manner in which parallel process (Doehrman, 1976) may impact the peer counseling relationship and their work with clients. The concept of parallel process comes from psychotherapy literature in which supervisory interactions impact client sessions between counselors and counselees. Hatcher et al. (1995b) state understanding this process may help college students as they work in the role of peer counselors. The concept is described through examples in which unconscious communication between peer counselors and clients is identified and tied back to interactions found in the supervisory relationship. For example, if the supervisor/supervisee relationship gets trapped in the directive teacher/passive learner role, the peer may re-create this relationship during the intervention, which is contrary to the MI stance of collaboration and elicitation. Hatcher and colleagues (1995b) believe awareness of this phenomenon is helpful in aiding peer counselors to provide more useful services for their clients. Supervisors have also found mirroring supervisees' treatment interventions can be helpful (Hart, 1982; Hawkins & Shohet, 1989). This can include modeling qualities and characteristics of the treatment (using open-ended questions, reflections, summaries, and expression of empathy) during supervision. In this way, supervision provides tools and insight allowing supervisees to incorporate their skills into future work (Tebb, Manning, & Klaumann, 1996).

To assure useful service to clients, the use of supervision is essential to client care and intervention fidelity (Hatcher et al., 1995b). In two randomized controlled trials, Mastroleo and colleagues (2010) implemented a model of peer counselor supervision that focused on MI and BASICS delivery skill building. Using audio-recorded sessions, peer counselors initially listen to a recorded session, during which they tally (code) their use of open and closed questions and simple and complex reflections using the Peer Proficiency Assessment (PEPA; Mastroleo et al., 2009; see Table 13.1 for skill definitions). Once tallied, the peer counselor met with the clinical supervisor, listened to the audio session together, and identified ways in which the peer counselor could improve his or her skills; for example, reducing the number of closed questions and improving on the use of complex reflections. Also discussed were methods in which peer counselors could more easily transition between intervention component sections (e.g., how to move from BAC to normative beliefs). Through individual coaching and listening to their own sessions, peer counselors were able to improve their use of complex reflections when compared to peer counselors who were not offered individual supervision (Mastroleo et al., under review). Although these procedures are time-intensive, such supervision supports effective skill delivery, which is an essential link to reducing drinking behaviors (Moyers et al., 2009; Tollison, Lee et al., 2008).

Group Supervision

Group supervision, "the regular meeting of a group of supervisees with a designated supervisor(s) in order to monitor the quality of their works and to further their understanding of themselves as clinicians, of the clients with whom they work, and of service delivery in general" (Bernard & Goodyear, 2004, p. 235), is a widely used alternative to one-on-one supervision given the limited resources (time and finances) in most brief intervention programs. A number of responsibilities fall to the group supervisor including the adequate balance of challenging and supporting each trainee, considering the level of development of the supervisee group, and staying in-tune to what is helpful or hindering to the supervisee group (Bernard & Goodyear, 2004). Factors including the supervisors' openness, the supervisory relationship, content of feedback, and contextual issues all facilitate or disrupt supervision depending on the supervisors' skill level (Hoffman, Hill, Holmes, & Freitas, 2005). There are several theories of group supervision that can be implemented depending on the preference of the supervisor. Some serve as supportive and process-focused groups, while others remain attentive to the acquisition of skills. Typically, in-group supervision focused on delivery of BMIs, skill acquisition and content delivery is the focus, however maintaining some connection to process and counselors' reactions to clients and sessions holds important value. It is important to note, however, if only self-report data is being used to discuss client cases and concerns, supervisors must be aware of the potential of both under and over reporting of skill delivery on the part of the counselor. If possible, use of audio-recorded sessions during group supervision will offer an important benefit to each member of the group. Another alternative is for the supervisor to listen to audio-recorded sessions prior to the group meeting to give appropriate feedback. Approaching the meeting with a team mentality in which counselors work together to find supportive methods to improve intervention delivery can be a useful tool in maintaining skills and intervention fidelity standards.

One question that often comes up is the optimal size for a group. Group size guidelines remain unclear, and have not yet been adequately investigated. However, some guidelines have been discussed in the general psychotherapy literature. The single study examining differences in training effects dependent upon the group size was inconclusive (Ray & Altekruse, 2000). Despite the lack of empirical evidence, there are several authors who have made suggestions. Aronson (1990) indicated that 5 to 6 is an optimal size allowing for individual attention to each trainee. On the other hand, authors have suggested including 6 to 12 (Chaiklin & Munson, 1983) and at least 7 (Schreiber & Frank, 1983) group members to decrease chances of disruption to the group process due to absences and/or dropouts may be optimal. These guidelines, however, are frequently not met in practice as the average supervision group for internship sites consists of three to five trainees (Riva & Comish, 1995), and university training centers can include up to 10 group members (Bernard & Goodyear, 2004).

Despite the theory used or the size of the group, supervision usually includes a didactic component, case conceptualization, skill development, constructive feedback, support, and encouragement. Again, little attention has been paid to the method and process of group supervision for delivery of college alcohol interventions, yet guidelines and processes have been discussed in the context of psychotherapy (Bernard & Goodyear, 2004; Tuckman & Jensen, 1977). Supervision begins with the supervisor establishing group ground rules (e.g., confidentiality) and structure (e.g., frequency of meetings, expectation of regular attendance, and guidelines for the presentation of case material). Often, supervisees have a need to feel and appear competent. In these instances, it is important that the supervisor works to avoid between-member competition and encourages supervisees to identify challenging clinical areas without becoming defensive or guarded. Overall goals are for group members to become comfortable working with one another. The supervisor must work to shape the groups norms to model behaviors that are most productive for the group. As members continue to work together, they will develop a shared responsibility and trust, at which point the supervisor can give more leadership to the group. A final aspect of group supervision is when the group ends, often specified by a training calendar (e.g., the end of the semester or academic year). At this stage, it is crucial that the supervisor help group members highlight the accomplished individual and group goals and skills acquired within the group. It is also becoming increasingly important for the group to provide the supervisor with feedback. Published studies have provided helpful feedback tools including the Group Supervisory Behavior Scale (White & Rudolph, 2000), the Group Supervision Scale (Arcinue, 2002), and the Group Supervision Impact Scale (Getzelmon, 2003).

In past studies utilizing group supervision for delivery of brief alcohol interventions with college students group sizes ranged from 3 to 12 members (e.g., Barnett et al., 2007; Larimer et al., 2001; Mastroleo et al., under review, Turrisi et al., 2009). Group processes varied as well and included discussion over client cases based on counselor self-report, listening to audio-recorded session segments followed by specific coaching around improved skill and content delivery, and continued role-play of intervention components. No research to date has empirically examined the effective aspects of group supervision. When using group supervision as a training and compliance modality, incorporating some tape review and consultation has the potential to improve intervention delivery and counselor confidence. Further, discussing challenging clients and brainstorming with group members about ways in which to work with similar clients offers constructive feedback to support counselor growth and intervention fidelity.

Benefits and Disadvantages of Group Supervision

Despite a lack of supporting research, group supervision is widely practiced and believed to have many benefits (Bernard & Goodyear, 2004). Perhaps the most appealing characteristic of group supervision is its efficient use of time, money, and expertise (Hawkins & Shohet, 1989). Additionally, it offers the opportunity to minimize supervisee dependence (Getzel & Salmon, 1985; Parihar, 1983) and hierarchical issues between supervisor and supervisee due to more input from other supervisees during case analysis (Allen, 1976; Cohen, Gross, & Turner, 1976).

Some literature points to the enhanced learning benefits cultivated through group supervision. Regarding skill acquisition, Hillerbrand (1989) found that those who observed peers performing a skill were more likely to exhibit skill improvement as well as an increased sense of self-efficacy than those who observed an expert delivering the same skill. Further, the supervisee is exposed to a far greater variety of cases in group supervision (Linton & Hedstrom, 2006; Riva & Cornish, 1995, 2008), providing the environment for increased quantity and diversity of feedback. There is also a greater quality of feedback among groups due to supervisees' ability to communicate to their fellow peers in a more understandable way. Hillerbrand (1989) found other supervisees were better at using language that was more understandable to other novices and were better at decoding nonverbal cues of confusion relayed by a fellow supervisee than an expert.

Although there are undoubtedly many benefits to group supervision, there are also some drawbacks. First, it may be difficult for some individuals to get the attention and assistance they need. Additionally, groups may get side-tracked, devoting too much time to irrelevant or unimportant topics. There are also confidentiality concerns for both the clients who are the focus of attention and the supervisees, and steps should be taken to minimize this risk (e.g., clarifying rules regarding confidentiality from the onset). Finally, there are certain group processes that may impede learning such as between-supervisee competition or rejection of certain members of the group. These can impede the learning process, and derail the group progress. In light of these potential pitfalls, it is the responsibility of the supervisor to promote a healthy group dynamic while encouraging a productive learning environment. Enhancing skills through practice and seeking adequate consultation when needed will minimize the risk of these obstacles.

Becoming a Supervisor

Important, yet often not discussed, are the aspects of effective supervision practices and the necessary training and competency to become an effective supervisor of BMIs for college students. An initial first step is for the supervisor to be trained and supervised in the intervention approach for which they will be conducting supervision. There are a number of trainings available at the national level to learn MI skills, individual and group BMI implementation, and supervisory skills (see Table 13.3 for additional resources). Next, it is also helpful if the supervisors themselves deliver the intervention, and ideally, receive supervision themselves. The benefit of this experience is to more clearly understand potential concerns and difficulties counselors and treatment staff may encounter. Although it is not essential this take place, the level of understanding and empathy supervisors can develop for their supervisees can often greatly enhance the working relationship and their ability to give constructive feedback on skills and intervention delivery. Another helpful skill is the ability to critically evaluate intervention delivery through use of fidelity and evaluation tools. For example, tools such as the MISC, MITI, or PEPA (Mastroleo et al., 2009; W. R. Miller et al., 2003; Moyers et al., 2005) can be used to help evaluate counselor's use of MI skills when conducing individual BMIs. In using these evaluation tools, concrete feedback on MI skill delivery can be offered to the counselor. Although some of these trainings can be time consuming, the benefits of a supervisor learning how to critically evaluate BMIs has the potential to greatly improve overall delivery and fidelity. Learning to be a supervisor takes time, and may be more in line with being an educator and coach.

INTERVENTION FIDELITY

A final component of ensuring competent delivery of alcohol interventions for college students is using fidelity assessments. The majority of research studies implement some form of fidelity assessment to check that counselors are delivering all components effectively and that counselor skills (e.g., MI Skills) meet threshold competency levels. A secondary use of fidelity assessments can be for supervision purposes. Specifically, both counselors and supervisors can evaluate audio-recorded sessions using a fidelity instrument to gauge counselor skill and identify areas in need of improvement. A number of assessments exist, some of which require large time commitments for training and use (e.g., MISC; W. R. Miller et al., 2003), and others that require much less training time and allow for quick assessments of counselors skills and intervention delivery methods (e.g., PEPA; Mastroleo et al., 2009). Two examples of MI fidelity assessments are the MISC and the Motivational Interviewing Treatment Integrity (MITI; Moyers et al., 2005). These tools have been developed to code and evaluate counselor and client behaviors within counseling sessions. Specific behavior classifications for all client and therapist utterances (which represents a complete thought, and ends when one thought is completed and a new thought begun by the speaker, or when an utterance from the other speaker begins) are coded using transcripts or audio recordings of the sessions. Behavior counts (e.g., simple/complex reflections, open/closed questions), are determined by categorization and decision rules of utterances. Specific ratios of open to closed questions, complex to simple reflections, and reflections to questions are identified and used to determine if fidelity to MI has been met. In addition to behavior counts, these tools allow for overall evaluation of counselors' performance during the session using Global scores of MI Spirit, Empathy, and Acceptance. *Empathy* represents counselors' ability to show an active interest in the client's experiences and to make an effort to understand the client's perspective accurately. *Spirit* reflects the counselor's overall competence in delivering the intervention using MI and focuses on evocation (communicating understanding that motivation and ability to carry out change reside within the student), collaboration (working together as equal partners), and autonomy/support (encouraging and actively promoting perception of choice). *Acceptance* captures the extent to which unconditional positive regard for the client is communicated. Ratings are on a 7-point Likert scale, with scores of 5 or higher reflecting good MI adherence.

The PEPA (Mastroleo et al., 2009) was developed to measure the effectiveness of individual peer counseling sessions. This tool evaluates the initial 15 minutes of each audio-recorded session for peer counselor use of reflective listening statements and open- and closed-ended questions. Behavior counts of open- and closed-ended questions and simple and complex reflective statement are tallied. Closed questions include the number of yes/no questions and answers with restricted range (e.g., "How many drinks did you have?") that were asked in the 15-minute segment. Open-ended questions are questions that are designed to elicit open-ended responses. Simple reflections are statements that convey understanding but offer little or no meaning to client statements (e.g., repeat, rephrase; see Table 13.1). Complex reflections are defined as statements made by the peer counselor where substantial meaning is inferred or hypothesis testing is explored (e.g., paraphrase, double-sided reflection, reflection of feeling). Complex reflections are used to convey a deeper meaning to the picture the client is developing and are used to assist the client in developing discrepancy and engaging in change talk (see Table 13.1 for examples). Training required to use the PEPA as a fidelity tool is typically 2 hours after which coders (or supervisors) have reliably coded brief alcohol intervention sessions with reliability (Mastroleo et al., 2010; Mastroleo et al., under review). This tool may also be used by peer counselors to evaluate their own sessions and identify areas in which they can more closely adhere to MI microskills.

Finally, additional project specific fidelity tools have been developed to identify counselor's delivery of specific intervention components and their adherence to protocol (e.g., Barnett et al., 2007; Borsari et al., under review; Wood et al., 2007).

In one study, intervention fidelity was measured by two independent raters (intra-class correlation scores ranging from .55 to .88), using an intervention checklist to identify adherence session component completion (Barnett et al., 2007). Intervention components were identified and the intervention fidelity checklist was evaluated on a 1 (below expectations) to 3 (above expectations) (see Barnett et al., 2007, for a description of this system). These evaluations were done as raters listened to audio-recorded sessions. This procedure of establishing adherence to session components is an important step in the delivery of brief alcohol interventions and is recommended to ensure that fidelity standards are being met consistently.

CONCLUSION

Comprehensive training and supervision are necessary components of successful counselor-delivered prevention and intervention efforts to reduce hazardous and harmful drinking among college students. Research has supported a range of intervention approaches, particularly those that incorporate MI, to be effective in promoting a shift away from risky alcohol use. These studies have provided us with the components that appear to be important in the implementation of brief alcohol interventions. However, training and supervision guidelines are less clear. Here, we emphasize the importance of adequate training, ongoing supervision and skill development, and maximizing treatment fidelity. It is important to acknowledge that counselor-delivered approaches, while brief, do require a commitment of resources (for both counselor and supervisor time) on the part of the university.

Crucial factors for successful training and supervision include weekly supervision meetings (individual- and/or group-based) to improve MI skills, discussion of client cases and concerns, and review of session audio/video recordings. Furthermore, practicing skills through roleplays and a combination of written and verbal feedback for the supervisee is invaluable. Finally, implementing ongoing fidelity assessments ensures competent delivery of the alcohol intervention. These measures are useful prior to trainees working with clients to ensure that they are ready, and during intervention implementation to ensure continued proper delivery. Overall, we can expect that a successful training program and supervisory process will increase the likelihood that interventions will successfully reduce alcohol use and associated consequences among college student drinkers.

REFERENCES

Allen, J. (1976). Peer group supervision in family therapy. *Child Welfare, 55,* 183–189.

Allen, N. J. (1993). A case study of a successful health advocate program. *Journal of American College Health, 41*(6), 293–295.

Arcinue, F. (2002). *The development and validation of the group supervision scale. Unpublished doctoral dissertation.* University of Southern California.

Aronson, M. L. (1990). A group therapist's perspectives on the use of supervisory groups in the training of psychotherapists. *Psychoanalysis and Psychotherapy, 8,* 88–94.

Baer, J. S., Marlatt, G. A., Kivlahan, D. R., Fromme, K., Larimer, M. E., & Williams, E. (1992). An experimental test of three methods of alcohol risk reduction with young adults. *Journal of Consulting and Clinical Psychology, 60*(6), 974–979.

Baer, J. S., Rosengren, D. B., Dunn, C. W., Wells, E. A., Ogle, R. L., & Hartzler, B. (2004). An evaluation of workshop training in motivational interviewing for addiction and mental health clinicians. [Print Electronic; Print]. *Drug and Alcohol Dependence, 73*(1), 99–106.

Barnett, N. P., Murphy, J. G., Colby, S. M., & Monti, P. M. (2007). Efficacy of counselor vs. computer-delivered intervention with mandated college students. *Addictive Behaviors, 32*(11), 2529–2548.

Bergen-Cico, D. (2000). Patterns of substance abuse and attrition among first-year students. *Journal of the First-Year Experience, 12*(1), 61–75.

Bernard, J. M., & Goodyear, R. K. (2004). *Fundamentals of clinical supervision* (3rd ed.). Needham Heights, MA: Allyn & Bacon.

Beutler, L. E. (1988). Introduction: Training to competency in psychotherapy. *Journal of Consulting and Clinical Psychology, 56,* 651–652.

Borsari, B., & Carey, K. B. (2005). Two brief alcohol interventions for mandated college students. *Psychology of Addictive Behaviors, 19*(3), 296–302.

Borsari, B., Hustad, J. T. P., Mastroleo, N. R., O'Leary Tevyaw, T., Barnett, N. P., Kahler, C. W., Short, E. E., & Monti, P. M. (in press). Addressing Alcohol Use and Problems in Mandated College Students: A Randomized Clinical Trial Using Stepped Care. *Journal of Consulting* and *Clinical Psychology.*

Carey, K. B., Henson, J. M., Carey, M. P., & Maisto, S. A. (2009). Computer versus in-person intervention for students violating campus alcohol policy. [Electronic Electronic; Print]. *Journal of Consulting and Clinical Psychology, 77*(1), 74–87.

Carroll, K. M. (2002). One size cannot fit all: A stage model for psychotherapy manual development. *Clinical Psychology: Science and Practice, 9,* 396–406.

Chaiklin, H., & Munson, C. E. (1993). Peer consultation in social work. *Clinical Supervisor, 1,* 21–34.

Cohen, M., Gross, S., & Turner, M. (1976). A note on a developmental model for training family therapists through group supervision. *Journal of Marriage and Family Counseling, 2,* 48–56.

Conant Sloane, B., & Zimmer, C. G. (1993). The power of peer health education. *Journal of American College Health, 41,* 241–245.

D'Andrea, V. J., & Salovey, P. (1996). *Peer counseling: Skills, ethics and perspectives* (2nd ed.). Palo Alto, CA: Science and Behavior Books.

Dimeff, L. A., Baer, J. S., Kivlahan, D. R., & Marlatt, G. A. (1999). *Brief alcohol screening and intervention for college students: A harm reduction approach*: New York, NY: Guilford Press.

Doehrman, M. J. (1976). Parallel process in supervision and psychotherapy. *Bulletin of the Menninger Clinic, 40,* 3–14.

Edelstein, M. E., & Gonyer, P. (1993). Planning for the future of peer education. *Journal of American College Health, 41,* 255–257.

Ender, S. C., & Winston, R. W. (1984). *Students as paraprofessional staff.* San Francisco, CA: Jossey-Bass.

Frayn, D. H. (1991). Supervising the supervisors: The evolution of a psychotherapy supervisors' group. [Print]. *American Journal of Psychotherapy, 45*(1), 31–42.

Freud, S. (1986). On the history of the pscyhoanalytic movement (first published in 1914). *Historical and Expository Works on Psychoanalysis.* Harmondsworth, England: Penguin.

Fromme, K., & Corbin, W. (2004). Prevention of heavy drinking and associated negative consequences among mandated and voluntary college students. *Journal of Consulting and Clinical Psychology, 72*(6), 1038–1049. doi: 2004–21587–014 [pii]

Getzel, G. S., & Salmon, R. (1985). Group supervision: An organizational approach. *Clinical Supervisor, 3,* 27–43.

Getzelmon, M. (2003). *Development and validation of the group supervision impact scale. Unpublished dissertation.* University of Southern California.

Goodyear, R. K., & Bernard, J. M. (1998). Clinical supervision: Lessons from the literature. [Print]. *Counselor Education and Supervision, 38*(1), 6–22.

Guindon, M. H. (2011). *A counseling primer: An introduction to the profession.* New York, NY: Routledge.

Hart, G. (1982). *The process of clinical supervision.* Baltimore, MD: University Park Press.

Hatcher, S. L. (1995). *Peer programs on college campuses: Theory, training, and "voice of the peers."* San Jose, CA: Resource.

Hatcher, S. L., Walsh, L., Reynolds, M., & Sullivan, J. (1995a). Rationale for an academic course in peer counseling. In S. L. Hatcher (Ed.), *Peer programs on the college campus* (pp. 20–30). San Jose, CA: Resource.

Hatcher, S. L., Walsh, L., Reynolds, M., & Sullivan, J. (1995b). The peer counseling course for college students. In S. L. Hatcher (Ed.), *Peer programs on the college campus* (pp. 31–80). San Jose, CA: Resource.

Hawkins, P., & Shohet, R. (1989). *Supervision in the helping professions.* Milton Keynes, United Kingdom: Open University Press.

Hill, C. E., Charles, D., & Reed, K. G. (1981). A longitudinal analysis of changes in counseling skills during doctoral training in counseling psychology. *Journal of Counseling Psychology, 28,* 428–436.

Hillerbrand, E. T. (1989). Cognitive differences between experts and novices: Implications for group supervision. *Journal of Counseling and Development, 67,* 293–296.

Hingson, R. W., Zha, W., & Weitzman, E. R. (2009). Magnitude of and trends in alcohol-related mortality and morbidity among U. S. college students ages 18–24, 1998-2005. *Journal of Studies on Alcohol and Drugs, 70 (Suppl 16),* 12–20.

Hoffman, M. A., Hill, C. E., Holmes, S. E., & Freitas, G. F. (2005). Supervisor perspective on the process and outcome of giving easy, difficult, or no feedback to supervisees. *Journal of Counseling Psychology, 53,* 3–13.

Holloway, E. L., & Neufeldt, S. A. (1995). Supervision: Its contributions to treatment efficacy. *Journal of Consulting and Clinical Psychology, 63,* 207–213.

Ivey, A. E. (1971). *Microcounseling: Innovations in interviewing training.* Springfield, IL: Thomas.

Ivey, A. E., & Ivey, M. B. (2008). *Essentials of intentional interviewing: Counseling in a multicultural world.* Belmont, CA: Thomson Brooks/Cole.

Karno, M. P., & Longabaugh, R. (2004). What do we know? Process analysis and the search for a better understanding of Project MATCH's anger-by-treatment matching effect. *Alcoholism: Clinical and Experimental Research, 65*(4), 501–512.

Karno, M. P., & Longabaugh, R. (2005). An examination of how therapist directiveness interacts with patient anger and reactance to predict alcohol use. *Journal of Studies on Alcohol, 66*(6), 825–832.

Keeling, R. P., & Engstrom, E. L. (1993). Refining your peer education program. *Journal of American College Health, 41,* 259–263.

Kivlahan, D. R., Marlatt, G. A., Fromme, K., Coppel, D. B., & Williams, E. (1990). Secondary prevention with college drinkers: Evaluation of an alcohol skills training program. *Journal of Consulting and Clinical Psychology, 58*(6), 805–810.

Klepp, K. I., Halper, A., & Perry, C. L. (1986). The efficacy of peer leaders in drug abuse prevention. *Journal of School Health, 56,* 407–411.

LaBrie, J. W., Lamb, T. F., Pedersen, E. R., & Quinlan, T. (2006). A group motivational interviewing intervention reduces drinking and alcohol-related consequences in adjudicated college students. *Journal of College Student Development, 47,* 267–280.

LaChance, H., Feldstein Ewing, S. W., Bryan, A. D., & Hutchison, K. E. (2009). What makes group MET work? A randomized controlled trial of college student drinkers in mandated alcohol diversion. *Psychology of Addictive Behaviors, 23*(4), 598–612.

Larimer, M. E., & Cronce, J. M. (2002). Identification, prevention and treatment: A review of individual-focused strategies to reduce problematic alcohol consumption by college students. *Journal of Studies on Alcohol, Suppl 14,* 148–163.

Larimer, M. E., & Cronce, J. M. (2007). Identification, prevention, and treatment revisited: Individual-focused college drinking prevention strategies 1999–2006. *Addictive Behaviors, 32*(11), 2439–2468. doi: S0306-4603(07)00147-5 [pii] 10.1016/j.addbeh.2007.05.006

Larimer, M. E., Turner, A. P., Anderson, B. K., Fader, J. S., Kilmer, J. R., Palmer, R. S. & Cronce, J. M. (2001). Evaluating a brief alcohol intervention with fraternities. *Journal of Studies on Alcohol, 62*(3), 370–380.

Larson, L. M., Suzuki, L. A., Gillespie, K. N., Potenza, M. T., Bechtel, M. A., & Toulouse, A. L. (1992). Development and validation of the counseling self-estimate inventory. [Print]. *Journal of Counseling Psychology, 39*(1), 105–120.

Leddick, G. R., & Bernard, J. M. (1980). The history of supervision. *Counselor Education and Supervision, 19*(3), 186–196.

Linton, J. M., & Hedstrom, S. M. (2006). An exploratory qualitative investigation of group processes in group supervision: Perceptions of master's level practicum students. *Journal for Specialists in Group Work, 31*, 51–72.

Marlatt, G. A., Baer, J. S., Kivlahan, D. R., Dimeff, L. A., Larimer, M. E., Quigley, L. A., ...Williams, E. (1998). Screening and brief intervention for high-risk college student drinkers: Results from a two-year follow-up assessment. *Journal of Clinical and Consulting Psychology, 66*(4), 604–615.

Martens, M. P., Cimini, M. D., Barr, A. R., Rivero, E. M., Vellis, P. A., Desemone, G. A., & Horner, K. J. (2007). Implementing a screening and brief intervention for high-risk drinking in university-based health and mental health care settings: Reductions in alcohol use and correlates of success. *Addictive Behaviors, 32*(11), 2563–2572. doi: S0306-4603(07)00146-3 [pii] 10.1016/j.addbeh.2007.05.005

Martino, S., Ball, S. A., Nich, C., Frankforter, T. L., & Carroll, K. M. (2008). Community program therapist adherence and competence in motivational enhancement therapy. [Electronic Electronic; Print]. *Drug and Alcohol Dependence, 96*(1–2), 37–48.

Mastroleo, N. R., Magill, M., Barnett, N. P., & Borsari, B. (under review). *A brief peer-led alcohol intervention with mandated college students: A pilot study.*

Mastroleo, N. R., Mallett, K. A., Ray, A. E., & Turrisi, R. (2008). The process of delivering peer-based alcohol intervention programs in college settings. *Journal of College Student Development, 49*(3), 255–259.

Mastroleo, N. R., Mallett, K. A., Turrisi, R., & Ray, A. E. (2009). Psychometric properties of the peer proficiency assessment (PEPA): A tool for evaluation of undergraduate peer counselors' motivational interviewing fidelity. *Addictive Behaviors, 34*, 717–722.

Mastroleo, N. R., Turrisi, R., Carney, J. V., Ray, A. E., & Larimer, M. E. (2010). Examination of posttraining supervision of peer counselors in a motivational enhancement intervention to reduce drinking in a sample of heavy-drinking college students. *Journal of Substance Abuse Treatment, 39*(3), 289–297. doi: S0740-5472(10)00132-7 [pii] 10.1016/j.jsat.2010.06.005

Miller, B. A., & Downs, W. R. (1993). The impact of family violence on the use of alcohol by women. *Alcohol Health and Research World, 17*(2), 137–143.

Miller, E. T., Kilmer, J. R., Kim, E. L., Weingardt, K. R., & Marlatt, G. A. (2001). Alcohol skills training for college students. In P. Monti, S. M. Colby, & T. O'Leary (Eds.), *Adolescents, alcohol, and substance abuse* (pp. 183–215). New York, NY: Guilford Press.

Miller, E. T., & Marlatt, A. (1998). *An acceptance-based intervention aimed at reducing the harm associated with high risk alcohol use.* Paper presented at the 32nd annual meeting of the Association for the Advancement of Behavior Therapy.

Miller, W. R., Benefield, R. G., & Tonigan, J. S. (1993). Enhancing motivation for change in problem drinking: A controlled comparison of two therapist styles. *Journal of Consulting and Clinical Psychology, 61*(3), 455–461.

Miller, W. R., Moyers, T. B., Ernst, D., & Amrhein, P. (2003). Manual for the motivational interviewing skills code (MISC) Version 2.0 Retrieved April 19, 2009, from http://www.motivationalinterview.org/training/MISC2.pdf

Miller, W. R., & Rollnick, S. (2002). *Motivational interviewing: Preparing people to change addictive behavior* (2nd ed.). New York, NY: Guilford Press.

Miller, W. R., Yahne, C. E., Moyers, T. B., Martinez, J., & Pirritano, M. (2004). A randomized trial of methods to help clinicians learn motivational interviewing. *Journal of Consulting and Clinical Psychology, 72*(6), 1050–1062. doi: 2004-21587-015 [pii]

Mitchell, D. R. (2008). *The impact of perceptions of clinical supervision on clinician self-efficacy in community behavioral health.* Dissertation. Northern Arizona University.

Moyers, T. B., Martin, T., Houck, J. M., Christopher, P. J., & Tonigan, J. S. (2009). From in-session behaviors to drinking outcomes: A causal chain for motivational interviewing. *Journal of Consulting and Clinical Psychology, 77*, 1113–1124.

Moyers, T. B., Martin, T., Manuel, J. K., Hendrickson, S. M. L., & Miller, W. R. (2005). Assessing competence in the use of motivational interviewing. [Electronic Electronic; Print]. *Journal of Substance Abuse Treatment, 28*(1), 19–26.

Murasky, D., & Sevig, T. (1995). A peer counseling phone line. In S. L. Hatcher (Ed.), *Peer programs on the college campus* (pp. 83–133). San Jose, CA: Resource.

O'Malley, P. M., & Johnston, L. D. (2002). Epidemiology of alcohol and other drug use among American college students. *Journal of Studies on Alcohol, Suppl 14*, 23–39.

Palmer, R. S. (2004). *Efficacy of the alcohol skills training program in mandated and nonmandated heavy drinking college students*. Dissertation. University of Washington.

Palmer, R. S., Kilmer, J. R., Ball, S. A., & Larimer, M. E. (2010). Intervention defensiveness as a moderator of drinking outcome among heavy-drinking mandated college students. *Addictive Behaviors, 35*(12), 1157–1160.

Parihar, B. (1983). Group supervision: A naturalistic field study in a specialty unit. *Clinical Supervisor, 1*, 3–14.

Pitts, M. A. (1996). *The effectiveness of peer counseling for resolving interpersonal problem distress in college students. Unpublished doctoral dissertation*. University of Idaho.

Prochaska, J. O., & DiClemente, C. C. (1982). Transtheoretical therapy: Toward a more integrative model of change. *Psychotherapy: Theory, Research, and Practice, 19*, 276–288.

Pyle, R. R., & Snyder, F. A. (1971). Students as paraprofessional counselors at community colleges. *Journal of College Student Personnel, 12*, 259–262.

Ray, D., & Altekruse, M. (2000). Effectiveness of group supervision versus combined group and individual supervision. *Counselor Education and Supervision, 40*, 19–30.

Riva, M. T., & Comish, J. A. E. (1995). Group supervision practices at psychology predoctoral internship programs: A national survey. *Professional Psychology: Research and Practice, 26*, 523–525.

Riva, M. T., & Cornish, J. A. E. (2008). Group supervision practices and psychology predoctoral internship programs: 15 years later. *Training and Education in Professional Psychology, 2*, 18–25.

Schoener, E. P., Madeja, C. L., Henderson, M. J., Ondersma, S. J., & Janisse, J. J. (2006). Effects of motivational interviewing training on mental health therapist behavior. *Drug and Alcohol Dependence, 82*, 269–275.

Schreiber, P., & Frank, E. (1983). The use of a peer supervision group by social work clinicians. *Clinical Supervisor, 1*, 29–36.

Tebb, S., Manning, D. W., & Klaumann, T. K. (1996). A renaissance of group supervision in practicum. *Clinical Supervisor, 14*, 39–51.

Tollison, S. J., Lee, C. M., Neighbors, C., Neil, T. A., Olson, N. D., & Larimer, M. E. (2008). Questions and reflections: the use of motivational interviewing microskills in a peer-led brief alcohol intervention for college students. *Behavior Therapy, 39*(2), 183–194.

Tollison, S. J., Mastroleo, N. R., Witkiewitz, K., Mallett, K., Ray, A. E., Grossbard, J. R., …& Larimer, M. E. (2008, June). *Motivational interviewing microskills and changes in alcohol use among college students attending an alcohol intervention: A replication*. Paper presented at the Research Society on Alcoholism, Washington, DC.

Tuckman, B. W., & Jensen, M. A. C. (1977). Stages of small group development revisited. *Group and Organizational Studies, 2*, 419–427.

Turrisi, R., Larimer, M. E., Mallett, K. A., Kilmer, J. R., Ray, A. E., Mastroleo, N. R., . . . Montoya, H. (2009). A randomized clinical trial evaluating a combined alcohol intervention for high-risk college students. *Journal of Studies on Alcohol and Drugs, 70*(4), 555–567.

Turrisi, R., Mallett, K. A., Mastroleo, N. R., & Larimer, M. E. (2006). Heavy drinking in college students: who is at risk and what is being done about it? *The Journal of General Psychology, 133*(4), 401–420.

Walters, S.T. & Baer, J. (2006). *Talking with college students about alcohol: Motivational strategies for reducing abuse*. New York, NY: Guilford Press

White, H. D., & Rudolph, B. A. (2000). A pilot investigation of the reliability and validity of the group supervisory behavior scale (GBS). *Clinical Supervisor, 19*, 161–171.

White, H. R., Mun, E. Y., Pugh, L., & Morgan, T. J. (2007). Long-term effects of brief substance use interventions for mandated college students: Sleeper effects of an in-person personal feedback intervention. *Alcoholism: Clinical and Experimental Research, 31*(8), 1380–1391.

Wiley, M., & Ray, P. (1986). Counseling supervision by developmental level. *Journal of Counseling Psychology, 33,* 439–445.

Williams, A. (1995). *Visual and active supervision: Role, focus, technique.* New York, NY: Norton.

Wood, M. D., Capone, C., Laforge, R., Erickson, D. J., & Brand, N. H. (2007). Brief motivational intervention and alcohol expectancy challenge with heavy drinking college students: A randomized factorial study. *Addictive Behaviors, 32*(11), 2509–2528.

14

Future Directions in College Student Alcohol Abuse Research and Prevention

James G. Murphy, Nancy P. Barnett, and Christopher J. Correia

The contents of this book reflect the significant advances that have been made in our understanding of college student alcohol abuse over the past 20 years. The increased attention to this significant social problem on the part of behavioral scientists, medical and mental health practitioners, college administrators and student affairs personnel, funding agencies, student and nonstudent members of university communities, parents of college students, and the media have resulted in a remarkable increase in knowledge related to the nature and causes of college student alcohol abuse (Ham & Hope, 2003; Hingson & White, this volume; National Institute on Alcohol Abuse and Alcoholism [NIAAA], 2002, 2007). Importantly, this knowledge has been directly applied to develop sophisticated prevention and intervention approaches—ranging from social norms campaigns, to campus/community coalitions to reduce the availability of alcohol and enforce relevant laws, to individual computerized and counselor-administered brief interventions—which have been tested in rigorous controlled trials and found to be generally efficacious (Carey, this volume; Fairlie, Erickson, & Wood, this volume; Hester & Campbell, this volume; Neighbors, Foster, Fossos, & Lewis, this volume).

Compared to older adult drinkers, college students tend to drink episodically (1 to 3 days per week), in relatively large social groups, outside of the context of meals, and often in large (i.e., binge) quantities over short periods. However, significant physical dependence—as evidenced by escalating daily drinking due to increasing tolerance and to avoid withdrawal—is rare, as are the chronic and extreme social or health problems that tend to precipitate help seeking in adult drinkers. Even so, in the past many college alcohol-prevention programs were influenced by disease models of alcoholism and were generally extensions of traditional adult treatments for severe alcohol dependence, often attempting to reduce drinking by educational approaches that highlighted risk for progression to severe alcoholism and the need for abstinence or significant treatment involvement. More recent perspectives recognize nondependent, episodic drinking as a problem in its own right, and associated (and more effective) approaches with college students place a relatively greater emphasis on reducing the acute risk for harm associated with heavy consumption on specific occasions more so than the long-term risk for developing alcohol dependence (see Kilmer & Logan, this volume). Indeed, retaining a focus on the risk of alcoholism or severe dependence in prevention could result in many students rightly concluding that such a prevention message does not apply to them. In contrast, the prevention approaches developed over the past 20 years are derived from up-to-date knowledge on the unique nature, course, developmental context, motives, and risk factors associated with college student drinking (Hingson & White, this volume).

Not surprisingly, these interventions are generally more efficacious and well received by students than previous approaches. The primary goal of this book is to detail the knowledge base that has led to the development of these prevention and intervention approaches, and to provide specific information on available approaches that we hope will facilitate effective college drinking prevention practices and continued research. Indeed, despite the considerable advances in our understanding of college drinking and in prevention and intervention approaches, college drinking remains a significant problem (Hingson & White, this volume). The goal of this brief concluding chapter is to provide suggestions for future directions in college student alcohol abuse research and prevention that we hope will help the field continue to progress toward the goal of understanding and reducing the harmful consequences associated with college drinking.

SUGGESTIONS FOR FUTURE RESEARCH

Delineate the specific drinking patterns and risk factors uniquely associated with both harmful alcohol-related consequences and risk for developmentally persistent problem drinking among college students. Particular attention should be paid to differentiating the various types of acute and long-term problematic outcomes associated with drinking. These include relatively mild acute negative outcomes such as hangovers or arguments with friends, to significant acute negative outcomes such as blackouts, injuries, or drinking and driving, to protracted negative outcomes such as academic or social impairment, to the development of tolerance, impaired control over drinking, and dependence symptoms. As noted by Martens, Arterberry, Cadigan, and Smith (this volume), these various phenomena have often been lumped together through the use of unidimensional "alcohol problem" measures (Kahler, Strong, & Read, 2005; Kahler, Strong, Read, Palfai, & Wood, 2004). This is unfortunate because these drinking consequences may be associated with somewhat distinct etiological factors and drinking patterns, and may also portend different levels of risk for developmentally persistent drinking and require different prevention and intervention approaches.

For example, a student who drinks to excess on 2 to 3 weekend evenings per month may be at relatively low risk for significant social or academic impairment or a developmentally persistent pattern of drinking, but may be at high risk for an acute negative outcome and require an intervention approach that focuses specifically on that risk (e.g., provides information about blood alcohol levels and specific protective behavioral strategies related to avoiding intoxication). Another student might typically drink below the binge level but may drink on 4 to 5 evenings per week, in part to deal with stress, which may lead him or her to neglect academic responsibilities and/or leisure pursuits that do not entail drinking. This student may be at relatively low risk for negative acute outcomes resulting from significant intoxication but may be at high risk for developing dependence and might benefit from an intervention approach that focuses on managing stress, learning about dependence, and setting limits on the number of drinking days per week. Increasingly refined assessment approaches are required to differentiate between relevant drinking patterns so potentially unique etiological risk factors can be identified. For example, behavioral economic measures have been developed that quantify the relative value of alcohol compared to alternatives using demand curve and relative behavioral allocation indices (MacKillop & Murphy, 2007; Murphy, Correia, & Barnett, 2007; Murphy, Correia, Colby, & Vuchinich, 2005 Tucker, Roth, Vignolo, & Westfall, 2009). These measures provide an alternative to traditional measures of negative consequences that may more specifically measure the extent to which a student value alcohol and their long-term risk for developmentally persistent problem drinking.

Investigate college student drug use. As noted by Simons, Gaher, Wray, and Reed (this volume), rates of drug use have increased among college students and many students combine drugs and alcohol in ways that can increase risk for overdose and a variety of other negative outcomes. Yet, relatively little is known about the unique risks associated with drug use among college students, and few intervention approaches address drug use or the combined use of different substances (Grossbard et al., 2010; Lee, Neighbors, Kilmer, & Larimer, 2010; McCambridge & Strang, 2004; White et al., 2006; see also Terlecki, Ecker, Copeland, & Buckner, this volume). We cannot assume, for example, that brief motivational interventions will be as successful in reducing marijuana use as they are in reducing alcohol use in college students, although few such investigations have been conducted. Similarly, the increase in the use of prescription drugs on college campuses requires a response, but we are aware of no interventions that address, for example, the use of prescription stimulants (also known as *study drugs*). Given that the motivation for using stimulants may be different from the motivation for using alcohol and marijuana (academic performance vs. recreational effects), and the behavioral response different as well (alertness and cognitive focus versus intoxication; McCabe & Teter, 2007), new approaches to address stimulant use may need to be developed. Future research should continue to develop and evaluate interventions for illicit drug use among college students.

Examine the relations between drinking and brain development among college students. In the past decade there has been a dramatic increase in knowledge about the developing human brain, including information that the brain continues to develop after traditional adolescent age, that there are specific characteristics of the adolescent brain that increase the risk of using alcohol and that inhibit the behavioral response to alcohol, and that alcohol has a significant negative effect on the developing brain (Spear, 2002). Much of this work has used animal models, but increasingly researchers are able to investigate the adolescent brain and its functions using technologies such as magnetic resonance imaging (MRI), magnetic resonance spectroscopic imaging (MRSI), and functional magnetic resonance imaging (fMRI). Studies using these approaches indicate, among other things, that heavy-drinking teens have smaller hippocampal volumes and prefrontal white matter relative to controls (Hanson, Cummins, Tapert, & Brown, 2011; Medina et al., 2008). The further development of these methods and their inclusion in research with adolescents and young adults is critical for understanding how alcohol use affects brain development and vice versa.

Evaluate the relations between college drinking and the development and progression of other significant health risk behaviors and outcomes. Although alcohol use has been consistently linked with health risk behaviors including cigarette smoking, drug use, and risky sexual behavior, relatively little research has examined the relations between alcohol use and diet, exercise and weight gain among college students (Buscemi, Martens, Murphy, Yurasek, & Smith, 2011; Vickers et al., 2004). Given the obesity epidemic and the fact that college is a crucial period for the development of healthy or unhealthy nutrition, physical activity habits, and weight gain, future research should examine the potential role of alcohol in these weight-related health behaviors. More generally, little is known about the impact of alcohol interventions on these other health behavior outcomes (including cigarette smoking and drug use; Magill, Barnett, Apodaca, Rohsenow, & Monti, 2009; White et al., 2006), or the potential to develop intervention approaches that address multiple health risk behaviors (Werch et al., 2007).

Develop an improved understanding of peer behaviors that influence the substance use of college students. In college, alcohol and other substances are often provided by and/or consumed with same-age peers. Peer drinking and peer approval/ disapproval of drinking have been established as important correlates of alcohol in college students (Borsari & Carey, 2001, 2003), but the mechanisms of this influence are not known. Field research on natural drinking groups (Lange, Johnson, & Reed, 2006) and investigations of the influence of social networks (Barnett et al., 2011; Reifman, Watson, & McCourt, 2006) are examples of research that uses peer behavioral reports (rather than participant perceptions of peer behavior) and measures of interpersonal dynamics to understand peer influences on substance use risk behaviors.

Develop inexpensive interventions that incorporate technology. The Internet is the primary source of health information for college students, and it is essential that colleges and universities capitalize on this modality for conveying information about behavioral risks associated with alcohol and drug use and related university policies. Similarly, mobile phones or smartphones are almost ubiquitous in their use by college students. Effective intervention approaches delivered via computer or the Internet are available (see Hester & Campbell, this volume), and future research should attempt to develop and refine increasingly brief and inexpensive interventions such as text-messaging based interventions (Suffoletto, Callaway, Kristan, Kraemer, & Clark, 2012) and smartphone "apps" (Dimeff, Rizvi, Contreras, Skutch, & Carroll; Rizvi, Dimeff, Skutch, Carroll, & Linehan, 2011). Other technologies for measuring alcohol use (e.g., ecological momentary assessment, alcohol biosensors) and for transmitting information (e.g., smartphones, social network websites) are particularly applicable to college student populations, but for the most part are still emerging. For interventions, stepped care approaches may be especially promising (see Borsari, this volume), as the first intervention applied will presumably be the least expensive approach, yet will be effective with some portion of the target population.

Identify risk factors for lack of response to brief interventions and develop additional intervention elements to address those specific risk factors. Although there has been considerable progress in developing brief and inexpensive interventions that can be administered with minimal or no counselor contact (Borsari, this volume; Hester & Campbell, this volume; Neighbors et al., this volume), research suggests that counselor-administered interventions appear to be slightly more effective (Walters et al., 2009). Nevertheless, in-person interventions such as BASICS are generally only associated with small effect sizes that tend to diminish over time (Carey, this volume). Interventions such as BASICS typically entail an assessment plus a single intervention session but may need to be enhanced with additional intervention content that is based on the unique risk factors (including personality and cognitive/executive functioning characteristics), drinking motives, and drinking patterns of the student (Conrad, Stewart, Comeau, & Maclean et al., 2006). Consistent with a stepped care approach, students who do not respond to initial interventions, might respond to extended interventions for alcohol misuse that might include repeated web-based personalized feedback administration (Neighbors et al., 2010), and/or components such as cognitive behavioral skills training (e.g., mood management, copings skills training, cue reactivity) and family or significant other involvement. Moderation and mediation analyses may also help to identifying particular groups of students who may benefit from particular intervention approaches (Carey, Henson, Carey, & Maisto, 2007; Mastroleo, Murphy, Colby, Monti, & Barnett, 2011) as well as the mechanism of change associated with the various interventions (Apodaca & Longabaugh, 2009). One recently developed intervention approach combined a standard BASICS session with a supplemental "substance-free activity session" that is based on behavioral economic theory and attempts to increase engagement in constructive alternatives to drinking including academics, community activities, and substance-free social/leisure activities (Murphy et al., in press). A recently completed clinical trial suggests that this combination of BASICS and the substance-free activity session resulted in significantly greater reductions in alcohol problems than BASICS plus a relaxation control session (Murphy et al., 2011).

Increase understanding of the unique risk factors and intervention approaches that are appropriate for diverse subgroups of college students. The overwhelming majority of intervention research with college students has focused on 18- to 22-year-old Caucasian students who attend large state or private residential colleges. Relatively little research has examined drinking or response to intervention among part-time or nontraditional students across a wider range of academic settings including community colleges, ethnic minority students, LGBTQ students, and students who are military veterans or involved with ROTC. One study found that African-American college students showed a greater response to in-person compared to computerized interventions (Murphy et al., 2010). Students with significant mental health or psychiatric difficulties are another high-risk group that may require unique intervention approaches (Bachrach & Read, this volume; Conrad, Stewart, Comeau, & Maclean et al., 2006; Geisner, Neighbors, Lee, & Larimer, 2007).

Develop and evaluate intervention approaches for students who are graduating or withdrawing from college. Although several studies have developed and evaluated interventions for the transition to college (Marlatt et al., 1998), we are unaware of any studies that have attempted to address risky drinking during the important developmental transition from college to the work force. Although drinking typically decreases during the postcollege years, this decrease is generally gradual and is not universal (Johnston et al., 2010). Interventions delivered prior to or shortly after graduation might be able to accelerate the developmental decline in drinking.

Increase dissemination of evidence-based approaches and include alternative providers. Despite the development of efficacious substance use prevention and intervention approaches, and a greater ease of dissemination of empirically based interventions, many colleges continue to use approaches that have not been empirically evaluated or have been determined to be ineffective. In some cases, this may be due to a lack of exposure to or trust of research findings, in other cases it may be due to a lack of resources. The efforts of the NIAAA Task Force a decade ago (NIAAA, 2002, 2007) provide guidance and resources for college campuses, but it can be difficult for college administrators to change policies and practices, or to avoid the pull to use untested but attractive programs. Furthermore, there have been numerous efficacy studies of alcohol interventions (i.e., those that use experimental methods and rigorous training of providers to evaluate the efficacy of an intervention), but few effectiveness studies (e.g., those that use providers in the intervention settings, with fewer methodological controls). It will be important for researchers, national organizations, and funders to prioritize effectiveness studies and dissemination research. Future research should attempt to increase the dissemination of effective individual-level interventions by:

(a) developing strategies to increase problem recognition and help-seeking among college drinkers, (b) developing increasingly flexible and appealing interventions that students will seek out, (c) teaching peers, parents, and student leaders to deliver interventions, and (d) developing incentives or contingencies/mandates to increase participation in brief interventions.

REFERENCES

Apodaca T. R. & Longabaugh R. (2009). Mechanisms of change in motivational interviewing: A review and preliminary evaluation of the evidence. *Addiction, 104,* 705–715. doi: 10.1111/j.1360-0443.2009.02527.x

Barnett, N. P., Ott, M., Linkletter, C., Rogers, M., Loxley, M., & Clark, M. (2011, October). *Alcohol use in one university dormitory: A social network analysis.* Paper presented at the annual meeting of the Society for the Study of Emerging Adulthood, Providence, RI.

Borsari, B., & Carey, K. B. (2001). Peer influences on college drinking: A review of the research. *Journal of Substance Abuse, 13*(4), 391–424.

Borsari, B., & Carey, K. B. (2003). Descriptive and injunctive norms in college drinking: A meta-analytic integration. *Journal of Studies on Alcohol and Drugs, 64*(3), 331–341.

Buscemi, J., Martens, M. P., Murphy, J. G., Yurasek, A. M., & Smith, A. E. (2011). Moderators of the relationship between physical activity and alcohol consumption in college students. *Journal of American College Health, 59,* 503–509.

Carey, K. B., Henson, J. M., Carey, M. P., & Maisto, S. A. (2007). Which heavy drinking college students benefit from a brief motivational intervention? *Journal of Consulting and Clinical Psychology, 75,* 663–669. doi: 10.1037/0022-006X.75.4.663

Conrad, P. J., Stewart, S. H., Comeau, N., & Maclean, A. M. (2006). Preventative efficacy of cognitive behavioral strategies matched to the motivational bases of alcohol misuse in at-risk youth. *Journal of Clinical Child and Adolescent Psychology, 35,* 490–504. Retrieved from http://www.clinicalchildpsychology.org/journal/

Dimeff, L. A., Rizvi, S. L., Contreras, I. S., Skutch, J. M., & Carroll, D. (2011, September). The mobile revolution and the DBT coach. *Behavior Therapist.*

Geisner, I., Neighbors, C., Lee, C. M., & Larimer, M. E. (2007). Evaluating personal alcohol feedback as a selective prevention for college students with depressed mood. *Addictive Behaviors, 32*(12), 2776–2787. doi: 10.1016/j.addbeh.2007.04.014

Grossbard, J. R., Mastroleo, N. R., Kilmer, J. R., Lee, C. M., Turrisi, R., Larimer, M. E., & Ray, A. (2010). Substance use patterns among first-year college students: Secondary effects of a combined alcohol intervention. *Journal of Substance Abuse Treatment, 39*(4), 384–390. doi: 10.1016/j.jsat.2010.07.001

Ham, L., & Hope, D. (2003). College students and problematic drinking: A review of the literature. *Clinical Psychology Review, 23*(5), 719–759. doi: 10.1016/S0306-4603(01)00230-1

Hanson, K. L., Cummins, K., Tapert, S. F., & Brown, S. A. (2011). Changes in neuropsychological functioning over 10 years following adolescent substance abuse treatment. *Psychology of Addictive Behaviors, 25*(1), 127–142. doi: 10.1037/a0022350

Johnston, L. D., O'Malley, P. M., Bachman, J. G., & Schulenberg, J. E. (2010). *Monitoring the future national survey results on drug use, 1975–2009: Volume II, College students and adults ages 19–50* (NIH Publication No. 10-7585). Bethesda, MD: National Institute on Drug Abuse.

Kahler, C. W., Strong, D. R., & Read, J. P. (2005). Toward efficient and comprehensive measurement of the alcohol problems continuum in college students: The brief young adult alcohol consequences questionnaire. *Alcoholism: Clinical and Experimental Research, 29,* 1180–1189.

Kahler, C. W., Strong, D. R., Read, J. P., Palfai, T. P., & Wood, M. D. (2004). Mapping the continuum of alcohol problems in college students: A Rasch model analysis. *Psychology of Addictive Behaviors, 18,* 322–333.

Lange, J. E., Johnson, M. B., & Reed, M. B. (2006). Drivers within natural drinking groups: An exploration of role selection, motivation, and group influence on driver sobriety. *American Journal of Drug and Alcohol Abuse, 32*(2), 261–274.

Lee, C., Neighbors, C., Kilmer, J., & Larimer, M. (2010). A brief, web-based personalized feedback selective intervention for college student marijuana use: A randomized clinical trial. *Psychology of Addictive Behaviors, 24*(2), 265–273. doi: 10.1037/a0018859

MacKillop, J., & Murphy, J. G. (2007). A behavioral economic measure of demand for alcohol predicts brief intervention outcomes. *Drug and Alcohol Dependence, 89*, 227–233. doi: 10.1016/j.drugalcdep.2007.01.002

Magill, M., Barnett, N. P., Apodaca, T. R., Rohsenow, D. J., & Monti, P. M. (2009). The role of marijuana use in brief motivational intervention with young adult drinkers treated in an emergency department. *Journal of Studies on Alcohol and Drugs, 70*(3), 409–413.

Marlatt, G. A., Baer, J. S., Kivlahan, D. R., Dimeff, L. A., Larimer, M. E., Quigley, L. A . . .. & Williams, E. (1998). Screening and brief intervention for high-risk college student drinkers: Results from a two-year follow-up assessment. *Journal of Consulting and Clinical Psychology, 66*, 604–615.

Mastroleo, N. R., Murphy, J. G., Colby, S. M., Monti, P. M., & Barnett, N. P. (2011). Incident-specific and individual level moderators of brief intervention effects with mandated college students. *Psychology of Addictive Behaviors, 25*, 616–624.

McCabe, S.E., & Teter C. J. (2007). Drug use related problems among nonmedical users of prescription stimulants: a web-based survey of college students from a Midwestern university. *Drug and Alcohol Dependence, 91*, 69–76.

McCambridge, J., & Strang, J. (2004). The efficacy of single-session motivational interviewing in reducing drug consumption and perceptions of drug-related risk and harm among young people: Results from a multi-site cluster randomized trial. *Addiction, 99*, 39–52.

Medina, K. L., McQueeny, T., Nagel, B. J., Hanson, K. L., Schweinsburg, A. D., & Tapert, S. F. (2008). Prefrontal cortex volumes in adolescents with alcohol use disorders: Unique gender effects. *Alcoholism: Clinical and Experimental Research, 32*, 386–394.

Murphy, J. G., & Correia, C. J., & Barnett, N. P. (2007). Behavioral economic approaches to reducing college student drinking. *Addictive Behaviors, 32*, 2573–2585. doi: 10.1016/j.addbeh.2007.05.015

Murphy, J., Correia, C., Colby, S., & Vuchinich, R. (2005). Using behavioral theories of choice to predict drinking outcomes following a brief Intervention. *Experimental and Clinical Psychopharmacology, 13*, 93–101. doi: 10.1037/1064-1297.13.2.93

Murphy, J. G., Skidmore, J. R., Dennhardt, A. A., Martens, M. P., Borsari, B., Barnett, N. P., & Colby, S. M. (*in press*). A behavioral economic supplement to brief motivational interventions for college drinking. Addiction Research and Theory. doi:10.3109/16066359.2012.665965

Murphy, J. G., Skidmore, J. R., Dennhardt, A. A., Martens, M. P., Barnett, N. P., Borsari, B., & Colby, S. M. (2011, June). Improving the efficacy of brief alcohol interventions with a behavioral economic supplement. In M. Martens (Chair), Innovative brief interventions for college student drinking. Symposium presented at the 2011 Research Society on Alcoholism Annual Convention. Atlanta, GA.

National Institute on Alcohol Abuse and Alcoholism. (2002). *High-risk drinking in college: What we know and what we need to learn. Final report on the panel on contexts and consequences.* National Advisory Council on Alcohol Abuse and Alcoholism Task Force on College Drinking. USDHHS.

National Institute on Alcohol Abuse and Alcoholism. (2007). *What colleges need to know now: An update on college drinking research.* National Advisory Council on Alcohol Abuse and Alcoholism Task Force on College Drinking.

Neighbors, C., Lewis, M. A., Atkins, D. C., Jensen, M. M., Walter, T., Fossos, N., . . . Larimer, M. E. (2010). Efficacy of web-based personalized normative feedback: A two-year randomized controlled trial. *Journal of Consulting and Clinical Psychology, 78*, 898-911. doi: 10.1037/a0020766

Reifman, A., Watson, W. K., & McCourt, A. (2006). Social networks and college drinking: Probing processes of social influence and selection. *Personality and Social Psychology Bulletin, 32*(6), 820–832.

Rizvi, S., Dimeff, L. A., Skutch, J., Carroll, D., & Linehan, M. M. (2011). A pilot study of the DBT coach: An interactive mobile phone application for individuals with borderline personality disorder and substance use disorder. *Behavior Therapy, 42*, 589–600.

Spear, L.P. (2002). The adolescent brain and the college drinker: Biological basis of the propensity to use and misuse alcohol. *Journal of Studies on Alcohol, Supplement,* 14, 71–81.

Suffoletto, B., Callaway, C., Kristan, J., Kraemer, K., & Clark, D. B. (2012). Text-message-based drinking assessments and brief interventions for young adults discharged from the emergency department. *Alcoholism: Clinical and Experimental Research, 36,* 552–560.

Tucker, J. A., Roth, D. L., Vignolo, M. J., & Westfall, A. O. (2009). A behavioral economic reward index predicts drinking resolutions: Moderation revisited and compared with other outcomes. *Journal of Consulting and Clinical Psychology, 77,* 219–228. doi: 10.1037/a0014968

Vickers, K. S., Patten, C. A., Bronars, C., Lane, K., Stevens, S. R., Croghan, I.T., . . . & Clark, M.M. (2004). Binge drinking in female college students: the association of physical activity, weight concern, and depressive symptoms. *Journal of American College Health, 53*(3), 133–140.

Walters, S. T., Vader, A. M., Harris, T. R., Field, C. A., & Jouriles, E. N. (2009). Dismantling motivational interviewing and feedback for college drinkers: A randomized clinical trial. *Journal of Consulting and Clinical Psychology, 77*(1), 64–73. doi: 2009–00563–015 [pii] 10.1037/a0014472

Werch, C. E., Bian, H., Moore, M. J., Ames, S., DiClemente, C. C., & Weiler, R.M. (2007). Brief multiple behavior interventions in college student health care clinic. *Journal of Adolescent Health, 41,* 577–585.

White, H. R., Morgan, T. J., Pugh, L. A., Celinska, K., Labouvie, E. W., & Pandina, R. J. (2006). Evaluating two brief substance-use interventions for mandated college students. *Journal of Studies on Alcohol, 67*(2), 309–317.

About the Editors

Dr. Christopher J. Correia is an associate professor in the Department of Psychology at Auburn University, where he has won a number of awards in recognition of outstanding research, teaching, and mentoring. He received his PhD in Clinical Psychology from Syracuse University and completed a NIDA-sponsored postdoctoral research fellowship in behavioral pharmacology at the Johns Hopkins University School of Medicine. He has published numerous journal articles and chapters on addictive behaviors, the majority of which studied substance use among college students. Recent interests include the behavioral economics of substance use and the development of laboratory models to study alcohol use and alcohol-related decision making. His research on substance use among college students has been supported by the National Institutes of Health. He is a consulting editor for *Psychology of Addictive Behaviors* and reviews for several other top journals in the field. In addition to teaching classes and conducting research on addictive behaviors, he is a licensed clinical psychologist and serves as the primary clinical supervisor for the Auburn University Health Behavior Assessment Center, which provides brief alcohol assessment and intervention services to college students.

Dr. James G. Murphy is an associate professor of psychology at the University of Memphis who has published numerous papers and chapters related to college student drinking, addiction, brief motivational interventions, and behavioral economics. After graduating from Seton Hall University with his bachelor degree, he completed his PhD in clinical psychology at Auburn University in 2003 and a clinical internship and NIAAA-sponsored postdoctoral research fellowship at Brown University. He has conducted numerous clinical trials of brief motivational interventions for college student drinkers. He has also developed and evaluated a novel behavioral economic supplement to brief motivational interventions that attempts to increase students' engagement in constructive alternatives to drinking that are associated with delayed reinforcement. His research also explores novel behavioral economic predictors of substance abuse problem severity, treatment outcome, and mechanisms of behavior change. These predictors include measures of alcohol reinforcement value derived from demand curves and relative behavioral allocation. Dr. Murphy's research has been funded by the National Institute on Alcohol Abuse and Alcoholism, the U.S. Department of Education, and the Alcohol Research Foundation (ABMRF). He is currently an assistant editor for the journal *Addiction* and a consulting editor for the journal *Psychology of Addictive Behaviors.* He is also actively involved with teaching, research mentoring, and clinical supervision related to substance abuse and health behavior change for graduate students in clinical psychology at the University of Memphis.

Dr. Nancy P. Barnett is an associate professor (research) in the Department of Behavioral and Social Sciences at Brown University. She received her PhD in Clinical Psychology from the University of Washington, after which she completed an NIAAA-sponsored postdoctoral fellowship at the Center for Alcohol and Addiction Studies at Brown University. Her primary research area is the development and evaluation of brief interventions for substance use, including motivational, computer-delivered, and Web-based interventions for adolescents and adults. She has conducted seminal work with college students mandated to alcohol interventions, and completed the first trial that incorporated an alcohol biosensor into a clinical intervention for alcohol use reduction. Her other research includes evaluations of mediators and moderators of brief interventions, predictors of behavior change following alcohol-related consequences, and behavioral economics constructs. Dr. Barnett's research on alcohol use in college students has been funded by the National Institute of Alcohol Abuse and Alcoholism. She has served in several roles for the Research Society on Alcoholism, is a frequent reviewer for clinical psychology and addiction journals, and is actively involved as a mentor in the Brown Center for Alcohol and Addiction Studies Postdoctoral Training Program.

Author Index

Subject Index